Summary of Contents

M000310042

Foreword xxi

Preface xxiii

1. Introducing ASP.NET and the .NET Platform 1

2. ASP.NET Basics 27

3. VB and C# Programming Basics 47

4. Constructing ASP.NET Web Pages 97

5. Building Web Applications 159

6. Using the Validation Controls 235

7. Database Design and Development 273

8. Speaking SQL 317

9. ADO.NET 363

10. Displaying Content Using Data Lists 435

11. Managing Content Using `GridView` and `DetailsView` 463

12. Advanced Data Access 507

13. Security and User Authentication 569

14. Working with Files and Email 615

15. Introduction to LINQ 655

16. Introduction to MVC 671

17. ASP.NET AJAX 701

A. Web Control Reference 723

B. Deploying ASP.NET Websites 763

Index 775

BUILD YOUR OWN
ASP.NET 4 WEBSITE
USING C# & VB

BY **CRISTIAN DARIE**
WYATT BARNETT
TIM POSEY
4TH EDITION

iv

Build Your Own ASP.NET 4 Website Using C# & VB

by Cristian Darie, Wyatt Barnett, and Tim Posey

Copyright © 2011 SitePoint Pty. Ltd.

Expert Reviewer: Pranav Rastogi
Product Editor: Simon Mackie
Technical Editor: Ricky Onsman
Printing History:
    First Edition: April 2004
    Second Edition: October 2006
    Third Edition: September 2008

Editor: Sarah Broomhall
Index Editor: Michelle Combs
Cover Design: Alex Walker
Latest Update: Fourth Edition: September 2011

Notice of Rights

All rights reserved. No part of this book may be reproduced, stored in a retrieval system or transmitted in any form or by any means, without the prior written permission of the publisher, except in the case of brief quotations embodied in critical articles or reviews.

Notice of Liability

The author and publisher have made every effort to ensure the accuracy of the information herein. However, the information contained in this book is sold without warranty, either express or implied. Neither the authors and SitePoint Pty. Ltd., nor its dealers or distributors, will be held liable for any damages to be caused either directly or indirectly by the instructions contained in this book, or by the software or hardware products described herein.

Trademark Notice

Rather than indicating every occurrence of a trademarked name as such, this book uses the names only in an editorial fashion and to the benefit of the trademark owner with no intention of infringement of the trademark.

Published by SitePoint Pty. Ltd.

48 Cambridge Street Collingwood
VIC Australia 3066.
Web: www.sitepoint.com
Email: business@sitepoint.com

ISBN 978-0-9870908-6-7 (print)

ISBN 978-0-9871530-3-6 (ebook)
Printed and bound in the United States of America

About the Authors

Cristian Darie is a software engineer with experience in a wide range of modern technologies, and the author of numerous technical books, including the popular *Beginning E-Commerce* series. He initially tasted programming success with a prize in his first programming contest at the age of 12. From there, Cristian moved on to many other similar achievements, and is now studying distributed application architectures for his PhD.

Wyatt Barnett leads the in-house development team for a major industry trade association in Washington DC. When not slinging obscene amounts of C# and SQL at a few exceedingly large monitors, he is most often spotted staring at HDTV and other forms of entertainment in local watering holes.

Tim Posey is a long-time developer and a passionate educator. Armed with a B.S. in Computer Science and an M.B.A. in Finance, he has traversed many industries, consulting for multiple corporations in banking, insurance, energy, and various e-commerce industries. As a serial entreprenuer, he mentors local startups and non-profit organizations. He serves as a senior software engineer at a Fortune 1000 company and an Adjunct Professor of Finance for the American Public University System. His favorite pastime is watching Alabama football. He may be contacted at tim@timposey.net.

About the Technical Editor

Ricky Onsman is an Australian freelance web designer and jack of all trades. With a background in information and content services, he built his first website in 1994 for a disability information service and has been messing about on the web ever since. He is the president of the Web Industry Professionals Association.

About SitePoint

SitePoint specializes in publishing fun, practical, and easy-to-understand content for web professionals. Visit http://www.sitepoint.com/ to access our books, newsletters, articles, and community forums.

To my family and friends.

—Cristian Darie

To my Father, whose guidance got me this far.

—Wyatt Barnett

For LJ and Erin.

—Tim Posey

Table of Contents

Foreword xxi

Preface xxiii

  Who Should Read This Book xxiii
  What's in This Book xxiv
  Where to Find Help xxviii
    The SitePoint Forums xxviii
    The Book's Website xxviii
  The SitePoint Newsletters xxix
  The SitePoint Podcast xxix
  Your Feedback xxix
  Acknowledgments xxx
  Conventions Used in This Book xxx
    Code Samples xxx
    Tips, Notes, and Warnings xxxi

Chapter 1 **Introducing ASP.NET and the .NET Platform** 1

  What is ASP.NET? 2
  Installing the Required Software 5
    Installing Visual Web Developer 2010 Express Edition 6
    Installing SQL Server Management Studio Express 8
  Writing Your First ASP.NET Page 11
  Getting Help 25
  Summary 25

Chapter 2   ASP.NET Basics 27

ASP.NET Page Structure 28

Directives 32

Code Declaration Blocks 33

Code Render Blocks 35

ASP.NET Server Controls 37

Server-side Comments 37

Literal Text and HTML Tags 39

View State 40

Working with Directives 44

ASP.NET Languages 45

Visual Basic 46

C# 46

Summary 46

Chapter 3   VB and C# Programming Basics 47

Programming Basics 47

Control Events and Subroutines 48

Page Events 53

Variables and Variable Declaration 56

Arrays 60

Functions 63

Operators 67

Conditional Logic 69

Loops 71

Object Oriented Programming Concepts 77

Objects and Classes 78

Properties 80

Methods 81

Classes 82

Constructors 82

Scope 83

Events 84

Understanding Inheritance 84

Objects in .NET 85

Namespaces 87

Using Code-behind Files 88

Summary 94

Chapter 4   Constructing ASP.NET Web Pages

Chapter 4   Constructing ASP.NET Web Pages 97

Web Forms 98

HTML Server Controls 99

Using the HTML Server Controls 101

Web Server Controls 107

Standard Web Server Controls 109

List Controls 117

Advanced Controls 119

Web User Controls 135

Creating a Web User Control 136

Master Pages 144

Using Cascading Style Sheets (CSS) 149

Types of Styles and Style Sheets 150

Summary 157

Chapter 5   Building Web Applications

Chapter 5   Building Web Applications 159

Introducing the Dorknozzle Project 160

Using Visual Web Developer 162

Meeting the Features 163

Executing Your Project 172

Core Web Application Features 175

    Web.config 176

    Global.asax 180

    Using Application State 182

    Working with User Sessions 191

    Using the Cache Object 192

    Using Cookies 195

Starting the Dorknozzle Project 197

    Preparing the Sitemap 198

    Using Themes, Skins, and Styles 200

    Building the Master Page 206

    Using the Master Page 210

Extending Dorknozzle 215

Debugging and Error Handling 217

    Debugging with Visual Web Developer 218

    Other Kinds of Errors 224

    Custom Errors 226

    Handling Exceptions Locally 227

Summary 232

Chapter 6   Using the Validation Controls 235

Client-side Validation and Server-side Validation 236

Introducing the ASP.NET Validation Controls 236

    Enforcing Validation on the Server 240

Using Validation Controls 246

    RequiredFieldValidator 247

    CompareValidator 248

    RangeValidator 251

    ValidationSummary 252

    `RegularExpressionValidator` 254

    `CustomValidator` 258

  Validation Groups 261

  Updating Dorknozzle 266

  Summary 270

Chapter 7   Database Design and Development

Chapter 7   **Database Design and Development** 273

  What Is a Database? 274

  Creating Your First Database 276

    Creating a New Database Using Visual Web Developer 277

    Creating a New Database Using SQL Server Management Studio 278

  Creating Database Tables 280

    Data Types 285

    Column Properties 287

    Primary Keys 288

    Creating the Employees Table 290

    Creating the Remaining Tables 293

    Populating the Data Tables 296

  Relational Database Design Concepts 299

    Foreign Keys 301

    Using Database Diagrams 304

    Implementing Relationships in the Dorknozzle Database 308

    Diagrams and Table Relationships 312

  Summary 316

Chapter 8   **Speaking SQL** 317

  Reading Data from a Single Table 318

Using the SELECT Statement 321

Selecting Certain Fields 324

Selecting Unique Data with DISTINCT 326

Row Filtering with WHERE 329

Selecting Ranges of Values with BETWEEN 330

Matching Patterns with LIKE 331

Using the IN Operator 332

Sorting Results Using ORDER BY 333

Limiting the Number of Results with TOP 334

Reading Data from Multiple Tables 335

Subqueries 336

Table Joins 337

Expressions and Operators 338

Transact-SQL (T-SQL) Functions 341

Arithmetic Functions 342

String Functions 343

Date and Time Functions 346

Working with Groups of Values 347

The COUNT Function 348

Grouping Records Using GROUP BY 349

Filtering Groups Using HAVING 350

The SUM, AVG, MIN, and MAX Functions 351

Updating Existing Data 352

The INSERT Statement 352

The UPDATE Statement 353

The DELETE Statement 354

Stored Procedures 355

Summary 360

Chapter 9   ADO.NET 363

Introducing ADO.NET 364

Importing the SqlClient Namespace 366

Defining the Database Connection 367

Preparing the Command 368

Executing the Command 369

Setting Up Database Authentication 371

Reading the Data 375

Using Parameters with Queries 377

Bulletproofing Data Access Code 385

Using the Repeater Control 387

Creating the Dorknozzle Employee Directory 393

More Data Binding 398

Inserting Records 405

Updating Records 411

Deleting Records 428

Using Stored Procedures 431

Summary 433

Chapter 10   Displaying Content Using Data
             Lists 435

DataList Basics 436

Handling DataList Events 440

Editing DataList Items and Using Templates 448

DataList and Visual Web Developer 457

Styling the DataList 458

Summary 461

Chapter 11 Managing Content Using `GridView` and `DetailsView` 463

Using the `GridView` Control 464

Customizing the `GridView` Columns 471

Styling the `GridView` with Templates, Skins, and CSS 472

Selecting Grid Records 477

Using the `DetailsView` Control 482

Styling the `DetailsView` 486

`GridView` and `DetailsView` Events 488

Entering Edit Mode 492

Using Templates 496

Updating `DetailsView` Records 500

Summary 505

Chapter 12 Advanced Data Access 507

Using Data Source Controls 508

Binding the `GridView` to a `SqlDataSource` 510

Binding the `DetailsView` to a `SqlDataSource` 519

Displaying Lists in `DetailsView` 531

More on `SqlDataSource` 534

Working with Data Sets and Data Tables 535

What Is a Data Set Made From? 538

Binding `DataSets` to Controls 540

Implementing Paging 546

Storing Data Sets in View State 548

Implementing Sorting 551

Filtering Data 562

Updating a Database from a Modified `DataSet` 563

Summary 567

Chapter 13 **Security and User Authentication** 569

Basic Security Guidelines 570
Securing ASP.NET Applications 572
    Working with Forms Authentication 574
ASP.NET Memberships and Roles 588
    Creating the Membership Data Structures 588
    Using Your Database to Store Membership Data 590
    Using the ASP.NET Web Site Configuration Tool 596
    Creating Users and Roles 599
    Changing Password Strength Requirements 600
    Securing Your Web Application 603
    Using the ASP.NET Login Controls 605
Summary 613

Chapter 14 **Working with Files and Email** 615

Writing and Reading Text Files 616
    Setting Up Permissions 617
    Writing Content to a Text File 620
    Reading Content from a Text File 624
Accessing Directories and Directory Information 628
    Working with Directory and File Paths 632
Uploading Files 635
Sending Email with ASP.NET 639
    Sending a Test Email 641
    Creating the Company Newsletters Page 643
Summary 653

Chapter 15 **Introduction to LINQ** 655

    Extension Methods 657

        LINQ to SQL 657

        Updating Data 661

        Relationships 662

        Directly Executing Queries from the DataContext 663

        Stored Procedures with LINQ-to-SQL 665

        Using ASP.NET and LINQ-to-SQL 667

Chapter 16 **Introduction to MVC** 671

    Summary 698

Chapter 17 **ASP.NET AJAX** 701

    What is Ajax? 702

    ASP.NET AJAX 703

    Using the `UpdatePanel` Control 704

        Managing the `ScriptManager` Control 708

    Using Triggers to Update an `UpdatePanel` 709

    The ASP.NET AJAX Control Toolkit 713

        The `ValidatorCalloutExtender` Control Extender 715

        Getting Started with Animation 718

    jQuery 720

    Summary 721

Appendix A **Web Control Reference** 723

    The `WebControl` Class 723

        Properties 723

        Methods 724

    Standard Web Controls 725

AdRotator 725

BulletedList 725

Button 726

Calendar 727

CheckBox 729

CheckBoxList 729

DropDownList 730

FileUpload 731

HiddenField 732

HyperLink 732

Image 732

ImageButton 733

ImageMap 733

Label 734

LinkButton 734

ListBox 735

Literal 736

MultiView 736

Panel 736

PlaceHolder 737

RadioButton 737

RadioButtonList 738

TextBox 739

Wizard 740

Xml 744

Validation Controls 744

CompareValidator 745

CustomValidator 746

RangeValidator 747

RegularExpressionValidator 748

`RequiredFieldValidator` 748

`ValidationSummary` 749

Navigation Web Controls 750

`SiteMapPath` 750

`Menu` 751

`TreeView` 756

Ajax Web Extensions 760

`ScriptManager` 760

`Timer` 761

`UpdatePanel` 761

`UpdateProgress` 762

Appendix B Deploying ASP.NET Websites 763

ASP.NET Hosting Considerations 763

Using Visual Web Developer Express to Deploy ASP.NET Websites 764

Deploying MVC Sites and Web Applications 767

ASP.NET Deployment "Gotchas" 769

Using the SQL Server Hosting Toolkit 770

Dealing with SQL Security 772

Index 775

Foreword

Before you go much further in reading this book, give yourself a small pat on the back for investing the money, time and effort in learning ASP.NET. Perhaps it is a new technology to you, or perhaps you are familiar with ASP or other programming in .NET. Either way, it's a great skill to add to your toolbox and increase your value as a developer.

ASP.NET is useful in more ways than one. If you aren't already a .NET developer, it's the gateway to learning the framework, and the languages that you can use to program against it. The most common languages, and the ones covered in this book, are C# and VB.NET. Skills in these languages and framework go way beyond web development. You can use them for mobile development with Silverlight, which uses the .NET framework for Windows Phone 7 Desktop development; or .NET on Windows Power Desktop development with the Windows Presentation Foundation (WPF), part of the .NET Framework Workflow development for business processes using the Workflow Foundation (WF)—which is also part of the .NET Framework Connected systems development using the Windows Communication Foundation (WCF).

Beyond these, the skills continue to grow in relevance as the industry matures and develops. Time invested in .NET development will reap benefits with cloud-scalable applications using Windows Azure, as well as the new Windows 8 client applications. But you have to start somewhere, and starting with the web is a wise choice. ASP.NET allows you to build dynamic websites, web applications and web services. As a developer, you know and understand that there as many different types of web application as there are web applications themselves, and you need a powerful and flexible framework that will allow you to build them, without having to reinvent the wheel each time.

ASP.NET is this framework, and with its Web Forms and Controls technologies, you can use rapid development methodologies to get your application up and running quickly. Being fully standards-compliant, you can also make it beautiful using CSS. Beyond this, particularly for professional, commercial applications, you'll need tools that allow database connectivity to be smart, secure, and efficient, and ASP.NET with its ADO.NET technology provides this for you.

And of course it wouldn't be Web 2.0 if you didn't have the ability to use Ajax. ASP.NET gives you simple but effective ways to use AJAX with server-side controls that do a lot of the hard work of handling asynchronous page updates for you. Indeed, server-side coding is something that you'll do a lot of with ASP.NET. It's amazing how simple it can make writing distributed applications, where the server is smart enough to manage sessions, connectivity, presentation and more on your behalf.

This book provides you with everything you need to know to skill up in ASP.NET development with Web Forms technology. It's a fantastic learning tool, written in an approachable and informative way. I strongly recommend you pick up your copy of this book, download the free Visual Web Developer Express tools, and start coding in ASP.NET. You'll be amazed at what you can build, quickly and easily.

Laurence Moroney, technologist and author

August 2011

Preface

Web development is very exciting. There's nothing like the feeling you have after you place your first dynamic web site online, and see your little toy in action while other people are actually using it!

Web development with ASP.NET is particularly exciting. If you've never created a dynamic web site before, I'm sure you'll fall in love with this area of web development. If you've worked with other server-side technologies, I expect you'll be a little shocked by the differences.

ASP.NET really is a unique technology, and it provides new and extremely efficient ways to create web applications using the programming language with which you feel most comfortable. Though it can take some time to learn, ASP.NET is simple to use. Whether you want to create simple web forms, feature-rich shopping carts, or even complex enterprise applications, ASP.NET can help you do it. All the tools you'll need to get up and running are immediately available and easy to install, and require very little initial configuration.

This book will be your gentle introduction to the wonderful world of ASP.NET, teaching you the foundations step by step. First, you'll learn the theory; then, you'll put it into practice as we work through practical exercises together. Finally, we'll stretch your abilities by introducing the MVC Framework and other advanced topics. To demonstrate some of the more complex functionality, and to put the theory into a cohesive, realistic context, we'll develop a project through the course of this book. The project—an intranet site for a company named Dorknozzle—will allow us to see the many components of .NET in action, and to understand through practice exactly how .NET works in the real world.

We hope you'll find reading this book an enjoyable experience that will significantly help you with your future web development projects!

Who Should Read This Book

This book is aimed at beginner, intermediate, and advanced web designers looking to make the leap into server-side programming with ASP.NET. We expect that you'll already feel comfortable with HTML, CSS, and a little knowlegable about database design although we will cover quite a few databatse topics along the way. Developers in open-source web development languages such as PHP, Java, or Ruby will make an excellent transition to learning ASP.NET.

By the end of this book, you should be able to successfully download and install Visual Web Developer 2010 Express Edition, and use it to create basic ASP.NET pages. You'll also learn how to install and run Microsoft SQL Server 2008 R2 Express Edition, create database tables, and work with advanced, dynamic ASP.NET pages that query, insert, update, and delete information within a database.

All examples provided in the book are written in both Visual Basic and C#, the two most popular languages for creating ASP.NET websites. The examples start at beginners' level and proceed to more advanced levels. As such, no prior knowledge of either language is required in order to read, understand, learn from, and apply the knowledge provided in this book. Experience with other programming or scripting languages (such as JavaScript) will certainly grease the wheels, though, and should enable you to grasp fundamental programming concepts more quickly.

What's in This Book

This book comprises the following chapters. Read them from beginning to end to gain a complete understanding of the subject, or skip around if you feel you need a refresher on a particular topic.

Chapter 1: Introducing ASP.NET

Before you can start building your database-driven web presence, you must ensure that you have the right tools for the job. In this first chapter, you'll install Visual Web Developer 2010 Express Edition and Microsoft SQL Server 2008 R2 Express Edition. Finally, you'll create a simple ASP.NET page to make sure that everything's running and properly configured.

Chapter 2: ASP.NET Basics

In this chapter, you'll create your first useful ASP.NET page. We'll explore all the components that make up a typical ASP.NET page, including directives, controls, and code. Then, we'll walk through the process of deployment, focusing specifically on allowing the user to view the processing of a simple ASP.NET page through a web browser.

Chapter 3: VB and C# Programming Basics

In this chapter, we'll look at two of the programming languages that are used to create ASP.NET pages: VB and C#. You'll learn about the syntax of the two languages as we explore the concepts of variables, data types, conditionals, loops, arrays, functions, and more. Finally, we'll see how these languages accommodate object oriented programming principles by allowing you to work with classes, methods, properties, inheritance, and so on.

Chapter 4: Constructing ASP.NET Web Pages

ASP.NET web pages are known as web forms, but, as we'll see, the process of building ASP.NET web forms is a lot like creating a castle with Lego bricks! ASP.NET is bundled with hundreds of controls—including HTML controls, web controls, and so on—that are designed for easy deployment within your applications. This chapter will introduce you to these building blocks and show how to lock them together. You'll also learn about master pages, which are a very exciting feature of ASP.NET.

Chapter 5: Building Web Applications

A web application is basically a group of web forms, controls, and other elements that work together to achieve complex functionality. So it's no surprise that when we build web applications, we must consider more aspects than when we build individual web forms. This chapter touches on those aspects. You'll configure your web application; learn how to use the application state, user sessions, and cookies; explore the process for debugging errors in your project; and more.

Chapter 6: Using the Validation Controls

This chapter introduces validation controls. With validation controls, Microsoft basically eliminated the headache of fumbling through and configuring tired, reused client-side validation scripts. First, you'll learn how to implement user input validation on both the client—and server sides—of your application using Microsoft's ready-made validation controls. Then, you'll learn how to perform more advanced validation using regular expressions and custom validators.

Chapter 7: Database Design and Development

Undoubtedly, one of the most important chapters in the book, Chapter 7 will prepare you to work with databases in ASP.NET. We'll cover the essentials you'll need to know in order to create a database using SQL Server 2008 R2

Express Edition. As well, you'll begin to build the database for the Dorknozzle intranet project.

Chapter 8: Speaking SQL

This chapter will teach you to speak the language of the database: Structured Query Language, or SQL. After a gentle introduction to the basic concepts of SQL, which will teach you how to write `SELECT`, `INSERT`, `UPDATE`, and `DELETE` queries, we'll move on to more advanced topics such as expressions, conditions, and joins. Finally, we'll take a look at how you can reuse queries quickly and easily by writing stored procedures.

Chapter 9: ADO.NET

The next logical step in building database-driven web applications is to roll up our sleeves and dirty our hands with a little ADO.NET—the technology that facilitates communication between your web application and the database server. This chapter explores the essentials of the technology, and will have you reading database data directly from your web applications in just a few short steps. You'll then help begin the transition from working with static applications to those that are database driven.

Chapter 10: Displaying Content Using `DataLists`

Taking ADO.NET further, this chapter shows you how to utilize the `DataList` control provided within the .NET Framework. `DataLists` play a crucial role in simplifying the presentation of information with ASP.NET. In learning how to present database data within your applications in a cleaner and more legible format, you'll gain an understanding of the concepts of data binding at a high level.

Chapter 11: Managing Content Using `GridView` and `DetailsView`

This chapter explores two of the most powerful data presentation controls of ASP.NET: `GridView` and `DetailsView`. `GridView` is a very dynamic control that automates almost all tasks that involve displaying grids of data. `DetailsView` completes the picture by offering the functionality needed to display the details of a single grid item.

Chapter 12: Advanced Data Access

This chapter explores a few of the more advanced details involved in data access, retrieval, and manipulation. We'll start by looking at direct data access using

ADO.NET's data source controls. We'll then compare this approach with that of using data sets to access data in a disconnected fashion. In this section, you'll also learn to implement features such as paging, filtering, and sorting, using custom code.

Chapter 13: Security and User Authentication

This chapter will show you how to secure your web applications with ASP.NET. We'll discuss the various security models available, including IIS, Forms, Windows, and Windows Live ID, and explore the roles that the **Web.config** and XML files can play. This chapter will also introduce you to the ASP.NET membership model and login controls.

Chapter 14: Working with Files and Email

In this chapter, we'll look at the task of accessing your server's file system, including drives, files, and the network. Next, I'll will show you how to work with file streams to create text files, write to text files, and read from text files stored on your web server. Finally, you'll gain first-hand experience in sending emails using ASP.NET.

Chapter 15: Introduction to LINQ

Here we learn about LINQ, a language construct that allows us to query relational data from different sources and interact with it just like any other object or class. With LINQ we get access to compile-time syntax checking, the use of IntelliSense, and the ability to access other data sources such as XML or just about any custom data sources.

Chapter 16: Introduction to MVC

In this chapter we familiarise ourselves with the Model-View-Controller architecture to solve problems in software development and maintenance, separating our business logic, user interface and control flow.

Chapter 17: ASP.NET AJAX

In our final chapter, you'll learn all about the Ajax features that are built into ASP.NET 3.5. We'll spice up the Dorknozzle project with a few Ajax features that'll show how simple ASP.NET AJAX is to use. We'll also explore the ASP.NET AJAX Control Toolkit, and see how it can enhance existing features.

Appendix A: Web Control Reference

Included in this book is a handy web control reference, which lists the most common properties and methods of the most frequently used controls in ASP.NET.

Appendix B: Deploying ASP.NET Websites

Here you'll be shown, step by step, how to use Visual Web Developer and how to move your website from your development environment to a web hosting service and make it live on the Internet. It also covers tips for choosing a reliable web host, ASP.NET deployment gotchas, and hints for using the SQL Server Hosting Toolkit to migrate your database.

Where to Find Help

SitePoint had a thriving community of web designers and developers ready and waiting to help you out if you run into trouble. We also manintain a list of known errat for the book, which you can consult for the latest updates.

The SitePoint Forums

The SitePoint Forums are [1]discussion forums where you can ask questions about anything related to web development. You may, of course, answer questions too. That's how a forum site works—some people ask, some people answer, and most people do a bit of both. Sharing your knowledge benefits others and strenghtens the community. A lot of interesting and experienced web designers and developers hang out there. It's a good way to learn new stuff, have questions answered in a hurry, and generally have a blast.

The Book's Website

Located at http://www.sitepoint.com/books/aspnet4/, the website that supports this book will give you access to the following facilities:

The Code Archive

As you progress through this book, you'll note a number of references to the code archive. This is a downloadable ZIP archive that contains every line of example source code printed in this book. If you want to cheat (or save yourself from carpal

---

[1] http://www.sitepoint.com/forums/

tunnel syndrome), go ahead and download the archive. [2]The archive contains one folder for each chapter of this book. Each folder may contain a **LearningASP** folder for the stand-alone examples in that chapter and a **Dorknozzle** folder for files associated with the Dorknozzle intranet application, the project that we'll work on throughout the book. Each folder will contain **CS** and **VB** subfolders, which contain the C# and VB versions of all the code examples for that chapter. Incremental versions of each file are represented by a number in the file's name.

Updates and Errata

No book is perfect, and we expect that watchful readers will be able to spot at least one or two mistakes before the end of this one. The Errata page [3]on the book's website will always have the latest information about known typographical and code errors.

The SitePoint Newsletters

In addition to books like this one, SitePoint publishes free email newsletters including *The SitePoint Tribune* and *The SitePoint Tech Times*. In them, you'll read about the latest news, product releases, trends, tips, and techniques for all aspects of web development. If nothing else, you'll gain useful ASP.NET articles and tips, but if you're interested in learning other technologies, you'll find them especially valuable. You can subscribe at http://www.sitepoint.com/newsletter/.

The SitePoint Podcast

Join the SitePoint Podcast team for news, interviews, opinion, and fresh thinking for web developers and designers. We discuss the latest web industry topics, present guest speakers, and interview some of the best minds in the industry. You can catch up on the latest and previous podcasts at http://www.sitepoint.com/podcast/, or subscribe via iTunes.

Your Feedback

If you 're unable to find an answer through the forums, or if you wish to contact us for any other reason, the best place to write is books@sitepoint.com. We have a

---

[2] http://www.sitepoint.com/books/aspnet4/code.php
[3] http://www.sitepoint.com/books/aspnet4/errata.php

well-staffed email support system set up to track your inquiries, and if our support team members are unable to answer your question, they'll send it straight to us. Suggestions for improvements, as well as notices of any mistakes you may find, are especially welcome.

Acknowledgments

I'd like to thank the many folks at SitePoint, including Tom, Ricky, Sarah, and Simon, for giving me the opportunity for this book and helping to produce a magnificent product. Special thanks to Pranav Rastogi from Microsoft for giving me detailed technical insight into the many behind-the-scenes details and undocumented features to help make this book a success. Finally, I would like to extend special thanks to my wife for enduring many long nights of having to put our child to bed while I worked on this project.

—Tim Posey

Conventions Used in This Book

You'll notice that we've used certain typographic and layout styles throughout this book to signify different types of information. Look out for the following items.

Code Samples

Code in this book will be displayed using a fixed-width font, like so:

```
<h1>A Perfect Summer's Day</h1>
<p>It was a lovely day for a walk in the park. The birds
were singing and the kids were all back at school.</p>
```

If the code is to be found in the book's code archive, the name of the file will appear at the top of the program listing, like this:

```
example.css
.footer {
  background-color: #CCC;
  border-top: 1px solid #333;
}
```

If only part of the file is displayed, this is indicated by the word *excerpt*:

```
                                                    example.css (excerpt)

border-top: 1px solid #333;
```

If additional code is to be inserted into an existing example, the new code will be displayed in bold:

```
function animate() {
  new_variable = "Hello";
}
```

Where existing code is required for context, rather than repeat all the code, a vertical ellipsis will be displayed:

```
function animate() {
    ⋮
  return new_variable;
}
```

Some lines of code are intended to be entered on one line, but we've had to wrap them because of page constraints. A ➥ indicates a line break that exists for formatting purposes only, and should be ignored:

```
URL.open("http://www.sitepoint.com/blogs/2007/05/28/user-style-she
➥ets-come-of-age/");
```

Tips, Notes, and Warnings

Hey, You!

Tips will give you helpful little pointers.

Ahem, Excuse Me ...

Notes are useful asides that are related—but not critical—to the topic at hand. Think of them as extra tidbits of information.

Make Sure You Always ...

... pay attention to these important points.

Watch Out!

Warnings will highlight any gotchas that are likely to trip you up along the way.

Chapter 1

Introducing ASP.NET and the .NET Platform

By now, ASP.NET is one of the most popular web development technologies on the planet. The first version was released in 2002, and since then, Microsoft has continued the tradition of releasing a powerful web development framework that allows web developers to do more with less. ASP.NET has experienced rapid growth among the established corporate world, as well as becoming the choice for many freelance developers. ASP.NET has many advantages, including a well-established IDE (Integrated Development Environment) called Microsoft Visual Studio, and advanced security and performance frameworks that handle many of the mundane tasks automatically on the server side, freeing the developer to create more full-fledged web applications and websites.

ASP.NET 4 is the latest iteration in the .NET framework, introducing many new features that build upon its predecessor to improve performance, security, and interoperability with the latest browsers. Best of all, it comes available with new development tools, including Visual Web Developer 2010 Express Edition and SQL

Server 2008 R2 Express Edition, both of which are free! These tools enable the rapid application development (RAD) of web applications.

The goal of this book is to enable you to use all these technologies together in order to produce fantastic results. We'll take you step by step through each task, showing you how to get the most out of each technology and tool. Let's begin!

What is ASP.NET?

ASP.NET is a sophisticated and powerful web development framework. If you've never used ASP.NET before, it's likely to take you some time and patience to grow accustomed to it. Development with ASP.NET requires not only an understanding of HTML and web design, but a firm grasp of the concepts of object oriented programming and development. Fortunately, we believe you'll find the benefits amply reward the learning effort!

In the next few sections, we'll introduce you to the basics of ASP.NET. We'll walk through the process of installing it on your web server, and look at a simple example that demonstrates how ASP.NET pages are constructed. But first, let's define what ASP.NET actually *is*.

ASP.NET is a server-side technology for developing web applications based on the Microsoft .NET Framework. Okay, let's break that jargon-filled sentence down.

ASP.NET is a server-side technology. That is, it runs on the web server. Most web designers cut their teeth learning client-side technologies such as HTML, JavaScript, and Cascading Style Sheets (CSS). When a web browser requests a web page created with only client-side technologies, the web server simply grabs the files that the browser (or client) requests and sends them down the line. The client is entirely responsible for reading the markup in those files and interpreting that markup to display the page on the screen.

Server-side technologies such as ASP.NET, however, are a different story. Instead of being interpreted by the client, server-side code (for example, the code in an ASP.NET page) is interpreted by the web server. In the case of ASP.NET, the code in the page is read by the server and used to generate the HTML, JavaScript, and CSS, which is then sent to the browser. Since the processing of the ASP.NET code occurs on the server, it's called a server-side technology. As Figure 1.1 shows, the client only sees the HTML, JavaScript, and CSS. The server is entirely responsible for processing the server-side code.

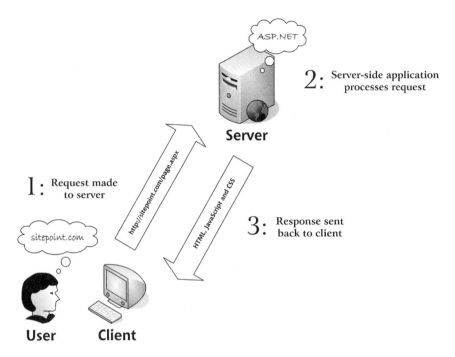

Figure 1.1. A user interacting with a web application

User   The transaction starts and ends with the user. The user operates the web client software and interprets the results.

Web client   This is the software program that the person uses to interact with the web application. The client is usually a web browser, such as Internet Explorer or Firefox.

Web server   This is the software program located on the server. It processes requests made by the web client.

ASP.NET is a technology for developing web applications. A web application is just a fancy name for a dynamic website. A "website" can be thought of as a static page, where the content rarely changes or is purely informational only. Your local dentist or high school probably has a "website". A web application is dynamic in nature, and often considered to be a web version of standard desktop software. Google Mail is an excellent example of a web application. Web applications usually (but not always) store information in a database, and allow visitors to the site to access and change that information. Many different programming technologies and supported languages have been developed to create web applications; PHP, JSP, Ruby on Rails, CGI, and ColdFusion are just a few of the more popular ones. However, rather than tying you to a specific technology and language, ASP.NET lets you write web applications in a variety of familiar programming. We will focus only on the two most popular .NET languages, Visual Basic.NET (often referred to simply as VB.NET or VB) and C# (pronounced "See-Sharp").

ASP.NET uses the Microsoft .NET Framework. The .NET Framework collects all the technologies needed for building Windows desktop applications, web applications, web services, and so on into a single package, and makes them available to many programming languages. To say that ASP.NET uses the .NET Framework is really a huge understatement. ASP.NET is essentially the web version of what the .NET Framework is to the Windows desktop application world. For instance, if your friend wrote a really neat encryption library using .NET for a Windows desktop application, that code could be easily used within an ASP.NET web application with almost little to no changes.

Even with all the jargon explained, you're probably still wondering what makes ASP.NET so good. The truth is that there are many server-side technologies around, each of which has its own strengths and weaknesses. Yet ASP.NET has a few unique features:

- ASP.NET lets you write the server-side code using your favorite programming language— or at least the one you prefer from the long list of supported languages. The .NET Framework currently supports over 40 languages, and many of these may be used to build ASP.NET websites.

- ASP.NET pages are *compiled*, not interpreted. In ASP.NET's predecessor, ASP ("classic ASP"), pages were interpreted: every time a user requested a page, the server would read the page's code into memory, figure out how to execute the code, and execute it. In ASP.NET, the server need only figure out how to execute the code once. The code is compiled into efficient binary files, which can be run very quickly, again and again, without the overhead involved in rereading the page each time. This allows a big jump in performance, compared to the old days of ASP.

- ASP.NET has full access to the functionality of the .NET Framework. Support for XML, web services, database interaction, email, regular expressions, and many other technologies are built right into .NET, which saves you from having to reinvent the wheel.

- ASP.NET allows you to separate the server-side code in your pages from the HTML layout. When you're working with a team composed of programmers and design specialists, this separation is a great help, as it lets programmers modify the server-side code without stepping on the designers' carefully crafted HTML—and vice versa.

- ASP.NET makes it easy to reuse common User Interface elements in many web forms, as it allows us to save those components as independent web user controls. During the course of this book, you'll learn how to add powerful features to your website, and reuse them in many places with a minimum of effort.

- You can get excellent tools that assist in developing ASP.NET web applications. Visual Studio 2010 Express is a powerful, free visual editor that includes features such as a visual HTML editor, code autocompletion, code formatting, database integration functionality, debugging, and more. In the course of this book, you'll learn how to use this tool to build the examples we discuss.

- Security mechanisms such as membership roles and logins, as well as SQL Injection attack prevention, are automatically enabled out-of-the-box with an ASP.NET web app.

Still with us? Great! It's time to gather our tools and start building.

Installing the Required Software

If you're going to learn ASP.NET, you first need to make sure you have all the necessary software components installed and working on your system. Let's take care of this before we move on.

Visual Web Developer 2010 Express Edition

This is a powerful, free web development environment for ASP.NET 4.0. It includes features such as a powerful code, HTML and CSS editor, project debugging, IntelliSense (Microsoft's code autocompletion technology), database integration with the ability to design databases and data structures visually, and much more. You're in for a lot of Visual Web Developer fun during the course of this book.

.NET Framework 3.5 and the .NET Framework Software Development Kit (SDK)
As we've already discussed, the .NET Framework drives ASP.NET. You're likely to have the .NET Framework already, as it installs automatically through the Windows Update service. Otherwise, it'll be installed together with Visual Studio.

Microsoft SQL Server 2008 R2 Express Edition
This is the free, but still fully functional, version of SQL Server 2008. This software is a Relational Database Management System whose purpose is to store, manage, and retrieve data as quickly and reliably as possible. You'll learn how to use SQL Server to store and manipulate the data for the DorkNozzle application you'll build in this book.

SQL Server Management Studio Express
Because the Express Edition of SQL Server doesn't ship with any visual management tools, you can use this free tool, also developed by Microsoft, to access your SQL Server 2008 database.

Installing Visual Web Developer 2010 Express Edition

Install Visual Web Developer 2010 Express Edition by following these simple steps:

1. Browse to http://www.microsoft.com/express/ and select **Microsoft Visual Studio**

2. Select the link for **Visual Web Developer 2010 Express** and click **Install Now**

3. On the Microsoft.com web page; click **Install Now**

4. .Execute the downloaded file, **vwd.exe**. This will begin the process for the Web Platform Installer.

5. As part of the installation of Visual Web Developer, you will install SQL Server 2008 R2 Express edition, which is identified as a dependency and automatically installed. The entire download is about 770MB.

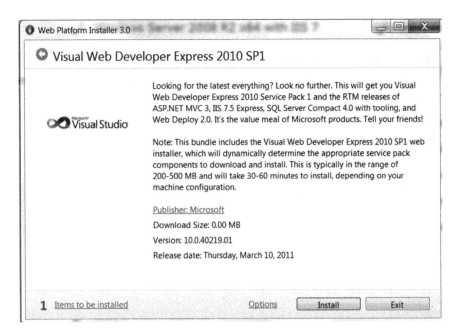

Figure 1.2. Installing Visual Web Developer 2010 Express Edition

6. In the next setup screen, you'll be asked to select the authentication mode for SQL Server 2008 R2 Express Edition. Here we choose to use Windows Authentication for simplicity going forward. Advanced users may choose to use mixed mode to set up their own account management with SQL Server, however, this book will assume the use of Windows Authentication mode.

7. The installer may prompt you to reboot your computer and possibly download more updates depending on your computer configuration. Please follow the on-screen instructions to ensure you have the latest versions.

8. Start Visual Web Developer to ensure it has installed correctly for you. Its welcome screen should look like Figure 1.3

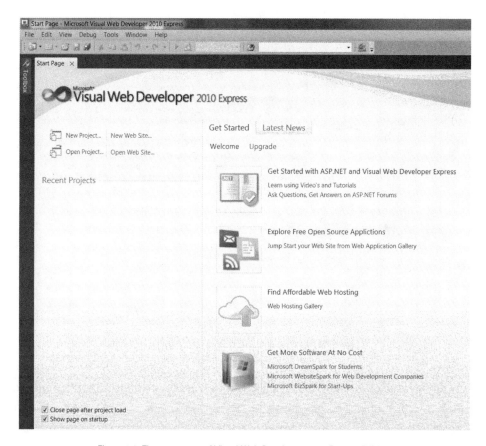

Figure 1.3. The start page of Visual Web Developer 2008 Express Edition

Installing SQL Server Management Studio Express

You've just installed Visual Web Developer and SQL Server 2008 R2 Express Editions. You won't use SQL Server until later in the book when we discuss relational databases, but we'll install all the required software here so that when the time comes, you'll have the complete environment set up.

In order to use your SQL Server 2008 instance effectively, you'll need an administration tool to work with your databases. SQL Server Management Studio Express is a free tool provided by Microsoft that allows you to manage your instance of SQL Server 2008. To install it, follow these steps:

1. Navigate to http://www.microsoft.com/express (or by using your favorite web search engine) and click the **Download** link under the **SQL Server Management Studio Express** section.

2. Download the file. After the download completes, execute the file and follow the steps to install the product. Be sure to choose the appropriate edition, whether 32-bit or 64-bit depending on your computer, with database tools. Be sure to choose to do a full install and under **Feature Selection** you check all boxes.

Once it's installed, SQL Server Manager Express can be accessed from **Start > All Programs > Microsoft SQL Server 2008 > SQL Server Management Studio Express**. When executed, it will first ask for your credentials, asFigure 1.4 illustrates.

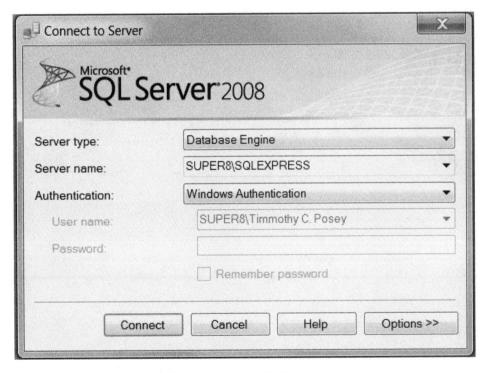

Figure 1.4. Connecting to SQL Server

By default, when installed, SQL Server 2008 Express Edition will only accept connections that use Windows Authentication, which means that you'll use your Windows user account to log into the SQL Server. Since you're the user that installed SQL Server 2008, you'll already have full privileges to the SQL Server. Click **Connect** to connect to your SQL Server 2008 instance.

After you're authenticated, you'll be shown the interface in Figure 1.5, which offers you many ways to interact with, and manage, your SQL Server 2008 instance.

SQL Server Management Studio lets you browse through the objects that reside on your SQL Server, and even modify their settings. For example, you can change the security settings of your server by right-clicking **COMPUTER\SQLEXPRESS** (where *COMPUTER* is the name of your computer), choosing **Properties**, and selecting **Security** from the panel, as shown in Figure 1.6. Here we've modified the **Server authentication** mode to `SQL Server and Windows Authentication` mode. We'll need this setting a bit later in the book, but you can set it now if you want, and then click **OK**.

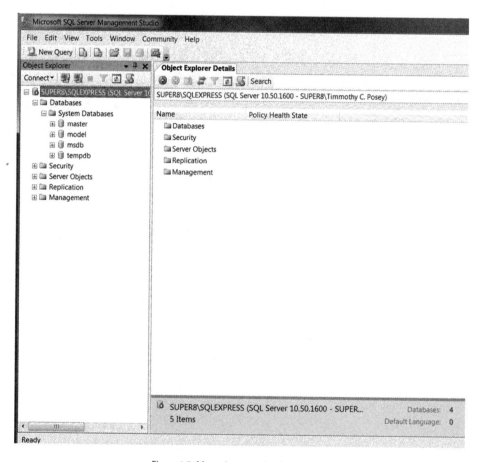

Figure 1.5. Managing your database server

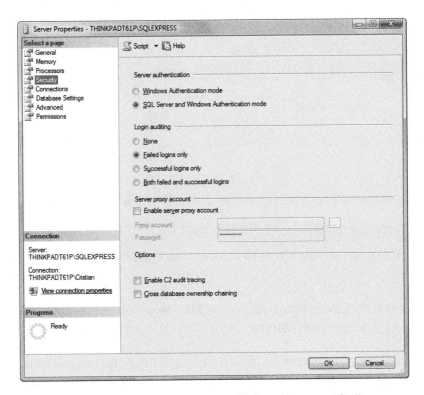

Figure 1.6. Changing server settings with SQL Server Management Studio

That's it. Your machine is now ready to build ASP.NET web projects and SQL Server databases. Now the fun starts—it's time to create your very first ASP.NET page!

Writing Your First ASP.NET Page

For your first ASP.NET exercise, we'll create the simple example shown in Figure 1.7. We'll go though the process of creating this page step by step.

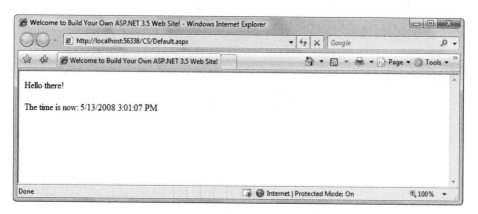

Figure 1.7. An exciting preview of your first ASP.NET page!

To create this page in Visual Web Developer, you'll need to follow a few simple steps:

1. Start Visual Web Developer, and choose **File** > **New Web Site** (or hit the default keyboard shortcut, **Shift+Alt+N**).

2. Choose `ASP.NET Web Site` for the template and `File System` for the location type. This location type tells Visual Web Developer to create the project in a physical folder on your disk, and execute that project using the integrated web server.

3. Choose the language in which you prefer to code your pages. Although ASP.NET allows you to code different pages inside a project in different languages, for the sake of simplicity we'll generally assume you work with a single language.

4. If you chose C# for the language, type `C:\LearningASP\CS\` for the folder location where you want to store the files for this exercise. If you prefer VB.NET, choose `C:\LearningASP\VB\`. You can choose any location you like. Figure 1.8 shows the C# version of the selection.

Figure 1.8. Starting a new ASP.NET Web Site project with Visual Web Developer

5. After clicking **OK**, Visual Web Developer will create the project along with several files to ease your transition into the ASP.NET development world. Your project will also come with a **Site.master** file, which represents a template applied to your entire site automatically. Your Project contains an empty **App_Data** folder, a **Scripts** folder which includes jQuery files, **Styles** which contains a basic **Site.css** stylesheet, a basic **Default.aspx** file, and a basic configuration file, **Web.config**—see Figure 1.9. We will discuss all of these files in Chapter 5, along with the purpose of the Account directory in detail. For now, let's jump right in to create our first ASP.NET web page.

Figure 1.9. Your new project in Visual Web Developer

You may notice that the HTML source is different than standard HTML. This is normal. You should also notice that there are two content areas one for "Header Content" and one for "Main Content". Again, we will discuss templating and Master Pages in just a bit, but let's get immediately going. To do so, we can just overwrite the sample file provided to us.

The main panel in the Visual Web Developer interface is the page editor, in which you'll see the HTML source of the **Default.aspx** web page. Edit the title of the page to something more specific than Home Page, such as **Welcome to Build Your Own ASP.NET 4 Website!**:

```
<html xmlns="http://www.w3.org/1999/xhtml">
  <head runat="server">
    <title>Welcome to Build Your Own ASP.NET 3.5 Website!
    </title>
  </head>
```

Loading the **Default.aspx** page in a web browser now opens the sample page that was created when Visual Web Developer created the project; this makes sense, since we didn't add any content to this page! Because we don't care for any of the sample page, we will simply modify the entire source code for the **default.aspx** page as follows:

```
<body>
  <form id="form1" runat="server">
  <div>
    <p>Hello there!</p>
    <p>
      The time is now:
      <asp:Label ID="myTimeLabel" runat="server" />
    </p>
  </div>
  </form>
</body>
</html>
```

Although our little page isn't yet finished (our work with the Label control isn't over), let's execute the page to ensure we're on the right track. Hit **F5** or go to **Debug** menu.

How a Web Server Control Works

You've just added a Web Server Control to the page by adding an `<asp:Label/>` element to the page. You'll learn all about Web Server Controls in Chapter 2, but for now you need to learn how this simple control works so that you can understand the exercise.

The `Label` control is one of the simplest controls in .NET, which lets you insert dynamic content into the page. The `asp:` part of the tag name identifies it as a built-in ASP.NET tag. ASP.NET comes with numerous built-in tags, and `<asp:Label/>` is probably one of the most frequently used.

The `runat="server"` attribute value identifies the tag as something that needs to be handled on the server. In other words, the web browser will never see the `<asp:Label/>` tag; when the page is requested by the client, ASP.NET sees it and converts it to regular HTML tags *before* the page is sent to the browser. It's up to us to write the code that will tell ASP.NET to replace this particular tag with something meaningful to the user loading the page.

The first time you do this, Visual Web Developer will let you know that your project isn't configured for debugging, and it'll offer to make the necessary change to the configuration (**Web.config**) file for you—see Figure 1.10. Confirm the change by clicking **OK**.

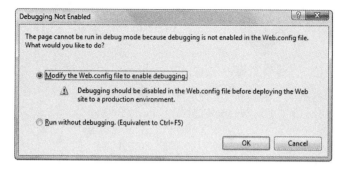

Figure 1.10. Enabling project debugging in Visual Web Developer

If `Script Debugging` is not enabled in Internet Explorer, you'll get the dialog shown in Figure 1.11. Check the **Don't show this dialog again** checkbox, and click **Yes**.

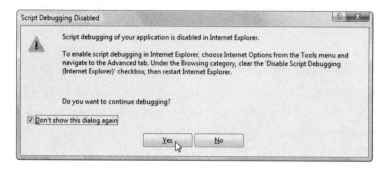

Figure 1.11. Enabling script debugging in Internet Explorer

After all the notifications are out of the way, you should have a page like that in Figure 1.12:

Figure 1.12. Executing your first ASP.NET web page

You can now close the Internet Explorer window. Visual Web Developer will automatically detect this action and will cancel debugging mode, allowing you to start editing the project again. Now let's do something with that Label control.

Set Your Default Browser to Internet Explorer

When executing the project, the website is loaded in your system's default web browser. For the purposes of developing ASP.NET applications, we recommend configuring Visual Web Developer to use Internet Explorer, even if this is not your preferred web browser. We recommend Internet Explorer because it integrates better with Visual Web Developer's .NET and JavaScript debugging features. For example, Visual Web Developer knows to automatically stop debugging the project when the Internet Explorer window is closed. To change the default browser to be used by Visual Web Developer, right-click the root node in **Solution Explorer**, choose **Browse With**, select a browser from the **Browsers** tab, and click **Set as Default**.

For our first dynamic web page using ASP.NET, let's write some code that will display the current time inside the Label control. That mightn't sound very exciting, but it's only for the purposes of this simple demonstration; don't worry, we'll reach the good stuff before too long. To programmatically manipulate the Label control, you'll have to write some C# or VB.NET code, depending on the language you've chosen when creating the project. As suggested earlier in this chapter, ASP.NET allows **web forms** (.aspx pages) to contain C# or VB.NET code, or they can use separate files—named **code-behind files**—for storing this code. The **Default.aspx** file that was generated for you when creating the project was generated with a code-behind file, and we want to edit that file now. There are many ways in which you can open that file. You can click the **View Code** icon at the top of the **Solution Explorer** window, right-click the **Default.aspx** file in **Solution Explorer** and choose **View Code**, or click the + symbol to expand the **Default.aspx** entry. No matter how you open this file, it should look like Figure 1.13 if you're using C#, or Figure 1.14 if you're using VB.NET.

Figure 1.13. Default.aspx.cs in Visual Web Developer

C#, VB.NET, and Visual Web Developer

You may be slightly alarmed, at first, by the fact that the code-behind file template that Visual Web Developer generates for the **Default.aspx** file in a new project when you're using C# is completely different from the one it generates when you're using VB.NET. They're based on the same platform and use the same data types and features, so C# and VB.NET are fundamentally very similar. However, there are still large differences between the languages' syntax. VB.NET is frequently preferred by beginners because its syntax is perceived to be easier to read and understand than C#. While the differences can be intimidating initially, after we discuss their details in Chapter 3, you'll see that it can be relatively easy to understand both.

Figure 1.14. Default.aspx.vb in Visual Web Developer

Looking at Figure 1.13 and Figure 1.14 you can see that the C# version contains a definition for a method called Page_Load, while the VB.NET version doesn't. This is the method that executes automatically when the project is executed, and we want to use it to write the code that will display the current time inside the Label control.

If you're using VB.NET, you'll need to generate the Page_Load method first. The easiest way to have Visual Web Developer generate Page_Load for you is to open **Default.aspx**—*not* its code-behind file—and switch to **Design** view (as shown in Figure 1.15). If you double-click on an empty place on the form, an empty Page_Load method will be created in the code-behind file for **Default.aspx**.

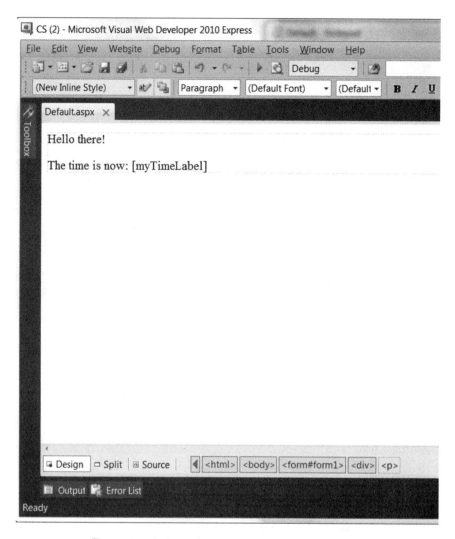

Figure 1.15. **Default.aspx** in **Design** view in Visual Web Developer

Now edit the `Page_Load` method so that it looks like this, selecting the version that applies to your chosen language:

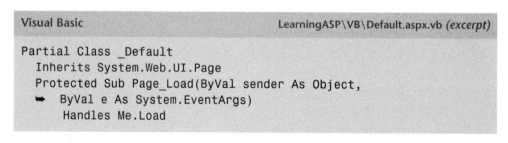

Visual Basic   LearningASP\VB\Default.aspx.vb *(excerpt)*

```
Partial Class _Default
  Inherits System.Web.UI.Page
  Protected Sub Page_Load(ByVal sender As Object,
➥    ByVal e As System.EventArgs)
    Handles Me.Load
```

```
    myTimeLabel.Text = DateTime.Now.ToString()
  End Sub
End Class
```

| C# | LearningASP\CS\Default.aspx.cs *(excerpt)* |

```csharp
public partial class _Default : System.Web.UI.Page
{
  protected void Page_Load(object sender, EventArgs e)
  {
    myTimeLabel.Text = DateTime.Now.ToString();
  }
}
```

C# is Case Sensitive

C#, unlike VB, is case sensitive. If you type the case of a letter incorrectly, the page won't load. If these languages look complicated, don't worry: you'll learn more about them in Chapter 3.

If you've never done any server-side programming before, the code may look a little scary. But before we analyze it in detail, let's load the page and test that it works for real. To see your dynamically generated web page content in all its glory, hit **F5** to execute the project again, and see the current date and time, as depicted in Figure 1.16.

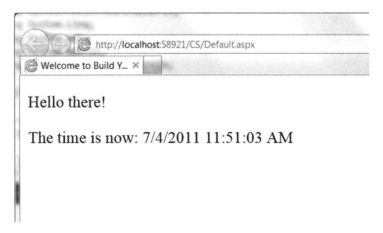

Figure 1.16. Loading **Default.aspx** with a Label element with dynamically generated content

Both versions of the page achieve exactly the same thing. You can even save them both, giving each a different filename, and test them separately. Alternatively, you can create two Visual Web Developer projects—one for C# code, in **C:\LearningASP\CS**, and one for VB.NET code, in **C:\LearningASP\VB**.

 No Time?

If the time isn't displayed in the page, chances are that you opened the file directly in your browser instead of loading it through your web server. Because ASP.NET is a server-side language, your web server needs to process the file before it's sent to your browser for display. If it doesn't gain access to the file, the ASP.NET code is never converted into HTML that your browser can understand, so make sure you load the page by executing it in Visual Web Developer. Loading the page in your browser directly from Windows Explorer will not execute the code, and consequently the time won't display.

So how does the code work? Let's break down some of the elements that make up the page. We're defining a method called Page_Load, in both languages:

Visual Basic   LearningASP\VB\Default.aspx.vb *(excerpt)*

```
Protected Sub Page_Load(ByVal sender As Object,
➥   ByVal e As System.EventArgs)
    Handles Me.Load
```

C#   LearningASP\CS\Default.aspx.cs *(excerpt)*

```
protected void Page_Load(object sender, EventArgs e)
{
```

I won't go into too much detail here. For now, all you need to know is that you can write script fragments that are run in response to different events, such as a button being clicked or an item being selected from a drop-down. What the first line of code basically says is, "execute the following script whenever the page is loaded." Note that C# groups code into blocks with curly braces ({ and }), while Visual Basic uses statements such as End Sub to mark the end of a particular code sequence. So, the curly brace ({) in the C# code above marks the start of the script that will be executed when the page loads for the first time.

Here's the line that actually displays the time on the page:

Visual Basic	LearningASP\VB\Default.aspx.vb *(excerpt)*

```vb
myTimeLabel.Text = DateTime.Now.ToString()
```

C#	LearningASP\CS\Default.aspx.cs *(excerpt)*

```csharp
myTimeLabel.Text = DateTime.Now.ToString();
```

As you can see, these .NET languages have much in common, because they're both built on the .NET Framework. In fact, the only difference between the ways the two languages handle the above line is that C# ends lines of code with a semicolon (;). In plain English, here's what this line says:

```
Set the Text of myTimeLabel to the current date and time, expressed
as text
```

Note that myTimeLabel is the value we gave for the id attribute of the <asp:Label/> tag where we want to show the time. So, myTimeLabel.Text, or the Text property of myTimeLabel, refers to the text that will be displayed by the tag. DateTime is a class that's built into the .NET Framework; it lets you perform all sorts of useful functions with dates and times. The .NET Framework has thousands of these classes, which do countless handy things. The classes are collectively known as the **.NET Framework Class Library**.

The DateTime class has a property called Now, which returns the current date and time. This Now property has a method called ToString, which expresses that date and time as text (a segment of text is called a **string** in programming circles). Classes, properties, and methods: these are all important words in the vocabulary of any programmer, and we'll discuss them in more detail a little later in the book. For now, all you need to take away from this discussion is that DateTime.Now.To-String() will give you the current date and time as a text string, which you can then tell your <asp:Label/> tag to display.

The rest of the script block simply ties up loose ends. The End Sub in the VB code, and the } in the C# code, mark the end of the script that's to be run when the page is loaded:

Visual Basic	LearningASP\VB\Default.aspx.vb *(excerpt)*

```
    End Sub
```

C#	LearningASP\CS\Default.aspx.cs *(excerpt)*

```
    }
```

One final thing that's worth investigating is the code that ASP.NET generated for you. It's clear by now that your web browser receives only HTML (no server-side code!), so what kind of HTML was generated for that label? The answer is easy to find! With the page displayed in your browser, you can use the browser's **View Source** feature to view the page's HTML code. In the middle of the source, you'll see something like this:

```html
<!DOCTYPE html PUBLIC "-//W3C//DTD XHTML 1.0 Transitional//EN"
    "http://www.w3.org/TR/xhtml1/DTD/xhtml1-transitional.dtd">

<html xmlns="http://www.w3.org/1999/xhtml">
  <head>
    <title>
      Welcome to Build Your Own ASP.NET 3.5 Web Site!
    </title>
  </head>
  <body>
    <form name="form1" method="post" action="Default.aspx"
        id="form1">
    <div>
      <input type="hidden" name="__VIEWSTATE" id="__VIEWSTATE"
        value="…" />
    </div>
    <div>
      <p>Hello there!</p>
      <p>
        The time is now:
        <span id="myTimeLabel">5/13/2008 3:10:38 PM</span>
      </p>
    </div>
    </form>
  </body>
</html>
```

Notice that all the ASP.NET code has gone? Even the `<asp:Label/>` tag has been replaced by a `<span>` tag (which has the same id attribute as the `<asp:Label/>` tag we used) that contains the date and time. There's a mysterious hidden `input` element named __VIEWSTATE that is used by ASP.NET for certain purposes, but we'll ignore it for now. (Don't worry, we'll discuss it a bit later in the book!)

That's how ASP.NET works. From the web browser's point of view, there's nothing special about an ASP.NET page; it's just plain HTML like any other. All the ASP.NET code is run by your web server and converted to plain HTML that's sent to the browser. So far, so good, but the example above was fairly simple. The next chapter will be a bit more challenging as we investigate some valuable programming concepts.

Getting Help

As you develop ASP.NET web applications, you'll undoubtedly have questions that need answers, and problems that need to be solved. Help is at hand—Microsoft has developed the ASP.NET support website.[1] This portal provides useful information for the ASP.NET community, such as news, downloads, articles, and discussion forums. You can also ask questions of the experienced community members in the SitePoint Forums.[2]

Summary

In this chapter, you learned about .NET, including the benefits of ASP.NET, and that it's a part of the .NET Framework.

First, we covered the components of ASP.NET. Then we explored the software that's required not only to use this book, but also in order to progress with ASP.NET development.

You've gained a solid foundation in the basics of ASP.NET. The next chapter will build on this knowledge as we begin to introduce you to ASP.NET in more detail, covering page structure, the languages that you can use, various programming concepts, and the finer points of form processing.

---

[1] http://www.asp.net/
[2] http://www.sitepoint.com/forums/

ASP.NET Basics

So far, you've learned what ASP.NET is, and what it can do. You've installed the software you need to get going, and you even know how to create a simple ASP.NET page. Don't worry if it all seems a little bewildering right now: as this book progresses, you'll learn how easy it is to use ASP.NET at more advanced levels.

As the next few chapters unfold, we'll explore some more advanced topics, including the use of controls and various programming techniques. But before you can begin to develop applications with ASP.NET, you'll need to understand the inner workings of a typical ASP.NET page—with this knowledge, you'll be able to identify the parts of the ASP.NET page referenced in the examples we'll discuss throughout this book. So in this chapter, we'll talk about some key mechanisms of an ASP.NET page, specifically:

- page structure
- view state
- namespaces
- directives

We'll also cover more of VB and C#, two of the "built-in" languages supported by the .NET Framework: VB and C#. As this section progresses, we'll explore the differences and similarities between them, and form a clear idea of the power that they provide for those creating ASP.NET applications.

So, what exactly makes up an ASP.NET page? The next few sections will give you an in-depth understanding of the constructs of a typical ASP.NET page.

ASP.NET Page Structure

ASP.NET pages are simply text files that have the **.aspx** file name extension, and can be placed on any web server equipped with ASP.NET.

When a client requests an ASP.NET page, the web server passes the page to the **ASP.NET runtime**, a program that runs on the web server that's responsible for reading the page and compiling it into a .NET class. This class is then used to produce the HTML that's sent back to the user. Each subsequent request for this page avoids the compilation process: the .NET class can respond directly to the request, producing the page's HTML and sending it to the client until such time as the **.aspx** file changes. This process is illustrated in Figure 2.1.

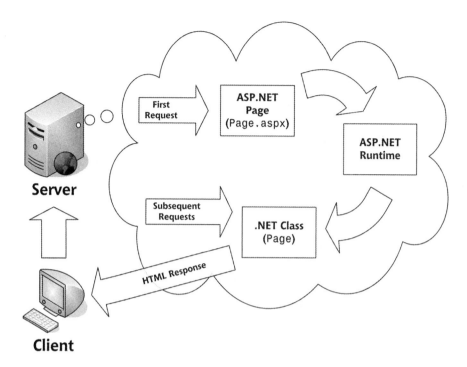

Figure 2.1. The life cycle of the ASP.NET page

An ASP.NET page consists of the following elements:

- directives
- code declaration blocks
- code render blocks
- ASP.NET server controls
- server-side comments
- literal text and HTML tags

For the purpose of examining all the elements that can make up an ASP.NET page, we will not be using any code-behind files as we did in Chapter 1. Code-behind files are useful for separating layout from code by breaking a web form into two files, but here all we're interested in seeing is all the pieces of a web form in one place. This will make it easier to understand the structure of the web form.

The code below represents a version of the page you wrote in Chapter 1, which does not use a code-behind file. You'll notice the server-side script code now resides in a script element:

Visual Basic	LearningASP\VB\Hello.aspx *(excerpt)*

```
<%@ Page Language="VB" %>

<!DOCTYPE html PUBLIC "-//W3C//DTD XHTML 1.0 Transitional//EN"
    "http://www.w3.org/TR/xhtml1/DTD/xhtml1-transitional.dtd">

<script runat="server">
  Protected Sub Page_Load(ByVal sender As Object,
  ➥  ByVal e As System.EventArgs)
    myTimeLabel.Text = DateTime.Now.ToString()
  End Sub
</script>

<html xmlns="http://www.w3.org/1999/xhtml">
  <head runat="server">
    <title>Welcome to Build Your Own ASP.NET 3.5 Web Site!</title>
  </head>
  <body>
    <form id="form1" runat="server">
    <div>
      <p>Hello there!</p>
      <p>
        The time is now:
        <%-- Display the current date and time --%>
        <asp:Label ID="myTimeLabel" runat="server" />
      </p>
      <p>
        <%-- Declare the title as string and set it --%>
        <% Dim Title As String = "This is generated by a code
            render block."%>
        <%= Title %>
      </p>
    </div>
    </form>
  </body>
</html>
```

C#	LearningASP\CS\Hello.aspx *(excerpt)*

```
<%@ Page Language="C#" %>

<!DOCTYPE html PUBLIC "-//W3C//DTD XHTML 1.0 Transitional//EN"
    "http://www.w3.org/TR/xhtml1/DTD/xhtml1-transitional.dtd">
```

```
<script runat="server">
  protected void Page_Load(object sender, EventArgs e)
  {
    myTimeLabel.Text = DateTime.Now.ToString();
  }
</script>

<html xmlns="http://www.w3.org/1999/xhtml">
  <head runat="server">
    <title>Welcome to Build Your Own ASP.NET 3.5 Web Site!</title>
  </head>
  <body>
    <form id="form1" runat="server">
    <div>
      <p>Hello there!</p>
      <p>
        The time is now:
        <%-- Display the current date and time --%>
        <asp:Label ID="myTimeLabel" runat="server" />
      </p>
      <p>
        <%-- Declare the title as string and set it --%>
        <% string Title = "This is generated by a code render
            block."; %>
        <%= Title %>
      </p>
    </div>
    </form>
  </body>
</html>
```

If you like, you can save this piece of code in a file named **Hello.aspx** within the
LearningASP\CS or **LearningASP\VB** directory you created in Chapter 1. You can open
a new file in Visual Web Developer by selecting **Website > Add New Item....** Use a
Web Form template, and, since we are not using a code-behind file for this example,
you need to deselect the **Place code in a separate file** checkbox. Alternatively, you
can copy the file from the source code archive.

Executing the file (by hitting **F5**) should render the result shown in Figure 2.2.

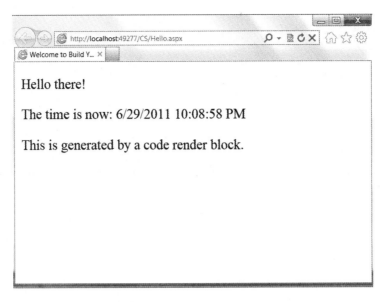

Figure 2.2. Sample page in action

This ASP.NET page contains examples of all the above components (except server-side includes) that make up an ASP.NET page. You won't often use every single element in a given page, but it's important that you're familiar with these elements, their purposes, and how and when it's appropriate to use them.

Directives

The directives section is one of the most important parts of an ASP.NET page. Directives control how a page is compiled, specify how a page is cached by web browsers, aid debugging (error-fixing), and allow you to import classes to use within your page's code. Each directive starts with <%@. This is followed by the directive name, plus any attributes and their corresponding values. The directive then ends with %>.

There are many directives that you can use within your pages, and we'll discuss them in greater detail later. For the moment, however, know that the Import and Page directives are the most useful for ASP.NET development. Looking at our sample ASP.NET page, **Hello.aspx**, we can see that a Page directive was used at the top of the page like so:

Visual Basic	LearningASP\VB\Hello.aspx *(excerpt)*

```
<%@ Page Language="VB" %>
```

C#	LearningASP\CS\Hello.aspx *(excerpt)*

```
<%@ Page Language="C#" %>
```

In this case, the Page directive specifies the language that's to be used for the application logic by setting the Language attribute. The value provided for this attribute, which appears in quotes, specifies that we're using either VB or C#. A whole range of different directives is available; we'll see a few more later in this chapter.

ASP.NET directives can appear anywhere on a page, but they're commonly included at its very beginning.

Code Declaration Blocks

In Chapter 3, we'll talk more about code-behind pages and how they let us separate our application logic from an ASP.NET page's HTML. However, if you're not working with code-behind pages, you must use code declaration blocks to contain all the application logic of your ASP.NET page. This application logic defines variables, subroutines, functions, and more. In our sample page, we've placed the code inside <script> tags with the runat="server" attribute, like so:

Visual Basic	LearningASP\VB\Hello.aspx *(excerpt)*

```
<script runat="server">
  Protected Sub Page_Load(ByVal sender As Object,
➥   ByVal e As System.EventArgs)
    'set the label text to the current time
    myTimeLabel.Text = DateTime.Now.ToString()
  End Sub
</script>
```

C#	LearningASP\CS\Hello.aspx *(excerpt)*

```
<script runat="server">
  protected void Page_Load(object sender, EventArgs e)
  {
    //set the label text to the current time
```

```
      myTimeLabel.Text = DateTime.Now.ToString();
   }
</script>
```

Comments in VB and C# Code

Both of these code snippets contain comments—explanatory text that will be ignored by ASP.NET, but which serves to describe to us how the code works.

In VB code, a single quote or apostrophe (') indicates that the remainder of the line is to be ignored as a comment, while in C# code, two slashes (//) achieve the same end:

Visual Basic	LearningASP\VB\Hello.aspx *(excerpt)*

```
    'set the label text to the current time
```

C#	LearningASP\CS\Hello.aspx *(excerpt)*

```
    //set the label text to the current time
```

C# code also lets us span a comment over multiple lines if we begin it with /* and end it with */, as in this example:

```
/*set the label text
  to the current time */
```

`<script>` Tag Attributes

Before .NET emerged, ASP also supported such script tags using a `runat="server"` attribute. However, they could only ever contain VBScript and, for a variety of reasons, they failed to find favor among developers.

The `<script runat="server">` tag accepts two other attributes: `language` and . We can set the language that's used in this code declaration block via the `language` attribute:

Visual Basic	

```
<script runat="server" language="VB">
```

```
C#
<script runat="server" language="C#">
```

If you don't specify a language within the code declaration block, the ASP.NET page will use the language provided by the `language` attribute of the `Page` directive. Each page's code must be written in a single language; for instance, it's not possible to mix VB and C# in the same page.

`src`The second attribute that's available to us is `src`; this lets us specify an external code file for use within the ASP.NET page:

```
Visual Basic
<script runat="server" language="VB" src="mycodefile.vb">
```

```
C#
<script runat="server" language="C#" src="mycodefile.cs">
```

We also can use these `<script>` blocks to write JavaScript code. This is especially useful for making our web pages more dynamic.

Code Render Blocks

You can use code render blocks to define inline code or expressions that will execute when a page is rendered. Code within a code render block is executed immediately when it is encountered during page rendering. On the other hand, code within a code *declaration* block (within `<script>` tags) is executed only when it is called or triggered by user or page interactions. There are two types of code render blocks—inline code, and inline expressions—both of which are typically written within the body of the ASP.NET page.

Inline code render blocks execute one or more statements, and are placed directly inside a page's HTML between `<%` and `%>` delimiters. In our example, the following is a code render block:

Visual Basic	LearningASP\VB\Hello.aspx *(excerpt)*

```
<% Dim Title As String = "This is generated by a code render
➥ block." %>
```

C#	LearningASP\CS\Hello.aspx *(excerpt)*

```
<% string Title = "This is generated by a code render block."; %>
```

These code blocks simply declare a String variable called Title, and assign it the value This is generated by a code render block.

Inline expression render blocks can be compared to Response.Write in classic ASP. They start with <%= and end with %>, and are used to display the values of variables and the results of methods on a page. In our example, an inline expression appears immediately after our inline code block:

Visual Basic	LearningASP\VB\Hello.aspx *(excerpt)*

```
<%= Title %>
```

C#	LearningASP\CS\Hello.aspx *(excerpt)*

```
<%= Title %>
```

If you're familiar with classic ASP, you'll know what this code does: it simply outputs the value of the variable Title that we declared in the previous inline code block.

As a new feature of the ASP.NET 4 release, you can also use code render blocks to "HTML Encode" your output. Html encoding is a fancy term for ensuring your text is output so it can be safely read by the browser instead of having it interpreted as HTML code itself. For instance, if you wanted to put a less-than < or greater-than sign >, these would automatically be interpreted by the browser as HTML tags. Html encoding ensures the actual characters are displayed. Consider the following example:

```
<%: "5 is > 3" %>
```

ASP.NET Server Controls

At the heart of any ASP.NET page lie server controls, which represent dynamic elements with which your users can interact. There are three basic types of server control: ASP.NET controls, HTML controls, and web user controls.

Usually, an ASP.NET control must reside within a `<form runat="server">` tag in order to function correctly. Controls offer the following advantages to ASP.NET developers:

- They give us the ability to access HTML elements easily from within our code: we can change these elements' characteristics, check their values, or even update them dynamically from our server-side programming language of choice.

- ASP.NET controls retain their properties thanks to a mechanism called **view state**. We'll be covering view state later in this chapter. For now, you need to know that view state prevents users from losing the data they've entered into a form once that form has been sent to the server for processing. When the response comes back to the client, text box entries, drop-down list selections, and so on are all retained through view state.

- With ASP.NET controls, developers are able to separate a page's presentational elements (everything the user sees) from its application logic (the dynamic portions of the ASP.NET page), so that each can be maintained separately.

- Many ASP.NET controls can be "bound" to the data sources from which they will extract data for display with minimal (if any) coding effort.

ASP.NET is all about controls, so we'll be discussing them in greater detail as we move through this book. In particular, Chapter 4 explains many of the controls that ship with ASP.NET. For now, though, let's continue our dissection of an ASP.NET page.

Server-side Comments

Server-side comments allow you to include within the page comments or notes that won't be processed by ASP.NET. Traditional HTML uses the `<!--` and `-->` character sequences to delimit comments; any information included between these tags won't be displayed to the user. ASP.NET comments look very similar, but use the sequences `<%--` and `--%>`.

Our ASP.NET example contains two server-side comment blocks, the first of which is:

LearningASP\VB\Hello.aspx *(excerpt)*

```
<%-- Display the current date and time --%>
```

The difference between ASP.NET comments and HTML comments is that ASP.NET comments are not sent to the client at all; HTML comments are, so they're not suited to commenting out ASP.NET code. Consider the following example:

```
C#

<!--
<% string Title = "This is generated by a code render block."; %>
<%= Title %>
-->
```

Here, it looks as though a developer has attempted to use an HTML comment to stop a code render block from being executed. Unfortunately, HTML comments will only hide information from the browser, not the ASP.NET runtime. So in this case, although we won't see anything in the browser that represents these two lines, they will be processed by ASP.NET, and the value of the variable `Title` will be sent to the browser inside an HTML comment, as shown here:

```
<!--

This is generated by a code render block.
-->
```

The code could be modified to use server-side comments very simply:

```
C#

<%--
<% string Title = "This is generated by a code render block."; %>
<%= Title %>
--%>
```

The ASP.NET runtime will ignore the contents of this comment, and the value of the `Title` variable will not be output.

Literal Text and HTML Tags

The final elements of an ASP.NET page are plain old text and HTML. Generally, you can't do without these elements—after all, HTML allows the display of the information in your ASP.NET controls and code in a way that's suitable for users and their browsers. Let's take a look at the literal text and HTML tags that were used to produce the display in the Visual Basic version of our sample page (the text and HTML in the C# version is identical):

Visual Basic   *LearningASP\VB\Hello.aspx (excerpt)*

```
<%@ Page Language="VB" %>

<!DOCTYPE html PUBLIC "-//W3C//DTD XHTML 1.0 Transitional//EN"
    "http://www.w3.org/TR/xhtml1/DTD/xhtml1-transitional.dtd">

<script runat="server">
  Protected Sub Page_Load(ByVal sender As Object,
➥    ByVal e As System.EventArgs)
    myTimeLabel.Text = DateTime.Now.ToString()
  End Sub
</script>

<html xmlns="http://www.w3.org/1999/xhtml">
  <head runat="server">
    <title>Welcome to Build Your Own ASP.NET 3.5 Web Site!</title>
  </head>
  <body>
    <form id="form1" runat="server">
    <div>
      <p>Hello there!</p>
      <p>
        The time is now:
        <%-- Display the current date and time --%>
        <asp:Label ID="myTimeLabel" runat="server" />
      </p>
      <p>
        <%-- Declare the title as string and set it --%>
        <% Dim Title As String = "This is generated by a code
           render block."%>
        <%= Title %>
```

```
      </p>
    </div>
    </form>
  </body>
</html>
```

The bold code above highlights the fact that literal text and HTML tags provide the structure for presenting our dynamic data. Without these elements, this page would have no format, and the browser would be unable to understand it.

By now, you should have a clearer understanding of the structure of an ASP.NET page. As you work through the examples in this book, you'll begin to realize that, in many cases, you won't need to use all of these elements. For the most part, your development will be modularized within code-behind files or code declaration blocks, and all of the dynamic portions of your pages will be contained within code render blocks or controls located inside a `<form runat="server">` tag.

In the following sections, we'll explore view state, discuss working with directives, and shine a little light on the languages that can be used within ASP.NET.

View State

ASP.NET controls automatically retain their data when a page is sent to the server in response to an event (such as a user clicking a button). Microsoft calls this persistence of data **view state**. In the past, developers would've had to resort to hacks to have the application remember the item a user had selected in a drop-down menu, or store the content entered into a text box; typically, these hacks would have relied on hidden form fields.

This is no longer the case. Once they're submitted to the server for processing, ASP.NET pages automatically retain all the information contained in text boxes and drop-down lists, as well as radio button and checkbox selections. They even keep track of dynamically generated tags, controls, and text. Consider the following code written in the "ancient" ASP (not ASP.NET!) framework:

```
<!DOCTYPE html PUBLIC "-//W3C//DTD XHTML 1.0 Strict//EN"
    "http://www.w3.org/TR/xhtml1/DTD/xhtml1-strict.dtd">
<html>
  <head>
```

```
    <title>Sample Page using VBScript</title>
  </head>
  <body>
    <form method="post" action="sample.asp">
      <input type="text" name="nameTextBox"/>
      <input type="submit" name="submitButton"
          value="Click Me" />
      <%
      If Request.Form("nameTextBox") <> "" Then
        Response.Write(Request.Form("nameTextBox"))
      End If
      %>
    </form>
  </body>
</html>
```

Loading this page through an ASP-enabled web server (such as IIS) would reveal that the view state is not automatically preserved. When the user submits the form, the information that was typed into the text box is cleared, although it's still available in the `Request.Form("nameTextBox")` property. The equivalent page in ASP.NET demonstrates this data persistence using view state:

Visual Basic   LearningASP\VB\ViewState.aspx

```
<%@ Page Language="VB" %>

<!DOCTYPE html PUBLIC "-//W3C//DTD XHTML 1.0 Transitional//EN"
    "http://www.w3.org/TR/xhtml1/DTD/xhtml1-transitional.dtd">

<script runat="server">
  Sub Click(ByVal s As Object, ByVal e As EventArgs)
    messageLabel.Text = nameTextBox.Text
  End Sub
</script>

<html xmlns="http://www.w3.org/1999/xhtml">
<head runat="server">
  <title>View State Example</title>
</head>
<body>
  <form id="form1" runat="server">
  <div>
    <asp:TextBox ID="nameTextBox" runat="server" />
    <asp:Button ID="submitButton" runat="server"
```

```
        Text="Click Me" OnClick="Click" />
      <asp:Label ID="messageLabel" runat="server" />
    </div>
    </form>
  </body>
  </html>
```

C#   LearningASP\CS\ViewState.aspx

```
<%@ Page Language="C#" %>

<!DOCTYPE html PUBLIC "-//W3C//DTD XHTML 1.0 Transitional//EN"
    "http://www.w3.org/TR/xhtml1/DTD/xhtml1-transitional.dtd">

<script runat="server">
  void Click(Object s, EventArgs e)
  {
    messageLabel.Text = nameTextBox.Text;
  }
</script>

<html xmlns="http://www.w3.org/1999/xhtml">
<head runat="server">
  <title>View State Example</title>
</head>
<body>
  <form id="form1" runat="server">
    <div>
      <asp:TextBox id="nameTextBox" runat="server" />
      <asp:Button id="submitButton" runat="server"
          Text="Click Me" OnClick="Click" />
      <asp:Label id="messageLabel" runat="server" />
    </div>
  </form>
</body>
</html>
```

In this case, the code uses ASP.NET controls with the runat="server" attribute. As you can see in Figure 2.3, the text from the box appears on the page when the button is clicked, but also notice that the data remains in the text box! The data in this example is preserved by view state.

Figure 2.3. ASP.NET maintaining the state of the controls

You can see the benefits of view state already. But where's all that information stored?

ASP.NET pages maintain view state by encrypting the data within a hidden form field. View the source of the page after you've submitted the form, and look for the following code:

```
<input type="hidden" name="__VIEWSTATE" id="__VIEWSTATE"
    value="/wEPDwUKLTEwNDY1NzgOMQ9...OfMCR+FN5P6v5pkTQwNEl5xhBk" />
```

This is a standard HTML hidden form field. All information that's relevant to the view state of the page is stored within this hidden form field as an encrypted string.

View state is enabled for every page by default.Using view state comes with a slight performance penalty due to the additional HTML being emitted by the server. If you don't intend to use view state, it is recommended that you disable it. To do this, set the EnableViewState property of the Page directive to false:

```
<%@ Page EnableViewState="False" %>
```

Disabling View State, Control by Control

View state can also be disabled for particular controls in a page: simply set their EnableViewState property to false. We'll see working examples of this in the following chapters.

Another new feature in ASP.NET 4 is the `ViewStateMode` feature. This allows you to turn off view state for an entire page, but allows for a control to override it. `ViewStateMode` is enabled in the page directive, and it only works if `EnableViewState` is set to true. If `EnableViewState` is set to false, all view state is disabled, regardless of the setting of the `ViewStateMode`. `ViewStateMode` has three settings—Inherit, Enabled, or Disabled. Consider the following code:

```
<%@ Page EnableViewState="True" ViewStateMode="Disabled" %>
<asp:Label id="messageLabel" runat="server" ViewStateMode="Enabled"
  />

<asp:Label id="errorLabel" runat="server" ViewStateMode="Inherit" />
<asp:Label id="copyrightLabel" runat="server" ViewStateMode=➥
  "Disabled" />
```

Because view state is enabled through the page directive (`EnableViewState="true"`), the ViewStateMode directive is allowed to be used. In our example, it is set to Disabled. Therefore, all controls on the page will have their view states disabled unless it is specifically overridden. The `messageLabel` control does just so, and it will have view state. The next control, `errorLabel`, is chosen to inherit the settings of the parent, which is the page's directive of Disabled: therefore, it will not have view state enabled. Inherit is also the default option of all controls if an option isn't specifically chosen. The final `copyrightLabel` control has its view state specifically disabled. This allows finer control over your view state. You can now disable view state for your entire page except for one control without having to change every single control on your page. Speaking of page directives, it's time to take a closer look at these curious beasts!

Working with Directives

For the most part, ASP.NET pages resemble traditional HTML pages with a few additions. In essence, just using the **.aspx** extension for an HTML file will ensure that IIS passes the page to the .NET Framework for processing. However, before you can work with certain, more advanced features, you'll need to know how to use directives.

We talked a little about directives and what they can do earlier in this chapter. You learned that directives control how a page is created and cached, help with bugfixing, and allow us to import advanced functionality for use within our code. Three of the most commonly used directives are:

Page

> This directive defines page-specific attributes for the ASP.NET page, such as the language used for server-side code. We've already seen this `Page` in use.

Import

> The `Import` directive makes functionality that's been defined elsewhere available in a given page. The following example, for instance, imports functionality from the `System.Web.Mail` namespace, which you could use to send email from a page. Namespaces are simply .NET's way of keeping all its functionality neatly organized (we'll see how they work in Chapter 3):

```
<%@ Import Namespace="System.Web.Mail" %>
```

> You'll become very familiar with this directive as you work through this book.

Register

> This directive allows you to register a user control for use on your page. We'll cover `Register` in Chapter 4, but the directive looks something like this:

```
<%@ Register TagPrefix="uc" TagName="footer"
    Src="footer.ascx" %>
```

ASP.NET Languages

As we saw in the previous chapter, .NET supports many different languages. If you're used to writing ASP 2.0 or ASP 3.0, you may think the choice of VBScript or JScript would be an obvious one. But, with ASP.NET, Microsoft did away with VBScript, merging it with Visual Basic. ASP.NET's support for C# is likely to find favor with developers from other backgrounds. By the end of this section, you'll likely agree that the similarities between the two are astonishing—any differences are minor and, in most cases, easy to figure out.

Traditional server technologies are much more constrained in terms of the development languages they offer. For instance, old-style CGI scripts were typically written with Perl or C/C++, JSP uses Java, Coldfusion uses CFML, and PHP is a technology and a language rolled into one. .NET's support for many different languages lets developers choose the ones they prefer. To keep things simple, this book will consider the two most popular: VB and C#. You can choose the language that feels more comfortable to you, or stick with your current favorite if you have one.

Visual Basic

The latest version of Visual Basic is the result of a dramatic overhaul of Microsoft's hugely popular Visual Basic language. With the inception of Rapid Application Development (RAD) in the 1990s, Visual Basic became extremely popular, allowing in-house teams and software development shops to bang out applications hand over fist. The latest version of VB has many advantages over older versions, most notably the fact that it has now became a fully object oriented language. At last, it can call itself a true programming language that's on a par with the likes of Java and C++. Despite the changes, VB generally stays close to the structured, legible syntax that has always made it so easy to read, use, and maintain.

C#

The official line is that Microsoft created C# in an attempt to produce a programming language that coupled the simplicity of Visual Basic with the power and flexibility of C++. However, there's little doubt that its development was at least hurried along by Microsoft's legal disputes with Sun. After Microsoft's treatment (some would say abuse) of Sun's Java programming language, Microsoft was forced to stop developing its own version of Java, and instead develop C# and another now defunct language, J#. C# is currently one of the most popular in-demand languages by employers because the syntax is very much like what is taught in universities, as well as being easy to pick up by C++ developers.

Summary

In this chapter, we started out by introducing key aspects of an ASP.NET page including directives, code declaration blocks, code render blocks, includes, comments, and controls. We took a closer look at the two most popular languages that ASP.NET supports, which we'll be using throughout this book. In the next chapter, we'll create a few more ASP.NET pages to demonstrate form processing techniques and programming basics, before we turn our attention to the topic of object oriented programming for the Web.

3

VB and C# Programming Basics

One of the great things about using ASP.NET is that we can pick and choose which of the various .NET languages we like. In this chapter, we'll look at the key programming principles that will underpin our use of Visual Basic and C#. We'll start by discussing some of the fundamental concepts of programming ASP.NET web applications using these two languages. We'll explore programming fundamentals such as variables, arrays, functions, operators, conditionals, loops, and events, and work through a quick introduction to object oriented programming (OOP). Next, we'll dive into namespaces and address the topic of classes—seeing how they're exposed through namespaces, and which ones you'll use most often.

The final sections of the chapter cover some of the ideas underlying modern, effective ASP.NET design, including code-behind and the value it provides by helping us separate code from presentation. We finish with an examination of how object oriented programming techniques impact upon the ASP.NET developer.

Programming Basics

One of the building blocks of an ASP.NET page is the application logic: the actual programming code that allows the page to function. To get anywhere with ASP.NET, you need to grasp the concept of **events**. Most ASP.NET pages will contain controls such as text boxes, checkboxes, and lists. Each of these controls allow the user to interact with the application in some way: checking checkboxes, scrolling through lists, selecting list items, and so on. Whenever one of these actions is performed, the control will raise an event. It's by handling these events within our code that we get ASP.NET pages to do what we want.

For example, imagine that a user clicks a button on an ASP.NET page. That button (or, more specifically, the ASP.NET `Button` control) raises an event (in this case, it will be the `Click` event). A method called an **event handler** executes automatically when an event is raised—in this case, the event handler code performs a specific action for that button. For instance, the `Click` event handler could save form data to a file, or retrieve requested information from a database. Events really are the key to ASP.NET programming, which is why we'll start this chapter by taking a closer look at them.

It wouldn't be practical, or even necessary, to cover *all* aspects of VB and C# in this book, so we're going to discuss enough to get you started, and then complete this chapter's projects and samples using both languages. Moreover, the programming concepts you'll learn here will be more than adequate to complete the great majority of day-to-day web development tasks using ASP.NET.

Control Events and Subroutines

As I just mentioned, an event (sometimes more than one) is raised, and handler code is called, in response to a specific action on a particular control. For instance, the code below creates a server-side button and label. Note the use of the `OnClick` attribute on the `Button` control. If you want to test the code, save the file in the **LearningASP** directory you've been using for the other examples. Here's the VB version:

```
Visual Basic                                    LearningASP\VB\ClickEvent.aspx

<%@ Page Language="VB" %>

<!DOCTYPE html PUBLIC "-//W3C//DTD XHTML 1.0 Transitional//EN"
    "http://www.w3.org/TR/xhtml1/DTD/xhtml1-transitional.dtd">

<script runat="server">
  Public Sub button_Click(ByVal s As Object, ByVal e As EventArgs)
```

```
      messageLabel.Text = "Hello World"
    End Sub
</script>

<html xmlns="http://www.w3.org/1999/xhtml">
  <head runat="server">
    <title>Click the Button</title>
  </head>
  <body>
    <form id="form1" runat="server">
    <div>
      <asp:Button ID="button" runat="server"
          OnClick="button_Click" Text="Click Me" />
      <asp:Label ID="messageLabel" runat="server" />
    </div>
    </form>
  </body>
</html>
```

Here's an excerpt from the C# version:

```
C#                                    LearningASP\CS\ClickEvent.aspx (excerpt)

<%@ Page Language="C#" %>
⋮
<script runat="server">
  public void button_Click(Object s, EventArgs e)
  {
    messageLabel.Text = "Hello World";
  }
</script>
⋮
```

The HTML and ASP.NET elements in the page are the same for both the C# and VB versions of the code, so I've shown only the differences in the code listing for the C# version above. This approach will be used for the other examples in this chapter, too. The complete C# version can be found in the code archive.

When the button's clicked, it raises the Click event, and ASP.NET checks the button's OnClick attribute to find the name of the handler subroutine for that event. In the previous code, we instruct ASP.NET to call the button_Click routine. You'll see the code for the button_Click routine within the <script> code declaration block:

Visual Basic	LearningASP\VB\ClickEvent.aspx *(excerpt)*

```
<script runat="server">
  Public Sub button_Click(ByVal s As Object, ByVal e As EventArgs)
    messageLabel.Text = "Hello World"
  End Sub
</script>
```

C#	LearningASP\CS\ClickEvent.aspx *(excerpt)*

```
<script runat="server">
  public void button_Click(Object s, EventArgs e)
  {
    messageLabel.Text = "Hello World";
  }
</script>
```

This code simply sets a message to display on the Label element that we declared with the button. So, when this page is run, and users click the button, they'll see the message "Hello World" appear next to it, as shown in Figure 3.1.

Figure 3.1. Handling the Click event

By now, you'll be starting to come to grips with the idea of events, and the ways in which they're used to call particular subroutines. In fact, there are many events that your controls can use, though some of them are found only on certain controls.

Here's the complete set of attributes that the Button control supports for handling events:

OnClick

As we've seen, the subroutine indicated by this attribute is called for the Click event, which occurs when the user clicks the button.

OnCommand

As with OnClick, the subroutine indicated by this attribute is called when the button is clicked.

OnLoad

The subroutine indicated by this attribute is called when the button is loaded for the first time—usually when the page first loads.

OnInit

When the button is initialized, any subroutine given in this attribute will be called.

OnPreRender

We can use this attribute to run code just before the button is rendered.

OnDisposed

The subroutine specified by this attribute is executed when the button is released from memory.

OnDataBinding

This attribute fires when the button is bound to a data source.

Don't worry too much about the details of all these events and when they occur; we just want you to understand that a single control can produce a number of different events. In the case of the Button control, you'll almost always be interested in the Click event; the others are only useful in rather obscure circumstances.

When a control raises an event, the specified subroutine (if one is specified) is executed. Let's take a look at the structure of a typical subroutine that interacts with a web control:

```
Visual Basic
```

```vbnet
Public Sub mySubName(s As Object, e As EventArgs)
  : subroutine code...
End Sub
```

```
C#
```

```csharp
public void mySubName(Object s, EventArgs e)
{
  : subroutine code...
}
```

Let's take a moment to break down all the components that make up a typical subroutine:

Public (Visual Basic)
public (C#)

> This keyword defines the level of visibility the subroutine has in relation to the rest of the page. There are a few different options to choose from, the most frequently used being `Public` (for a global subroutine that can be used anywhere within the entire page) and `Private` (for subroutines that are available for the specific class only). We'll analyze these options in more detail a bit later in the chapter.

Sub (Visual Basic)
void (C#)

> This keyword defines the chunk of code as a subroutine. A subroutine is a named block of code that doesn't return a result; thus, in C#, we use the `void` keyword, which means exactly what the name says. We don't need this in VB, though, because the `Sub` keyword implies that no value is returned.

mySubName(…)

> This part gives the name we've chosen for the subroutine. The parameters and their data types are mentioned in the parentheses.

s As Object (Visual Basic)

Object s (C#)

> When we write a subroutine that will function as an event handler, it must accept two parameters. The first is a reference to the control that fired the event. Each control has a particular type, such as `Label` or `TextBox`, but `Object` is a generic type that can be used to reference any kind of object in .NET—even basic type, such as numbers or strings. Here, we're putting that `Object` in a variable named s (again, we'll talk more about variables later in this chapter). We can then use that variable to access features and settings of the specific control from our subroutine.

e As EventArgs (Visual Basic)

EventArgs e (C#)

> This, the second parameter, contains certain information that's specific to the event that was raised. Note that, in many cases, you won't need to use either of these two parameters, so you don't need to worry about them too much at this stage.

As this chapter progresses, you'll see how subroutines that are associated with particular events by the appropriate attributes on controls can revolutionize the way your user interacts with your application.

Page Events

Until now, we've considered only events that are raised by controls. However, there is another type of event: the **page event**. Technically, a page is simply another type of control, so its events follow the same principles as those of controls.

The idea is the same as for control events, except that here, it's the page as a whole that generates the events.[1] You've already used one of these events: the `Page_Load` event, which is fired when the page loads for the first time. Note that we don't need to associate handlers for page events as we did for control events; instead, we just place our handler code inside a subroutine with a preset name.

The following list outlines the most frequently used page event subroutines:

---

[1] Strictly speaking, a page is simply another type of control, so page events *are* actually control events. But when you're first learning ASP.NET, it can be helpful to think of page events as being different, especially since you don't usually use `OnEventName` attributes to assign subroutines to handle them.

Page_Init

called when the page is about to be initialized with its basic settings

Page_Load

called once the browser request has been processed, and all the controls in the page have their updated values

Page_PreRender

called once all objects have reacted to the browser request and any resulting events, but before any response has been sent to the browser

Page_UnLoad

called when the page is no longer needed by the server, and is ready to be discarded

The order in which the events are listed above is also the order in which they're executed. In other words, the Page_Init event is the first event raised by the page, followed by Page_Load, Page_PreRender, and finally Page_UnLoad.

The best way to illustrate how these events work is through an example. Create the following **PageEvents.aspx** file in your **LearningASP** directory:

```
Visual Basic                                    LearningASP\VB\PageEvents.aspx

<%@ Page Language="VB" %>

<!DOCTYPE html PUBLIC "-//W3C//DTD XHTML 1.0 Transitional//EN"
    "http://www.w3.org/TR/xhtml1/DTD/xhtml1-transitional.dtd">

<script runat="server">
  Sub Page_Init(ByVal s As Object, ByVal e As EventArgs)
    messageLabel.Text = "1. Page_Init <br/>"
  End Sub
  Sub Page_Load(ByVal s As Object, ByVal e As EventArgs)
    messageLabel.Text += "2. Page_Load <br/>"
  End Sub
  Sub Page_PreRender(ByVal s As Object, ByVal e As EventArgs)
    messageLabel.Text += "3. Page_PreRender <br/>"
  End Sub
  Sub Page_UnLoad(ByVal s As Object, ByVal e As EventArgs)
    messageLabel.Text += "4. Page_UnLoad <br/>"
  End Sub
```

```
</script>

<html xmlns="http://www.w3.org/1999/xhtml">
  <head runat="server">
    <title>Page Events</title>
  </head>
  <body>
    <form id="form1" runat="server">
    <div>
      <asp:Label ID="messageLabel" runat="server" />
    </div>
    </form>
  </body>
</html>
```

C#	LearningASP\CS\PageEvents.aspx *(excerpt)*

```
<%@ Page Language="C#" %>
⋮
<script runat="server">
  void Page_Init(Object s, EventArgs e)
  {
    messageLabel.Text = "1. Page_Init <br/>";
  }
  void Page_Load(Object s, EventArgs e)
  {
    messageLabel.Text += "2. Page_Load <br/>";
  }
  void Page_PreRender(Object s, EventArgs e)
  {
    messageLabel.Text += "3. Page_PreRender <br/>";
  }
  void Page_UnLoad(Object s, EventArgs e)
  {
    messageLabel.Text += "4. Page_UnLoad <br/>";
  }
</script>
⋮
```

You can see that the event handlers (the functions that are executed to handle the events) aren't specifically defined anywhere. There's no need to define them, because these events are generated by default by the ASP.NET page, and their handlers have the default names that we've used in the code (Page_Init, Page_Load, and so on). As the page loads, it will generate a number of events. We've added a text message to the `Label` control within each event's event handler; this will give us visual proof that the events actually fire in order. No matter which version of the code you execute (C# or VB), the output should look like Figure 3.2.

As you can see, `Page_UnLoad` doesn't generate any output. Why not? At that point, the HTML output has already been generated and sent to the browser.

Popular `Page_Load`

The event you'll make the most use of in your code is `Page_Load`. However, in certain situations the other events will be helpful as well. It's also worth noting that ASP.NET supports other events, which we haven't covered here. You'll only need those when it comes to certain complex applications that aren't within the scope of this book.

Variables and Variable Declaration

Variables are fundamental to programming, and you're almost certain to have come across the term before. Basically, variables let you give a name, or identifier, to a specific piece of data; we can then use that identifier to store, modify, and retrieve the data in question.

VB and C# have access to the same basic data types, which are defined as foundation classes of the .NET Framework. However, they can be named differently, as each language defines its own aliases. There are many different kinds of data types, including strings, integers (whole numbers), and floating point numbers (fractions or decimals). Before you can use a variable in VB or C#, you must specify the types of data it can contain using keywords such as `Integer` and `Decimal`, like this:

Visual Basic

```
Dim name As String
Dim age As Integer
```

C#

```
string name;
int age;
```

Figure 3.2. Handling ASP.NET events

These lines declare the types of data we want our variables to store, and are therefore known as **variable declarations**. In VB, we use the keyword `Dim`, which is short for "dimension," while in C#, we simply precede the variable name with the appropriate data type.

Sometimes, we want to set an initial value for variables that we declare; we can do this using a process known as **initialization**, which simply involves declaring a variable and setting its initial value:

Visual Basic

```
Dim carType As String = "BMW"
```

C#

```
string carType = "BMW";
```

We can declare and/or initialize a group of variables of the same type simultaneously using a comma-delimited list. This practice isn't recommended, though, as it makes the code more difficult to read. I know you're curious, so here's how it would look:

Visual Basic

```
Dim carType As String, carColor As String = "blue"
```

C#

```
string carType, carColor = "blue";
```

Table 3.1 lists the most useful data types available in VB and C#.

Table 3.1. Commonly Used Data Types

VB	C#	Description
Integer	int	whole numbers in the range -2,147,483,648 to 2,147,483,647
Decimal	decimal	numbers up to 28 decimal places; this command is used most often when dealing with costs of items
String	string	any text value
Char	char	a single character (letter, number, or symbol)
Boolean	bool	true or false
Object	object	a generic type that can be used to refer to objects of any type

You'll encounter many other data types as you progress, but this list provides an overview of the ones you'll use most often.

Many Aliases Are Available

These data types are the VB- and C#-specific aliases for types of the .NET Framework. For example, instead of Integer or int, you could use `System.Int32` in any .NET language; likewise, instead of Boolean or bool, you could use `System.Boolean`, and so on.

To sum up, once you've declared a variable as a given type, it can only hold data of that type: you can't put a string into an integer variable, for instance. However, there are frequently times when you'll need to convert one data type to another. Have a look at this code:

Visual Basic

```
Dim intX As Integer
Dim strY As String = "35"
intX = strY + 6
```

```
C#
int intX;
string strY = "35";
intX = strY + 6;
```

Now, you'd be forgiven for assuming that this could make sense—after all, the string strY contains a number, so we may wish to add it to another number. Well, this isn't so simple for a computer!

VB performs some conversions for us. The VB version of the code will execute without a hitch, because the string will be converted to a number before the mathematical operation is applied. C#, on the other hand, will throw an error, as it's more strict than VB about conversions.

As a rule of thumb, it's better to stay on the safe side and avoid mixing types wherever possible.

VB and VB and C#: Strongly Typed Languages

Both VB and C# are **strongly typed** languages, which means that they're very strict about data types. Many other languages—mostly scripting languages such as JavaScript—are loosely typed, which means that they're more flexible when it comes to dealing with data types, but can cause unintended behaviour if you're not careful. For example, if you try to calculate the sum of a number and a string, as we did in the previous code snippet, the JavaScript interpreter would make the conversion for you automatically ... but what does it convert? It would convert the integer **6** into a string and join it with the string **35** to make **356**—not what you intended at all! At times, despite being a strongly typed language at heart, VB does a bit of background work for you, which makes it slightly easier to work with.

In .NET, you can (and sometimes need to) explicitly convert the string into an integer before you're able to add them up:

```
Visual Basic
Dim intX As Integer
Dim strY As String = "35"
intX = Int32.Parse(strY) + 6
```

```
C#
int intX;
string strY = "35";
intX = Convert.ToInt32(strY) + 6;
```

Now, both of these examples can be executed successfully—the server ends up adding two numbers, rather than a number and a string, which we tried initially, because the string value is converted to a number value before the addition occurs. This principle holds true whenever we're mixing types in a single expression.

Arrays

Arrays are a special kind of variable that's tailored for storing related items of the same data type. Any one item in an array can be accessed using the array's name, followed by that item's position in the array (its offset). Let's create a sample page to see how it's done:

```
Visual Basic                                          LearningASP\VB\Arrays.aspx
<%@ Page Language="VB" %>

<!DOCTYPE html PUBLIC "-//W3C//DTD XHTML 1.0 Transitional//EN"
    "http://www.w3.org/TR/xhtml1/DTD/xhtml1-transitional.dtd">

<script runat="server">
  Sub Page_Load()
    Dim drinkList(4) As String
    drinkList(0) = "Water"
    drinkList(1) = "Juice"
    drinkList(2) = "Soda"
    drinkList(3) = "Milk"
    drinkLabel.Text = drinkList(1)
  End Sub
</script>

<html xmlns="http://www.w3.org/1999/xhtml">
  <head runat="server">
    <title>Arrays</title>
  </head>
  <body>
    <form id="form1" runat="server">
```

```
    <div>
      <asp:Label ID="drinkLabel" runat="server" />
    </div>
    </form>
  </body>
</html>
```

| C# | LearningASP\CS\Arrays.aspx *(excerpt)* |

```
<%@ Page Language="C#" %>
⋮
<script runat="server">
  void Page_Load()
  {
    string[] drinkList = new string[4];
    drinkList[0] = "Water";
    drinkList[1] = "Juice";
    drinkList[2] = "Soda";
    drinkList[3] = "Milk";
    drinkLabel.Text = drinkList[1];
  }
</script>
⋮
```

The results of this code are shown in Figure 3.3.

Figure 3.3. Reading an element from an array

There are some important points to pick up from this code. First, notice how we declare an array. In VB, it looks like a regular declaration for a string, except that the number of items we want the array to contain is provided in parentheses after the name:

Visual Basic	LearningASP\VB\Arrays.aspx *(excerpt)*

```
Dim drinkList(4) As String
```

In C#, it's a little different. First, we declare that drinkList is an array by following the data type with two empty square brackets. We then use the new keyword to specify that this is an array of four items:

C#	LearningASP\CS\Arrays.aspx *(excerpt)*

```
string[] drinkList = new string[4];
```

A crucial point to realize here is that, in both C# and VB, these arrays are known as **zero-based** arrays. In a zero-based array, the first item has position 0, the second has position 1, and so on through to the last item, which has a position that's one less than the size of the array (3, in this case). So, we specify each item in our array like this:

Visual Basic	LearningASP\VB\Arrays.aspx *(excerpt)*

```
drinkList(0) = "Water"
drinkList(1) = "Juice"
drinkList(2) = "Soda"
drinkList(3) = "Milk"
```

C#	LearningASP\CS\Arrays.aspx *(excerpt)*

```
drinkList[0] = "Water";
drinkList[1] = "Juice";
drinkList[2] = "Soda";
drinkList[3] = "Milk";
```

Note that C# uses square brackets for arrays, while VB uses standard parentheses. We have to remember that arrays are zero-based when we set the label text to the value of the second array item, as shown here:

Visual Basic	LearningASP\VB\Arrays.aspx *(excerpt)*

```
drinkLabel.Text = drinkList(1)
```

C#	LearningASP\CS\Arrays.aspx *(excerpt)*

```
drinkLabel.Text = drinkList[1];
```

To help this fact sink in, you might like to try changing this code to show the third item in the list, instead of the second. Can you work out what change you'd need to make? That's right—you need only to change the number in the brackets to reflect the new item's position in the array (don't forget to start at zero). In fact, it's this ability to select one item from a list using only its numerical location that makes arrays so useful in programming. We'll experience this benefit first-hand as we get further into the book.

Functions

Functions are very similar to subroutines, but for one key difference: they return a value. In VB, we declare a function using the Function keyword in place of Sub, while in C#, we simply have to specify the return type in place of void. The following code shows a simple example:

Visual Basic	LearningASP\VB\Functions.aspx

```
<%@ Page Language="VB" %>

<!DOCTYPE html PUBLIC "-//W3C//DTD XHTML 1.0 Transitional//EN"
    "http://www.w3.org/TR/xhtml1/DTD/xhtml1-transitional.dtd">

<script runat="server">
  Function getName() As String
    Return "John Doe"
  End Function

  Sub Page_Load(ByVal s As Object, ByVal e As EventArgs)
    messageLabel.Text = getName()
  End Sub
</script>

<html xmlns="http://www.w3.org/1999/xhtml">
  <head runat="server">
```

```
    <title>ASP.NET Functions</title>
  </head>
  <body>
    <form id="form1" runat="server">
    <div>
        <asp:Label id="messageLabel" runat="server" />
    </div>
    </form>
  </body>
</html>
```

```
<%@ Page Language="C#" %>
⋮
<script runat="server">
  string getName()
  {
    return "John Doe";
  }

  void Page_Load()
  {
    messageLabel.Text = getName();
  }
</script>
⋮
```

When the page above is loaded in the browser, the Load event will be raised, causing the Page_Load event handler to be called; in turn, it will call the getName function. The getName function returns a simple string that we can assign to our label. Figure 3.4 shows the result in the browser.

Figure 3.4. Executing an ASP.NET function

In this simple example, we're merely returning a fixed string, but the function could just as easily retrieve the name from a database (or some other location). The point is that, regardless of how the function gets its data, we call it in just the same way.

When we're declaring our function, we must remember to specify the correct return type. Take a look at this code:

Visual Basic

```
Function addUp(x As Integer, y As Integer) As Integer
  Return x + y
End Function

Sub Page_Load(s As Object, e As EventArgs)
  messageLabel.Text = addUp(5, 2).ToString()
End Sub
```

C#

```
int addUp(int x, int y)
{
  return x + y;
}

void Page_Load()
```

```
{
  messageLabel.Text = addUp(5, 2).ToString();
}
```

You can easily adapt the previous example to use this new code so that you can see the results in your browser—just replace the code inside the <script> tags within **Functions.aspx** with the code above.

We can readily use the parameters inside the function or subroutine just by using the names we gave them in the function declaration (here, we've chosen x and y, but we could have selected any names).

The other difference between this function and the function declaration we had before is that we now declare our function with a return type of Integer or int, rather than String, because we want it to return a whole number.

When we call the new function, we simply have to specify the values for the required parameters, and remember that the function will return a value with the type we specified in the function definition. In this case, we have to convert the integer value that the function returns to a string, so that we can assign it to the label.

The simplest way to convert an integer to a string is to append .ToString() to the end of the variable name. In this case, we appended ToString to the function call that returns an integer during execution. Converting numbers to strings is a very common task in ASP.NET, so it's good to get a handle on it early.

Converting Numbers to Strings

There are more ways to convert numbers to strings in .NET, as the following lines of VB code illustrate:

Visual Basic

```
messageLabel.Text = addUp(5, 2).ToString()
messageLabel.Text = Convert.ToString(addUp(5, 2))
```

If you prefer C#, these lines of code perform the same operations as the VB code above:

C#

```
messageLabel.Text = addUp(5, 2).ToString();
messageLabel.Text = Convert.ToString(addUp(5, 2));
```

Don't be concerned if you're a little confused by how these conversions work, though—the syntax will become clear once we discuss object oriented concepts later in this chapter.

Operators

Throwing around values with variables and functions isn't very handy—unless you can use them in some meaningful way. To do that, we need operators. An **operator** is a symbol that has a certain meaning when it's applied to a value. Don't worry—operators are nowhere near as scary as they sound! In fact, in the last example, where our function added two numbers, we were using an operator: the addition operator, or + symbol. Most of the other operators are just as well known, although there are one or two that will probably be new to you. Table 3.2 outlines the operators that you'll use most often in your ASP.NET development.

Operators Abound!

The list of operators in Table 3.2 is far from complete. You can find detailed lists of the differences between VB and C# operators on the Code Project website.[2]

---

[2] http://www.codeproject.com/dotnet/vbnet_c__difference.asp

Table 3.2. Common ASP.NET Operators

VB	C#	Description
>	>	greater than
>=	>=	greater than or equal to
<	<	less than
<=	<=	less than or equal to
<>	!=	not equal to
=	==	equals
=	=	assigns a value to a variable
OrElse	||	or
AndAlso	&&	and
&	+	concatenate strings
New	new	create an object or array
*	*	multiply
/	/	divide
+	+	add
-	-	subtract

The following code uses some of these operators:

Visual Basic

```
If (user = "John" AndAlso itemsBought  <>  0) Then
  messageLabel.Text = "Hello John! Do you want to proceed to " & _
    "checkout?"
End If
```

C#

```
if (user  ==  "John" && itemsBought  != 0)
{
  messageLabel.Text = "Hello John! Do you want to proceed to " +
    "checkout?";
}
```

Here, we use the equality, inequality (not equal to), and logical "and" operators in an If statement to print a tailored message for a given user who has put a product in his electronic shopping cart. Of particular note is the C# equality operator, ==, which is used to compare two values to see if they're equal. Don't use a single equals sign in C# unless you're assigning a value to a variable; otherwise, your code will have a very different meaning than you expect!

Breaking Long Lines of Code

Since the message string in the above example was too long to fit on one line in this book, we used the **string concatenation operator** to combine two shorter strings on separate lines to form the complete message: & in VB and + in C#. In VB, we also had to break one line of code into two using the **line continuation symbol (_)**, an underscore at the end of the line to be continued). Since C# marks the end of each command with a semicolon (;), you can split a single command over two lines in this language without having to do anything special.

We'll use these techniques throughout this book to present long lines of code within our limited page width. Feel free to recombine the lines in your own code if you like—there are no length limits on lines of VB and C# code.

Conditional Logic

As you develop ASP.NET applications, there will be many instances in which you'll need to perform an action only if a certain condition is met; for instance, if the user has checked a certain checkbox, selected a certain item from a DropDownList control, or typed a certain string into a TextBox control. We check for such occurrences using **conditionals**—statements that execute different code branches based upon a specified condition, the simplest of which is probably the If statement. This statement is often used in conjunction with an Else statement, which specifies what should happen if the condition is not met. So, for instance, we may wish to check whether or not the name entered in a text box is Zak, redirecting the user to a welcome page if it is, or to an error page if it's not:

Visual Basic

```
If (userName.Text = "Zak") Then
  Response.Redirect("JohnsPage.aspx")
Else
  Response.Redirect("ErrorPage.aspx")
End If
```

C#

```
if (userName.Text == "Zak")
{
  Response.Redirect("JohnsPage.aspx");
}
else
{
  Response.Redirect("ErrorPage.aspx");
}
```

 Take Care with Case Sensitivity

Instructions are case sensitive in both C# and VB, so be sure to use if in C# code, and If in VB code. On the other hand, variable and function names are case sensitive only in C#. So, in C#, two variables called x and X would be considered to be different; in VB, they would be considered to be the same variable.

Often, we want to check for many possibilities, and specify that our application perform a particular action in each case. To achieve this, we use the Select Case (VB) or switch (C#) construct, as follows:

Visual Basic

```
Select Case userName
  Case "John"
    Response.Redirect("JohnsPage.aspx")
  Case "Mark"
    Response.Redirect("MarksPage.aspx")
  Case "Fred"
    Response.Redirect("FredsPage.aspx")
```

```
  Case Else
    Response.Redirect("ErrorPage.aspx")
End Select
```

C#

```
switch (userName)
{
  case "John":
    Response.Redirect("JohnsPage.aspx");
    break;
  case "Mark":
    Response.Redirect("MarksPage.aspx");
    break;
  case "Fred":
    Response.Redirect("FredsPage.aspx");
    break;
  default:
    Response.Redirect("ErrorPage.aspx");
    break;
}
```

Loops

As you've just seen, an If statement causes a code block to execute once if the value
of its test expression is true. **Loops**, on the other hand, cause a code block to execute
repeatedly for as long as the test expression remains true. There are two basic kinds
of loop:

▪ While loops, also called Do loops (which sounds like something Betty Boop might
  say!)
▪ For loops, including For Next and For Each

A While loop is the simplest form of loop; it makes a block of code repeat for as
long as a particular condition is true. Here's an example:

```
Visual Basic                                        LearningASP\VB\Loops.aspx

<%@ Page Language="VB" %>

<!DOCTYPE html PUBLIC "-//W3C//DTD XHTML 1.0 Transitional//EN"
    "http://www.w3.org/TR/xhtml1/DTD/xhtml1-transitional.dtd">

<script runat="server">
  Sub Page_Load(ByVal s As Object, ByVal e As EventArgs)
    Dim counter As Integer = 0
    Do While counter <= 10
      messageLabel.Text = counter.ToString()
      counter += 1
    Loop
  End Sub
</script>

<html xmlns="http://www.w3.org/1999/xhtml">
  <head runat="server">
    <title>Loops</title>
  </head>
  <body>
    <form id="form1" runat="server">
    <div>
      <asp:Label id="messageLabel" runat="server" />
    </div>
    </form>
  </body>
</html>
```

```
C#                                                  LearningASP\CS\Loops.aspx

<%@ Page Language="C#" %>
⋮
<script runat="server">
  void Page_Load()
  {
    int counter = 0;
    while (counter <= 10)
    {
      messageLabel.Text = counter.ToString();
      counter++;
    }
```

```
  }
</script>
```

If you load this page, you'll get the result illustrated in Figure 3.5.

Figure 3.5. Results of a `While` loop

When you open the page, the label will be set to show the number 0, which will increment to 1, then 2, all the way to 10. Of course, since all this happens in `Page_Load` (that is, before any output is sent to the browser), you'll only see the last value assigned: 10.

These examples also demonstrate the use of two new operators: += (supported by both VB and C#) and ++ (which is supported only by C# and is a shortcut for += 1). The += operator adds the value on the left-hand side of the operator to the value on the right-hand side of the operator, and then assigns the total to the variable on the left-hand side of the operator. This operator is also available in C#, but all we want to do here is increment a value by 1, and C# offers a more convenient operator for that purpose: the ++ operator.

The above page demonstrates that the loop repeats until the condition is no longer met. Try changing the code so that the `counter` variable is initialized to 20 instead of 0. When you open the page now, you won't see anything on the screen, because the loop condition was never met.

The other form of the `While` loop, called a `Do While` loop, checks whether or not the condition has been met at the end of the code block, rather than at the beginning. Here's what the above loops would look like if we changed them into `Do While` loops:

Visual Basic

```vb
Sub Page_Load(s As Object, e As EventArgs)
  Dim counter As Integer = 0
  Do
    messageLabel.Text = counter.ToString()
    counter += 1
  Loop While counter <= 10
End Sub
```

C#

```csharp
void Page_Load()
{
  int counter = 0;
  do
  {
    messageLabel.Text = counter.ToString();
    counter++;
  }
  while (counter <= 10);
}
```

If you run this code, you'll see it provides exactly the same output we obtained when we tested the condition before the code block. However, we can see the crucial difference if we change the code so that the `counter` variable is initialized to 20. In this case, **20** will, in fact, be displayed, because the loop code is executed once before the condition is even checked! There are some instances when this is just what we want, so being able to place the condition at the end of the loop can be very handy.

A `For` loop is similar to a `While` loop, but we typically use it when we know in advance how many times we need it to execute. The following example displays the count of items within a `DropDownList` control called `productList`:

Visual Basic

```
Dim i As Integer
For i = 1 To productList.Items.Count
  messageLabel.Text = i.ToString()
Next
```

C#

```
int i;
for (i = 1; i <= productList.Items.Count; i++)
{
  messageLabel.Text = i.ToString();
}
```

In VB, the loop syntax specifies the starting and ending values for our counter variable within the For statement itself.

In C#, we assign a starting value (i = 1) along with a condition that will be tested each time we move through the loop (i <= productList.Items.Count), and lastly, we identify how the counter variable should be incremented after each loop (i++). While this allows for some powerful variations on the theme in our C# code, it can be confusing at first. In VB, the syntax is considerably simpler, but it can be a bit limiting in exceptional cases.

The other type of For loop is For Each (foreach in C#), which loops through every item within a collection. The following example loops through an array called arrayName:

Visual Basic

```
For Each item In arrayName
  messageLabel.Text = item
Next
```

```
C#

foreach (string item in arrayName)
{
   messageLabel.Text = item;
}
```

The important difference between a `For` loop and a `For Each` loop involves what happens to the variable we supply to the loop. In a `For` loop, the variable (we supplied `i` in the previous example) represents a counter—a number which starts at a predefined initial value and is incremented until it reaches a predefined maximum value. The counter is incremented every time the code in the `For` loop is executed.

In a `For Each` loop, the variable (we supplied `item` in the above example) represents the current object from the given collection. It's not necessarily an integer, like the counter in a `For` loop—it can be any kind of object, including a string, date, or custom object that you created (more about these a bit later!). The object reference changes to the next item in the collection each time the code in the `For Each` loop executes. So if we were looping over an array of string values, the variable `item` would start by containing the string value for the first item in the array, then it would receive the next item of the array, and so on, until there were no items left in the array.

You may also come across instances in which you need to exit a loop prematurely. In these cases, you can use `Exit`, if your code is in VB, or the equivalent (`break`) statement in C#, to terminate the loop:

```
Visual Basic

Dim i As Integer
For i = 0 To 10
   If (i = 5) Then
      Response.Write("Oh no! Not the number 5!!")
      Exit For
   End If
Next
```

```
C#
int i;
for (i = 0; i <= 10; i++)
{
  if (i == 5)
  {
    Response.Write("Oh no! Not the number 5!!");
    break;
  }
}
```

In this case, as soon as our For loop hits the condition i = 5, it displays a warning message using the Response.Write method (which will be familiar to those with past ASP experience), and exits the loop so that no further passes will be made through the loop.

Although we've only scratched the surface, VB and C# provide a great deal of power and flexibility to web developers, and the time you spend learning the basics now will more than pay off in the future.

Object Oriented Programming Concepts

VB and C# are modern programming languages that give you the tools to write structured, extensible, and maintainable code. The code can be separated into modules, each of which defines classes that can be imported and used in other modules. Both languages are relatively simple to get started with, yet they offer sophisticated features for writing complex, large-scale enterprise applications.

One of the reasons why these languages are so powerful is that they facilitate **object oriented programming** (OOP). In this section, we'll explain the fundamentals of OOP and learn how adopting a good OOP style now can help you to develop better, more versatile web applications down the road. This section will provide a basic OOP foundation angled towards the web developer. In particular, we'll cover the following concepts:

- objects
- properties
- methods

- classes
- scope
- events
- inheritance

In the pages that follow, we'll discuss these concepts briefly, and from Chapter 4 onwards, you'll see some practical examples of OOP in action.

Objects and Classes

So what does object oriented programming really mean? Basically, as the name suggests, it's an approach to development that puts objects at the center of the programming model. The object is probably the most important concept in the world of OOP; an **object** is a self-contained entity that has *state* and *behavior*, just like a real-world object.

In programming, an object's state is described by its **fields** and **properties**, while its behavior is defined by its **methods** and **events**. An important part of OOP's strength comes from the natural way it allows programmers to conceive and design their applications.

We often use objects in our programs to describe real-world objects—we can have objects that represent a car, a customer, a document, or a person. Each object has its own state and behavior.

It's very important to have a clear understanding of the difference between a class and an object. A class acts like a blueprint for the object, while an object represents an instance of the class. I just said that you could have objects of type `Car`, for example. If you did, `Car` would be the class, or the type, and we could create as many `Car` objects as we wanted, calling them `myCar`, `johnsCar`, `davesCar`, and so on.

The class defines the behavior of all objects of that type. So all objects of type `Car` will have the same *behavior*—for example, the ability to change gear. However, each individual `Car` object may be in a different gear at any particular time; thus, each object has its own particular *state*.

Let's take another example: think of `Integer` (or `int`) as a class, and `age` and `height` as objects of type `Integer`. The class defines the behavior of the objects—they're numeric, and we can perform mathematical operations on them. The instances of objects (age and height) have their behavior defined by the class to which they belong, but they also hold state (so age could be 20).

Take a look at the following code:

```
Visual Basic

Dim age As Integer
Dim name As String
Dim myCar As Car
Dim myOtherCar As Car
```

```
C#

int age;
string name;
Car myCar;
Car myOtherCar;
```

As you can see, the syntax for declaring an object is the same as that for declaring a simple integer or string variable. In C#, we first mention the type of the object, then we name that particular instance. In VB, we use the Dim keyword.

Rayne is your average friendly, loving, playful mutt. You might describe him in terms of his physical properties: he's gray, white, brown, and black; he stands roughly one-and-a-half-feet high; and he's about three-feet long. You might also describe some methods to make him do things: he sits when he hears the command "Sit," lies down when he hears the command "Lie down," and comes when his name is called.

So, if we were to represent Rayne in an OOP program, we'd start by creating a class called Dog. A class describes how certain types of objects look from a programming point of view. When we define a class, we must define the following two items:

Properties   Properties hold specific information that's relevant to that class of object. You can think of properties as characteristics of the objects that they represent. Our Dog class might have properties such as Color, Height, and Length.

Methods   Methods are actions that objects of the class can be told to perform. Methods are subroutines (if they don't return a value) or functions (if they do) that are specific to a given class. So the Dog class could have methods such as Sit and LieDown.

Once we've defined a class, we can write code that creates objects of that class, using the class a little like a template. This means that objects of a particular class expose (or make available) the methods and properties defined by that class. So, we might create an instance of our Dog class called rayne, set its properties accordingly, and use the methods defined by the class to interact with rayne, as shown in Figure 3.6.

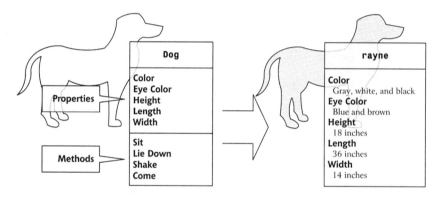

Figure 3.6. An instance of Dog

This is just a simple example to help you visualize what OOP is all about. In the next few sections, we'll cover properties and methods in greater detail, and talk about classes and class instances, scope, events, and inheritance.

Properties

As we've seen, properties are characteristics shared by all objects of a particular class. In the case of our example, the following properties might be used to describe any given dog:

- color
- height
- length

In the same way, the more useful ASP.NET `Button` class exposes properties including:

- `Width`
- `Height`
- `ID`
- `Text`
- `ForeColor`
- `BackColor`

Unfortunately, if I get sick of Rayne's color, I can't change it in real life. However, if Rayne was a .NET object, we could change any of his properties in the same way that we set variables (although a property can be read-only or write-only). For instance, we could make him brown very easily:

Visual Basic

```
rayne.Color = "Brown"
```

C#

```
rayne.Color = "Brown";
```

In this example, we're using an instance of our `Dog` class called `rayne`. We use the dot operator (`.`) to access the `Color` property that the object exposes, and set it to the string `"Brown."`

Methods

Within our dog example, we can expect to make a particular dog do things by calling commands. If I want Rayne to sit, I tell him to sit. If I want Rayne to lie down, I tell him to lie down. In object oriented terms, I tell him what I want him to do by calling a predefined command or method, and an action results. For example, if we wanted to make Rayne sit, we would use the following code to call his `Sit` method:

Visual Basic

```
rayne.Sit()
```

```
C#
```
```
rayne.Sit();
```

Given that `rayne` is an instance of our `Dog` class, we say that the `Sit` method is exposed by the `Dog` class.

Classes

You can think of a class as a template for building as many objects of a particular type as you like. When you create an instance of a class, you're creating an object of that class, and that new object will have all the characteristics and behaviors (that is, properties and methods) defined by the class.

In our dog example, `rayne` was an instance of the `Dog` class, as Figure 3.6 illustrated. In our code, we can create a new instance of the `Dog` class called `rayne`, as shown below:

```
Visual Basic
```
```
Dim rayne As New Dog()
```

```
C#
```
```
Dog rayne = new Dog();
```

Constructors

Constructors are methods that are used to initialize the object. In OOP, when we create new instances of a class, we say we're **instantiating** that class. The constructor is a method of a class that's executed automatically when a class is instantiated.

At least one constructor will be defined for most of the classes you will write (though we can define more than one constructor for a class, as we'll see shortly), since it's likely that some data will need to be initialized for each class at the time of creation.

In C# and VB, the constructor is defined as a method that has the same name as the class, and has no return type.

Scope

You should now understand programming objects to be entities that exist in a program and are manipulated through the methods and properties they expose. However, in some cases, we want to create methods for use inside our class that are not available to code outside that class.

Imagine we're writing the `Sit` method inside this class, and we realize that before the dog can sit, it has to shuffle its back paws forward a little (bear with me on this one!). We could create a method called `ShufflePaws`, and then call that method from inside the `Sit` method. However, we don't want code in an ASP.NET page or in some other class to call this method—it'd just be silly. We can prevent that from happening by controlling the scope of the `ShufflePaws` method.

The careful control of which members of a class are accessible from outside that class is fundamental to the success of object oriented programming. You can control the visibility of a class member using a special set of keywords called **access modifiers**:

`Public`   Defining a property or method of a class as public allows that property or method to be called from outside the class itself. In other words, if an instance of this class is created inside another object (remember, too, that ASP.NET pages themselves are objects), public methods and properties are freely available to the code that created that instance of the class. This is the default scope for VB and C# classes.

`Private`   If a property or method of a class is private, it cannot be used from outside the class itself. So, if an instance of this class is created inside an object of a different class, the creating object has no access to private methods or properties of the created object.

`Protected`   A protected property or method sits somewhere between public and private. A protected member is accessible from the code within its class, or to the classes derived from it. We'll learn more about derived classes a bit later.

Deciding which access modifier to use for a given class member can be a very difficult decision—it affects not only your class, but also the other classes and programs that use your class. Of special importance are the class's public members, which together form the class's **public interface**. The public interface acts like a contract between your class and the users of your class, and if it's designed properly, it shouldn't change over time. If, for example, you mark the Sit method as public, and later decide to make it private, all the other classes that use this method will have to change accordingly, which is not good. For an extreme scenario, imagine that in a year's time, Microsoft decided to remove the ToString method from its classes—obviously, this would wreak havoc with your code.

Keep Everything Private Until You Need It

As a simple guideline for designing your classes, remember that it's often easier just to make all the members private, and make public only those that really need to be public. It's much easier to add to a public interface than it is to remove from it.

Events

We've covered events in some depth already. To sum up, events occur when a control object sends a message as a result of some change that has been made to it. Generally, these changes occur as the result of user interaction with the control via the browser. For instance, when a button is clicked, a Click event is raised, and we can handle that event to perform some action. The object that triggers the event is referred to as the **event sender**, while the object that receives the event is referred to as the **event receiver**. You'll learn more about these objects in Chapter 4.

Understanding Inheritance

The term **inheritance** refers to the ability of a specialized class to refine the properties and methods exposed by another, more generalized class.

In our dog example, we created a class called Dog, and then created instances of that class to represent individual dogs such as Rayne. However, dogs are types of animals, and many characteristics of dogs are shared by all (or most) animals. For instance, Rayne has four legs, two ears, one nose, two eyes, and so on. It might be better, then, for us to create a base class called Animal. When we then defined the Dog class, it would inherit from the Animal class, and all public properties and methods of Animal would be available to instances of the Dog class.

Similarly, we could create a new class based on the Dog class. In programming circles, this is called **deriving a subclass** from Dog. For instance, we might create a class for Rayne called `AustralianShepherd`, and one for my other dog, Amigo, called `Chihuahua`, both of which would inherit the properties and methods of the `Dog` base class, and define new classes specific to each breed.

Don't worry too much if this is still a little unclear. The best way to appreciate inheritance is to see it used in a real program. The most obvious use of inheritance in ASP.NET is in the technique called code-behind, and we'll build plenty of examples using inheritance and code-behind in Chapter 4.

Objects in .NET

If this is the first book in which you've read about object oriented programming, you're probably starting to dream about objects! Don't worry, the effects of the first exposure to objects doesn't usually last for more than a week. Even though this is yet another discussion about objects, I promise it won't be boring. Moreover, in the course of this section, we'll cover some important concepts that every serious .NET programmer must know.

So far, we've explored various concepts that apply in one form or another to almost any truly object oriented language. Every language has its peculiarities, but the general concepts are the same in all of these languages.

You may already have heard the common mantra of object oriented programmers: everything is an object. This has two meanings. First of all, in C#, every program consists of a class. In all stages of application development, from design to implementation, decisions must be made in regard to the way we design and relate objects and classes to each other. Yes, objects are everywhere.

If you look at the documentation for the ASP.NET `Page` class, you can see the list of classes from which this class inherits, as shown in Figure 3.7.

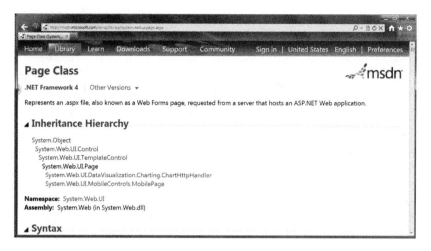

Figure 3.7. The Page class's documentation

You'll remember from the last section that we said our hypothetical
`AustralianShepherd` class would inherit from the more general `Dog` class, which,
in turn, would inherit from the even more general `Animal` class. This is exactly the
kind of relationship that's being shown in Figure 3.7—`Page` inherits methods and
properties from the `TemplateControl` class, which in turn inherits from a more
general class called `Control`. In the same way that we say that an Australian Shep-
herd is an `Animal`, we say that a `Page` is a `Control`. `Control`, like all .NET classes,
inherits from `Object`.

Since `Object` is so important that every other class derives from it, either directly
or indirectly, it deserves a closer look. `Object` contains the basic functionality that
the designers of .NET felt should be available in any object. The `Object` class contains
these public members:

- `Equals`
- `ReferenceEquals`
- `GetHashCode`
- `GetType`
- `ToString`

The only member we're really interested in at the moment is `ToString`, which returns
the text representation of an object. This method is called automatically when
conversions to string are needed, as is the case in the following code, which joins
a number and a string:

Visual Basic

```
Dim age As Integer = 5
Dim message As String = "Current Age: " & age
```

C#

```
int age = 5;
string message = "Current Age: " + age;
```

Namespaces

As ASP.NET is part of the .NET Framework, we have access to all the goodies that are built into it in the form of the .NET Framework Class Library. This library represents a huge resource of tools and features in the form of classes, which are organized in a hierarchy of namespaces. When we want to use certain features that .NET provides, we have only to find the namespace that contains the desired functionality, and import that namespace into our ASP.NET page. Once we've done that, we can make use of the .NET classes in that namespace to achieve our own ends.

For instance, if we wanted to access a database from a page, we would import the namespace that contains classes for this purpose, which could be `System.Data.SqlClient`. You can view the namespace of a class when visiting its page in the .NET documentation. For example, the `Button` control's class can be found in `System.Web.UI.WebControls`.

To use a class that's part of a namespace, but which isn't available to you by default, you either need to import the namespace (for example `System.Web.UI.WebControls`), or reference the class using its **fully qualified name** (such as `System.Web.UI.Web-Controls.Button`). To import a namespace page, we use the `Imports` directive in VB, and `using` in C#:

Visual Basic

```
Imports System.Data.SqlClient
```

```
C#
```

```
using System.Data.SqlClient;
```

As we've imported that namespace, we have access to all the classes that it contains.

Using Code-behind Files

Most companies that employ web development teams usually split projects into two groups—visual design and functional development—because software engineers are usually poor designers, and designers are often poor engineers. However, the two groups still need to contribute code and markup to the project. The best approach is to keep programmers' code separate from the designers' page markup as much as possible. Some of the ASP.NET pages we've worked on so far have contained code render blocks that place VB or C# code directly into the ASP.NET page. The problem with this approach is that there's no separation of the presentational elements of the page from the application logic. The old versions of ASP were infamous for creating "spaghetti" code—snippets of code that were scattered throughout the presentation elements. This made it very tricky to manage the code between development teams, as you'll know if you've ever tried to pick apart someone else's ASP code. In response to these problems, ASP.NET introduced a new development approach that allows code developers to work separately from the presentation designers who lay out individual pages.

This new approach, called **code-behind**, keeps all of your presentational elements (controls) inside the **.aspx** file, but moves all of your code to a separate class in a **.vb** or **.cs** code-behind file. Consider the following ASP.NET page, which displays a simple button and label:

```
Visual Basic                                    LearningASP\VB\HelloWorld.aspx
<%@ Page Language="VB" %>

<!DOCTYPE html PUBLIC "-//W3C//DTD XHTML 1.0 Transitional//EN"
    "http://www.w3.org/TR/xhtml1/DTD/xhtml1-transitional.dtd">

<script runat="server">
  Sub Click(ByVal s As Object, ByVal e As EventArgs)
    messageLabel.Text = "Hello World!"
```

```
      End Sub
</script>

<html xmlns="http://www.w3.org/1999/xhtml">
  <head runat="server">
    <title>Hello World!</title>
  </head>
  <body>
    <form id="form1" runat="server">
    <div>
      <asp:Button ID="submitButton" Text="Click Me"
          runat="server" OnClick="Click" />
      <asp:Label ID="messageLabel" runat="server" />
    </div>
    </form>
  </body>
</html>
```

C#	LearningASP\CS\HelloWorld.aspx

```
<%@ Page Language="C#" %>
⋮
<script runat="server">
  void Click(Object s, EventArgs e)
  {
    messageLabel.Text = "Hello World!";
  }
</script>
⋮
```

Let's see how this example could be separated into the following distinct files:

HelloWorldCodeBehind.aspx
   layout, presentation, and static content

HelloWorldCodeBehind.aspx.vb or HelloWorldCodeBehind.aspx.cs
   code-behind files containing a custom page class

Since there isn't a lot of code to type, you could create these files with any text editor, including Notepad. Visual Web Developer makes things easier for you, though. When adding a new Web Form file to the project, you have the option—which you've already noticed when creating new pages—to **Place code in separate file**.

Create a new Web Form for your project by clicking **Website > Add New Item...** and choosing the **Web Form** template. Check the **Place code in a separate file** checkbox, type `HelloWorldCodeBehind.aspx` for the filename, and click **Add**. The default code Visual Web Developer generates for the Web Form and its code-behind file is very similar to the code of the **Default.aspx** form it created for your new Website project, back in Chapter 1.

We'll start with the ASP.NET Web Form file **HelloWorldCodeBehind.aspx**. All we have to do is change the page title and insert the ASP.NET controls—a `Button` and a `Label`:

Visual Basic   LearningASP\VB\HelloWorldCodeBehind.aspx *(excerpt)*

```
<%@ Page Language="VB" AutoEventWireup="false"
    CodeFile="HelloWorldCodeBehind.aspx.vb"
    Inherits="HelloWorldCodeBehind" %>

<!DOCTYPE html PUBLIC "-//W3C//DTD XHTML 1.0 Transitional//EN"
    "http://www.w3.org/TR/xhtml1/DTD/xhtml1-transitional.dtd">

<html xmlns="http://www.w3.org/1999/xhtml">
<head runat="server">
    <title>Hello World!</title>
</head>
<body>
    <form id="form1" runat="server">
    <div>
      <asp:Button ID="submitButton" Text="Click Me"
          runat="server" OnClick="Click" />
      <asp:Label ID="messageLabel" runat="server" />
    </div>
    </form>
</body>
</html>
```

C#   LearningASP\CS\HelloWorldCodeBehind.aspx *(excerpt)*

```
<%@ Page Language="C#" AutoEventWireup="true"
    CodeFile="HelloWorldCodeBehind.aspx.cs"
    Inherits="HelloWorldCodeBehind" %>

<!DOCTYPE html PUBLIC "-//W3C//DTD XHTML 1.0 Transitional//EN"
    "http://www.w3.org/TR/xhtml1/DTD/xhtml1-transitional.dtd">
```

```
<html xmlns="http://www.w3.org/1999/xhtml">
  <head runat="server">
    <title>Hello World!</title>
  </head>
  <body>
    <form id="form1" runat="server">
    <div>
      <asp:Button ID="submitButton" Text="Click Me"
          runat="server" OnClick="Click" />
      <asp:Label ID="messageLabel" runat="server" />
    </div>
    </form>
  </body>
</html>
```

As you can see, without code blocks, the main ASP.NET page becomes a bit simpler. You might also notice that the only line that differs between these **.aspx** pages is the Page directive. Since the **.aspx** pages now contain only HTML layout, the contents are identical no matter what language you use for the code.

You'll also notice that the code-behind file (**HelloWorldCodeBehind.aspx.vb** or **HelloWorldCodeBehind.aspx.cs**) has been generated automatically, as it was for the **Default.aspx** file back in Chapter 1. This is a pure code file, and contains no HTML or other markup tags. Nevertheless, we can still access presentation elements from this file using their IDs (such as messageLabel).

Change the code to look like this:

Visual Basic	LearningASP\VB\HelloWorldCodeBehind.aspx.vb

```
Imports System
Imports System.Web.UI
Imports System.Web.UI.WebControls
Partial Class HelloWorldCodeBehind
  Inherits System.Web.UI.Page
  Sub Click(ByVal s As Object, ByVal e As EventArgs)
    messageLabel.Text = "Hello World!"
  End Sub
End Class
```

C#	LearningASP\CS\HelloWorldCodeBehind.aspx.cs

```csharp
using System;
using System.Collections;
using System.Configuration;
using System.Data;
using System.Linq;
using System.Web;
using System.Web.Security;
using System.Web.UI;
using System.Web.UI.HtmlControls;
using System.Web.UI.WebControls;
using System.Web.UI.WebControls.WebParts;
using System.Xml.Linq;

public partial class HelloWorldCodeBehind : System.Web.UI.Page
{
  protected void Page_Load(object sender, EventArgs e)
  {

  }
  public void Click(Object s, EventArgs e)
  {
    messageLabel.Text = "Hello World!";
  }
}
```

The code in the code-behind file is written differently than the code we've written using <script> tags. Instead of the simple functions we wrote in Chapter 2, we have a class definition. In our VB example, we added three lines that import namespaces for use within the code. We can achieve the same end using page directives (as shown in Chapter 2), but when you're using code-behind files, it's easier to type the namespace reference in the code-behind file:

Visual Basic	LearningASP\VB\HelloWorldCodeBehind.aspx.vb *(excerpt)*

```vb
Imports System
Imports System.Web.UI
Imports System.Web.UI.WebControls
```

Note that, in VB projects, you won't find any Import statements in the default code-behind files, although you'll find them in C# projects. For some reason, the designers of Visual Web Developer thought that most VB developers would prefer not to be bothered with this kind of detail, so they "hid" the namespace references in the **Web.config** configuration file. Here are the `using` statements that were automatically added for you when you created the code-behind file for the C# version:

C#	LearningASP\CS\HelloWorldCodeBehind.aspx.cs

```csharp
using System;
using System.Collections;
using System.Configuration;
using System.Data;
using System.Linq;
using System.Web;
using System.Web.Security;
using System.Web.UI;
using System.Web.UI.HtmlControls;
using System.Web.UI.WebControls;
using System.Web.UI.WebControls.WebParts;
using System.Xml.Linq;
```

The following lines create a new class, named `HelloWorldCodeBehind`. Since our code-behind page contains code for an ASP.NET page, our class inherits from the `Page` class:

Visual Basic	LearningASP\VB\HelloWorldCodeBehind.aspx.vb *(excerpt)*

```vb
Partial Class HelloWorldCodeBehind
  Inherits System.Web.UI.Page
    ⋮
End Class
```

C#	LearningASP\CS\HelloWorldCodeBehind.aspx.cs

```csharp
public partial class HelloWorldCodeBehind : System.Web.UI.Page
{
    ⋮
}
```

This is the practical application of inheritance that we mentioned earlier. The `HelloWorldCodeBehind` class inherits from `Page`, borrowing all its functionality, and extending it according to the particular needs of the page.

But what does `Partial` mean? A feature that was introduced in .NET 2.0, **partial classes** allow a class to be spread over multiple files. ASP.NET uses this feature to make programmers' lives easier. We write one part of the class in the code-behind file, and ASP.NET generates the other part of the class for us, adding the object declarations for all the user interface elements.

Take a look at the `Click` subroutine, through which we access the `messageLabel` object without defining it anywhere in the code:

Visual Basic	LearningASP\VB\HelloWorldCodeBehind.aspx.vb

```vb
Sub Click(ByVal s As Object, ByVal e As EventArgs)
  messageLabel.Text = "Hello World!"
End Sub
```

C#	LearningASP\CS\HelloWorldCodeBehind.aspx.cs

```csharp
public void Click(Object s, EventArgs e)
{
  messageLabel.Text = "Hello World!";
}
```

That's pretty handy! However, don't be fooled into thinking that you can use objects that haven't been declared—the `messageLabel` object has been declared in another partial class file that the ASP.NET runtime generates for us. The file contains declarations for all of the controls referenced in **HelloWorldCodeBehind.aspx**.

As I hope you can see, code-behind files are easy to work with, and they can make managing and using your pages much more straightforward than keeping your code in code declaration blocks. You'll find yourself using code-behind files in most of the real-world projects that you build, but for simplicity's sake, we'll stick with code declaration blocks for one more chapter.

Summary

Phew! We've covered quite a few concepts over the course of this chapter. Be sure to reference this chapter again if you have trouble grasping the language concepts until they become second nature to you. We hope you leave this chapter with a basic understanding of programming concepts as they relate to the ASP.NET web developer.

The next chapter will begin to put all the concepts that we've covered so far into practice. We'll begin by working with HTML Controls, Web Forms, and Web Controls, before launching into our first hands-on project!

Constructing ASP.NET Web Pages

If you've ever built a model from Lego bricks, you're well prepared to start building real ASP.NET web pages. ASP.NET offers features that allow web developers to build parts of web pages independently, then put them together later to form complete pages.

The content we're creating through our work with ASP.NET is almost never static. At design time, we tend to think in terms of templates that contain placeholders for the content that will be generated dynamically at runtime. And to fill those placeholders, we can either use one of the many controls ASP.NET provides, or build our own.

In this chapter, we'll discuss many of the objects and techniques that give life and color to ASP.NET web pages, including:

- web forms
- HTML server controls
- web server controls
- web user controls
- master pages

- handling page navigation
- styling pages and controls with CSS

If the list looks intimidating, don't worry—all of this is far easier to understand than it might first appear.

Web Forms

As you know, there's always new terminology to master when you're learning new technologies. The term used to describe an ASP.NET web page is **web form**, and this is the central object in ASP.NET development. You've already met web forms—they're the **.aspx** files you've worked with so far in this book. At first glance, web forms look much like HTML pages, but in addition to static HTML content they also contain ASP.NET-specific elements, and code that executes on the server side.

Every web form includes a `<form runat="server">` tag, which contains the ASP.NET-specific elements that make up the page. Multiple `forms` aren't supported. The basic structure of a web form is shown here:

```
<%@ Page Language="language" %>

<!DOCTYPE html PUBLIC "-//W3C//DTD XHTML 1.0 Transitional//EN"
    "http://www.w3.org/TR/xhtml1/DTD/xhtml1-transitional.dtd">

<script runat="server">
  ⋮ code block…
</script>

<html xmlns="http://www.w3.org/1999/xhtml">
<head runat="server">
  <title>Page Title</title>
</head>
<body>
  <form id="form1" runat="server">
    ⋮ user interface elements…
  </form>
</body>
</html>
```

To access and manipulate a web form programmatically, we use the `System.Web.UI.Page` class. You might recognize this class from the code-behind example we saw in Chapter 3. We must mention the class explicitly in the code-behind file. In situations in which we're not using code-behind files (that is, we're writing all the code inside the **.aspx** file instead), the `Page` class is still used—we just don't see it.

We can use a range of user interface elements inside the form—including typical, static HTML code—but we can also use elements whose values or properties can be generated or manipulated on the server either when the page first loads, or when the form is submitted. These elements—which, in ASP.NET parlance, are called **controls**—allow us to reuse common functionality, such as the page header, a calendar, a shopping cart summary, or a "Today's Quote" box, for example, across multiple web forms. There are several types of controls in ASP.NET:

- HTML server controls
- web server controls
- web user controls
- master pages

There are significant technical differences between these types of controls, but what makes them similar is the ease with which we can integrate and reuse them in our web sites. Let's take a look at them one by one.

HTML Server Controls

HTML server controls are outwardly identical to plain old HTML tags, but include a `runat="server"` attribute. This gives the ASP.NET runtime control over the HTML server controls, allowing us to access them programmatically. For example, if we have an `<a>` tag in a page and we want to be able to change the address to which it links dynamically, using VB or C# code, we use the `runat="server"` attribute.

A server-side HTML server control exists for each of HTML's most common elements. Creating HTML server controls is easy: we simply stick a `runat="server"` attribute on the end of a normal HTML tag to create the HTML control version of that tag. The complete list of current HTML control classes and their associated tags is given in Table 4.1.

Table 4.1. HTML control classes

Class	Associated Tags
HtmlAnchor	`<a runat="server">`
HtmlButton	`<button runat="server">`
HtmlForm	`<form runat="server">`
HtmlImage	`<img runat="server">`
HtmlInputButton	`<input type="submit" runat="server">`
	`<input type="reset" runat="server">`
	`<input type="button" runat="server">`
HtmlInputCheckBox	`<input type="checkbox" runat="server">`
HtmlInputFile	`<input type="file" runat="server">`
HtmlInputHidden	`<input type="hidden" runat="server">`
HtmlInputImage	`<input type="image" runat="server">`
HtmlInputRadioButton	`<input type="radio" runat="server">`
HtmlInputText	`<input type="text" runat="server">`
	`<input type="password" runat="server">`
HtmlSelect	`<select runat="server">`
HtmlTable	`<table runat="server">`
HtmlTableRow	`<tr runat="server">`
HtmlTableCell	`<td runat="server">`
	`<th runat="server">`
HtmlTextArea	`<textarea runat="server">`
HtmlGenericControl	`<span runat="server">`
	`<div runat="server">`
	All other HTML tags

All the HTML server control classes are contained within the System.Web.UI.Htm-
lControls namespace. As they're processed on the server side by the ASP.NET
runtime, we can access their properties through code elsewhere in the page. If you're
familiar with JavaScript, HTML, and CSS, you'll know that manipulating text
within HTML tags, or even manipulating inline styles within an HTML tag, can be
cumbersome and error-prone. HTML server controls aim to solve these problems

by allowing you to manipulate the page easily with your choice of .NET language—for instance, using VB or C#.

Using the HTML Server Controls

Nothing explains the theory better than a simple, working example. Let's create a simple survey form that uses the following HTML server controls:

- `HtmlForm`
- `HtmlButton`
- `HtmlInputText`
- `HtmlSelect`

We'll begin by creating a new file named `Survey.aspx`. Create the file in the **LearningASP\VB** or **LearningASP\CS** folder you created in Chapter 1. For the purpose of the exercises in this chapter we won't be using a code-behind file, so don't check the **Place code in a separate file** checkbox when you create the form.

Update the automatically generated file with the following code to create the visual interface for the survey:

Visual Basic	LearningASP\VB\Survey_01.aspx *(excerpt)*

```
<%@ Page Language="VB" %>

<!DOCTYPE html PUBLIC "-//W3C//DTD XHTML 1.0 Transitional//EN"
    "http://www.w3.org/TR/xhtml1/DTD/xhtml1-transitional.dtd">

<script runat="server">

</script>

<html xmlns="http://www.w3.org/1999/xhtml">
  <head runat="server">
    <title>Using ASP.NET HTML Server Controls</title>
  </head>
  <body>
    <form id="form1" runat="server">
    <div>
      <h1>Take the Survey!</h1>
      <!-- Display user name -->
      <p>
```

```
      Name:<br />
      <input type="text" id="name" runat="server" />
    </p>
    <!-- Display email -->
    <p>
      Email:<br />
      <input type="text" id="email" runat="server" />
    </p>
    <!-- Display technology options -->
    <p>
      Which server technologies do you use?<br />
      <select id="serverModel" runat="server" multiple="true">
        <option>ASP.NET</option>
        <option>PHP</option>
        <option>JSP</option>
        <option>CGI</option>
        <option>ColdFusion</option>
      </select>
    </p>
    <!-- Display .NET preference options -->
    <p>
      Do you like .NET so far?<br />
      <select id="likeDotNet" runat="server">
        <option>Yes</option>
        <option>No</option>
      </select>
    </p>
    <!-- Display confirmation button -->
    <p>
      <button id="confirmButton" OnServerClick="Click"
          runat="server">Confirm</button>
    </p>
    <!-- Confirmation label -->
    <p>
      <asp:Label id="feedbackLabel" runat="server" />
    </p>
  </div>
  </form>
</body>
</html>
```

The C# version is identical except for the first line—the page declaration:

```
C#                                          LearningASP\CS\Survey_01.aspx (excerpt)

<%@ Page Language="C#" %>
    ⋮
```

From what we've already seen of HTML controls, you should have a good idea of the classes we'll be working with in this page. All we've done is place some `HtmlInputText` controls, an `HtmlButton` control, and an `HtmlSelect` control inside the obligatory `HtmlForm` control. We've also added a `Label` control, which we'll use to give feedback to the user.

HTML Server Controls in Action

Remember, HTML server controls are essentially HTML tags with the `runat="server"` attribute. In most cases, you'll also need to assign them IDs, which will enable you to use the controls in your code.

Validation Warnings

You may notice that Visual Web Developer will display a validation warning about the `multiple="true"` attribute value on the `select` element. In XHTML 1.0, the select element only supports `multiple="multiple"` and the IDE dutifully reports the problem. However, since this is a server control—it has a `runat="server"` attribute—you must specify `multiple="true"`, otherwise the page will not compile and execute.

When you eventually test this page, you'll be happy to note that ASP.NET will change the attribute value to `multiple="multiple"` when the HTML is generated and the page is displayed.

When it's complete, and you view it in Visual Web Developer's **Design** mode, the **Survey.aspx** web form will resemble Figure 4.1. Note that you can't execute the form yet, because it's missing the button's `Click` event handler that we've specified using the `OnServerClick` attribute on the `HtmlButton` control.

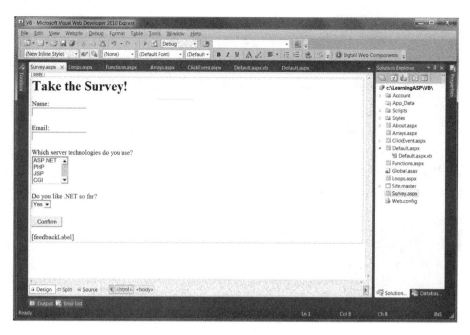

Figure 4.1. A simple form that uses HTML server controls

When a user clicks on the **Confirm** button, we'll display the submitted responses in the browser. In a real application, we'd probably be more likely to save this inform-ation to a database, and perhaps show the results as a chart. Keeping it simple for now, the code for the Click event handler method below shows how we'd access the properties of the HTML controls:

Visual Basic   LearningASP\VB\Survey_02.aspx *(excerpt)*

```
<script runat="server">
  Sub Click(ByVal s As Object, ByVal e As EventArgs)
    Dim i As Integer
    feedbackLabel.Text = "Your name is: " & name.Value & "<br />"
    feedbackLabel.Text += "Your email is: " & email.Value & _
        "<br />"
    feedbackLabel.Text += "You like to work with:<br />"
    For i = 0 To serverModel.Items.Count - 1
      If serverModel.Items(i).Selected Then
        feedbackLabel.Text += " - " & _
            serverModel.Items(i).Text & "<br />"
      End If
    Next i
```

```
      feedbackLabel.Text += "You like .NET: " & likeDotNet.Value
    End Sub
</script>
```

C#   LearningASP\CS\Survey_02.aspx *(excerpt)*

```
<script runat="server">
  void Click(Object s, EventArgs e)
  {
    feedbackLabel.Text = "Your name is: " + name.Value + "<br />";
    feedbackLabel.Text += "Your email is: " + email.Value +
        "<br />";
    feedbackLabel.Text += "You like to work with:<br />";
    for (int i = 0; i <= serverModel.Items.Count - 1; i++)
    {
      if (serverModel.Items[i].Selected)
      {
        feedbackLabel.Text += " - " + serverModel.Items[i].Text +
            "<br />";
      }
    }
    feedbackLabel.Text += "You like .NET: " + likeDotNet.Value;
  }
</script>
```

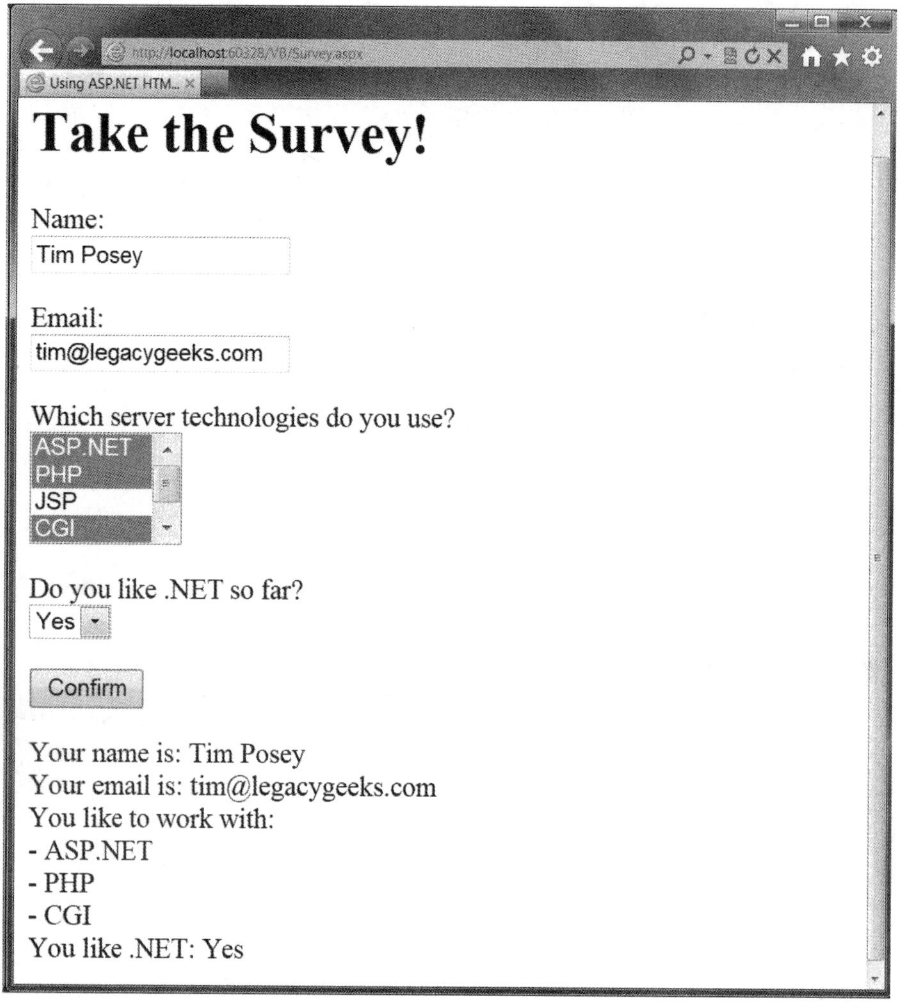

Figure 4.2. Viewing the survey results

Once you've written the code, save your work and test the results in your browser. Enter some information and click the button. To select multiple options in the `serverModel` option box, hold down **Ctrl** as you click on your preferences. The information you enter should appear at the bottom of the page when the **Confirm** button is clicked, as shown in Figure 4.2.

In conclusion, working with HTML server controls is really simple. All you need to do is assign each control an ID, and add the `runat="server"` attribute. Then, you can simply access and manipulate the controls using VB or C# code on the server side.

Web Server Controls

Web server controls can be seen as advanced versions of HTML server controls. Web server controls are those that generate content for you—you're no longer in control of the HTML being used. While having good knowledge of HTML is useful, it's not a necessity for those working with web server controls.

Let's look at an example. We can use the `Label` web server control to place simple text inside a web form. To change the `Label`'s text from within our C# or VB code, we simply set its `Text` property like so:

Visual Basic

```
myLabel.Text = "Mickey Mouse"
```

Similarly, to add a text box to our form, we use the `TextBox` web server control. Again, we can read or set its text using the `Text` property:

C#

```
username = usernameTextBox.Text;
```

Though we're applying the `TextBox` control, ASP.NET still uses an `input` element behind the scenes; however, we no longer have to worry about this detail. With web server controls, you no longer need to worry about translating the needs of your application into elements you can define in HTML—you can let the ASP.NET framework do the worrying for you.

Unlike HTML server controls, web server controls don't have a direct, one-to-one correspondence with the HTML elements they generate. For example, we can use either of two web server controls—the `DropDownList` control, or the `ListBox` control—to generate a `select` element.

Web server controls follow the same basic pattern as HTML tags, but the tag name is preceded by `asp:`, and is capitalized using Pascal Casing. Pascal Casing is a form that capitalizes the first character of each word (such as `TextBox`). The object IDs are usually named using Camel Casing, where the first letter of each word *except the first* is capitalized (e.g. `usernameTextBox`).

Consider the following HTML `input` element, which creates an input text box:

```
<input type="text" name="usernameTextBox" size="30" />
```

The equivalent web server control is the `TextBox` control, and it looks like this:

```
<asp:TextBox id="usernameTextBox" runat="server" Columns="30">
</asp:TextBox>
```

Remember that, unlike any normal HTML that you might use in your web forms, web server controls are first processed by the ASP.NET engine, where they're transformed to HTML. A side effect of this approach is that you must be very careful to always include closing tags (the `</asp:TextBox>` part above). The HTML parsers of most web browsers are forgiving about badly formatted HTML code, but ASP.NET is not. Remember that you can use the shorthand syntax (`/>`) if nothing appears between your web server control's opening and closing tags. As such, you could also write this `TextBox` like so:

```
<asp:TextBox id="usernameTextBox" runat="server" Columns="30" />
```

To sum up, the key points to remember when you're working with web server controls are:

- Web server controls must be placed within a `<form runat="server">` tag to function properly.

- Web server controls require the `runat="server"` attribute to function properly.

- We include web server controls in a form using the `asp:` prefix.

There are more web server controls than HTML controls. Some offer advanced features that simply aren't available using HTML alone, and some generate quite complex HTML code for you. We'll meet many web server controls as we work through this and future chapters.

For more information on web server controls, including the properties, methods, and events for each, have a look at Appendix A.

Standard Web Server Controls

The standard set of web server controls that comes with ASP.NET mirrors the HTML server controls in many ways. However, web server controls offer some new refinements and enhancements, such as support for events and view state, a more consistent set of properties and methods, and more built-in functionality. In this section, we'll take a look as some of the controls you're most likely to use in your day-to-day work.

Remember to use the .NET Framework SDK Documentation whenever you need more details about any of the framework's classes (or controls). You can access the documentation from the **Help > Index** menu item in Visual Web Developer. To find a class, simply search for the class's name. If there are many classes with a given name in different namespaces, you'll be able to choose the one you want from the **Index Results** window. For example, you'll find that there are two classes named Label, located in the System.Web.UI.WebControls and System.Windows.Forms namespaces, as Figure 4.3 illustrates. You'll most likely be interested in the version of the class situated in the WebControls namespace.

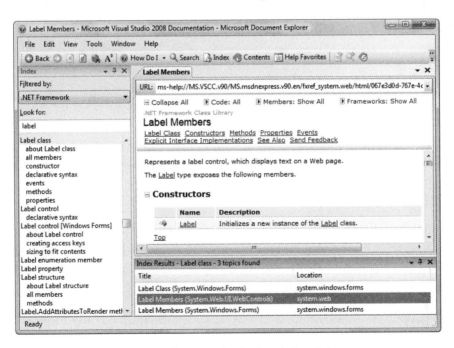

Figure 4.3. Documentation for the Label control

Label

The easiest way to display static text on your page is simply to add the text to the body of the page without enclosing it in a tag. However, if you want to modify the text displayed on a page using ASP.NET code, you can display your text within a Label control. Here's a typical example:

```
<asp:Label id="messageLabel" Text="" runat="server" />
```

The following code sets the Text property of the Label control to display the text "Hello World":

Visual Basic

```
Public Sub Page_Load()
  messageLabel.Text = "Hello World"
End Sub
```

C#

```
public void Page_Load()
{
  messageLabel.Text = "Hello World";
}
```

Reading this Page_Load handler code, we can see that when the page first loads, the Text property of the Label control with the id of message will be set to "Hello World."

Literal

This is perhaps the simplest control in ASP.NET. If you set Literal's Text property, it will simply insert that text into the output HTML code without altering it. Unlike Label, which has similar functionality, Literal doesn't wrap the text in <span> tags that would allow the setting of style information.

TextBox

The TextBox control is used to create a box in which the user can type or read standard text. You can use the TextMode property to set this control to display text in a single line, across multiple lines, or to hide the text being entered (for instance, in HTML password fields). The following code shows how we might use it in a simple login page:

```
<p>
  Username: <asp:TextBox id="userTextBox" TextMode="SingleLine"
      Columns="30" runat="server" />
</p>
<p>
  Password: <asp:TextBox id="passwordTextBox"
      TextMode="Password" Columns="30" runat="server" />
</p>
<p>
  Comments: <asp:TextBox id="commentsTextBox"
      TextMode="MultiLine" Columns="30" Rows="10"
      runat="server" />
</p>
```

In each of the instances above, the TextMode attribute dictates the kind of text box that's to be rendered.

HiddenField

HiddenField is a simple control that renders an input element whose type attribute is set to hidden. We can set its only important property, Value. These are sometimes used to pass information through to another website, such as transferring user name information to another site to perform auto-login functionality.

Button

By default, the Button control renders an input element whose type attribute is set to submit. When a button is clicked, the form containing the button is submitted to the server for processing, and both the Click and Command events are raised.

The following markup displays a Button control and a Label:

```
<asp:Button id="submitButton" Text="Submit" runat="server"
    OnClick="WriteText" />
<asp:Label id="messageLabel" runat="server" />
```

Notice the OnClick attribute on the control. When the button is clicked, the Click event is raised, and the WriteText subroutine is called. The WriteText subroutine will contain the code that performs the intended function for this button, such as displaying a message to the user:

Visual Basic

```
Public Sub WriteText(s As Object, e As EventArgs)
  messageLabel.Text = "Hello World"
End Sub
```

C#

```
public void WriteText(Object s, EventArgs e)
{
  messageLabel.Text = "Hello World";
}
```

It's important to realize that events are associated with most web server controls, and the basic techniques involved in using them, are the same events and techniques we used with the Click event of the Button control. All controls implement a standard set of events because they all inherit from the WebControl base class.

ImageButton

An ImageButton control is similar to a Button control, but it uses an image that we supply in place of the typical system button graphic. Take a look at this example:

```
<asp:ImageButton id="myImgButton" ImageUrl="myButton.gif"
    runat="server" OnClick="WriteText" />
<asp:Label id="messageLabel" runat="server" />
```

The Click event of the ImageButton receives the coordinates of the point at which the image was clicked:

Visual Basic

```
Public Sub WriteText(s As Object, e As ImageClickEventArgs)
  messageLabel.Text = "Coordinate: " & e.X & "," & e.Y
End Sub
```

```
C#

public void WriteText(Object s, ImageClickEventArgs e)
{
   messageLabel.Text = "Coordinate: " + e.X + "," + e.Y;
}
```

LinkButton

A LinkButton control renders a hyperlink that fires the Click event when it's clicked. From the point of view of ASP.NET code, LinkButtons can be treated in much the same way as buttons, hence the name. Here's LinkButton in action:

```
<asp:LinkButton id="myLinkButon" Text="Click Here"
    runat="server" />
```

HyperLink

The HyperLink control creates on your page a hyperlink that links to the URL in the NavigateUrl property. Unlike the LinkButton control, which offers features such as Click events and validation, HyperLinks are meant to be used to navigate from one page to the next:

```
<asp:HyperLink id="myLink" NavigateUrl="http://www.sitepoint.com/"
    ImageUrl="splogo.gif" runat="server">SitePoint</asp:HyperLink>
```

If it's specified, the ImageUrl attribute causes the control to display the specified image, in which case the text is demoted to acting as the image's alternate text.

CheckBox

You can use a CheckBox control to represent a choice that can have only two possible states—checked or unchecked:

```
<asp:CheckBox id="questionCheck" Text="Yep, ASP.NET is cool!"
    Checked="True" runat="server" />
```

The main event associated with a CheckBox is the CheckChanged event, which can be handled with the OnCheckChanged attribute. The Checked property is True if the checkbox is checked, and False otherwise.

RadioButton

A `RadioButton` is a lot like a `CheckBox`, except that `RadioButtons` can be grouped to represent a set of options from which only one can be selected. Radio buttons are grouped together using the `GroupName` property, like so:

```
<asp:RadioButton id="sanDiego" GroupName="City" Text="San Diego"
    runat="server" /><br />
<asp:RadioButton id="boston" GroupName="City" Text="Boston"
    runat="server" /><br />
<asp:RadioButton id="phoenix" GroupName="City" Text="Phoenix"
    runat="server" /><br />
<asp:RadioButton id="seattle" GroupName="City" Text="Seattle"
    runat="server" />
```

Like the `CheckBox` control, the main event associated with `RadioButtons` is the `CheckChanged` event, which can be handled with the `OnCheckChanged` attribute. The other control we can use to display radio buttons is `RadioButtonList`, which we'll also meet in this chapter.

Image

An `Image` control creates an image that can be accessed dynamically from code; it equates to the `<img>` tag in HTML. Here's an example:

```
<asp:Image id="myImage" ImageUrl="mygif.gif" runat="server"
    AlternateText="description" />
```

ImageMap

The `ImageMap` control generates HTML to display images that have certain clickable regions called **hot spots**. Each hot spot reacts in a specific way when it's clicked by the user.

These areas can be defined using three controls, which generate hot spots of different shapes: `CircleHotSpot`, `RectangleHotSpot`, and `PolygonHotSpot`. Here's an example that defines an image map with two circular hot spots:

```
<asp:ImageMap ID="myImageMap" runat="server" ImageUrl="image.jpg">
  <asp:CircleHotSpot AlternateText="Button1"
      Radius="20" X="50" Y="50" />
```

```
    <asp:CircleHotSpot AlternateText="Button2"
        Radius="20" X="100" Y="50" />
</asp:ImageMap>
```

Table 4.2. Possible values of `HotSpotMode`

`HotSpotMode` value	Behavior when hot spot is clicked
Inactive	none
Navigate	The user is navigated to the specified URL.
NotSet	When this value is set for a `HotSpot`, the behavior is inherited from the parent `ImageMap`; if the parent `ImageMap` doesn't specify a default value, `Navigate` is set.
	When it's set for an `ImageMap`, this value is effectively equivalent to `Navigate`.
PostBack	The hot spot raises the `Click` event that can be handled on the server side to respond to the user action.

To configure the action that results when a hot spot is clicked by the user, we set the `HotSpotMode` property of the `ImageMap` control, or the `HotSpotMode` property of the individual hot spot objects, or both, using the values shown in Table 4.2. If the `HotSpotMode` property is set for the `ImageMap` control as well as for an individual hot spot, the latter property will override that set for the more general `ImageMap` control.

The Microsoft .NET Framework SDK Documentation for the `ImageMap` class and HotSpotMode enumeration contains detailed examples of the usage of these values.

PlaceHolder

The `PlaceHolder` control lets us add elements at a particular place on a page at any time, dynamically, through our code. Here's what it looks like:

```
<asp:PlaceHolder id="myPlaceHolder" runat="server" />
```

The following code dynamically adds a new `HtmlButton` control within the place-holder:

```
Visual Basic

Public Sub Page_Load()
  Dim myButton As HtmlButton = New HtmlButton()
  myButton.InnerText = "My New Button"
  myPlaceHolder.Controls.Add(myButton)
End Sub
```

```
C#

public void Page_Load()
{
  HtmlButton myButton = new HtmlButton();
  myButton.InnerText = "My New Button";
  myPlaceHolder.Controls.Add(myButton);
}
```

Panel

The Panel control functions similarly to the div element in HTML, in that it allows the set of items that resides within the tag to be manipulated as a group. For instance, the Panel could be made visible or hidden by a Button's Click event:

```
<asp:Panel id="myPanel" runat="server">
  <p>Username: <asp:TextBox id="usernameTextBox" Columns="30"
    runat="server" /></p>
  <p>Password: <asp:TextBox id="passwordTextBox"
    TextMode="Password" Columns="30" runat="server" /></p>
</asp:Panel>
<asp:Button id="hideButton" Text="Hide Panel" OnClick="HidePanel"
  runat="server" />
```

The code above places two TextBox controls within a Panel control. The Button control is outside of the panel. The HidePanel subroutine would then control the Panel's visibility by setting its Visible property to False:

```
Visual Basic

Public Sub HidePanel(s As Object, e As EventArgs)
  myPanel.Visible = False
End Sub
```

```
C#
public void HidePanel(Object s, EventArgs e)
{
  myPanel.Visible = false;
}
```

In this case, when the user clicks the button, the `Click` event is raised and the `HidePanel` subroutine is called, which sets the `Visible` property of the `Panel` control to `False`.

List Controls

Here, we'll meet the ASP.NET controls that display simple lists of elements: `ListBox`, `DropDownList`, `CheckBoxList`, `RadioButtonList`, and `BulletedList`.

DropDownList

A `DropDownList` control is similar to the HTML `select` element. The `DropDownList` control allows you to select one item from a list using a drop-down menu. Here's an example of the control's code:

```
<asp:DropDownList id="ddlFavColor" runat="server">
  <asp:ListItem Text="Red" value="red" />
  <asp:ListItem Text="Blue" value="blue" />
  <asp:ListItem Text="Green" value="green" />
</asp:DropDownList>
```

The most useful event that this control provides is `SelectedIndexChanged`. This event is also exposed by other list controls, such as the `CheckBoxList` and `RadioButtonList` controls, allowing for easy programmatic interaction with the control you're using. These controls can also be bound to a database and used to extract dynamic content into a drop-down menu.

ListBox

A `ListBox` control equates to the HTML `select` element with either the `multiple` or `size` attribute set (`size` would need to be set to a value of 2 or more). If you set the `SelectionMode` attribute to `Multiple`, the user will be able to select more than one item from the list, as in this example:

```
<asp:ListBox id="listTechnologies" runat="server"
    SelectionMode="Multiple">
  <asp:ListItem Text="ASP.NET" Value="aspnet" />
  <asp:ListItem Text="JSP" Value="jsp" />
  <asp:ListItem Text="PHP" Value="php" />
  <asp:ListItem Text="CGI" Value="cgi" />
  <asp:ListItem Text="ColdFusion" Value="cf" />
</asp:ListBox>
```

RadioButtonList

Like the RadioButton control, the RadioButtonList control represents radio buttons. However, the RadioButtonList control represents a list of radio buttons and uses more compact syntax. Here's an example:

```
<asp:RadioButtonList id="favoriteColor" runat="server">
  <asp:ListItem Text="Red" Value="red" />
  <asp:ListItem Text="Blue" Value="blue" />
  <asp:ListItem Text="Green" Value="green" />
</asp:RadioButtonList>
```

CheckBoxList

As you may have guessed, the CheckBoxList control represents a group of check boxes; it's equivalent to using several CheckBox controls in a row:

```
<asp:CheckBoxList id="favoriteFood" runat="server">
  <asp:ListItem Text="Pizza" Value="pizza" />
  <asp:ListItem Text="Tacos" Value="tacos" />
  <asp:ListItem Text="Pasta" Value="pasta" />
</asp:CheckBoxList>
```

BulletedList

The BulletedList control displays bulleted or numbered lists, using <ul> (unordered list) or <ol> (ordered list) tags. Unlike the other list controls, the BulletedList doesn't allow the selection of items, so the SelectedIndexChanged event isn't supported.

The first property you'll want to set is DisplayMode, which can be Text (the default), or HyperLink, which will render the list items as links. When DisplayMode is set to HyperLink, you can use the Click event to respond to a user's click on one of the items.

The other important property is BulletStyle, which determines the style of the bullets. The accepted values are:

- Numbered (1, 2, 3, …)
- LowerAlpha (a, b, c, …)
- UpperAlpha (A, B, C, …)
- LowerRoman (i, ii, iii, …)
- UpperRoman (I, II, III, …)
- Circle
- Disc
- Square
- CustomImage

If the style is set to CustomImage, you'll also need to set the BulletStyleImageUrl to specify the image to be used for the bullets. If the style is one of the numbered lists, you can also set the FirstBulletNumber property to specify the first number or letter that's to be generated.

Advanced Controls

These controls are advanced in terms of their usage, the HTML code they generate, and the background work they do for you. Some of these controls aren't available to older versions of ASP.NET; we'll learn more about many of them (as well as others that aren't covered in this chapter) as we progress through this book.

Calendar

The Calendar is a great example of the reusable nature of ASP.NET controls. The Calendar control generates markup that displays an intuitive calendar in which the user can click to select, or move between, days, weeks, months, and so on.

The Calendar control requires very little customization. In Visual Web Developer, select **Website > Add New Item…**, and make the changes indicated:

Visual Basic	LearningASP\VB\Calendar_01.aspx

```
<%@ Page Language="VB" %>

<!DOCTYPE html PUBLIC "-//W3C//DTD XHTML 1.0 Transitional//EN"
    "http://www.w3.org/TR/xhtml1/DTD/xhtml1-transitional.dtd">

<script runat="server">

</script>

<html xmlns="http://www.w3.org/1999/xhtml">
  <head runat="server">
    <title>Calendar Test</title>
  </head>
  <body>
    <form id="form1" runat="server">
    <div>
      <asp:Calendar ID="myCalendar" runat="server" />
    </div>
    </form>
  </body>
</html>
```

Again, the C# version is the same, except for the Page declaration:

C#	LearningASP\CS\01_Calendar.aspx *(excerpt)*

```
<%@ Page Language="C#" %>
⋮
```

If you save this page in your working folder and load it, you'll see the output shown in Figure 4.4.

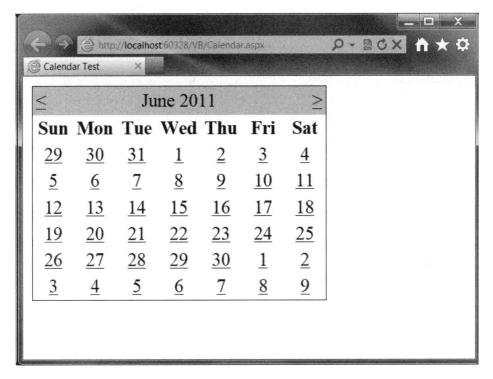

Figure 4.4. Displaying the default calendar

The Calendar control contains a wide range of properties, methods, and events, including those listed in Table 4.3.

Table 4.3. Some of the `Calendar` control's properties

Property	Description
DayNameFormat	This property sets the format of the day names. Its possible values are `FirstLetter`, `FirstTwoLetters`, `Full`, and `Short`. The default is `Short`, which displays the three-letter abbreviation.
FirstDayOfWeek	This property sets the day that begins each week in the calendar. By default, the value of this property is determined by your server's region settings, but you can set this to `Sunday` or `Monday` if you want to control it.
NextPrevFormat	Set to `CustomText` by default, this property can be set to `ShortMonth` or `FullMonth` to control the format of the next and previous month links.
SelectedDate	This property contains a DateTime value that specifies the highlighted day. You'll use this property often, to determine which date the user has selected.
SelectionMode	This property determines whether days, weeks, or months can be selected; its possible values are `Day`, `DayWeek`, `DayWeekMonth`, and `None`, and the default is `Day`. When `Day` is selected, a user can only select a day; when `DayWeek` is selected, a user can select a day or an entire week; and so on.
SelectMonthText	This property controls the text of the link that's displayed to allow users to select an entire month from the calendar.
SelectWeekText	This property controls the text of the link that's displayed to allow users to select an entire week from the calendar.
ShowDayHeader	If `True`, this property displays the names of the days of the week. The default is `True`.
ShowGridLines	If `True`, this property renders the calendar with grid lines. The default is `True`.
ShowNextPrevMonth	If `True`, this property displays **next month** and **previous month** links. The default is `True`.
ShowTitle	If `True`, this property displays the calendar's title. The default is `False`.
TitleFormat	This property determines how the month name appears in the title bar. Possible values are `Month` and `MonthYear`. The default is `MonthYear`.
TodaysDate	This DateTime value sets the calendar's current date. By default, this value is not highlighted within the `Calendar` control.
VisibleDate	This DateTime value controls which month is displayed.

Let's take a look at an example that uses some of these properties, events, and methods to create a `Calendar` control which allows users to select days, weeks, and months. Modify the calendar in **Calendar.aspx** (both the VB and C# versions), and add a label to it, as follows:

```
                                    LearningASP\VB\Calendar_02.aspx (excerpt)

  <form id="form1" runat="server">
  <div>
    <h1>Pick your dates:</h1>
    <asp:Calendar ID="myCalendar" runat="server"
        DayNameFormat="Short" FirstDayOfWeek="Sunday"
        NextPrevFormat="FullMonth" SelectionMode="DayWeekMonth"
        SelectWeekText="Select Week"
        SelectMonthText="Select Month" TitleFormat="Month"
        OnSelectionChanged="SelectionChanged" />
    <h1>You selected these dates:</h1>
    <asp:Label ID="myLabel" runat="server" />
  </div>
  </form>
```

Now edit the `<script runat="server">` tag to include the `SelectionChanged` event handler referenced by your calendar:

```
Visual Basic                        LearningASP\VB\Calendar_02.aspx (excerpt)

<script runat="server">
  Sub SelectionChanged(ByVal s As Object, ByVal e As EventArgs)
    myLabel.Text = ""
    For Each d As DateTime In myCalendar.SelectedDates
      myLabel.Text &= d.ToString("D") & "<br />"
    Next
  End Sub
</script>
```

```
C#                                  LearningASP\CS\Calendar_02.aspx (excerpt)

<script runat="server">
  void SelectionChanged(Object s, EventArgs e)
  {
    myLabel.Text = "";
```

```
    foreach (DateTime d in myCalendar.SelectedDates)
    {
      myLabel.Text += d.ToString("D") + "<br />";
    }
  }
</script>
```

Save your work and test it in a browser. Try selecting a day, week, or month. The selection will be highlighted in a similar way to the display shown in Figure 4.5.

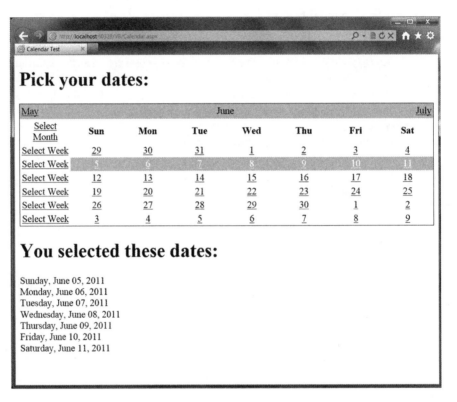

Figure 4.5. Using the `Calendar` control

In `SelectionChanged`, we loop through each of the dates that the user has selected, and append each to the `Label` we added to the page.

AdRotator

The `AdRotator` control allows you to display a list of banner advertisements at random within your web application. However, it's more than a mere substitute for creating a randomization script from scratch. Since the `AdRotator` control gets its content from an XML file, the administration and updating of banner advertisement files and their properties is a snap. Also, the XML file allows you to control the banner's image, link, link target, and frequency of appearance in relation to other banner ads.

The benefits of using this control don't stop there, though. Most of the `AdRotator` control's properties reside within an XML file, so, if you wanted to, you could share that XML file on the Web, allowing value added resellers (VARS), or possibly your companies' partners, to use your banner advertisements on their web sites.

What Is XML?

In essence, XML is simply a text-based format for the transfer or storage of data; it contains no details about how that data should be presented. XML is very easy to start with because of its close resemblance to your old friend HTML: both are largely comprised of tags inside angle brackets (< and >), and any tag may contain attributes that are specific to that tag. The biggest difference between XML and HTML is that, rather than providing a fixed set of tags as HTML does, XML allows us to create our own tags to describe the data we wish to represent.

Take a look at the following HTML element:

```
<h1>Star Wars Episode I: The Phantom Menace</h1>
```

This example describes the content between the tags as a level one heading. This is fine if all we want to do is display the heading "Star Wars Episode I: The Phantom Menace" on a web page. But what if we want to access those words as data?

Like HTML, XML's purpose is to describe the content of a document. But where HTML is a very generic markup language for documents—headings, paragraphs and lists, for example—XML can, very specifically, describe *what the content is*. Using XML, the web author can mark up the contents of a document, describing that content in terms of its relevance as data.

We can use XML to mark up the words "Star Wars Episode I: The Phantom Menace" in a way that better reflects this content's significance as data:

```
<film>
  <title>Star Wars Episode I: The Phantom Menace</title>
</film>
```

Here, the XML tag names we've chosen best describe the contents of the element. We also define our own attribute names as necessary. For instance, in the example above, you may decide that you want to differentiate between the VHS version and the DVD version of the film, or record the name of the movie's director. This can be achieved by adding attributes and elements, as shown below:

```
<film format="DVD">
    <title>Star Wars Episode I: The Phantom Menace</title>
    <director>George Lucas</director>
</film>
```

If you want to test this control out, create a file called **ads.xml** in your **LearningASP\VB** or **LearningASP\CS** folder (or both), and insert the content presented below. Feel free to create your own banners, or to use those provided in the code archive for this book:

LearningASP\VB\Ads.xml

```xml
<?xml version="1.0" encoding="utf-8" ?>
<Advertisements>
  <Ad>
    <ImageUrl>workatdorknozzle.gif</ImageUrl>
    <NavigateUrl>http://www.example.com</NavigateUrl>
    <TargetUrl>_blank</TargetUrl>
    <AlternateText>Work at Dorknozzle!</AlternateText>
    <Keyword>HR Sites</Keyword>
    <Impressions>2</Impressions>
  </Ad>
  <Ad>
    <ImageUrl>getthenewsletter.gif</ImageUrl>
    <NavigateUrl>http://www.example.com</NavigateUrl>
    <TargetUrl>_blank</TargetUrl>
    <AlternateText>Get the Nozzle Newsletter!</AlternateText>
    <Keyword>Marketing Sites</Keyword>
    <Impressions>1</Impressions>
  </Ad>
</Advertisements>
```

As you can see, the Advertisements element is the root node, and in accordance with the XML specification, it appears only once. For each individual advertisement, we simply add an Ad child element. For instance, the above advertisement file contains details for two banner advertisements.

As you've probably noticed by now, the **.xml** file enables you to specify properties for each banner advertisement by inserting appropriate elements inside each of the Ad elements. These elements include:

ImageURL

the URL of the image to display for the banner ad

NavigateURL

the web page to which your users will navigate when they click the banner ad

AlternateText

the alternative text to display for browsers that don't support images

Keyword

the keyword to use to categorize your banner ad

If you use the KeywordFilter property of the AdRotator control, you can specify the categories of banner ads to display.

Impressions

the relative frequency with which a particular banner ad should be shown in relation to other banner advertisements

The higher this number, the more frequently that specific banner will display in the browser. The number provided for this element can be as low as one, but cannot exceed 2,048,000,000; if it does, the page throws an exception.

Except for ImageURL, all these elements are optional. Also, if you specify an Ad without a NavigateURL, the banner ad will display without a hyperlink.

To make use of this **Ads.xml** file, create a new ASP.NET page called **AdRotator.aspx**, and add the following code to it:

Visual Basic	LearningASP\VB\AdRotator.aspx

```
<%@ Page Language="VB" %>

<!DOCTYPE html PUBLIC "-//W3C//DTD XHTML 1.0 Transitional//EN"
```

```
        "http://www.w3.org/TR/xhtml1/DTD/xhtml1-transitional.dtd">

<script runat="server">

</script>

<html xmlns="http://www.w3.org/1999/xhtml">
  <head runat="server">
    <title>Using the AdRotator Control</title>
  </head>
  <body>
    <form id="form1" runat="server">
    <div>
      <asp:AdRotator ID="adRotator" runat="server"
          AdvertisementFile="Ads.xml" />
    </div>
    </form>
  </body>
</html>
```

Figure 4.6. Displaying ads using **AdRotator.aspx**

As with most of our examples, the C# version of this code is the same except for
the Page declaration. You'll also need to copy the **workatdorknozzle.gif** and
getthenewsletter.gif image files from the code archive and place them in your
working folder in order to see these ad images. Save your work and test it in the
browser; the display should look something like Figure 4.6.

Refresh the page a few times, and you'll notice that the first banner appears more
often than the second. This occurs because the Impression value for the first Ad is
double the value set for the second banner, so it will appear twice as often.

TreeView

The `TreeView` control is a very powerful control that's capable of displaying a complex hierarchical structure of items. Typically, we'd use it to view a directory structure or a site navigation hierarchy, but it could be used to display a family tree, a corporate organizational structure, or any other hierarchical structure.

The `TreeView` can pull its data from various sources. We'll talk more about the various kinds of data sources later in the book; here, we'll focus on the `SiteMapDataSource` class, which, as its name suggests, contains a hierarchical sitemap. By default, this sitemap is read from a file called **Web.sitemap** that's located in the root of your project (you can easily create this file using the **Site Map** template in Visual Web Developer). **Web.sitemap** is an XML file that looks like this:

LearningASP\VB\Web.sitemap

```
<siteMap
    xmlns="http://schemas.microsoft.com/AspNet/SiteMap-File-1.0">
  <siteMapNode title="Home" url="~/Default.aspx"
      description="Home">
    <siteMapNode title="SiteMapPath" url="~/SiteMapPath.aspx"
        description="TreeView Example" />
    <siteMapNode title="TreeView" url="~/TreeViewSitemap.aspx"
        description="TreeView Example" />
    <siteMapNode title="ClickEvent" url="~/ClickEvent.aspx"
        description="ClickEvent Example" />
    <siteMapNode title="Loops"  url="~/Loops.aspx"
        description="Loops Example" />
  </siteMapNode>
</siteMap>
```

 A Web.sitemap Limitation

An important limitation to note when you're working with **Web.sitemap** files is that they must contain only one `siteMapNode` as the direct child of the root `siteMap` element.

In the example above, the `siteMapNode` with the title Home is this single `siteMapNode`. If we added another `siteMapNode` alongside (rather than inside) this element, the **Web.sitemap** file would no longer be valid.

To use this file, you'll need to add a `SiteMapDataSource` control to the page, as well as a `TreeView` control that uses this data source, like this:

```
Visual Basic                                    LearningASP\VB\TreeViewSiteMap.aspx

<%@ Page Language="VB" %>

<!DOCTYPE html PUBLIC "-//W3C//DTD XHTML 1.0 Transitional//EN"
    "http://www.w3.org/TR/xhtml1/DTD/xhtml1-transitional.dtd">

<script runat="server">

</script>

<html xmlns="http://www.w3.org/1999/xhtml">
  <head runat="server">
    <title>TreeView Demo</title>
  </head>
  <body>
    <form id="form1" runat="server">
    <div>
      <asp:SiteMapDataSource ID="mySiteMapDataSource"
          runat="server" />
      <asp:TreeView ID="myTreeView" runat="server"
          DataSourceID="mySiteMapDataSource" />
    </div>
    </form>
  </body>
</html>
```

Note that although the `SiteMapDataSource` is a control, it doesn't generate any HTML within the web page. There are many data source controls like this; we'll delve into them in more detail later.

When combined with the example **Web.sitemap** file above, this web form would generate an output like that shown in Figure 4.7.

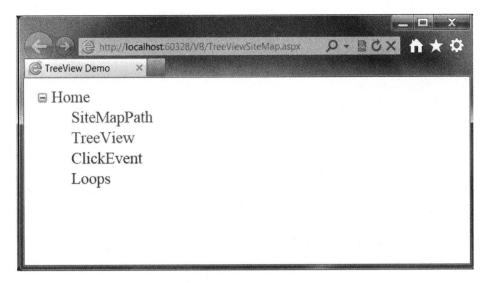

Figure 4.7. A simple `TreeView` control

As you can see, the `TreeView` control generated the tree for us. The root **Home** node can even be collapsed or expanded.

In many cases, we won't want to show the root node; we can hide it from view by setting the `ShowStartingNode` property of the `SiteMapDataSource` to `false`:

```
<asp:SiteMapDataSource ID="mySiteMapDataSource" runat="server"
    ShowStartingNode="false" />
```

SiteMapPath

The `SiteMapPath` control provides the functionality to generate a **breadcrumb** navigational structure for your site. Breadcrumb systems help to orientate users, giving them an easy way to identify their current location within the site, and providing handy links to the current location's ancestor nodes. An example of a breadcrumb navigation system is shown in Figure 4.8.

The `SiteMapPath` control will automatically use any `SiteMapDataSource` control that exists in a web form, such as the `TreeView` control in the previous example, to display a user's current location within the site. For example, you could simply add the following code to a new web form to achieve the effect shown in Figure 4.8:

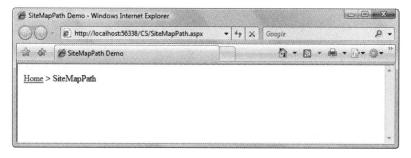

Figure 4.8. A breadcrumb created using the `SiteMapPath` control

Visual Basic	LearningASP\VB\SiteMapPath.aspx

```
<%@ Page Language="VB" %>

<!DOCTYPE html PUBLIC "-//W3C//DTD XHTML 1.0 Transitional//EN"
    "http://www.w3.org/TR/xhtml1/DTD/xhtml1-transitional.dtd">

<script runat="server">

</script>

<html xmlns="http://www.w3.org/1999/xhtml">
  <head runat="server">
    <title>SiteMapPath Demo</title>
  </head>
  <body>
    <form id="form1" runat="server">
    <div>
      <asp:SiteMapDataSource ID="mySiteMapDataSource"
          runat="server" />
      <asp:SiteMapPath ID="mySiteMapPath" runat="server"
          DataSourceID="mySiteMapDataSource"
          PathSeparator=" > " />
    </div>
    </form>
  </body>
</html>
```

Note that the `SiteMapPath` control allows you to customize the breadcrumbs' separator character via the `PathSeparator` property. Also note that if you don't have a file named **Default.aspx** in the directory, the root node link won't work.

Menu

The Menu control is similar to TreeView in that it displays hierarchical data from a data source; the ways in which we work with both controls are also very similar. The most important differences between the two lie in their appearances, and the fact that Menu supports templates for better customization, and displays only two levels of items (menu items and submenu items).

MultiView

The MultiView control is similar to Panel in that it doesn't generate interface elements itself, but contains other controls. However, a MultiView can store more pages of data (called **views**), and lets you show one page at a time. You can change the active view (the one that's being presented to the visitor) by setting the value of the ActiveViewIndex property. The first page corresponds to an ActiveViewIndex of 0; the value of the second page is 1; the value of the third page is 2; and so on.

The contents of each template are defined inside child View elements. Consider the following code example, which creates a Button control and a MultiView control:

```
Visual Basic                                    LearningASP\VB\MultiView.aspx

<%@ Page Language="VB" %>

<!DOCTYPE html PUBLIC "-//W3C//DTD XHTML 1.0 Transitional//EN"
  "http://www.w3.org/TR/xhtml1/DTD/xhtml1-transitional.dtd">

<script runat="server">
  Sub SwitchPage(s as Object, e as EventArgs)
    myMultiView.ActiveViewIndex = _
        (myMultiView.ActiveViewIndex + 1) Mod 2
  End Sub
</script>

<html xmlns="http://www.w3.org/1999/xhtml">
  <head runat="server">
    <title>MultiView Demo</title>
  </head>
  <body>
    <form id="form1" runat="server">
    <div>
      <p>
        <asp:Button ID="myButton" Text="Switch Page"
```

```
            runat="server" OnClick="SwitchPage" />
    </p>
    <asp:MultiView ID="myMultiView" runat="server"
        ActiveViewIndex="0">
      <asp:View ID="firstView" runat="server">
        <p>... contents of the first view ...</p>
      </asp:View>
      <asp:View ID="secondView" runat="server">
        <p>... contents of the second view ...</p>
      </asp:View>
    </asp:MultiView>
    </div>
    </form>
  </body>
</html>
```

C#   LearningASP\CS\MultiView.aspx *(excerpt)*

```
<%@ Page Language="C#" %>
⋮
<script runat="server">
  public void SwitchPage(Object s, EventArgs e)
  {
    myMultiView.ActiveViewIndex =
        (myMultiView.ActiveViewIndex + 1) % 2;
  }
</script>
⋮
```

As you can see, by default, the ActiveViewIndex is 0, so when this code is first executed, the MultiView will display its first template, which is shown in Figure 4.9.

Clicking on the button will cause the second template to be displayed. The SwitchPage event handler uses the modulo operator, Mod in VB and % in C#, to set the ActiveViewIndex to 1 when its original value is 0, and vice versa

The MultiView control has a number of other handy features, so be sure to check the documentation for this control if you're using it in a production environment.

Figure 4.9. Using the MultiView control

Wizard

The Wizard control is a more advanced version of the MultiView control. It can display one or more pages at a time, but also includes additional built-in functionality such as navigation buttons, and a sidebar that displays the wizard's steps.

FileUpload

The FileUpload control allows you to let visitors upload files to your server. You'll learn how to use this control in Chapter 14.

Web User Controls

As you build real-world projects, you'll frequently encounter pieces of the user interface that appear in multiple places—headers or footers, navigation links, and login boxes are just a few examples. Packaging their forms and behaviors into your own controls will allow you to reuse these components just as you can reuse ASP.NET's built-in controls.

Building your own web server controls involves writing advanced VB or C# code, and is not within the scope of this book, but it's good to know that it's possible. Creating customized web server controls makes sense when you need to build more complex controls that provide a high level of control and performance, or you want to create controls that can be integrated easily into many projects.

Those of us without advanced coding skills can develop our own controls by creating **web user controls**. These are also powerful and reusable within a given project; they can expose properties, events, and methods, just like other controls; and they're easy to implement.

A web user control is represented by a class that inherits from `System.Web.UI.UserControl`, and contains the basic functionality that you need to extend to create your own controls. The main drawback to using web user controls is that they're tightly integrated into the projects in which they're implemented. As such, it's more difficult to distribute them, or include them in other projects, than it is to distribute or reuse web server controls.

Web user controls are implemented very much like normal web forms—they're comprised of other controls, HTML markup, and server-side code. The file extension of a web user control is **.ascx**.

Creating a Web User Control

Let's get a feel for web user controls by stepping through a simple example. Let's say that in your web site, you have many forms consisting of pairs of `Label` and `TextBox` controls, like the one shown in Figure 4.10.

All the labels must have a fixed width of 100 pixels, and the text boxes must accept a maximum of 20 characters.

Rather than adding many labels and text boxes to the form, and then having to set all their properties, let's make life easier by building a web user control that includes a `Label` of the specified width, and a `TextBox` that accepts 20 characters; you'll then be able to reuse the web user control wherever it's needed in your project.

Create a new file in you working project using the Web User Control template, as shown in Figure 4.11.

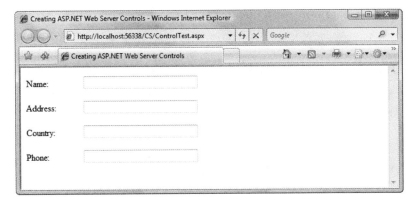

Figure 4.10. A simple form

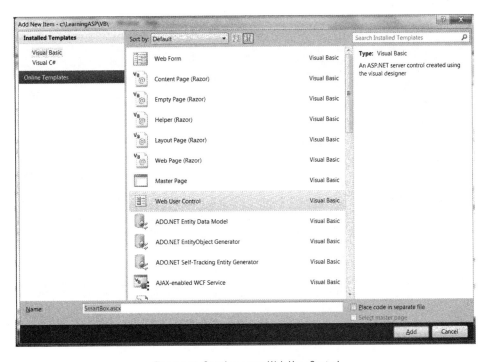

Figure 4.11. Creating a new Web User Control

Name the file SmartBox.ascx. Then, add the control's constituent controls—a Label control and a TextBox control—as shown below (for both VB and C# versions):

```
Visual Basic                              LearningASP\VB\SmartBox.ascx (excerpt)

<%@ Control Language="VB" ClassName="SmartBox" %>

<script runat="server">
⋮
</script>

<p>
  <asp:Label ID="myLabel" runat="server" Text="" Width="100" />
  <asp:TextBox ID="myTextBox" runat="server" Text="" Width="200"
      MaxLength="20" />
</p>
```

 Label Widths in Firefox

Unfortunately, setting the Width property of the Label control doesn't guarantee that the label will appear at that width in all browsers. The current version of Firefox, for example, will not display the above label in the way it appears in Internet Explorer.

To get around this pitfall, you should use a CSS style sheet and the CssClass property, which we'll take a look at later in this chapter.

In Chapter 3 we discussed properties briefly, but we didn't explain how you could create your own properties within your own classes. So far, you've worked with many properties of the built-in controls. For example, you've seen a lot of code that sets the Text property of the Label control.

As a web user control is a class, it can also have methods, properties, and so on. Our SmartBox control extends the base System.Web.UI.UserControl class by adding two properties:

- LabelText is a write-only property that allows the forms using the control to set the control's label text.

- Text is a read-only property that returns the text the user typed into the text box.

Let's add a server-side script element that will give our control two properties—one called Text, for the text in the TextBox, and one called LabelText, for the text in the Label:

Visual Basic   **LearningASP\VB\SmartBox.ascx** *(excerpt)*

```
<%@ Control Language="VB" ClassName="SmartBox" %>

<script runat="server">
  Public WriteOnly Property LabelText() As String
    Set(ByVal value As String)
      myLabel.Text = value
    End Set
  End Property

  Public ReadOnly Property Text() As String
    Get
      Text = myTextBox.Text
    End Get
  End Property
</script>

<p>
  <asp:Label ID="myLabel" runat="server" Text="" Width="100" />
  <asp:TextBox ID="myTextBox" runat="server" Text="" Width="200"
      MaxLength="20" />
</p>
```

C#   **LearningASP\CS\SmartBox.ascx** *(excerpt)*

```
<%@ Control Language="C#" ClassName="SmartBox" %>

<script runat="server">
  public string LabelText
  {
    set
    {
      myLabel.Text = value;
    }
  }
  public string Text
  {
    get
    {
      return myTextBox.Text;
    }
  }
</script>
```

```
<p>
  <asp:Label ID="myLabel" runat="server" Text="" Width="100" />
  <asp:TextBox ID="myTextBox" runat="server" Text="" Width="200"
      MaxLength="20" />
</p>
```

When you use the SmartBox control in a form, you can set its label and have the text entered by the user, like this:

Visual Basic

```
mySmartBox.LabelText = "Address:"
userAddress = mySmartBox.Text
```

C#

```
mySmartBox.LabelText = "Address:";
userAddress = mySmartBox.Text;
```

Let's see how we implemented this functionality. In .NET, properties can be read-only, write-only, or read-write. In many cases, you'll want to have properties that can be both readable and writeable, but in this case, we want to be able to set the text of the inner Label, and to read the text from the TextBox.

To define a write-only property in VB, you need to use the WriteOnly modifier. Write-only properties need only define a special block of code that starts with the keyword Set. This block of code, called an **accessor**, is just like a subroutine that takes as a parameter the value that needs to be set. The block of code uses this value to perform the desired action—in the case of the LabelText property, the action sets the Text property of our Label control, as shown below:

Visual Basic   LearningASP\VB\SmartBox.ascx *(excerpt)*

```
Public WriteOnly Property LabelText() As String
  Set(ByVal value As String)
    myLabel.Text = value
  End Set
End Property
```

Assuming that a form uses a `SmartBox` object called `mySmartBox`, we could set the `Text` property of the `Label` like this:

Visual Basic

```
mySmartBox.LabelText = "Address:"
```

When this code is executed, the `Set` accessor of the `LabelText` property is executed with its *value* parameter set to `Address:`. The `Set` accessor uses this value to set the `Text` property of the `Label`.

The other accessor you can use when defining properties is `Get`, which allows us to read values instead of writing them. Obviously, you aren't allowed to add a `Get` accessor to a `WriteOnly` property, but one is required for a `ReadOnly` property, such as `Text`:

Visual Basic   LearningASP\VB\SmartBox.ascx *(excerpt)*

```
Public ReadOnly Property Text() As String
  Get
    Text = myTextBox.Text
  End Get
End Property
```

The `Text` property is `ReadOnly`, but it doesn't need to be. If you wanted to allow the forms using the control to set some default text to the `TextBox`, you'd need to add a `Set` accessor, and remove the `ReadOnly` modifier.

When you're defining a property in C#, you don't need to set any special modifiers, such as `ReadOnly` or `WriteOnly`, for read-only or write-only properties. A property that has only a `get` accessor will, by default, be considered read-only:

C#   LearningASP\CS\SmartBox.ascx *(excerpt)*

```
public string Text
{
  get
  {
    return myTextBox.Text;
  }
}
```

Likewise, a property that has only a `set` accessor will be considered to be write-only:

```
C#                                          LearningASP\CS\SmartBox.ascx (excerpt)

public string LabelText
{
  set
  {
    myLabel.Text = value;
  }
}
```

Using the Web User Control

Once the user control has been created, it can be referenced from any ASP.NET page using the `Register` directive, as follows:

```
<%@ Register TagPrefix="prefix" TagName="name"
    Src="source.ascx" %>
```

The `Register` directive requires three attributes:

TagPrefix

the prefix for the user control, which allows you to group related controls together, and avoid naming conflicts

TagName

the control's tag name, which will be used when the control is added to the ASP.NET page

Src

the path to the **.ascx** file that describes the user control

After we register the control, we create instances of it using the `<TagPrefix:TagName>` format. Let's try an example that uses the `SmartBox` control. Create a Web Form named **ControlTest.aspx** in your project folder, and give it this content:

Visual Basic	LearningASP\VB\ControlTest.aspx

```
<%@ Page Language="VB" %>
<%@ Register TagPrefix="sp" TagName="SmartBox"
    Src="SmartBox.ascx" %>
<!DOCTYPE html PUBLIC "-//W3C//DTD XHTML 1.0 Transitional//EN"
    "http://www.w3.org/TR/xhtml1/DTD/xhtml1-transitional.dtd">

<script runat="server">

</script>

<html xmlns="http://www.w3.org/1999/xhtml">
  <head runat="server">
    <title>Creating ASP.NET Web Server Controls</title>
  </head>
  <body>
    <form id="form1" runat="server">
    <div>
      <sp:SmartBox ID="nameSb" runat="server"
          LabelText="Name:" />
      <sp:SmartBox ID="addressSb" runat="server"
          LabelText="Address:" />
      <sp:SmartBox ID="countrySb" runat="server"
          LabelText="Country:" />
      <sp:SmartBox ID="phoneSb" runat="server"
          LabelText="Phone:" />
    </div>
    </form>
  </body>
</html>
```

Creating this page by hand will really help you to understand the process of building a web form. In time, you'll learn how to use Visual Web Developer to do part of the work for you. For example, you can drag a user control from **Solution Explorer** and drop it onto a web form; Visual Web Developer will register the control and add an instance of the control for you. Loading this page will produce the output we saw in Figure 4.10.

Now, this is a very simple example indeed, but we can easily extend it for other purposes. You can see in the above code snippet that we set the LabelText property directly using the control's attributes; however, we could have accessed the properties from our code instead. Here's an example in which we set the `LabelText` properties of each of the controls using VB and C#:

Visual Basic

```
<script runat="server">
  Protected Sub Page_Load()
    nameSb.LabelText = "Name:"
    addressSb.LabelText = "Address:"
    countrySb.LabelText = "Country:"
    phoneSb.LabelText = "Phone:"
  End Sub
</script>
```

C#

```
<script runat="server">
  protected void Page_Load()
  {
    nameSb.LabelText = "Name:";
    addressSb.LabelText = "Address:";
    countrySb.LabelText = "Country:";
    phoneSb.LabelText = "Phone:";
  }
</script>
```

Master Pages

Master pages are an important feature that was introduced in ASP.NET 2.0. Master pages are similar to web user controls in that they, too, are composed of HTML and other controls; they can be extended with the addition of events, methods, or properties; and they can't be loaded directly by users—instead, they're used as building blocks to design the structure of your web forms. forms. You got a taste of master pages when you created your first ASP.NET project in Chapter 1, since the Visual Web Developer IDE automatically includes a sample master page when you created your project file.

A master page is a page template that can be applied to give many web forms a consistent appearance. For example, a master page can set out a standard structure containing the header, footer, and other elements that you expect to display in multiple web forms within a web application.

Master page files have the **.master** extension, and, just like web forms and web user controls, they support code-behind files. All master pages inherit from the class `System.Web.UI.MasterPage`.

Designing a site structure using master pages and web user controls gives you the power to modify and extend the site easily. If your site uses these features in a well-planned way, it can be very easy to modify certain details of the layout or functionality of your site, because updating a master page or a web user control takes immediate effect on all the web forms that use the file.

As we've already mentioned, a master page is built using HTML and controls, including the special `ContentPlaceHolder` control. As its name suggests, the `ContentPlaceHolder` is a placeholder that can be filled with content that's relevant to the needs of each web form that uses the master page. In creating a master page, we include all of the basic structure of future pages in the master page itself, including the <html>, <head>, and <body> tags, and let the web forms specify the content that appears in the placeholders.

Let's see how this works with a simple example. Suppose we have a site with many pages, all of which contain a standard header, footer, and navigation menu, laid out as per the wireframe shown in Figure 4.12.

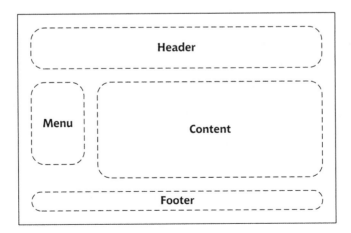

Figure 4.12. A simple web site layout

If all the pages in the site have the same header, footer, and navigation menu, it makes sense to include these components in a master page, and to build several web forms that customize only the content areas on each page. We'll begin to create such a site in Chapter 5, but let's work through a quick example here.

To keep this example simple, we won't include a menu here: we'll include just the header, the footer, and the content placeholder. Add a new file to your project using the **Master Page** template in Visual Web Developer. Name the file **FrontPages.master**, as shown in Figure 4.13, and select the appropriate language. You'll notice that some <asp:ContentPlaceHolder> tags have been created for you already, one in the <head>, and one in the page body. You can remove them and modify the page like this:

```
Visual Basic                                    LearningASP\VB\FrontPages.master

<%@ Master Language="VB" %>

<!DOCTYPE html PUBLIC "-//W3C//DTD XHTML 1.0 Transitional//EN"
    "http://www.w3.org/TR/xhtml1/DTD/xhtml1-transitional.dtd">

<script runat="server">

</script>

<html xmlns="http://www.w3.org/1999/xhtml">
  <head runat="server">
    <title>Untitled Page</title>
  </head>
  <body>
    <form id="form1" runat="server">
    <div>
      <h1>Welcome to SuperSite Inc!</h1>
      <asp:ContentPlaceHolder ID="FrontPageContent"
          runat="server" />
      <p>Copyright 2006</p>
    </div>
    </form>
  </body>
</html>
```

Again, the C# version is identical except for the Master declaration at the top of the page:

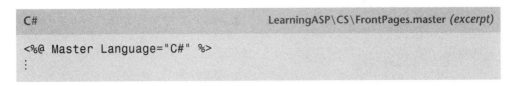

```
C#                                          LearningASP\CS\FrontPages.master (excerpt)

<%@ Master Language="C#" %>
⋮
```

Figure 4.13. Creating a Master Page

The master page looks almost like a web form, except for one important detail: it has an empty `ContentPlaceHolder` control. If you want to build a web form based on this master page, you just need to reference the master page using the `Page` directive in the web form, and add a `Content` control that includes the content you want to insert.

Let's try it. Create a web form in Visual Web Developer called **FrontPage.aspx**, and check the **Select master page** option. This option will allow you to choose a master page for the form; Visual Web Developer will then use that master page to generate the code for you. Edit it to match this code snippet:

Visual Basic   *LearningASP\VB\FrontPage.aspx (excerpt)*

```
<%@ Page Language="VB" MasterPageFile="~/FrontPages.master"
    Title="Front Page" %>

<script runat="server">

</script>

<asp:Content ID="Content1" ContentPlaceHolderID="FrontPageContent"
    Runat="Server">
  <p>
    Welcome to our web site! We hope you'll enjoy your visit.
  </p>
</asp:Content>
```

The VB and C# versions of this code are the same except for the Language attribute on the Page declaration, but because Visual Web Developer generates all the code for you automatically, you don't need to worry about it—instead, you can focus on the content.

You're all set now! Executing **FrontPage.aspx** will generate the output shown in Figure 4.14.

Figure 4.14. Using a master page to set the header and footer

Although the example is simplistic, it's easy to see the possibilities: you can create many web forms based on this template very easily. In our case, the master page contains a single `ContentPlaceHolder`, but it could have more. Also, we can define within the master page default content for display inside the `ContentPlaceHolder` on pages whose web forms don't provide a `Content` element for that placeholder.

We'll explore Visual Web Developer's capabilities in more depth in the following chapters, but for now you can play around with it yourself, using **Design** mode to visually edit web forms that are based on master pages. Looking at Figure 4.15, you can see that the content of the master page is read-only, and that you can edit only the content areas of the page.

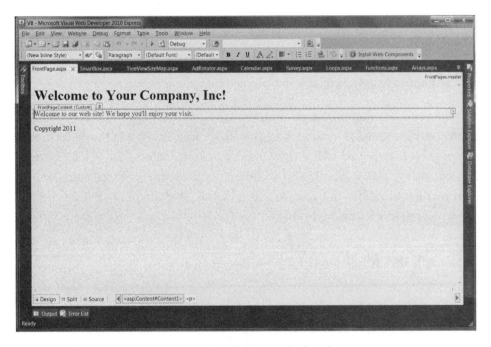

Figure 4.15. **Design** mode shows the editable areas of a form that uses a master page

Using Cascading Style Sheets (CSS)

It's clear that controls make it easy for us to reuse pieces of functionality in multiple locations. For example, I can't imagine an easier way to add calendars to many web forms than to use the `Calendar` web server control.

However, controls don't solve the problem of defining and managing the visual elements of your web site. Modern web sites need constant updating to keep them fresh, and it's not much fun editing hundreds of pages by hand just to change a border color, for example, and then having to check everything to ensure that your changes are consistent. The process is even more painful if your client wants a more serious update, like a rearrangement of the components on the pages.

The good news is that this maintenance work can be made a lot easier if you plan ahead, correctly follow a few basic rules, and efficiently use the tools that HTML and ASP.NET offer you.

An essential tool for building reusable visual styles is **Cascading Style Sheets (CSS)**. HTML was initially designed to deliver simple text content, and didn't address the specifics of how particular items appeared in the browser. HTML left it to the individual browsers to work out these intricacies, and tailor the output to the limitations and strengths of users' machines. While we can change font styles, sizes, colors, and so on using HTML tags, this practice can lead to verbose code and pages that are very hard to restyle at a later date.

CSS gives web developers the power to create one set of styles in a single location, and to apply those styles to all of the pages in our web site. All of the pages to which the style sheet is applied will display the same fonts, colors, and sizes, giving the site a consistent feel. Regardless of whether our site contains three pages or 300, when we alter the styles in the style sheet, our changes are immediately applied to all the pages that use that style sheet.

 Look Out for Themes and Skins

> ASP.NET provides extra value and power to those building reusable visual elements through offerings like themes and skins. You'll learn more about these features in Chapter 5.

Types of Styles and Style Sheets

There are three ways in which you can associate styles with the elements of a particular web page:

using an external style sheet
> If you place your **style rules** in an external style sheet, you can link this file to any web page on which you want those styles to be used, which makes updating a web site's overall appearance a cakewalk.

To reference an external style sheet from a web form, place the following markup inside the head element:

```
<link rel="stylesheet" type="text/css" href="file.css" />
```

In the above example, **file.css** would be a text file containing CSS rules, much like the example shown below, which sets the background and foreground color of all <a> elements:

```
a {
  background-color: #ff9;
  color: #00f;
}
```

using an embedded style sheet

You can place style rules for a page between <style type="text/css"> tags inside that page's head element, like so:

```
<style type="text/css">
  a {
    background-color: #ff9;
    color: #00f;
  }
</style>
```

The problem with using embedded styles is that we can't reuse those styles in another page without typing them in again—an approach that makes global changes to the site very difficult to manage.

using inline style rules

Inline styles allow us to set the styles for a single element using the style attribute. For instance, we'd apply the style declarations from our previous example to a specific <a> tag like this:

```
<a href="/" style="background-color: #ff9; color: #00f;">
  Home
</a>
```

When it's used in embedded or external style sheets, a style rule has a selector, followed by a declaration block that contains one or more style declarations. Consider this example:

```
a {
  background-color: #ff9;
  color: #00f;
}
```

Here we have a style rule with a selector, a, followed by a declaration block that contains two style declarations: one for the background-color property, and one for the color property. A declaration block is delimited by curly braces: {…}. A style declaration consists of a property, a colon (:) and a value. Multiple declarations are delimited by semicolons (;), but it's a good practice to put a semicolon at the end of all your declarations.

The **selector** in a style rule determines the elements to which that rule will apply. In ASP.NET, we typically use two types of selectors:

element type selectors

An element type selector targets every single instance of the specified element. For example, if we wanted to change the colour of all second-level headings in a document, we'd use an element type selector to target all <h2>s:

```
h2 {
  color: #369;
}
```

class selectors

Arguably the most popular way to use styles within your pages is to give each element a class attribute, then target elements that have a certain class value. For example, the following markup shows a paragraph whose class attribute is set to pageinfo:

```
<p class="pageinfo">
  Copyright 2006
</p>
```

Now, given that any element with the class `pageinfo` should be displayed in fine print, we can create a style rule that will reduce the size of the text in this paragraph, and any other element with the attribute `class="pageinfo"`, using a class selector. The class selector consists of a dot (.) and the class name:

```
.pageinfo {
  font-family: Arial;
  font-size: x-small;
}
```

Whether you're building external style sheets, embedded style sheets, or inline style rules, style declarations use the same syntax.

Now that you have a basic understanding of some of the fundamental concepts behind CSS, let's look at the different types of styles that can be used within our ASP.NET applications.

Style Properties

You can specify many different types of properties within style sheets. Here's a list of the most common property types:

font

This category of properties gives you the ability to format text-level elements, including their font faces, sizes, decorations, weights, colors, and so on.

background

This category allows you to customize backgrounds for objects and text. These values give you control over the background, including whether you'd like to use a color or an image for the background, and whether or not you want to repeat a background image.

block

This category allows you to modify the spacing between paragraphs, between lines of text, between words, and between letters.

box

The box category allows us to customize tables. If you need to modify borders, padding, spacing, and colors on a table, row, or cell, use the elements within this category.

border

> This category lets you draw borders of different colors, styles, and thicknesses around page elements.

list

> This category allows you to customize the way ordered and unordered lists are displayed.

positioning

> Modifying positioning allows you to move and position tags and controls freely.

These categories outline the aspects of a page design that can typically be modified using CSS. As we progress through the book, the many types of style properties will become evident.

The `CssClass` Property

Once you've defined a class in a style sheet (be it external or internal), you'll want to begin to associate that class with elements in your web forms. You can associate classes with ASP.NET web server controls using the `CssClass` property. In most cases, the value you give the `CssClass` property will be used as the value of the resulting element's `class` attribute.

Let's see an example. First, use the **Style Sheet** template to create within your working folder (**LearningASP\VB** or **LearningASP\CS**) a file named **Styles.css**. You'll notice that Visual Web Developer adds an empty style rule to the newly created style sheet file with the selector `body`. We don't need that rule for this example, so just insert this code after it:

Styles.css

```css
body {
}
.title {
  font-family: Arial, Helvetica, sans-serif;
  font-size: 19px;
}
.dropdownmenu {
  font-family: Arial;
  background-color: #0099FF;
}
```

```
.textbox {
  font-family: Arial;
  background-color: #0099FF;
  border: 1px solid
}
.button {
  font-family: Arial;
  background-color: #0099FF;
  border: 1px solid
}
```

Then, create a new web form named **UsingStyles.aspx**, containing this code:

Visual Basic	LearningASP\VB\UsingStyles.aspx

```
<%@ Page Language="VB" %>

<!DOCTYPE html PUBLIC "-//W3C//DTD XHTML 1.0 Transitional//EN"
    "http://www.w3.org/TR/xhtml1/DTD/xhtml1-transitional.dtd">

<script runat="server">

</script>

<html xmlns="http://www.w3.org/1999/xhtml">
  <head runat="server">
    <title>Testing CSS</title>
    <link rel="Stylesheet" type="text/css" href="Styles.css" />
  </head>
  <body>
    <form id="form1" runat="server">
    <div>
      <p class="title">
        Please select a product:</p>
      <p>
        <asp:DropDownList ID="productsList" CssClass="dropdownmenu"
            runat="server">
          <asp:ListItem Text="Shirt" Selected="true" />
          <asp:ListItem Text="Hat" />
          <asp:ListItem Text="Pants" />
          <asp:ListItem Text="Socks" />
        </asp:DropDownList>
      </p>
      <p>
        <asp:TextBox ID="quantityTextBox" CssClass="textbox"
```

```
        runat="server" />
    </p>
    <p>
      <asp:Button ID="addToCartButton" CssClass="button"
          Text="Add To Cart" runat="server" />
    </p>
  </div>
  </form>
  </body>
</html>
```

Loading this page should produce the output shown in Figure 4.16. (We know it doesn't look great—we're programmers, not designers—and it shows! But as far as you understand the principles of using CSS with ASP.NET, you've successfully met the goal of this exercise.)

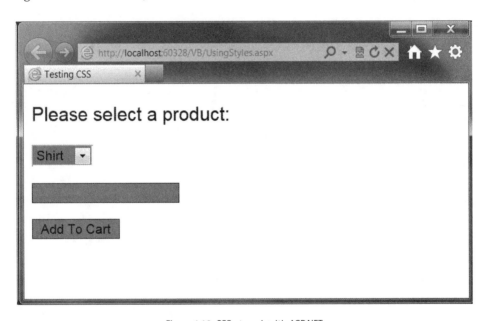

Figure 4.16. CSS at work with ASP.NET

In the next chapter, we'll learn to use Visual Web Developer to create CSS definitions through a simple visual interface.

Summary

In this chapter, we discussed web forms, HTML server controls, web server controls, web user controls, master pages, and CSS. All these elements can be combined to create powerful structures for your web sites.

In the next chapter, we'll start building "real" web applications, putting into practice most of the theory you've learned so far, and using a professional development environment that will do part of the work for you.

5

Building Web Applications

In the previous chapters, we discussed the different pieces of ASP.NET in some detail. In this chapter, you'll start putting together everything you've learned in a larger context. That's right: it's time to build your own web application!

Microsoft defines a **web application** as the collection of all files, pages, handlers, modules, and executable code that can be invoked or run within a given directory on a web server. As we embark on developing a web application, we'll continue using Visual Web Developer 2010 Express Edition, and you'll explore more of the useful features it has in store for ASP.NET developers.

It's worth keeping in mind that you don't have to use Visual Web Developer, or any other specialized tool, to develop ASP.NET web applications: any old text editor will do. However, we recommend using Visual Web Developer for any real-world project that's more complex than a simple, "Hello World"-type example, because this tool can do a lot of the work for you as you build web applications.

In this chapter, you'll learn about much of the functionality Visual Web Developer offers as we start to create an intranet for a company called Dorknozzle. Along the way, we'll also explore many interesting ASP.NET features:

■ We'll use Visual Web Developer to create a new Web Application.

■ We'll work with **Web.config**, **Global.asax**, and the special ASP.NET folders.

■ We'll use the application state, user sessions, the application cache, and cookies.

■ We'll debug your project and handle potential coding errors.

Introducing the Dorknozzle Project

While most books give you a series of simple, isolated examples to illustrate particular techniques, this book is a little different. Most of the examples provided in these pages will see us working on a single project: an intranet application for a fictional company called Dorknozzle. We'll build on this application as we move through the remaining chapters of this book—the Dorknozzle intranet will give us a chance to investigate and grasp the many different concepts that are important to developers of any type of web application.

Now, real-world web development projects are built according to a detailed specification document which, among other information, includes specific details of the site's layout. We'll assume that the pages in the Dorknozzle intranet will be laid out as shown in Figure 5.1.

The menu on the left suggests that the site will have more pages than this homepage. They'll all have the same structure: the menu will sit on the left, and the header will be identical to the one shown here. Only the contents of each individual page will be different from the others. (As mentioned in Chapter 4, you'll already have realized that this is a scenario in which it makes sense to use master pages.)

The intranet application we'll develop will offer the following functionality:

homepage   You can customize this page by including news about the Dorknozzle company.

help desk   This page allows Dorknozzle employees to report problems they experience with software, hardware, or their computers, as help desk tickets that are sent to an IT administrator.

employee directory   Employees will likely want to call each other to discuss important, company-related affairs ... such as last night's television viewing! The employee directory should let

Figure 5.1. The Dorknozzle company intranet site

employees find other staff members' details quickly and easily.

address book   While the employee directory houses handy information for staff use, the purpose of the address book is to provide more detailed information about every employee within the company.

departments   The Departments page displays information about Dorknozzle's various departments.

admin tools   Administrators will need the ability to perform various administrative tasks, such as updating users' information. The Admin Tools section will provide the interface for these kinds of interactions.

admin newsletter   This page will allow administrators to send email newsletters to the company employees.

You'll learn new techniques when building each of these pages. However, before you can begin to create all these smaller applications, we'll need to build the framework that will act as a template for the site as a whole. You've already worked with Visual Web Developer in the previous chapters, but we'll quickly review its features before moving on.

Using Visual Web Developer

We'll start by creating the Dorknozzle project, which will be your working folder for the exercises to come. Start Visual Web Developer, then Select **File** > **New Web Site**….

In the dialog that appears, which is shown in Figure 5.2, select the **ASP.NET Web Site** template, choose your preferred programming language in the **Language** box, and identify the location at which the web site should be created—preferably **C:\Dorknozzle\VB** if you use VB or **C:\Dorknozzle\CS** if you use C#. Feel free to choose the language with which you feel most comfortable, and remember that you can choose different languages for use in different files, so if you're not sure which language is your favorite just yet, don't worry. It's also okay to create two projects, and work with both VB and C# at the same time: Visual Web Developer allows you to run two instances of the application at the same time to facilitate this approach.

Figure 5.2. Creating the Dorknozzle web site project

Choosing Your App's Location

Remember that setting the **Location** drop-down menu to **File System** tells Visual Web Developer to execute the project in that folder using its integrated web server. You can create a new web project in IIS by changing the **Location** to **HTTP**. In that case, you'd need to specify an HTTP location for your application, such as **http://localhost/Dorknozzle**, and IIS would take care of creating a physical folder for you.

Meeting the Features

Once you click **OK**, your project will be created, along with a few default files, and you'll be presented with the first page of your project. It should look something like the one shown in Figure 5.3.

Figure 5.3. Your new Dorknozzle web application

Don't be daunted by the many forms and windows around your screen—each has something to offer! Visual Web Developer is very flexible, so you can resize, relocate, or regroup the interface elements that appear. We'll spend the next few pages taking a brief tour of these windows, though we'll discover even more as we progress through the chapters of this book.

The Solution Explorer

The Solution Explorer, whose default location is the upper right-hand part of the Visual Web Developer window, provides the main view of your project, and displays the files of which your project is composed. As Figure 5.4 shows, the root node is the location of your project; beneath the root node you can see that Visual Web Developer has already created other elements for you.

The files that are created for you will differ depending on the type of project you're working on, and the language you've chosen.

Let's investigate the functions of the three child nodes shown in Figure 5.4:

- **Account** is a folder that is automatically created by Visual Web Developer to manage security and user authentication. The included files allow out-of-the-box user management such as `registration`, login, and change of password. We will keep this folder for discussion in Chapter 13.

- **App_Data** is a special folder that ASP.NET uses to store database files. You'll learn more about this folder in Chapter 13.

- **Script** is a folder that by default contains the latest jQuery JavaScript files for use within your application. jQuery will be discussed in Chapter 17.

- **Styles** is a folder for the containment of (you guessed it) CSS styles.

- **About.aspx** is a web form created by Visual Web Developer that serves as an "About Us" page. We won't need this so feel free to delete this page.

- **Default.aspx** is the default web form that Visual Web Developer creates for you. If you look closely, you'll see that you can expand the **Default.aspx** node by clicking the + sign to its left. If you expand the node, you'll find a code-behind file named **Default.aspx.vb**, or **Default.aspx.cs**, depending on the language you selected when you started the project. Visual Web Developer can work with web forms that use a code-behind file, as well as with those that don't.

- **Global.asax** is a global configuration file to manage special events related to the application and session management. We will discuss its use within this chapter.

■ **Site.master** is a pre-defined Master Page created by Visual Web Developer to give programmers an example of how Master Pages and templates apply within a website. Because we will use our own template, this file isn't necessary.

■ **Web.config** is your web application's configuration file. By editing **Web.config**, you can set numerous predefined configuration options for your project (for instance, you can enable debug mode). You can also define your own custom project-wide settings that can then be read from your code (such as the administrator's email address, the project name, your favorite color, or any other simple value you'd like to store in a central place). We'll come back to this file later in the chapter.

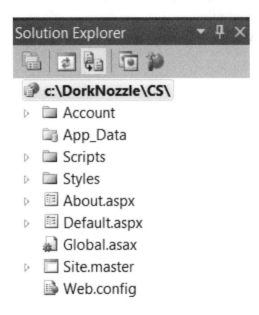

Figure 5.4. The Solution Explorer

An icon sits beside each node, reflecting its type. If you right-click on each node, a list of options that are specific to that particular node type will appear. For example, right-click on the root node, and you'll see a list of options that affect the project as a whole. Double-click on a file, and that file will open in an appropriate editor (for instance, double-clicking on a web form will open that file in the Web Forms Designer).

The Web Forms Designer

The Web Forms Designer is the place where you'll spend most of your time working with Visual Web Developer. The Web Forms Designer is a very powerful tool that allows you to edit web forms, web user controls, and master pages. You can edit these files in **Source** view, where you can see their code, or in **Design** view, which provides a WYSIWYG (what you see is what you get) interface. Visual Web Developer 2008 introduced the **Split** view mode, which combines the other two views in a single view.

By default, when you start a new web site project, the Web Forms Designer will display the contents of **Default.aspx**. Figure 5.5 shows the default form in **Split** view, where I've started to edit the content of the page in the WYSIWYG editor. As you can see, the WYSIWYG editor is similar to those of Dreamweaver, FrontPage, and other similar tools.

Tabbed quick links to the currently open files or windows appear at the top of the interface. In Figure 5.5, only **Default.aspx**, and the **Start Page** (the window that was initially loaded when Visual Web Developer started) are open. Each kind of file is opened by a different editor or designer, so when you open a database table or a CSS file, for example, you'll see a different view from the one shown in Figure 5.5.

The Code Editor

As well as editing HTML code, ASP.NET web developers also edit those forms' associated VB or C# code, regardless of whether that code is written inside the **.aspx** file or inside its code-behind file. (We'll be using code-behind files when we develop the Dorknozzle intranet—this approach is recommended for developing any non-trivial page.)

If you've opened a web form that uses a code-behind file in the Web Forms Designer, you can easily switch to that code-behind file: click the **View Code** icon in the Solution Explorer, right-click the Web Form in Solution Explorer, and select **View Code**; alternatively, expand the Web Form's node in Solution Explorer and double-click its code-behind file.

Do this to open the code-behind file for **Default.aspx**. If you chose VB as your preferred language when you created the project, the code-behind file will be called De-fault.aspx.vb, and will look like the one shown in Figure 5.6.

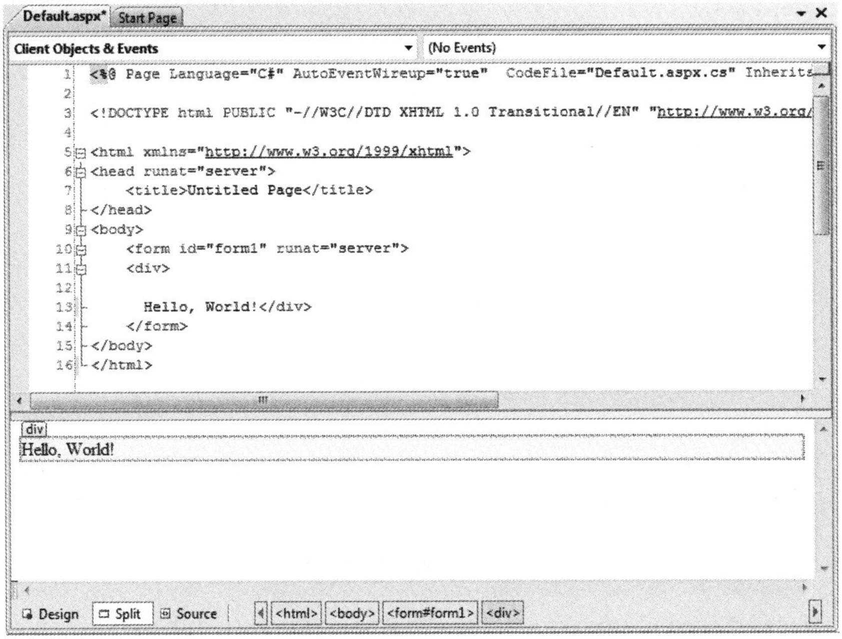

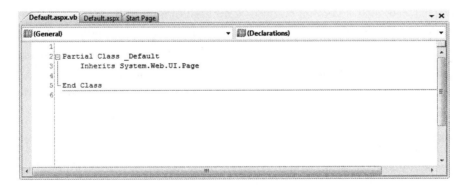

Figure 5.5. Viewing **Default.aspx** in Web Forms Designer's Source view

Figure 5.6. Editing **Default.aspx.vb**

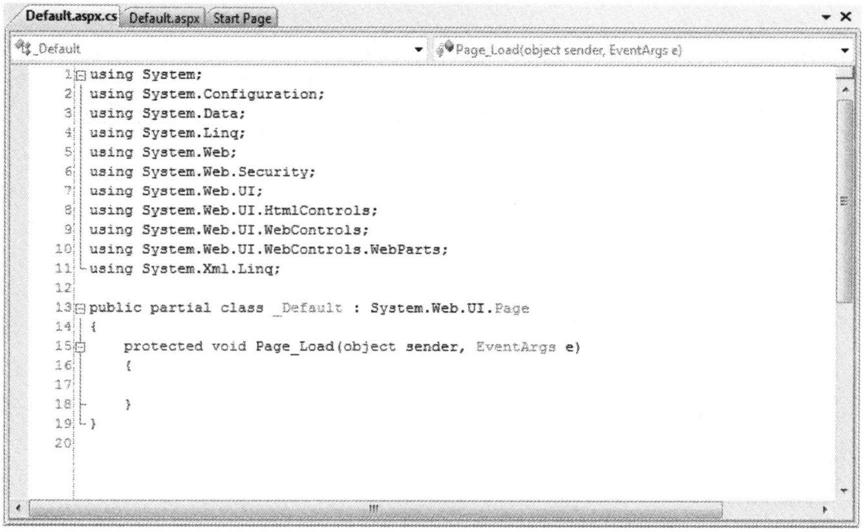

Figure 5.7. Editing **Default.aspx.cs**

If you chose C# as your preferred language when you started the project, you'll see a slightly different code-behind file—something like the one pictured in Figure 5.7.

As you can see, the C# version contains a number of namespace references. For the VB template, Visual Web Developer adds these references to the **Web.config** file, thereby applying them to the whole project. This difference makes **Default.aspx.vb** look less scary than **Default.aspx.cs** to a beginner, but in the end the functionality of the default CS and VB templates is very similar. Of course, it's possible to add the namespace references to **Web.config** yourself if you're using C#.

The – icons to the left of certain sections of your file (such as the starting points of classes and methods) allow you to collapse those sections, which can help you to manage larger code files. In Figure 5.8, I've collapsed the section of **Default.aspx.cs** that contains the namespace references—you can see that the `using` statements have been collapsed into a single ellipsis. If you hover your cursor over the ellipsis, you'll see a preview of the hidden text.

Visual Web Developer also allows the use of code regions. These are blocks of code that can be used to collapse/expand large portions into "regions" for ease of readability. These are created with the #region and #endregion lines.

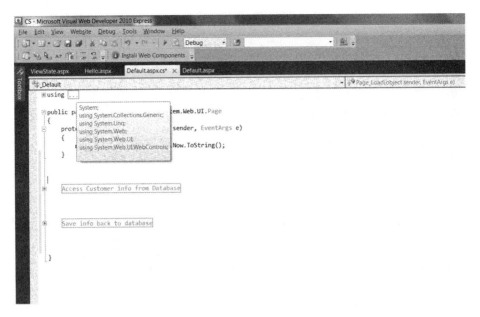

Figure 5.8. Playing around with Visual Web Developer

IntelliSense

IntelliSense is a fantastic code autocompletion feature that Microsoft has included in the Visual Studio line for some time. In its latest incarnation as part of Visual Web Developer 2010 Express Edition, IntelliSense is pretty close to perfection. This feature alone makes it more worthwhile to use Visual Web Developer than simpler code editors.

Let's do a quick test. If you're using VB, delete a character from the end of the `Inherits System.Web.UI.Page` line in **Default.aspx.vb**. As Figure 5.9 shows, IntelliSense will automatically display other words that could be used in that position.

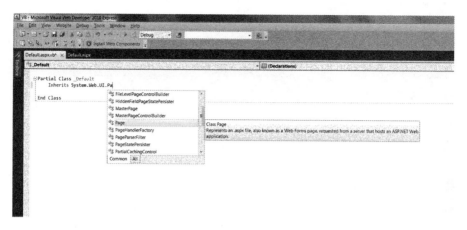

Figure 5.9. IntelliSense displaying possible word autocompletions

IntelliSense behaves slightly differently depending on the language you've chosen to use. For example, if you're using C#, IntelliSense isn't triggered as frequently as it is for those using VB. You can activate IntelliSense yourself by pressing **Ctrl+Space**. Then, once you've selected the correct entry, press **Tab** or **Enter** to have the word completed for you.

The Toolbox

When you're editing a web form, web user control, or master page visually, the Toolbox comes in very handy. The Toolbox contains most of the popular ASP.NET controls, which you can drag directly from the toolbox and drop into your form. You must be viewing a form in the Web Forms Designer to see the proper controls in the Toolbox. If you can't see the toolbox, which is shown in Figure 5.10, select **View** > **Toolbox** to make it appear.

Let's give it a test-drive: double-click on the **TextBox** entry, or drag it from the Toolbox to the form, to have a `TextBox` control added to your form.

The controls listed in the Toolbox are grouped within tabs that can be expanded and collapsed. In the **Standard** tab of the Toolbox, you'll find the standard web server controls we discussed in Chapter 4. In the other tabs, you'll find other controls, including the validation controls we'll discuss in Chapter 6, which can be found in the **Validation** tab. Figure 5.11 shows the toolbox with all its tabs in the collapsed state.

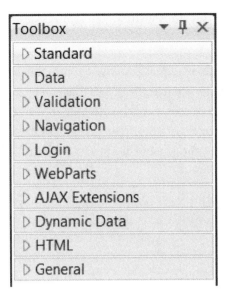

Figure 5.10. The Toolbox

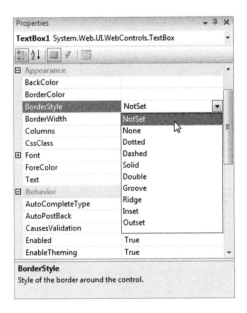

Figure 5.11. The collapsed Toolbox tabs

The Properties Window

When you select a control in the web forms designer, its properties are displayed automatically in the Properties window. For example, if you select the TextBox control we added to the form earlier, the properties of that TextBox will display in the Properties window. If it's not visible, you can make it appear by selecting **View** > **Properties Window.**

The Properties window doesn't just allow you to see the properties—it also lets you set them. Many properties—such as the colors that can be chosen from a palette—can be set visually, but in other cases, complex dialogs are available to help you establish the value of a property. In Figure 5.12, the properties of the `TextBox` are displayed in the **Properties** window, and the `BorderStyle` property is being altered.

By default, the control's properties are listed by category, but you can order them alphabetically by clicking the **A-Z** button. Other buttons in the window allow you to switch between Properties view and Events view.

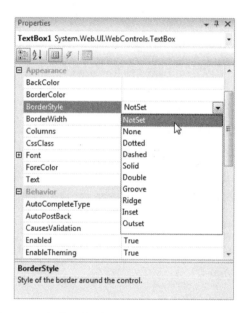

Figure 5.12. Setting a border style using the Properties window

Executing Your Project

As you already know, every time you pressed **F5** or selected **Debug** > **Start Debugging** to load a web page, the page was executed through Visual Web Developer's integrated web server, also known as **Cassini**. The debugging features of Visual Web Developer enable you to find and fix errors in your code, execute a block of code line by line, inspect the values of the variables while the code runs, and much more—you'll learn more about these features later in this chapter. When you don't need to use the debugging features, you can execute a page by selecting **Debug** > **Start Without Debugging**, or using the keyboard shortcut **Ctrl+F5**.

To run an ASP.NET project with debugging enabled, you'll need to enable that feature in the project's **Web.config** file. This is why the first time you try to debug the project in Visual Web Developer, it will offer to alter **Web.config** for you.

When you execute a project through Cassini, it will automatically start on a random port. When you ran the examples in the previous chapters, you may have noticed that the URL looked something like this: **http://localhost:52481/CS/Default.aspx**. You can see that the integrated web server was running with the host name `localhost` on port **52481**. The last part of the URL (**/CS/Default.aspx**) includes a reference to the folder in which the application file is located—either **CS** or **VB** for the examples in this book. Visual Web Developer's web server displays one small icon in the Windows system tray for each web server instance that's running. If you run multiple projects at the same time, one web server instance will be created for each project and more icons will appear. If you double-click on any of those icons, you'll be presented with a dialog that contains the web server details, and looks very much like the window shown in Figure 5.13.

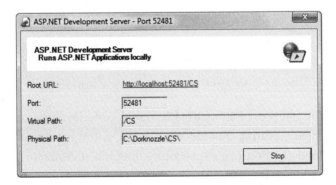

Figure 5.13. Visual Web Developer's web server in action

As it executes the project, Visual Web Developer will launch your system's default web browser, but you can make it use another browser if you wish (we showed you how to do that in the section called "Writing Your First ASP.NET Page" in Chapter 1). For the purpose of running and debugging your ASP.NET web applications, you might find it easier to use Internet Explorer as your default browser—it works a little better with Visual Web Developer than other browsers. For example, if you close the Internet Explorer window while your project runs in debug mode, Visual

Web Developer will stop the application automatically. Otherwise, you'd need to stop it manually by selecting **Debug** > **Stop Debugging**, or clicking the **Stop** button shown in Figure 5.14.

Figure 5.14. Stopping debug mode

To change the browser that's used to execute your web applications, first make sure that none of your projects are running. Then, right-click the root node in **Solution Explorer**, and select **Browse With** to display the dialog shown in Figure 5.15. Select **Internet Explorer**, click **Set as Default**, and click **Browse**.

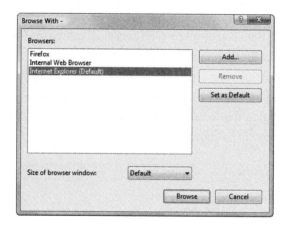

Figure 5.15. Setting the default browser in Visual Web Developer

By default, when you press **F5** or **Ctrl+F5**, Visual Web Developer will execute the page you're currently editing. Frequently, though, you'll have a single start page that you want loaded when you're executing the project. You can set the default page by right-clicking a web form in **Solution Explorer**, and selecting **Set As Start Page**.

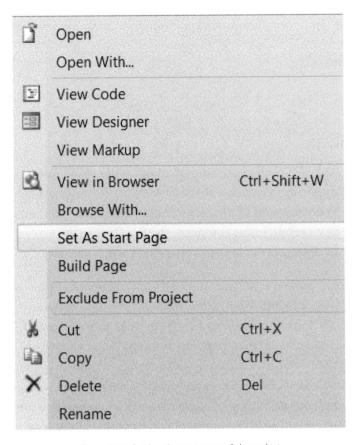

Figure 5.16. Setting the start page of the project

Core Web Application Features

Let's continue our exploration of the key topics related to developing ASP.NET web applications. We'll put them into practice as we move through the book, but in this quick introduction, we'll discuss:

- **Web.config**
- **Global.asax**
- user sessions
- caching
- cookies

Web.config

Almost every ASP.NET web application contains a file named **Web.config**, which stores various application settings. By default, all .NET web applications are configured in the **Machine.config** file, which contains machine-wide settings. This file should rarely be changed, but if you must, the file lives in the **C:\WINDOWS\Microsoft.NET\Framework**_version_**\CONFIG** directory.

For the most part, all your configuration settings will be part of the **web.config** file in the root directory of your application. You won't want to make any modifications to this file. Microsoft has gone to great lengths to make the **web.config** file in ASP.NET 4 much simpler and cleaner than previous versions. Such versions of ASP.NET had the **web.config** file at about 125 lines by default, this is now only about 12 lines in the 4.0 version. The **web.config** file is included by default when creating a new project in Visual Web Developer, but if any reason you need to re-create the file (after accidentally deleting it for example) you can add it by accessing **Website > Add New Item…**, then selecting **Web Configuration File** from the dialog that appears.

The **Web.config** file is an XML file that can hold configuration settings for the application in which the file resides. One of the most useful settings that **Web.config** controls is ASP.NET's debug mode. If Visual Web Developer hasn't enabled debug mode for you, you can do it yourself by opening **Web.config** and editing the compilation element, which looks like this:

Dorknozzle\VB\01_web.config *(excerpt)*

```
<!--
    Set compilation debug="true" to insert debugging
    symbols into the compiled page. Because this
    affects performance, set this value to true only
    during development.

    Visual Basic options:
    Set strict="true" to disallow all data type conversions
```

```
    where data loss can occur.
    Set explicit="true" to force declaration of all variables.
-->
<compilation debug="true" strict="false" explicit="true" />
```

Enabling debug mode is as simple as changing the value of the debug attribute to true. The other attributes listed here were added by Visual Web Developer to offer a helping hand to VB developers migrating from older versions. For example, strict="false" makes the compiler forgive some of the mistakes we might make, such as using the wrong case in variable names. They don't appear if your project uses C#. Lastly the targetFramework attribute is a directive to ASP.NET to use the 4.0 version of the .NET Framework.

Web.config can also be used to store custom information for your application in a central location that's accessible from all the pages of your site. For example, if you want to store the email address of someone in your technical support team so that it can be changed easily, you might take the approach shown here:

```
<configuration>
  <appSettings>
    <add key="SupportEmail" value="support@dorknozzle.com" />
  </appSettings>
</configuration>
```

This way, whenever you need to display or use an email address for technical support within the site, you can simply read the SupportEmail key using the WebConfigurationManager class. And, if you wanted to change the email address you used for technical support, you'd just need to change this setting in **Web.config**.

Dorknozzle\VB\01_web.config *(excerpt)*

```
<pages>
  <namespaces>
    <clear/>
    <add namespace="System"/>
    <add namespace="System.Collections"/>
    <add namespace="System.Collections.Generic"/>
    <add namespace="System.Collections.Specialized"/>
    <add namespace="System.Configuration"/>
    <add namespace="System.Text"/>
    <add namespace="System.Text.RegularExpressions"/>
```

```
    <add namespace="System.Linq"/>
    <add namespace="System.Xml.Linq"/>
    <add namespace="System.Web"/>
    <add namespace="System.Web.Caching"/>
    <add namespace="System.Web.SessionState"/>
    <add namespace="System.Web.Security"/>
    <add namespace="System.Web.Profile"/>
    <add namespace="System.Web.UI"/>
    <add namespace="System.Web.UI.WebControls"/>
    <add namespace="System.Web.UI.WebControls.WebParts"/>
    <add namespace="System.Web.UI.HtmlControls"/>
  </namespaces>
    ⋮
</pages>
```

You'll learn more about working with **Web.config** as you progress through this book, so if you wish, you can skip the rest of these details for now, and come back to them later as you need them.

The **Web.config** file's root element is always `configuration`, and it can contain three different types of elements:

configuration section groups

As ASP.NET and the .NET Framework are so configurable, the configuration files could easily become jumbled if we didn't have a way to break them into groups of related settings. A number of predefined section grouping tags let you do just that. For example, settings specific to ASP.NET must be placed inside a `system.web` section grouping element, while settings that are relevant to .NET's networking classes belong inside a `system.net` element.

General settings, like the `appSettings` element we saw above, stand on their own, outside the section grouping tags. In this book, though, our configuration files will also contain a number of ASP.NET-specific settings, which live inside the `system.web` element.

configuration sections

These are the actual setting tags in our configuration file. Since a single element can contain a number of settings (for example, the `appSettings` element we saw earlier could contain a number of different strings for use by the application), Microsoft calls each of these tags a **configuration section**. ASP.NET provides a wide range of built-in configuration sections to control the various aspects of your web applications.

The following list outlines some of the commonly used ASP.NET configuration sections, all of which must appear within the `system.web` section grouping element:

authentication

outlines configuration settings for user authentication, and is covered in detail in Chapter 13

authorization

specifies users and roles, and controls their access to particular files within an application; discussed more in Chapter 13

compilation

contains settings that are related to page compilation, and lets you specify the default language that's used to compile pages

customErrors

used to customize the way errors display

globalization

used to customize character encoding for requests and responses

pages

handles the configuration options for specific ASP.NET pages; allows you to disable session state, buffering, and view state, for example

sessionState

contains configuration information for modifying session state (that is, variables associated with a particular user's visit to your site)

trace

contains information related to page and application tracing

configuration section handler declarations

ASP.NET's configuration file system is so flexible that it allows you to define your own configuration sections. For most purposes, the built-in configuration sections will do nicely, but if we want to include some custom configuration sections, we need to tell ASP.NET how to handle them. To do so, we declare a configuration section handler for each custom configuration section we want to create. This is fairly advanced stuff, so we won't worry about it in this book.

Global.asax

Global.asax is another special file that can be added to the root of an application. It defines subroutines that are executed in response to application-wide events. For instance, `Application_Start` is executed the first time the application runs (or just after we restart the server). This makes this method the perfect place to execute any initialization code that needs to run when the application loads for the first time. Another useful method is `Application_Error`, which is called whenever an unhandled error occurs within a page. The following is a list of the handlers that you'll use most often within the `Global.asax` file:

Application_Start

called immediately after the application is created; this event occurs once only

Application_End

called immediately before the end of all application instances

Application_Error

called by an unhandled error in the application

Application_BeginRequest

called by every request to the server

Application_EndRequest

called at the end of every request to the server

Application_PreSendRequestHeaders

called before headers are sent to the browser

Application_PreSendRequestContent

called before content is sent to the browser

Application_AuthenticateRequest

called before authenticating a user

`Application_AuthorizeRequest`

    called before authorizing a user

The **Global.asax** file is created in the same way as the **Web.config** file—just select **File** > **New File…**, then choose the **Global Application Class** template, as depicted in Figure 5.17.

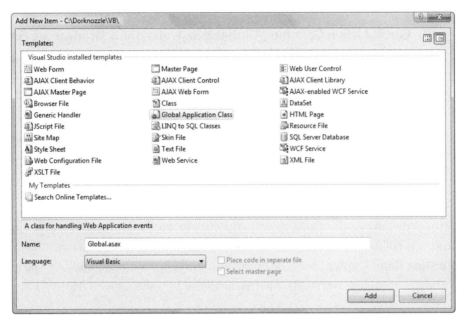

Figure 5.17. Creating **Global.asax**

Since our project comes with an existing **Global.asax** file, we can double click on the file within Solution Explorer to view the contents of the file. **Global.asax** contains empty stubs for a number of event handlers, and comments that explain their roles. A typical event handler in a **Global.asax** file looks something like this:

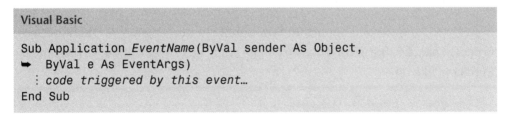

```
Visual Basic

Sub Application_EventName(ByVal sender As Object,
➥   ByVal e As EventArgs)
    ⋮ code triggered by this event…
End Sub
```

```
C#

void Application_EventName(Object sender, EventArgs e)
{
  : code triggered by this event…
}
```

 Be Careful when Changing Global.asax,web.config, or machine.config

Be cautious when you add and modify code within the **Global.asax**, **web.config**, or **machine.config** file. Any additions or modifications you make within this file will cause the application to restart, so you'll lose any data stored in application state, as well as any users on your site will experience a session reset. This can be incredibly troubling for instance if you have a user half-way through the checkout process on an e-commerce site.

Using Application State

You can store the variables and objects you want to use throughout an entire application in a special object called `Application`. The data stored in this object is called **application state**. The `Application` object also provides you with methods that allow you to share application state data between all the pages in a given ASP.NET application very easily.

Application state is closely related to another concept: **session state**. The key difference between the two is that session state stores variables and objects for one particular user for the duration of that user's current visit, whereas application state stores objects and variables that are shared between all users of an application at the same time. Thus, application state is ideal for storing data that's used by all users of the same application.

In ASP.NET, session and application state are both implemented as **dictionaries**, or sets of name-value pairs. You can set the value of an application variable named `SiteName` like this:

```
Visual Basic

Application("SiteName") = "Dorknozzle Intranet Application"
```

```
C#

Application["SiteName"] = "Dorknozzle Intranet Application";
```

With SiteName set, any pages in the application can read this string:

```
Visual Basic

Dim appName As String = Application("SiteName")
```

```
C#

string appName  = (string)Application["SiteName"];
```

You might have noticed the term (string) in the C# code example above. This is an example of the task of casting a variable to a specific type. **Casting** is the act of ensuring that a value is converted to a specific data type so that it can be stored in a variable of a matching data type. In the above example the value stored in Application["SiteName"] is actually one of type object and must be cast to a string in order to be able to be stored in a string variable. We don't have to worry about such issues in the VB code example above, because the data type conversion takes place automatically although for readability and code maintenance, it is recommended.

Using the cast above, an exception will be thrown if the object can not be cast to the data type requested. To fix this, C# has introduced the as keyword. This allows the compiler to automatically cast the object as the type specified. If the cast can not be performed, a null will be returned. Therefore it makes good habit to check for a null before using a variable being cast.

```
string appName = Application["SiteName"] as string;

if (appName != null)
{
  // it is now safe to use the appName variable.
}
```

We can remove an object from application state using the Remove method, like so:

Visual Basic

```
Application.Remove("SiteName")
```

C#

```
Application.Remove("SiteName");
```

If you find you have multiple objects and application variables lingering in application state, you can remove them all at once using the `RemoveAll` method:

Visual Basic

```
Application.RemoveAll()
```

C#

```
Application.RemoveAll();
```

It's important to be cautious when using application variables. Objects remain in application state until you remove them using the `Remove` or `RemoveAll` methods, or shut down the application in IIS. If you continue to save objects into the application state without removing them, you can place a heavy demand on server resources and dramatically decrease the performance of your applications.

Let's take a look at application state in action. Application state is very commonly used to maintain hit counters, so our first task in this example will be to build one! Let's modify the **Default.aspx** page that Visual Web Developer created for us. Double-click **Default.aspx** in Solution Explorer, and add a `Label` control inside the `form` element. You could drag the control from the Toolbox (in either Design view or Source view) and modify the generated code, or you could simply enter the new code by hand. We'll also add a bit of text to the page, and change the `Label`'s ID to `myLabel`, as shown below (the VB and C# versions are identical):

Dorknozzle\VB\02_Default.aspx *(excerpt)*

```
  <form id="form1" runat="server">
    <div>
      The page has been requested
      <asp:Label ID="myLabel" runat="server" />
      times!
    </div>
  </form>
```

In Design view, you should see your label appear inside the text, as shown in Figure 5.18.

Now, let's modify the code-behind file to use an application variable that will keep track of the number of hits our page receives. As we mentioned in the section called "Writing Your First ASP.NET Page" in Chapter 1, if your site uses, C# the `Page_Load` method is already present in the code-behind file. If your site uses VB, double-click in any empty space on your form; Visual Web Developer will create a `Page_Load` method automatically, and display it in the code editor. The method will look like this:

Visual Basic   Dorknozzle\VB\03_Default.aspx.vb *(excerpt)*

```
Partial Class _Default
    Inherits System.Web.UI.Page

Protected Sub Page_Load(ByVal sender As Object,
➡  ByVal e As System.EventArgs) Handles Me.Load

End Sub
End Class
```

C#   Dorknozzle\CS\03_Default.aspx.cs *(excerpt)*

```
public partial class _Default : System.Web.UI.Page
{
    protected void Page_Load(object sender, EventArgs e)
    {
```

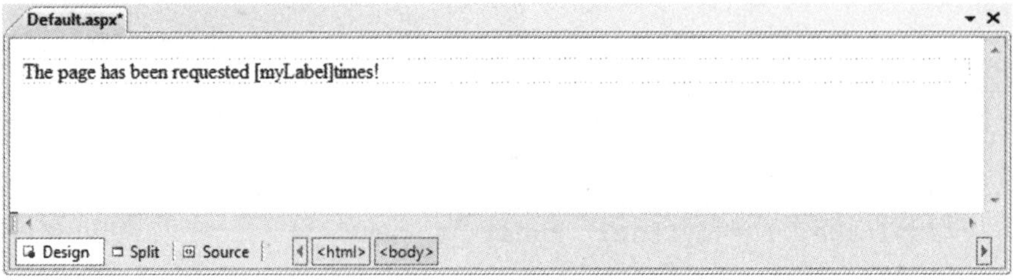

Figure 5.18. The new label appearing in Design view

```
    }
}
```

Now, let's modify the automatically generated method by adding the code that we want to run every time the page is loaded. Modify Page_Load as shown below:

Visual Basic   Dorknozzle\VB\04_Default.aspx.vb *(excerpt)*

```
Protected Sub Page_Load(ByVal sender As Object,
➥  ByVal e As System.EventArgs) Handles Me.Load
  If Application("PageCounter") >= 10 Then
    Application.Remove("PageCounter")
  End If
  If Application("PageCounter") Is Nothing Then
    Application("PageCounter") = 1
  Else
    Application("PageCounter") += 1
  End If
  myLabel.Text = Application("PageCounter")
End Sub
```

C#   Dorknozzle\CS\04_Default.aspx.cs *(excerpt)*

```
protected void Page_Load(object sender, EventArgs e)
{
  if (Application["PageCounter"] != null &&
      (int)Application["PageCounter"] >= 10)
  {
    Application.Remove("PageCounter");
  }
  if (Application["PageCounter"] == null)
  {
    Application["PageCounter"] = 1;
```

```
  }
  else
  {
    Application["PageCounter"] =
        (int)Application["PageCounter"] + 1;
  }
  myLabel.Text = Convert.ToString(Application["PageCounter"]);
}
```

Before analyzing the code, press **F5** to run the site and ensure that everything works properly. Every time you refresh the page, the hit counter should increase by one until it reaches ten, when it starts over. Now, shut down your browser altogether, and open the page in another browser. We've stored the value within application state, so when you restart the application, the page hit counter will remember the value it reached in the original browser, as Figure 5.19 shows.

If you play with the page, reloading it over and over again, you'll see that the code increments PageCounter every time the page is loaded. First, though, the code verifies that the counter hasn't reached or exceeded ten requests. If it has, the counter variable is removed from the application state:

Visual Basic	Dorknozzle\VB\04_Default.aspx.vb *(excerpt)*

```
If Application("PageCounter") >= 10 Then
  Application.Remove("PageCounter")
End If
```

C#	Dorknozzle\CS\04_Default.aspx.cs *(excerpt)*

```
if (Application["PageCounter"] != null &&
    (int)Application["PageCounter"] >= 10)
{
  Application.Remove("PageCounter");
}
```

Notice that the C# code has to do a little more work than the VB code. You may remember from Chapter 3 that C# is more strict than VB when it comes to variable types. As everything in application state is stored as an Object, C# requires that we cast the value to an integer, by using (int), before we make use of it. This conversion won't work if PageCounter hasn't been added to application state, so we also need to check that it's not equal to null.

Figure 5.19. Using the Application object

Next, we try to increase the hit counter. First of all, we to need verify that the counter variable exists in the application state. If it doesn't, we set it to 1, reflecting that the page is being loaded. To verify that an element exists in VB, we use Is Nothing:

Visual Basic   Dorknozzle\VB\04_Default.aspx.vb *(excerpt)*

```
If Application("PageCounter") Is Nothing Then
  Application("PageCounter") = 1
Else
  Application("PageCounter") += 1
End If
```

As we've already seen, we compare the value to null in C#:

C#   Dorknozzle\CS\04_Default.aspx.cs *(excerpt)*

```
if (Application["PageCounter"] == null)
{
  Application["PageCounter"] = 1;
}
else
{
  Application["PageCounter"] =
      (int)Application["PageCounter"] + 1;
}
```

The last piece of code simply displays the hit counter value in the Label.

There's one small problem with our code: if two people were to open the page simultaneously, the value could increment only by one, rather than two. The reason for this has to do with the code that increments the counter:

```
C#                                            Dorknozzle\CS\04_Default.aspx.cs (excerpt)
Application["PageCounter"] =
    (int)Application["PageCounter"] + 1;
```

The expression to the right of the = operator is evaluated first; to do this, the server must read the value of the PageCounter value stored in the application. It adds one to this value, then stores the updated value in application state.

Now, let's imagine that two users visit this page at the same time, and that the web server processes the first user's request a fraction of a second before the other request. The web form that's loaded for the first user might read PageCounter from application state and obtain a value of 5, to which it would add 1 to obtain 6. However, before the web form had a chance to store this new value into application state, another copy of the web form, running for the second user, might read PageCounter and also obtain the value 6. Both copies of the page will have read the same value, and both will store an updated value of 6! This tricky situation is illustrated in Figure 5.20.

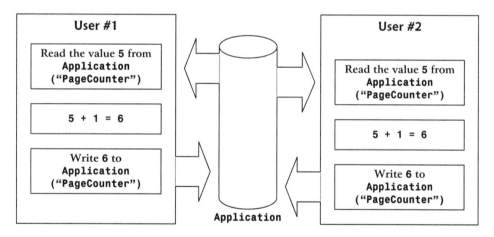

Figure 5.20. Two users updating application state simultaneously

To avoid this kind of confusion, we should develop the application so that each user locks application state, updates the value, and then unlocks application state so that other users can do the same thing. This process is depicted in Figure 5.21.

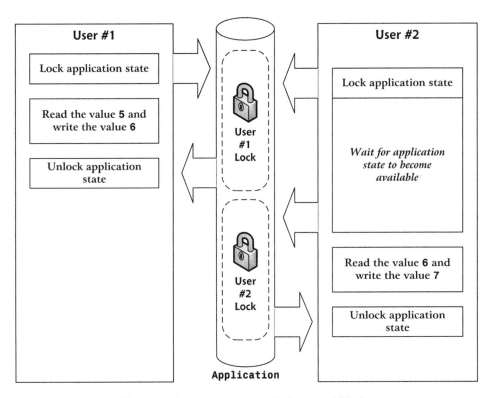

Figure 5.21. Two users updating application state with locks

Let's modify our code slightly to create these locks:

Visual Basic	Dorknozzle\CS\05_Default.aspx.vb *(excerpt)*

```
⋮
If Application("PageCounter") Is Nothing Then
  Application("PageCounter") = 1
Else
  Application.Lock()
  Application("PageCounter") += 1
  Application.UnLock()
End If
⋮
```

C#	Dorknozzle\CS\05_Default.aspx.cs *(excerpt)*

```
⋮
if (Application["PageCounter"] == null)
{
```

```
    Application["PageCounter"] = 1;
}
else
{
  Application.Lock();
  Application["PageCounter"] =
      (int)Application["PageCounter"] + 1;
  Application.UnLock();
}
⋮
```

In this case, the Lock method guarantees that only one user can work with the application variable at any time. Next, we call the UnLock method to unlock the application variable for the next request. Our use of Lock and UnLock in this scenario guarantees that the application variable is incremented by one for each visit that's made to the page.

Working with User Sessions

Like application state, session state is an important way to store temporary information across multiple page requests. However, unlike application state, which is accessible to all users, each object stored in session state is associated with a particular user's visit to your site. Stored on the server, session state allocates each user free memory on that server for the temporary storage of objects (strings, integers, or any other kinds of objects).

The process of reading and writing data into session state is very similar to the way we read and write data to the application state: instead of using the Application object, we use the Session object. However, the Session object doesn't support locking and unlocking like the Application object does.

To test session state, you could simply edit the Page_Load method to use Session instead of Application, and remove the Lock and UnLock calls if you added them. The easiest way to replace Application with Session is by selecting **Edit** > **Find and Replace** > **Quick Replace**.

In the page hit counter example that we created earlier in this chapter, we stored the count in the application state, which created a single hit count that was shared by all users of the site. Now, if you load the page in multiple browsers, you'll see that each increments its counter independently of the others.

Like objects stored in application state, session state objects linger on the server even after the user leaves the page that created them. However, unlike application variables, session variables disappear after a certain period of user inactivity. Since web browsers don't notify web servers when a user leaves a web site, ASP.NET can only assume that a user has left your site after a period in which it hasn't received any page requests from that user. By default, a user's session will expire after 20 minutes of inactivity. We can change this timeframe simply by increasing or decreasing the `Timeout` property of the `Session` object, as follows:

Visual Basic

```
Session.Timeout = 15
```

You can do this anywhere in your code, but the most common place to set the `Timeout` property is in the **Global.asax** file. If you open **Global.asax**, you'll see that it contains an event handler named `Session_Start`. This method runs before the first request from each user's visit to your site is processed, and gives you the opportunity to initialize their session variables before the code in your web form has a chance to access them.

Here's a `Session_Start` that sets the **Timeout** property to 15 minutes:

Visual Basic   Dorknozzle\VB\06_Global.asax *(excerpt)*

```
Sub Session_Start(sender As Object, e As EventArgs)
  Session.Timeout = 15
End Sub
```

C#   Dorknozzle\CS\06_Global.asax *(excerpt)*

```
void Session_Start(Object sender, EventArgs e)
{
  Session.Timeout = 15;
}
```

Using the `Cache` Object

In traditional ASP, developers used application state to cache data. Although there's nothing to prevent you from doing the same thing here, ASP.NET provides a new object, `Cache`, specifically for that purpose. `Cache` is also a collection, and we access its contents similarly to the way we accessed the contents of `Application`. Another similarity is that both have application-wide visibility, being shared between all users who access a web application.

Let's assume that there's a list of employees that you'd normally read from the database and store in a variable called `employeesTable`. To spare the database server's resources, after you read the table from the database the first time, you might save it into the cache using a command like this:

Visual Basic

```
Cache("Employees") = employeesTable
```

C#

```
Cache["Employees"] = employeesTable;
```

By default, objects stay in the cache until we remove them, or server resources become low, at which point ASP.NET will automatically remove items to free resources. The `Cache` object also lets us control expiration—if, for example, we want to add an object to the cache for a period of ten minutes, we can use the `Insert` method to do so. Here's an example:

Visual Basic

```
Cache.Insert("Employees", employeesTable, Nothing,
➥   DateTime.MaxValue, TimeSpan.FromMinutes(10))
```

C#

```
Cache.Insert("Employees", employeesTable, null,
    DateTime.MaxValue, TimeSpan.FromMinutes(10));
```

The third parameter, which in this case is `Nothing` or `null`, can be used to add cache dependencies. A cache dependency is an external change indicator to tell ASP.NET to remove that item from the cache. This is useful for instance if you want to cache the Employees table, but have it automatically removed if there have been changes to the Employees table. This kind of task is a little beyond the scope of this discussion.

Later in the code, we could use the cached object as follows:

Visual Basic

```
employeesTable = Cache("Employees")
```

C#

```
employeesTable = Cache["Employees"];
```

Because ASP.NET automatically manages the items in the Cache as well as its removal, it's good practice to verify that the object you're expecting does actually exist, to avoid any surprises:

Visual Basic

```
employeesTable = Cache("Employees")
If employeesTable Is Nothing Then
  : Read the employees table from another source…
  Cache("Employees") = employeesTable
End If
```

C#

```
employeesTable = Cache["Employees"];
if (employeesTable  == null)
{
  : Read the employees table from another source…
  Cache["Employees"] = employeesTable;
}
```

This sample code checks to see if the data you're expecting exists in the cache. If not, it means that this is the first time the code has been executed, or that the item has been removed from the cache. Thus, we can populate `employeesTable` from the database, remembering to store the retrieved data into the cache. The trip to the database server is made only if the cache is empty or not present.

Using Cookies

If you want to store data related to a particular user, you could use the Session object, but this approach has an important drawback: its contents are lost when the user closes the browser window.

To store user data for longer periods of time, you need to use **cookies**. Cookies are pieces of data that your ASP.NET application can save on the user's browser, to be read later by your application. Cookies aren't lost when the browser is closed (unless the user deletes them), so you can save data that helps identify your user in a cookie.

In ASP.NET, a cookie is represented by the HttpCookie class. We read the user's cookies through the Cookies property of the Request object, and we set cookies though the Cookies property of the Response object. Cookies expire by default when the browser window is closed (much like session state), but their points of expiration can be set to dates in the future; in such cases, they become **persistent cookies**.

Let's do a quick test. First, open **Default.aspx** and remove the text surrounding myLabel:

Visual Basic	Dorknozzle\VB\07_Default.aspx *(excerpt)*

```
<form id="form1" runat="server">
  <div>
    <asp:Label ID="myLabel" runat="server" />
  </div>
</form>
```

Then, modify Page_Load in the code-behind file as shown here:

Visual Basic	Dorknozzle\VB\08_Default.aspx.vb *(excerpt)*

```
Protected Sub Page_Load(ByVal sender As Object,
➥  ByVal e As System.EventArgs) Handles Me.Load
  Dim userCookie As HttpCookie
  userCookie = Request.Cookies("UserID")
  If userCookie Is Nothing Then
    myLabel.Text = "Cookie doesn't exist! Creating a cookie now."
    userCookie = New HttpCookie("UserID", "Joe Black")
    userCookie.Expires = DateTime.Now.AddMonths(1)
    Response.Cookies.Add(userCookie)
```

```
  Else
    myLabel.Text = "Welcome back, " & userCookie.Value
  End If
End Sub
```

C#   Dorknozzle\CS\08_Default.aspx.cs *(excerpt)*

```csharp
protected void Page_Load(object sender, EventArgs e)
{
  HttpCookie userCookie;
  userCookie = Request.Cookies["UserID"];
  if (userCookie == null)
  {
    myLabel.Text =
        "Cookie doesn't exist! Creating a cookie now.";
    userCookie = new HttpCookie("UserID", "Joe Black");
    userCookie.Expires = DateTime.Now.AddMonths(1);
    Response.Cookies.Add(userCookie);
  }
  else
  {
    myLabel.Text = "Welcome back, " + userCookie.Value;
  }
}
```

In the code above, the userCookie variable is initialised as an instance of the HttpCookie class and set to the value of the UserID cookie. The existence of the cookie is checked by testing if the userCookie object is equal to Nothing in VB or null in C#. If it is equal to Nothing or null, then it must not exist yet—an appropriate message is displayed in the Label and the cookie value is set, along with an expiry date that's one month from the current date. The cookie is transferred back to the browser using the Response.Cookies.Add method. If the cookie value already existed, a Welcome Back message is displayed.

The result of this code is that the first time you load the page, you'll be notified that the cookie doesn't exist and a new cookie is being created, via a message like the one shown in Figure 5.22.

Figure 5.22. Creating a new cookie

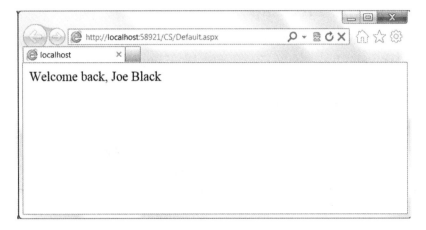

Figure 5.23. A persistent cookie

If you reload the page, the cookie will be found, and you'll get a different message, as Figure 5.23 shows. What's interesting to observe is that you can close the browser window, or even restart your computer—the cookie will still be there, and the application will be able to identify that you're a returning visitor because the cookie is set to expire one month after its creation.

Be aware, however, that visitors can choose to reject your cookies, so you can't rely on them for essential features of your application.

Starting the Dorknozzle Project

You're now prepared to start developing a larger project! We were introduced to Dorknozzle at the beginning of the chapter, and you've already created a project for it. Now, it's time to add some real functionality to the project! In the next few pages, we will:

- Prepare the sitemap for your site.
- Create a default theme that defines the common styles.
- Create a master page that will contain the layout for all the pages of Dorknozzle.
- Create a web form that uses the master page.
- Learn how to debug your project in case you encounter errors.

The star of the show will be the master page, but because it needs to have the sitemap and the theme in place, we'll deal with these first.

Preparing the Sitemap

As we saw in Figure 5.1, on the left of every page of our Dorknozzle site will sit a menu that contains links to the site's pages. We'll implement that list using the SiteMapPath control, which will require a sitemap file.

Adding Files to Your Project

If the project is running in debug mode, you can't add new files to it, so you must first stop debugging. You can do this by closing the browser window (if you're using Internet Explorer), by selecting **Debug > Stop Debugging**, or by clicking the **Stop** icon on the debug toolbar.

In **Solution Explorer**, right-click the root node and select **Add New Item…**.

From the templates list, choose **Site Map**, as depicted in Figure 5.24, and leave the filename as **Web.sitemap**.

Figure 5.24. Adding a sitemap file

Click **Add** to have the file created and added to your project. You'll be presented with a default, empty sitemap that you can start modifying. For now, you need only add a few nodes; you can add the rest later on. Change its contents as shown below—this is the VB version, but the C# version is exactly the same:

Dorknozzle\VB\09_Web.sitemap

```
<?xml version="1.0" encoding="utf-8" ?>
<siteMap
    xmlns="http://schemas.microsoft.com/AspNet/SiteMap-File-1.0" >
  <siteMapNode url="~/" title="Root" description="Root">
    <siteMapNode url="~/Default.aspx" title="Home"
        description="Dorknozzle Home" />
    <siteMapNode url="~/HelpDesk.aspx" title="Help Desk"
        description="Dorknozzle Help Desk" />
    <siteMapNode url="~/EmployeeDirectory.aspx"
        title="Employee Directory"
        description="Dorknozzle Employee Directory" />
    <siteMapNode url="~/AddressBook.aspx" title="Address Book"
        description="Dorknozzle Address Book" />
    <siteMapNode url="~/Departments.aspx" title="Departments"
```

```
          description="Dorknozzle Departments" />
    <siteMapNode url="~/AdminTools.aspx" title="Admin Tools"
          description="Admin Tools" />
    <siteMapNode url="~/AdminNewsletter.aspx"
          title="Admin Newsletter"
          description="Dorknozzle Admin Newsletter" />
  </siteMapNode>
</siteMap>
```

Great! Your sitemap file is ready to be used.

Using Themes, Skins, and Styles

We'll be using CSS to build the layout of our Dorknozzle interface. CSS provides developers with flexibility and control over the look of their web applications, and makes it very simple to keep the appearance of the website consistent.

In ASP.NET, style sheets can be managed through a mechanism called **themes**. Themes can be used to do much more than simply select which style sheets are applied to an application, as we'll see shortly. But first up, let's add a style sheet to our Dorknozzle site.

Creating a New Theme Folder

Right-click the root node in Solution Explorer, and select **Add ASP.NET Folder > Theme**. You'll then be able to type in a name for the new theme. Type **Blue**, then hit **Return**. If everything worked as planned, you should have a brand new folder called **App_Themes** in the root of your project, with a subfolder called **Blue**, as Figure 5.25 illustrates.

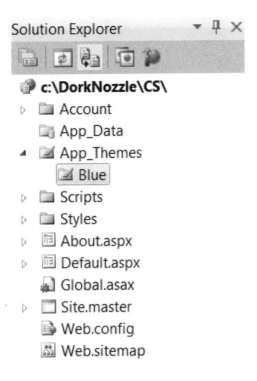

Figure 5.25. Viewing your new theme in Solution Explorer

We'll keep all the files related to the default appearance of Dorknozzle in this **Blue** folder.

Creating a New Style Sheet

We'll start by adding a new CSS file to the Blue theme. CSS files can be created independently of themes, but it's easier in the long term to save them to themes—this way, your solution becomes more manageable, and you can save different versions of your CSS files under different themes. Any files with the **.css** extension in a theme's folder will automatically be linked to any web form that uses that theme.

Right-click the **Blue** folder, and select **Add New Item....** Select the **Style Sheet** template to create a new file named **Dorknozzle.css**, and click **Add**. By default, **Dorknozzle.css** will be almost empty, containing a single empty CSS rule with the selector body.

Let's make this file more useful by adding more styles to it. We'll use these styles soon, when we build the first page of Dorknozzle. Again the same file used for VB and C#:

Dorknozzle\VB\10_Dorknozzle.css *(excerpt)*

```
body {
  font-family: Tahoma, Helvetica, Arial, sans-serif;
  font-size: 12px;
}
h1 {
  font-size: 25px;
}
a:link, a:visited {
  text-decoration: none;
  color: Blue;
}
a:hover {
  color: Red;
}
.Header {
  top: 0px;
  left: 0px;
  position: absolute;
  width: 800px;
  background-image: url(../../Images/header_bg.gif);
  background-repeat: repeat-x;
}
.Menu {
  top: 160px;
  left: 15px;
  width: 195px;
  position: absolute;
}
.Content {
  top: 160px;
  left: 170px;
  position: absolute;
  width: 600px;
}
```

Remember, we're not limited to using these styles. If, during the development of our application, we decide to add more styles, we'll simply need to open the **Dorknozzle.css** file and add them as necessary.

While you're editing the CSS, take a quick look at the built-in features that Visual Web Developer offers for building and editing styles. Right-click on any style rule in the CSS code editor, and in the context menu that appears (which is shown in Figure 5.26), you'll see one very handy item: **Build Style**....

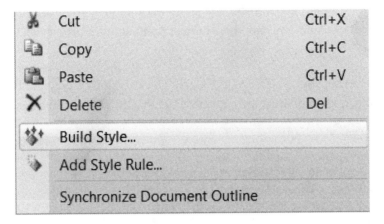

Figure 5.26. Choosing to edit a style visually

If you choose **Build Style**..., you'll access the very useful **Style Builder** tool, shown in Figure 5.27, which lets you set the properties of the selected style.

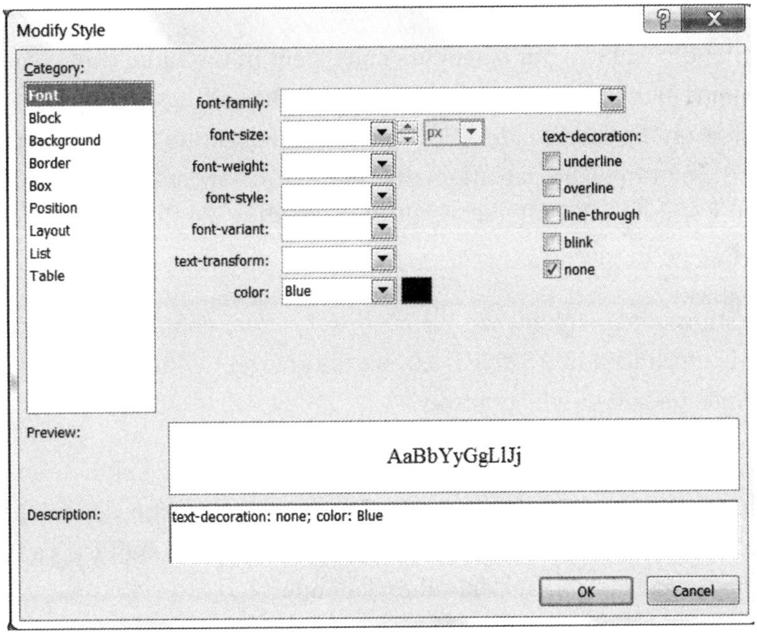

Figure 5.27. Using the Style Builder

Styling Web Server Controls

CSS styles can apply only to HTML elements—they can't really be used to keep the appearance of web server controls consistent. In Chapter 4, you learned about many ASP.NET controls, and you saw that some of them contain properties that affect their output.

Take the `Calendar` control, for example. Say you use many calendars throughout your web site, and all of them are supposed to have the same properties as this one:

```
<asp:Calendar id="myCalendar" runat="server" DayNameFormat="Short"
    FirstDayOfWeek="Sunday" NextPrevFormat="FullMonth"
    SelectionMode="DayWeekMonth" SelectWeekText="Select Week"
    SelectMonthText="Select Month" TitleFormat="Month"
    OnSelectionChanged="SelectionChanged" />
```

Now, given that you have many calendars, you decide that you'd like to have the common set of properties saved in a central place. This way, if you decided to change the format later, you'd need to make changes in one place, rather than all over your web site.

So, can CSS help us keep our calendars consistent in the same way it can keep our headings consistent? Unfortunately, it can't. All the settings in the above calendar are processed on the server side, and are used to determine the actual HTML that's output by the control. CSS can affect the final output by setting the colors or other details of the resulting HTML code, but it can't influence the way the `Calendar` control works on the server.

So the question remains: how can we keep web server controls consistent? **Skins**, which were introduced in ASP.NET 2.0, are the answer to this question. They define default values for server-side controls.

Skin definitions are saved into files with the **.skin** extension. A skin definition looks like the markup for a normal web server control, except that it doesn't have an ID, and it can't set event handlers. This makes sense, since the skin isn't an actual control. Here's an example of a skin for a calendar:

```
<asp:Calendar runat="server" DayNameFormat="Short"
    FirstDayOfWeek="Sunday" NextPrevFormat="FullMonth"
    SelectionMode="DayWeekMonth" SelectWeekText="Select Week"
    SelectMonthText="Select Month" TitleFormat="Month" />
```

Now, provided this skin is part of the theme that's applied to the current page, all Calendar controls will inherit all of these property values automatically. These values can be overridden for any specific calendar, but the skin provides the default values.

A skin can also contain a SkinId property, and if it does, it becomes a **named skin**. A named skin doesn't apply automatically to all controls of its type: it affects only those that specify that the skin applies to them. This allows you to define many skins for the same control (for instance, a SmallCalendar and a BlueCalendar).

Adding a Skin

The truth is, we don't really need skins for our simple site, but we'll add one so that you can get an idea of their functionality. Right-click again on the **Blue** node in Solution Explorer, and select **Add New Item...**. Choose the **Skin File** template, leave its name as **SkinFile.skin**, and click **Add**.

Visual Web Developer adds a comment to the file; this comment contains default text that briefly describes skins. A theme can contain one or many skin files, and each skin file can contain one or more skin definitions. ASP.NET will automatically read all the files with the **.skin** extension.

Let's say we want all TextBox controls to have the default ForeColor property set to blue. Without skins, we'd need to set this property manually on all **TextBox** controls in your site. However, you can achieve the same effect by adding this line to your **SkinFile.skin** file:

Dorknozzle\VB\11_SkinFile.skin *(excerpt)*

```
<%--
  :
--%>
<asp:TextBox runat="server" ForeColor="blue" />
```

Once the theme containing this skin has been applied, the new skin will give all `TextBox` controls on your site the default `ForeColor` of `blue`.

Applying the Theme

In order for your CSS—and the skin—to take effect, you'll need to apply the theme to your web page. Once the new theme has been created, applying it is a piece of cake. You can apply a new theme using the **Web.config** configuration file, or through your code.

For now we'll use **Web.config**. The theme can be set using the `theme` attribute of the `pages` element, which should be located inside the `system.web` element.

The `pages` element already exists in **Web.config**—you just need to add the `theme` attribute:

```
                                          Dorknozzle\VB\12_web.config (excerpt)
<system.web>
  ⋮
  <pages theme="Blue">
    ⋮
  </pages>
  ⋮
<system.web>
```

Building the Master Page

This is where the real fun begins! All of the pages in Dorknozzle have a common structure, with the same header on the top, and the same menu on the left, so it makes sense to build a master page. With this master page in place, we'll be able to create pages for the site by writing only the content that makes them different, rather than writing the header and the menu afresh for each page.

Right-click again on the root node in Solution Explorer and select **Add New Item**…. There, select the **Master Page** template from the list of available templates, and name it **Dorknozzle.master**. Choose the language in which you want to program the master page from the **Language** drop-down list, and check the **Place code in a separate file** checkbox, as illustrated in Figure 5.28. This latter option will instruct Visual Web Developer to generate a code-behind file for the master page.

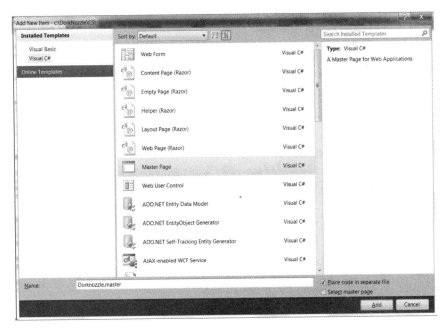

Figure 5.28. Creating a new master page

Upon the master page's creation Visual Web Developer will open the
Dorknozzle.master file (not its code-behind file) for you to edit. You'll find that
Visual Web Developer has given you a very simple default master page. Edit the
markup inside the `form` element as shown below:

```
                                    Dorknozzle\VB\13_Dorknozzle.master (excerpt)

<body>
    <form id="form1" runat="server">
      <!-- Header -->
      <div class="Header">
        <asp:Image id="Image1" runat="server"
            ImageUrl="~/Images/header.gif" Width="450" Height="174"
            AlternateText="The Official Dorknozzle Company
            Intranet" />
      </div>
      <!-- Menu -->
      <div class="Menu">
        <asp:SiteMapDataSource id="dorknozzleSiteMap" runat="server"
            ShowStartingNode="false" />
        <asp:Menu id="dorknozzleMenu" runat="server"
            DataSourceID="dorknozzleSiteMap">
```

```
        <StaticItemTemplate>
          <img src="Images/book_closed.gif" alt="+"
              width="16" height="16" style="border-width: 0;" />
          <%# Eval("Text") %>
        </StaticItemTemplate>
      </asp:Menu>
    </div>
    <!-- Content -->
    <div class="Content">
      <asp:ContentPlaceHolder id="ContentPlaceHolder1"
          runat="server" />
    </div>
  </form>
</body>
```

The code is pretty simple, and it's identical regardless of whether you're using VB or C#: basically, it defines the layout of all the Dorknozzle pages. Each of the three sections defined here starts with a comment that identifies the section as being the header, the menu on the left, or the content area. These elements are positioned on the page using the CSS styles you added earlier to the Dorknozzle.css file, so you may want to have another look at that file to refresh your memory.

We saw in Chapter 4 that the TreeView and Menu controls know how to read data from a SiteMapDataSource class, which reads the **Web.sitemap** file located in the root of your project (unless you specify otherwise). To build the menu on the left-hand side of the page, we create a **Web.sitemap** file, then add a SiteMapDataSource control to our web form or master page:

Dorknozzle\VB\13_Dorknozzle.master *(excerpt)*

```
<asp:SiteMapDataSource id="dorknozzleSiteMap" runat="server"
    ShowStartingNode="false" />
```

You might recall that the **Web.sitemap** file forces us to add a root siteMapNode element, but we can suppress this root element using the SiteMapDataSource: we set its ShowStartingNode property to False.

To have the Menu control simply display the list of nodes, it's sufficient to set its DataSourceID to the ID of the SiteMapDataSource. However, the Menu control also gives us the potential to customize the look of each menu item through **templates**.

Here, we used the `StaticItemTemplate` to add a little book image to the left of each menu item:

```
                              Dorknozzle\VB\13_Dorknozzle.master (excerpt)
<asp:Menu id="dorknozzleMenu" runat="server"
    DataSourceID="dorknozzleSiteMap">
  <StaticItemTemplate>
    <img src="Images/book_closed.gif" alt="+"
        width="16" height="16" style="border-width: 0;" />
    <%# Eval("Text") %>
  </StaticItemTemplate>
</asp:Menu>
```

After you write **Dorknozzle.master**, copy the **Images** folder from the code archive to your **Dorknozzle** folder (**C:\Dorknozzle\VB** or **C:\Dorknozzle\CS**).[1] Once this is done, you should have a **Dorknozzle\Images** folder that contains a few image files. To make the Images folder appear in Solution Explorer, right-click the root node and choose **Refresh Folder**.

The master page is now in place. Click the **Design** button at the base of the editor window to see a preview of the page. Does yours look like the page shown in Figure 5.29?

---

[1] Remember that all code and images used in building the Dorknozzle project are available in the code archive, which is available for download from sitepoint.com.

Figure 5.29. Viewing **Dorknozzle.master** in Design view

Note that the CSS styles don't apply at design time, so you'll have to hang on a little longer to see that code in action.

Using the Master Page

It's time for our moment of glory, when we assemble all the pieces we've been building and put them to work! We'll start by re-creating the **Default.aspx** web form, but this time, we'll use the master page. Start by deleting your current **Default.aspx** file by right-clicking that file in Solution Explorer, and choosing **Delete**. You'll be warned that **Default.aspx** is about to be deleted (see Figure 5.30)—choose **OK**.

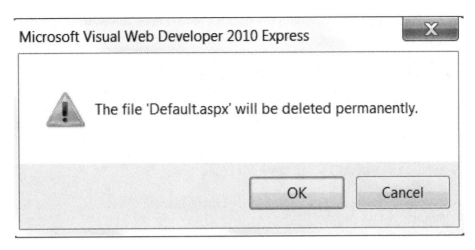

Figure 5.30. Deleting **Default.aspx**

Click the root node in Solution Explorer, then select **File** > **New File…** (or right-click the root node in Solution Explorer and select **Add New Item…** from the context menu).

Figure 5.31. Creating the new **Default.aspx**

Once you click **Add**, you'll be asked to select the master page you want to use. Choose **Dorknozzle.master**, and click **OK**.

Our new form inherits everything from its master page, so its code is minimal:

Visual Basic   Dorknozzle\VB\14_Default.aspx *(excerpt)*

```
<%@ Page Language="VB" MasterPageFile="~/Dorknozzle.master"
    AutoEventWireup="false" CodeFile="Default.aspx.vb"
    Inherits="_Default" title="Untitled Page" %>

<asp:Content ID="Content1" ContentPlaceHolderID="head"
    Runat="Server">
</asp:Content>
<asp:Content ID="Content2"
    ContentPlaceHolderID="ContentPlaceHolder1" Runat="Server">
</asp:Content>
```

C#   Dorknozzle\CS\14_Default.aspx *(excerpt)*

```
<%@ Page Language="C#" MasterPageFile="~/Dorknozzle.master"
    AutoEventWireup="true" CodeFile="Default.aspx.cs"
    Inherits="_Default" Title="Untitled Page" %>

<asp:Content ID="Content1" ContentPlaceHolderID="head"
    Runat="Server">
</asp:Content>
<asp:Content ID="Content2"
    ContentPlaceHolderID="ContentPlaceHolder1" Runat="Server">
</asp:Content>
```

This file is almost exactly the same when it's written in C#—the only differences are the `Language`, `AutoEventWireup`, and `CodeFile` attributes in the `Page` directive. Let's modify the file by adding some content to the `ContentPlaceHolder`, and altering the page title. Edit the file to reflect the highlighted sections here:

Visual Basic   Dorknozzle\VB\15_Default.aspx *(excerpt)*

```
<%@ Page Language="VB" MasterPageFile="~/Dorknozzle.master"
    AutoEventWireup="false" CodeFile="Default.aspx.vb"
    Inherits="_Default" title="Welcome to Dorknozzle!" %>

<asp:Content ID="Content1" ContentPlaceHolderID="head"
```

```
    Runat="Server">
</asp:Content>
<asp:Content ID="Content2"
    ContentPlaceHolderID="ContentPlaceHolder1" Runat="Server">
  <h1>Company News</h1>
  <p>We'll add some news later.</p>
  <h1>Company Events</h1>
  <p>We'll add company events later.</p>
</asp:Content>
```

Switch to Design view to see a preview of the whole page, like the one shown in Figure 5.32. The master page areas will be grayed out, and only the content placeholder will be editable.

By default, when you select **Debug** > **Start Debugging** or press **F5**, Visual Web Developer executes the page that's being edited. However, if you prefer, you can set a particular page to execute whenever you start debugging. To make sure that **Default.aspx** is the page that's loaded when the project is executed, right-click De-fault.aspx in Solution Explorer, and select **Set As Start Page**.

Now, execute **Default.aspx** by hitting **F5**. It should appear as per the page in Figure 5.33, with all the CSS applied.

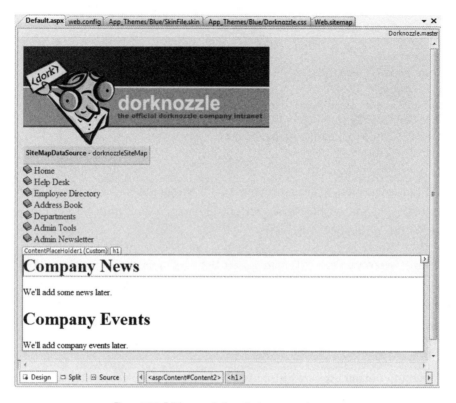

Figure 5.32. Editing a web form that uses a master page

Figure 5.33. Welcome to Dorknozzle!

Extending Dorknozzle

We'll extend the Dorknozzle site by adding an employee help desk request web form. This form will allow our fictitious employees to report hardware, software, and workstation problems to the help desk. The web form will be arranged into a series of simple steps that users will work through to report their problems. The process will include the following stages:

- Choose from a predefined list of potential problem areas.
- Choose from a range of predetermined subjects that are related to the problem area.
- Enter a description of the problem.
- Submit the request.

As we already have a master page that defines the layout of the site's pages, adding a new page to the site is now a trivial task. In this example, we'll see how simple it is to add new pages to an ASP.NET web site once the structure has been created correctly.

Create a web form in the same way you created **Default.aspx**, but this time, name it **HelpDesk.aspx**. Be sure to check both the **Place code in separate file** and **Select master page** checkboxes. Next, modify the default code that will be generated to reflect the edits shown below:

Visual Basic   Dorknozzle\VB\16_HelpDesk.aspx *(excerpt)*

```
<%@ Page Language="VB" MasterPageFile="~/Dorknozzle.master"
    AutoEventWireup="false" CodeFile="HelpDesk.aspx.vb"
    Inherits="HelpDesk" title="Dorknozzle Help Desk" %>

<asp:Content ID="Content1" ContentPlaceHolderID="head"
    Runat="Server">
</asp:Content>
<asp:Content ID="Content2"
    ContentPlaceHolderID="ContentPlaceHolder1" Runat="Server">
  <h1>Employee Help Desk Request</h1>
  <p>
    Station Number:<br />
    <asp:TextBox id="stationTextBox" runat="server"
        CssClass="textbox" />
  </p>
  <p>
    Problem Category:<br />
    <asp:DropDownList id="categoryList" runat="server"
        CssClass="dropdownmenu" />
  </p>
  <p>
    Problem Subject:<br />
    <asp:DropDownList id="subjectList" runat="server"
        CssClass="dropdownmenu" />
  </p>
  <p>
    Problem Description:<br />
    <asp:TextBox id="descriptionTextBox" runat="server"
        CssClass="textbox" Columns="40" Rows="4"
        TextMode="MultiLine" />
  </p>
  <p>
    <asp:Button id="submitButton" runat="server"
        CssClass="button" Text="Submit Request" /></p>
</asp:Content>
```

Don't worry that the `DropDownList` controls don't have items associated with them—eventually, the categories and subjects will be retrieved from a database. When you're finished, save your work, execute the project, and click the **Help Desk** link from the menu. You should see the display shown in Figure 5.34.

Figure 5.34. The Help Desk page up and running

This page gives us the opportunity to test the skin file we created earlier. If you type text into the text boxes, you'll see that the color of the text is blue. True, this effect could have been achieved just as easily through CSS, but in future, when you're working on projects that utilize more complex controls and properties, skins might be your only choice. As such, it's important that you know how to use them.

Debugging and Error Handling

Your work with Dorknozzle for this chapter is over, but now that we've started to create a real-world application, it's time to consider the real-world problems that might occur as we're developing that application. A constant truth in the life of any programmer is that programming mistakes do happen, and they happen no matter how experienced the programmer is. For this reason, it's beneficial to know what you can do when you encounter an error, and to learn how ASP.NET and Visual Web Developer can help you analyze and debug your code.

Debugging with Visual Web Developer

Create a new web form in Visual Web Developer that uses a code-behind file in your **C:\LearningASP\VB** or **C:\LearningASP\CS** folder, and call it **ErrorTest.aspx**. Then add the code below to the Page_Load method (remember, if you're using VB, to double-click the page in design mode to generate the method) in the code-behind file:

Visual Basic   LearningASP\VB\ErrorTest_01.aspx.vb *(excerpt)*

```
Protected Sub Page_Load(ByVal sender As Object,
➥  ByVal e As System.EventArgs) Handles Me.Load
  Dim a(10) As Integer
  Dim i As Integer
  For i = 1 To 11
    a(i) = i
  Next
End Sub
```

C#   LearningASP\CS\ErrorTest_01.aspx.cs *(excerpt)*

```
protected void Page_Load(object sender, EventArgs e)
{
  int[] a = new int[10];
  int i;
  for (i = 0; i < 11; i++)
  {
    a[i] = i;
  }
}
```

The code above creates an array of ten elements, then uses a For loop to assign values to them. The problem is that it doesn't stop at the tenth element: it also tries to assign a value to the 11th element, which doesn't exist.

If you execute the page without debugging (using the **CTRL+F5** shortcut), the page will generate an error in your web browser, as shown in Figure 5.35.

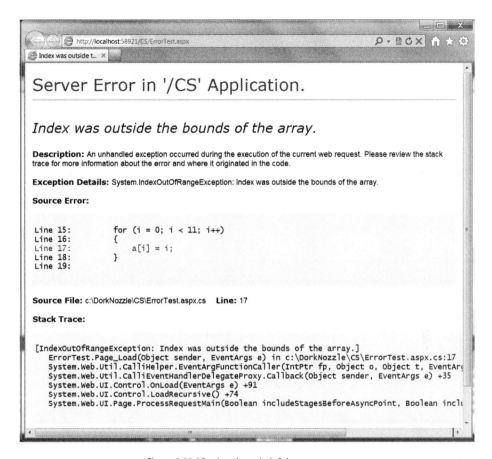

Figure 5.35. Viewing the unhelpful error message

You can obtain more details by executing the project in debug mode (by pressing **F5** in Visual Web Developer).

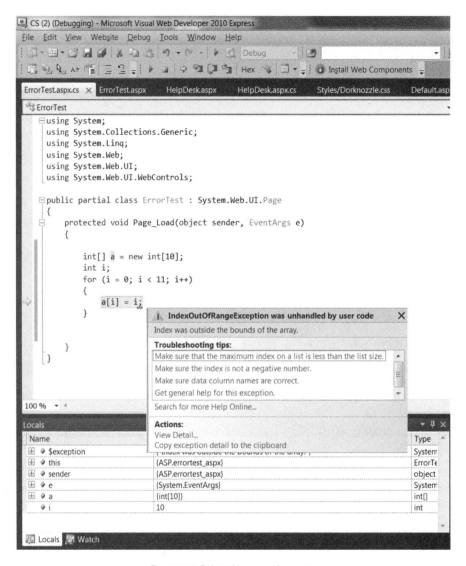

Figure 5.36. Debugging a run-time error

Executing the page once again—this time, with debugging enabled—takes you straight to the error in Visual Web Developer, as Figure 5.36 illustrates.

This interface tells you that the code has thrown an **exception** of type `IndexOutOfRangeException`. In .NET, exceptions are the standard means by which errors are generated and propagated. An exception is a .NET class (in this case, the `IndexOutOfRangeException` class) that contains the details of an error. As you'll see a little later, you can **catch** the error in your code using the `Try-Catch-Finally` construct. If the error isn't caught and handled, as in this case, it's finally caught by the ASP.NET runtime, which generates an error message.

In Figure 5.36, the debugger has paused execution at the moment the exception was raised. Let's see what your options are at this moment. One very useful window is the Watch window, which appears by default when your application is being debugged. If it's not displayed, you can open it by accessing **Debug > Windows > Watch**. You can type the names of the objects in your code into the Watch window; in response, it will display their values and types. Try typing **a(5)** (or **a[5]** if you're using C#) into the Watch window; you should see a display like the one in Figure 5.37.

Figure 5.37. Inspecting values using the Watch window

You could even type just **a**, then explore its members via the display shown in Figure 5.38.

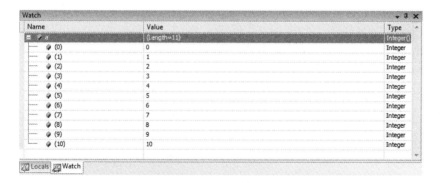

Figure 5.38. The Watch window showing the contents of an array

Arrays and VB

This example reveals an interesting aspect of this array. The Watch window reports that the array's length is 11, yet we defined it as a(10). In all .NET languages, arrays are zero-based, which means that the first element of an array is a(0), the second is a(1), and so on. So an array called a that had ten elements would have as its first element a(0), and a(9) as its last.

However, VB offers extra assistance for developers who are experienced with pre-.NET versions of the language (which used one-based arrays in which the first element would have been a(1), and the last would have been a(10)): it adds an element for you. In other words, if you declare an array of ten elements in VB, you'll get an array of 11 elements.

C# has always had zero-based arrays, so an array defined as a[10] will have ten elements.

In more complex scenarios, if you enter the name of an object, the Watch window will let you explore its members as we just saw.

If you switch to the Locals window (**Debug** > **Windows** > **Locals**) shown in Figure 5.39, you can see the variables or objects that are visible from the line of code at which the execution was paused.

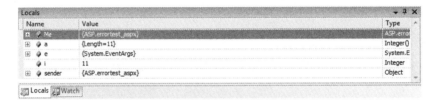

Figure 5.39. The Locals window

Another nice feature of Visual Web Developer is that when you hover your cursor over a variable, the editing window shows you at-a-glance information about that variable.

Sometimes, you'll want to debug your application even if it doesn't generate an exception. For example, you may find that your code isn't generating the output you expected. In such cases, it makes sense to execute pieces of code line by line, and see in detail what happens at each step.

The most common way to get started with this kind of debugging is to set a **breakpoint** in the code. In Visual Web Developer, we do this by clicking on the gray bar on the left-hand side of the editing window. When we click there, a red bullet appears, and the line is highlighted with red to indicate that it's a breakpoint, as Figure 5.40 illustrates.

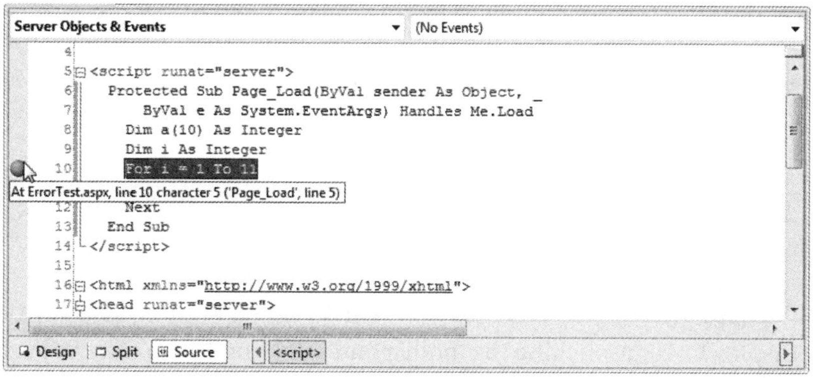

Figure 5.40. Setting a breakpoint

Once the breakpoint is set, we execute the code. When the execution pointer reaches the line you selected, execution of the page will be paused and Visual Web Developer will open your page in debug mode. In debug mode, you can perform a number of tasks:

▓ View the values of your variables or objects.

▓ Step into any line of code by selecting **Debug** > **Step Into**. This executes the currently highlighted line, then pauses. If the selected line executes another local method, the execution pointer is moved to that method so that you can execute it line by line, too.

▓ Step over any line of code by selecting **Debug** > **Step Over**. This makes the execution pointer move to the next line in the current method without stepping into any local methods that might be called by the current line.

▓ Step out of any method by selecting **Debug** > **Step Out**. This causes the current method to complete and the execution to be paused on the next line of the method that called the current method.

▓ Continue execution of the program normally by selecting **Debug** > **Continue**. Execution will stop again only if an exception is raised, or another breakpoint is met. If the execution is stopped as a result of an exception, choosing to continue the execution will allow the error to propagate to the ASP.NET runtime, which will cause the error message to display in the browser window.

▓ Stop execution by selecting **Debug** > **Stop Debugging**.

▓   Stop and restart the program by selecting **Debug** > **Restart**.

All these commands are also available from the Debug toolbar, which is shown in Figure 5.41.

Figure 5.41. The Debug toolbar

This toolbar appears by default when you're debugging, but if it doesn't, you can make it display by right-clicking the toolbar and selecting **Debug**. The Debug toolbar reflects the commands you can find in the **Debug** menu, which is depicted in Figure 5.42, and the button on the extreme right gives you easy access to the various debugging windows.

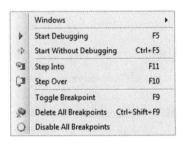

Figure 5.42. The debugging windows accessible from the toolbar

Other Kinds of Errors

Along with the runtime errors we've seen so far, ASP.NET can also throw the following kinds of errors:

configuration errors

These are caused by problems in the `Web.config` file. If you add an incorrect tag to `Web.config`, the next time you try to load the application, an error will occur.

parser errors

Parser errors are caused by the use of incorrect syntax in an ASP.NET script page; for instance, problems in the definitions of ASP.NET controls included in a web form will cause parser errors.

compilation errors

These errors are raised by the compiler when there's a syntax error in the page's C# or VB code, and will be caught by Visual Web Developer.

If you try to execute a page that contains compilation errors with Visual Web Developer, those errors will be signaled right away, as shown in Figure 5.43, and the page won't be loaded in the web browser.

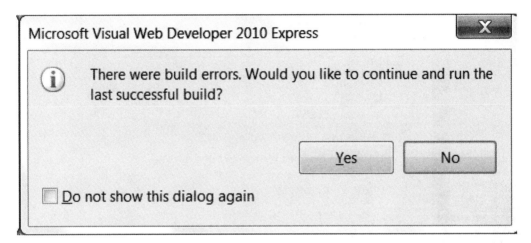

Figure 5.43. Visual Web Developer providing a compilation error warning

If you'd like to try this for yourself, write some VB code, but terminate one of the lines with a semicolon as if you were writing C# code, as shown in the snippet below:

```
Visual Basic

Sub Page_Load(s As Object, e As EventArgs)
   timeLabel.Text = DateTime.Now.ToString();
End Sub
```

If you try to run this code, Visual Web Developer will present you with the message shown in Figure 5.43. If you choose **Yes**, a previous version of the code that used to compile successfully will be executed. Usually, this isn't what you want: you'll prefer to investigate the problem and fix the error. If you choose **No**, Visual Web Developer will display a window called the Error List. Double-click the entry in the Error List, and the offending portion of code will be highlighted in the editor. Moreover, hovering your cursor over the highlighted code will display a tooltip containing a few details about the error, as Figure 5.44 illustrates.

After such a demonstration, I hope you agree that Visual Web Developer is a fantastic tool. What you've just seen is merely a common-sense feature in the world of Visual Web Developer, though—much more exciting and powerful features are available!

Figure 5.44. Visual Web Developer explaining an error in a tooltip

Custom Errors

If you're not running your application through Visual Web Developer, for example when your application has been deployed to a live web server, ASP.NET will report errors by displaying a message in the browser window, as we saw in Figure 5.35. The default error message that's shown to remote users doesn't contain code or other sensitive data, but you can customize the page that's displayed to visitors when errors occur using a **Web.config** element called `customErrors`.

We define the `customErrors` element as a child of the `system.web` element like so:

```
<configuration>
  <system.web>
    ⋮
    <customErrors mode="modeValue"
        defaultRedirect="errorPage.aspx" />
    ⋮
  </system.web>
</configuration>
```

The `defaultRedirect` attribute of the `customErrors` element is used to specify the page that's used to report errors. We can then choose whether this error page is shown to everybody, to nobody, or only to users who access the site from another network using the `mode` attribute. The possible values for the `mode` attribute are:

On When `mode` is `On`, ASP.NET uses user-defined custom error pages, instead of its default error page, for both local and remote users.

Off When `mode` has a value of `Off`, ASP.NET uses its default error page for both local and remote users. The `customErrors` element has no effect when `mode` is set to `Off`.

RemoteOnly When `mode` has the `RemoteOnly` value, the ASP.NET error page is shown only to local users, and the custom error page is shown to remote users. `RemoteOnly` is the default value, and is generally the safest option during development. If the `defaultRedirect` attribute is present, remote visitors will see the page mentioned; otherwise, they'll see a generic error that doesn't contain debugging information.

Handling Exceptions Locally

As you can see, unless you handle any exceptions that are raised in your code yourself, they'll be caught by the debugger. If you're not running the code within Visual Web Developer, the exceptions will be caught by the ASP.NET runtime, which displays the errors in the browser.

Additionally, C# and VB enable you to handle runtime errors using the `Try-Catch-Finally` construct.

The basic syntax of `Try-Catch-Finally` is as follows:

```
Visual Basic

Try
  : code block…
Catch ex As Exception
  : code block…
Finally
  : code block…
End Try
```

The equivalent C# syntax looks like this:

```
C#

try
{
  : code block…
}
catch (Exception ex)
{
  : code block…
}
finally
{
  : code block…
}
```

As a basic rule of thumb, we place inside a `Try` block any code that we suspect might generate errors that we'll want to handle. If an exception is generated, the code in the `Catch` block will be executed. We can access information about the error from the `ex` object, which contains the current exception—an instance of the `Exception` class. If the code in the `Try` block doesn't generate any exceptions, the code in the `Catch` block won't execute. In the end, whether an exception occurred or not, the code in the `Finally` block will execute.

That's an important point: the code in the `Finally` block will *always* execute, no matter what! As such, it's good practice to place any "mission-critical" code in that block. For example, if database operations are performed in the `Try` block, a good practice would be to close the database connection in the `Finally` block to ensure that no open connections remain active on the database server—consuming resources!—or to keep database objects locked.

Exceptions propagate from the point at which they were raised up through the **call stack** of your program. The call stack is the list of methods that are being executed. So, if method A calls a method B, which in turn calls method C, the call stack will be formed of these three methods, as Figure 5.45 illustrates.

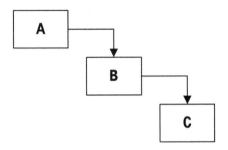

Figure 5.45. A simple call stack

In this scenario, an exception that's raised in method C can be handled within the same function, provided the offending code is inside a Try/Catch block. If this isn't the case, the exception will propagate to method B, which also has the opportunity to handle the exception, and so on. If no method handles the exception, it will be intercepted either by the Visual Web Developer debugger or the ASP.NET runtime.

In the Try-Catch-Finally construct, both the Finally and Catch blocks are optional. You can use only the Try and Catch blocks if there's no need for a Finally block; you might use only Try and Finally blocks if you want your code always to perform a particular action when an exception is thrown, but you want the exception to propagate up the call stack.

In more complex scenarios, you can use more layers of error handling. In these scenarios, you'll want to handle the error partially in the place in which it occurred, but you'll still want to let it propagate so that the upper layers take note of it, and perform further processing. Exceptions are thrown using the Throw keyword (throw in C#), like so:

Visual Basic

```
Try
  : code block…
Catch ex As Exception
```

```
  ⋮ code block…
  Throw ex
End Try
```

```
C#
```

```
try
{
  ⋮ code block…
}
catch (Exception ex)
{
  ⋮ code block…
  throw ex;
}
```

If an error is thrown in the Try block, we can use the Catch block to optionally execute some code and then Throw the exception again so that it's caught higher up the stack. We could modify our array example to include Try and Catch blocks like this:

Visual Basic   **LearningASP\VB\ErrorTest_02.aspx.vb** *(excerpt)*

```
Protected Sub Page_Load(ByVal sender As Object,
➡  ByVal e As System.EventArgs) Handles Me.Load
  Dim a(10) As Integer
  Dim i As Integer
  Try
    For i = 1 To 11
      a(i) = i
    Next
  Catch ex As Exception
    messageLabel.Text = "Exception!<br />" & ex.Message
  End Try
End Sub
```

C#   **LearningASP\CS\ErrorTest_02.aspx.cs** *(excerpt)*

```
protected void Page_Load(object sender, EventArgs e)
{
  int[] a = new int[10];
  int i;
```

```
try
{
  for (i = 0; i < 11; i++)
  {
    a[i] = i;
  }
}
catch(Exception ex)
{
  messageLabel.Text = "Exception!<br />" + ex.Message;
}
}
```

Provided you have a `Label` control named `messageLabel` in your web form, you'll see the message shown in Figure 5.46 when you run this code.

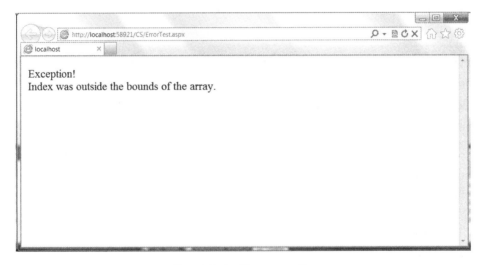

Figure 5.46. Catching an exception

In the code above, we can see that the `Catch` block receives an `Exception` object, `ex`, as a parameter. This object describes the exception that has caused the `Catch` block to execute. In our code, we use one of the `Exception` object's many properties—in this case, `Message`—to display some information about the error. In a realistic scenario, you may want to use this opportunity within the `Catch` block to possibly redirect a custom error page that will display a more friendly error message.

In .NET, all exceptions are .NET classes derived from the `Exception` class. This means that, in fact, each exception is a different class (in our case, `ex` is an

`IndexOutOfRangeException` object), but we can treat `ex` as the generic `Exception` class to access the generic details of any error.

The `Exception` class contains the following properties:

Message
> the error message

Source
> the name of the exception's source

StackTrace
> the names of the methods that were called just before the error occurred

TargetSite
> an instance of the `MethodBase` class that represents the method that caused the error

Specialized exception classes can contain additional members. For example, the `SqlException` class, which is raised when database-related errors occur, includes a collection of error messages (`SqlError` objects) in its `Errors` property. You could use a `For Each` loop to iterate through these errors.

In complex application scenarios, you could even create your own exception classes as specialized versions of `Exception`. You could then throw these exceptions as needed, and catch them in a class or method that was situated in the upper levels of the hierarchy, and would handle these errors properly.

Summary

In this chapter, you've learned just how powerful Visual Web Developer can be. We've seen most of its basic features in action, and we've experimented with some of the really useful features you'll find yourself using every day, such as automatic code generation and debugging. We also used Visual Web Developer to make a start on our exciting new project: Dorknozzle!

We've taken a close look at **Web.config**, which is where your web application's configuration settings will be stored, and **Global.asax**, which is where application-wide events can be handled. We've also discussed the `Application` and `Cache` objects, which can be used to store data that's available to all pages within an application; the `Session` object, which can be used to store user-specific data across requests; and cookies, which can be sent to the user's browser, then read on subsequent visits.

Finally, we took a look at themes and master pages, which are powerful ways of managing your site's look and feel.

In Chapter 6, we'll discuss data validation, and learn how ASP.NET's validation controls can help us ensure that our back-end systems are as secure as possible.

Using the Validation Controls

Ever needed to ensure that a user typed an email address into a text box? Or wanted to make sure that a user typed numbers only into a phone number field? Validation involves checking that the data your application's users have entered obeys a number of predefined rules. To help developers with the most common data validation tasks, ASP.NET provides a set of validation controls that ease the problems that troubled web developers in the past. This chapter will show you how to use them.

More specifically, in this chapter you will:

- Learn the difference between client-side and server-side data validation.
- Use the .NET validation controls to restrict the data your visitors can submit.
- Create validation groups to form groups of controls that need to be validated together.
- Update Dorknozzle to validate the data submitted by its users.

Client-side Validation and Server-side Validation

There are two kinds of form validation, and they're differentiated by the location in which the validation takes place. You could write client-side JavaScript code that validates the data typed by the user directly into the browser (**client-side validation**), or you could use server-side VB or C# code to validate the user input once the form has been submitted to the server (**server-side validation**).

Client-side validation has its benefits, chief among them being the fact that it provides instant feedback to users. If users fail to enter their names into a text box, the page automatically displays an error message. The users know immediately that they need to enter their names—they don't need to wait for a response from the server to tell them so. The process is quick and efficient, and good for the overall user experience.

However, there's one big drawback with client-side validation: users must have JavaScript enabled in their browsers, or validation simply will not occur. Some browsers, such as those built into PDAs and mobile telephones, don't support JavaScript, so client-side validation doesn't work. Although client-side validation is a great way to increase the usability of your site, it's not a foolproof way to ensure that the data entered into your form will pass all your rules.

While client-side validation is optional, server-side validation is not. For this reason, developers frequently choose to implement only server-side validation methods. Server-side validation is necessary because it's our last line of defense against bogus user data. The downside to server-side validation is that the application has to make a trip to the server before users can be alerted to any errors in their data.

Introducing the ASP.NET Validation Controls

ASP.NET includes controls that make validation a snap. The ASP.NET validation controls, while primarily useful for implementing client-side validation, make it easier to implement server-side validation as well. The ASP.NET validation controls generate the JavaScript required for basic validation tasks for you (so you don't need to deal with any JavaScript code yourself); then, once the page is submitted, you can use the controls to check on the server whether or not the client-side validation was successful.

ASP.NET's validation controls provide client-side validation capabilities while virtually eliminating the need for developers to know JavaScript. Better still, they don't require complex server-side scripting. To use ASP.NET validation controls, we just add an object to the page and configure some simple properties.

As our first step towards demonstrating the ASP.NET validation controls, we'll create a number of simple pages in the **LearningASP** folder we worked with in previous chapters. Then we'll update the Dorknozzle intranet, adding validation features to the Help Desk page.

To start with, let's create a simple login web form. Create a file named **Login.aspx** (with no code-behind file) in your **C:\LearningASP\VB** or **C:\LearningASP\CS** folder and modify it as shown below:

Visual Basic   LearningASP\VB\Login_01.aspx *(excerpt)*

```
<%@ Page Language="VB" %>

<!DOCTYPE html PUBLIC "-//W3C//DTD XHTML 1.0 Transitional//EN"
  "http://www.w3.org/TR/xhtml1/DTD/xhtml1-transitional.dtd">

<script runat="server">

</script>

<html xmlns="http://www.w3.org/1999/xhtml">
  <head runat="server">
    <title>Simple Login Page</title>
  </head>
  <body>
    <form id="form1" runat="server">
      <div>
        <!-- Username -->
        <p>
          Username:<br />
          <asp:TextBox id="usernameTextBox" runat="server" />
          <asp:RequiredFieldValidator id="usernameReq"
              runat="server"
              ControlToValidate="usernameTextBox"
              ErrorMessage="Username is required!" />
```

```
      </p>
      <!-- Password -->
      <p>
        Password:<br />
        <asp:TextBox id="passwordTextBox" runat="server"
            TextMode="Password" />
        <asp:RequiredFieldValidator id="passwordReq"
            runat="server"
            ControlToValidate="passwordTextBox"
            ErrorMessage="Password is required!" />
      </p>
      <!-- Submit Button -->
      <p>
        <asp:Button id="submitButton" runat="server"
            Text="Submit" />
      </p>
    </div>
  </form>
 </body>
</html>
```

The VB version is displayed above, but the C# version is identical except for the
Page declaration. Here, we've added two RequiredFieldValidator controls, which
force the user to type some data into the referenced controls before the form can be
submitted. Let's have a closer look at the first RequiredFieldValidator to see that
it does its job. It sets a couple of properties, whose names are fairly descriptive
(ControlToValidate and ErrorMessage):

LearningASP\VB\Login_01.aspx *(excerpt)*

```
<asp:RequiredFieldValidator id="usernameReq" runat="server"
    ControlToValidate="usernameTextBox"
    ErrorMessage="Username is required!" />
```

Load this page and immediately click the **Submit** button without entering text into
either field. The page should display as shown in Figure 6.1. When we click the
Submit button, we instantly see the error messages that tell us we forgot to type in
a username and password.

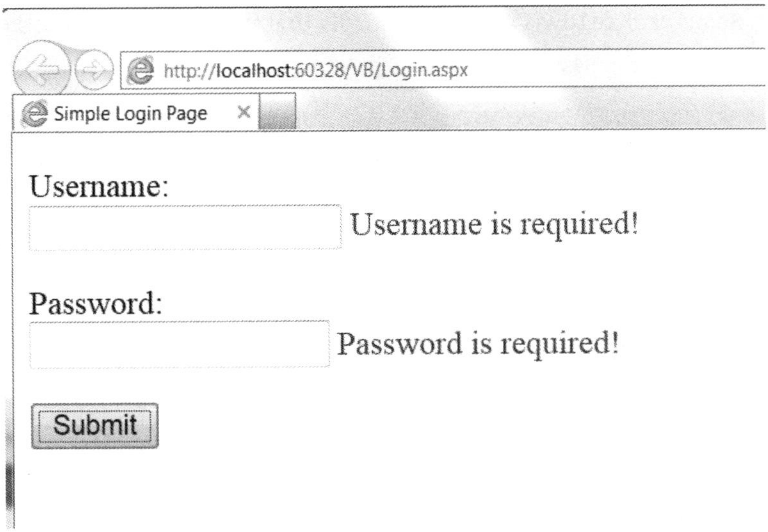

Figure 6.1. Validation controls at work

The beauty of ASP.NET validation controls is that they determine whether or not the browser is capable of supporting client-side validation. If it is, ASP.NET automatically includes the necessary client-side JavaScript; if not, it's omitted and the form is validated on the server.

ASP.NET and Client–side Validation

In older versions of ASP.NET, these controls demonstrated a tendency to assume that non-Microsoft browsers, such as Firefox, did not support JavaScript. As ASP.NET's client-side validation relies on JavaScript, client-side validation was not supported in those browsers, and users had to rely on these controls' server-side validation.

However, from version 2.0 on, ASP.NET recognized the JavaScript capabilities of these browsers, so client-side validation is now available to all modern browsers, including Opera, Firefox, and others. Support is even better now in ASP.NET 4.0. That said, it's important not to forget that JavaScript can be disabled in any browser, so client-side validation cannot be relied upon—we must always validate any submitted data on the server.

A nice feature of ASP.NET is that we can make it set the focus automatically to the first input control that causes a validation error. We activate this feature by setting the SetFocusOnError property of the validation control to True. Our simple example offers two `RequiredFieldValidation` controls that we can update. Let's do that now:

```
LearningASP\VB\Login_02.aspx (excerpt)

<!-- Username -->
<p>
  Username:<br />
  <asp:TextBox id="usernameTextBox" runat="server" />
  <asp:RequiredFieldValidator id="usernameReq" runat="server"
      ControlToValidate="usernameTextBox"
      ErrorMessage="Username is required!"
      SetFocusOnError="True" />
</p>
<!-- Password -->
<p>
  Password:<br />
  <asp:TextBox id="passwordTextBox" runat="server"
      TextMode="Password" />
  <asp:RequiredFieldValidator id="passwordReq" runat="server"
      ControlToValidate="passwordTextBox"
      ErrorMessage="Password is required!"
      SetFocusOnError="True" />
</p>
```

If you make the changes highlighted in bold above, and load the page again, pressing the **Submit** button when a text box is empty will cause that text box to gain focus. If both text boxes are empty, the first one will receive focus.

Enforcing Validation on the Server

Validation is critical in circumstances in which users' submission of invalid data could harm your application. There are many circumstances where processing bad input data could have negative effects—for instance, it could produce runtime errors, or cause bad data to be stored in your database.

To get a clear idea of these implications, let's add to the login page some server-side code that uses the data input by the visitor. The typical point at which visitor data is used in a login page is the `Click` event handler of the **Submit** button. Add the `OnClick` property to the `Button` control, and give it the value `submitButton_Click`. This property mimics what Visual Web Developer would give the control if you double-clicked the button in Design view:

LearningASP\VB\Login_03.aspx *(excerpt)*

```
<!-- Submit Button -->
<p>
  <asp:Button id="submitButton" runat="server" Text="Submit"
    OnClick="submitButton_Click" />
</p>
```

Next, create the `submitButton_Click` subroutine. You can add this between the `<script runat="server">` and `</script>` tags, like so:

Visual Basic   LearningASP\VB\Login_03.aspx *(excerpt)*

```
Protected Sub submitButton_Click(s As Object, e As EventArgs)
  submitButton.Text = "Clicked"
End Sub
```

C#   LearningASP\CS\Login_03.aspx *(excerpt)*

```
protected void submitButton_Click(object sender, EventArgs e)
{
  submitButton.Text = "Clicked";
}
```

You can have Visual Web Developer help you generate the method signatures by switching the form to **Design** view and double-clicking the button.

Now, if you're trying to submit invalid data using a browser that has JavaScript enabled, this code will never be executed. However, if you disable your browser's JavaScript, you'll see the label on the Button control change to **Clicked**! Obviously, this is not an ideal situation—we'll need to do a little more work to get validation working on the server side.

 Disabling JavaScript in Firefox

To disable JavaScript in Firefox, go to **Tools > Options...**, click the **Content** tab, and uncheck the **Enable JavaScript** checkbox.

Disabling JavaScript in Opera

To disable JavaScript in Opera, go to **Tools** > **Preferences...**, click the **Advanced** tab, select **Content** in the list on the left, and uncheck the **Enable JavaScript** checkbox.

Disabling JavaScript in Internet Explorer

To disable JavaScript in Internet Explorer, go to **Tools** > **Internet Options...** and click the **Security** tab. There, select the zone for which you're changing the settings (the zone will be shown on the right-hand side of the browser's status bar—it will likely be **Local Intranet Zone** if you're developing on the local machine) and press **Custom Level....** Scroll down to the **Scripting** section, and check the **Disable** radio button for **Active Scripting**.

ASP.NET makes it easy to verify on the server side if the submitted data complies to the validator rules without our having to write very much C# or VB code at all. All we need to do is to check the `Page` object's `IsValid` property, which only returns `True` if all the validators on the page are happy with the data in the controls they're validating. This approach will always work, regardless of which web browser the user has, or the settings he or she has chosen.

Let's make use of this property in our `Click` event handler:

Visual Basic	LearningASP\VB\Login_04.aspx *(excerpt)*

```vb
Protected Sub submitButton_Click(s As Object, e As EventArgs)
  If Page.IsValid Then
    submitButton.Text = "Valid"
  Else
    submitButton.Text = "Invalid!"
  End If
End Sub
```

C#	LearningASP\CS\Login_04.aspx *(excerpt)*

```csharp
protected void submitButton_Click(object s, EventArgs e)
{
  if(Page.IsValid)
  {
    submitButton.Text = "Valid";
  }
```

```
  else
  {
    submitButton.Text = "Invalid!";
  }
}
```

Load the page again after you disable JavaScript, and press the **Submit** button without entering any data in the text boxes. The text label on the button should change, as shown in Figure 6.2.

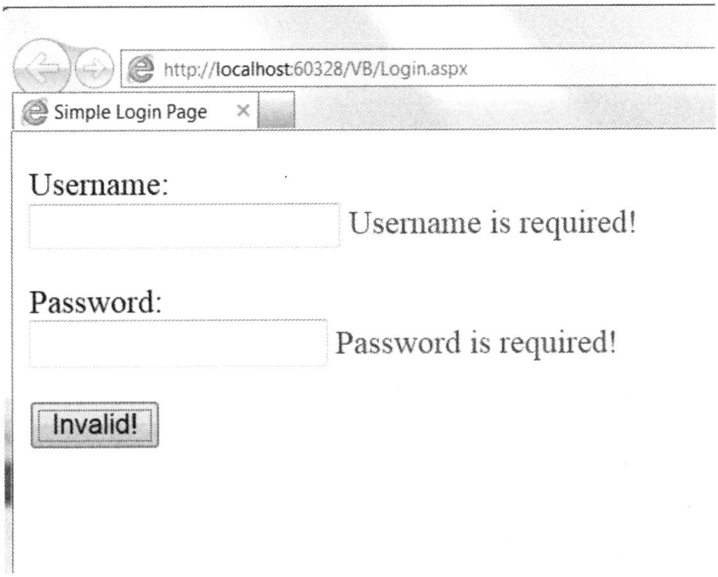

Figure 6.2. Server validation failed

As you can see, the text on the button changed to a message that reflects the fact that `Page.IsValid` returned `False`. The validator controls also display the error messages, but only after a round-trip to the server. If JavaScript was enabled, the validator controls would prevent the page from submitting, so the code that changes the `Button`'s text wouldn't execute.

If you use validation controls, and verify on the server that `Page.IsValid` is `True` before you use any of the validated data, you have a bulletproof solution that's guaranteed to avoid bad data entering your application through any browser. JavaScript-enabled browsers will deliver an improved user experience by allowing client-side validation to take place, but server-side validation ensures that, ultimately, the functionality is the same regardless of your users' browser settings.

 Using `CausesValidation`

There are cases in which you might decide to disable validation when a certain event is triggered. For example, imagine you have a registration page that contains two buttons: **Submit** and **Cancel**. You'll probably want the **Cancel** button to work regardless of whether valid data has been entered, otherwise users won't be able to cancel the process before typing in some valid data! You can make **Cancel** work at all times by setting the `CausesValidation` property of the button to `False`.

One thing to note about validator controls is that, by default, they take up space in your web form. To illustrate this point, let's add a password confirmation text box just after the password text box's `RequiredFieldValidator`:

```
                                    LearningASP\VB\Login_05.aspx (excerpt)

⋮
<!-- Password -->
<p>
  Password and Confirmation:<br />
  <asp:TextBox id="passwordTextBox" runat="server"
      TextMode="Password" />
  <asp:RequiredFieldValidator id="passwordReq" runat="server"
      ControlToValidate="passwordTextBox"
      ErrorMessage="Password is required!"
      SetFocusOnError="True" />
  <asp:TextBox id="confirmPasswordTextBox" runat="server"
      TextMode="Password" />
  <asp:RequiredFieldValidator id="confirmPasswordReq"
      runat="server" ControlToValidate="confirmPasswordTextBox"
      ErrorMessage="Password confirmation is required!"
      SetFocusOnError="True" />
</p>
⋮
```

Load this page and you'll see that the new `confirmPasswordTextBox` control appears after the space that's reserved for the `RequiredFieldValidator` control, as Figure 6.3 illustrates.

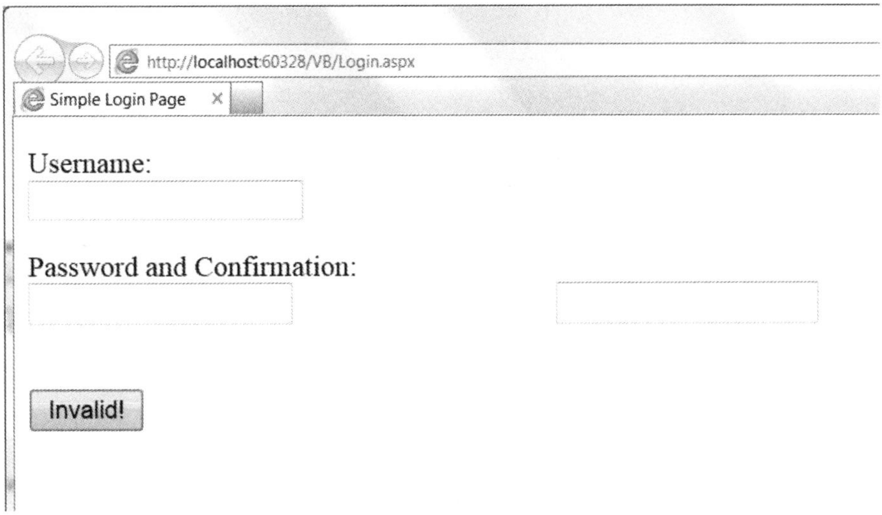

Figure 6.3. Displaying the `RequiredValidatorControlRequiredFieldValidator` control ?

As you can see, ASP.NET reserves space for its validator controls by default. However, we can change this behavior using the `Display` property, which can take any one of the values `None`, `Static`, or `Dynamic`:

None

> None makes the validator invisible—no space is reserved, and the error message is never shown. You may want to set this option when using the `ValidationSummary` control (which we'll cover later) to display a list of validation errors for the entire page, in which case you won't want each validation control to display its own error message separately.

Static

> `Static` is the default display mode. With this mode, the validator occupies space on the generated form even if it doesn't display anything.

Dynamic

> The `Dynamic` mode causes the validation control to display if any validation errors occur, but ensures that it doesn't generate any output (including the whitespace shown in Figure 6.3) if the validation is passed.

In the code below, the `Display` property is set to `Dynamic`. If we set this property for all of the validation controls in our page, the two password `TextBox` controls will appear side by side until one of them fails validation:

```
                                    LearningASP\VB\Login_06.aspx (excerpt)
  ⋮
<!-- Password -->
<p>
  Password and Confirmation:<br />
  <asp:TextBox id="passwordTextBox" runat="server"
      TextMode="Password" />
  <asp:RequiredFieldValidator id="passwordReq" runat="server"
      ControlToValidate="passwordTextBox"
      ErrorMessage="Password is required!"
      SetFocusOnError="True" Display="Dynamic" />
  <asp:TextBox id="confirmPasswordTextBox" runat="server"
      TextMode="Password" />
  <asp:RequiredFieldValidator id="confirmPasswordReq"
      runat="server" ControlToValidate="confirmPasswordTextBox"
      ErrorMessage="Password confirmation is required!"
      SetFocusOnError="True" Display="Dynamic" />
</p>
  ⋮
```

Using Validation Controls

Now that you have an understanding of what validation controls can do, let's have
a look at the different controls that are available in ASP.NET:

- RequiredFieldValidator
- RangeValidator
- RegularExpressionValidator
- CompareValidator
- CustomValidator
- ValidationSummary

In general, most controls can be validated. The Calendar control is the exception
to the rule.

If you're working with Visual Web Developer, you can see the validation controls
in the **Validation** tab of the Toolbox, as Figure 6.4 illustrates.

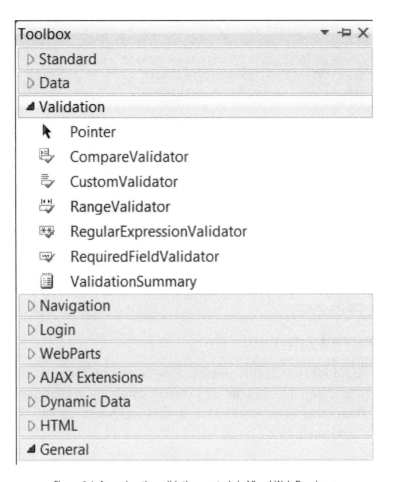

Figure 6.4. Accessing the validation controls in Visual Web Developer

Validation controls, like other web server controls, are inserted as tags with the asp: prefix. Once a validation control is inserted, it validates an existing control elsewhere on the page, and presents an error message to the user if necessary. To validate a field, all you have to do is insert a control—there's no JavaScript or clumsy server-side code to write by hand! Let's take a look at these ASP.NET validation controls in detail now.

RequiredFieldValidator

The RequiredFieldValidator control is the simplest of the validation controls. It does exactly what its name suggests: it makes sure that a user enters a value into a web control. We used the RequiredFieldValidator control in the login page example presented earlier:

LearningASP\VB\Login_06.aspx *(excerpt)*

```
<asp:RequiredFieldValidator id="passwordReq" runat="server"
    ControlToValidate="passwordTextBox"
    ErrorMessage="Password is required!"
    SetFocusOnError="True" Display="Dynamic" />
```

The `ControlToValidate` property contains the ID of the web control that the `RequiredFieldValidator` control is assigned to. The `ErrorMessage` property contains the error message that will be displayed when the user fails to enter a value into each control. Lastly, we apply red font coloring to bring the note to the user's attention. By default, ASP.NET 4 does not apply any styling to the error messages, a break from previous versions. To perform styling on your own using CSS, there is a `CssClass` attribute that can be used to have ASP.NET use the styling based on the CSS class of your choice. Going forward we will use the `errorMsg` class that we add to our Dorknozzle.css file:

CompareValidator

One of the most useful validation controls is the `CompareValidator` control, which performs a comparison between the data entered into a given control and some other value. That other value can be a fixed value, such as a number, or a value entered into another control.

Let's look at an example that builds on the login example we saw in the previous section. Here, we'll validate that the data entered into both the password fields is identical. Make the following changes to **Login.aspx**:

LearningASP\VB\Login_07.aspx *(excerpt)*

```
<p>
  Password and Confirmation:<br />
  ⋮
  <asp:CompareValidator id="comparePasswords" runat="server"
      ControlToCompare="passwordTextBox"
      ControlToValidate="confirmPasswordTextBox"
      ErrorMessage="Your passwords do not match up!"
      Display="Dynamic" />
</p>
```

Run the page and enter a different password into each field. The **CompareValidator** control will appear as soon as you move on from the two fields whose data doesn't match, as Figure 6.5 shows.

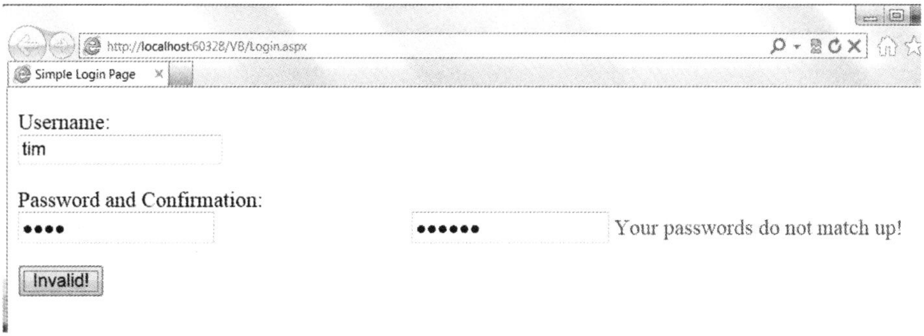

Figure 6.5. A `CompareValidator` control in action

As you've probably noticed, the `CompareValidator` control differs very little from the `RequiredFieldValidator` control:

```
                                          LearningASP\VB\Login_07.aspx (excerpt)

<asp:RequiredFieldValidator id="confirmPasswordReq"
    runat="server" ControlToValidate="confirmPasswordTextBox"
    ErrorMessage="Password confirmation is required!"
    SetFocusOnError="True" Display="Dynamic" />
<asp:CompareValidator id="comparePasswords" runat="server"
    ControlToCompare="passwordTextBox"
    ControlToValidate="confirmPasswordTextBox"
    ErrorMessage="Your passwords do not match up!"
    Display="Dynamic" />
```

The only difference is that in addition to a `ControlToValidate` property, the `CompareValidator` has a `ControlToCompare` property. We set these two properties to the IDs of the controls we want to compare. So, in our example, the `ControlToValidate` property is set to the `confirmPasswordTextBox`, and the `ControlToCompare` property is set to the `passwordTextBox`.

The `CompareValidator` can be used to compare the value of a control to a fixed value, too. `CompareValidator` can check whether the entered value is equal to, less than, or greater than any given value. As an example, let's add an "age" field to our login form:

LearningASP\VB\Login_08.aspx *(excerpt)*

```
<!-- Age -->
<p>
  Age:<br />
  <asp:TextBox id="ageTextBox" runat="server" />
  <asp:RequiredFieldValidator id="ageReq" runat="server"
      ControlToValidate="ageTextBox"
      ErrorMessage="Age is required!"
      SetFocusOnError="True" Display="Dynamic" />
  <asp:CompareValidator id="ageCheck" runat="server"
      Operator="GreaterThan" Type="Integer"
      ControlToValidate="ageTextBox" ValueToCompare="15"
      ErrorMessage="You must be 16 years or older to log in" />
</p>
```

In this case, the CompareValidator control is used to check that the user is old enough to log in to our fictitious web application. Here, we set the Operator property of the CompareValidator to GreaterThan. This property can take on any of the values Equal, NotEqual, GreaterThan, GreaterThanEqual, LessThan, LessThanEqual, or DataTypeCheck, which we'll look at shortly. Next, we tell the CompareValidator control to compare the two values by setting the Type property to Integer, which will cause the CompareValidator to treat the values as whole numbers (this property can also be set to Currency or Date, among other options). Finally, we use the ValueToCompare property to make sure that the user's age is greater than 15. If you load this page in your web browser now, you'll see that the form is only validated when the user enters an age of 16 or more.

We can also use the CompareValidator control to perform data type checks. To see how this works, let's replace the age TextBox control with a date-of-birth text box, whose value must be a valid date:

LearningASP\VB\Login_09.aspx *(excerpt)*

```
<!-- Birth Date -->
<p>
  Birth Date:<br />
  <asp:TextBox id="birthDateTextBox" runat="server" />
  <asp:CompareValidator id="birthDateCheck" runat="server"
      Operator="DataTypeCheck" Type="Date"
      ControlToValidate="birthDateTextBox"
```

```
         ErrorMessage="You must enter the date in a valid format!"
         SetFocusOnError="True" Display="Dynamic" />
   </p>
```

As you can see, the `Operator` property of the `CompareValidator` control is set to perform a `DataTypeCheck`, and the `Type` property is set to `Date`. Load the page, and you'll see that you can't enter anything other than a valid date into this field. The constituents of a "valid" date will depend on the regional settings on your web server.

RangeValidator

The `RangeValidator` control checks whether the value of a form field falls between minimum and maximum values. For instance, we could make sure that users who visit our web site were born in a certain decade. If they enter values that don't fit into the range we specify, the validator will return an "invalid" message.

birth date, validatingLet's continue by expanding **Login.aspx** even further:

```
                                          LearningASP\VB\Login_10.aspx (excerpt)

<!-- Birth Date -->
<p>
  Birth Date:<br />
  <asp:TextBox id="birthDateTextBox" runat="server" />
  <asp:RangeValidator id="birthDateRangeTest" runat="server"
      Type="Date" ControlToValidate="birthDateTextBox"
      MinimumValue="1/1/1970" MaximumValue="12/31/1979"
      ErrorMessage="You must've been born in the 1970s to use
      this web site!" />
</p>
```

 Take Care when Specifying Dates

If you're located outside of the US, you may need to modify the above example. In the US, dates are specified in month-day-year format. In the UK and Australia, they're specified in day-month-year order, and in other countries, the year is specified first. The ASP.NET runtime will be expecting you to specify dates in your local format, so adjust the values of the `MinimumValue` and `MaximumValue` properties accordingly.

Here, we've added a `RangeValidator` to validate the `birthDateTextBox` control. Our `RangeValidator` control checks whether the date entered falls within the 1970s, and shows an error message similar to Figure 6.6 if it doesn't.

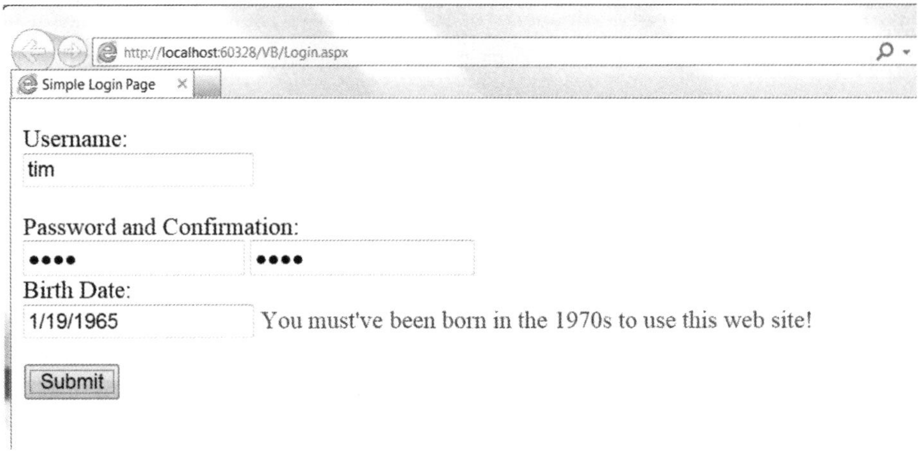

Figure 6.6. Using the `RangeValidator` control

Note that the `Type` property of the `RangeValidator` control specifies the data type that's expected in the control with which it's associated; if some other data type is entered into this field, it fails validation. As such, we've removed the `CompareValidator` we added for this purpose.

ValidationSummary

Imagine we have a form that contains many form fields. If that page contains errors, it could be difficult for users to figure out which control caused a given error, because the page is so big. The `ValidationSummary` control can alleviate this problem by presenting the user with a list of error messages in one place on the page. Let's see the `ValidationSummary` control in use. Add it to the end of your **Login.aspx** file, like so:

LearningASP\VB\Login_11.aspx *(excerpt)*

```
<!-- Submit Button -->
<p>
  <asp:Button id="submitButton" runat="server" Text="Submit"
    OnClick="submitButton_Click" />
</p>
<!-- Validation Summary -->
```

```
<p>
  <asp:ValidationSummary id="vSummary" runat="server" />
</p>
```

When the user clicks the **Submit** button, the ValidationSummary is populated automatically with a list of all the errors on the page, as we can see in Figure 6.7.

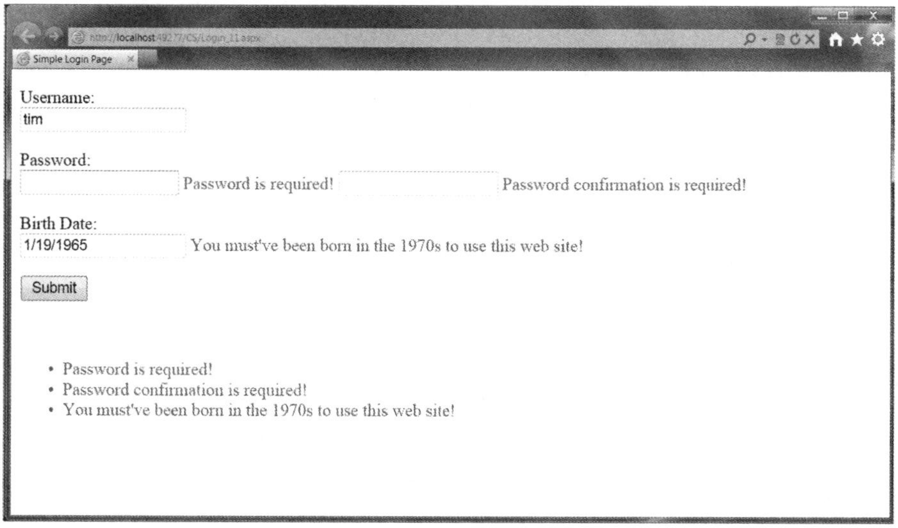

Figure 6.7. Using the ValidationSummary control

This control isn't particularly good looking, but you can see its potential. If you set the Display properties of all of the other validation controls on the page to None, you could use a ValidationSummary to show all the errors in one place.

If you set the ShowMessageBox property of the ValidationSummary control to True, the list of errors will be shown in a JavaScript alert box similar to Figure 6.8. The server-side list will still be shown to users who don't have JavaScript-enabled browsers.

Figure 6.8. Showing validation errors in a dialog

RegularExpressionValidator

The `RegularExpressionValidator` lets you specify a regular expression that describes all the allowable values for a field. Regular expressions are powerful tools for manipulating strings, and are supported by many programming languages. They're commonly used to check for patterns inside strings. Consider, for instance, the following regular expression:

```
^\S+@\S+\.\S+$
```

In plain English, this expression will match any string that begins with one or more non-whitespace characters followed by the @ character, then one or more non-whitespace characters, then a dot (.), then one or more non-whitespace characters, followed by the end of the string.

This regular expression describes any one of these email addresses:

- books@sitepoint.com
- zac@host.modulemedia.com
- joe_bloggs@yahoo.co.uk

However, the regular expression would fail if the user typed in one of these entries:

▒ `books@sitepoint`

▒ `joe bloggs@yahoo.co.uk`

Although regular expressions cannot check to see if the email address itself is valid, they can, at the very least, provide a means for us to determine whether or not the user has entered a string of characters that has all the key components of a valid email address.

Let's change the username field in our login form to an email address field, and validate it using the `RegularExpressionValidator` control.

```
                                          LearningASP\VB\Login_12.aspx (excerpt)

<!-- Email Address -->
<p>
  Email address:<br />
  <asp:TextBox id="emailTextBox" runat="server" />
  <asp:RequiredFieldValidator id="emailReq" runat="server"
      ControlToValidate="emailTextBox"
      ErrorMessage="Email address is required!"
      SetFocusOnError="True" Display="Dynamic" />
  <asp:RegularExpressionValidator id="emailValidator"
      runat="server" ControlToValidate="emailTextBox"
      ValidationExpression="^\S+@\S+\.\S+$"
      ErrorMessage="You must enter a valid email address!" />
</p>
```

The important property within this control is `ValidationExpression`, to which we assign the regular expression that's appropriate for handling our custom validation functionality. Figure 6.9 shows the error message that appears when a user enters an incorrect email address.

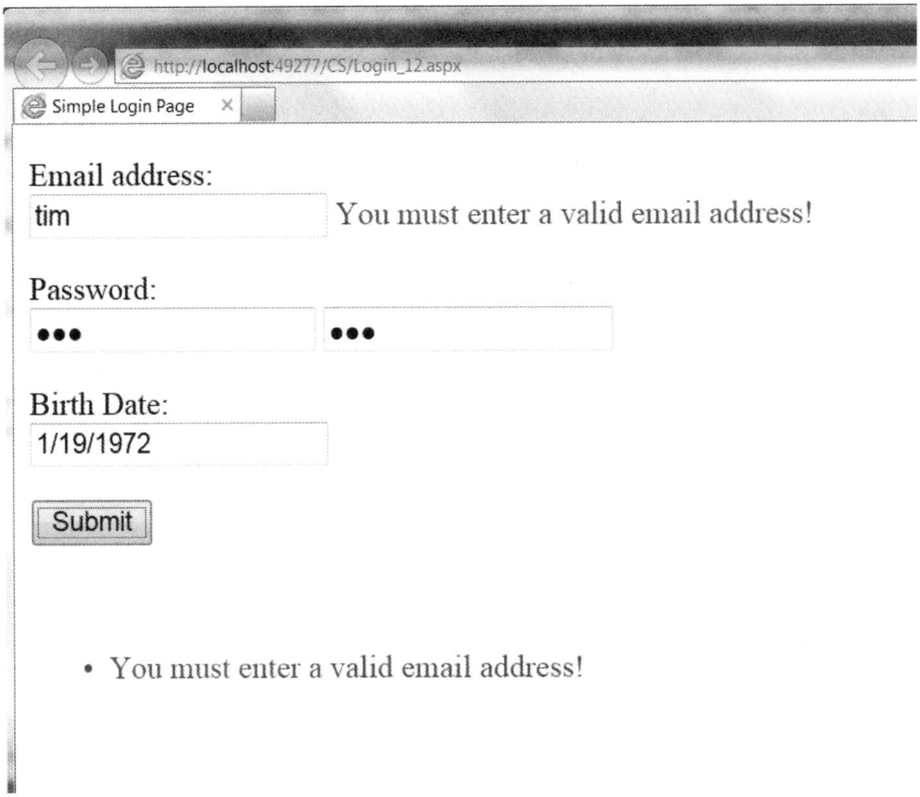

Figure 6.9. Using the `RegularExpressionValidator` control

Some Useful Regular Expressions

Writing regular expressions can be tricky, and a comprehensive discussion of the topic is outside the scope of this book. Many of the regular expressions presented here are nowhere near as rigorous as they could be, but they're still quite useful. The book *Mastering Regular Expressions*, by Jeffrey E. F. Friedl, contains a single expression for checking email addresses that tops 6,000 characters![1]

Table 6.1 outlines the usage of some simple regular expressions.

---

[1] Jeffrey E. F. Friedl, *Mastering Regular Expressions*, Third Edition (Sebastopol: O'Reilly Media), 2006.

Table 6.1. Some simple regular expressions

Description	Regular Expression
email address	`^\S+@\S+\.\S+$`
web URL	`^https?://\S+\.\S+$`
US phone numbers ((555) 555-5555 or 555-555-5555)	`^\(?\d{3}\)?(\s|-)\d{3}-\d{4}$`
international phone numbers (begins with a digit, followed by between seven and 20 digits and/or dashes)	`^\d(\d|-){7,20}$`
five-digit ZIP code	`^\d{5}$`
nine-digit ZIP code	`^\d{5}-\d{4}$`
either five-digit or nine-digit ZIP code	`^(\d{5})|(\d{5}\-\d{4})$`
US social security number	`^\d{3}-\d{2}-\d{4}$`

Take a close look at the components of the regular expressions in Table 6.2, and you should begin to see how they work. If you'd like more information on regular expressions, try the following resources:

Regular Expression Library[2]
a searchable library of regular expressions

Using Regular Expressions in PHP[3]
a great article on the use of regular expressions and PHP

Regular Expressions in JavaScript[4]
another great article, this time on the use of regular expressions with JavaScript

---

[2] http://www.regexlib.com/
[3] http://www.sitepoint.com/article/regular-expressions-php
[4] http://www.sitepoint.com/article/expressions-javascript

Table 6.2. Common regular expression components and their descriptions

Special Character	Description
.	any character
^	beginning of string
$	end of string
\d	numeric digit
\s	whitespace character
\S	non-whitespace character
(abc)	the string abc as a group of characters
?	preceding character or group is optional
+	one or more of the preceding character or group
*	zero or more of the preceding character or group
{n}	exactly n of the preceding character or group
{n,m}	n to m of the preceding character or group
(a|b)	either a or b
\$	a dollar sign (as opposed to the end of a string). We can **escape** any of the special characters listed above by preceding it with a backslash. For example, \. matches a period character, \? matches a question mark, and so on.

You'll find a complete guide and reference to regular expressions and their components in the .NET Framework SDK Documentation.

CustomValidator

The validation controls included with ASP.NET allow you to handle many kinds of validation, yet certain types of validation cannot be performed with these built-in controls. For instance, imagine that you needed to ensure that a new user's login details were unique by checking them against a list of existing usernames on the server. The CustomValidator control can be helpful in this situation, and others like it. Let's see how:

```vb
<%@ Page Language="VB" %>

<!DOCTYPE html PUBLIC "-//W3C//DTD XHTML 1.0 Transitional//EN"
    "http://www.w3.org/TR/xhtml1/DTD/xhtml1-transitional.dtd">

<script runat="server">
  Sub CheckUniqueUserName(ByVal s As Object,
  ➥  ByVal e As ServerValidateEventArgs)
    Dim username As String = e.Value.ToLower
    If (username = "andrei" Or username = "cristian") Then
      e.IsValid = False
    End If
  End Sub

  Sub submitButton_Click(ByVal s As Object, ByVal e As EventArgs)
    If Page.IsValid Then
      submitButton.Text = "Valid"
    Else
      submitButton.Text = "Invalid!"
    End If
  End Sub
</script>

<html xmlns="http://www.w3.org/1999/xhtml">
  <head runat="server">
    <title>Custom Validator</title>
  </head>
  <body>
    <form id="form1" runat="server">
      <div>
        <p>
          New Username:<br />
          <asp:TextBox ID="usernameTextBox" runat="server" />
          <asp:CustomValidator ID="usernameUnique" runat="server"
              ControlToValidate="usernameTextBox"
              OnServerValidate="CheckUniqueUserName"
              ErrorMessage="This username already taken!" />
        </p>
        <p>
          <asp:Button ID="submitButton" runat="server"
              OnClick="submitButton_Click" Text="Submit" />
        </p>
      </div>
```

```
      </form>
    </body>
</html>
```

```
<%@ Page Language="C#" %>

<!DOCTYPE html PUBLIC "-//W3C//DTD XHTML 1.0 Transitional//EN"
    "http://www.w3.org/TR/xhtml1/DTD/xhtml1-transitional.dtd">

<script runat="server">
  void CheckUniqueUserName(Object s, ServerValidateEventArgs e)
  {
    string username = e.Value.ToLower();
    if (username == "andrei" || username == "cristian")
    {
      e.IsValid = false;
    }
  }

  void submitButton_Click(Object s, EventArgs e)
  {
    if (Page.IsValid)
    {
      submitButton.Text = "Valid";
    }
    else
    {
      submitButton.Text = "Invalid!";
    }
  }
</script>

<html xmlns="http://www.w3.org/1999/xhtml">
  <head runat="server">
    <title>Custom Validator</title>
  </head>
  <body>
    <form id="form1" runat="server">
      <div>
        <p>
          New Username:<br />
          <asp:TextBox ID="usernameTextBox" runat="server" />
          <asp:CustomValidator ID="usernameUnique" runat="server"
```

```
                ControlToValidate="usernameTextBox"
                OnServerValidate="CheckUniqueUserName"
                ErrorMessage="This username already taken!" />
         </p>
         <p>
           <asp:Button ID="submitButton" runat="server"
                OnClick="submitButton_Click" Text="Submit" />
         </p>
       </div>
     </form>
   </body>
</html>
```

When this form is submitted, the `CustomValidator` control raises the `ServerValid-ate` event, and the `CheckUniqueUserName` method is called as a result. At the moment, our list of usernames is limited to `andrei` and `cristian`. If the new username matches either of these, `e.IsValid` is set to `False`, and the error message is displayed; otherwise, we assume that the username is valid. When our `submitButton_Click` event handler checks the `Page.IsValid` property, `e.IsValid` returns `False` if the user entered `andrei` or `cristian`, and `True` if the new username is anything else.

Although this example shows a very simple `CustomValidator`, you can certainly imagine the possibilities this class makes available. For example, while we won't explore it in this book, you could create a client-side validation function for your `CustomValidator` controls by means of the `ClientValidationFunction` property. For details, refer to the .NET Framework SDK Documentation for the `CustomValidator` control.

Validation Groups

A very useful feature of ASP.NET, validation groups allow us to validate individual parts of a web page independently of its other sections. This capability proves particularly handy when you're working with complex pages that contain many functional components. For example, consider the scenario of a single page that contains a login form *and* a quick registration form, each with its own **Submit** button and its own set of validation controls. Certainly we don't want the functionality of the login form's **Submit** button to be affected by the data in the registration form; nor can we allow the login form's data to affect submission of the registration form.

The solution to this problem is to set the controls in each of the boxes within different validation groups. You can assign a control to a validation group using its ValidationGroup property, as shown in the following code:

```
                                    LearningASP\VB\ValidationGroups.aspx (excerpt)
<%@ Page Language="VB" %>

<!DOCTYPE html PUBLIC "-//W3C//DTD XHTML 1.0 Transitional//EN"
    "http://www.w3.org/TR/xhtml1/DTD/xhtml1-transitional.dtd">

<script runat="server">

</script>

<html xmlns="http://www.w3.org/1999/xhtml">
  <head runat="server">
    <title>Untitled Page</title>
  </head>
<body>
  <form id="form1" runat="server">
    <div>
      <!-- Login Controls -->
      <h1>Login</h1>
      <!-- Username -->
      <p>
        Username:<br />
        <asp:TextBox ID="usernameTextBox" runat="server" />
        <asp:RequiredFieldValidator ID="usernameReq"
            runat="server" ControlToValidate="usernameTextBox"
            ErrorMessage="Username is required!"
            SetFocusOnError="True" ValidationGroup="Login" />
      </p>
      <!-- Password -->
      <p>
        Password:<br />
        <asp:TextBox ID="passwordTextBox" runat="server"
            TextMode="Password" />
        <asp:RequiredFieldValidator ID="passwordReq"
            runat="server" ControlToValidate="passwordTextBox"
            ErrorMessage="Password is required!"
            SetFocusOnError="True" ValidationGroup="Login" />
      </p>
      <p>
        <asp:Button ID="loginButton" runat="server" Text="Log In"
```

```
                    ValidationGroup="Login" />
      </p>
      <!-- Login Controls -->
      <h1>
        Register</h1>
      <!-- Username -->
      <p>
        Username:<br />
        <asp:TextBox ID="newUserNameTextBox" runat="server" />
        <asp:RequiredFieldValidator ID="newUserNameReq"
             runat="server" ControlToValidate="newUserNameTextBox"
             ErrorMessage="Username is required!"
             SetFocusOnError="True" ValidationGroup="Register" />
      </p>
      <!-- Password -->
      <p>
        Password:<br />
        <asp:TextBox ID="newPasswordTextBox" runat="server"
             TextMode="Password" />
        <asp:RequiredFieldValidator ID="newPasswordReq"
             runat="server" ControlToValidate="newPasswordTextBox"
             ErrorMessage="Password is required!"
             SetFocusOnError="True" ValidationGroup="Register" />
      </p>
      <p>
        <asp:Button ID="registerButton" runat="server"
             Text="Register" ValidationGroup="Register" />
      </p>
    </div>
  </form>
</body>
</html>
```

Executing this page reveals the two sets of controls: one for logging in an existing user, and another for registering a new user. To keep things simple, the only validation we've implemented in this example is achieved through RequiredFieldValidator controls.

Clicking the **Log In** button triggers only those validators that share that button's ValidationGroup setting, as Figure 6.10 indicates.

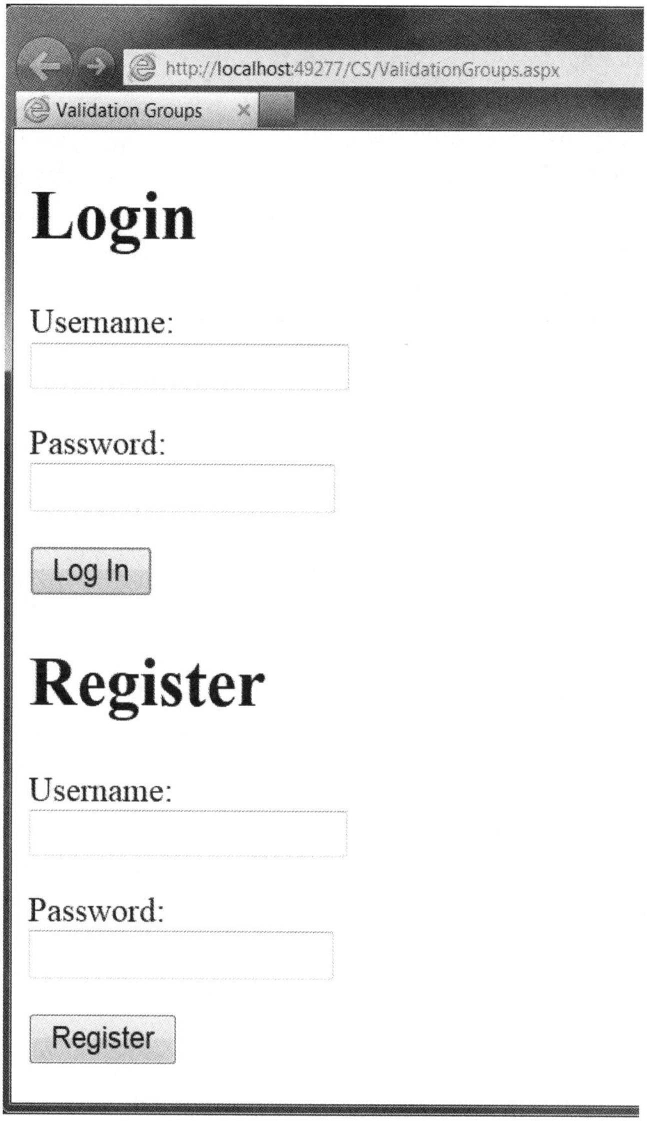

Figure 6.10. Triggering the `Login` `ValidationGroup`

Likewise, clicking the **Register** button triggers the second set of validators, and de-activates the first, as Figure 6.11 shows.

Default Validation Groups

Controls that aren't specifically assigned to any validation group are aggregated into a default validation group. In other words, a button that isn't assigned to any

validation group will trigger only those validation controls that aren't assigned
to any groups.

Finally, remember that `Page.IsValid` returns the results of the current validation
group (that is, the one that caused the server-side event). To verify the validity of
another group on the page, we use the `Page.Validate` method, which can receive
as a parameter the name of the validation group to be validated.

Figure 6.11. Activating the `RegisterValidationGroup`

Updating Dorknozzle

Now that you've spent some time with validation controls, let's use them to update Dorknozzle's Help Desk page. The following rules must be met before the user can submit a new help desk request:

- The station number text box cannot be empty.
- The station number must be a valid number.
- The station number must be a numeral between 1 and 50.
- A description of the problem must be entered.

To make changes to the Help Desk page, you first need to load the Dorknozzle project in Visual Web Developer. Go to **File > Open Web Site…** and select the Dorknozzle project.

 Loading Multiple Projects

Did you know that you can work with several projects at the same time? You can launch multiple instances of Visual Web Developer and load a different web application in each of them.

After Dorknozzle loads, open **HelpDesk.aspx** in the editor, and make the following changes to the file:

Dorknozzle\VB\01_HelpDesk.aspx (excerpt)

```
<%@ Page Language="VB" MasterPageFile="~/Dorknozzle.master"
    AutoEventWireup="false" CodeFile="HelpDesk.aspx.vb"
    Inherits="HelpDesk" title="Dorknozzle Help Desk" %>

<asp:Content ID="Content1" ContentPlaceHolderID="head"
    Runat="Server">
</asp:Content>
<asp:Content ID="Content2"
    ContentPlaceHolderID="ContentPlaceHolder1" Runat="Server">
  <h1>Employee Help Desk Request</h1>
  <p>
    Station Number:<br />
    <asp:TextBox id="stationTextBox" runat="server"
        CssClass="textbox" />
    <asp:RequiredFieldValidator id="stationNumReq" runat="server"
```

```
              ControlToValidate="stationTextBox"
              ErrorMessage="<br />You must enter a station number!"
              Display="Dynamic" />
         <asp:CompareValidator id="stationNumCheck" runat="server"
              ControlToValidate="stationTextBox"
              Operator="DataTypeCheck" Type="Integer"
              ErrorMessage="<br />The value must be a number!"
              Display="Dynamic" />
         <asp:RangeValidator id="stationNumRangeCheck" runat="server"
              ControlToValidate="stationTextBox"
              MinimumValue="1" MaximumValue="50" Type="Integer"
              ErrorMessage="<br />Number must be between 1 and 50."
              Display="Dynamic" />
    </p>
    <p>
      Problem Category:<br />
      <asp:DropDownList id="categoryList" runat="server"
          CssClass="dropdownmenu" />
    </p>
    <p>
      Problem Subject:<br />
      <asp:DropDownList id="subjectList" runat="server"
          CssClass="dropdownmenu" />
    </p>
    <p>
      Problem Description:<br />
      <asp:TextBox id="descriptionTextBox" runat="server"
          CssClass="textbox" Columns="40" Rows="4"
          TextMode="MultiLine" />
         <asp:RequiredFieldValidator id="descriptionReq" runat="server"
          ControlToValidate="descriptionTextBox"
          ErrorMessage="<br />You must enter a description!"
          Display="Dynamic" />
    </p>
    <p>
      <asp:Button id="submitButton" runat="server"
          CssClass="button" Text="Submit Request" /></p>
</asp:Content>
```

Now execute the project, and select the **Help Desk** page from the menu. Clicking **Submit** without entering valid data triggers the validation controls, as Figure 6.12 shows.

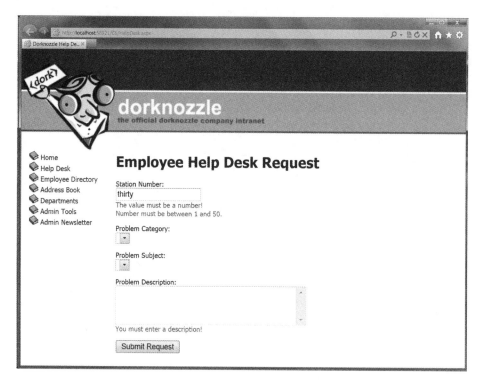

Figure 6.12. Validation controls in action on the Dorknozzle Help Desk

Right now, we're not doing anything with the data that's been entered, but we'll take care of that in following chapters. When we finally do something with this data, we don't want our server-side code to try to work with invalid data. So let's add the safety check to the server side as well, to make sure we have a solid foundation from which to start developing our server-side functionality in the coming chapters.

Stop the project from within Visual Web Developer, and open **HelpDesk.aspx** in **Design** view. There, double-click the **Submit Request** button to have its Click event handler generated for you.

Complete the automatically generated code as shown below:

Visual Basic	Dorknozzle\VB\02_HelpDesk.aspx.vb *(excerpt)*

```
Protected Sub submitButton_Click(ByVal sender As Object,
➥    ByVal e As System.EventArgs) Handles submitButton.Click
  If Page.IsValid Then
```

```
    ' Code that uses the data entered by the user
  End If
End Sub
```

C#   Dorknozzle\CS\02_HelpDesk.aspx.cs *(excerpt)*

```
protected void submitButton_Click(object sender, EventArgs e)
{
  if (Page.IsValid)
  {
    // Code that uses the data entered by the user
  }
}
```

Up to this point, we've only discussed one way of tying a control's event to an event handler method. This approach involves setting a property, such as OnClick, on the control, as shown here:

C#   Dorknozzle\CS\03_HelpDesk.aspx *(excerpt)*

```
<asp:Button id="submitButton" runat="server" CssClass="button"
    Text="Submit Request" OnClick="submitButton_Click" />
```

This property causes ASP.NET to call a method named submitButton_Click whenever this button is clicked. If you're using C#, you'll see that Visual Web Developer added this property to the submitButton control when you double-clicked the **Submit Request** button in Design view and it generated your event handler, as is shown above.

However, if you're using VB, this property is not added. Instead, Visual Web Developer uses the VB-specific keyword Handles, followed by the name of the control that's responsible for raising the event, and finally the name of the event that's being handled (in our case, submitButton.Click). This generated code is shown below:

Visual Basic   Dorknozzle\VB\02_HelpDesk.aspx.vb *(excerpt)*

```
Protected Sub submitButton_Click(ByVal sender As Object,
➥   ByVal e As System.EventArgs) Handles submitButton.Click
```

This is simply an alternative way of tying this method to the submitButton control's Click event.

Event Handling Code and the Examples In this Book

Now is probably a good time to mention that the examples in this book will assume that you'll double-click ASP.NET controls in Visual Web Developer Design view to have the event handling code generated for you, instead of entering it manually. This is particularly important to remember if you are using C# because example code listings that contain web form markup may not include properties like `OnClick` that are automatically generated.

Double-clicking controls in Design view will ensure all the correct event handling code is generated regardless of whether you're using VB or C#.

We'll expand the code inside this `submitButton_Click` method in later chapters, but for the time being, you can rest assured that you've put the validation mechanism in place.

Summary

As we've seen, the validation controls available through ASP.NET are very powerful. This chapter explained how to validate required form fields with the `RequiredFieldValidator` control, compare form fields with the `CompareValidator` control, check for a numeric range within form fields with the `RangeValidator` control, provide a user with a summary of errors using the `ValidationSummary` control, check for email addresses with the `RegularExpressionValidator` control, and perform your own custom validation with the `CustomValidator` control.

If you disabled JavaScript during this chapter to test server-side validation, don't forget to turn it back on before proceeding. And lastly, don't forget styling! ASP.NET 4.0 doesn't automatically require validators to be the color red. Styling of validation error messages and summary groups can be done through CSS for ultimate flexibility using the CssClass attribute.

In the next chapter, we'll begin to introduce you to the challenges—and rewards!—involved in working with databases. This is a skill you'll almost certainly need when building any non-trivial, real-world web application, so roll up your sleeves and let's get into it!

7

Database Design and Development

As you begin to build dynamic web applications, it will become increasingly obvious that you need to store data and allow users to access it through your application. Whether you're building a company-wide intranet that can only be accessed by employees, or a feature-rich ecommerce site that will be visited by millions of people, you'll need a system for storing information. Enter: the database.

In 1970, E.F. Codd, an employee of IBM, proposed his idea for what would become the first relational database design model. His model, which offered new methods for storing and retrieving data in large applications, far surpassed any idea or system that was in place at the time. The concept of relational data stemmed from the fact that data was organized in tables, and relationships were defined between those tables.

In this chapter, you'll learn:

- what a database is, and why it's useful
- what a database is made of
- what kind of relationships can exist between database elements
- how to use database diagrams

What Is a Database?

Before we become mired in techno-speak, let's take a step back to consider the project at hand—the Dorknozzle Intranet—and how it can benefit from a relational database. By the end of this book, our site will be able to do all sorts of things, but besides these bells and whistles, our company intranet will need to perform one core task: keeping track of the employees in our company. The employee directory we plan to build would be a sorry sight indeed without a list of employees!

So, how will we go about building that information into our site? Experience with static web design might lead you to create a web page named Employee Directory, which would display a table or list of some kind, and type in the details of each of the employees in the company. But, unless Dorknozzle is a very small company, a single page containing all the details of every employee destined to become unusably large. Instead, you might only list the employees' names, and link each to an individual profile page. Sure, this approach might mean there's a bit of typing to do, but it's the kind of job you can assign to the boss's son on his summer internship.

Now, imagine that, a month or two down the track, Dorknozzle undergoes a corporate rebranding exercise (a bright idea undoubtedly proposed by the boss's son one night at the dinner table), and the entire website needs to be updated to match the "new look" of the company. By now, Dorknozzle Jr is back at school, and the mind-numbing job of manually updating each of the employee profile pages falls right in your lap. Lucky you!

This is the time when you realize that life would be a lot easier if a database was added to the mix. A database is a collection of data organized within a framework that can be accessed by programs such as your ASP.NET website. For example, you could have the Dorknozzle intranet site look into a database to find a list of employees that you want to display on the employee directory page.

Such a collection of data needs to be managed by some kind of software—that software is called a **database server**. The database server we'll use in this book is SQL Server 2008 R2 Express Edition, which is a free but powerful database engine created by Microsoft. Other popular database server software products include Oracle, DB2, PostgreSQL, MySQL, and more.

In our Dorknozzle scenario, the employee records would be stored entirely in the database, which would provide two key advantages over the manual maintenance of a list of employees. First, instead of having to write an HTML file for each employee profile page, you could write a single ASP.NET web form that would fetch any employee's details from the database and display them as a profile. This single form could be updated quite easily in the event of corporate rebranding or some other disaster. Second, adding an employee to the directory would be a simple matter of inserting a new record into the database. The web form would take care of the rest, automatically displaying the new employee profile along with the others when it fetched the list from the database.

As a bonus, since this slick, ultra-manageable system reduces the burden of data entry and maintenance, you could assign the boss's son to clean the coffee machine to fill his time!

Let's run with this example as we look at how data is stored in a database. A database is composed of one or more **tables**. For our employee database, we'd probably start with a table called Employees that would contain—you guessed it—a list of employees. Each table in a database has one or more **columns** (or **fields**). Each column holds a certain piece of information about each item in the table. In our example, the Employees table might have columns for the employees' names, network usernames, and phone numbers. Each employee whose details were stored in this table would then be said to be a **row** (or **record**) in the table. These rows and columns would form a table that looks like the one shown in Figure 7.1.

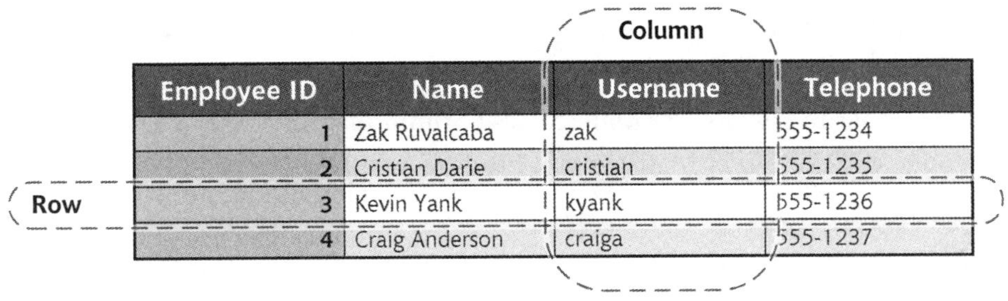

	Employee ID	Name	Username	Telephone
	1	Zak Ruvalcaba	zak	555-1234
	2	Cristian Darie	cristian	555-1235
Row	3	Kevin Yank	kyank	555-1236
	4	Craig Anderson	craiga	555-1237

Figure 7.1. Structure of a typical database table

Notice that, in addition to columns for the employees' names, usernames, and telephone numbers, we included a column named Employee ID. As a matter of good design, a database table should always provide a way to identify each of its rows uniquely. In this particular case, you may consider using an existing piece of data as the unique identifier—after all, it's unlikely that two employees will share the same network username. However, that's something for our network administrator to worry about. Just in case he or she slips up somewhere along the line, we include the Employee ID column, the function of which is to assign a unique number to each employee in the database. This gives us an easy way to refer to each person, and allows us to keep track of which employee is which. We'll discuss such database design issues in greater depth shortly.

So, to review, Figure 7.1 shows a four-column table with four rows, or entries. Each row in the table contains four fields, one for each column in the table: the employee's ID, name, username, and telephone number.

Now, with this basic terminology under your belt, you're ready to roll up your sleeves and build your first database!

Creating Your First Database

The SQL Server engine does a great job of storing and managing your databases, but in order to be able to do anything meaningful with the data, we first need to connect to SQL Server. There are many ways to interact with SQL Server, but for starters we're just interested in using it as a visual tool to facilitate basic administrative tasks. The tools you'll use to interact with your database are:

- Visual Web Developer 2010 Express Edition
- SQL Server Management Studio Express Edition

Visual Web Developer has everything you need to get started with SQL Server; however, we'll use SQL Server Management Studio for most database tasks. Most tasks are easier in SQL Server Management Studio than they are in Visual Web Developer, as SQL Server Management Studio's interface has been designed specifically for working with databases.

We'll name the database that will store the data for our sample project "Dorknozzle." In this chapter, you'll learn how to create its structure, and in the next chapter, we'll begin to work with the database. You can use either Visual Web Developer or SQL Server Management Studio to create the Dorknozzle database. Let's look at both approaches, so that you're comfortable with both options.

Creating a New Database Using Visual Web Developer

Visual Web Developer's Database Explorer window gives you access to most database-related features. You can make this window appear by selecting **View** > **Database Explorer**. Right-click the **Data Connections** node and select **Add Connection...** from the context menu, as shown in Figure 7.2.

Figure 7.2. Adding a new database connection

If you correctly checked the SQL Server Express Edition option during the installation of Visual Web Developer back in Chapter 1, select **Microsoft SQL Server** from the **Choose Data Source** dialog that appears, and click **Continue**. You'll then be asked to enter the details for your data connection. Enter the following data:

1. Set **Server name** to **localhost\SqlExpress**.

2. Leave the **Use Windows Authentication** option selected.

3. Click **Test Connection** to ensure you can successfully connect to SQL Server using the data you've provided.

4. Enter **Dorknozzle** in the **Select or enter a database name** field. Click **OK**.

5. You'll be asked to confirm the creation of a new database called Dorknozzle. Click **Yes**.

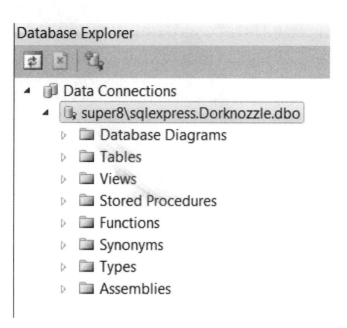

Figure 7.3. Exploring the Dorknozzle database

Once you click **Yes**, the new database will be created, and a link to it will be added to the Data Connections node in Database Explorer. You can expand it to view its contents, as Figure 7.3 illustrates.

Creating a New Database Using SQL Server Management Studio

To start SQL Server Management Studio, which we installed in Chapter 1, select **Start > All Programs > Microsoft SQL Server > SQL Server Management Studio Express**. In the dialog that appears, enter **localhost\SqlExpress** into the **Server Name** box, and leave **Authentication mode** to **Windows Authentication**, as Figure 7.4 illustrates. (The local computer name may be used instead of **localhost**.)

Figure 7.4. Connecting to a SQL Server instance

After you connect to SQL Server, expand the **Databases** node to see the current databases. If you've just installed SQL Server, you'll only have installed the system databases, which are grouped under a **System Databases** node. In Figure 7.5, you can see that there's another database, named `BalloonShop`, on the SQL Server. If you added the Dorknozzle database using Visual Web Developer, you'll see that listed there too.

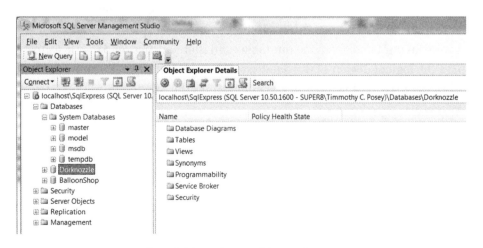

Figure 7.5. Inspecting your SQL server instance

If you haven't done so yet, you should go ahead and create the Dorknozzle database. To create a new database, right-click the **Databases** node, and select **New Database...** from the context menu. In the dialog that appears, enter `Dorknozzle` into the **Database name** field, click **OK**.

Congratulations, you have a brand new database to play with!

Creating Database Tables

Let's launch into creating the tables for our intranet application. It's helpful to think of tables as the drawers in a filing cabinet: just as we can separate different information into different drawers, we can break down information about employees, departments, and help desk requests into different tables. Tables can also be compared to spreadsheets, as they have rows and columns, but they have many other useful features. They know what kinds of data they're allowed to store, can relate to data contained in other tables, and can be searched and manipulated with a very effective language called SQL (which you'll learn about in Chapter 8).

You can organize the tables in your database using either Visual Web Developer or SQL Server Management Studio, depending on your preference. While SQL Server Management Studio is more powerful, both tools can be used for basic tasks such as creating database tables.

In just a minute, we'll dive in and create our first table. Before we do, it's worth giving some thought to how many tables our application will need, and exactly what they'll contain. We can think of tables as lists of **entities**. Entities are the rows or records in our table. Drawing our tables and their entities on paper is a great way to plan the **logical design** of the database. The logical design shows what kinds of data our database will need to store, and outlines the relationships that we want to exist between specific pieces of data.

However, unlike a typical spreadsheet file, the tables defined in the logical design do *not* usually represent the way we'll store the data in the database. This is taken care of in the **physical design** phase, in which we create a practical blueprint that allows us to improve database speed, enable relationships between different tables, or implement other advanced features—basically, to optimize our database in various ways.

Your database's design has important consequences in terms of the way your application works, and how easy it is to extend, so it's important to take the logical and physical design phases seriously. Let's take a look at an example, so that you can see what this means in practice.

Let's say that, in addition to a name, username, and telephone number, you wanted to keep track of the departments in which employees work at Dorknozzle. To do so, it may seem logical to simply add a column to the Employees table we discussed above; Figure 7.6 shows how this would look.

Employee ID	Name	Username	Telephone	Department
1	Zak Ruvalcaba	zak	555-1234	Executive
2	Cristian Darie	cristian	555-1235	Marketing
3	Kevin Yank	kyank	555-1236	Engineering
4	Craig Anderson	craiga	555-1237	Engineering

Figure 7.6. The Employees table

It looks good, right? Well, it's okay in theory. However, if you went ahead and implemented this structure in your database, you'd likely end up in trouble, because this approach presents a couple of potential problems:

- Every time you insert a new employee record, you'll have to provide the name of the department in which that employee works. If you make even the slightest spelling error, then, as far as the database is concerned, you've created a new department. Now, I don't know about you, but I'd be fairly upset if my employee record showed me as the only person working in a department called "Enineering." And what if Dorknozzle Sr. decides to rename one of the departments? You may try to update all the affected employee records with the new department name, but, even if you miss just one record, your database will contain inconsistent information. Database design experts refer to this sort of problem as an **update anomaly**.

- It would be natural for you to rely on your database to provide a list of all the departments in the company so you could, for example, choose to view a list of employees in a particular department. But if, for some reason, you deleted the records of all the employees in that department (don't ask me why—your human resources issues aren't *my* problem!), you'd remove any record that the depart-

ment had ever existed (although, if you really *did* have to fire everyone, that
might be a good thing …). Database design experts call this a **delete anomaly**.

These problems—and more—can be dealt with very easily. Instead of storing the
information for the departments in the Employees table, let's create an entirely new
table for our list of departments. Similarly to the Employees table, the new Departments table will include a column called Department ID, which will identify each
of our departments with a unique number. We can use those department IDs in our
Employees table to associate departments with employees. This new database layout
is shown in Figure 7.7.

Employees				
Employee ID	Name	Username	Telephone	Department ID
1	Zak Ruvalcaba	zak	555-1234	1
2	Cristian Darie	cristian	555-1235	2
3	Kevin Yank	kyank	555-1236	3
4	Craig Anderson	craiga	555-1237	3

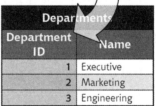

Departments	
Department ID	Name
1	Executive
2	Marketing
3	Engineering

Figure 7.7. The Employees table with a new Department ID field

The Difference between Design and Implementation

As this example has shown, the way you'd naturally draw your database design
on paper, and the best way to implement the design in practice, can be quite distinct. However, keep in mind that there are no absolute rules in database design,
and expert database designers sometimes bend or break rules to meet the requirements of particular circumstances.

What these tables show are four employees and three departments. The Department
ID column of the Employees table provides a **relationship** between the two tables,
indicating that Zak Ruvalcaba works in Department 1, while Kevin Yank and Craig
Anderson work in Department 3. Notice also that, as each department appears only

once in the database, and appears independently of the employees who work in it, we've avoided the potential problems outlined before.

However, the most important characteristic of this database design is that, since we're storing information about two types of entities (employees and departments), we're using two tables. This approach illustrates an important rule of thumb that we must keep in mind when designing databases:

Each type of entity about which we want to be able to store information should be given its own table.

With this rule in mind, we can sit back and think about the Dorknozzle application we want to build, as it was described in Chapter 5. We need to think of the design in terms of the entities that we want to track, and come up with a preliminary list of tables. You'll become more comfortable with this kind of task as you gain experience in database design, but it's worth giving it a try on your own at this stage. When you're done, compare your list to the one below, and see how you did. Here are the entities we think we'll want to track:

Employees

    This table keeps track of our company's employees, each of which is associated with a department.

Departments

    This table lists the departments in our company.

Help Desk Problem Reports

    This table stores the problem reports that have been filed at Dorknozzle's employee help desk. A category, subject, and status will be associated with each problem report.

Help Desk Categories

    The categories that are available for help desk items ("Hardware," "Software," and so on) are stored in this table.

Help Desk Subjects

    The subjects that are available for help desk items ("Computer crashes," "My chair is broken," and the like) are stored in this table.

Help Desk States

This table stores the various states in which a help desk item can exist ("open" or "closed").

Breaking down and analyzing the items of information that need to be saved is the first step in determining the database's design—this process represents the *logical design* phase that I mentioned earlier. Through this process, we work to build a high-level definition of the data that needs to be saved. This definition can then be transformed into a *physical design* structure, which contains the details required to implement the database.

As you analyze the data that needs to be stored, you may come across items that we overlooked when we designed the site in Chapter 5, such as help desk item categories, subjects, and states, which aren't obvious entities in our application's current design. However, remember that whenever you predict that your database will contain a field that should only accept values from a specific list, it makes sense to create a table to hold that list. This approach makes it easy to execute changes to the list in future; it also reduces the amount of disk space required by your database, and helps you to avoid redundancy, as you store only single instances of department names, strings like "I can't print," and so on.

This process of planning out the entities, tables, and relationships between the tables to eliminate maintenance problems and redundant data is called database **normalization**. Although we'll talk a bit more about normalization before the end of this chapter, we'll only ever discuss it in an informal, hands-on way. As any computer science major will tell you, database design is a serious area of research, with tested and mathematically provable principles that, while useful, are beyond the scope of this book.

So, we have our list of tables. In the next section, we'll look at the columns within those tables, and discuss how we can ascertain their characteristics. Although we won't go over the creation of all the tables for the Dorknozzle database, we will create one as an example: the Employees table. Once you understand how to create a new table, you can create the rest of the tables for the Dorknozzle application in your own time, based on the descriptions we'll provide. Or, if you prefer, you can simply grab the finished database from the code archive.

Once you've outlined all your tables, the next step is to decide what pieces of information will be included within those tables. For instance, you may want to include a first name, last name, phone number, address, city, state, zip code, and so on, for all employees in the Employees table. Let's see how we can define these columns as we create the Employees table for the Dorknozzle database.

Data Types

One of the differences between logical design and physical design is that when we're planning the database's physical design, we have to deal with details such as data types. That's right—as with the data we're storing in our VB.NET and C# variables, the data we store in each table's columns has a particular data type.

SQL Server knows many data types—in fact, it knows too many to list here—but it's worth our while to take a look at the most common ones. Below is a list of the common data types that we'll use in this book:

int

> Use the int data type when you need to store whole integers. This data type can store numbers from -2,147,483,648 to 2,147,483,647.

float

> Use the float data type when you're working with very large numbers or very small numbers. float can be used for fractions, but they're prone to rounding errors.

money

> The money data type should be used to store monetary data, such as prices for a product catalog. This data type is closely related to the int data type.

bit

> Use the bit data type when a condition is either true (represented as 1) or false (represented as 0).

datetime

> As you might have guessed, the datetime data type is used to store dates and times. It's very useful when you want to sort items in your table chronologically.

nvarchar(*n*)

The nvarchar data type stores strings of text. It's the most commonly used data type because it stores names, descriptions, and the like. When we're defining a column of this type, we also need to specify a maximum size in parentheses; longer strings will be trimmed to fit the defined size. For example, nvarchar(50) specifies a field that can hold up to 50 characters. The *var* part of the nvarchar name indicates that this data type can store strings of *variable* length up to the specified maximum.

nchar(*n*)

The nchar data type is similar to nvarchar in that it stores strings, but a field of this type will always store strings of the defined size. If the string you're saving is shorter, it's padded with spaces until the specified size is reached. For example, if you're working with an nchar(6) field (where the 6 in parentheses indicates that the field can hold six characters), and you add the word "test" to the field, two space characters will be appended to the end of the word so that all six characters are used. This data type is useful when you're storing strings that have a predefined size—in such cases, it may be more efficient to use the nchar(*n*) type than nvarchar.

money, money, money

Sometimes, you may see poorly designed databases use float to store monetary data. As float is susceptible to rounding errors, this is a bad idea. money, on the other hand, is not susceptible to these errors and is a much better choice.

The SQL Server data types, as with the other SQL Server keywords, aren't case-sensitive. nvarchar and nchar have non-Unicode cousins named varchar and char, which you can use if you're sure you won't need to store Unicode data. You may need to use Unicode (or a language-specific form of encoding) when storing non-English text, such as Chinese, Arabic, and others. Unicode is a very widely supported standard, so it's strongly recommended you stick with nvarchar and nchar.

The type of a column defines how that column behaves. For example, sorting data by a datetime column will cause the records to be sorted chronologically, rather than alphabetically or numerically.

Column Properties

Other than a column's data type, we can define a number of additional properties for a column. Other properties you'll use frequently include:

NULL

In database speak, NULL means "undefined." Although we talk about it as if it's a value, NULL actually represents the lack of a value. If you set an employee's mobile telephone number to NULL, for example, it could indicate that the employee doesn't have a mobile telephone.

However, it's important to realize that allowing NULLs is often inappropriate. For instance, you might create a department with the name NULL to represent a mysterious department with no name, but this is far from ideal. As you create a table, you can specify which columns are allowed to store NULL, and which aren't. In our example, we'd like every department to have a name, so we shouldn't allow the Name column to allow NULLs.

DEFAULT

SQL Server is capable of supplying a default value for a certain column if you don't supply one when you add a new row. We won't be using this feature when we create Dorknozzle, but it's good to know you have this option.

IDENTITY

Identity columns are numbered automatically. If you set a column as an IDENTITY column, SQL Server will generate numbers automatically for that column as you add new rows to it. The first number in the column is called the **identity seed**. To generate subsequent numbers, the identity column adds a given value to the seed; the value that's added is called the **identity increment**. By default, both the seed and increment have a value of 1, in which case the generated values are 1, 2, 3, and so on. If the identity seed were 5 and the identity increment were 10, the generated numbers would be 5, 15, 25, and so on.

IDENTITY is useful for ID columns, such as Department ID, for which you don't care what the values are, as long as they're unique. When you use IDENTITY, the generated values will always be unique. By default, you can't specify values manually for an IDENTITY column. Note also that the column can never contain NULL.

Understanding NULL

Be sure not to see NULL as equivalent to 0 (in numerical columns), or an empty string (in the case of string columns). Both 0 and an empty string *are* values; NULL defines the lack of a value.

NULL and Default Values

I've often heard people say that when we set a default value for a column, it doesn't matter whether or not we set it to accept NULLs. Many people seem to believe that columns with default values won't store NULL.

That's incorrect. You can modify a record after it was created, and change any field that will allow it to NULL. Your columns' ability to store NULL is important for the integrity of your data, and it should reflect the purpose of that data. A default value does make things easier when we create new rows, but it's not as vital as is correctly allowing (or disallowing) NULL in columns.

Primary Keys

Primary keys are the last fundamental concept that you need to understand before you can create your first data table. In the world of relational databases, each row in a table *must* be identified uniquely by a column called a **key**, on which all database operations are based.

The tables in your databases could contain hundreds or even thousands of rows of similar data—you could have several hundred employees in your Employees table alone. Imagine that your program needs to update or delete the record for John Smith, and there are several people with that name in your organization. You couldn't rely on the database to find the record for the particular John Smith that you were trying to work with—it might end up updating or deleting the wrong record.

We can avoid these kinds of problems only by using a system that uniquely identifies each row in the table. The first step toward achieving this goal is to add to the table an ID column that provides a unique identifier for each employee, as did the Employee ID column that we saw in Figure 7.1.

Remember that when we discussed this Employees table, we noted that you may be tempted to use each employee's username to uniquely identify each employee.

After all, that's what the network administrator uses them for, so why shouldn't you? It's true that this column uniquely identifies each row in the table, and we call such a column a **candidate key**. However, it's not a good idea to use this column in our database operations for a number of reasons. First, network usernames have been known to change, and such a change would wreak havoc on any database of more than a couple of tables. As we'll see later, keys are fundamental to establishing relationships between tables, and these relationships rely keys never changing. Second, non-numeric keys require much more processing power than simple numeric ones. Using a nvarchar field to uniquely identify rows in your table will bring your SQL Server to a grinding halt much faster than if you chose a standard, numeric key.

The column that we use to uniquely identify a row in a table in practice is called the **primary key**. In the case of our Employee table, the Employee ID will always be unique, so it would be a suitable primary key.

Multi-column Keys

To make the concept of keys easier to understand, we have kept the definition simple, although, technically, it's not 100% correct. A key isn't necessarily formed by a single column—it can be formed by two or more columns. If the key is made up of multiple columns, the set of values in those columns must be unique for any given record. We'll see an example of such a key in a moment.

Although we usually refer to *primary keys* as if they were columns, technically they're **constraints** that we apply to the existing columns of a table. Constraints impose restrictions on the data we can enter into our tables, and the primary key is a particular kind of constraint. When the primary key constraint is set on a column, the database will refuse to store duplicate values in that column.

Constraints in general, and primary keys in particular, represent a means by which the database can maintain the integrity and consistency of data.

Primary keys composed of a single column, such as Employee ID, are frequently used in conjunction with the IDENTITY property. The primary key constraint guarantees that duplicate values cannot be inserted into the table. The IDENTITY property helps us by always generating a new value that hasn't already been used in the primary key.

Primary Keys and the IDENTITY Property

Using the IDENTITY property for a column doesn't mean we can avoid specifying a primary key. It's true that the IDENTITY property always *generates* unique values, but it doesn't necessarily *enforce* them.

For example, say we have a table with a number of columns, one of which has the IDENTITY property set. This table contains three records that are likely to contain the automatically generated values 1, 2, and 3 in the IDENTITY column. Provided the IDENTITY_INSERT property for this table is enabled (by default it's disabled, but it's easy to enable), it's quite simple to insert another record with the value 2. The IDENTITY column will continue to generate unique values (4, 5, 6, and so on), but it doesn't guarantee the column remains unique.

Creating the Employees Table

In this section, we'll show you how to use Visual Web Developer or SQL Server Management Studio, but to create a new data table. If you're using Visual Web Developer, expand the database node in Database Explorer, right-click **Tables**, and select **Add New Table**, as shown in Figure 7.8.

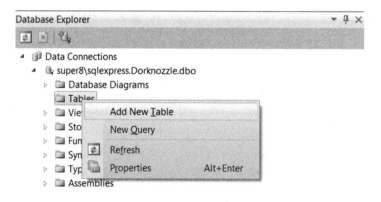

Figure 7.8. Adding a new table in Visual Web Developer

If you prefer SQL Server Management Studio, you need to follow a similar procedure. Expand the **Dorknozzle** database node, right-click **Tables**, and select **New Table...**, as illustrated in Figure 7.9.

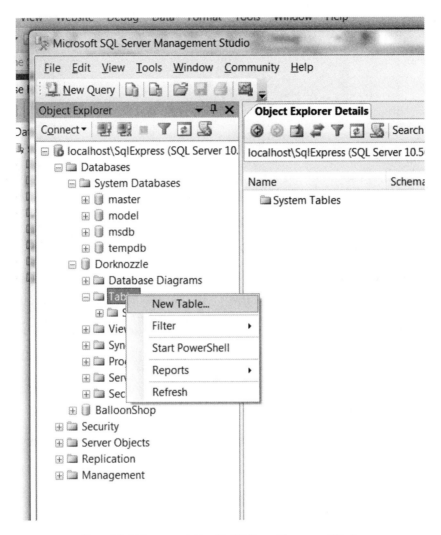

Figure 7.9. Adding a new table with SQL Server Management Studio

The window that appears as a result of either procedure is shown in Figure 7.10—it looks the same in both Visual Web Developer and SQL Server Management Studio. The main editing window lets you specify the column's three main properties: **Column Name**, **Data Type**, and **Allow Nulls**. To set additional properties, you need to use the **Column Properties** pane.

To add the IDENTITY property to a column, locate the **Identity Specification** row in the **Column Properties** pane and expand it. This will reveal the **(Is Identity)** drop-down list, which should be set to **Yes** for an IDENTITY column, as Figure 7.10 indicates.

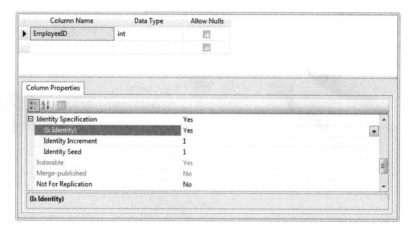

Figure 7.10. Specifying column properties

To set a column as the primary key, we can select **Table Designer** > **Set Primary Key**, or click the little golden key icon in the Table Designer toolbar when the column is selected. When a column is set as a primary key, a little golden key appears next to it, as Figure 7.11 illustrates.

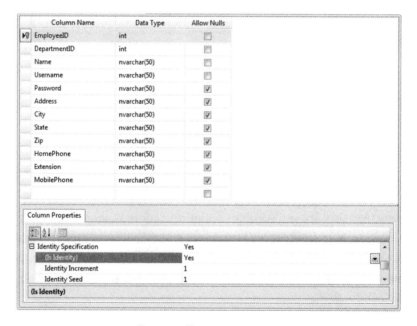

Figure 7.11. The Employees table

Now, let's create a table called Employees by adding the columns described in Table 7.1.

Table 7.1. The structure of the `Employees` table

Column Name	SQL Data Type	Identity	Allow Nulls	Primary Key
EmployeeID	int	Yes	No	Yes
DepartmentID	int	No	No	No
Name	nvarchar(50)	No	No	No
Username	nvarchar(50)	No	No	No
Password	nvarchar(50)	No	Yes	No
Address	nvarchar(50)	No	Yes	No
City	nvarchar(50)	No	Yes	No
State	nvarchar(50)	No	Yes	No
Zip	nvarchar(50)	No	Yes	No
HomePhone	nvarchar(50)	No	Yes	No
Extension	nvarchar(50)	No	Yes	No
MobilePhone	nvarchar(50)	No	Yes	No

After you enter this information, press **Ctrl+S** to save the table. When you're asked to name the table, type **Employees** and click **OK**. When you're done, your table will resemble Figure 7.11.

After you create the table, you'll see it appear under the **Tables** node in the **Object Explorer**, in SQL Server Management, or **Database Explorer** in Visual Web Developer. SQL Server Management Studio prepends dbo. to the table's name; dbo is the default "database owner" user. Don't worry about this for now—we'll explore the topic of database users in some detail later.

If you close the table designer window, you can open it later by right-clicking the `Employees` table and selecting **Open Table Definition** in Visual Web Developer, or **Modify** in SQL Server Management Studio. You'll be taken back to the screen that shows the structure of the table (shown in Figure 7.11).

Creating the Remaining Tables

Let's create the rest of the database tables. Apply the process you used to build the `Employee` table to create the new data tables, using the data presented in Table 7.2

to Table 7.6. Later in this chapter, we'll discuss how these tables work. For starters, though, you need to insert them into your database.

Table 7.2. The Departments table

Column Name	SQL Data Type	Identity	Allow Null	Primary Key
DepartmentID	int	Yes	No	Yes
Department	nvarchar(50)	No	No	No

Table 7.3. The HelpDesk table

Column Name	SQL Data Type	Identity	Allow Null	Primary Key
RequestID	int	Yes	No	Yes
EmployeeID	int	No	No	No
StationNumber	int	No	Yes	No
CategoryID	int	No	No	No
SubjectID	int	No	No	No
Description	nvarchar(50)	No	Yes	No
StatusID	int	No	No	No

Table 7.4. The HelpDeskCategories table

Column Name	SQL Data Type	Identity	Allow Null	Primary Key
CategoryID	int	Yes	No	Yes
Category	nvarchar(50)	No	No	No

Table 7.5. The HelpDeskSubjects table

Column Name	SQL Data Type	Identity	Allow Null	Primary Key
SubjectID	int	Yes	No	Yes
Subject	nvarchar(50)	No	No	No

Table 7.6. The `HelpDeskStatus` table

Column Name	SQL Data Type	Identity	Allow Null	Primary Key
StatusID	int	Yes	No	Yes
Status	nvarchar(50)	No	No	No

 Using SQL Scripts

Yes, there's a lot of data to type in! Whilst we recommend that you create the tables yourself by defining the fields outlined here, you can achieve the same goal using an SQL script that's included in this book's code archive. This script contains SQL code that SQL Server understands, and has instructions that create data structures (you'll learn about SQL in Chapter 8). If you want to use the download-able script, we recommend you have a look over the following tables to get an idea of the structures we'll be creating, then read the section called "Executing SQL Scripts" that follows.

We already have a clear idea of the data we'll store in the `Employees` and `Depart-ments` tables. The other tables will be used to store help desk requests; we'll discuss these in more detail in the following pages.

Executing SQL Scripts

If you prefer not to create the data tables manually, you can use the **CreateTables.sql** script included in the book's code archive to create the tables for you. This script is most easily used with SQL Server Management Studio. After you log in, click the **New Query** button on the toolbar (or select **File > New > Query with Current Connection**). Paste the contents of the **CreateTables.sql** script into the window that displays, and press **F5** to execute the commands. Note that if you have already created the `Employ-ees` table, you should remove the `CREATE TABLE` command that creates this table *before* you hit **F5**.

The SQL script included in the code archive contains all the commands required for this chapter; it even creates the sample data and table references that we'll cover later.

Populating the Data Tables

If tables represent drawers in a filing cabinet, rows represent individual paper records in those drawers. Let's imagine for a moment that our intranet web application is a real application. As people begin to register and interact with the application, rows are created within the various tables, and are filled up with information about those people.

Once the data structures are in place, adding rows of data is as easy as typing information into the cells in the **Datasheet View** of a table, which looks a bit like a spreadsheet. To access it, right-click on the table and select **Show Table Data** in Visual Web Developer, or **Open Table** in SQL Server Management Studio. You can use the dialog that opens to start adding data. Let's add some sample data to the tables you've just created, so that we can test the Dorknozzle database as we develop the application. Table 7.7 to Table 7.11 represent the tables and data you should add.

 Inserting Data and Identity Columns

If you correctly set the ID column as an identity column, you won't be allowed to specify the values manually—the ID values will be generated for you automatically. You need to be careful, because an ID value will never be generated twice on the same table. So even if you delete all the rows in a table, the database will not generate an ID with the value of 1; instead, it will continue creating new values from the last value that was generated for you.

Keep in mind that a new row is saved to the database at the moment that you move on to the next row. It's very important that you remember this when you reach the last row, as you'll need to move to an empty row even if you aren't adding any more records.

Table 7.7. The **Departments** table

DepartmentID (Primary Key)	Department
1	Accounting
2	Administration
3	Business Development
4	Customer Support
5	Executive
6	Engineering
7	Facilities
8	IT
9	Marketing
10	Operations

Table 7.8. The **Employees** table

Emp'ID (Primary Key)	Dep'tID	Name	U'name	P'word	City	State	M'Phone
1	5	Zak Ruvalcaba	zak	zak	San Diego	CA	555-555-5551
2	9	Jessica Ruvalcaba	jessica	jessica	San Diego	CA	555-555-5552
3	6	Ted Lindsey	ted	ted	San Diego	CA	555-555-5555
4	6	Shane Weebe	shane	shane	San Diego	CA	555-555-5554
5	9	David Levinson	david	david	San Diego	CA	555-555-5553
6	1	Geoff Kim	geoff	geoff	San Diego	CA	555-555-5556

The `Employees` table contains a few more columns than those outlined here, but, due to the size constraints of this page, I've left them out. Feel free to add your own data to the rest of the cells, or you could leave the remaining cells empty, as they're marked to accept NULL.

Table 7.9. The `HelpDeskCategories` table

CategoryID (Primary Key)	Category
1	Hardware
2	Software
3	Workstation
4	Other/Don't Know

Table 7.10. The `HelpDeskStatus` table

StatusID (Primary Key)	Status
1	Open
2	Closed

Table 7.11. The `HelpDeskSubjects` table

SubjectID (Primary Key)	Subject
1	Computer won't start
2	Monitor won't turn on
3	Chair is broken
4	Office won't work
5	Windows won't work
6	Computer crashes
7	Other

What IDENTITY Columns Are *Not* For

In our examples, as in many real-world scenarios, the ID values are sequences that start with 1 and increment by 1. This makes many beginners assume that they can use the ID column as a record-counter of sorts, but this is incorrect. The ID is really an arbitrary number that we know to be unique; no other information should be discerned from it.

Relational Database Design Concepts

It is said that data becomes information when we give significance to it. When we draw tables on paper to decide the logical design of a database, we actually include significant information about our application (and about the business for which the application is used). In Figure 7.12, for example, we can see that the employee Zak Ruvalcaba works in the Executive department.

Employee ID	Name	Username	Telephone	Department
1	Zak Ruvalcaba	zak	555-1234	Executive
2	Cristian Darie	cristian	555-1235	Marketing
3	Kevin Yank	kyank	555-1236	Engineering
4	Craig Anderson	craiga	555-1237	Engineering

Figure 7.12. Information about employees

We've seen how, in order to optimize data storage and better protect the integrity of our data, we can extract independent pieces of data, such as department names, and save them in separate tables, such as the Department table. However, as we did so, we kept the significance of the original information intact by including references to the new tables in our existing table. For example, in the Employees table, we have a DepartmentID column that specifies the department in which each employee works, as Figure 7.13 illustrates.

This separation of data helps us to eliminate redundant information—for example, we'd expect to have many employees in each department, but we don't need to replicate the department name for each of those employees. Instead, each employee record refers to the ID of the appropriate department. The benefits of this approach would be more obvious if more data (such as a department description) were associated with each department; copying all that data for each employee would generate even more redundancy.

Employees				
Employee ID	Name	Username	Telephone	Department ID
1	Zak Ruvalcaba	zak	555-1234	1
2	Cristian Darie	cristian	555-1235	2
3	Kevin Yank	kyank	555-1236	3
4	Craig Anderson	craiga	555-1237	3

Departments	
Department ID	Name
1	Executive
2	Marketing
3	Engineering

Figure 7.13. Related data about employees and departments

These kinds of relationships exist between the HelpDesk, HelpDeskCategories, HelpDeskStatus, and HelpDeskSubjects tables. Each record in HelpDesk will store a help desk request. Now, if we stored all the request information in a single table, its records would look like those shown in Figure 7.14.

Employee	Station No.	Category	Subject	Description	Status
Kevin Yank	5	Software	Office won't work	Crashes when I open documents	Open
Craig Anderson	7	Software	Windows won't work	Crashes when I start Solitaire	Open

Figure 7.14. Information about help desk requests

In order to eliminate redundant data here, we've decided to store pieces of this data in separate tables, and to reference those tables from the HelpDesk table. The only items of data in the table in Figure 7.14 that aren't likely to repeat very frequently are the descriptions and the station numbers. We want users to enter their station numbers manually, rather than choosing them from a predefined list, so we wouldn't gain any benefits from creating a separate table for this item.

Given these requirements, we split the information from Figure 7.14 into four tables:

- HelpDeskCategories contains the possible help desk request categories.
- HelpDeskSubject contains the possible request subjects.
- HelpDeskStatus contains the possible request statuses.

■ The `HelpDesk` table stores the help desk requests by referencing records from the other tables, and adding only two original pieces of data itself: the help desk request description and the station number.

The relationships between these tables are critical, because without them the original significance of the information would be lost. The relationships are so important that the database has tools to protect them. Primary keys were used to ensure the integrity of the records within a table (by guaranteeing their uniqueness); in a moment, we'll meet foreign keys, which protect the integrity of data spread over multiple tables.

In our database's `HelpDesk` table, the data depicted in Figure 7.14 would be stored physically as shown in Table 7.12.

Table 7.12. Sample data from the `HelpDesk` table

RequestID (Primary Key)	Emp'ID	StationN'ber	Cat'ID	Subj'ID	Description	StatusID
1	3	5	2	4	Crashes when I open documents	1
2	4	7	2	5	Crashes when I start Solitaire	1

Note that, apart from storing data about the request itself, the `HelpDesk` table also has an ID column, named `RequestID`, which acts as the table's primary key.

Foreign Keys

Technically speaking, a **foreign key** is a constraint that applies to a column that refers to the primary key of another table. In practice, we'll use the term "foreign key" to refer to the column to which the constraint applies.

Unlike primary key columns, a foreign key column can contain `NULL`, and almost always contains repeating values. The numeric columns in the `HelpDesk` table that reference data from other tables (`EmployeeID`, `CategoryID`, `SubjectID`, and `StatusID`), and the `DepartmentID` column in the `Employees` table, are perfect candidates for the application of a foreign key constraint. Take a look at the examples shown in Table 7.13 and Table 7.14.

The `DepartmentID` column in the `Employees` table references the `DepartmentID` primary key in the `Departments` table. Notice that the `DepartmentID` primary key in the `Departments` table is unique, but the `DepartmentID` foreign key within the `Employees` table may repeat.

As they stand, these tables already have an established relationship, and all the data in the `DepartmentID` column of the `Employees` table correctly matches existing departments in the `Department` table. However, as with primary keys, just having the correct fields in place doesn't mean that our data is guaranteed to be correct.

For example, try setting the `DepartmentID` field for one of the employees to `123`. SQL Server won't mind making the change for you, so if you tried this in practice, you'd end up storing invalid data. However, after we set the foreign keys correctly, SQL Server will be able to ensure the integrity of our data—specifically, it will forbid us to assign employees to nonexistent departments, or to delete departments with which employees are associated.

The easiest way to create foreign keys using Visual Web Developer or SQL Server Management Studio is through database diagrams, so let's learn about them.

Table 7.13. The Departments table's primary key

DepartmentID (Primary Key)	Department
1	Accounting
2	Administration
3	Business Development
4	Customer Support
5	Executive
6	Engineering
7	Facilities
8	IT
9	Marketing
10	Operations

Table 7.14. The Employees table referencing records from the Departments table

Emp'ID (Primary Key)	Dep'tID	Name	U'name	P'word	City	State	M'Phone
1	5	Zak Ruvalcaba	zak	zak	San Diego	CA	555-555-5551
2	9	Jessica Ruvalcaba	jessica	jessica	San Diego	CA	555-555-5552
3	6	Ted Lindsey	ted	ted	San Diego	CA	555-555-5555
4	6	Shane Weebe	shane	shane	San Diego	CA	555-555-5554
5	9	David Levinson	david	david	San Diego	CA	555-555-5553
6	1	Geoff Kim	geoff	geoff	San Diego	CA	555-555-5556

Using Database Diagrams

To keep the data consistent, the Dorknozzle database really should contain quite a few foreign keys. The good news is that you have access to a great feature called **database diagrams**, which makes it a cinch to create foreign keys. You can define the table relationships visually using the database diagrams tool in Visual Web Developer or SQL Server Management Studio, and have the foreign keys generated for you.

Database diagrams weren't created specifically for the purpose of adding foreign keys. The primary use of diagrams is to offer a visual representation of the tables in your database and the relationships that exist between them, to help you to design the structure of your database. However, the diagrams editor included in Visual Web Developer and SQL Server Management Studio is very powerful, so you can use the diagrams to create new tables, modify the structure of existing tables, or add foreign keys.

Let's start by creating a diagram for the Dorknozzle database. To create a database diagram in Visual Web Developer, right-click the **Database Diagrams** node, and select **Add New Diagram**, as shown in Figure 7.15.

The process is similar in SQL Server Management Studio, which, as Figure 7.16 illustrates, has a similar menu.

The first time you try to create a diagram, you'll be asked to confirm the creation of the database structures that support diagrams. Select **Yes** from the dialog, which should look like the one shown in Figure 7.17.

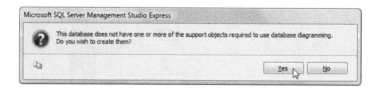

Figure 7.17. Adding support for database diagrams

Next, a dialog like the one in Figure 7.18 will ask you which of your database tables you want included in the diagram. If you're working with a database that comprises many tables, you may want to have diagrams built to represent specific pieces of

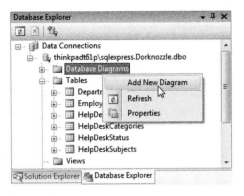

Figure 7.15. Creating a database diagram with Visual Web Developer

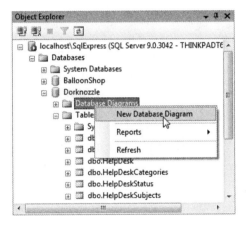

Figure 7.16. Creating a database diagram with SQL Server Management Studio

functionality, but we want to create a diagram that includes all the tables in our database.

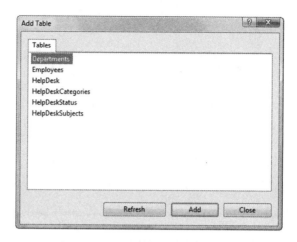

Figure 7.18. Adding tables to the diagram

Click **Add** until all the tables are added to the diagram. As you click **Add**, the tables will be removed from the list and will appear in the diagram. Once you've added all the tables, click **Close**. You'll see a window in which all the tables are clearly displayed—something like Figure 7.19.

You'll probably need to tweak their positioning and dimensions that so they fit nicely into the window. The zooming feature may prove useful here! Select **File > Save Diagram1** (or similar) to save your new diagram. Enter **Dorknozzle** for the diagram's name.

Now, if you right-click any table in the diagram, you'll gain access to a plethora of possibilities, as Figure 7.20 reveals. This menu, along with the other diagramming features, is identical in Visual Web Developer and SQL Server Management Studio.

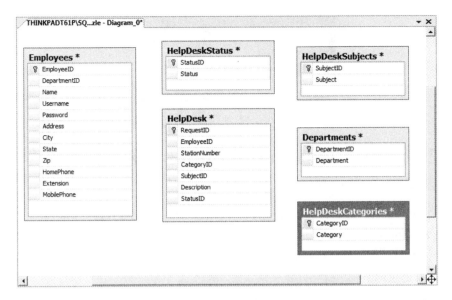

Figure 7.19. Visualizing data tables using a diagram

Figure 7.20. The many features of the diagram editor

Expanding the **Table View** submenu gives you more options for displaying your table. If you choose **Standard**, you'll see a full-blown version of the table definition; as Figure 7.21 shows, you can change the table structure directly in the diagram. The diagramming features provided for free are extremely useful.

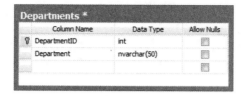

Figure 7.21. The standard table view

Implementing Relationships in the Dorknozzle Database

Every table in the Dorknozzle database has a relationship with another table. To create a foreign key using the diagram, click the gray square to the left-hand side of the column for which you want to create the foreign key, and drag it over the table to which you want it to relate.

Let's give it a try. Start by dragging the DepartmentID column of the Employees table over the DepartmentID column of the Departments table, as illustrated in Figure 7.22.

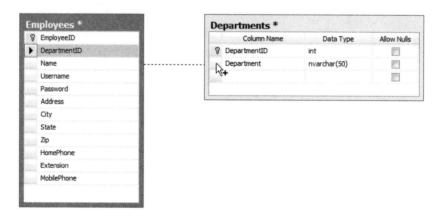

Figure 7.22. Creating a link between Employees and Departments

The designer will open a dialog that shows the details of the new foreign key, like the one shown in Figure 7.23.

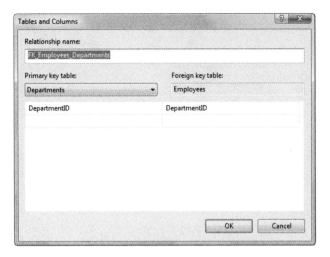

Figure 7.23. Adding a foreign key

Ensure that your data matches that shown in Figure 7.23, and click **OK**. A new dialog like the one shown in Figure 7.24 will appear, allowing you to tweak numerous options that relate to the new foreign key. Leave the default options as they are for now (though we'll discuss them shortly), and click **OK** to finish up.

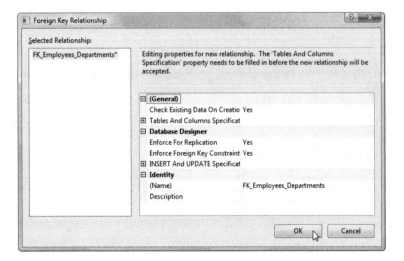

Figure 7.24. Editing the foreign key options

After creating the foreign key, make a quick test to ensure that the relationship is indeed enforced. Try adding an employee, but set the person's `DepartmentID` to `123`. You should see an error like the one pictured in Figure 7.25.

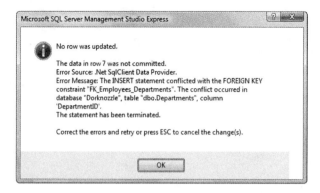

Figure 7.25. The foreign key disallowing the addition of invalid data

If you tried to delete a department with which employees were associated, you'd generate a similar error.

Table 7.15 shows the foreign keys that we need to establish in the Dorknozzle database. In our project, the foreign key column has the same name as its corresponding primary key column. Go ahead and create all the foreign keys outlined in Table 7.15.

Table 7.15. The relationships in the Dorknozzle database

Primary Key	Foreign Key
DepartmentID in the table Departments	DepartmentID in the table Employees
EmployeeID in the table Employees	EmployeeID in the table HelpDesk
CategoryID in the table HelpDeskCategories	CategoryID in the table HelpDesk
SubjectID in the table HelpDeskSubjects	SubjectID in the table HelpDesk
StatusID in the table HelpDeskStatus	StatusID in the table HelpDesk

When it's complete, your relationship diagram should resemble Figure 7.26. After you add the relationships, save your changes by selecting **File** > **Save Dorknozzle**.

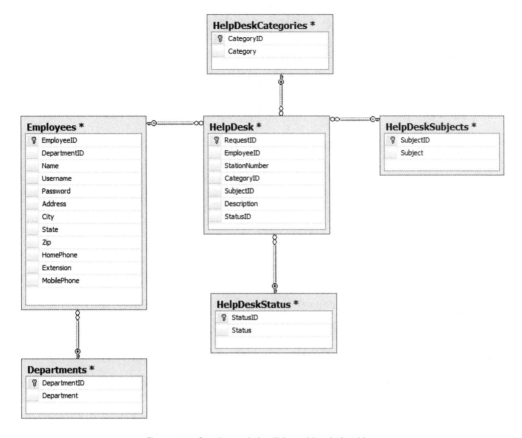

Figure 7.26. Creating and visualizing table relationships

When you're asked to confirm the changes to the database tables you're altering, click **Yes**.

Now that you've created these foreign keys, you can be sure that all the data stored in your tables will obey the enforced table relationships. The DepartmentID column in the Employees table will always reference valid departments, and the HelpDesk records will always reference valid employees, help desk categories, help desk subjects, and help desk status codes.

In Chapter 8, you'll start learning how to use your new database. Before then, let's take a moment to analyze the diagram, and learn more about the information it shows us.

Diagrams and Table Relationships

Relationships describe how data in one table is linked to data in other tables. In fact, it's because relationships are so crucial that these types of databases are given the name "relational databases." Relationships exist for the sole purpose of associating one table with one or more other tables using primary keys and foreign keys.

There are three types of relationships that can occur between the tables in your database:

- one-to-one relationships
- one-to-many relationships
- many-to-many relationships

One-to-one Relationships

A one-to-one relationship means that for each record in one table, only one other related record can exist in another table.

One-to-one relationships are rarely used, since it's usually more efficient just to combine the two records and store them together as columns in a single table. For example, every employee in our database will have a phone number stored in the `HomePhone` column of the `Employees` table. In theory, we could store the phone numbers in a separate table and link to them via a foreign key in the `Employees` table, but this would be of no benefit to our application, since we assume that one phone number can belong to only one employee. As such, we can leave this one-to-one relationship (along with any others) out of our database design.

One-to-many Relationships

The one-to-many relationship is by far the most common relationship type. Within a one-to-many relationship, each record in a table can be associated with multiple records from a second table. These records are usually related on the basis of the primary key from the first table. In the employees/departments example, a one-to-many relationship exists between the `Employees` and `Departments` tables, as one department can be associated with many employees.

When a foreign key is used to link two tables, the table that contains the foreign key is on the "many" side of the relationship, and the table that contains the primary key is on the "one" side of the relationship. In database diagrams, one-to-many relationships are signified by a line between the two tables; a golden key symbol appears next to the table on the "one" side of the relationship, and an infinity sign is displayed next to the table that could have many items related to each of its records. In Figure 7.27, those icons appear next to the `Employees` and `Departments` tables.

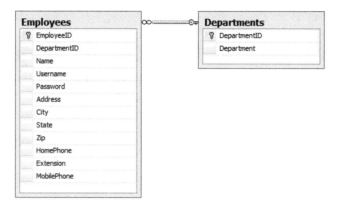

Figure 7.27. Database diagram showing a one-to-many relationship

As you can see, one-to-many relationships are easy to spot if you have a diagram at hand—just look for the icons next to the tables. Note that the symbols don't show the exact columns that form the relationship; they simply identify the tables involved.

Select the line that appears between two related tables to view the properties of the foreign key that defines that relationship. The properties display in the **Properties** window (you can open this by selecting **View > Properties Window**). As Figure 7.28 illustrates, they're the same options we saw earlier in Figure 7.24.

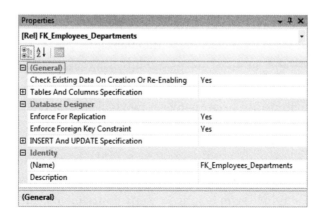

Figure 7.28. The properties of a foreign key

Advanced Foreign Key Options

Unless you really know what you're doing, we recommend that you use the default foreign key options for now. However, it's good to have some idea of the features available through the Properties window, as they may well come in handy later in your database development career.

The most significant setting here is **Enforce Foreign Key Constraint**, which, when set to **Yes**, prevents users or applications from entering inconsistent data into our database (for example, by inserting into the `Employees` table a `DepartmentID` value that doesn't have a matching entry in the `Departments` table). In our application, every user must be associated with a valid department, so we'll leave this option enabled.

The options available under **INSERT And UPDATE Specification** can be used to tell your database to update the tables itself in order to keep the data valid at times when a change in a given table would affect a related table. If, for some reason, we changed the ID of a department in the `Departments` table, we could set the database to propagate this change to all the tables related to that department, keeping the relationships intact. Similarly, we can set the database to automatically delete all the employees related to a department that has been removed. However, these are quite sensitive options, and it's best to avoid them unless you have good reason not to. The cases in which an ID changes are very uncommon (the ID doesn't have any special meaning itself, other than being a unique identifier), and letting the database delete data for you is a risky approach (it's safer to delete the related records yourself).

If these concepts sound a bit advanced at the moment, don't worry; it will all become clear as you spend some time working with databases.

Many-to-many Relationships

Many-to-many relationships occur between two tables, when records from either table can be associated with multiple records in the other table.

Imagine that you wanted a single employee to be able to belong to more than one department—someone who works in "Engineering" could also be an "Executive," for example. *One* employee can belong to *many* departments, and *one* department can contain *many* employees, so this is a many-to-many relationship.

How do we represent it in our database? Faced with this question, many less-experienced developers begin to think of ways to store several values in a single column, because the obvious solution is to change the `DepartmentID` column in the Employees table so that it contains a list of the IDs of those departments to which each employee belongs. One of those good old rules of thumb we discussed previously applies here:

If you need to store multiple values in a single column, your design is probably flawed.

The correct way to represent a many-to-many relationship is to add a third table, named a **mapping table**, to the database. A mapping table is a table that contains no data other than the definitions of the pairs of entries that are related. Figure 7.29 shows the database design for our employees and departments.

Figure 7.29. Using a mapping table to implement a many-to-many relationship

The `EmployeeDepartment` table associates employee IDs with department IDs. If we added this table to our database, we could add Zak Ruvalcaba to both the "Executive" and "Engineering" departments.

A mapping table is created in much the same way as any other table. The only difference lies in the choice of the primary key. Every table we've created so far has had a column named *something*`ID` that was designed to be that table's primary key. Designating a column as a primary key tells the database not to allow two entries in that column to have the same value. It also speeds up database searches based on that column.

In the case of a mapping table, there's no single column that we want to force to have unique values. Each employee ID may appear more than once, as an employee may belong to more than one department, and each department ID may appear more than once, as a department may contain many employees. What we *don't* want to allow is the same *pair* of values to appear in the table twice (it wouldn't make sense to associate a particular employee with a particular department more than once). For this reason, we usually create mapping tables with a multicolumn primary key.

In this example, the primary key for the `EmployeeDepartment` table would consist of the `EmployeeID` and `DepartmentID` columns. This enforces the uniqueness that is appropriate to a look-up table, and prevents a particular employee from being assigned to a particular department more than once.

If you'd like to learn more about many-to-many relationships, or about anything else related to SQL Server programming, I recommend you download and use the product's excellent documentation, SQL Server Books Online.[1]

Summary

This chapter has introduced the fundamental concepts of relational databases. You learned about the underlying structure of a modern relational database, which is composed of tables, columns, and rows, and about crucial concepts that can aid in database performance, maintenance, and efficiency. You've also learned how to implement and enforce table relationships, and you have a solid understanding of good relational database design.

Chapter 8 goes beyond data storage and introduces you to the language used to access and manipulate the data you hold in your tables. That language is the Structured Query Language, or SQL.

---

[1] http://msdn2.microsoft.com/en-us/library/ms130214.aspx

Chapter

8

Speaking SQL

So your database has been created, and you've defined all the tables you'll need, and all the columns for your tables—you've even defined the relationships between your tables. The question now is, "How will you get to that data?" Sure, you can open the database, look at the data contained in the tables, and manually insert and delete records, but that does little to help your web users interact with that data. Mary in Accounting isn't going to want to download and learn to use SQL Server Management Studio just so she can retrieve an employee's mobile phone number—this functionality has to be provided by the Dorknozzle intranet website, which, after all, is supposed to enable staff members to access data easily. In fact, the functionality can be created using web forms, web controls, a little code, and a useful database programming language known as Structured Query Language (or SQL).

SQL has its origins in a language developed by IBM in the 1970s called SEQUEL (which stood for Structured English QUEry Language), and is still often referred to as "sequel" or "ess-que-el." It represents a very powerful way of interacting with current database technologies and the tables that constitute our databases. SQL has roughly 30 keywords, and is the language of choice for simple and complex database operations alike. The queries you'll construct with these keywords range from the very basic to extremely complex strings of subqueries and table joins.

SQL is an international standard, and almost all database products, including SQL Server, Oracle, DB2, and so on, support the standard to a certain degree. The dialect of SQL supported by SQL Server is named Transact-SQL (or T-SQL). This chapter cannot begin to cover all there is to know on the subject, but we hope it will provide you with an introduction to beginner and advanced SQL concepts.

In this chapter, you'll learn:

▨ basic SQL commands
▨ expressions that SQL supports
▨ the most important SQL functions
▨ how to perform table joins and subqueries
▨ how to create stored procedures

This may sound like a lot of work, but you're certain to enjoy it! Let's get started.

Reading Data from a Single Table

Information that's contained within a database is useless unless we have a way to extract it. SQL is that mechanism; it allows quick but sophisticated access to database data through the use of **queries**. Queries pose questions to the database server, which returns the answer to your application.

Table 8.1. Sample contents from the `Employees` table

EmployeeID (Primary Key)	Dep'tID	Name	Username	City
1	5	Zak Ruvalcaba	zak	San Diego
2	9	Jessica Ruvalcaba	jessica	San Diego
3	6	Ted Lindsey	ted	San Diego
4	6	Shane Weebe	shane	San Diego
5	9	David Levinson	david	San Diego
6	1	Geoff Kim	geoff	San Diego

For example, imagine that you're trying to extract the information shown in Table 8.1 from the Employees table of the Dorknozzle database.

How do we make this kind of data available to our website? The first step is to learn how to read this data using SQL. Then, in the next chapter, we'll learn to access the data from ASP.NET web applications.

In the following sections, we'll learn to write queries that will let us view existing data, insert new data, modify existing data, and delete data. Once you've learned how to write these fundamental SQL queries, the next step is to put everything together, and build the web forms with which your users will interact.

Let's begin: first up, open SQL Server Management Studio. Visual Web Developer can also be used to test SQL queries, but SQL Server Management Studio is slightly easier to use for our purposes. Log in to your SQL Server instance, and select the Dorknozzle database in the **Object Explorer** pane, as illustrated in Figure 8.1.

Figure 8.1. Using SQL Server Management Studio Express

Having selected the Dorknozzle database, go to **File > New > Database Engine Query**, or simply click the **New Query** button on the toolbar. A new query window, like the one shown in Figure 8.2, should open in the right-hand pane.

Figure 8.2. A new query window

In the query window, type your first command:

```
SELECT Name
FROM Employees
```

Click the **Execute** button, or press **F5**. If everything works as planned, the result will appear similar to Figure 8.3.

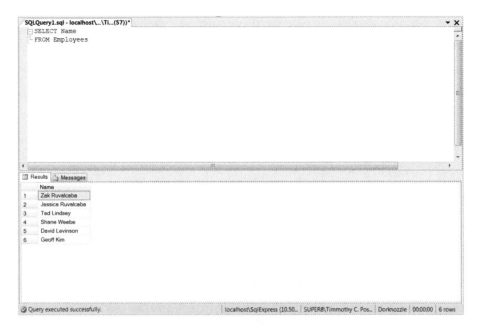

Figure 8.3. Executing a simple query

Nice work! Now that we've taken our first look at SQL, let's talk more about SQL queries.

Using the SELECT Statement

The most common of all SQL queries is the SELECT query. This query is generally constructed using a SELECT clause and a FROM clause. To understand this concept more clearly, take a look at the following statement, which retrieves all columns of all records in the Departments table:

```
SELECT *
FROM Departments
```

In this case, the SELECT clause lists the columns that you want to retrieve. In this case, we used *, which means "all columns." The FROM clause specifies the table from which you want to pull the records. Together, these two clauses create an SQL statement that extracts all data from the Departments table.

You've probably noticed that the two clauses appear on separate lines. If you wanted to keep the entire statement on one line, that's fine, but SQL lets you separate the statements on multiple lines to make complex queries easier to read. Also note that although SQL is not actually a case-sensitive language, we'll capitalize the keywords (such as SELECT and FROM) according to the popular convention.

To sum up, here's the basic syntax used in a SELECT query:

SELECT

This keyword indicates that we want to retrieve data, rather than modify, add, or delete data—these activities use the UPDATE, INSERT, and DELETE keywords, respectively, in place of SELECT.

columns

We must provide the names of one or more columns in the database table from which we want to retrieve data. We can list multiple columns by separating the column names with commas, or we can use * to select all columns. We can also prefix each column name with the table name, as shown here:

```
SELECT Employees.Name, Employees.Username
FROM Employees
```

This approach is mandatory when two or more of the tables we're dealing with contain columns that have the same names. We'll learn to read data from multiple tables a little later in the chapter.

FROM

The FROM keyword ends the SELECT clause and starts the FROM clause, which identifies the tables from which the data will be extracted. This clause is required in all SELECT statements.

tables

We need to identify the names of the tables from which we want to extract data. To list multiple tables, separate their names with commas. Querying multiple tables is called a *table join*—we'll cover this a bit later.

Armed with this knowledge, we can see that the preceding sample statement would retrieve all records from the Departments table, producing a set of results like that shown in Figure 8.4.

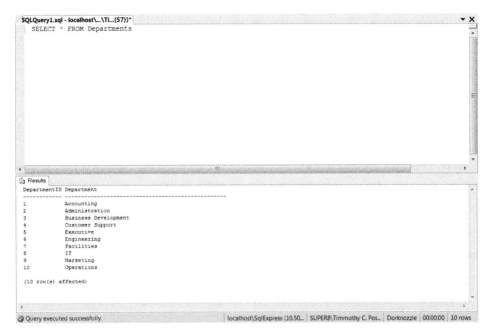

Figure 8.4. Reading the list of departments

See how easy it is? The SELECT query is probably the one you'll use most.

Viewing Results in Text Format

By default, the query editor of SQL Server Management Studio displays the results in a grid like the one shown in Figure 8.3. As you work with SQL Server, you may start to find this view a little impractical; in particular, it makes viewing longer strings of text painful because each time you run the query, you need to resize the columns in the grid. Personally, I prefer the plain text view, shown in Figure 8.4. You can enable this mode by selecting **Query > Results To > Results To Text**.

The Number of Affected Rows

As you can see in Figure 8.4, SQL Server reports the number of records that have been affected by a certain query. This report doesn't indicate that those records were modified. Instead, the figure represents the number of rows that were read, modified, deleted, or inserted by a certain query.

Let's move on and take a look at some variations of the SELECT query. Then we'll see how easy it is to insert, modify, and delete items from the database using other keywords.

Selecting Certain Fields

If you didn't want to select all the fields from the database table, you'd include the names of the specific fields that you wanted in place of the * in your query. For example, if you're interested only in the department names—not their IDs—you could execute the following query:

```
SELECT Department
FROM Departments
```

This statement would retrieve data from the Department field only. Rather than specifying the *, which would return all the fields within the database table, we specify only the fields that we need.

 Selecting All Columns Using *

To improve performance in real-world development scenarios, it's better to ask only for the columns that are of interest, rather than using *. Moreover, even when you need all the columns in a table, it's better to specify them by nam; this safeguards against the possibility of future changes, which cause more columns to be added to the table, affect the queries you're writing now.

It's important to note that the order of the fields in a table determines the order in which the data will be retrieved. Take this query, for example:

```
SELECT DepartmentID, Department
FROM Departments
```

You could reverse the order in which the columns are returned with this query:

```
SELECT Department, DepartmentID
FROM Departments
```

Executing this query would produce the result set shown in Figure 8.5.

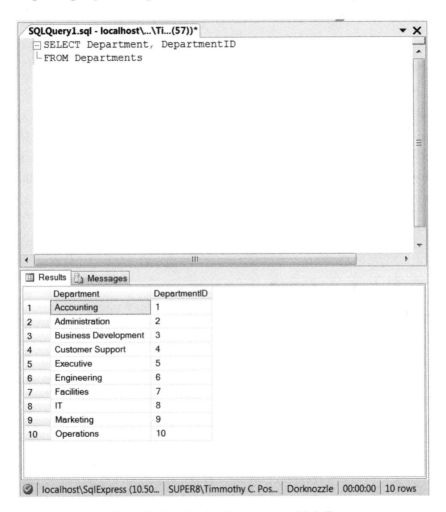

Figure 8.5. Retrieving department names and their IDs

Try it for yourself!

Selecting Unique Data with DISTINCT

Say you want to find out which cities your employees hail from. It's most likely
that this sort of query would generate multiple results:

```
SELECT City
FROM Employees
```

If this query were applied to the Dorknozzle application, the same city location
would appear six times in the results—once for every employee in our database.
Figure 8.6 illustrates this point.

That's not usually what we want to see in our results. Typically, we prefer to see
the *unique* cities in the list—a task that, fortunately enough, is easy to achieve.
Adding the DISTINCT keyword immediately after the SELECT clause extracts only
the unique instances of the retrieved data. Take a look at the following SQL statement:

```
SELECT DISTINCT City
FROM Employees
```

This query will produce the result shown in Figure 8.7.

Figure 8.6. Reading the employees' cities

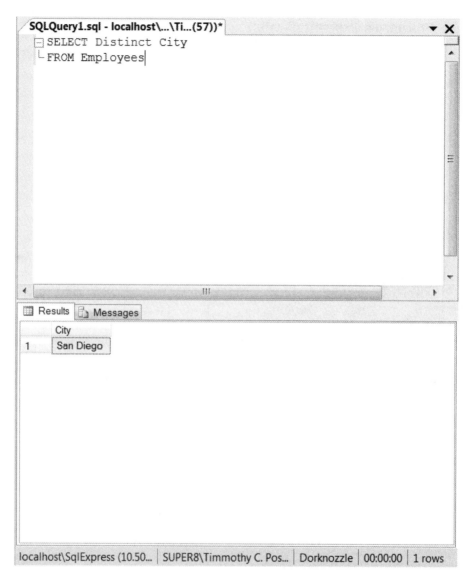

Figure 8.7. Selecting distinct cities

In this case, because only the City column was included within the SQL query, unique instances within the City column were returned.

Note that the uniqueness condition applies to the whole of the returned rows. If, for example, we asked for the name of each employee as well, all the rows would be considered unique (because no two employees have the same name) and no row would be eliminated by DISTINCT. To see for yourself, execute this query:

```
SELECT DISTINCT Name, City
FROM Employees
```

The results of this code are pictured in Figure 8.8. As we expected, the DISTINCT clause doesn't have any effect, since each row is unique.

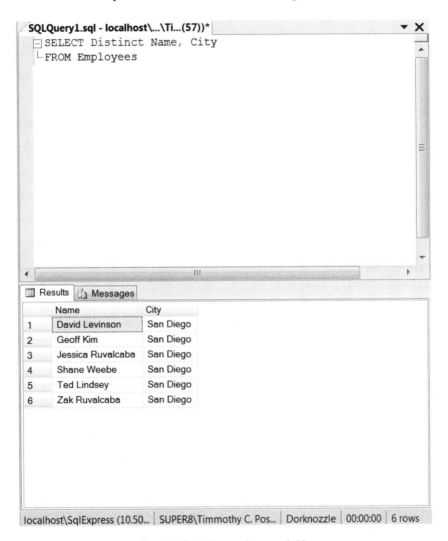

Figure 8.8. Retrieving employees and cities

Row Filtering with WHERE

The WHERE clause is used in conjunction with SQL queries, including the SELECT query, to deliver more refined search results based on individual field criteria. The following example could be used to extract all employees that work in the Department whose ID is 6:

```
SELECT Name, DepartmentID
FROM Employees
WHERE DepartmentID = 6
```

This query returns the results shown below:

```
Name                                                  DepartmentID
----------------------------------------------------  ------------
Ted Lindsey                                           6
Shane Weebe                                           6

(2 row(s) affected)
```

But wait! How do I know the name of the department with the ID of 6? Well, you could use a similar query to find out. Try this:

```
SELECT Department
FROM Departments
WHERE DepartmentID = 6
```

Executing this query reveals that the department with the ID of 6 is Engineering:

```
Department
--------------------------------------------------------
Engineering

(1 row(s) affected)
```

Selecting Ranges of Values with BETWEEN

There may be times when you'll want to search within a database table for rows that fall within a certain range of values. For instance, if you wanted to retrieve from the Departments table all departments that have IDs between 2 and 5, you could use the BETWEEN keyword like so:

```
SELECT DepartmentID, Department
FROM Departments
WHERE DepartmentID BETWEEN 2 AND 5
```

As we requested, all departments whose IDs are between 2 and 5 are returned. Note that the range is inclusive, so departments with IDs of 2 and 5 will also be retrieved.

Keep in mind that any conditions that use BETWEEN could easily be rewritten by combining two "greater than or equal" and "less than or equal" conditions:

```
SELECT DepartmentID, Department
FROM Departments
WHERE DepartmentID >= 2 AND DepartmentID <= 5
```

We could also use the NOT keyword before the BETWEEN keyword to specify all items that fall outside the range, as follows:

```
SELECT DepartmentID, Department
FROM Departments
WHERE DepartmentID NOT BETWEEN 2 AND 5
```

In this example, all rows whose DepartmentIDs are less than 2 or greater than 5 are returned.

Matching Patterns with LIKE

As we've just seen, the WHERE clause allows us to filter results based on criteria that we specify. The example we discussed earlier filtered rows by comparing two numbers, but SQL also knows how to handle strings. For example, if we wanted to search the company's Employees table for all employees named Zak Ruvalcaba, we'd use the following SQL statement:

```
SELECT EmployeeID, Username
FROM Employees
WHERE Name = 'Zak Ruvalcaba'
```

However, we won't see many such queries in reality. In real-world scenarios, most record matching is done by matching the primary key of the table to some specific value. When an arbitrary string such as a name is used (as in the previous example), it's likely that we're searching for data based on partially complete information.

A more realistic example is one in which we want to find all employees with the surname Ruvalcaba. The LIKE keyword allows us to perform pattern matching with the help of **wildcard characters**. The wildcard characters supported by SQL Server are the percentage symbol (%), which matches any sequence of zero or more characters, and the underscore symbol (_), which matches exactly one character.

If we wanted to find all names within our `Employees` table with the surname of `Ruvalcaba`, we could modify the SQL query using a wildcard, as follows:

```
SELECT EmployeeID, Name
FROM Employees
WHERE Name LIKE '%Ruvalcaba'
```

With this query, all records in which the `Name` column ends with `Ruvalcaba` are returned, as shown below.

```
EmployeeID  Name
----------- ---------------------------------------------------------
1           Zak Ruvalcaba
2           Jessica Ruvalcaba

(2 row(s) affected)
```

As we knew that the last name was Ruvalcaba, we only needed to place a wildcard immediately before the last name. But what would happen if we didn't know how to spell the entire last name? That name *is* fairly difficult to spell! You could solve the problem by modifying your SQL statement to use two wildcards as follows:

```
SELECT EmployeeID, Name
FROM Employees
WHERE Name LIKE '%Ruv%'
```

In this case, the wildcard is placed before and after the string `Ruv`. Although this statement would return the same values we saw in the results table above, it would also return any employees whose names (first or last) contain the sequence `Ruv`. As SQL is case-insensitive, this would include the names Sarah Ruvin, Jonny Noruvitch, Truvor MacDonald, and so on.

Using the IN Operator

We use the `IN` operator in `SELECT` queries primarily to specify a list of values that we want to match in our `WHERE` clause. Let's say we want to find all employees who live in California, Indiana, and Maryland. You could write the following SQL statement to accomplish this task:

```
SELECT Name, State
FROM Employees
WHERE State = 'CA' OR State = 'IN' OR State = 'MD'
```

A better way to write this statement uses the IN operator as follows:

```
SELECT Name, State
FROM Employees
WHERE State IN ('CA', 'IN', 'MD')
```

If you execute this query, you'll get the expected results. Since our database only contains employees living in CA, only those records will be displayed:

```
Name                              State
------------------------------    ------------------------------
Zak Ruvalcaba                     Ca
Jessica Ruvalcaba                 Ca
Ted Lindsey                       Ca
Shane Weebe                       Ca
David Levinson                    Ca
Geoff Kim                         Ca

(6 row(s) affected)
```

Sorting Results Using ORDER BY

Unless you specify some sorting criteria, SQL Server can't guarantee to return the results in a particular order. We'll most likely receive the results sorted by the primary key, because it's easier for SQL Server to present the results in this way than any other, but this ordering isn't guaranteed. This explains why, in some of the examples we've completed so far, the order of the results you see on your machine may differ from what you see in this book. The ORDER BY clause provides you with a quick way to sort the results of your query in either ascending or descending order. For instance, to retrieve the names of your employees in alphabetical order, you'd need to execute this command:

```
SELECT EmployeeID, Name
FROM Employees
ORDER BY Name
```

Looks simple, doesn't it?

```
EmployeeID  Name
----------- ---------------------------------------------------------
5           David Levinson
6           Geoff Kim
2           Jessica Ruvalcaba
4           Shane Weebe
3           Ted Lindsey
1           Zak Ruvalcaba

(6 row(s) affected)
```

Note that the default ordering here is ascending (that is, it runs from A to Z). You could add the DESC designation (for descending) to the end of the statement, to order the results backwards:

```
SELECT EmployeeID, Name
FROM Employees
ORDER BY Name DESC
```

If you execute this query, you'll achieve the results we saw above, listed in reverse order. You could also order the results on the basis of multiple columns—simply add a comma after the field name and enter a second field name, as follows:

```
SELECT EmployeeID, Name, City
FROM Employees
ORDER BY City, Name
```

In this case, the results are returned in alphabetical order by city, and any tying records (that is, any records that have the same city) will appear sorted by name.

Limiting the Number of Results with TOP

Another useful SQL keyword is TOP, which can be used together with SELECT to limit the number of returned rows. For example, if we want to retrieve the first five departments, and have the list ordered alphabetically, we'd use this command:

```
SELECT TOP 5 Department
FROM Departments
ORDER BY Department
```

Here are the results:

```
Department
-------------------------------------------------------
Accounting
Administration
Business Development
Customer Support
Engineering

(5 row(s) affected)
```

Reading Data from Multiple Tables

Until now, we've primarily focused on extracting data from a single table. Yet in many real-world applications, you'll need to extract data from multiple tables simultaneously. To do so, you'll need to use subqueries or joins.

Let's learn about subqueries and joins by looking closely at a typical example. Say you're asked to build a report that displays all the employees in the Engineering department. To find employee data, you'd normally query the Employees table, and apply a WHERE filter on the ID of the department. That approach would work fine in this case, except for one element: you don't know the ID of the Engineering department!

The solution? First, execute this query to find the ID of the Engineering department:

```
SELECT DepartmentID
FROM Departments
WHERE Department = 'Engineering'
```

The result of this query will show that the ID of the Engineering department is 6. Using this data, you can make a new query to find the employees in that department:

```
SELECT Name
FROM Employees
WHERE DepartmentID = 6
```

This query retrieves the same list of employees we saw earlier in this chapter.

So everything's great … except that you had to execute two queries in order to do the job! There *is* a better way: SQL is very flexible and allows you to retrieve the intended results using a single command. You could use either subqueries or joins to do the job, so let's take a look at them in turn.

Subqueries

A **subquery** is a query that's nested inside another query, and can return data that's used by the main query. For example, you could retrieve details of all the employees who work in the Engineering department like this:

```
SELECT Name
FROM Employees
WHERE DepartmentID IN
   (SELECT DepartmentID
   FROM Departments
   WHERE Department LIKE '%Engineering')
```

In this case, the subquery (highlighted in bold) returns the ID of the Engineering department, which is then used to identify the employees who work in that department. An embedded SELECT statement is used when you want to perform a second query within the WHERE clause of a primary query.

Note that we're using the IN operator instead of the equality operator (=). We do so because our subquery could return a list of values. For example, if we added another department with the name "Product Engineering," or accidentally added another Engineering record to the Departments table, our subquery would return two IDs. So, whenever we're dealing with subqueries like this, we should use the IN operator unless we're *absolutely certain* that the subquery will return only one record.

Querying Multiple Tables

When using queries that involve multiple tables, it's useful to take a look at the database diagram you created in Chapter 7 to see what columns exist in each table, as well as gain an idea of the relationships between the tables.

Table Joins

An **inner join** allows you to read and combine data from two tables between which a relationship is established. In Chapter 7, we created such a relationship between the Employees table and the Departments table using a foreign key.

Let's make use of this now, to obtain a list of all employees in the engineering department:

```
SELECT Employees.Name
FROM Departments
INNER JOIN Employees ON Departments.DepartmentID =
    Employees.DepartmentID
WHERE Departments.Department LIKE '%Engineering'
```

The first point to notice here is that we qualify our column names by preceding them with the name of the table to which they belong, and a period character (.). We use Employees.Name rather than Name, and Departments.DepartmentID instead of DepartmentID. We need to specify the name of the table whenever the column name exists in more than one table (as is the case with DepartmentID); in other cases (such as with Employees.Name), adding the name of the table is optional.

As an analogy, imagine that you have two colleagues at work named John. John Smith works in the same department as you, and his desk is just across the aisle. John Thomas, on the other hand, works in a different department on a different floor. When addressing a large group of colleagues, you'd use John Smith's full name, otherwise people could become confused. However, it would quickly become tiresome if you always used John Smith's full name when dealing with people in your own department on a day-to-day basis. In exactly the same way, you could always refer to a column in a database using the *Table.Column* form, but it's only necessary when there's the potential for confusion.

As for the join itself, the code is fairly clear: we're joining the `Departments` table and the `Employees` table into a single, virtual table by matching the values in the `Departments.DepartmentID` column with those in the `Employees.DepartmentID` column. From this virtual table, we're only interested in the names of the employees whose records match the filter `Departments.Department LIKE '%Engineering'`.

By eliminating the `WHERE` clause and adding the department's name to the column list, we could generate a list that contained the details of all the employees and their associated departments. Try this query:

```
SELECT Employees.Name, Departments.Department
FROM Departments
INNER JOIN Employees ON Departments.DepartmentID =
    Employees.DepartmentID
```

The results are as you'd expect:

```
Name                               Department
---------------------------------  ------------------------------------
Zak Ruvalcaba                      Executive
Jessica Ruvalcaba                  Marketing
Ted Lindsey                        Engineering
Shane Weebe                        Engineering
David Levinson                     Marketing
Geoff Kim                          Accounting

(6 row(s) affected)
```

Expressions and Operators

In the wonderful world of programming, an **expression** is any piece of code that, once evaluated, results in a value. For instance, 1 + 1 is a very simple expression. In SQL, expressions work in much the same way, though they don't necessarily have to be mathematical. For a simple example, let's create a list that contains employees and their cities as single strings. Try this query:

```
SELECT EmployeeID, Name + ', ' + City AS NameAndCity
FROM Employees
```

The results are shown below:

```
EmployeeID NameAndCity
---------- ------------------------------------------------------------
1          Zak Ruvalcaba, San Diego
2          Jessica Ruvalcaba, San Diego
3          Ted Lindsey, San Diego
4          Shane Weebe, San Diego
5          David Levinson, San Diego
6          Geoff Kim, San Diego

(6 row(s) affected)
```

Note that the results of the expression are used to create a virtual column. This column doesn't exist in reality, but is calculated using the values of other columns. We give this column the name NameAndCity using the AS keyword.

Expressions would be quite useless if we didn't have operators. Over the course of the previous sections, you've seen the operators =, AND, >=, <=, LIKE, and IN at work. Here's a list of operators that you'll need to know to use SQL effectively:

+   The addition operator adds two numbers or combines two strings.

−   The subtraction operator subtracts one number from another.

*   The multiplication operator multiplies one number with another.

/   The division operator divides one number by another.

>   The greater-than operator is used in WHERE clauses to determine whether the first value is greater than the second. For example, the following query would return all the records from the table whose EmployeeID is greater than ten (that is, 11 and up):

```
SELECT Name
FROM Employees
WHERE EmployeeID > 10
```

<   The less-than operator is used in WHERE clauses to determine whether the first value is less than the second. The result of the following query would return from the table all records whose EmployeeID is less than ten (that is, nine and lower):

```
SELECT Name
FROM Employees
WHERE EmployeeID < 10
```

>=   The greater-than or equal-to operator is used in WHERE clauses to determine whether the first value is greater than, or equal to, the second. The following query would return the record with an EmployeeID of ten, and every one after that:

```
SELECT Name
FROM Employees
WHERE EmployeeID >= 10
```

<=   The less-than or equal-to operator is used in WHERE clauses to determine whether the first value is less than, or equal to, the second. The result of the following query would be the record with EmployeeID of ten, and every one before that:

```
SELECT Name
FROM Employees
WHERE EmployeeID <= 10
```

<>, !=   This operator is used to check whether a value is not equal to a second value.

OR   This operator is used with the WHERE clause in the SELECT statement. The OR operator can be used when a certain condition needs to be met, or when only one of two conditions needs to be met. For example, the following query's results would return the employees with employee IDs of 1 or 2:

```
SELECT Name
FROM Employees
WHERE EmployeeID = 1 OR EmployeeID = 2
```

AND This operator works just like OR, except that it requires *all* the conditions to be satisfied, not just any of them.

NOT Typically used in conjunction with the LIKE operator, the NOT operator is used when we're looking for values that are not like the value we specify. For example, the following query would return all employees whose names do not begin with "Jess":

```
SELECT Name
FROM Employees
WHERE Name NOT LIKE 'Jess%'
```

_, ? The underscore operator is used by SQL Server in WHERE clauses, and matches any single character in a string. For instance, if you weren't sure of the first letter of Geoff Kim's surname, you could use the following query:

```
SELECT Name
FROM Employees
WHERE Name LIKE 'Geoff _im'
```

This would return Geoff Kim's record, as well as Geoff Sim's, Geoff Lim's, and so on, were there such employees in the database. Note that the _ character only matches a single character, so Geoff Sirrim would not be returned. To match zero or more characters, you'd use the % or * operator.

%, * The multiple character operator is similar to the underscore operator, except that it matches multiple or zero characters, whereas the underscore operator only matches one.

IN This operator is used in WHERE clauses to specify that an expression's value must be one of the values specified in a list.

Transact-SQL (T-SQL) Functions

As well as using operators to construct expressions manually, SQL Server provides us with some functions that we can use within our queries. For the most part, SQL has sufficient functions to handle almost all of the day-to-day tasks that you'll undertake. So let's take a look at some of the most useful and common functions you're likely to use in your queries.

Getting More Information

Note that the complete list of built-in functions supported by T-SQL is much longer than that presented here. You can find the complete lists by searching for, say, "string functions" or "date and time functions" in the free SQL Server documentation, SQL Server Books Online, which can be downloaded from Microsoft's TechNet site.[1] Additionally, SQL Server allows you to create your own user-defined functions either in SQL, or a language such as VB or C#. However, this is an advanced topic that we won't be covering in this book.

Arithmetic Functions

SQL supports many arithmetic functions. Although the commonly preferred solution is to perform such calculations in VB or C# code, SQL's arithmetic functions can prove handy at times.

ABS

This function returns the absolute value. Both of the following queries will return the value 5:

```
SELECT ABS(5)
```

```
SELECT ABS(-5)
```

CEILING

CEILING returns the smallest integer that's greater than the value that was passed in. In other words, this function rounds up the value passed in. The following query will return 6:

```
SELECT CEILING(5.5)
```

---

[1] http://www.microsoft.com/technet/prodtechnol/sql/2005/downloads/books.mspx

FLOOR

This function returns the largest integer that's less than the value that was passed in—in other words—it rounds down the value that was passed in. The following query will return the value 5:

```
SELECT FLOOR(5.5)
```

MOD

MOD returns the remainder of one value divided by another. The following query would return the value 2:

```
SELECT MOD(8, 3)
```

SIGN

This function returns -1, 0, or 1, to indicate the sign of the argument.

POWER

This function returns the result of one value raised to the power of another. The following query returns the result of 2^3:

```
SELECT POWER(2, 3)
```

SQRT

SQRT returns the non-negative square root of a value.

Many, many more mathematical functions are available—check SQL Server Books Online[2] for a full list.

String Functions

String functions work with literal text values rather than numeric values.

UPPER, LOWER

This function returns the value passed in as all uppercase or all lowercase, respectively. Take the following example:

---

[2] http://msdn.microsoft.com/en-us/library/ms130214.aspx

```
SELECT LOWER(Username), UPPER(State)
FROM Employees
```

The query above will return a list of usernames in lowercase, and a list of states in uppercase.

LTRIM, RTRIM

This function trims whitespace characters, such as spaces, from the left- or right-hand side of the string, respectively.

REPLACE

Use the REPLACE function to change a portion of a string to a new sequence of characters that you specify:

```
SELECT REPLACE('I like chocolate', 'like', 'love')
```

This query will search the string "I like chocolate" for the word "like" and replace it with the word "love," as shown in the output below:

```
--------------------------------------------------------------
I love chocolate

(1 row(s) affected)
```

SUBSTRING

This function returns the sequence of characters within a given value, beginning at a specified start position and spanning a specified number of characters:

```
SELECT SUBSTRING('I like chocolate', 8, 4)
```

The above query will take four characters from the string "I like chocolate" starting from the eighth character, as shown in the output below:

```
----
choc

(1 row(s) affected)
```

LEN

This function returns the length of a string. Thus, the following query would return a list of all usernames, and how many characters were in each username:

```
SELECT Username, LEN(Username) AS UsernameLength
FROM Employees
```

CHARINDEX

This function returns the first position in which a substring can be found in a string.

It's also worth noting that these functions can be used in conjunction with other functions, often to create quite powerful results. For example, the following SQL query would return the first name of every employee within the Employees table:

```
SELECT SUBSTRING(Name, 1, CHARINDEX(' ', Name)) AS FirstName
FROM Employees
```

Here, we're using two string functions. CHARINDEX is used to locate the first space within the Name column. If we assume that the first space indicates the end of the first name, we can then use SUBSTRING to extract the first name from the name string. The results, shown in Figure 8.9, are as we'd expect.

Figure 8.9. Employees' first names

Note that the query isn't bulletproof—it's only suitable for western-style names. If employees had no spaces in their names (for instance, Cher or Madonna), the CHARINDEX function would return -1, indicating that there was no space character in the name. The SUBSTRING function would then return NULL, so the list of results would be flawed.

Date and Time Functions

Date and time functions facilitate the manipulation of dates and times that are stored within your database. These functions work with arguments of the datetime type. Here are some of the most useful ones:

GETDATE

Returns the current date and time

DATEADD

Adds an interval to an existing date (a number of days, weeks, and so on) in order to obtain a new date

DATEDIFF

Calculates the difference between two specified dates

DATEPART

Returns a part of a date (such as the day, month, or year)

DAY

Returns the day number from a date

MONTH

Returns the month number from a date

YEAR

Returns the year from a date

We won't be working with these functions in our example application, but it's good to keep them in mind. Here's a quick example that displays the current year:

```
SELECT YEAR(GETDATE())
```

The result (assuming it's still 2008, of course) is shown below:

```
CurrentYear
-----------
2008

(1 row(s) affected)
```

Working with Groups of Values

Transact-SQL includes two very useful clauses that handle the grouping of records and the filtering of these groups: GROUP BY and HAVING. These clauses can help you find answers to questions like, "Which are the departments in my company that have at least three employees?" and "What is the average salary in each department?"[3]

When working with groups of data, you'll usually need to use **aggregate functions**. Earlier, you learned about simple functions, which receive fixed numbers of parameters as their inputs. Aggregate functions, on the other hand, can handle a variable number of parameters, and can perform a range of tasks with these parameters.

The typical example for an aggregate function is COUNT, which is used when we want to count how many records are returned by a SELECT query. In the following pages, we'll learn about the GROUP BY and HAVING clauses, which are useful when working with aggregate functions; we'll also explore the COUNT, SUM, AVG, MIN, and MAX functions.

The COUNT Function

The COUNT function returns the number of records selected by a query. If you wanted to retrieve the total count of employees in your Employees table, you could run the following query:

```
SELECT COUNT(Name) AS NumberOfEmployees
FROM Employees
```

Running this query with your current sample data would return the number of employees stored in the database, as follows:

```
NumberOfEmployees
-----------------
6

(1 row(s) affected)
```

The COUNT function becomes far more useful when it's combined with a GROUP BY clause.

---

[3] Assuming, of course, that your Employees table has a Salary column, or some other way of keeping track of salaries.

Grouping Records Using GROUP BY

Let's imagine that you need to find out how many employees work in each department. We already know how to get a list of employees and their departments:

```
SELECT Departments.Department, Employees.Name
FROM Employees
INNER JOIN Departments ON Departments.DepartmentID =
    Employees.DepartmentID
```

The results of this query are shown below:

```
Department                          Name
- - - - - - - - - - - - - - - - - - - - - - - -    - - - - - - - - - - - - - - - - - - - - - - - - - -
Executive                           Zak Ruvalcaba
Marketing                           Jessica Ruvalcaba
Engineering                         Ted Lindsey
Engineering                         Shane Weebe
Marketing                           David Levinson
Accounting                          Geoff Kim


(6 row(s) affected)
```

Now, let's build on this query to find out how many employees work in each department. Let's start by adding the COUNT aggregate function:

```
SELECT Departments.Department, COUNT(Employees.Name) AS
    HowManyEmployees
FROM Employees
INNER JOIN Departments ON Departments.DepartmentID =
    Employees.DepartmentID
```

If we execute this query as is, we receive the following error message:

```
Msg 8120, Level 16, State 1, Line 1
Column 'Departments.Department' is invalid in the select list
because it is not contained in either an aggregate function or the
GROUP BY clause.
```

Yikes! What this error message is trying to tell us is that SQL Server is confused. It knows that we want to count employees, but it doesn't understand how the Depart-

ments.Department field relates to this query. We can tell SQL Server to count the
employees based on their departments by adding a GROUP BY clause, like so:

```
SELECT Departments.Department, COUNT(Employees.Name) AS
    HowManyEmployees
FROM Employees
INNER JOIN Departments ON Departments.DepartmentID =
    Employees.DepartmentID
GROUP BY Departments.Department
```

When we run the query now, we get the result we were expecting:

```
Department                                              HowManyEmployees
------------------------------------------------------- ----------------
Accounting                                              1
Engineering                                             2
Executive                                               1
Marketing                                               2

(4 row(s) affected)
```

Filtering Groups Using HAVING

Let's say that we're interested only in the members of the Ruvalcaba family that
work at Dorknozzle, and that we want to know how many of them work in each
department. We can filter out those employees using a WHERE clause, as shown below:

```
SELECT Departments.Department, COUNT(Employees.Name) AS
    HowManyEmployees
FROM Employees
INNER JOIN Departments ON Departments.DepartmentID =
    Employees.DepartmentID
WHERE Employees.Name LIKE '%Ruvalcaba'
GROUP BY Departments.Department
```

While this query is a little complicated, the WHERE clause by itself is fairly simple—it
includes only employees whose names end with Ruvalcaba. These records are the
only ones that are included in the count, as you can see here:

```
Department                                              HowManyEmployees
- - - - - - - - - - - - - - - - - - - - - - - - - - - - - - - - - - - - -    - - - - - - - - - - - - - - - -
Executive                                               1
Marketing                                               1

(2 row(s) affected)
```

When SQL Server processes this query, it uses the WHERE clause to remove records before counting the number of employees in each department. The HAVING clause works similarly to the WHERE clause, except that it removes records *after* the aggregate functions have been applied. The following query builds on the previous example. It seeks to find out which of the departments listed in the Dorknozzle database have at least two employees:

```
SELECT Departments.Department, COUNT(Employees.Name) AS
    HowManyEmployees
FROM Employees
INNER JOIN Departments ON Departments.DepartmentID =
    Employees.DepartmentID
GROUP BY Departments.Department
HAVING COUNT(Employees.Name) >= 2
```

The results show us that there are two departments that have at least two employees:

```
Department                                              HowManyEmployees
- - - - - - - - - - - - - - - - - - - - - - - - - - - - - - - - - - - - -    - - - - - - - - - - - - - - - -
Engineering                                             2
Marketing                                               2

(2 row(s) affected)
```

The SUM, AVG, MIN, and MAX Functions

Other common aggregate functions you're likely to need when you're building more complex applications include:

SUM

Unlike the COUNT function, which returns a value that reflects the number of rows returned by a query, the SUM function performs a calculation on the data within those returned rows.

AVG

The AVG function receives a list of numbers as its arguments, and returns the average of these numbers.

MIN, MAX

The MIN and MAX functions enable you to find the smallest and largest values in a group, respectively.

These functions are great for conducting a statistical analysis of records within the database. For example, it would be quite easy to use them to put together a web-based accounting application that monitored daily sales, giving us totals, averages, and the minimum and maximum values for certain products sold.

Updating Existing Data

Okay, so SQL is great for querying existing data. Fantastic! But how are we supposed to add data to the tables in the first place? We can't exactly ask Dorknozzle employees to add data to our tables using SQL Server Management Studio, can we? We need to learn how to add, update, and delete data inside our database programmatically.

The basic SQL statements that handle these actions are INSERT, UPDATE, and DELETE. Let's put them to work!

The INSERT Statement

Here's a very simple example of INSERT in action:

```
INSERT INTO Departments (Department)
VALUES ('Cool New Department')
```

Executing this command adds a new department, named Cool New Department, to our database. When we add a new row to a table, we must supply data for all the columns that don't accept NULL, don't have a default value, and aren't IDENTITY columns that are automatically filled by the database (as in this example).

If, in Chapter 7, you used the database scripts to create database structures and insert data, you probably noticed that the script contained many INSERT commands, which populated the tables with the sample data.

The INSERT statement generally consists of the following components:

INSERT INTO

> These keywords indicate that this statement will add a new record to the data-base. The INTO part is optional, but it can make your commands easier to read.

Table name

> We provide the name of the table into which we want to insert the values.

Column names

> We also list the names of the columns for which we'll be supplying data in this statement. We separate these column names with commas and enclose the list in parentheses.

VALUES

> This keyword comes between the list of columns and their values.

Values

> We provide a list of values that we wish to supply for the columns listed above.

Try the above SQL statement. Then, to read the new list of records, execute the following query:

```
SELECT DepartmentID, Department
FROM Departments
```

All records in the Departments table will be displayed, along with our Cool New Department and its automatically generated DepartmentID.

 Identity Values

> To obtain programmatically the identity value that we just generated, we can use the scope_identity function like this:
>
> ```
> SELECT scope_identity()
> ```

The **UPDATE** Statement

We use the UPDATE statement to make changes to existing records within our database tables. The UPDATE statement requires certain keywords, and usually a WHERE clause, in order to modify particular records. Consider this code:

```
UPDATE Employees
SET Name = 'Zak Christian Ruvalcaba'
WHERE EmployeeID = 1
```

This statement would change the name of the employee whose EmployeeID is 1. Let's break down the UPDATE statement's syntax:

UPDATE

This clause identifies the statement as one that modifies the named table in the database.

Table name

We provide the name of the table we're updating.

SET

The SET clause specifies the columns we want to modify, and gives their new values.

Column names and values

We provide a list of column names and values, separated by commas.

WHERE condition(s)

This condition specifies which records are being updated.

 Updating Records

Be sure to always include a WHERE clause in your UPDATE statement. If you fail to do so, *all* the records will be updated, which is not usually what you want!

The DELETE Statement

The DELETE statement removes records from the database. You could use it to delete all records from the Departments table, like so:

```
DELETE
FROM Departments
```

Fortunately, executing this command will throw an error if the foreign key that links the Departments and Employees tables is in place, because removing the departments records would leave the employee records referencing nonexistent departments, which would make your data inconsistent (note that the reverse *isn't* true, you *could* delete all the employees if you wanted to, but please don't!).

In case you're curious, here's the error message that would be generated by the DE-LETE command above:

```
Msg 547, Level 16, State 0, Line 1
The DELETE statement conflicted with the REFERENCE constraint
    "FK_Employees_Departments". The conflict occurred in database
    "Dorknozzle", table "dbo.Employees", column 'DepartmentID'.
The statement has been terminated.
```

You could also delete that new department you created earlier:

```
DELETE
FROM Departments
WHERE Department = 'Cool New Department'
```

The command above would execute successfully because there aren't any employees linked to the new department.

Real-world References

Remember that in real-world scenarios, items should be referenced by their IDs, not by name (as shown in the previous above). Note also that if you mistype the name of a department when you're executing that command, no rows will be affected.

Deleting Records

Like the UPDATE command, the WHERE clause is best used together with DELETE; otherwise, you can end up deleting all the records in the table inadvertently!

Stored Procedures

Stored procedures are database objects that group one or more T-SQL statements. Much like VB or C# functions, stored procedures can take parameters and return values.

Stored procedures are used to group SQL commands that form a single, logical action. For example, let's say that you want to add to your website functionality that allows departments to be deleted. However, as you know, you must delete all the department's employees before you can delete the department itself.

To help with such management issues, you could have a stored procedure that copies the employees of that department to another table (called `EmployeesBackup`), deletes those employees from the main `Employees` table, then removes the department from the `Department` table. As you can imagine, having all this logic saved as a stored procedure can make working with databases much easier.

We'll see a more realistic example of a stored procedure in the next chapter, when we start to add more features to the Dorknozzle project, but until then, let's learn how to create a stored procedure in SQL Server, and how to execute it.

The basic form of a stored procedure is as follows:

```
CREATE PROCEDURE ProcedureName
(
  @Parameter1 DataType,
  @Parameter2 DataType,
    ⋮
)
AS
  -- an optional comment
  ⋮ SQL Commands
```

The leading "--" marks a comment. The parameter names, as well as the names of variables we can declare inside stored procedures, start with @. As you might expect, their data types are the same data types supported by SQL Server.

The stored procedure shown below creates a new department whose name is specified through the first parameter. It then creates a new employee whose name is specified as the second parameter, assigns the new employee to the new department, and finally deletes both the new employee and the new department. Now, such a stored procedure would make little sense in reality, but this example allows you to learn a few interesting details that you'll be using frequently as you develop applications, and it uses much of the theory you've learned in this chapter. Take a look at it now:

```
CREATE PROCEDURE DoThings
(
  @NewDepartmentName VARCHAR(50),
  @NewEmployeeName VARCHAR(50),
  @NewEmployeeUsername VARCHAR(50)
)
AS
-- Create a new department
INSERT INTO Departments (Department)
VALUES (@NewDepartmentName)
-- Obtain the ID of the created department
DECLARE @NewDepartmentID INT
SET @NewDepartmentID = scope_identity()
-- Create a new employee
INSERT INTO Employees (DepartmentID, Name, Username)
VALUES (@NewDepartmentID, @NewEmployeeName, @NewEmployeeUsername)
-- Obtain the ID of the created employee
DECLARE @NewEmployeeID INT
SET @NewEmployeeID = scope_identity()
-- List the departments together with their employees
SELECT Departments.Department, Employees.Name
FROM Departments
INNER JOIN Employees ON Departments.DepartmentID =
    Employees.DepartmentID
-- Delete the new employee
DELETE FROM Employees
WHERE EmployeeID = @NewEmployeeID
-- Delete the new department
DELETE FROM Departments
WHERE DepartmentID = @NewDepartmentID
```

Execute this code to have the DoThings stored procedure saved to your Dorknozzle database. You can now execute your new stored procedure by supplying the required parameters as follows:

```
EXECUTE DoThings 'Research', 'Cristian Darie', 'cristian'
```

If you execute the procedure multiple times, you'll achieve the same results, since any data that's created as part of the stored procedure is deleted at the end of the stored procedure:

```
(1 row(s) affected)

(1 row(s) affected)
Department                          Name
-------------------------------     ----------------------------
Executive                           Zak Ruvalcaba
Marketing                           Jessica Ruvalcaba
Engineering                         Ted Lindsey
Engineering                         Shane Weebe
Marketing                           David Levinson
Accounting                          Geoff Kim
Research                            Cristian Darie

(7 row(s) affected)

(1 row(s) affected)

(1 row(s) affected)
```

So, what does the stored procedure do? Let's take a look at the code step by step.

The beginning of the stored procedure code specifies its name and its parameters:

```
CREATE PROCEDURE DoThings
(
   @NewDepartmentName VARCHAR(50),
   @NewEmployeeName VARCHAR(50),
   @NewEmployeeUsername VARCHAR(50)
)
AS
```

The parameters include a department name, an employee name, and an employee username.

 CREATE PROCEDURE and ALTER PROCEDURE

> To modify an existing stored procedure, you'll need to use ALTER PROCEDURE instead of CREATE PROCEDURE. Feel free to play with your existing procedure, to get and idea of how this works.

The code of the stored procedure starts by creating a new department with the name specified by the *@NewDepartmentName* parameter:

```
-- Create a new department
INSERT INTO Departments (Department)
VALUES (@NewDepartmentName)
```

Immediately after it creates the department, the stored procedure stores the value generated for the IDENTITY primary key column (DepartmentID). This value is returned by the scope_identity function, which returns the most recently generated identity value. Keep in mind that it's good practice to store this identity value right after the INSERT query that generated it; if we don't store this value immediately, a second INSERT query may generate another identity value, and that second identity value would then be returned by scope_identity. The value is saved into a new variable named @NewDepartmentID.

Next, you can see how we use the DECLARE statement to declare a new variable in an SQL stored procedure:

```
-- Obtain the ID of the created department
DECLARE @NewDepartmentID INT
SET @NewDepartmentID = scope_identity()
```

The stored procedure continues by creating a new employee using the name and username it received as parameters; it assigns this employee to the department that was created earlier:

```
-- Create a new employee
INSERT INTO Employees (DepartmentID, Name, Username)
VALUES (@NewDepartmentID, @NewEmployeeName, @NewEmployeeUsername)
```

Again, right after creating the new employee, we store its ID into a variable named @NewEmployeeID. Earlier, we needed to store the generated DepartmentID so that we could assign the new employee to it; this time, we're storing the new employee ID so we can delete the employee later:

```
-- Obtain the ID of the created employee
DECLARE @NewEmployeeID INT
SET @NewEmployeeID = scope_identity()
```

Finally, with the new department and employee in place, the stored procedure selects the list of departments together with their employees:

```
-- List the departments together with their employees
SELECT Departments.Department, Employees.Name
FROM Departments
INNER JOIN Employees ON Departments.DepartmentID =
    Employees.DepartmentID
```

For the purposes of this example, we'd prefer to keep the database tidy, which is why we're deleting the new records at the end of the stored procedure:

```
-- Delete the new employee
DELETE FROM Employees
WHERE EmployeeID=@NewEmployeeID
-- Delete the new department
DELETE FROM Departments
WHERE DepartmentID=@NewDepartmentID
```

In the code above, the department and employee IDs that we saved earlier come in very handy: without them, we wouldn't have any way to guarantee that we were deleting the right records!

As you can see, a stored procedure is similar to a function in VB or C#: just like functions in VB or C# code, stored procedures can accept parameters, perform calculations based on those parameters, and return values. SQL also allows for some of the other programming constructs we've seen in the preceding chapters, such as If statements, While loops, and so on, but advanced stored procedure programming is a little beyond the scope of this book.

Summary

Robust, reliable data access is crucial to the success of any application, and SQL meets those needs. As you have seen, SQL not only returns simple results from individual tables, but can produce complex data queries complete with filtering, sorting, expressions, and even nested statements.

In the latter part of this chapter, we learned how to group T-SQL statements and save them together as stored procedures. In Chapter 9, you'll begin to use the knowledge you've gained about databases, and the language that connects those databases together, to create a real, working application.

Chapter 9

ADO.NET

Through the preceding chapters, you've made major strides into the world of dynamic web development using ASP.NET. You've learned about interface development using web forms and web controls and about modeling and structuring your data within the framework of a database—you've even learned about the SQL language that's used to access the data stored within your database. What you're yet to learn is how to access that data through your web applications.

The next step is to learn how to access a database using VB or C# code. This, of course, is what we've been working towards from the beginning of our adventures in ASP.NET. The whole purpose of data store is to support an application. In our case, that application is the Dorknozzle Intranet website, which offers an easy-to-use interface to company data.

ADO.NET (*ActiveX Data Objects .NET*) is a modern Microsoft technology that permits us to access a relational database from an application's code. With ADO.NET, we'll be able to display lists of employees and departments, and allow users to add data to the data store, directly from the Dorknozzle application.

In this chapter, you'll learn how to:

- connect to your database using ADO.NET
- execute SQL queries and retrieve their results using ADO.NET
- display data that is read from a database
- handle data access errors

Introducing ADO.NET

In previous chapters, we learned how to use Visual Web Developer and SQL Management Studio to connect to a database and execute SQL queries. Now, it's time to apply this knowledge. Within our web application, we'll use ADO.NET's classes to connect to the database. Once that connection is established, we'll be in a position where we can execute SQL queries.

In order to use ADO.NET, we must first decide which kind of database we'll use. Once we have made that choice, we can import the namespaces that contain classes that will work with the database. Since we're using SQL Server, you'll need to import the `System.Data.SqlClient` namespace. This contains all the required `Sql` classes, the most important of which are:

SqlConnection

This class exposes properties and methods for connecting to an SQL Server database.

SqlCommand

This class holds data about the SQL queries and stored procedures that you intend to run on your SQL Server database.

SqlDataReader

Data is returned from the database in an `SqlDataReader` class. This class comes with properties and methods that let you iterate through the data it contains. Traditional ASP developers can think of the `SqlDataReader` as being similar to a forward-only `RecordSet`, in which data can only be read forward, one record at a time, and we can't move back to the beginning of the data stream.

The `System.Data.SqlClient` namespace exposes many more than the few classes listed above. We'll discuss some of the more advanced classes in the next few chapters.

ADO.NET and Generic Data Access

ADO.NET is able to use different types of data connections, depending on the kind of database to which the application is trying to connect. The ADO.NET classes whose names start with `Sql` (such as the previously mentioned `SqlConnection`, `SqlCommand`, and so on) are specifically built to connect to SQL Server.

Similar classes are provided for other databases—for example, if you're working with Oracle, you can use classes such as `OracleConnection`, `OracleCommand`, and so on. If, on the other hand, you're working with database systems for which such classes aren't specifically designed, you can use generic low-level interfaces; most databases can be accessed through the OLE DB interface (using classes such as `OleDbConnection` and `OleDbCommand`), or the older ODBC interface (using classes such as `OdbcConnection` and `OdbcCommand`).

In this book, we'll use only the `Sql` classes, but it's good to know that you have options!

Once you're ready to begin working with ADO.NET, the task of establishing a link between the database and your application is a straightforward, six-step process:

1. Import the necessary namespaces.

2. Define a connection to your database with an `SqlConnection` object.

3. When you're ready to manipulate your database, set up the appropriate query in an `SqlCommand` object.

4. Open the connection and execute the SQL query to return the results into a `SqlDataReader` object.

5. Extract relevant database data from the `SqlDataReader` object and display it on your web page.

6. Close the database connection.

Let's walk through this process, discussing each step.

Importing the `SqlClient` Namespace

It's been a while since we've written some VB or C# code! Let's fire up our old friend, Visual Web Developer, and load the `LearningASP` project. We'll use this application to create a few simple scripts; then we'll move to `Dorknozzle`, adding more functionality to the project site.

Open the `LearningASP` project and go to **File > New File…** to create a new file. Select the **Web Form** template, and name it **AccessingData.aspx**. Uncheck the **Place code in separate file** and **Select master page** checkboxes, as shown in Figure 9.1.

Figure 9.1. Creating the **AccessingData.aspx** web form

Once the form is created, we can import the `SqlClient` namespace:

LearningASP\VB\AccessingData_01.aspx (excerpt)

```
<%@ Page Language="VB" %>
<%@ Import Namespace = "System.Data.SqlClient" %>
<!DOCTYPE html PUBLIC "-//W3C//DTD XHTML 1.0 Transitional//EN"
    "http://www.w3.org/TR/xhtml1/DTD/xhtml1-transitional.dtd">
```

Defining the Database Connection

With our import of the SqlClient namespace complete, we can create a new instance of the SqlConnection, which will facilitate our connection to the database. To initialize this connection, we need to specify a **connection string**—a string in which we specify the database we want to connect to, and provide any required authentication details. A typical connection string for an SQL Server Express database looks like this:

```
Server=computer\SqlExpress;Database=database;
➡  User ID=username;Password=password
```

The connection string must specify the name of the computer on which the database is located (you can always use localhost to refer to the local machine), and the name assigned to the database server instance (SqlExpress is the default for SQL Server Express). Also required are the name of the database (such as Dorknozzle), the user ID, and the password for that user account.

SQL Server supports two methods of authentication: **SQL Server Authentication** and **Windows Authentication**. The form of authentication we've used in previous chapters to connect to SQL Server was Windows Authentication, which doesn't require you to supply a SQL Server name and password, but instead uses the credentials of your Windows user account. To tell SQL Server that we're logging in using Windows Authentication, we'd use a connection string that included Integrated Security=True, rather than a username and password, as shown here:

```
Server=computer\SqlExpress;Database=database;
➡  Integrated Security=True
```

 SQL Server Authentication

> Be aware that, when the ASP.NET web application is run by ASP.NET through IIS, it authenticates to SQL Server using a special account named ASPNET. We'll discuss more about configuring SQL Server authentication a little later; for now, let's assume that your code can access your database successfully.

Let's put this approach into practice by creating an SqlConnection in the Page_Load event handler. To have Visual Web Developer create an empty Page_Load event handler for you, switch to **Design** view, and double-click somewhere within the form. This should take you back to **Source** view, where you can see the Page_Load method that was created for you. If you're using VB, enter the code shown in bold below:

Visual Basic	LearningASP\VB\AccessingData_02.aspx *(excerpt)*

```
Protected Sub Page_Load(ByVal sender As Object,
➥   ByVal e As System.EventArgs)
    Dim conn As New SqlConnection("Server=localhost\SqlExpress;" & _
        "Database=Dorknozzle;Integrated Security=True")
End Sub
```

If you're sick of typing quotes, ampersands, and underscores, you can combine the three bold strings in the above code into a single string. However, I'll continue to present connection strings this way throughout this book—not only are they more readable that way, but they fit on the page, too!

If you're using C#, your code should look like this:

C#	LearningASP\CS\AccessingData_02.aspx *(excerpt)*

```
protected void Page_Load(object sender, EventArgs e)
{
    SqlConnection conn = new SqlConnection(
        "Server=localhost\\SqlExpress;Database=Dorknozzle;" +
        "Integrated Security=True");
}
```

Be aware that, in C#, the backslash (\) character has a special meaning when it's contained inside a string; so, when we wish to use one, we have to use the double backslash (\\) shown above.

Preparing the Command

Now we're at step three, in which we create an SqlCommand object and pass in our SQL statement. The SqlCommand object accepts two parameters. The first is the SQL statement, and the second is the connection object that we created in the previous step:

Visual Basic	LearningASP\VB\AccessingData_03.aspx *(excerpt)*

```vb
Protected Sub Page_Load(ByVal sender As Object,
➥ ByVal e As System.EventArgs)
  Dim conn As New SqlConnection("Server=localhost\SqlExpress;" & _
      "Database=Dorknozzle;Integrated Security=True")
  Dim comm As New SqlCommand("SELECT EmployeeID, Name " & _
      "FROM Employees", conn)
End Sub
```

C#	LearningASP\CS\AccessingData_03.aspx *(excerpt)*

```csharp
protected void Page_Load(object sender, EventArgs e)
{
  SqlConnection conn = new SqlConnection(
      "Server=localhost\\SqlExpress;Database=Dorknozzle;" +
      "Integrated Security=True");
  SqlCommand comm = new SqlCommand(
      "SELECT EmployeeID, Name FROM Employees", conn);
}
```

Executing the Command

When we're ready to run the query, we open the connection and execute the command. The SqlCommand class has three methods that we can use to execute a command; we simply choose the one that meets the specific needs of our query. The three methods are as follows:

ExecuteReader

ExecuteReader is used for queries or stored procedures that return one or more rows of data. ExecuteReader returns an SqlDataReader object that can be used to read the results of the query one by one, in a forward-only, read-only manner. Using the SqlDataReader object is the fastest way to retrieve records from the database, but it can't be used to update the data or to access the results in random order.

The SqlDataReader keeps the database connection open until all the records have been read. This can be a problem, as the database server will usually have a limited number of connections—people who are using your application simultaneously may start to see errors if you leave these connections open. To alleviate this problem, we can read all the results from the SqlDataReader object into an object such as a `DataTable`, which stores the data locally without needing a database connection. You'll learn more about the `DataTable` object in Chapter 12.

ExecuteScalar

`ExecuteScalar` is used to execute SQL queries or stored procedures that return a single value, such as a query that counts the number of employees in a company. This method returns an `Object`, which you can convert to a specific data type depending on the kind of data you expect to receive. This is the fastest of the execution methods, helpful if you only want the first column of the first row in a result set.

ExecuteNonQuery

`ExecuteNonQuery` is an oddly named method that's used to execute stored procedures and SQL queries that insert, modify, or update data. The return value will be the number of affected rows.

As we're reading a list of employees, we'll be using `ExecuteReader`. After we execute this method, we'll follow standard practice, reading the data from the returned `SqlDataReader` as quickly as possible; we'll then close both the `SqlDataReader` and the `SqlConnection`, to ensure we don't keep any database resources tied up for longer than is necessary:

Visual Basic	LearningASP\VB\AccessingData_04.aspx *(excerpt)*

```
Protected Sub Page_Load(ByVal sender As Object,
➥   ByVal e As System.EventArgs)
  Dim conn As New SqlConnection("Server=localhost\SqlExpress;" & _
      "Database=Dorknozzle;Integrated Security=True")
  Dim comm As New SqlCommand("SELECT EmployeeID, Name " & _
      "FROM Employees", conn)
  conn.Open()
  Dim reader As SqlDataReader = comm.ExecuteReader()
  : we'll do something with the data here...
  reader.Close()
  conn.Close()
End Sub
```

```
C#                              LearningASP\CS\AccessingData_04.aspx (excerpt)

protected void Page_Load(object sender, EventArgs e)
{
  SqlConnection conn = new SqlConnection(
      "Server=localhost\\SqlExpress;Database=Dorknozzle;" +
      "Integrated Security=True");
  SqlCommand comm = new SqlCommand(
      "SELECT EmployeeID, Name FROM Employees", conn);
  conn.Open();
  SqlDataReader reader = comm.ExecuteReader();
  : we'll do something with the data here…
  reader.Close();
  conn.Close();
}
```

Let's take a look at a few of the methods that are being introduced here. Before we can query our database, a connection must be opened, so we need to call the Open method of our SqlConnection object: conn. Once the connection is opened, we call the ExecuteReader method of our SqlCommand object—comm—to run our query. ExecuteReader will retrieve a list of all employees and return the list in an open SqlDataReader object.

At this point, we would typically use the data in reader, but for now, we've left a comment to remind ourselves that this method doesn't produce any output.

Immediately after we've done something with the data, we close the SqlDataReader and SqlConnection objects using their Close methods. Keeping the connection open for longer than necessary can waste database resources, which can be an issue in real-world applications where hundreds or more users might be accessing the same database at once. As such, it's best practice to keep the connection open for the minimum time.

The aforementoned code lacks any "real" functionality, as it doesn't actually display anything for the user; however, it does open a connection to your database, it executes a SQL query, and finally closes the connection.

Setting Up Database Authentication

Quite frequently, when using Integrated Windows Authentication (by setting "Integrated Security=True" in the connection string), programmers find that their applications are unable to access the database. If you receive a `login failed` error when executing the **AccessingData.aspx** file, you'll find the solution to the problem in this section. If you don't get this error, you can safely skip to the next section —come back only if you get into trouble when you're connecting to SQL Server.

Such database authentication and authorization problems can be solved easily with SQL Server authentication. When you use this authentication method, your application doesn't use a Windows account to log in to the SQL Server database; instead, it uses an SQL Server username and password. This is also the authentication method you'll use when you deploy applications to a production server.

To be able to use SQL Server authentication with your database, you first need to enable the feature in SQL Server by setting the **Server authentication** mode to `SQL Server and Windows Authentication` mode as we did in the section called "Installing SQL Server Management Studio Express" in Chapter 1. You then need to create an SQL Server username that has access to the Dorknozzle database. To do that, start SQL Server Management Studio, expand the **Security** > **Logins** node in **Object Explorer**, right-click the **Logins** node, and select **New Login**.... In the dialog that displays, select **SQL Server authentication** and type `dorknozzle` as the username and `dorknozzle` as the password. Deselect the **Enforce password policy** checkbox. Though these options are very important in a real-world scenario, we're deactivating them for the exercises in this book. Finally, change the **Default database** to `Dorknozzle`. The required settings are shown in Figure 9.2.

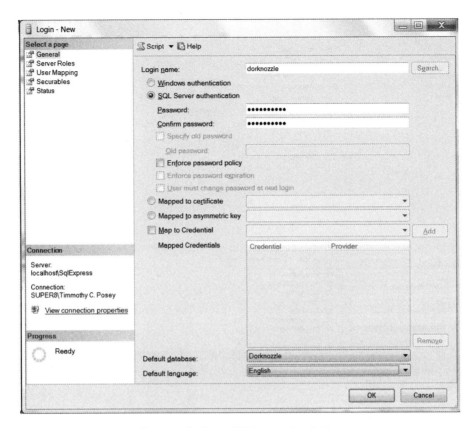

Figure 9.2. Setting up SQL Server authentication

We also want our new user to have full access to the Dorknozzle database. You can modify this user permission when you're creating the new user, or after the fact. To make the user `dorknozzle` the owner of the Dorknozzle database, select **User Mapping** from the **Select a page** pane, check the **Dorknozzle** table in the list, and check the **db_owner** role, as depicted in Figure 9.3. To return to this page after you create the user, right-click the **dorknozzle** user in SQL Server Management Studio and select **Properties**.

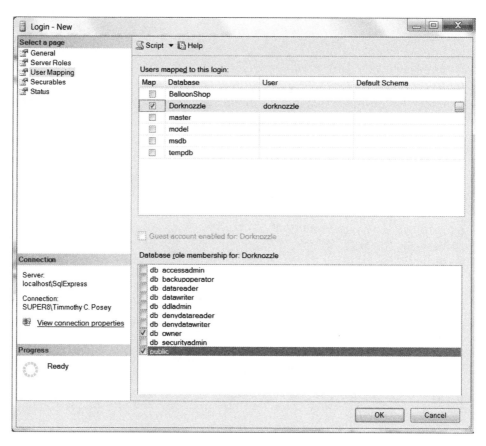

Figure 9.3. Setting the database owner

Once the new user is in place, you can employ this user account to connect to your database. The code to do this in VB and C# is shown below. Be sure to replace *ServerName*, *InstanceName*, *DatabaseName*, *Username*, and *Password* with the appropriate details for your server:

Visual Basic

```
Dim conn As New SqlConnection("Server=ServerName\InstanceName;" & _
    "Database=DatabaseName;User ID=Username;" & _
    "Password=Password")
```

```
C#
```

```
SqlConnection conn = new SqlConnection(
    "Server=ServerName\\InstanceName;" +
    "Database=DatabaseName;User ID=Username;" +
    "Password=Password");
```

Reading the Data

Okay, so you've opened the connection and executed the command. Let's do something with the returned data!

A good task for us to start with is to display the list of employees we read from the database. To do so, we'll simply use a `While` loop to add the data to a `Label` control that we'll place in the form. Start by adding a `Label` named `employeesLabel` to the **AccessingData.aspx** web form. We'll also change the title of the page to **Using ADO.NET**:

LearningASP\VB\AccessingData_05.aspx *(excerpt)*

```
  ⋮
  <head runat="server">
    <title>Using ADO.NET</title>
  </head>
  <body>
    <form id="form1" runat="server">
      <div>
        <asp:Label ID="employeesLabel" runat="server" />
      </div>
    </form>
  </body>
  ⋮
```

Now, let's use the `SqlDataReader`'s `Read` method to loop through the data items held in the reader; we'll display them by adding their text to the `employeesLabel` object as we go:

Visual Basic   LearningASP\VB\AccessingData_06.aspx *(excerpt)*

```
Protected Sub Page_Load(ByVal sender As Object,
➥    ByVal e As System.EventArgs)
    : create the SqlConnection and SqlCommand objects…
    conn.Open()
```

```vb
    Dim reader As SqlDataReader = comm.ExecuteReader()
    While reader.Read()
      employeesLabel.Text &= reader.Item("Name") & "<br />"
    End While
    reader.Close()
    conn.Close()
  End Sub
```

C#   LearningASP\CS\AccessingData_06.aspx *(excerpt)*

```csharp
protected void Page_Load(object sender, EventArgs e)
{
  ⋮ create the SqlConnection and SqlCommand objects…
  conn.Open();
  SqlDataReader reader = comm.ExecuteReader();
  while (reader.Read())
  {
    employeesLabel.Text += reader["Name"] + "<br />";
  }
  reader.Close();
  conn.Close();
}
```

We know that the SqlDataReader class reads the data one row at a time, in a forward-only fashion. When we call reader.Read, our SqlDataReader reads the next row of data from the database. If there's data to be read, it returns True; otherwise—if we've already read the last record returned by the query—the Read method returns False. If we view this page in the browser, it should look like Figure 9.4.

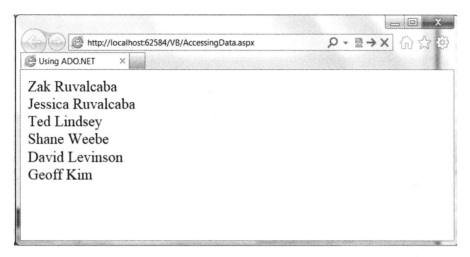

Figure 9.4. Displaying the list of employees

Using Parameters with Queries

What if the user doesn't want to view information for all employees, but instead, wants to see details for one specific employee?

To get this information from our **Employees** table, we'd run the following query, replacing *EmployeeID* with the ID of the employee in which the user was interested:

```
SELECT EmployeeID, Name, Username, Password
FROM Employees
WHERE EmployeeID = EmployeeID
```

Let's build a page like the one shown in Figure 9.5 to display this information.

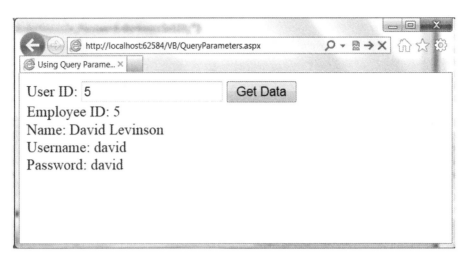

Figure 9.5. Retrieving the details of a specific employee

Create a new web form called **QueryParameters.aspx** and alter it to reflect the code shown here:

```
LearningASP\VB\QueryParameters_01.aspx (excerpt)

<%@ Page Language="VB" %>
<%@ Import Namespace="System.Data.SqlClient" %>
<!DOCTYPE html PUBLIC "-//W3C//DTD XHTML 1.0 Transitional//EN"
    "http://www.w3.org/TR/xhtml1/DTD/xhtml1-transitional.dtd">

<script runat="server">

</script>

<html xmlns="http://www.w3.org/1999/xhtml">
  <head runat="server">
    <title>Using Query Parameters</title>
  </head>
  <body>
    <form id="form1" runat="server">
      <div>
        User ID:
        <asp:TextBox ID="idTextBox" runat="server" />
        <asp:Button ID="submitButton" runat="server"
            Text="Get Data" onclick="submitButton_Click" /><br />
        <asp:Label ID="userLabel" runat="server" />
      </div>
```

```
    </form>
  </body>
</html>
```

With these amendments, we've added a `Textbox` control into which users can enter the ID of the employee whose information they want to see. We've also added a `Button` that will be used to submit the form and retrieve the data.

Next, we need to add a `Click` event handler to the `Button` control. When this button is clicked, our web form will need to execute the following tasks:

1.   Read the ID typed by the user in the `idTextBox` control.

2.   Prepare an SQL query to retrieve data about the specified employee.

3.   Execute the query and read the results.

Now, we *could* perform this query using the following code:

Visual Basic

```
comm = New SqlCommand( _
    "SELECT EmployeeID, Name, Username, Password " & _
    "FROM Employees WHERE EmployeeID = " & idTextBox.Text , conn)
```

If the user entered the number **5** into the text box and clicked the button, the following query would be run:

```
SELECT EmplyeeID, Name, Username, Password
FROM Employees
WHERE EmployeeID = 5
```

The database would run this query without complaint, and your program would execute as expected. However, if—as is perhaps more likely—the user entered an employee's name, your application would attempt to run the following query:

```
SELECT EmployeeID, Name, Username, Password
FROM Employees
WHERE EmployeeID = Zac Ruvalcaba
```

This query would cause an error in the database, which would, in turn, cause an exception in your web form. As a safeguard against this eventuality, ADO.NET allows you to define parameters in your query, and give each of those parameters a type. Inserting parameters into your query is a reasonably simple task:

Visual Basic

```
comm = New SqlCommand( _
    "SELECT EmployeeID, Name, Username, Password " & _
    "FROM Employees WHERE EmployeeID = @EmployeeID", conn)
```

We've added a placeholder to the query for our parameter; it comprises the @ symbol, followed by an identifier for the parameter (in this case, we have used EmployeeID). Next, we need to add this parameter to the SqlCommand object, and give it a value:

Visual Basic

```
comm.Parameters.Add("@EmployeeID", System.Data.SqlDbType.Int)
comm.Parameters("@EmployeeID").Value = idTextBox.Text
```

C#

```
comm.Parameters.Add("@EmployeeID", System.Data.SqlDbType.Int);
comm.Parameters["@EmployeeID"].Value = idTextBox.Text;
```

Here, we call the Add method of comm.Parameters, passing in the name of the parameter (EmployeeID) and the parameter's type; we've told ADO.NET that we're expecting an int to be passed to the database, but we could specify any of the SQL Server data types here.

One of the most common SQL Server data types is nvarchar. If your query involved an nvarchar parameter named @Username, for example, you could set its value with the following code:

Visual Basic

```
comm.Parameters.Add("@Username", Data.SqlDbType.NVarChar, 50)
comm.Parameters("@Username").Value = username
```

```csharp
comm.Parameters.Add("@Username", SqlDbType.NVarChar, 50);
comm.Parameters["@Username"].Value = username;
```

Notice that we've included an additional parameter in our call to the Add method. This optional parameter tells the SqlCommand object the maximum allowable size of the nvarchar field in the database. We've given the Username field in our Employees table a maximum size of 50 characters, so our code should reflect this limit.

For a list of all the types you can use when calling conn.Parameters.Add, see the entry on System.Data.SqlDbType enumeration in the .NET Framework's SDK Documentation.

Let's put parameters into action in **QueryParameters.aspx**. First, create a Click event handler for the Button control by double-clicking it in Design view. Next, fill the event handler with the code shown:

Visual Basic   LearningASP\VB\QueryParameters_02.aspx *(excerpt)*

```vbnet
Protected Sub submitButton_Click(ByVal sender As Object,
➥  ByVal e As System.EventArgs)
  Dim conn As SqlConnection
  Dim comm As SqlCommand
  Dim reader As SqlDataReader
  conn = New SqlConnection("Server=localhost\SqlExpress;" & _
      "Database=Dorknozzle;Integrated Security=True")
  comm = New SqlCommand( _
      "SELECT EmployeeID, Name, Username, Password " & _
      "FROM Employees WHERE EmployeeID=@EmployeeID", conn)
  Dim employeeID As Integer
  If (Not Integer.TryParse(idTextBox.Text, employeeID)) Then
    userLabel.Text = "Please enter a numeric ID!"
  Else
    comm.Parameters.Add("@EmployeeID", System.Data.SqlDbType.Int)
    comm.Parameters("@EmployeeID").Value = employeeID
    conn.Open()
    reader = comm.ExecuteReader()
    If reader.Read() Then
      userLabel.Text = "Employee ID: " & _
          reader.Item("EmployeeID") & "<br />" & _
          "Name: " & reader.Item("Name") & "<br />" & _
```

```
          "Username: " & reader.Item("Username") & "<br />" & _
          "Password: " & reader.Item("Password")
    Else
      userLabel.Text = _
          "There is no user with this ID: " & employeeID
    End If
    reader.Close()
    conn.Close()
  End If
End Sub
```

C#   LearningASP\CS\QueryParameters_02.aspx *(excerpt)*

```csharp
protected void submitButton_Click(object sender, EventArgs e)
{
  SqlConnection conn;
  SqlCommand comm;
  SqlDataReader reader;
  conn = new SqlConnection("Server=localhost\\SqlExpress;" +
      "Database=Dorknozzle;Integrated Security=True");
  comm = new SqlCommand(
      "SELECT EmployeeID, Name, Username, Password " +
      "FROM Employees WHERE EmployeeID=@EmployeeID", conn);
  int employeeID;
  if (!int.TryParse(idTextBox.Text, out employeeID))
  {
    userLabel.Text = "Please enter a numeric ID!";
  }
  else
  {
    comm.Parameters.Add("@EmployeeID", System.Data.SqlDbType.Int);
    comm.Parameters["@EmployeeID"].Value = employeeID;
    conn.Open();
    reader = comm.ExecuteReader();
    if (reader.Read())
    {
      userLabel.Text = "Employee ID: " +
          reader["EmployeeID"] + "<br />" +
          "Name: " + reader["Name"] + "<br />" +
          "Username: " + reader["Username"] + "<br />" +
          "Password: " + reader["Password"];
    }
    else
    {
      userLabel.Text =
```

```
          "There is no user with this ID: " + employeeID;
    }
    reader.Close();
    conn.Close();
  }
}
```

Now, when the user clicks the button, the Click event is raised, and the event
handler is executed. In that method, we grab the Employee ID from the Text property
of the TextBox control, and check that it's a valid integer. This check can be done
with the Integer.TryParse method in VB, or the int.TryParse method in C#:

Visual Basic	LearningASP\VB\QueryParameters_02.aspx *(excerpt)*

```
⋮
Dim employeeID As Integer
If (Not Integer.TryParse(idTextBox.Text, employeeID)) Then
    ⋮
```

C#	LearningASP\CS\QueryParameters_02.aspx *(excerpt)*

```
⋮
int employeeID;
if (!int.TryParse(idTextBox.Text, out employeeID))
{
    ⋮
```

This method verifies whether or not the string we pass as the first parameter can
be cast to an integer; if it can, the integer is returned through the second parameter.
Note that in C#, this second parameter is an out parameter. **Out parameters** are
parameters that are used to retrieve data from a function, rather than send data to
that function. Out parameters are similar to return values, except that we can supply
multiple out parameters to any method. The return value of TryParse is a Boolean
value that specifies whether or not the supplied value could be properly converted.

If the ID entered isn't a valid number, we notify the user, as Figure 9.6 illustrates.

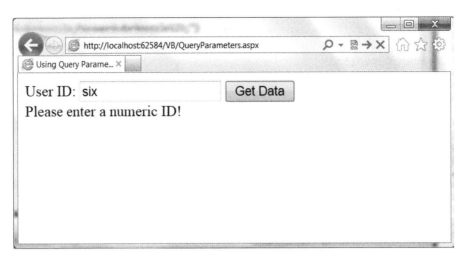

Figure 9.6. Invalid input data generating a warning

We also want to notify the user if the query doesn't return any results. This feature is simple to implement, because `reader.Read` only returns `True` if the query returns a record:

Visual Basic	LearningASP\VB\QueryParameters_02.aspx *(excerpt)*

```
⋮
If reader.Read() Then
  userLabel.Text = "Employee ID: " & reader.Item("EmployeeID") & _
  ⋮
```

C#	LearningASP\CS\QueryParameters_02.aspx *(excerpt)*

```
⋮
if (reader.Read())
{
  userLabel.Text = "Employee ID: " + reader["EmployeeID"] +
  ⋮
```

Figure 9.7 shows the message you'll see if you enter an ID that doesn't exist in the database.

There are still a couple of details that we could improve in this system. For example, if an error occurs in the code, the connection will never be closed. Let's look at this problem next.

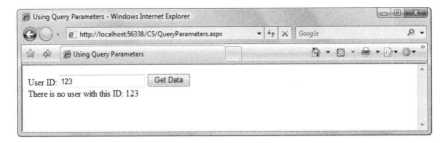

Figure 9.7. An invalid ID warning

Bulletproofing Data Access Code

Right now, the code in **QueryParameters.aspx** seems to be perfect, right? Well, not quite. While the code does its job most of the time, it still has one important weakness: it doesn't take into account potential errors that could occur in the data access code. It's very good practice to enclose such code in Try-Catch-Finally blocks, and to always use the Finally block to close any open data objects. We learned about Try-Catch-Finally in Chapter 5; now we're going to use that theory in a real-world scenario.

Take a look at the following code samples:

Visual Basic   LearningASP\VB\QueryParameters_03.aspx *(excerpt)*

```
Protected Sub submitButton_Click(ByVal sender As Object,
➥  ByVal e As System.EventArgs)
  Dim conn As SqlConnection
  Dim comm As SqlCommand
  Dim reader As SqlDataReader
  conn = New SqlConnection("Server=localhost\SqlExpress;" & _
      "Database=Dorknozzle;Integrated Security=True")
  comm = New SqlCommand( _
      "SELECT EmployeeID, Name, Username, Password " & _
      "FROM Employees WHERE EmployeeID=@EmployeeID", conn)
  Dim employeeID As Integer
  If (Not Integer.TryParse(idTextBox.Text, employeeID)) Then
    userLabel.Text = "Please enter a numeric ID!"
  Else
    comm.Parameters.Add("@EmployeeID", System.Data.SqlDbType.Int)
    comm.Parameters("@EmployeeID").Value = employeeID
    Try
      conn.Open()
      reader = comm.ExecuteReader()
```

```
      If reader.Read() Then
        userLabel.Text = "Employee ID: " & _
            reader.Item("EmployeeID") & "<br />" & _
            "Name: " & reader.Item("Name") & "<br />" & _
            "Username: " & reader.Item("Username") & "<br />" & _
            "Password: " & reader.Item("Password")
      Else
        userLabel.Text = _
            "There is no user with this ID: " & employeeID
      End If
      reader.Close()
    Catch
      userLabel.Text = "Error retrieving user data."
    Finally
      conn.Close()
    End Try
  End If
End Sub
```

C#   LearningASP\CS\QueryParameters_03.aspx *(excerpt)*

```
protected void submitButton_Click(object sender, EventArgs e)
{
  SqlConnection conn;
  SqlCommand comm;
  SqlDataReader reader;
  conn = new SqlConnection("Server=localhost\\SqlExpress;" +
      "Database=Dorknozzle;Integrated Security=True");
  comm = new SqlCommand(
      "SELECT EmployeeID, Name, Username, Password " +
      "FROM Employees WHERE EmployeeID=@EmployeeID", conn);
  int employeeID;
  if (!int.TryParse(idTextBox.Text, out employeeID))
  {
    userLabel.Text = "Please enter a numeric ID!";
  }
  else
  {
    comm.Parameters.Add("@EmployeeID", System.Data.SqlDbType.Int);
    comm.Parameters["@EmployeeID"].Value = employeeID;
    try
    {
      conn.Open();
      reader = comm.ExecuteReader();
      if (reader.Read())
```

```
      {
        userLabel.Text = "Employee ID: " +
            reader["EmployeeID"] + "<br />" +
            "Name: " + reader["Name"] + "<br />" +
            "Username: " + reader["Username"] + "<br />" +
            "Password: " + reader["Password"];
      }
      else
      {
        userLabel.Text =
            "There is no user with this ID: " + employeeID;
      }
      reader.Close();
    }
    catch
    {
      userLabel.Text = "Error retrieving user data.";
    }
    finally
    {
      conn.Close();
    }
  }
}
```

So, what's new in this version of the event handler, apart from the fact that it has
become larger? First of all—and most importantly—we have the Try-Catch-Finally
block in place. Everything that manipulates the database is in the Try block. If an
error arises, we display a message for the user through the Catch block. In the Finally block, which is guaranteed to execute, we close the database connection.

Using the Repeater Control

The .NET Framework comes bundled with a few controls that can help us to display
more complex lists of data: Repeater, DataList, GridView, DetailsView, and
FormView. These controls allow you to format database data easily within an
ASP.NET page.

In this chapter, you'll learn how to work with the Repeater; we'll cover the other
controls in the next few chapters. Note that these controls aren't part of ADO.NET,
but we're presenting them together with ADO.NET because they're frequently used
in work with databases.

The `Repeater` control is a lightweight ASP.NET control that allows the easy presentation of data directly from a data source, usually in just a handful of code. Let's look at a quick example of how a `Repeater` control can be added to a page:

```
<asp:Repeater id="myRepeater" runat="server">
  <ItemTemplate>
    <%# Eval("Name") %>
  </ItemTemplate>
</asp:Repeater>
```

As you can see, the `Repeater` control looks a little different from the other web controls we've used thus far. The difference with this control is that an `<ItemTemplate>` subtag—otherwise known as a **child tag**—is located within the control's main `<asp:Repeater>` tag, or **parent tag**. This child tag contains a code render block that specifies the particular data item that we want to appear in the `Repeater`. However, before this data can be displayed, we have to bind an `SqlDataReader` object (which contains the results of an SQL query) to the `Repeater` control using the process known as **data binding**. This task is achieved from a code block like so:

Visual Basic

```
myRepeater.DataSource = reader
myRepeater.DataBind()
```

Yes, it's that easy! In a moment, we'll display the code within the framework of a new example. But first, let's discuss what's happening here in more detail.

True to its name, the `Repeater` control lets us output some markup for each record in an `SqlDataReader`, inserting values from those records wherever we like in this repeated markup. The markup that's to be repeated is provided as **templates** for the `Repeater` to use. For example, if we wanted to display the results of a database query in an HTML table, we could use a `Repeater` to generate an HTML table row for each record in that results set. We'd provide a template containing `<tr>` and `</tr>` tags, as well as `<td>` and `</td>` tags, and we'd indicate where in that template we wanted the values from the results set to appear.

To gain greater flexibility in the presentation of our results, we can provide the `Repeater` control with a number of different templates, which the `Repeater` will use in the circumstances described in the templates list below. Each of these templates must be specified in a child tag of the `<asp:Repeater>` tag:

`<HeaderTemplate>`

This template provides a header for the output. If we're generating an HTML table, for example, we could include the opening `<table>` tag, provide a row of header cells (`th`), and even specify a `caption` for the table.

`<ItemTemplate>`

The only template that is actually required, `<ItemTemplate>` specifies the markup that should be output for each item in the data source. If we were generating an HTML table, this template would contain the `<td>` and `</td>` tags and their contents.

`<AlternatingItemTemplate>`

This template, if provided, will be applied instead of `ItemTemplate` to every second record in the data source, making it easy to produce effects such as alternating table row colors.

`<SeparatorTemplate>`

This template provides markup that will appear between the items in the data source. It will not appear before the first item or after the last item.

`<FooterTemplate>`

This template provides a footer for the control's output, which will appear after all the items in the data source. If you're generating an HTML table, you could include the closing `</table>` tag in this template.

Let's take a look at a repeater control that displays a table of employees. If you want to test this code, create a new web form named **UsingRepeater.aspx** in the Learning application. Don't use a code-behind file or a master page. Import the `System.Data.SqlClient` namespace just as you did for the two forms we created earlier in this chapter.

The following code will set up a `Repeater` that can be used to display a table of employees, listing their employee IDs, names, usernames, and passwords:

```
<%@ Page Language="VB" %>
<%@ Import Namespace="System.Data.SqlClient" %>
<!DOCTYPE html PUBLIC "-//W3C//DTD XHTML 1.0 Transitional//EN"
    "http://www.w3.org/TR/xhtml1/DTD/xhtml1-transitional.dtd">

<script runat="server">

</script>

<html xmlns="http://www.w3.org/1999/xhtml" >
<head runat="server">
    <title>Using the Repeater</title>
</head>
<body>
    <form id="form1" runat="server">
    <div>
      <asp:Repeater ID="myRepeater" runat="server">
        <HeaderTemplate>
          <table width="400" border="1">
            <tr>
              <th>Employee ID</th>
              <th>Name</th>
              <th>Username</th>
              <th>Password</th>
            </tr>
        </HeaderTemplate>
        <ItemTemplate>
            <tr>
              <td><%# Eval("EmployeeID") %></td>
              <td><%# Eval("Name") %></td>
              <td><%# Eval("Username") %></td>
              <td><%# Eval("Password") %></td>
            </tr>
        </ItemTemplate>
        <FooterTemplate>
          </table>
        </FooterTemplate>
      </asp:Repeater>
    </div>
    </form>
</body>
</html>
```

The Repeater control naturally lends itself to generating HTML tables, and that's just what we're doing here. First, we include a <HeaderTemplate>, which includes the opening <table> tag, along with the table's heading row.

Next, we provide a template for each item in the result set. The template specifies a table row containing four table cells, each of which contains a code render block that outputs the values taken from each record in the results set. In both VB and C#, we use Eval to retrieve database values. Alternatively, you could use the longer form, Container.DataItem("*FieldName*") in VB.NET or DataBinder.Eval(Container.DataItem, "*FieldName*") in C#, but we'll stick with Eval in this book.

Finally, here's the <FooterTemplate> that includes the closing </table> tag. To make the repeater display information, we need to bind a data source to it. Use Visual Web Developer to generate the web form's Page_Load event handler, and complete it like this:

Visual Basic	LearningASP\VB\UsingRepeater.aspx *(excerpt)*

```
Protected Sub Page_Load(ByVal sender As Object,
➥   ByVal e As System.EventArgs)
  Dim conn As SqlConnection
  Dim comm As SqlCommand
  Dim reader As SqlDataReader
  conn = New SqlConnection("Server=localhost\SqlExpress;" & _
      "Database=Dorknozzle;Integrated Security=True")
  comm = New SqlCommand( _
      "SELECT EmployeeID, Name, Username, Password " & _
      "FROM Employees", conn)
  Try
    conn.Open()
    reader = comm.ExecuteReader()
    myRepeater.DataSource = reader
    myRepeater.DataBind()
    reader.Close()
  Catch
    Response.Write("Error retrieving user data.")
  Finally
    conn.Close()
  End Try
End Sub
```

C#   LearningASP\CS\UsingRepeater.aspx *(excerpt)*

```csharp
protected void Page_Load(object sender, EventArgs e)
{
  SqlConnection conn;
  SqlCommand comm;
  SqlDataReader reader;
  conn = new SqlConnection("Server=localhost\\SqlExpress;" +
      "Database=Dorknozzle;Integrated Security=True");
  comm = new SqlCommand(
      "SELECT EmployeeID, Name, Username, Password " +
      "FROM Employees", conn);
  try
  {
    conn.Open();
    reader = comm.ExecuteReader();
    myRepeater.DataSource = reader;
    myRepeater.DataBind();
    reader.Close();
  }
  catch
  {
    Response.Write("Error retrieving user data.");
  }
  finally
  {
    conn.Close();
  }
}
```

As you can see, binding a control to a data source makes it very easy to display our data in the web form. In this case, we've used the Repeater control, which, in the server-side code, we bound to the SqlDataReader that contains our data. The results of this work are shown in Figure 9.8.

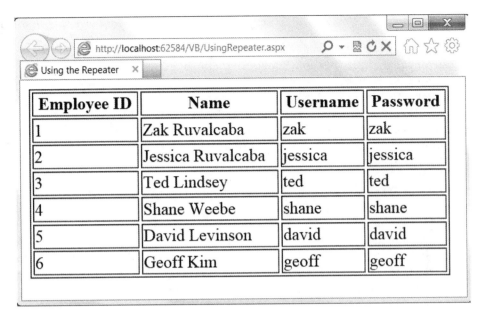

Figure 9.8. Using the Repeater control

Creating the Dorknozzle Employee Directory

Great work! You're presenting data in the browser window based on user interaction, and you have even allowed your users to filter that data in accordance with their own search parameters. Your code also takes care to close the database connection in case an error occurs along the way.

It's time to apply the theory we're learning directly to the Dorknozzle application. In the following pages, you'll insert, update, and delete database records in a new Dorknozzle Employee Directory web form. You'll also learn how to call stored procedures using ADO.NET.

Start by loading the Dorknozzle project and creating a new web form. Make sure you name it **EmployeeDirectory.aspx**, check that both the **Place code in separate file** and the **Select master page** checkboxes are checked, and confirm that your new page is based on the master page **Dorknozzle.master**. Then, modify the automatically generated code like this:

```
                                   Dorknozzle\VB\01_EmployeeDirectory.aspx (excerpt)
<%@ Page Language="VB" MasterPageFile="~/Dorknozzle.master"
    AutoEventWireup="true" CodeFile="EmployeeDirectory.aspx.vb"
    Inherits="EmployeeDirectory"
    title="Dorknozzle Employee Directory" %>

<asp:Content ID="Content1" ContentPlaceHolderID="head"
    Runat="Server">
</asp:Content>
<asp:Content ID="Content2"
    ContentPlaceHolderID="ContentPlaceHolder1" Runat="Server">
  <h1>Employee Directory</h1>
  <asp:Repeater id="employeesRepeater" runat="server">
    <ItemTemplate>
      Employee ID:
      <strong><%#Eval("EmployeeID")%></strong><br />
      Name: <strong><%#Eval("Name")%></strong><br />
      Username: <strong><%#Eval("Username")%></strong>
    </ItemTemplate>
    <SeparatorTemplate>
      <hr />
    </SeparatorTemplate>
  </asp:Repeater>
</asp:Content>
```

This Repeater includes item and separator templates. The item template contains code render blocks that will display the data from an SqlDataReader. When this repeater is properly populated with data, the employee directory page will look like the one shown in Figure 9.9.

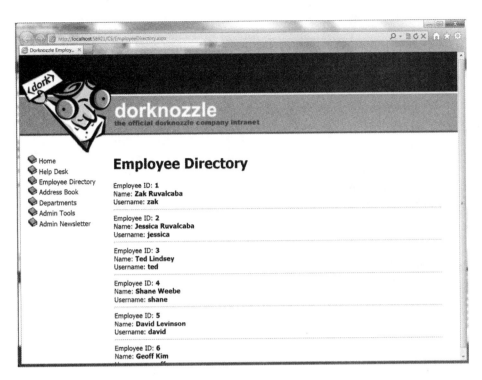

Figure 9.9. The completed Employee Directory page

First up, let's write the code that populates the repeater control. That code will take the form of a `Page_Load` method within our code-behind file. To have the method's signature generated for you, switch the form to **Design** view, and double-click an empty space on the form (not in the space of other controls such as the `Repeater`; a good place to double-click would be to the right of the Employee Directory header). Then, add this code:

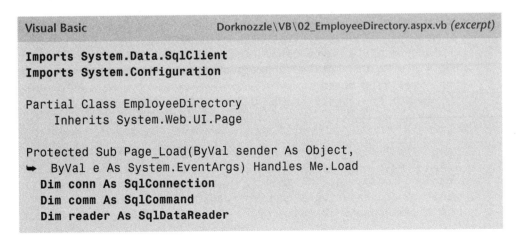

```vbnet
Imports System.Data.SqlClient
Imports System.Configuration

Partial Class EmployeeDirectory
    Inherits System.Web.UI.Page

Protected Sub Page_Load(ByVal sender As Object,
➥ ByVal e As System.EventArgs) Handles Me.Load
  Dim conn As SqlConnection
  Dim comm As SqlCommand
  Dim reader As SqlDataReader
```

Visual Basic · Dorknozzle\VB\02_EmployeeDirectory.aspx.vb *(excerpt)*

```vb
  Dim connectionString As String = _
      ConfigurationManager.ConnectionStrings( _
      "Dorknozzle").ConnectionString
  conn = New SqlConnection(connectionString)
  comm = New SqlCommand( _
      "SELECT EmployeeID, Name, Username FROM Employees", _
      conn)
  Try
    conn.Open()
    reader = comm.ExecuteReader()
    employeesRepeater.DataSource = reader
    employeesRepeater.DataBind()
    reader.Close()
  Finally
    conn.Close()
  End Try
End Sub
End Class
```

C#   Dorknozzle\CS\02_EmployeeDirectory.aspx.cs *(excerpt)*

```csharp
using System;
⋮
using System.Data.SqlClient;

public partial class EmployeeDirectory : System.Web.UI.Page
{
  protected void Page_Load(object sender, EventArgs e)
  {
    SqlConnection conn;
    SqlCommand comm;
    SqlDataReader reader;
    string connectionString =
        ConfigurationManager.ConnectionStrings[
        "Dorknozzle"].ConnectionString;
    conn = new SqlConnection(connectionString);
    comm = new SqlCommand(
        "SELECT EmployeeID, Name, Username FROM Employees",
        conn);
    try
    {
      conn.Open();
      reader = comm.ExecuteReader();
      employeesRepeater.DataSource = reader;
      employeesRepeater.DataBind();
```

```
      reader.Close();
    }
    finally
    {
      conn.Close();
    }
  }
}
```

Most of the code should look familiar, except for the following part, which reads the connection string:

Visual Basic   Dorknozzle\VB\02_EmployeeDirectory.aspx.vb *(excerpt)*

```
Dim connectionString As String = _
    ConfigurationManager.ConnectionStrings( _
    "Dorknozzle").ConnectionString
```

C#   Dorknozzle\CS\02_EmployeeDirectory.aspx.cs *(excerpt)*

```
string connectionString =
    ConfigurationManager.ConnectionStrings[
    "Dorknozzle"].ConnectionString;
```

Back in Chapter 5, you learned that you can store various configuration options in **Web.config**. Anticipating that many applications will use **Web.config** to store their connection strings, the designers of .NET reserved a special place in **Web.config** for database connection strings. If you open **Web.config** now, you'll see an empty connectionStrings element located inside the configuration element. Modify **Web.config** like this:

Dorknozzle\VB\03_web.config *(excerpt)*

```
<configuration>
  ⋮
  <connectionStrings>
    <add name="Dorknozzle"
        connectionString="Server=localhost\SqlExpress;
➥       Database=Dorknozzle;Integrated Security=True"
        providerName="System.Data.SqlClient"/>
```

```
    </connectionStrings>
      ⋮
  </configuration>
```

You can add more connection strings under the `connectionStrings` element by inserting add elements with three attributes: `connectionString` contains the actual connection string, `name` gives the connection string an identifier that we can reference within our code, and `providerName` indicates the type of data provider we want to use for the connection. In our case, `providerName="System.Data.SqlClient"` specifies that we're connecting to an SQL Server database.

To retrieve configuration data from **Web.config**, we use the `ConfigurationManager` class, which is located in the `System.Configuration` namespace.

You may have also noticed we're without a `Catch` block in our database handling code. When a `Catch` block is absent, any exceptions that are raised are not caught, although the code in the `Finally` block is still executed. In other words, we're choosing not to handle potential errors in **EmployeeDirectory.aspx**, but we still want to ensure that the database connection is properly closed if an error arises.

The rest of the code comprises the typical data access routine, involving a `SqlConnection` object, a `SqlCommand` object, and a `SqlDataReader` object. Once the reader has been filled with the database data, it is bound to the `Repeater` control's `DataSource` property, and from this point, the `repeater` takes control and reads all the data from the data source. If you save and run this page, it should appear as shown in Figure 9.9.

More Data Binding

The term **data binding** describes the act of associating a **data source** with a **data consumer**. In our previous examples, the data source was an `SqlDataReader` object, and the consumer was a `Repeater` control that read and displayed the data. Data binding typically involves setting the `DataSource` property of the consumer object to the data source object, and calling the `DataBind` method to apply the binding:

Visual Basic

```
employeesRepeater.DataSource = reader
employeesRepeater.DataBind()
```

```C#
C#

employeesRepeater.DataSource = reader;
employeesRepeater.DataBind();
```

As we discussed earlier, ASP.NET includes a few controls that specialize in display-ing data that comes from data sources, but you can also bind data to numerous other controls, including lists, menus, text boxes, and so on. To explore the process of control binding further, let's open the Help Desk page again. If you remember, we left the **Category** and **Subject** drop-down lists empty back in Chapter 5. We did so because we knew that, eventually, those items would have to be populated dy-namically through code. Sure, we could have hard-coded the values ourselves, but imagine what would happen if additions or deletions needed to be made to that list. In order to make the necessary changes to the controls, we would have to open every page that contained lists of categories and subjects.

It's preferable to store the lists of categories and subjects in database tables, and to bind this data to the drop-down lists in the Help Desk page. Whenever a change needs to be made, we can make it once within the database; all the controls that are bound to that database table will change automatically.

Let's go ahead and add the necessary code to Page_Load in **HelpDesk.aspx** to populate the DropDownList controls from the database. After the changes are made, the lists will be populated with the data you added to your database in Chapter 7, as illus-trated in Figure 9.10.

Figure 9.10. A drop-down list created with data binding

Open **HelpDesk.aspx** in Design view and double-click an empty space on the form to have the signature of the Page_Load method generated for you. First, we'll need to import some namespaces. You'll need two if you're using VB, but only one if you're using C#. Add the following to the top section of the file:

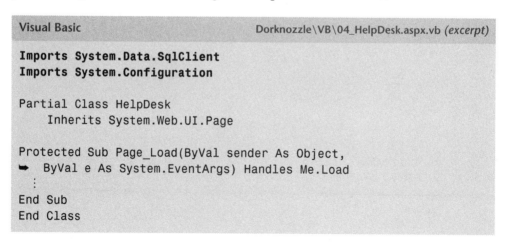

```vб
Imports System.Data.SqlClient
Imports System.Configuration

Partial Class HelpDesk
    Inherits System.Web.UI.Page


Protected Sub Page_Load(ByVal sender As Object,
➥   ByVal e As System.EventArgs) Handles Me.Load
    ⋮
End Sub
End Class
```

Visual Basic — Dorknozzle\VB\04_HelpDesk.aspx.vb *(excerpt)*

```
C#                              Dorknozzle\CS\04_HelpDesk.aspx.cs (excerpt)

using System;
⋮
using System.Data.SqlClient;

public partial class HelpDesk : System.Web.UI.Page
{
  protected void Page_Load(object sender, EventArgs e)
  {
    ⋮
  }
}
```

Then, add the following code to the Page_Load method:

```
Visual Basic                    Dorknozzle\VB\04_HelpDesk.aspx.vb (excerpt)

Protected Sub Page_Load(ByVal sender As Object,
➡   ByVal e As System.EventArgs) Handles Me.Load
  If Not IsPostBack Then
    Dim conn As SqlConnection
    Dim categoryComm As SqlCommand
    Dim subjectComm As SqlCommand
    Dim reader As SqlDataReader
    Dim connectionString As String = _
        ConfigurationManager.ConnectionStrings( _
        "Dorknozzle").ConnectionString
    conn = New SqlConnection(connectionString)
    categoryComm = New SqlCommand( _
        "SELECT CategoryID, Category FROM HelpDeskCategories", _
        conn)
    subjectComm = New SqlCommand( _
      "SELECT SubjectID, Subject FROM HelpDeskSubjects", conn)
    Try
      conn.Open()
      reader = categoryComm.ExecuteReader()
      categoryList.DataSource = reader
      categoryList.DataValueField = "CategoryID"
      categoryList.DataTextField = "Category"
      categoryList.DataBind()
      reader.Close()
      reader = subjectComm.ExecuteReader()
      subjectList.DataSource = reader
      subjectList.DataValueField = "SubjectID"
```

```
      subjectList.DataTextField = "Subject"
      subjectList.DataBind()
      reader.Close()
    Finally
      conn.Close()
    End Try
  End If
End Sub
```

```csharp
protected void Page_Load(object sender, EventArgs e)
{
  if (!IsPostBack)
  {
    SqlConnection conn;
    SqlCommand categoryComm;
    SqlCommand subjectComm;
    SqlDataReader reader;
    string connectionString =
        ConfigurationManager.ConnectionStrings[
        "Dorknozzle"].ConnectionString;
    conn = new SqlConnection(connectionString);
    categoryComm = new SqlCommand(
        "SELECT CategoryID, Category FROM HelpDeskCategories",
        conn);
    subjectComm = new SqlCommand(
        "SELECT SubjectID, Subject FROM HelpDeskSubjects", conn);
    try
    {
      conn.Open();
      reader = categoryComm.ExecuteReader();
      categoryList.DataSource = reader;
      categoryList.DataValueField = "CategoryID";
      categoryList.DataTextField = "Category";
      categoryList.DataBind();
      reader.Close();
      reader = subjectComm.ExecuteReader();
      subjectList.DataSource = reader;
      subjectList.DataValueField = "SubjectID";
      subjectList.DataTextField = "Subject";
      subjectList.DataBind();
      reader.Close();
    }
    finally
```

```
    {
      conn.Close();
    }
  }
}
```

You'll notice that the guts of Page_Load are enclosed in an If statement, which tests to see if IsPostBack is not True. But just what *is* this IsPostBack?

Earlier, in Chapter 2, we explored the view state mechanism that ASP.NET uses to remember the data in its controls. View state allows your user controls to remember their states across page loads. Every time an event that needs to be handled on the server is raised, the form in the page is submitted to the server—a process known as a **post back**. For example, when a button with a server-side Click event handler is clicked, a post back occurs so that the server-side code can respond to the Click event.

After such an event occurs, all the controls in the web form retain their values, but the Page_Load method is executed again regardless. In consequence, if you click the **Submit Request** button ten times, Page_Load will be executed ten times. If the data access code that fills the form with values is in Page_Load, the database will be queried ten times, even though the data that needs to be displayed on the page won't change!

It's here that IsPostBack comes into play. IsPostBack returns False if the web form is being loaded for the first time; it returns True if the page is being loaded, because the form has been posted back to the server.

Referring to IsPostBack

IsPostBack is actually a property of the Page class, but since our web form is a class that inherits from Page, we can refer to IsPostBack directly. If we wanted to, we could refer to this property as Me.IsPostBack in VB, or this.IsPostBack in C#.

Using the IsPostBack Property Appropriately

It's not always appropriate to use IsPostBack as we're using it here. We're loading the form with data only the first time the page is loaded, because we know that the data in the drop-down lists won't change in response to other changes in the form. In cases in which the data in the drop-down lists may change, it may be appropriate to access the database and refill the form with data every time the form is loaded. For example, we might want to take such action in a car search form in which, when users select a car manufacturer, their selection triggers a request to the server to load a list of all models of car made by that manufacturer.

Once it has been established that this is the first time the page has been loaded, the code continues in a pattern similar to the previous code samples. We retrieve the connection string from **Web.config**, create a new connection to the database, and set up our `SqlCommand` objects. In this page, we retrieve two lists—a list of help desk request categories and a list of subjects—so we'll need to execute two queries. These queries are stored in two `SqlCommand` objects: `categoryComm` and `subjectComm`.

Next, inside a `Try` block, we execute the commands and bind the data in our `SqlDataReader` to the existing controls. First, we execute `categoryComm` to retrieve a list of categories; then, we bind that list to `categoryList`:

Visual Basic   Dorknozzle\VB\04_HelpDesk.aspx.vb *(excerpt)*

```
reader = categoryComm.ExecuteReader()
categoryList.DataSource = reader
categoryList.DataValueField = "CategoryID"
categoryList.DataTextField = "Category"
categoryList.DataBind()
reader.Close()
```

C#   Dorknozzle\CS\04_HelpDesk.aspx.cs *(excerpt)*

```
reader = categoryComm.ExecuteReader();
categoryList.DataSource = reader;
categoryList.DataValueField = "CategoryID";
categoryList.DataTextField = "Category";
categoryList.DataBind();
reader.Close();
```

Note that not all controls handle their bindings in the same way. In this case, we want the `DropDownList` control to display the data from the `Category` column of the `HelpDeskCategories` table. The `DropDownList` control is cleverly designed, and it can also store an ID associated with each item in the list. This can be very helpful when we're performing database operations using the items selected from a Drop-

DownList, because the database operations are always carried out using the items' IDs.

The DataTextField property of the DropDownList needs to be set to the name of the column that provides the text to be displayed, and the DataValueField must be set to the name of the column that contains the ID. This allows us to pass the ID of the category or subject along to any part of the application when a user makes a selection from the drop-down lists.

When the page loads, all the categories and subjects will be loaded into their respective DropDownList controls, as shown previously in Figure 9.10.

Inserting Records

The code that inserts records from your application into a database isn't too different from what we've already seen. The main difference is that we need to retrieve data from the user input controls in the page, and use this data as the parameters to our INSERT query, rather than simply firing off a simple SELECT query. As we discussed earlier in this chapter, to execute an INSERT query, you'd need to use the ExecuteNonQuery method of the SqlCommand object, as INSERT queries don't return results.

When you're inserting user-entered data into the database, you need to be extra careful about validating that data, in case the users don't type whatever you expect them to (those pesky users always seem to find unimaginable ways to do things!).

A typical INSERT query is coded as follows:

```
Visual Basic

comm = New SqlCommand( _
  "INSERT INTO HelpDesk (Field1, Field2, …) " & _
  "VALUES (@Parameter1, @Parameter2, …)", conn)
```

Once the SqlCommand object has been created with a parameterized INSERT query, we simply pass in the necessary parameters, similarly to the process we followed for SELECT queries:

Visual Basic

```
comm.Parameters.Add("@Parameter1", System.Data.SqlDbType.Type1)
comm.Parameters("@Parameter1").Value = value1
comm.Parameters.Add("@Parameter2", System.Data.SqlDbType.Type2)
comm.Parameters("@Parameter2").Value = value2
```

Keep in mind that in C#, the syntax for accessing the `parameters` collection is slightly different:

C#

```
comm.Parameters.Add("@Parameter1", System.Data.SqlDbType.Type1);
comm.Parameters["@Parameter1"].Value = value1;
comm.Parameters.Add("@Parameter2", System.Data.SqlDbType.Type2);
comm.Parameters["@Parameter2"].Value = value2;
```

To demonstrate the process of inserting records into the database, let's finish the Help Desk page.

When employees visit the Help Desk page, they'll fill out the necessary information and click **Submit Request** to cause the information to be saved within the `HelpDesk` table. The `HelpDesk` table acts as a queue for IT personnel to review and respond to reported issues.

First, open **HelpDesk.aspx**, and add a label just below the page's heading:

Dorknozzle\VB\05_HelpDesk.aspx (excerpt)

```
⋮
<h1>Employee Help Desk Request</h1>
<asp:Label ID="dbErrorMessage" ForeColor="Red" runat="server" />
⋮
```

The form already contains numerous validation controls that display error messages if problems are found within the entered data. We're adding this `Label` control to display errors that arise when an exception is caught while the database query is executing. This is necessary because, although the validation controls prevent most of the errors that could occur, they can't guarantee that the database query will run flawlessly. For example, if the database server is rebooted, and we try to run a database query, we'll receive an error; this situation will persist until the database is up and running again. There could be other kinds of errors, too. An example of an error message is shown in Figure 9.11.

You already have a `Click` event handler for the **Submit Request** button in **HelpDesk.aspx**—we added it in the section called "Updating Dorknozzle" in Chapter 6, when we added validation controls to the page. Modify this method by adding code that inserts the user-submitted Help Desk Request into the database, as shown below:

Visual Basic	Dorknozzle\VB\06_HelpDesk.aspx.vb *(excerpt)*

```vb
Protected Sub submitButton_Click(ByVal sender As Object,
➥  ByVal e As System.EventArgs) Handles submitButton.Click
  If Page.IsValid Then
    Dim conn As SqlConnection
    Dim comm As SqlCommand
    Dim connectionString As String = _
        ConfigurationManager.ConnectionStrings( _
        "Dorknozzle").ConnectionString
    conn = New SqlConnection(connectionString)
    comm = New SqlCommand( _
        "INSERT INTO HelpDesk (EmployeeID, StationNumber, " & _
        "CategoryID, SubjectID, Description, StatusID) " & _
        "VALUES (@EmployeeID, @StationNumber, @CategoryID, " & _
        "@SubjectID, @Description, @StatusID)", conn)
    comm.Parameters.Add("@EmployeeID", System.Data.SqlDbType.Int)
    comm.Parameters("@EmployeeID").Value = 5
    comm.Parameters.Add("@StationNumber", _
        System.Data.SqlDbType.Int)
    comm.Parameters("@StationNumber").Value = stationTextBox.Text
    comm.Parameters.Add("@CategoryID", System.Data.SqlDbType.Int)
    comm.Parameters("@CategoryID").Value = _
        categoryList.SelectedItem.Value
    comm.Parameters.Add("@SubjectID", System.Data.SqlDbType.Int)
    comm.Parameters("@SubjectID").Value = _
        subjectList.SelectedItem.Value
    comm.Parameters.Add("@Description", _
        System.Data.SqlDbType.NVarChar, 50)
    comm.Parameters("@Description").Value = _
        descriptionTextBox.Text
    comm.Parameters.Add("@StatusID", System.Data.SqlDbType.Int)
    comm.Parameters("@StatusID").Value = 1
    Try
      conn.Open()
```

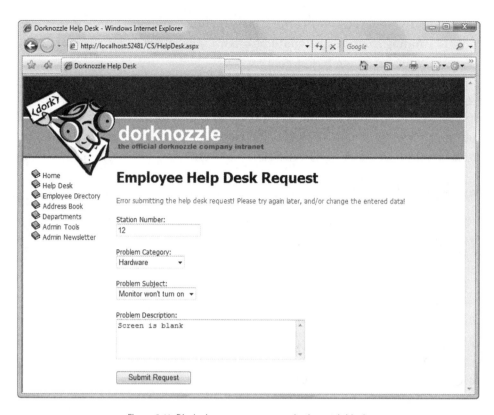

Figure 9.11. Displaying an error message in the catch block

```
      comm.ExecuteNonQuery()
      Response.Redirect("HelpDesk.aspx")
   Catch
     dbErrorMessage.Text = _
        "Error submitting the help desk request! Please " & _
        "try again later, and/or change the entered data!"
   Finally
     conn.Close()
   End Try
  End If
End Sub
```

| C# | Dorknozzle\CS\06_HelpDesk.aspx.cs *(excerpt)* |

```
protected void submitButton_Click(object sender, EventArgs e)
{
  if (Page.IsValid)
  {
```

```
SqlConnection conn;
SqlCommand comm;
string connectionString =
    ConfigurationManager.ConnectionStrings[
    "Dorknozzle"].ConnectionString;
conn = new SqlConnection(connectionString);
comm = new SqlCommand(
  "INSERT INTO HelpDesk (EmployeeID, StationNumber, " +
  "CategoryID, SubjectID, Description, StatusID) " +
  "VALUES (@EmployeeID, @StationNumber, @CategoryID, " +
  "@SubjectID, @Description, @StatusID)", conn);
comm.Parameters.Add("@EmployeeID", System.Data.SqlDbType.Int);
comm.Parameters["@EmployeeID"].Value = 5;
comm.Parameters.Add("@StationNumber",
    System.Data.SqlDbType.Int);
comm.Parameters["@StationNumber"].Value = stationTextBox.Text;
comm.Parameters.Add("@CategoryID", System.Data.SqlDbType.Int);
comm.Parameters["@CategoryID"].Value =
    categoryList.SelectedItem.Value;
comm.Parameters.Add("@SubjectID", System.Data.SqlDbType.Int);
comm.Parameters["@SubjectID"].Value =
    subjectList.SelectedItem.Value;
comm.Parameters.Add("@Description",
    System.Data.SqlDbType.NVarChar, 50);
comm.Parameters["@Description"].Value =
    descriptionTextBox.Text;
comm.Parameters.Add("@StatusID", System.Data.SqlDbType.Int);
comm.Parameters["@StatusID"].Value = 1;
try
{
  conn.Open();
  comm.ExecuteNonQuery();
  Response.Redirect("HelpDesk.aspx");
}
catch
{
  dbErrorMessage.Text =
      "Error submitting the help desk request! Please " +
      "try again later, and/or change the entered data!";
}
finally
{
  conn.Close();
```

```
      }
    }
  }
```

It may look intimidating, but most of this code is simply defining the SQL command parameter types and values that are to be inserted into the SQL statement.

 Make Sure You've Set the `Identity` Property!

Note that when we're inserting a new record into the `HelpDesk` table, we rely on the ID column, `RequestID`, to be generated automatically for us by the database. If we forget to set `RequestID` as an identity column, we'll receive an exception every time we try to add a new Help Desk Request!

You may have noticed the use of the `ExecuteNonQuery` method:

Visual Basic   Dorknozzle\VB\06_HelpDesk.aspx.vb *(excerpt)*

```
Try
  conn.Open()
  comm.ExecuteNonQuery()
  Response.Redirect("HelpDesk.aspx")
```

C#   Dorknozzle\CS\06_HelpDesk.aspx.cs *(excerpt)*

```
try
{
  conn.Open();
  comm.ExecuteNonQuery();
  Response.Redirect("HelpDesk.aspx");
}
```

As you know, we use this method when we're executing any SQL query that doesn't return a set of results, such as `INSERT`, `UPDATE`, and `DELETE` queries.

You'll remember that, in order to make the example simpler, we hard-coded the `EmployeeID` (to the value of 5), and the `Status` (to the value of 1). To make the application complete, you could add another drop-down list from which employees could select their names, and take the IDs from there. For now, just make sure that the `Employees` table has a record with an `EmployeeID` of 5, otherwise the query won't execute successfully.

The other potentially unfamiliar part of this code is the final line of the `Try` block, which uses `Response.Redirect`. This method should be quite familiar to developers who are experienced with ASP. `Response.Redirect` simply redirects the browser to another page.

In our Dorknozzle Help Desk request form script, we redirect the user back to the same web form. Why on earth would we want to do that? It's because of view state—if we didn't end our event handler this way, the same page would display in the browser, but ASP.NET would preserve all the values that the user had typed into the form fields. The user might not realize the form had even been submitted, and might submit the form repeatedly in his or her confusion. Redirecting the user in the way that's been outlined causes the browser to reload the page from scratch, clearing the form fields to indicate the completed submission.

Okay, save your work and run it in a browser. Now, we can enter help desk information, as shown in Figure 9.12, and click **Submit Request**.

Once we click **Submit Request**, the `Click` event is raised, the `submitButton_Click` method is called, all the parameters from the form are passed into the SQL statement, and the data is inserted into the `HelpDesk` table. To verify this, we can open the table in SQL Server Management Studio or Visual Web Developer; we'll see the view shown in Figure 9.13.

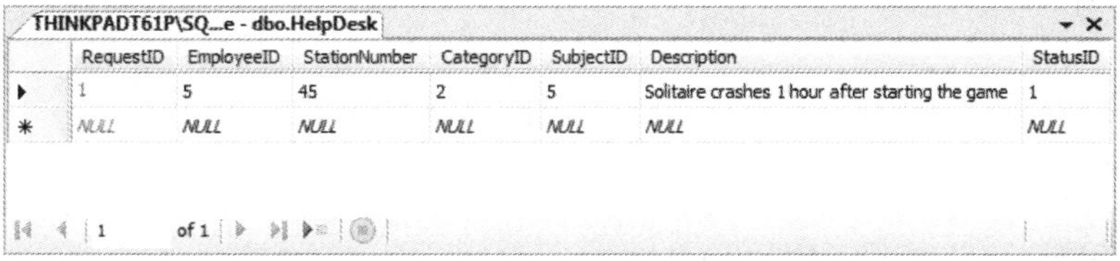

THINKPADT61P\SQ...e - dbo.HelpDesk							▾ ✕
RequestID	EmployeeID	StationNumber	CategoryID	SubjectID	Description	StatusID
▶ 1	5	45	2	5	Solitaire crashes 1 hour after starting the game	1
* NULL	NULL	NULL	NULL	NULL	NULL	NULL

`|◀ ◀ | 1    of 1 | ▶ ▶| ▶= | ⊛ |`

Figure 9.13. The new request appearing in the `HelpDesk` table

Updating Records

The major difference between inserting new database records and updating existing ones is that if a user wants to update a record, you'll usually want to display the information that already exists in the database table before allowing the user to update it. This gives the user a chance to review the data, make the necessary changes, and, finally, submit the updated values. Before we get ahead of ourselves, though, let's take a look at the code we'll use to update records within the database table:

Figure 9.12. Submitting the Help Desk Request form

Visual Basic

```
comm = New SqlCommand("UPDATE Table " & _
  "SET Field1=@Parameter1, Field2=@Parameter2, … " & _
  "WHERE UniqueField=@UniqueFieldParameter", conn)
comm.Parameters.Add("@Parameter1", System.Data.SqlDbType.Type1)
comm.Parameters("@Parameter1").Value = value1
comm.Parameters.Add("@Parameter2", System.Data.SqlDbType.Type2)
comm.Parameters("@Parameter2").Value = value2
```

C#

```
comm = new SqlCommand ("UPDATE Table " +
  "SET Field1=@Parameter1, Field2=@Parameter2, … " +
  "WHERE UniqueField=@UniqueFieldParameter", conn);
comm.Parameters.Add("@Parameter1", System.Data.SqlDbType.Type1);
comm.Parameters["@Parameter1"].Value = value1;
comm.Parameters.Add("@Parameter2", System.Data.SqlDbType.Type2);
comm.Parameters["@Parameter2"].Value = value2;
```

Once the `SqlCommand` object has been created using this UPDATE statement, we simply pass in the necessary parameters, as we did with the INSERT statement. The important thing to remember when you're updating records is that you must take care to perform the UPDATE on the correct record. To do this, you must include a WHERE clause that specifies the correct record using a value from a suitable unique column (usually the primary key), as shown.

Handle Updates with Care!

If you don't specify a WHERE clause when you're updating a table with new data, every record in the table will be updated with the new data, and (usually) there's no way to undo the action!

Let's put all this theory into practice as we build the Admin Tools page. The database doesn't contain a table that's dedicated to this page; however, we'll use the Admin Tools page as a centralized location for a number of tables associated with other pages, including the `Employees` and `Departments` tables. For instance, in this section, we'll allow an administrator to change the details of a specific employee.

Create a new web form named **AdminTools.aspx** in the same way you created the other web forms we've built so far in Dorknozzle. Use the **Dorknozzle.master** master page and a code-behind file. Then, add the following code to the content placeholder, and modify the page title as shown below:

Dorknozzle\VB\07_AdminTools.aspx *(excerpt)*

```
<%@ Page Language="VB" MasterPageFile="~/Dorknozzle.master"
    AutoEventWireup="true" CodeFile="AdminTools.aspx.vb"
    Inherits="AdminTools" title="Dorknozzle Admin Tools" %>
<asp:Content ID="Content1" ContentPlaceHolderID="head"
    Runat="Server">
</asp:Content>
<asp:Content ID="Content2"
    ContentPlaceHolderID="ContentPlaceHolder1" runat="Server">
  <h1>Admin Tools</h1>
  <p>
    <asp:Label ID="dbErrorLabel" ForeColor="Red" runat="server" />
    Select an employee to update:<br />
    <asp:DropDownList ID="employeesList" runat="server" />
    <asp:Button ID="selectButton" Text="Select" runat="server" />
  </p>
```

```
<p>
  <span class="widelabel">Name:</span>
  <asp:TextBox ID="nameTextBox" runat="server" />
  <br />
  <span class="widelabel">User Name:</span>
  <asp:TextBox ID="userNameTextBox" runat="server" />
  <br />
  <span class="widelabel">Address:</span>
  <asp:TextBox ID="addressTextBox" runat="server" />
  <br />
  <span class="widelabel">City:</span>
  <asp:TextBox ID="cityTextBox" runat="server" />
  <br />
  <span class="widelabel">State:</span>
  <asp:TextBox ID="stateTextBox" runat="server" />
  <br />
  <span class="widelabel">Zip:</span>
  <asp:TextBox ID="zipTextBox" runat="server" />
  <br />
  <span class="widelabel">Home Phone:</span>
  <asp:TextBox ID="homePhoneTextBox" runat="server" />
  <br />
  <span class="widelabel">Extension:</span>
  <asp:TextBox ID="extensionTextBox" runat="server" />
  <br />
  <span class="widelabel">Mobile Phone:</span>
  <asp:TextBox ID="mobilePhoneTextBox" runat="server" />
  <br />
</p>
<p>
  <asp:Button ID="updateButton" Text="Update Employee"
              Width="200" Enabled="False" runat="server" />
</p>
</asp:Content>
```

Now add the following CSS style rule to **Dorknozzle.css** (remember the **Dorknozzle.css** file is under the **Blue** theme, under the **App_Themes** folder):

Dorknozzle\VB\08_Dorknozzle.css *(excerpt)*

```css
.widelabel {
  display:-moz-inline-block;
  display:inline-block;
  width: 100px;
}
```

You can switch to **Design** view to ensure that you created your form correctly; it should look like the one shown in Figure 9.14.

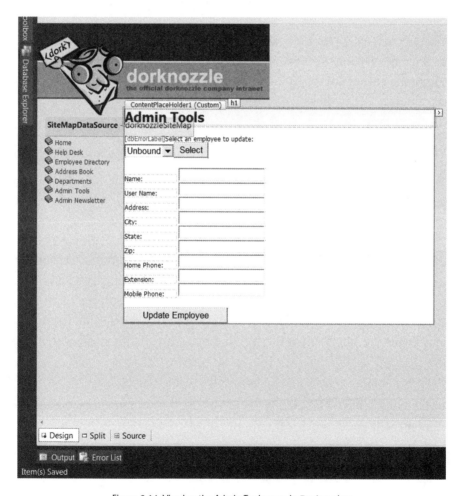

Figure 9.14. Viewing the Admin Tools page in **Design** view

We've added the following controls to our form:

employeesList

In order for administrators to select the record for the employee whose details they want to update, we'll first have to bind the Employees table to this DropDownList control.

selectButton

Once the users select the record for the aforementioned employee, they'll click this Button control. The Click event will be raised, and the Employee ID that's selected from employeesList will be passed to the web form—this will be used in an SqlCommand to retrieve the details for this employee.

nameTextBox, userNameTextBox, addressTextBox, cityTextBox, stateTextBox, zipTextBox, homePhoneTextBox, extensionTextBox, mobilePhoneTextBox

Within the selectButton's Click event handler, we'll add some code that binds user information to these TextBox controls.

updateButton

When the users make the desired changes to the TextBox controls listed above, they'll click this button to update the database.

dbErrorLabel

We use dbErrorLabel to display an error message if a database operation fails.

Our first task is to populate the employeesList control with the list of employees from our database. Use Visual Web Developer to generate the page's Page_Load event handler, add the following code. First, we need to import the required namespaces. If you're using VB these go right at the top of the file, but if you're using C# place the using statement at the end of the existing list of using statements:

```
Visual Basic                          Dorknozzle\VB\09_AdminTools.aspx.vb (excerpt)

Imports System.Data.SqlClient
Imports System.Configuration

Partial Class AdminTools
    Inherits System.Web.UI.Page
    ⋮
End Class
```

```
C#                                          Dorknozzle\CS\09_AdminTools.aspx.cs (excerpt)

using System;
⋮
using System.Data.SqlClient;

public partial class AdminTools : System.Web.UI.Page
{
⋮
}
```

Next, add the following to the Page_Load method:

```
Visual Basic                                Dorknozzle\VB\09_AdminTools.aspx.vb (excerpt

Protected Sub Page_Load(ByVal sender As Object,
➡  ByVal e As System.EventArgs) Handles Me.Load
  If Not IsPostBack Then
    LoadEmployeesList()
  End If
End Sub
```

```
C#                                          Dorknozzle\CS\09_AdminTools.aspx.cs (excerpt)

protected void Page_Load(object sender, EventArgs e)
{
  if (!IsPostBack)
  {
    LoadEmployeesList();
  }
}
```

You've probably noticed in this code that we've added a call to a separate subroutine called LoadEmployeeList. We'll place the code to populate the employeesList in this method. Later on, we'll need to reload the names in this list in case any of those names have been edited; we put this code into its own subroutine so that we don't need to repeat it. Our next task is to add the code for the LoadEmployeeList subroutine after the Page_Load method, but within the AdminTools partial class:

```
Partial Class AdminTools
    Inherits System.Web.UI.Page

  Protected Sub Page_Load(ByVal sender As Object,
  ➥   ByVal e As System.EventArgs) Handles Me.Load
    ⋮
  End Sub

  Private Sub LoadEmployeesList()
    Dim conn As SqlConnection
    Dim comm As SqlCommand
    Dim reader As SqlDataReader
    Dim connectionString As String = _
        ConfigurationManager.ConnectionStrings( _
        "Dorknozzle").ConnectionString
    conn = New SqlConnection(connectionString)
    comm = New SqlCommand( _
        "SELECT EmployeeID, Name FROM Employees", conn)
    Try
      conn.Open()
      reader = comm.ExecuteReader()
      employeesList.DataSource = reader
      employeesList.DataValueField = "EmployeeID"
      employeesList.DataTextField = "Name"
      employeesList.DataBind()
      reader.Close()
    Catch
      dbErrorLabel.Text = _
          "Error loading the list of employees!<br />"
    Finally
      conn.Close()
    End Try
    updateButton.Enabled = False
    nameTextBox.Text = ""
    userNameTextBox.Text = ""
    addressTextBox.Text = ""
    cityTextBox.Text = ""
    stateTextBox.Text = ""
    zipTextBox.Text = ""
    homePhoneTextBox.Text = ""
    extensionTextBox.Text = ""
```

```
      mobilePhoneTextBox.Text = ""
    End Sub
End Class
```

```csharp
public partial class AdminTools : System.Web.UI.Page
{
  protected void Page_Load(object sender, EventArgs e)
  {
    ⋮
  }
  private void LoadEmployeesList()
  {
    SqlConnection conn;
    SqlCommand comm;
    SqlDataReader reader;
    string connectionString =
        ConfigurationManager.ConnectionStrings[
        "Dorknozzle"].ConnectionString;
    conn = new SqlConnection(connectionString);
    comm = new SqlCommand(
        "SELECT EmployeeID, Name FROM Employees", conn);
    try
    {
      conn.Open();
      reader = comm.ExecuteReader();
      employeesList.DataSource = reader;
      employeesList.DataValueField = "EmployeeID";
      employeesList.DataTextField = "Name";
      employeesList.DataBind();
      reader.Close();
    }
    catch
    {
      dbErrorLabel.Text =
          "Error loading the list of employees!<br />";
    }
    finally
    {
      conn.Close();
    }
    updateButton.Enabled = false;
    nameTextBox.Text = "";
    userNameTextBox.Text = "";
```

```
    addressTextBox.Text = "";
    cityTextBox.Text = "";
    stateTextBox.Text = "";
    zipTextBox.Text = "";
    homePhoneTextBox.Text = "";
    extensionTextBox.Text = "";
    mobilePhoneTextBox.Text = "";
  }
}
```

In our `LoadEmployeeList` method, we use data binding to create the values in the drop-down list as we did in the section called "More Data Binding", and we clear all the form fields by setting their values to an empty string. You may have also noticed that we set the `Enabled` property of the `updateButton` to `False`. We have a good reason for doing this, as we'll explain shortly, when we come to write the code that updates the employee record in the database.

Load the page now, testing that the list of employees is bound to `employeeList`, and that the page displays as shown in Figure 9.15.

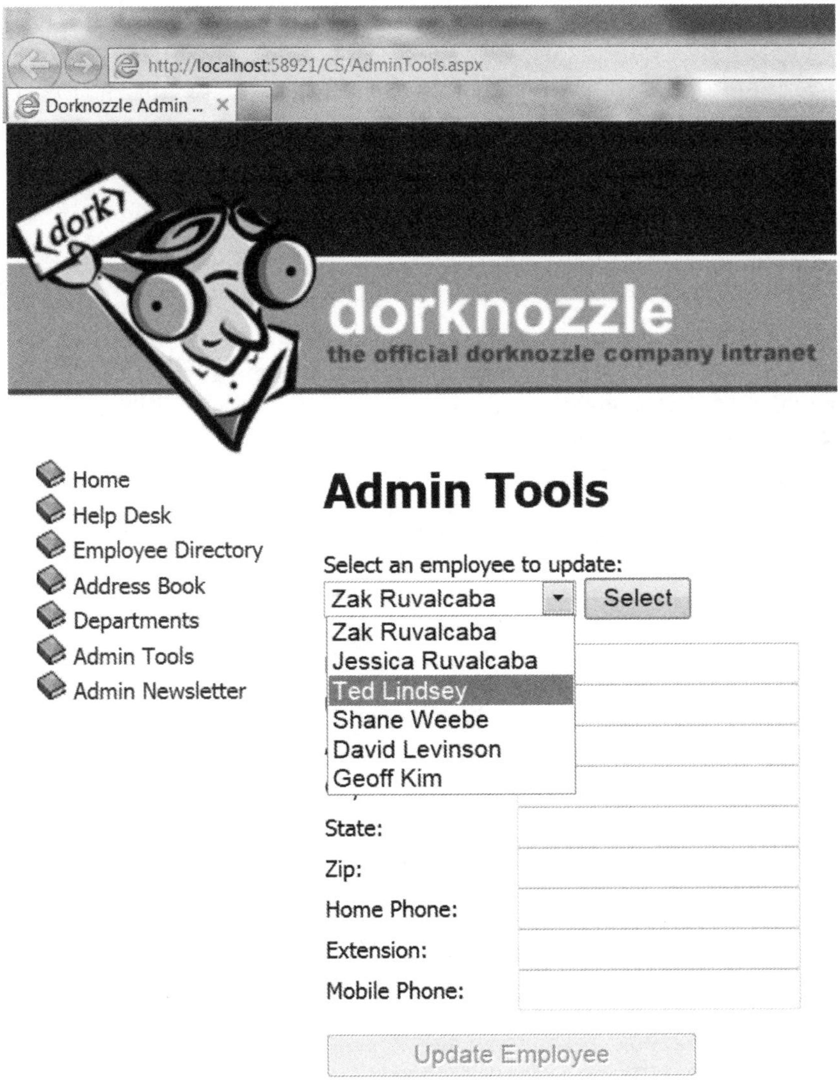

Figure 9.15. Displaying the list of employees in a drop-down list

As you can see, all the employees are listed within the drop-down menu. Again, the employees' names are shown because the Name field is bound to the DataTextField property of the DropDownList control. Similarly, the EmployeeID field is bound to the DataValueField property of the DropDownList control, ensuring that a selected employee's ID will be submitted as the value of the field.

We need to undertake two more tasks to complete this page's functionality. First, we need to handle the Click event of the Select button so that it will load the form with data about the chosen employee. Then, we'll need to handle the Click event of the Update button, to update the information for the selected employee. Let's start with the Select button. Double-click the button in Design view to have the Click event handler generated for you, and then insert the following code:

Visual Basic	Dorknozzle\VB\10_AdminTools.aspx.vb *(excerpt)*

```vb
Protected Sub selectButton_Click(ByVal sender As Object,
➥ ByVal e As System.EventArgs) Handles selectButton.Click
  Dim conn As SqlConnection
  Dim comm As SqlCommand
  Dim reader As SqlDataReader
  Dim connectionString As String = _
      ConfigurationManager.ConnectionStrings( _
      "Dorknozzle").ConnectionString
  conn = New SqlConnection(connectionString)
  comm = New SqlCommand( _
      "SELECT Name, Username, Address, City, State, Zip, " & _
      "HomePhone, Extension, MobilePhone FROM Employees " & _
      "WHERE EmployeeID = @EmployeeID", conn)
  comm.Parameters.Add("@EmployeeID", Data.SqlDbType.Int)
  comm.Parameters.Item("@EmployeeID").Value = _
      employeesList.SelectedItem.Value
  Try
    conn.Open()
    reader = comm.ExecuteReader()
    If reader.Read() Then
      nameTextBox.Text = reader.Item("Name").ToString()
      userNameTextBox.Text = reader.Item("Username").ToString()
      addressTextBox.Text = reader.Item("Address").ToString()
      cityTextBox.Text = reader.Item("City").ToString()
      stateTextBox.Text = reader.Item("State").ToString()
      zipTextBox.Text = reader.Item("Zip").ToString()
      homePhoneTextBox.Text = reader.Item("HomePhone").ToString()
      extensionTextBox.Text = reader.Item("Extension").ToString()
      mobilePhoneTextBox.Text = _
          reader.Item("MobilePhone").ToString()
    End If
    reader.Close()
    updateButton.Enabled = True
  Catch
    dbErrorLabel.Text = _
```

```
                "Error loading the employee details!<br />"
    Finally
      conn.Close()
    End Try
End Sub
```

```csharp
protected void selectButton_Click(object sender, EventArgs e)
{
  SqlConnection conn;
  SqlCommand comm;
  SqlDataReader reader;
  string connectionString =
      ConfigurationManager.ConnectionStrings[
      "Dorknozzle"].ConnectionString;
  conn = new SqlConnection(connectionString);
  comm = new SqlCommand(
      "SELECT Name, Username, Address, City, State, Zip, " +
      "HomePhone, Extension, MobilePhone FROM Employees " +
      "WHERE EmployeeID = @EmployeeID", conn);
  comm.Parameters.Add("@EmployeeID", System.Data.SqlDbType.Int);
  comm.Parameters["@EmployeeID"].Value =
      employeesList.SelectedItem.Value;
  try
  {
    conn.Open();
    reader = comm.ExecuteReader();
    if (reader.Read())
    {
      nameTextBox.Text = reader["Name"].ToString();
      userNameTextBox.Text = reader["Username"].ToString();
      addressTextBox.Text = reader["Address"].ToString();
      cityTextBox.Text = reader["City"].ToString();
      stateTextBox.Text = reader["State"].ToString();
      zipTextBox.Text = reader["Zip"].ToString();
      homePhoneTextBox.Text = reader["HomePhone"].ToString();
      extensionTextBox.Text = reader["Extension"].ToString();
      mobilePhoneTextBox.Text = reader["MobilePhone"].ToString();
    }
    reader.Close();
    updateButton.Enabled = true;
  }
  catch
  {
```

```
    dbErrorLabel.Text =
        "Error loading the employee details!<br />";
  }
  finally
  {
    conn.Close();
  }
}
```

In our **Select** button `Click` event code, we start by setting up our database connection and `command` objects, as well as the `command` parameter for the employee ID. Then, within the `Try` block we read the data from the `SqlDataReader` object to fill in the form fields. If you load the page, select an employee, and click the **Select** button, the form will be populated with the employee's details, as depicted in Figure 9.16.

The last thing we need to do is add code to handle the update interaction. You may have noticed that the `Button` control has an `Enabled` property, which is initially set to `False`. The reason for this is simple: you don't want your users updating information before they've selected an employee. You want them to use the **Update Employee** button only when data for an existing employee has been loaded into the `TextBox` controls. If you look again at the `selectButton_Click` method above, just before the `Catch` statement, you'll notice that we enable this button by setting its `Enabled` property to `True`, after binding the user data to the fields.

Now that these `TextBox` controls are populated and the **Update Employee** button is enabled, let's add some code to update an employee's details. Open **AdminTools.aspx** in **Design** view, and double-click the **Update Employee** button. Visual Web Developer will generate the signature for the `updateButton_Click` event handler automatically. Finally, let's add the code that handles the updating of the employee data:

Visual Basic   Dorknozzle\VB\11_AdminTools.aspx.vb *(excerpt)*

```
Protected Sub updateButton_Click(ByVal sender As Object,
➥  ByVal e As System.EventArgs) Handles updateButton.Click
  Dim conn As SqlConnection
  Dim comm As SqlCommand
  Dim connectionString As String = _
      ConfigurationManager.ConnectionStrings( _
      "Dorknozzle").ConnectionString
  conn = New SqlConnection(connectionString)
  comm = New SqlCommand( _
```

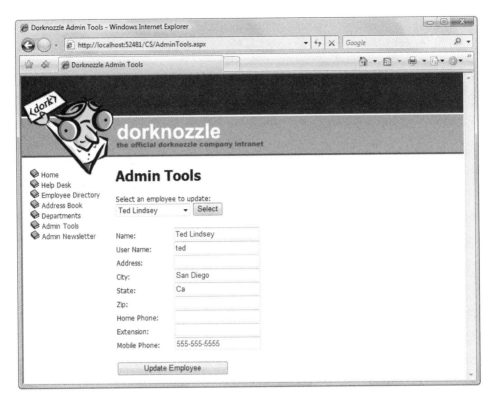

Figure 9.16. Displaying employee details in the update form

```
    "UPDATE Employees SET Name=@Name, Username=@Username, " & _
    "Address=@Address, City=@City, State=@State, Zip=@Zip," & _
    "HomePhone=@HomePhone, Extension=@Extension, " & _
    "MobilePhone=@MobilePhone " & _
    "WHERE EmployeeID=@EmployeeID", conn)
comm.Parameters.Add("@Name", System.Data.SqlDbType.NVarChar, 50)
comm.Parameters("@Name").Value = nameTextBox.Text
comm.Parameters.Add("@Username", _
    System.Data.SqlDbType.NVarChar, 50)
comm.Parameters("@Username").Value = userNameTextBox.Text
comm.Parameters.Add("@Address", _
    System.Data.SqlDbType.NVarChar, 50)
comm.Parameters("@Address").Value = addressTextBox.Text
comm.Parameters.Add("@City", _
    System.Data.SqlDbType.NVarChar, 50)
comm.Parameters("@City").Value = cityTextBox.Text
comm.Parameters.Add("@State", _
    System.Data.SqlDbType.NVarChar, 50)
comm.Parameters("@State").Value = stateTextBox.Text
```

```
  comm.Parameters.Add("@Zip", System.Data.SqlDbType.NVarChar, 50)
  comm.Parameters("@Zip").Value = zipTextBox.Text
  comm.Parameters.Add("@HomePhone", _
      System.Data.SqlDbType.NVarChar, 50)
  comm.Parameters("@HomePhone").Value = homePhoneTextBox.Text
  comm.Parameters.Add("@Extension", _
      System.Data.SqlDbType.NVarChar, 50)
  comm.Parameters("@Extension").Value = extensionTextBox.Text
  comm.Parameters.Add("@MobilePhone", _
      System.Data.SqlDbType.NVarChar, 50)
  comm.Parameters("@MobilePhone").Value = mobilePhoneTextBox.Text
  comm.Parameters.Add("@EmployeeID", System.Data.SqlDbType.Int)
  comm.Parameters("@EmployeeID").Value = _
      employeesList.SelectedItem.Value
  Try
    conn.Open()
    comm.ExecuteNonQuery()
  Catch
    dbErrorLabel.Text = _
        "Error updating the employee details!<br />"
  Finally
    conn.Close()
  End Try
  LoadEmployeesList()
End Sub
```

C#   Dorknozzle\CS\11_AdminTools.aspx.cs *(excerpt)*

```csharp
protected void updateButton_Click(object sender, EventArgs e)
{
  SqlConnection conn;
  SqlCommand comm;
  string connectionString =
    ConfigurationManager.ConnectionStrings[
    "Dorknozzle"].ConnectionString;
  conn = new SqlConnection(connectionString);
  comm = new SqlCommand(
      "UPDATE Employees SET Name=@Name, Username=@Username, " +
      "Address=@Address, City=@City, State=@State, Zip=@Zip, " +
      "HomePhone=@HomePhone, Extension=@Extension, " +
      "MobilePhone=@MobilePhone " +
      "WHERE EmployeeID=@EmployeeID", conn);
  comm.Parameters.Add("@Name",
      System.Data.SqlDbType.NVarChar,50);
  comm.Parameters["@Name"].Value = nameTextBox.Text;
```

```
comm.Parameters.Add("@Username",
    System.Data.SqlDbType.NVarChar, 50);
comm.Parameters["@Username"].Value = userNameTextBox.Text;
comm.Parameters.Add("@Address",
    System.Data.SqlDbType.NVarChar, 50);
comm.Parameters["@Address"].Value = addressTextBox.Text;
comm.Parameters.Add("@City",
    System.Data.SqlDbType.NVarChar, 50);
comm.Parameters["@City"].Value = cityTextBox.Text;
comm.Parameters.Add("@State",
    System.Data.SqlDbType.NVarChar, 50);
comm.Parameters["@State"].Value = stateTextBox.Text;
comm.Parameters.Add("@Zip",
    System.Data.SqlDbType.NVarChar, 50);
comm.Parameters["@Zip"].Value = zipTextBox.Text;
comm.Parameters.Add("@HomePhone",
    System.Data.SqlDbType.NVarChar, 50);
comm.Parameters["@HomePhone"].Value = homePhoneTextBox.Text;
comm.Parameters.Add("@Extension",
    System.Data.SqlDbType.NVarChar, 50);
comm.Parameters["@Extension"].Value = extensionTextBox.Text;
comm.Parameters.Add("@MobilePhone",
    System.Data.SqlDbType.NVarChar, 50);
comm.Parameters["@MobilePhone"].Value = mobilePhoneTextBox.Text;
comm.Parameters.Add("@EmployeeID", System.Data.SqlDbType.Int);
comm.Parameters["@EmployeeID"].Value =
    employeesList.SelectedItem.Value;
try
{
  conn.Open();
  comm.ExecuteNonQuery();
}
catch
{
  dbErrorLabel.Text =
      "Error updating the employee details!<br />";
}
finally
{
  conn.Close();
}
LoadEmployeesList();
}
```

As you can see, the only real differences between this and the help desk page are that here we're using an UPDATE query instead of an INSERT query, and we've had to let the user choose an entry from the database to update. We use that selection not only to populate the form fields with the existing database values, but to restrict our UPDATE query so that it only affects that one record.

You'll also notice that at the very end of this method, we call LoadEmployeesList to reload the list of employees, as the user may have changed the name of one of the employees. LoadEmployeesList also disables the **Update Employee** button and clears the contents of the page's TextBox controls. Once LoadEmployeesList has executed, the page is ready for the user to select another employee for updating.

As with all examples in this book, you can find this page's completed code in the code archive.

Deleting Records

Just as we can insert and update records within the database, so we can delete them. Again, most of the code for deleting records resembles that which we've already seen. The only major part that changes is the SQL statement within the command:

Visual Basic

```
comm = New SqlCommand("DELETE FROM Table " & _
    "WHERE UniqueField=@UniqueFieldParameter", conn)
```

C#

```
comm = new SqlCommand("DELETE FROM Table " +
    "WHERE UniqueField=@UniqueFieldParameter", conn)
```

Once we've created the DELETE query's SqlCommand object, we can simply pass in the necessary parameter:

Visual Basic

```
comm.Parameters.Add("@UniqueFieldParameter", _
    System.Data.SqlDbType.Type)
comm.Parameters("@UniqueFieldParameter").Value = UniqueValue
```

```
C#
```
```
comm.Parameters.Add("@UniqueFieldParameter",
    System.Data.SqlDbType.Type);
comm.Parameters["@UniqueFieldParameter"].Value = UniqueValue;
```

To demonstrate the process of deleting an item from a database table, we'll expand on the Admin Tools page. Since we're allowing administrators to update information within the Employees table, let's also give them the ability to delete an employee's record from the database. To do this, we'll place a new Button control for deleting the selected record next to our existing **Update Employee** button.

Start by adding the new control at the end of **AdminTools.aspx**:

```
                                    Dorknozzle\VB\12_AdminTools.aspx (excerpt)
```
```
<p>
  <asp:Button ID="updateButton" Text="Update Employee"
      Enabled="False" runat="server" />
  <asp:Button ID="deleteButton" Text="Delete Employee"
      Enabled="False" runat="server" />
</p>
```

Next, update the LoadEmployeesList method. Here, you need to ensure the **Delete Employee** button is disabled when the form loads, or after the **Update Employee** button has been clicked. Place it directly after the line in which you disable the updateButton:

```
Visual Basic                        Dorknozzle\VB\13_AdminTools.aspx.vb (excerpt)
```
```
updateButton.Enabled = False
deleteButton.Enabled = False
```

```
C#                                  Dorknozzle\CS\13_AdminTools.aspx.cs (excerpt)
```
```
updateButton.Enabled = false;
deleteButton.Enabled = false;
```

Perform the opposite action in the selectButton_Click method to enable the **Delete Employee** button when an employee is selected:

Visual Basic	Dorknozzle\VB\13_AdminTools.aspx.vb *(excerpt)*

```
updateButton.Enabled = True
deleteButton.Enabled = True
```

C#	Dorknozzle\CS\13_AdminTools.aspx.cs *(excerpt)*

```
updateButton.Enabled = true;
deleteButton.Enabled = true;
```

Next, write the code for its `Click` event handler. Remember that you can double-click the button in Visual Web Developer's Design view to have the signature generated for you:

Visual Basic	Dorknozzle\VB\14_AdminTools.aspx.vb *(excerpt)*

```
Protected Sub deleteButton_Click(ByVal sender As Object,
➥ ByVal e As System.EventArgs) Handles deleteButton.Click
  Dim conn As SqlConnection
  Dim comm As SqlCommand
  Dim connectionString As String = _
      ConfigurationManager.ConnectionStrings( _
      "Dorknozzle").ConnectionString
  conn = New SqlConnection(connectionString)
  comm = New SqlCommand( _
      "DELETE FROM Employees " & _
      "WHERE EmployeeID=@EmployeeID", conn)
  comm.Parameters.Add("@EmployeeID", System.Data.SqlDbType.Int)
  comm.Parameters("@EmployeeID").Value = _
      employeesList.SelectedItem.Value
  Try
    conn.Open()
    comm.ExecuteNonQuery()
  Catch
    dbErrorLabel.Text = "Error deleting employee!<br />"
  Finally
      conn.Close()
  End Try
  LoadEmployeesList()
End Sub
```

```
C#                              Dorknozzle\CS\14_AdminTools.aspx.cs (excerpt)

protected void deleteButton_Click(object sender, EventArgs e)
{
  SqlConnection conn;
  SqlCommand comm;
  string connectionString =
      ConfigurationManager.ConnectionStrings[
      "Dorknozzle"].ConnectionString;
  conn = new SqlConnection(connectionString);
  comm = new SqlCommand("DELETE FROM Employees " +
      "WHERE EmployeeID = @EmployeeID", conn);
  comm.Parameters.Add("@EmployeeID", System.Data.SqlDbType.Int);
  comm.Parameters["@EmployeeID"].Value =
      employeesList.SelectedItem.Value;
  try
  {
    conn.Open();
    comm.ExecuteNonQuery();
  }
  catch
  {
    dbErrorLabel.Text = "Error deleting employee!<br />";
  }
  finally
  {
    conn.Close();
  }
  LoadEmployeesList();
}
```

Save your work and test it within the browser. For testing purposes, feel free to add more records to the Employees table using SQL Server Management Studio Express; then delete them through the Dorknozzle application (if you do that, note you'll need to refresh the view of the Employees table manually in order to see the changes).

Using Stored Procedures

In the section called "Stored Procedures" in Chapter 8, you learned all about stored procedures. As far as ADO.NET is concerned, a stored procedure is much like a query that has parameters.

Let's assume you'd prefer to use a stored procedure to add help desk requests, rather than typing the SQL code in **HelpDesk.aspx.vb**, or **HelpDesk.aspx.cs**. Naturally, the first step would be to add a stored procedure to your `Dorknozzle` database. In SQL Server Management Studio Express, select the `Dorknozzle` database, go to **File > New > Database Engine Query**, or simply click the **New Query** button on the toolbar. Then, copy and paste the following code into the query window, and execute the query to create the stored procedure:

Dorknozzle\VB\15_InsertHelpDesk.sql *(excerpt)*

```
CREATE PROCEDURE InsertHelpDesk
(
  @EmployeeID int,
  @StationNumber int,
  @CategoryID int,
  @SubjectID int,
  @Description nvarchar(50),
  @StatusID int
)
AS
INSERT INTO HelpDesk (EmployeeID, StationNumber, CategoryID,
    SubjectID, Description, StatusID)
VALUES (@EmployeeID, @StationNumber, @CategoryID, @SubjectID,
    @Description, @StatusID)
```

To use this stored procedure, you'd need to modify the `submitButton_Click` method in **HelpDesk.aspx.vb** (or **HelpDesk.aspx.cs**). You can do this by replacing the line that creates a new `SqlCommand` object using an SQL query with one that does so using the name of the stored procedure, as shown here:

Visual Basic   HelpDesk.aspx.vb *(excerpt)*

```
Dim conn As SqlConnection
Dim comm As SqlCommand
Dim connectionString As String = _
    ConfigurationManager.ConnectionStrings( _
    "Dorknozzle").ConnectionString
conn = New SqlConnection(connectionString)
comm = New SqlCommand("InsertHelpDesk", conn)
comm.CommandType = System.Data.CommandType.StoredProcedure
: add command parameters
```

```
C#                                              HelpDesk.aspx.cs (excerpt)

SqlConnection conn;
SqlCommand comm;
string connectionString = ConfigurationManager.ConnectionStrings[
    "Dorknozzle"].ConnectionString;
conn = new SqlConnection(connectionString);
comm = new SqlCommand("InsertHelpDesk", conn);
comm.CommandType = System.Data.CommandType.StoredProcedure;
: add command parameters
```

You'll also notice that we've had to place an additional line of code to set the
CommandType property of the SqlCommand object to System.Data.CommandType.Stored-
Procedure, in order to specify that we are calling a stored procedure. If you now
load the Help Desk page, you'll see that it works just as it used to, but behind the
scenes, it's making use of a stored procedure. You can verify that this approach
works by adding a new Help Desk Request through the web form, and then opening
the HelpDesk table and checking for your new Help Desk Request.

That's it! As you can see, using stored procedures is very easy. Everything else is
the same as when working with a parameterized query.

Summary

In this chapter, you learned how to create simple web applications that interact
with databases. First, you learned about the various classes included with ADO.NET,
such as SqlConnection, SqlCommand, and SqlDataReader. Then, you learned how
to use these classes to create simple applications that query the database, insert records into a database, update records within a database, and delete records from a
database. You also learned important techniques for querying database data, including using parameters and control binding. Later in the chapter, you learned how to
use stored procedures.

The next chapter will expand on what we learned here, and introduce a new control
that's often used to display data from a database: the DataList.

Displaying Content Using Data Lists

Similar to the Repeater control, the DataList control allows you to bind and customize the presentation of database data. The fundamental difference is that while the Repeater requires building the template from scratch (allowing you to customize the generated HTML output in any way you like), the DataList control automatically generates a single-column HTML table for you, like the one shown below:

```
<table>
  <tr>
    <td>
      <p>Employee ID: 1</p>
      <p>Name: Zak Ruvalcaba</p>
      <p>Username: zak</p>
    </td>
  </tr>
  <tr>
    <td>
      <p>Employee ID: 2</p>
      <p>Name: Jessica Ruvalcaba</p>
      <p>Username: jessica</p>
    </td>
  </tr>
```

```
  <tr>
    <td>
      <p>Employee ID: 3</p>
      <p>Name: Ted Lindsey</p>
      <p>Username: ted</p>
    </td>
  </tr>
  ⋮
</table>
```

As you can see, `DataList` has, as the name implies, been designed to display lists of data; while it's less flexible than the `Repeater`, it contains more built-in functionality that can help make the implementation of certain features faster and easier. In the following pages, you'll learn:

- the basics of the `DataList` control
- how to handle `DataList` events
- how to edit `DataList` items
- how to handle the controls inside the `DataList` templates
- how to use Visual Web Developer to edit the `DataList`

Let's get started!

DataList Basics

To learn how to use the `DataList`, we'll update the Dorknozzle Employee Directory page to use a `DataList` control instead of a `Repeater` control. This update will be particularly easy to do because the Employee Directory already has a list-like format.

If you now open **EmployeeDirectory.aspx**, you'll see the `Repeater` control is used like this:

```
<asp:Repeater id="employeesRepeater" runat="server">
  <ItemTemplate>
    Employee ID:
    <strong><%#Eval("EmployeeID")%></strong><br />
    Name: <strong><%#Eval("Name")%></strong><br />
    Username: <strong><%#Eval("Username")%></strong>
  </ItemTemplate>
  <SeparatorTemplate>
```

```
    <hr />
  </SeparatorTemplate>
</asp:Repeater>
```

You can see the output of this code in Figure 9.9 in Chapter 9. Now, let's update the employee directory page to use a `DataList` instead of a `Repeater`. We can do this simply by replacing the `<asp:Repeater>` and `</asp:Repeater>` tags with the tags for a `DataList`:

Dorknozzle\VB\01_EmployeeDirectory.aspx *(excerpt)*

```
<asp:DataList id="employeesList" runat="server">
  <ItemTemplate>
    Employee ID:
    <strong><%#Eval("EmployeeID")%></strong><br />
    Name: <strong><%#Eval("Name")%></strong><br />
    Username: <strong><%#Eval("Username")%></strong>
  </ItemTemplate>
  <SeparatorTemplate>
    <hr />
  </SeparatorTemplate>
</asp:DataList>
```

As we've changed the ID for this control, we'll need to change the name of the control in the code-behind file as well. Locate the following lines of code and change `employeesRepeater` to `employeesList`, as shown here:

Visual Basic   Dorknozzle\VB\02_EmployeeDirectory.aspx.vb *(excerpt)*

```
    reader = comm.ExecuteReader()
    employeesList.DataSource = reader
    employeesList.DataBind()
    reader.Close()
```

C#   Dorknozzle\CS\02_EmployeeDirectory.aspx.cs *(excerpt*

```
    reader = comm.ExecuteReader();
    employeesList.DataSource = reader;
    employeesList.DataBind();
    reader.Close();
```

You can see that the changes required to use `DataList` instead of `Repeater` are minimal in this case. That's largely because the `Repeater` was displaying a basic list of data anyway.

As with the `Repeater` control, we can feed data into the `DataList` control by binding it to a data source. Both `Repeater` and `DataList` support the `ItemTemplate` and `SeparatorTemplate` templates, but in the case of the `DataList`, the templates specify the content that is to be inserted in the `td` elements of the table.

At the moment, the output appears very similar to the output we generated using the `Repeater`, as Figure 10.1 illustrates.

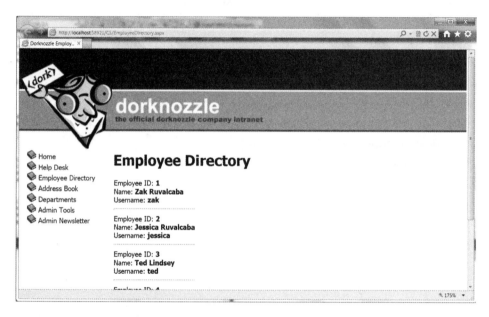

Figure 10.1. The Dorknozzle Employee Directory page

 Repeater versus DataList

As a rule of thumb, you'll use the `Repeater` when you need total control over the HTML output, and when you don't require features such as editing, sorting, formatting, or paging for the data you're displaying. Depending on the extra features needed, you can use either the `DataList` control (which is covered in this chapter), or the `GridView` or `DetailsView` controls (which you'll learn about in Chapter 12).

In this example, we've used the `ItemTemplate` of our `DataList`. The `DataList` offers a number of templates:

ItemTemplate

This template is replicated for each record that's read from the data source. The contents of the `ItemTemplate` are repeated for each record and placed inside td elements.

AlternatingItemTemplate

If this template is defined, it will be used instead of `ItemTemplate` to display every second element.

SelectedItemTemplate

This is used to display the selected list item. The `DataList` control doesn't automatically give the user a way to select an item in the list, but you can mark an item as selected by setting the `DataList` control's `SelectedIndex` property. Setting this property to 0 will mark the first item as selected; setting `SelectedIndex` to 1 will mark the second item as selected; and so on. Setting `SelectedIndex` to -1 deselects any selected item.

EditItemTemplate

Similar to `SelectedItemTemplate`, this template applies to an item that's being edited. We can set the item that's being edited using the `EditItemIndex` property of the `DataList`, which operates in the same way as the `SelectedIndex` property. Later on, you'll learn how to edit your `DataList` using the `EditItemTemplate`.

HeaderTemplate

This template specifies the content to be used for the list header.

FooterTemplate

This template defines the list footer.

SeparatorTemplate

This specifies the content to be inserted between two consecutive data items. The content will appear inside its own table cell.

Handling `DataList` Events

One problem you may encounter when working with container controls such as the `DataList` or the `Repeater` is that you can't access the controls inside their templates directly from your code. For example, consider this `ItemTemplate`, which contains a `Button` control:

```
<asp:DataList ID="employeesList" runat="server">
  <ItemTemplate>
    Employee ID: <strong><%#Eval("EmployeeID")%></strong>
    <asp:Button runat="server" ID="myButton" Text="Select" />
  </ItemTemplate>
</asp:DataList>
```

Although it may not be obvious at first glance, you can't access the `Button` easily through your code. So the following code would generate an error:

Visual Basic

```
' Don't try this at home
myButton.Enabled = False
```

It becomes even more complicated if you want to handle the `Button`'s `Click` event, because—you guessed it—you can't do so without jumping through some reasonably complicated hoops.

So, if we can't handle events raised by the buttons and links inside a template, how can we interact with the data in each template? To answer this question, we'll improve our employee directory by making a more basic view of the items, and adding a **View More** link that users can click in order to access more details about the employee. To keep it simple, for now, we'll hide only the employee ID from the standard view; we'll show it when the visitor clicks the **View More** link.

After we implement this feature, our list will appear as shown in Figure 10.2. You'll be able to view more details about any employee by clicking on the appropriate link.

Open **EmployeeDirectory.aspx**, and modify the `ItemTemplate` of the `DataList` as shown:

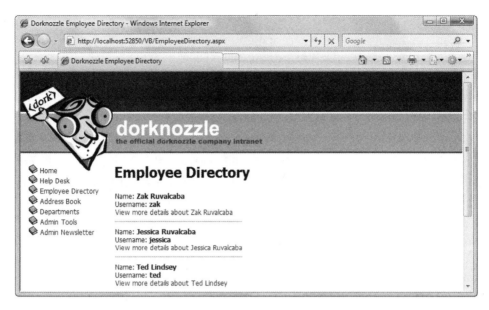

Figure 10.2. Hiding employee details

Visual Basic	Dorknozzle\VB\03_EmployeeDirectory.aspx *(excerpt)*

```
<asp:DataList id="employeesList" runat="server">
  <ItemTemplate>
    <asp:Literal ID="extraDetailsLiteral" runat="server"
        EnableViewState="false" />
    Name: <strong><%#Eval("Name")%></strong><br />
    Username: <strong><%#Eval("Username")%></strong><br />
    <asp:LinkButton ID="detailsButton" runat="server"
        Text=<%#"View more details about " & Eval("Name")%>
        CommandName="MoreDetailsPlease"
        CommandArgument=<%#Eval("EmployeeID")%> />
  </ItemTemplate>
  <SeparatorTemplate>
    <hr />
  </SeparatorTemplate>
</asp:DataList>
```

In C#, the string concatenation operator is + rather than &, so the Text property
definition of the Linkbutton should be as follows:

```
<asp:LinkButton ID="detailsButton" runat="server"
    Text=<%#"View more details about " + Eval("Name")%>
    CommandName="MoreDetailsPlease"
    CommandArgument=<%#Eval("EmployeeID")%> />
```

Here, we've added two controls. The first is a `Literal` control, which serves as a placeholder that we can replace with HTML later when the user clicks on the other control we've added—a `LinkButton`. Even though the `LinkButton` looks like a link, it really behaves like a button. When someone clicks this button, it generates an event that can be handled on the server side. If you prefer, you can change the `LinkButton` to a `Button`, and the functionality will remain identical. If you load the page now, it should appear as shown in Figure 10.2.

Now you have a button that's displayed for each employee in the list. In order to react to this `LinkButton` being clicked, you might think that you'd need to handle its `Click` event. Not this time! The button is located *inside* the `DataList`—it's part of its `ItemTemplate`—so it's not directly visible to your code. Additionally, when the code executes, the page will contain more instances of this button, so on the server side, you'll need a way to know which of them was clicked!

Luckily, ASP.NET provides an ingenious means of handling this scenario. When ever a button inside a `DataList` generates a `Click` event, the `DataList` generates itself an `ItemCommand` event. The `DataList` control *is* accessible in your code, so you can handle its `ItemCommand` event, whose arguments will give us information about which control was clicked.

Within the `ItemCommand` event handler, we can retrieve the data contained in the `LinkButton`'s `CommandName` and `CommandArgument` properties. We use these properties to pass the employee ID to the `ItemCommand` event handler, which can use the ID to get more data about that particular employee.

Take another look at the button definition from the `DataList`'s `ItemTemplate`:

| Visual Basic | Dorknozzle\VB\03_EmployeeDirectory.aspx *(excerpt)* |

```
<asp:LinkButton ID="detailsButton" runat="server"
    Text=<%#"View more details about " & Eval("Name")%>
    CommandName="MoreDetailsPlease"
    CommandArgument=<%#Eval("EmployeeID")%> />
```

Here, you can see that we're using `CommandArgument` to save the ID of the employee record with which it's associated. We're able to read this data from the `DataList`'s `ItemCommand` event handler.

Let's use Visual Web Developer to generate the `ItemCommand` event handler. Open **EmployeeDirectory.aspx** in **Design** view, select the `DataList`, and hit **F4** to open its **Properties** window. There, click the yellow lightning symbol to open the list of events, and double-click the `ItemCommand` event in that list. Visual Web Developer will generate an empty event handler, and take you to the event handler's code in the code-behind file.

If you were to open the `DataList`'s properties again, you'd see the event handler name appearing next to the event name, as depicted in Figure 10.3.

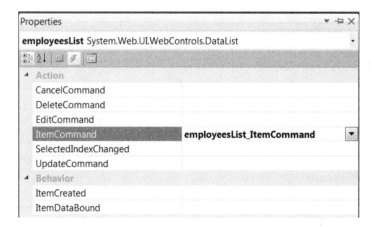

Figure 10.3. The `ItemCommand` event in the **Properties** window

If you're using C#, you will also notice that as well as the generation of the empty event handler in the code-behind file, the `onitemcommand` property has been added to the `DataList` element, as shown here:

```
C#

<asp:DataList id="employeesList" runat="server"
    onitemcommand="employeesList_ItemCommand">
    ⋮
</asp:DataList>
```

Modify the code in employeesList_ItemCommand like so:

```
Visual Basic                    Dorknozzle\VB\04_EmployeeDirectory.aspx.vb (excerpt)

Protected Sub employeesList_ItemCommand(ByVal source As Object,
➥  ByVal e As System.Web.UI.WebControls.DataListCommandEventArgs)
➥  Handles employeesList.ItemCommand
  If e.CommandName = "MoreDetailsPlease" Then
    Dim li As Literal
    li = e.Item.FindControl("extraDetailsLiteral")
    li.Text = "Employee ID: <strong>" & e.CommandArgument & _
        "</strong><br />"
  End If
End Sub
```

```
C#                              Dorknozzle\CS\04_EmployeeDirectory.aspx.cs (excerpt)

protected void employeesList_ItemCommand(object source,
    DataListCommandEventArgs e)
{
  if (e.CommandName == "MoreDetailsPlease")
  {
    Literal li;
    li = (Literal)e.Item.FindControl("extraDetailsLiteral");
    li.Text = "Employee ID: <strong>" + e.CommandArgument +
        "</strong><br />";
  }
}
```

Our code is almost ready to execute, but we should make one more minor tweak before we execute this page. Currently, the Page_Load event will cause the DataList to bind data on every page load. Not only is this bad for overall performance of our application, it is best practice to only data bind when there is not a PostBack event. Doing so may otherwise overwrite any changes the user requests on the page. We'll also move the data binding code into its own function, so that we can make use of it later. Modify the code as shown here, moving the current contents of `Page_Load` into a new method called `BindList`:

Visual Basic	Dorknozzle\VB\05_EmployeeDirectory.aspx.vb *(excerpt)*

```vb
Protected Sub Page_Load(ByVal sender As Object, _
    ByVal e As System.EventArgs) Handles Me.Load
  If Not IsPostBack Then
    BindList()
  End If
End Sub
Protected Sub BindList()
  Dim conn As SqlConnection
  Dim comm As SqlCommand
  Dim reader As SqlDataReader
  ⋮
End Sub
```

C#	Dorknozzle\CS\05_EmployeeDirectory.aspx.cs *(excerpt)*

```csharp
protected void Page_Load(object sender, EventArgs e)
{
    if (!IsPostBack)
    {
      BindList();
    }
}
protected void BindList()
{
  SqlConnection conn;
  SqlCommand comm;
  SqlDataReader reader;
  ⋮
}
```

Execute the project and click the **View more details** links to see the employee ID, as shown in Figure 10.4.

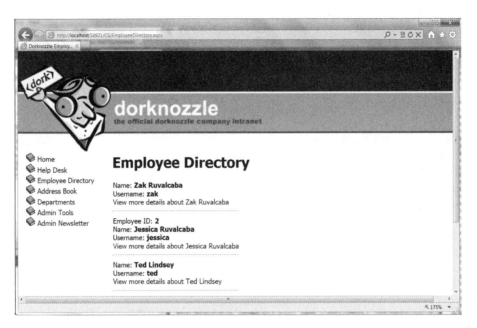

Figure 10.4. The Employee Directory showing employee IDs

The code in `employeesList_ItemCommand` shows how you can work with controls inside a `DataList` template, and how to handle their events. We determine which control was clicked by checking the value of `e.CommandName` in the event handler; it will be populated with the value of the `CommandName` property of the control that was clicked. Since our `LinkButton` has the `CommandName` value `MoreDetailsPlease`, we check for this value in the `ItemCommand` event handler, as shown below:

Visual Basic	Dorknozzle\VB\05_EmployeeDirectory.aspx.vb *(excerpt)*

```
If e.CommandName = "MoreDetailsPlease" Then
```

C#	Dorknozzle\CS\05_EmployeeDirectory.aspx.cs *(excerpt)*

```
if (e.CommandName == "MoreDetailsPlease")
{
```

Once we know the **View more details** button was clicked, we want to use the `extra-DetailsLiteral` control from our template to display the employee ID. But, given that this control is inside our template, how can we access it through code?

To use a control inside a `DataList`, we use the `FindControl` method of the object `e.Item`. Here, `e.Item` refers to the template that contains the control; the `FindControl` method will return a reference to any control within the template that has the supplied ID. So, in order to obtain a reference to the control with the ID `extraDetails-Literal`, we use `FindControl` like this:

Visual Basic	Dorknozzle\VB\05_EmployeeDirectory.aspx.vb *(excerpt)*

```vb
Dim li As Literal
li = e.Item.FindControl("extraDetailsLiteral")
```

Note that `FindControl` returns a generic `Control` object. If you're using VB, the returned `Control` is automatically converted to a `Literal` when you assign it to an object of type `Literal`. In C#, we need an explicit cast, or conversion, as shown here:

C#	Dorknozzle\CS\05_EmployeeDirectory.aspx.cs *(excerpt)*

```csharp
Literal li;
li = (Literal)e.Item.FindControl("extraDetailsLiteral");
```

Finally, once we have access to the `Literal` control in a local variable, setting its contents is a piece of cake:

Visual Basic	Dorknozzle\VB\05_EmployeeDirectory.aspx.vb *(excerpt)*

```vb
li.Text = "Employee ID: <strong>" & e.CommandArgument & _
    "</strong><br />"
```

C#	Dorknozzle\CS\05_EmployeeDirectory.aspx.cs *(excerpt)*

```csharp
li.Text = "Employee ID: <strong>" + e.CommandArgument +
    "</strong><br />";
```

Disabling View State

If you take a look at the definition of the `extraDetailsLiteral` control in **EmployeeDirectory.aspx**, you'll see that we set its `EnableViewState` property to `False`:

Dorknozzle\VB\03_EmployeeDirectory.aspx (excerpt)

```
<asp:Literal ID="extraDetailsLiteral" runat="server"
    EnableViewState="false" />
```

When this property is `False`, its contents aren't persisted during postback events. In our case, once the visitor clicks another **View more details** button, all the instances of that `Literal` control lose their values. This way, at any given moment, no more than one employee's ID will be displayed. If you change `EnableViewState` to `True` (the default value), and then click the **View more details** button, you'll see that all employee IDs remain in the form, as they're persisted by the view state mechanism.

Editing `DataList` Items and Using Templates

Continuing our journey into the world of the `DataList`, let's learn a little more about its templates, and see how you can use the `EditItemTemplate` to edit its contents. Our goal here is to allow users to change the name or username of any employee using this form.

Start by adding another button to the `ItemTemplate` of the `DataList`. This button will read **Edit employee *Employee Name*** and, when clicked, it will cause the item of which it's a part to become editable. It goes at the end of the `ItemTemplate` element:

Visual Basic　　　　　　　*Dorknozzle\VB\06_EmployeeDirectory.aspx (excerpt)*

```
<ItemTemplate>
  ⋮
  <br />
  <asp:LinkButton ID="editButton" runat="server"
      Text=<%#"Edit employee " & Eval("Name")%>
```

```
    CommandName="EditItem"
    CommandArgument=<%#Eval("EmployeeID")%> />
</ItemTemplate>
```

If you are using C#, don't forget to replace the & with a + in the Text property value.

When an **Edit employee** button is clicked, we will make the item enter edit mode. When one of the DataList items is in edit mode, the EditItemTemplate template of the DataList is used to generate the contents of that item. All the other items are generated by the ItemTemplate, as usual.

Modify **EmployeeDirectory.aspx** by adding the EditItemTemplate to the DataList. The EditItemTemplate contains TextBox controls into which the user can enter the employee's name and username, and two buttons: **Update Item** and **Cancel Editing**, whose names are self-explanatory:

Dorknozzle\VB\07_EmployeeDirectory.aspx *(excerpt)*

```
<EditItemTemplate>
  Name: <asp:TextBox ID="nameTextBox" runat="server"
      Text=<%#Eval("Name")%> /><br />
  Username: <asp:TextBox ID="usernameTextBox" runat="server"
      Text=<%#Eval("Username")%> /><br />
  <asp:LinkButton ID="updateButton" runat="server"
      Text="Update Item" CommandName="UpdateItem"
      CommandArgument=<%#Eval("EmployeeID")%> />
  or
  <asp:LinkButton ID="cancelButton" runat="server"
      Text="Cancel Editing" CommandName="CancelEditing"
      CommandArgument=<%#Eval("EmployeeID")%> />
</EditItemTemplate>
```

Finally, before you can see your new template, we need to handle the **Edit employee** button. Again, when that button is clicked, the DataList's ItemCommand event is fired. This time, the CommandName of the new button is EditItem, and when we discover that this button was clicked, we'll put the item into edit mode. To put a DataList item into edit mode, we set its EditItemIndex to the index of the item, and then bind the DataList to its data source again to refresh its contents. Add this code to the file:

```
Visual Basic                    Dorknozzle\VB\08_EmployeeDirectory.aspx.vb (excerpt)

Protected Sub employeesList_ItemCommand(ByVal source As Object,
➥   ByVal e As System.Web.UI.WebControls.DataListCommandEventArgs)
➥   Handles employeesList.ItemCommand
  If e.CommandName = "MoreDetailsPlease" Then
    Dim li As Literal
    li = e.Item.FindControl("extraDetailsLiteral")
    li.Text = "Employee ID: <strong>" & e.CommandArgument & _
        "</strong><br />"
  ElseIf e.CommandName = "EditItem" Then
    employeesList.EditItemIndex = e.Item.ItemIndex
    BindList()
  End If
End Sub
```

```
C#                              Dorknozzle\CS\08_EmployeeDirectory.aspx.cs (excerpt)

protected void employeesList_ItemCommand(object source,
    DataListCommandEventArgs e)
{
  if (e.CommandName == "MoreDetailsPlease")
  {
    Literal li;
    li = (Literal)e.Item.FindControl("extraDetailsLiteral");
    li.Text = "Employee ID: <strong>" + e.CommandArgument +
        "</strong><br />";
  }
  else if (e.CommandName == "EditItem")
  {
    employeesList.EditItemIndex = e.Item.ItemIndex;
    BindList();
  }
}
```

Execute the project now, load the employee directory, and enter one of your items
into edit mode, as shown in Figure 10.5.

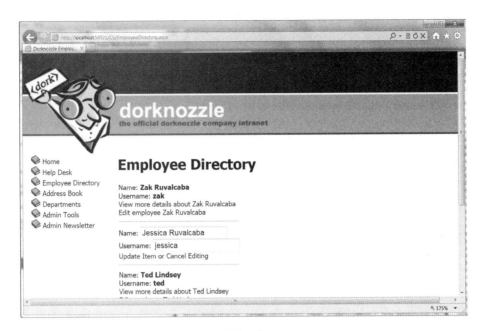

Figure 10.5. Editing the `DataList`

We need to implement functionality for two more buttons: **Update Item** and **Cancel Editing**. We'll take them one at a time, starting with **Cancel Editing**, which is easier to handle. Modify `employeesList_ItemCommand` like this:

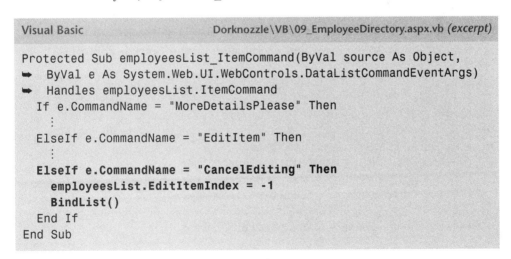

Visual Basic	Dorknozzle\VB\09_EmployeeDirectory.aspx.vb *(excerpt)*

```vb
Protected Sub employeesList_ItemCommand(ByVal source As Object,
➥  ByVal e As System.Web.UI.WebControls.DataListCommandEventArgs)
➥  Handles employeesList.ItemCommand
  If e.CommandName = "MoreDetailsPlease" Then
    ⋮
  ElseIf e.CommandName = "EditItem" Then
    ⋮
  ElseIf e.CommandName = "CancelEditing" Then
    employeesList.EditItemIndex = -1
    BindList()
  End If
End Sub
```

```
C#                                    Dorknozzle\CS\09_EmployeeDirectory.aspx.cs (excerpt)

protected void employeesList_ItemCommand(object source,
    DataListCommandEventArgs e)
{
  if (e.CommandName == "MoreDetailsPlease")
  {
    ⋮
  }
  else if (e.CommandName == "EditItem")
  {
    ⋮
  }
  else if (e.CommandName == "CancelEditing")
  {
    employeesList.EditItemIndex = -1;
    BindList();
  }
}
```

Execute your project again and check that your new button works. As you can see, exiting edit mode is really simple. You merely need to set the EditItemIndex property of the DataList to -1, and then refresh the DataList's contents.

Let's deal with the task of updating the record now. We read the ID of the employee whose details are being edited from the button's CommandArgument property, and we read that person's new name and username from the TextBox control:

```
Visual Basic                          Dorknozzle\VB\10_EmployeeDirectory.aspx.vb (excerpt)

Protected Sub employeesList_ItemCommand(ByVal source As Object,
➥   ByVal e As System.Web.UI.WebControls.DataListCommandEventArgs)
➥   Handles employeesList.ItemCommand
  If e.CommandName = "MoreDetailsPlease" Then
    ⋮
  ElseIf e.CommandName = "EditItem" Then
    ⋮
  ElseIf e.CommandName = "CancelEditing" Then
    ⋮
  ElseIf e.CommandName = "UpdateItem" Then
    Dim employeeId As Integer = e.CommandArgument
    Dim nameTextBox As TextBox = _
        e.Item.FindControl("nameTextBox")
    Dim newName As String = nameTextBox.Text
```

```
   Dim usernameTextBox As TextBox = _
       e.Item.FindControl("usernameTextBox")
   Dim newUsername As String = usernameTextBox.Text
   UpdateItem(employeeId, newName, newUsername)
   employeesList.EditItemIndex = -1
   BindList()
  End If
End Sub
```

C#   Dorknozzle\CS\10_EmployeeDirectory.aspx.cs *(excerpt)*

```csharp
protected void employeesList_ItemCommand(object source,
    DataListCommandEventArgs e)
{
  if (e.CommandName == "MoreDetailsPlease")
  {
    ⋮
  }
  else if (e.CommandName == "EditItem")
  {
    ⋮
  }
  else if (e.CommandName == "CancelEditing")
  {
    ⋮
  }
  else if (e.CommandName == "UpdateItem")
  {
    int employeeId = Convert.ToInt32(e.CommandArgument);
    TextBox nameTextBox =
        (TextBox)e.Item.FindControl("nameTextBox");
    string newName = nameTextBox.Text;
    TextBox usernameTextBox =
        (TextBox)e.Item.FindControl("usernameTextBox");
    string newUsername = usernameTextBox.Text;
    UpdateItem(employeeId, newName, newUsername);
    employeesList.EditItemIndex = -1;
    BindList();
  }
}
```

The techniques used in the above code are ones we have used earlier, but be sure to read the code carefully to ensure that you understand how it works. If you are using C#, you may have noticed that once again we need an explicit case for the

`TextBox` objects, whereas VB automatically converts the control to the proper type. This is also true of the `employeeId` variable; in VB this is automatically converted to an integer, but in C# we have to perform the conversion explicitly using the `Convert.ToInt32` method.

As you can see, we make a call to a mysterious method named `UpdateItem`. This method is used to perform the actual update. We've created it as a separate method to make the code easier to manage. Add this code to your code-behind file:

Visual Basic   Dorknozzle\VB\11_EmployeeDirectory.aspx.vb *(excerpt)*

```
Protected Sub UpdateItem(ByVal employeeId As Integer,
➥   ByVal newName As String, ByVal newUsername As String)
  Dim conn As SqlConnection
  Dim comm As SqlCommand
  Dim connectionString As String = _
      ConfigurationManager.ConnectionStrings( _
      "Dorknozzle").ConnectionString
  conn = New SqlConnection(connectionString)
  comm = New SqlCommand("UpdateEmployee", conn)
  comm.CommandType = System.Data.CommandType.StoredProcedure
  comm.Parameters.Add("@EmployeeID", Data.SqlDbType.Int)
  comm.Parameters("@EmployeeID").Value = employeeId
  comm.Parameters.Add("@NewName", Data.SqlDbType.NVarChar, 50)
  comm.Parameters("@NewName").Value = newName
  comm.Parameters.Add("@NewUsername", Data.SqlDbType.NVarChar, 50)
  comm.Parameters("@NewUsername").Value = newUsername
  Try
    conn.Open()
    comm.ExecuteNonQuery()
  Finally
    conn.Close()
  End Try
End Sub
```

C#   Dorknozzle\CS\11_EmployeeDirectory.aspx.cs *(excerpt)*

```
protected void UpdateItem(int employeeId, string newName,
    string newUsername)
{
  SqlConnection conn;
  SqlCommand comm;
  string connectionString =
      ConfigurationManager.ConnectionStrings[
```

```
      "Dorknozzle"].ConnectionString;
  conn = new SqlConnection(connectionString);
  comm = new SqlCommand("UpdateEmployee", conn);
  comm.CommandType = System.Data.CommandType.StoredProcedure;
  comm.Parameters.Add("@EmployeeID", SqlDbType.Int);
  comm.Parameters["@EmployeeID"].Value = employeeId;
  comm.Parameters.Add("@NewName", SqlDbType.NVarChar, 50);
  comm.Parameters["@NewName"].Value = newName;
  comm.Parameters.Add("@NewUsername", SqlDbType.NVarChar, 50);
  comm.Parameters["@NewUsername"].Value = newUsername;
  try
  {
    conn.Open();
    comm.ExecuteNonQuery();
  }
  finally
  {
    conn.Close();
  }
}
```

Once the parameters are prepared, the `UpdateItem` method calls the `UpdateEmployee` stored procedure, which performs the database operation.

Next, let's add the `UpdateEmployee` stored procedure to our database by executing the following script using SQL Server Management Studio:

Dorknozzle\VB\12_UpdateEmployee.sql *(excerpt)*

```
CREATE PROCEDURE UpdateEmployee
(
  @EmployeeID Int,
  @NewName nvarchar(50),
  @NewUsername nvarchar(50)
)
AS
UPDATE Employees
SET Name = @NewName, Username = @NewUsername
WHERE EmployeeID = @EmployeeID
```

Finally, execute the project again, load the Employee Directory page, and enter one of the employees into edit mode. You should see a display like the one shown in Figure 10.6.

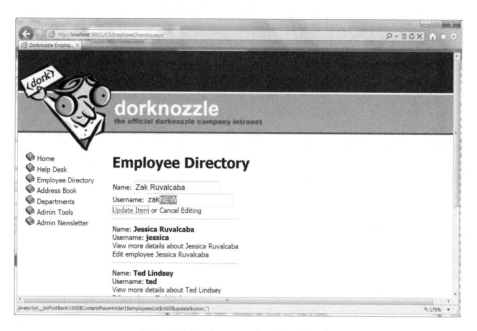

Figure 10.6. Viewing an employee in edit mode

Change the name or username, and click **Update Item** to see the listed data change. In Figure 10.7, you can see that I've changed Zak's username to zakNew.ch

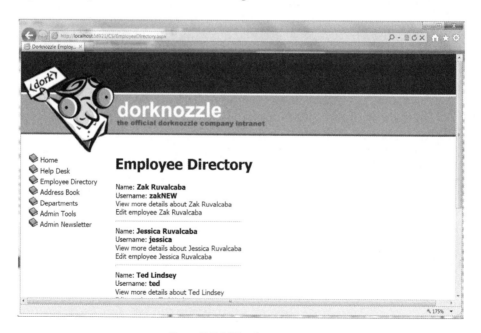

Figure 10.7. Editing the username

DataList and Visual Web Developer

Just like some of the more complex web server controls, DataLists offer a number of design-time features that are tightly integrated within Visual Web Developer. One of these slick features is the **smart tag**, which appears as a little arrow button in the upper-right part of the control when the cursor is hovered over the control in Design view.

You'll be working with these cool features in coming chapters, but we can't finish a chapter on DataLists without making ourselves aware of them. If you open **EmployeeDirectory.aspx** in Design view and click the smart tag, you'll see the menu depicted in Figure 10.8.

You can use this menu to apply predefined styles to your grid, choose a data source control (you'll learn more about these in the following chapters), or edit the grid's templates.

If you click **Edit Templates**, you can build the DataList's templates visually, shown in Figure 10.9.

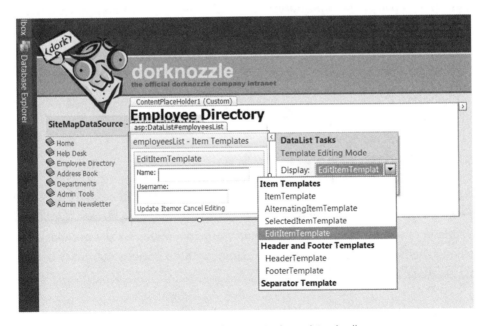

Figure 10.9. Building the DataList's templates visually

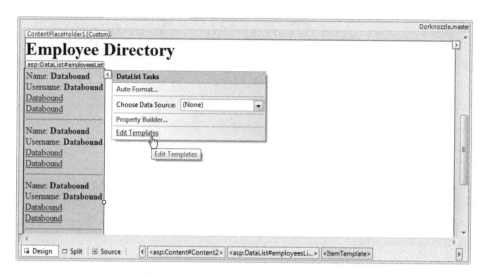

Figure 10.8. The smart tag options of `DataList`

Advanced users will probably want to code by hand, but the visual designer is still available. We will continue the rest of the way with coding manually so that we can gain a better understanding of the technology.

Choose the **Property Builder** from the smart tag's menu, and a window will display that lets us set various properties of a `DataList`. We can access the same settings through the **Properties** window, but the `DataList` gives us another way to set these properties.

The **Choose Data Source** item in the smart tag's menu lets us choose a data source control for our list. You'll learn a lot more about this in Chapter 12.

Styling the `DataList`

The **Auto Format** item in the smart tag menu is probably the most interesting. We left this discussion until the end of the chapter to give you the chance to play with it a little beforehand. When you select **Auto Format**, a dialog with a number of predefined schemes will appear; you can customize these options manually to suit your tastes, as Figure 10.10 illustrates.

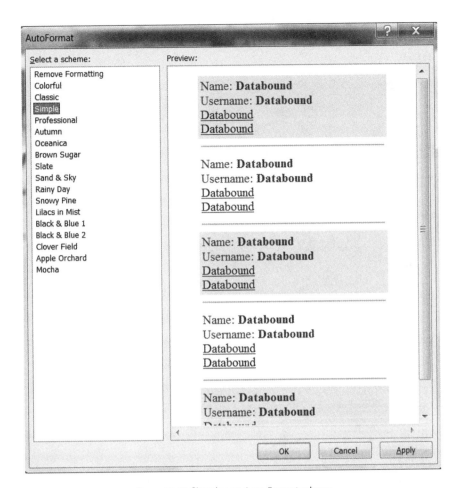

Figure 10.10. Choosing an **Auto Format** scheme

If you choose the **Simple** style, and then remove the `SeparatorTemplate` from your `DataList`, your Employee Directory page will look like the one shown in Figure 10.11.

So, what happened behind the scenes? If you look at the `DataList` definition in **EmployeeDirectory.aspx**, you'll see it contains a few new lines that Visual Web Developer generated for us after we chose the style:

```
<asp:DataList>
  ⋮
  <FooterStyle BackColor="#1C5E55" Font-Bold="True"
      ForeColor="White" />
  <SelectedItemStyle BackColor="#C5BBAF" Font-Bold="True"
```

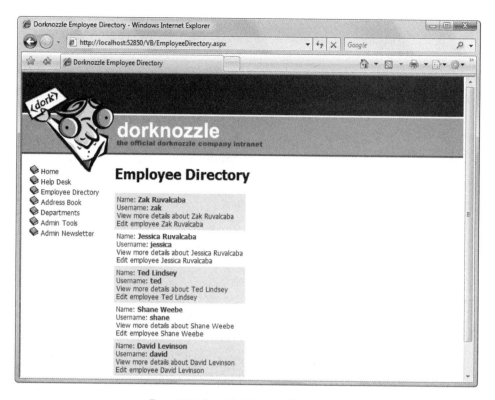

Figure 10.11. The styled Employee Directory list

```
        ForeColor="#333333" />
  <AlternatingItemStyle BackColor="White" />
  <ItemStyle BackColor="#E3EAEB" />
  <HeaderStyle BackColor="#1C5E55" Font-Bold="True"
      ForeColor="White" />
</asp:DataList>
```

The significance of these new elements is as follows:

HeaderStyle

Customizes the appearance of the DataList's heading

ItemStyle

Customizes the appearance of each item displayed within the DataList

AlternatingItemStyle

Customizes the appearance of every second item displayed within the DataList

FooterStyle

 Customizes the appearance of the `DataList`'s footer

SelectedItemStyle

 Customizes the appearance of a selected item within the `DataList`

EditItemStyle

 Customizes the appearance of the `DataList` in edit mode

In the next chapter, you'll learn how to use CSS styles and control skins to facilitate a more professional approach to styling your data controls. Until then, enjoy the benefits of having a modern-looking, functional employee directory!

Summary

As you've seen, `DataLists` provide flexibility and power in terms of presenting database data dynamically within the browser. In this chapter, you learned how to bind your data to `DataLists`, and how to customize appearance using templates and styles. You also learned how to edit data in your `DataList` control, and how to access controls located in the `DataList` templates.

The next chapter will introduce you to two more powerful controls: `GridView` and `DetailsView`.

11

Managing Content
Using `GridView` and `DetailsView`

In the previous chapters, you learned some of the important concepts surrounding data access and presentation. You learned that when connecting to a database, you have to establish a connection using the `SqlConnection` class. You also learned that in order to retrieve data from the database table, you must write an SQL statement within a command using the `SqlCommand` class. You discovered that we use the `SqlDataReader` class to place the database records into a virtual container of some sort. Finally, you learned that presenting the data within the `SqlDataReader` was simply a matter of binding the `SqlDataReader` to a data control such as the `Repeater` or `DataList` controls.

Here, we'll learn about two more controls that offer much more functionality and make it very easy for you to create a table: `GridView` and `DetailsView`. These controls, which form part of ASP.NET's set of data controls, are more complex and offer many more features than `Repeater` and `DataList`. Of course, these additional features come at a cost—they consume more memory and processing power on the server, so they should only be used when they deliver real benefits. Otherwise, it's best to stick to simpler controls.

In this chapter you'll learn how to:

▨ Create `GridView` controls and set up their columns.
▨ Style the data displayed by `GridView`.
▨ Display the details of a selected record using the `DetailsView` control.
▨ Customize the appearance of the `DetailsView` control.
▨ Use `GridView` and `DetailsView` to update your data.

Using the `GridView` Control

The `GridView` control solves a problem that has plagued developers for years: data presentation. The `GridView` control generates simple HTML tables, so information within a `GridView` is presented to the end user in a familiar, cleanly formatted, tabular structure. Similar to the `Repeater` control, the `GridView` can automatically display on a page all the content contained within an `SqlDataReader`, based on styles we set within its templates. However, unlike the `Repeater` control, the `GridView` offers several more advanced features, such as sorting and **paging** (that is, splitting a large result set into pages), and makes it easy to modify the data in the underlying data source.

To sum up, the `GridView` control provides the following functionality:

▨ database table-like presentation of data
▨ table headers and footers
▨ paging
▨ sorting
▨ style modification through templates
▨ customizable columns for advanced editing

You'll learn about some of these features in this chapter; we'll leave the more advanced ones (sorting, paging, and editing) for the next chapter.

As with any other ASP.NET server control, `GridView` controls are added to the page using a specific element:

```
<asp:GridView id="myGridView" runat="server" />
```

Once we add the `GridView` to the page, we can bind an `SqlDataReader` to it as follows:

Visual Basic

```
myGridView.DataSource = myDataReader
myGridView.DataBind()
```

The `GridView` doesn't seem to function very differently from the `Repeater` control, right? Think again! The `Repeater` control didn't work unless we specified content within the required `<ItemTemplate>` and `</ItemTemplate>` tags. The `GridView` takes the structure of the database table automatically, and presents the data to the user in a cleanly formatted HTML table.

Let's take a look at `GridView` in action as we develop the Dorknozzle intranet's address book page. Start by opening the Dorknozzle project, if it's not already open, and creating a new web form named **AddressBook.aspx**, based on the **Dorknozzle.master** master page. Also, make sure the new web form uses a code-behind file.

Now, open **AddressBook.aspx**, and complete its code as shown in the following snippet:

Dorknozzle\VB\01_AddressBook.aspx (excerpt)

```
<%@ Page Language="VB" MasterPageFile="~/Dorknozzle.master"
    AutoEventWireup="false" CodeFile="AddressBook.aspx.vb"
    Inherits="AddressBook" title="Dorknozzle Address Book" %>

<asp:Content ID="Content1" ContentPlaceHolderID="head"
    Runat="Server">
</asp:Content>
<asp:Content ID="Content2"
    ContentPlaceHolderID="ContentPlaceHolder1" Runat="Server">
  <h1>Address Book</h1>
  <asp:GridView id="grid" runat="server" />
</asp:Content>
```

Switch to Design view to see how your grid is represented in the designer. It should look something like Figure 11.1.

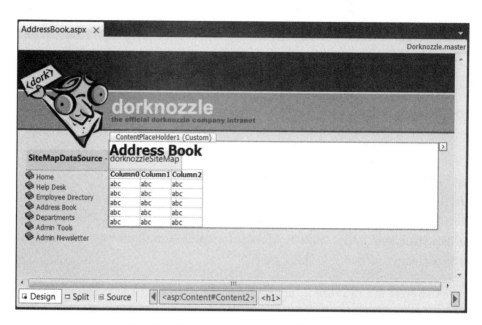

Figure 11.1. Viewing **AddressBook.aspx** in Design view

Now, double-click on an empty portion of the page to have the form's `Page_Load` event handler generated for you in the code-behind file. In `Page_Load`, we'll call a method named `BindGrid`, which will, in turn, create a database connection and a database command object, execute that command, and bind the resulting data reader to the grid, as shown below:

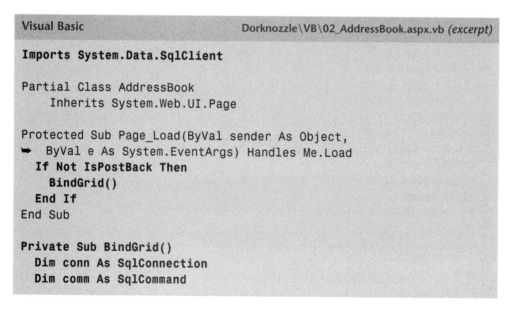

| Visual Basic | Dorknozzle\VB\02_AddressBook.aspx.vb *(excerpt)* |

```vb
Imports System.Data.SqlClient

Partial Class AddressBook
    Inherits System.Web.UI.Page

Protected Sub Page_Load(ByVal sender As Object,
➥   ByVal e As System.EventArgs) Handles Me.Load
  If Not IsPostBack Then
    BindGrid()
  End If
End Sub

Private Sub BindGrid()
  Dim conn As SqlConnection
  Dim comm As SqlCommand
```

```
  Dim reader As SqlDataReader
  Dim connectionString As String = _
      ConfigurationManager.ConnectionStrings( _
      "Dorknozzle").ConnectionString
  conn = New SqlConnection(connectionString)
  comm = New SqlCommand( _
      "SELECT EmployeeID, Name, City, State, MobilePhone " & _
      "FROM Employees", conn)
  Try
    conn.Open()
    reader = comm.ExecuteReader()
    grid.DataSource = reader
    grid.DataBind()
    reader.Close()
  Finally
    conn.Close()
  End Try
End Sub
End Class
```

```
C#                              Dorknozzle\CS\02_AddressBook.aspx.cs (excerpt)
```

```
using System;
⋮
using System.Data.SqlClient;

public partial class AddressBook : System.Web.UI.Page
{
  protected void Page_Load(object sender, EventArgs e)
  {
    if (!IsPostBack)
    {
      BindGrid();
    }
  }
  private void BindGrid()
  {
    SqlConnection conn;
    SqlCommand comm;
    SqlDataReader reader;
    string connectionString =
        ConfigurationManager.ConnectionStrings[
        "Dorknozzle"].ConnectionString;
    conn = new SqlConnection(connectionString);
    comm = new SqlCommand(
```

```
            "SELECT EmployeeID, Name, City, State, MobilePhone " +
            "FROM Employees", conn);
    try
    {
      conn.Open();
      reader = comm.ExecuteReader();
      grid.DataSource = reader;
      grid.DataBind();
      reader.Close();
    }
    finally
    {
      conn.Close();
    }
  }
}
```

What's going on here? If you disregard the fact that you're binding the `SqlDataReader` to a `GridView` instead of a `Repeater` or `DataList`, the code is almost identical to that which we saw in the previous chapter.

Now save your work and open the page in the browser. Figure 11.2 shows how the `GridView` presents all of the data within the `Employees` table in a cleanly formatted structure.

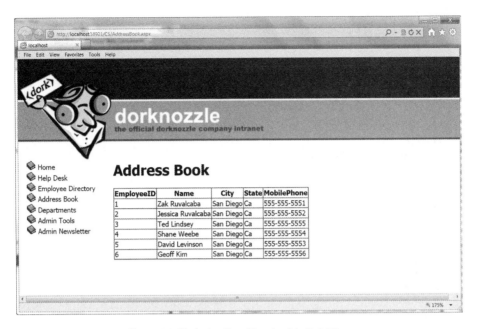

Figure 11.2. Displaying the address book in `GridView`

Okay, perhaps it doesn't look all that clean right now! One of the new features in ASP.NET 4 is the clean grid-styles that will allow the programmer to easily change CSS styles and how the grid can be displayed. By default, we see just a single-pixel black border for the table, a departure from previous version where ASP.NET would apply other styling that wasn't as configurable as we now have the ability to change. However, the display will change as we get some practice using the `GridView`'s powerful and intuitive formatting capabilities. You'll notice that the `GridView` closely resembles the structure of the query's result shown when you run a SELECT query directly from SQL Server Management Studio in the grid result format. All the names of the columns in the database table show as headers within the table, and all the rows from the database table are repeated down the page.

If you look at the generated page source (right-click the page in browser and choose **View Source** or similar), you'll see that the `GridView` indeed generated an HTML table for you:

```
<table cellspacing="0" rules="all" border="1"
    id="ctl00_ContentPlaceHolder1_grid"
    style="border-collapse:collapse;">
  <tr>
```

```
    <th scope="col">EmployeeID</th>
    <th scope="col">Name</th>
    <th scope="col">City</th>
    <th scope="col">State</th>
    <th scope="col">MobilePhone</th>
  </tr>
  <tr>
    <td>1</td>
    <td>Zak Ruvalcaba</td>
    <td>San Diego</td>
    <td>Ca</td>
    <td>555-555-5551</td>
  </tr>
  <tr>
    <td>2</td>
    <td>Jessica Ruvalcaba</td>
    <td>San Diego</td>
    <td>Ca</td>
    <td>555-555-5552</td>
  </tr>
    ⋮
</table>
```

 Formatted for Readability

The HTML generated by ASP.NET won't look exactly as it does above. You'll find that ASP.NET will output long, convoluted lines of **td** elements, each of which appears directly after the previous one. We've simply made the code a little easier to read; the two HTML tables are otherwise identical. ASP.NET 4 has also made it easier for newer browser and even mobile devices to easily read the HTML being output from the **GridView** control.

There's no doubt that the GridView's automatic presentation features are useful. The GridView automatically displays all columns retrieved from the database in the order in which they're sent from the database. While this is very useful, in some cases you'll want your grid to display only a subset of the information retrieved from the database, and in many cases you'll also want to change the order in which the columns of data are displayed.

Let's learn how to customize the GridView by selecting the columns we want to show in a given order. In this case, one of the columns that we want to retrieve from the database, but hide from users, is the `EmployeeID` column. We need to retrieve the table's primary key because it's required for any database operations that involve the unique identification of a record (including tasks such as editing or deleting an employee from the list). The user doesn't need to be overwhelmed with this information, though—after all, humans don't use numeric IDs to identify people in a list.

Customizing the `GridView` Columns

Our next task is to customize the columns displayed by the `GridView`. In this case, our goal is to prevent the `EmployeeID` column from appearing, but the techniques we'll learn here can be used to make all sorts of customizations.

Filtering Table Columns

This is rather obvious, but it has to be said: the columns you can display in the `GridView` must be a subset of the columns you're retrieving from the database. For example, unless you modify the database query to retrieve the employees' passwords, it's not possible to display them in the grid.

If you wish to restrict the information that appears within your `GridView`, you can select the columns you want to display by making a few simple modifications. When you simply bind an `SqlDataReader` to the `GridView`, you're presented with a quick, simple representation of the data you've retrieved from the database, with automatically generated column headers.

One of the properties available to `GridView` is `AutoGenerateColumns`, which is set to `True` by default. If you want to name the columns that your `GridView` displays manually, you must set this property to `False`.

If you set this property to `False` and test it in the browser, you'll find that the grid doesn't display any more. The reason for this is simple: as the `GridView` can't generate its own column headers, you must manually specify the columns that you want displayed. To do so, list the columns inside the `<asp:GridView>` and `</asp:GridView>` tags, as shown below:

Dorknozzle\VB\03_AddressBook.aspx (excerpt)

```
<asp:GridView ID="grid" runat="server" AutoGenerateColumns="False">
  <Columns>
    <asp:BoundField DataField="Name" HeaderText="Name" />
```

```
      <asp:BoundField DataField="City" HeaderText="City" />
      <asp:BoundField DataField="MobilePhone"
          HeaderText="Mobile Phone" />
    </Columns>
</asp:GridView>
```

Notice that each column that we want to display is created using a `BoundField` control inside a set of `<Columns>` and `</Columns>` tags. Each `BoundField` control has a `DataField` property, which specifies the name of the column, and a `HeaderText` property, which sets the name of the column as you want to display it to the user.

Now, save your work and view it in the browser. This time, only the columns that you specified to be bound are displayed in the `GridView`, as Figure 11.3 indicates.

Note that if you don't include the `HeaderText` property for any of the bound columns, those columns won't have a header.

We've now succeeded in displaying only the information we want to display, but the `GridView` still looks plain. In the next section, we'll use styles to customize the appearance of our `GridView`.

Styling the `GridView` with Templates, Skins, and CSS

The `GridView` control offers a number of design-time features that are tightly integrated with the Visual Web Developer designer. As with the `DataList` class, when you click the grid's smart tag, you get quick access to a number of very useful features, as Figure 11.4 illustrates.

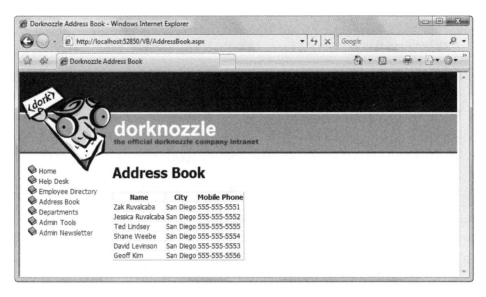

Figure 11.3. Displaying selected columns

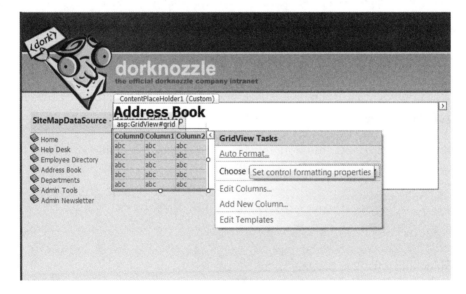

Figure 11.4. The smart tag options of GridView

If you click the **Auto Format…** link from the smart tag menu and choose one of the predefined styles, Visual Web Developer generates a number of template styles for you, like this:

```
<asp:GridView ID="grid" runat="server" AutoGenerateColumns="False"
    CellPadding="4" ForeColor="#333333" GridLines="None">
  <Columns>
    <asp:BoundField DataField="Name" HeaderText="Name" />
    <asp:BoundField DataField="City" HeaderText="City" />
    <asp:BoundField DataField="MobilePhone"
        HeaderText="Mobile Phone" />
  </Columns>
  <FooterStyle BackColor="#5D7B9D" Font-Bold="True"
      ForeColor="White" />
  <RowStyle BackColor="#F7F6F3" ForeColor="#333333" />
  <EditRowStyle BackColor="#999999" />
  <SelectedRowStyle BackColor="#E2DED6" Font-Bold="True"
      ForeColor="#333333" />
  <PagerStyle BackColor="#284775" ForeColor="White"
      HorizontalAlign="Center" />
  <HeaderStyle BackColor="#5D7B9D" Font-Bold="True"
      ForeColor="White" />
  <AlternatingRowStyle BackColor="White" ForeColor="#284775" />
</asp:GridView>
```

However, this time, let's not rely on the predefined templates; let's define our own styles through CSS. Additionally, we want to add a new skin definition for the GridView (you learned about skins back in Chapter 5), so that all the GridView controls throughout the site have a standard appearance.

Open your **Dorknozzle.css** file from the **App_Themes/Blue** folder and add these styles to it:

Dorknozzle\VB\04_Dorknozzle.css *(excerpt)*

```
.GridMain
{
  border-right: gainsboro thin solid;
  border-top: gainsboro thin solid;
  border-left: gainsboro thin solid;
  border-bottom: gainsboro thin solid;
  background-color: #333333;
  width: 400px;
}
.GridRow
{
  background-color: #FFFAFA;
```

```
}
.GridSelectedRow
{
  background-color: #E6E6FA;
}
.GridHeader
{
  background-color: #ADD8E6;
  font-weight: bold;
  text-align: left;
}
```

Now, modify the skin file **SkinFile.skin** in **App_Themes/Blue** by adding this skin definition:

Dorknozzle\VB\05_SkinFile.skin (excerpt)

```
<asp:GridView runat="server" CssClass="GridMain" CellPadding="4"
    GridLines="None">
  <RowStyle CssClass="GridRow" />
  <SelectedRowStyle CssClass="GridSelectedRow" />
  <HeaderStyle CssClass="GridHeader" />
</asp:GridView>
```

Finally, make sure that your `GridView` declaration in **AddressBook.aspx** doesn't contain any styling details. Your page declaration also should have the theme set to "Blue". It should look like the excerpt shown here:

Dorknozzle\VB\03_AddressBook.aspx (excerpt)

```
<%@ Page Title="" Language="C#" MasterPageFile="~/Dorknozzle.➥
  master" AutoEventWireup="true" CodeFile="AddressBook.aspx.cs"➥
  Theme="Blue" Inherits="AddressBook" %>

<asp:Content ID="Content1" ContentPlaceHolderID="head"
    Runat="Server">
</asp:Content>
<asp:Content ID="Content2"
    ContentPlaceHolderID="ContentPlaceHolder1" Runat="Server">

  <h1>Address Book</h1>
  <asp:GridView ID="grid" runat="server" AutoGenerateColumns=➥
    "false">
```

```
<Columns>
  <asp:BoundField DataField="Name" HeaderText="Name" />
  <asp:BoundField DataField="City" HeaderText="City" />
  <asp:BoundField DataField="MobilePhone"
      HeaderText="Mobile Phone" />
</Columns>
</asp:GridView>
```

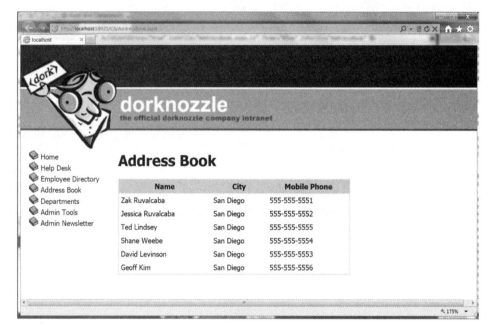

Figure 11.5. The styled address book

All the styling we need is already defined in the skin file; we'd only need to define new properties if we wanted to alter the default values provided through the skin file. Save your work and view the results in the browser. Do they look like the display in Figure 11.5?

Congratulations! You've harnessed the power of CSS and skin files, and combined it with the flexibility of GridView to create a good-looking address book. And it was easy, too!

As you can see, you can style the items in the GridView by altering their font types, colors, and sizes. You can also style the column headers and apply an alternating item style to the rows in the table. Now, when the GridView is viewed in the browser,

we see a little more room between cells, and the lines surrounding the `GridView`
are gone.

Selecting Grid Records

We've already made quite a few changes to the display of our `GridView`. The next
step will be to allow users to select any of the rows in the `GridView` so they can
view more information about the listed employees.

We can create several types of columns in a `GridView` in addition to the `BoundField`
columns we've already seen. For instance, we could create a `ButtonField` column,
which displays a button in each row. Here's a complete list of column controls and
their descriptions:

BoundField

> As you've already seen, the `BoundField` provides flexibility in presentation by
> allowing you to specify which columns will appear within the `GridView`. When
> the grid enters edit mode, this field renders itself as an editable text box, as
> we'll see later.

ButtonField

> Use the `ButtonField` to display a clickable button for each row within the
> `GridView`. When it's clicked, the button triggers a configurable event that you
> can handle within your code to respond to the user's action. A button can trigger
> the following event types: `Cancel`, `Delete`, `Edit`, `Select`, and `Update`.

CheckBoxField

> The `CheckBoxField` displays a checkbox in each row, allowing you to easily
> present Boolean data in the display.

CommandField

> The `CommandField` column automatically generates a `ButtonField` in your grid.
> The actions performed by these buttons depend on the grid's current state. For
> example, if `CommandField` is set to generate **Edit** buttons, it will display an **Edit**
> button when the grid is in non-editable mode, and will display **Update** and
> **Cancel** buttons when the grid is being edited.

HyperLinkField

Use the `HyperLinkField` to display a clickable link within the `GridView`. This link simply acts as a hyperlink to a URL; it raises no server-side events.

ImageField

This control displays an image inside your grid.

TemplateField

Use the `TemplateField` to display markup within the `GridView`.

If you're using Visual Web Developer, you can quickly and easily add a new column to your table in Design view. Click the `GridView`'s smart tag, and click the **Add New Column...** item, as shown in Figure 11.6.

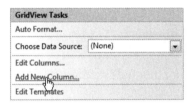

Figure 11.6. Adding a new `GridView` column

In the dialog that appears, change the field type to **ButtonField**, the command name to **Select**, and set the **Text** field to `Select`, so the dialog appears as it does in Figure 11.7.

Figure 11.7. Adding a new field

After clicking **OK**, your brand-new column shows up in Design view. If you switch to Source view, you can see it there, too:

> **Dorknozzle\VB\06_AddressBook.aspx** *(excerpt)*

```
<asp:GridView ID="grid" runat="server"
    AutoGenerateColumns="false">
  <Columns>
    <asp:BoundField DataField="Name" HeaderText="Name" />
    <asp:BoundField DataField="City" HeaderText="City" />
    <asp:BoundField DataField="MobilePhone"
        HeaderText="Mobile Phone" />
    <asp:ButtonField CommandName="Select" Text="Select" />
  </Columns>
</asp:GridView>
```

If you execute the project now, and click the new button, the row will become highlighted, as Figure 11.8 indicates. You'll have noticed that we didn't write any code to implement this feature. We're relying on the functionality provided by the `ButtonField` control when it's `CommandName` property is set to `Select`, combined with the style settings you set earlier, to produce this functionality.

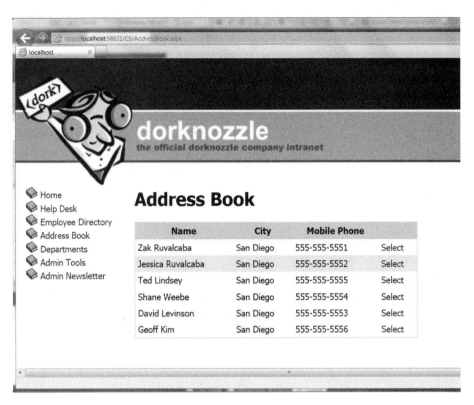

Figure 11.8. Highlighting the selected field in the Address Book

We usually want extra work—in addition to the row highlighting—to be performed when a user selects a row in the address book. When the Select button is pressed, the GridView fires the SelectedIndexChanged event, which we handle if we need to do any further processing. We can generate the GridView's SelectedIndexChanged event handler simply by double-clicking the GridView in the Visual Web Developer designer.

 Generating Default Event Handlers

Double-clicking a control in the designer causes Visual Web Developer to generate the handler of the control's default event. The default event of the GridView is SelectedIndexChanged, which explains why it's so easy to generate its signature. Remember that you can use the Properties window to have Visual Web Developer generate handlers for other events—just click the lightning icon in the Properties window, then double-click on any of the listed events.

Before we handle the `SelectedIndexChanged` event, let's add just below the `GridView` control in **AddressBook.aspx** a label that we can use to display some details of the selected record. You can use Visual Web Developer's designer to add the control, or you can write the code manually:

```
Dorknozzle\VB\07_AddressBook.aspx (excerpt)

⋮
  <asp:GridView id="grid" runat="server"
     AutoGenerateColumns="False">
     ⋮
  </asp:GridView>
  <br />
  <asp:Label ID="detailsLabel" runat="server" />
</asp:Content>
```

Now, generate the `SelectedIndexChanged` event handler by double-clicking the `GridView` control in Design view, then update the event handler to display a short message about the selected record:

```
Visual Basic                    Dorknozzle\VB\08_AddressBook.aspx.vb (excerpt)

Protected Sub grid_SelectedIndexChanged(ByVal sender As Object,
➥  ByVal e As System.EventArgs) Handles grid.SelectedIndexChanged
  Dim selectedRowIndex As Integer
  selectedRowIndex = grid.SelectedIndex
  Dim row As GridViewRow = grid.Rows(selectedRowIndex)
  Dim name As String = row.Cells(0).Text
  detailsLabel.Text = "You selected " & name & "."
End Sub
```

```
C#                              Dorknozzle\CS\08_AddressBook.aspx.cs (excerpt)

protected void grid_SelectedIndexChanged(object sender,
    EventArgs e)
  {
    int selectedRowIndex;
    selectedRowIndex = grid.SelectedIndex;
    GridViewRow row = grid.Rows[selectedRowIndex];
    string name = row.Cells[0].Text;
    detailsLabel.Text = "You selected " + name + ".";
  }
```

Execute the project, and select one of the records. You should see a display like the one in Figure 11.9.

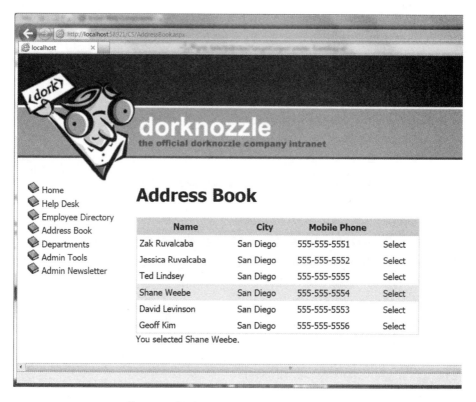

Figure 11.9. Displaying details about the selected row

It was easy to add this new feature, wasn't it?

Using the `DetailsView` Control

ASP.NET 2.0 introduced the `DetailsView` control, which can come in very handy when you want to display more details about one record in a grid. You'll find this control very useful when you need to display details about a record that contains many fields—so many, in fact, that the main grid can't display all of them.

The `DetailsView` control is commonly used to create a page that shows a list of items, and allows you to drill down to view the details of each item. For instance, an ecommerce site might initially present users with only a little information about all available products, to reduce download time and make the information more readable. Users could then select a product to see a more detailed view of that product.

Let's see how this works by using a `GridView` and a `DetailsView` in our Address Book web form. Replace `detailsLabel` with a `DetailsView` control, as shown in the following code snippet:

Dorknozzle\VB\09_AddressBook.aspx *(excerpt)*

```
⋮
<asp:GridView ID="grid" runat="server"
    AutoGenerateColumns="false">
  ⋮
</asp:GridView>
<br />
<asp:DetailsView id="employeeDetails" runat="server" />
</asp:Content>
```

Next, we'll modify the `BindGrid` method to specify the grid's **data key**. The data key feature of the `GridView` control basically allows us to store a piece of data about each row without actually displaying that data. We'll use it to store the `EmployeeID` of each record. Later, when we need to retrieve additional data about the selected employee, we'll be able to read the employee's ID from the data key, and use it in our `SELECT` query. Add this line to your code-behind file:

Visual Basic   Dorknozzle\VB\10_AddressBook.aspx.vb *(excerpt)*

```
Try
  conn.Open()
  reader = comm.ExecuteReader()
  grid.DataSource = reader
  grid.DataKeyNames = New String() {"EmployeeID"}
  grid.DataBind()
  reader.Close()
```

C#   Dorknozzle\CS\10_AddressBook.aspx.cs *(excerpt)*

```
try
{
  conn.Open();
  reader = comm.ExecuteReader();
  grid.DataSource = reader;
```

```
grid.DataKeyNames = new string[] { "EmployeeID" };
grid.DataBind();
reader.Close();
}
```

As you can see, we tell the `GridView` which keys to store by setting the `DataKeyNames` property. This property needs to be populated with an *array* of keys, because the `GridView` supports storing zero, one, or many keys for each row it displays. In this case, we create an array that contains just one value: `EmployeeID`. In the code you've just written, you can see the syntax that creates such an array on the fly, without declaring an array first.

After you make this change, you'll be able to access the `EmployeeID` value for any given row through the `GridView`'s `DataKeys` property.

With this new data to hand, loading the details of the selected employee into the `DetailsView` is a straightforward process. Within the `GridView`'s `SelectedIndex-Changed` event handler, we just need to make another database query to read the details we want to display for the selected employee, then simply feed the results into the `DetailsView` object, like this:

Visual Basic   Dorknozzle\VB\11_AddressBook.aspx.vb *(excerpt)*

```
Protected Sub grid_SelectedIndexChanged(ByVal sender As Object,
➡  ByVal e As System.EventArgs) Handles grid.SelectedIndexChanged
   BindDetails()
End Sub

Private Sub BindDetails()
  Dim selectedRowIndex As Integer = grid.SelectedIndex
  Dim employeeId As Integer = _
      grid.DataKeys(selectedRowIndex).Value
  Dim conn As SqlConnection
  Dim comm As SqlCommand
  Dim reader As SqlDataReader
  Dim connectionString As String = _
      ConfigurationManager.ConnectionStrings( _
      "Dorknozzle").ConnectionString
  conn = New SqlConnection(connectionString)
  comm = New SqlCommand( _
      "SELECT EmployeeID, Name, Address, City, State, Zip, " & _
      "HomePhone, Extension FROM Employees " & _
```

```
        "WHERE EmployeeID=@EmployeeID", conn)
  comm.Parameters.Add("EmployeeID", Data.SqlDbType.Int)
  comm.Parameters("EmployeeID").Value = employeeId
  Try
    conn.Open()
    reader = comm.ExecuteReader()
    employeeDetails.DataSource = reader
    employeeDetails.DataKeyNames = New String() {"EmployeeID"}
    employeeDetails.DataBind()
    reader.Close()
  Finally
    conn.Close()
  End Try
End Sub
```

C#   Dorknozzle\CS\11_AddressBook.aspx.cs *(excerpt)*

```
protected void grid_SelectedIndexChanged(object sender, EventArgs e)
{
  BindDetails();
}
private void BindDetails()
{
  int selectedRowIndex = grid.SelectedIndex;
  int employeeId = (int)grid.DataKeys[selectedRowIndex].Value;
  SqlConnection conn;
  SqlCommand comm;
  SqlDataReader reader;
  string connectionString =
      ConfigurationManager.ConnectionStrings[
      "Dorknozzle"].ConnectionString;
  conn = new SqlConnection(connectionString);
  comm = new SqlCommand(
      "SELECT EmployeeID, Name, Address, City, State, Zip, " +
      "HomePhone, Extension FROM Employees " +
      "WHERE EmployeeID=@EmployeeID", conn);
  comm.Parameters.Add("EmployeeID", SqlDbType.Int);
  comm.Parameters["EmployeeID"].Value = employeeId;
  try
  {
    conn.Open();
    reader = comm.ExecuteReader();
    employeeDetails.DataSource = reader;
    employeeDetails.DataKeyNames = new string[] { "EmployeeID" };
    employeeDetails.DataBind();
```

```
    reader.Close();
  }
  finally
  {
    conn.Close();
  }
}
```

Now, if you execute the project and select one of the employees, you should see a page like the one shown in Figure 11.10.

Styling the `DetailsView`

Displaying the data in the `DetailsView` control is easy enough, but you'll probably want to make it look a bit prettier. We'll start by changing the row headings in the left-hand column. Open **AddressBook.aspx** and modify the `DetailsView` control like this:

Dorknozzle\VB\12_AddressBook.aspx *(excerpt)*

```
<asp:DetailsView id="employeeDetails" runat="server"
    AutoGenerateRows="False">
  <Fields>
    <asp:BoundField DataField="Address" HeaderText="Address" />
    <asp:BoundField DataField="City" HeaderText="City" />
    <asp:BoundField DataField="State" HeaderText="State" />
    <asp:BoundField DataField="Zip" HeaderText="Zip" />
    <asp:BoundField DataField="HomePhone"
        HeaderText="Home Phone" />
    <asp:BoundField DataField="Extension"
        HeaderText="Extension" />
  </Fields>
  <HeaderTemplate>
    <%#Eval("Name")%>
  </HeaderTemplate>
</asp:DetailsView>
```

As you can see, we customize the `DetailsView` control in a similar way to the `GridView`, except that this time we're dealing with fields instead of rows. We set the `AutoGenerateRows` property to `False`. Then, we define the fields we want to show, and create a `HeaderTemplate` to display the name of the employee in the header—we'll see what this looks like in a minute.

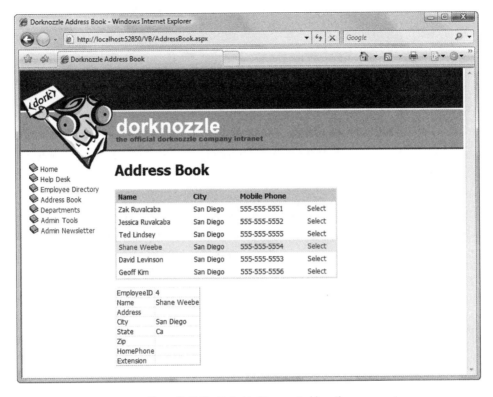

Figure 11.10. The DetailsView control in action

To further improve the appearance of the DetailsView, add this skin to **SkinFile.skin**:

Dorknozzle\VB\13_SkinFile.skin *(excerpt)*

```
<asp:DetailsView runat="server" CssClass="GridMain"
    CellPadding="4" GridLines="None">
  <RowStyle CssClass="GridRow" />
  <HeaderStyle CssClass="GridHeader" />
</asp:DetailsView>
```

Here, we've defined a style that's similar to the GridView control, which will ensure that our page has a consistent appearance. Save your work, open **AddressBook.aspx** in the browser, and select an employee. You should see something similar to Figure 11.11.

We're really making progress now. There's only one problem—our employee records don't include any addresses, and at this moment there's no way to add any! Let's take care of this next.

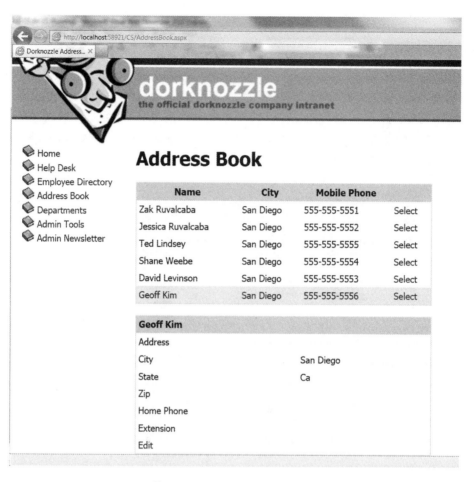

Figure 11.11. Viewing employee details

GridView and DetailsView Events

In order to use the GridView and DetailsView controls effectively, we need to know how to handle their events. In this section, we'll learn about the events raised by these controls. We'll focus on the events that relate to editing and updating data, as our next goal will be to allow users to edit employee details in the DetailsView.

Earlier, you learned how to respond to the user's clicking of the **Select** button by handling the GridView's SelectedIndexChanged event. Soon you'll implement editing functionality, which you'll achieve by adding an **Edit** button to the DetailsView control. The editing features of the GridView and the DetailsView are very similar, so you can apply the same principles—and almost the same code—to both of them.

Both the GridView and DetailsView controls support **Edit** command buttons, which will place **Edit** buttons in the control when the page loads. Once one of the **Edit** buttons has been clicked, the row (in case of GridView) or the entire form (in case of DetailsView) will become editable, and instead of an **Edit** button, users will see **Update** and **Cancel** buttons.

These features are fairly amazing, because you can achieve this "edit mode" without writing any HTML at all: the columns know how to render their editable modes by themselves. If you don't like their default edit mode appearances, you can customize them using templates.

Before we write any code, let's see what this edit mode looks like. Figure 11.12 shows a GridView control in which one row appears in edit mode.

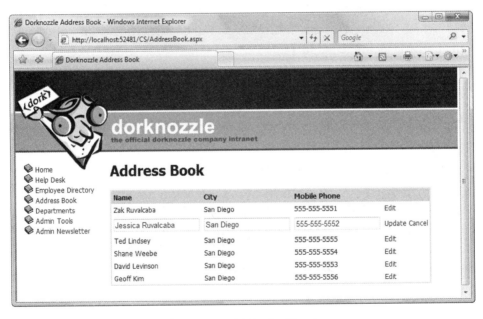

Figure 11.12. GridView in edit mode

Figure 11.13 shows a DetailsView control in edit mode.

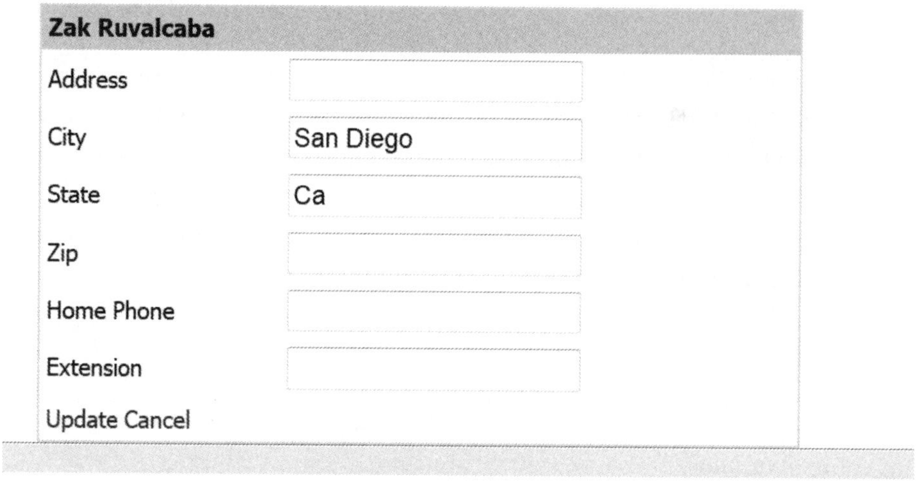

Figure 11.13. DetailsView in edit mode

When command buttons such as **Edit** are clicked, they raise events that we can handle on the server side. The GridView supports more kinds of command buttons, each of which triggers a certain event that we can handle. The action types and the events they trigger are listed in Table 11.1.

Table 11.1. GridView Action Types and the Events They Trigger

Action	Events Triggered When Clicked
Select	SelectedIndexChanging, SelectIndexChanged
Edit	RowEditing
Update	RowUpdating, RowUpdated
Cancel	RowCancelingEdit
Delete	RowDeleting, RowDeleted
(sorting buttons)	RowSorting, RowSorted
(custom action)	RowCommand

The DetailsView control, on the other hand, has buttons and events that refer to *items*, rather than *rows*, which makes sense when you realize that DetailsView is used to display the items in one record, while GridView displays a few items from many records. The DetailsView action types, and the events they generate, are listed in Table 11.2.

Table 11.2. DetailsView Action Types and the Events They Trigger

Action	Events triggered when clicked
(paging controls)	PageIndexChanging, PageIndexChanged
Delete	ItemDeleting, ItemDeleted
Insert	ItemInserting, ItemInserted
Edit	ModeChanging, ModeChanged
Update	ItemUpdating, ItemUpdated
Delete	RowDeleting, RowDeleted
(custom action)	ItemCommand

Notice that, except for the RowCommand (for the GridView) and the ItemCommand (for the DetailsView) events, we have some events that are named in the present tense (that is, those that end in "ing," such as SelectedIndexChanging and ItemUpdating), and other events that are named in the past tense (that is, those that end in "ed," such as SelectIndexChanged and ItemUpdated). The events that end in "ing" are fired just before their past-tense counterparts, and should be handled only if you want to implement some logic to determine whether the action in question should be performed.

The "ed" events, on the other hand, should perform the actual task of the button. We saw such an event handler when we handled the SelectIndexChanged event of our GridView control. In this handler, we queried the database to get the details of the selected employee, then displayed the result in a DetailsView control.

If we wanted to disallow the selection of a particular employee (say, the employee with the ID 1), we could do so by setting e.Cancel to True in the SelectIndexChanging event handler, as shown below:

Visual Basic

```
Protected Sub grid_SelectedIndexChanging(ByVal sender As Object,
➡    ByVal e As GridViewSelectEventArgs)
➡    Handles grid.SelectedIndexChanging
  Dim selectedRowIndex As Integer = grid.SelectedIndex
  Dim employeeId As Integer = _
      grid.DataKeys(selectedRowIndex).Value
  If employeeId = 1 Then
```

```
        e.Cancel = True
    End If
End Sub
```

```
C#

protected void grid_SelectedIndexChanging(object sender,
    GridViewSelectEventArgs e)
{
  int selectedRowIndex = grid.SelectedIndex;
  int employeeId = (int)grid.DataKeys[selectedRowIndex].Value;
  if (employeeId == 1)
  {
    e.Cancel = true;
  }
}
```

 ### Where's `RowEdited`?

Note that, in the case of the `Edit` action in the `GridView`, there's no `RowEdited` event. Why not? Well, it wouldn't make much sense to have one—`GridView` knows what to do when an editing action is approved to take place. More specifically, when a row enters edit mode, it's displayed using the default editing style of the column. The built-in column types (such as bound columns, check box columns, and so on) have built-in editing templates, which you can customize by providing custom templates.

Entering Edit Mode

To get a better grasp on all this theory, let's look at another example. Here, we'll modify the `DetailsView` control to let users update employee data. To implement `GridView` or `DetailsView` editing, we can use a `CommandField` column.

Let's get started. Open **AddressBook.aspx** in the designer, click the `DetailsView`'s smart tag, and choose **Add New Field…**. In the **Choose a field type** drop-down, select **CommandField**, and check the **Edit/Update** checkbox, as shown in Figure 11.14.

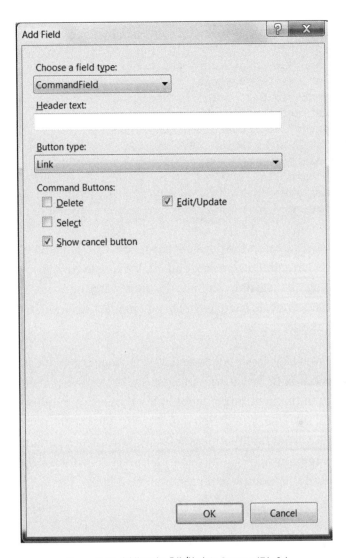

Figure 11.14. Adding the Edit/Update `CommandField`

If you'd prefer to add the new column by hand, do so by adding it to
AddressBook.aspx. Either way, you should end up with the following code:

```
                                    Dorknozzle\VB\14_AddressBook.aspx (excerpt)

<asp:DetailsView id="employeeDetails" runat="server"
    AutoGenerateRows="False">
  <Fields>
    <asp:BoundField DataField="Address" HeaderText="Address" />
    <asp:BoundField DataField="City" HeaderText="City" />
```

```
      <asp:BoundField DataField="State" HeaderText="State" />
      <asp:BoundField DataField="Zip" HeaderText="Zip" />
      <asp:BoundField DataField="HomePhone"
          HeaderText="Home Phone" />
      <asp:BoundField DataField="Extension"
          HeaderText="Extension" />
      <asp:CommandField ShowEditButton="True" />
    </Fields>
    <HeaderTemplate>
      <%#Eval("Name")%>
    </HeaderTemplate>
  </asp:DetailsView>
```

The new item will appear in the designer as an **Edit** link immediately below the list
of columns. If you execute the project and click that **Edit** link, an exception will be
thrown, telling you that you didn't handle the ModeChanging event. The DetailsView
control doesn't know how to switch itself to edit mode, but fortunately, it's extremely
easy to write the code yourself.

To have Visual Web Developer generate the ModeChanging event signature for you,
open **AddressBook.aspx** in Design view, select the DetailsView control, click the
yellow button with the lightning symbol in the Properties window to display the
list of the control's events, and double-click on the ModeChanging entry. This will
generate an empty event handler for you (as well as the onmodechanging property
on the DetailsView control if you're using C#), and take you straight to the function
in the code-behind file. Complete the generated code like this:

Visual Basic   Dorknozzle\VB\15_AddressBook.aspx.vb *(excerpt)*

```
Protected Sub employeeDetails_ModeChanging(ByVal sender As Object,
➥   ByVal e As System.Web.UI.WebControls.DetailsViewModeEventArgs)
➥   Handles employeeDetails.ModeChanging
  employeeDetails.ChangeMode(e.NewMode)
  BindDetails()
End Sub
```

C#   Dorknozzle\CS\15_AddressBook.aspx.cs *(excerpt)*

```
protected void employeeDetails_ModeChanging(object sender,
    DetailsViewModeEventArgs e)
  {
```

```
    employeeDetails.ChangeMode(e.NewMode);
    BindDetails();
}
```

Execute the project and click the **Edit** button. This will transform the control as shown in Figure 11.15.

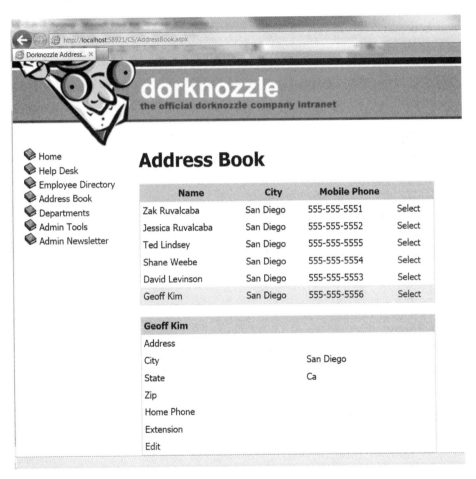

Figure 11.15. The `DetailsView` in edit mode

In order to understand the code in `employeeDetails_ModeChanging`, you need to know about the **display modes** of the `DetailsView` control. The `DetailsView` control supports three display modes. You can change the current mode using its `ChangeMode` method, providing as parameter one of these values:

DetailsViewMode.ReadOnly

This is the default mode, which is used to display data. When you execute your project, and load the details of an employee, you see those details in `ReadOnly` mode.

DetailsViewMode.Edit

This mode is used to edit an existing record. We saw this mode in action earlier, when we clicked the **Edit** button.

DetailsViewMode.Insert

We use this mode to insert a new record. It's similar to the edit mode, except all the controls are empty, so you can fill in data for a new item.

If you look at the `employeeDetails_ModeChanging`, you'll see it receives a parameter named e that is an object of class `DetailsViewModeEventArgs`. e's `NewMode` property tells us which display mode was requested by the user. Its value will be `Details-ViewMode.Edit` when the `ModeChanging` event is fired as a result of the **Edit** button being clicked. We pass this value to the `DetailsView` control's `ChangeMode` method, which does exactly as its name suggests: it changes the mode of the `DetailsView`. With this code, you've implemented the functionality to make both the **Edit** and **Cancel** buttons work correctly, as we'll see in an example shortly.

However, note that once you switch to edit mode, clicking the **Update** button will generate an error, because we still haven't handled the `ItemUpdating` event that's fired when the user tries to save changes to a record. We'll create the event handler later; next, we want to improve our existing solution using templates.

Using Templates

The built-in column types are sufficiently varied and configurable to provide for most of the functionality you're likely to need, but in cases where further customization is required, you can make the desired changes using templates. In the smart tag menu of the `GridView` and `DetailsView` controls, you'll see an option called **Edit Columns** (for the `GridView`) or **Edit Fields** (for the `DetailsView`). Select that option to open a dialog that provides us with a great deal of control over the options for each column or field.

You'll notice a **Convert this field into a TemplateField** link in the dialog. Let's see how this works. Click the smart tag of your `DetailsView` control, then click **Edit Fields**.

In the dialog that appears, select the **Address** field from the **Selected fields** list, as shown in Figure 11.16.

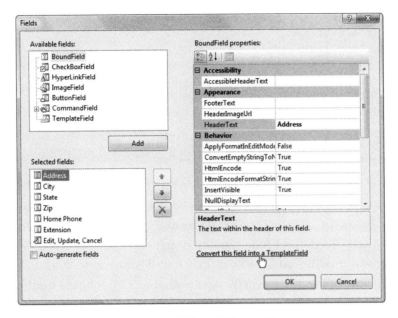

Figure 11.16. Editing a field's properties

Click the **Convert this field into a TemplateField** link to have Visual Web Developer create a template that simulates the current functionality of the field, then click **OK** to close the dialog.

So, what happened? Let's switch **AddressBook.aspx** to Source view. After you convert the field to a template field, its definition will look like this:

Dorknozzle\VB\16_AddressBook.aspx *(excerpt)*

```
<asp:DetailsView id="employeeDetails" runat="server"
    AutoGenerateRows="False">
  <Fields>
    <asp:TemplateField HeaderText="Address">
      <EditItemTemplate>
        <asp:TextBox ID="TextBox1" runat="server"
            Text='<%# Bind("Address") %>'></asp:TextBox>
      </EditItemTemplate>
      <InsertItemTemplate>
        <asp:TextBox ID="TextBox1" runat="server"
            Text='<%# Bind("Address") %>'></asp:TextBox>
```

```
      </InsertItemTemplate>
      <ItemTemplate>
        <asp:Label ID="Label1" runat="server"
            Text='<%# Bind("Address") %>'></asp:Label>
      </ItemTemplate>
    </asp:TemplateField>
    <asp:BoundField DataField="City" HeaderText="City" />
    ⋮
    <asp:CommandField ShowEditButton="True" />
  </Fields>
  ⋮
</asp:DetailsView>
```

Cool, huh? Visual Web Developer did a little bit of magic for us: it replaced the BoundField column that used to display the address with a TemplateField containing an ItemTemplate, an EditItemTemplate, and an InsertItemTemplate. Despite these alterations, the current functionality hasn't changed: you can still execute your project and load the address book, and it will continue to work as before. The difference is that now you can easily refer to these inner controls from your code, you can easily change their appearance using custom HTML code, and, if you wish, you can replace them with totally different controls. The power is in your hands. For example, you can widen the TextBox controls that are used to edit the fields, as well as performing other kinds of customizations. You can also give specific IDs to the inner template controls, rather than using their default generic names, so that you can find them easily when you need to.

Beware of ReadOnly

Note that if you set a column as read-only (by setting the column's ReadOnly property to True) prior to its conversion, Visual Web Developer will use a Label control instead of a TextBox control in the EditItemTemplate for that field. Thus, when the grid enters edit mode, that particular column won't be transformed into a TextBox, so its read-only behavior will be conserved.

Now, convert the other fields—except for CommandField—to template fields. Then, we'll modify the generated code by altering the TextBox controls, and assigning appropriate names to our controls. To keep things simple, we're only going to make changes to the **Address** and **City** fields in the code samples provided here—you can update the others yourself. Let's get started:[1]

Dorknozzle\VB\17_AddressBook.aspx *(excerpt)*

```
<asp:TemplateField HeaderText="Address">
  <EditItemTemplate>
    <asp:TextBox ID="editAddressTextBox" runat="server"
        Text='<%# Bind("Address") %>'></asp:TextBox>
  </EditItemTemplate>
  <InsertItemTemplate>
    <asp:TextBox ID="insertAddressTextBox" runat="server"
        Text='<%# Bind("Address") %>'></asp:TextBox>
  </InsertItemTemplate>
  <ItemTemplate>
    <asp:Label ID="addressLabel" runat="server"
        Text='<%# Bind("Address") %>'></asp:Label>
  </ItemTemplate>
</asp:TemplateField>
<asp:TemplateField HeaderText="City">
  <EditItemTemplate>
    <asp:TextBox ID="editCityTextBox" runat="server"
        Text='<%# Bind("City") %>'></asp:TextBox>
  </EditItemTemplate>
  <InsertItemTemplate>
    <asp:TextBox ID="insertCityTextBox" runat="server"
        Text='<%# Bind("City") %>'></asp:TextBox>
  </InsertItemTemplate>
  <ItemTemplate>
    <asp:Label ID="cityLabel" runat="server"
        Text='<%# Bind("City") %>'></asp:Label>
  </ItemTemplate>
</asp:TemplateField>
```

Execute your project, load the address book, select one employee, and click the **Edit** link to ensure everything works (and looks) as shown in Figure 11.17.

---

[1] If you're feeling lazy, you'll be pleased to hear that updating the other fields is optional for the purposes of this chapter.

Zak Ruvalcaba	
Address	
City	San Diego
State	Ca
Zip	
Home Phone	
Extension	
Update Cancel	

Figure 11.17. After the DetailsView's BoundFields have been converted to TemplateFields

Updating DetailsView Records

Now that you have your DetailsView control in place, let's complete its functionality by making the **Update** link functional. To begin, we'll generate the ItemUpdating event handler. The ItemUpdating event is triggered when the **Update** link is clicked—an action that will occur once the user enters new data into the text boxes and is ready to commit the updated data to the database.

 Updating Employee Details

To keep the code in this chapter short, we're only showing the code that's required to update a couple of the fields in the Employees table. Adding the code to update the rest of the fields is easy, so we've left it as a task for you to complete on your own. If you decide to have a go (and you should!), don't forget to update the stored procedure in the database as well as the code-behind file.

To take care of the actual database update, though, we will be using a stored procedure called UpdateEmployeeDetails. To create this stored procedure, run the following script in SQL Server Management Studio:

```
                    Dorknozzle\VB\18_UpdateEmployeeDetails.sql (excerpt)

CREATE PROCEDURE UpdateEmployeeDetails
(
  @EmployeeID Int,
  @NewAddress nvarchar(50),
  @NewCity nvarchar(50)
)
AS
UPDATE Employees
SET Address = @NewAddress, City = @NewCity
WHERE EmployeeID = @EmployeeID
```

Now that our stored procedure is in place, we can add the code for the **Update** link,
Open **AddressBook.aspx** in the designer, select the DetailsView control, and switch
to the events viewer by clicking the **Event** button (the little lightning symbol) in the
Properties window. There, double-click the ItemUpdating row to have the designer
generate the employeeDetails_ItemUpdating method for you (and of course the
onitemupdating property if you're using C#), and update the handler with the code
shown below:

```
Visual Basic            Dorknozzle\VB\19_AddressBook.aspx.vb (excerpt)

Protected Sub employeeDetails_ItemUpdating(ByVal sender As Object,
➡   ByVal e As System.Web.UI.WebControls.DetailsViewUpdateEventArgs)
➡   Handles employeeDetails.ItemUpdating
  Dim employeeId As Integer = employeeDetails.DataKey.Value
  Dim newAddressTextBox As TextBox = _
      employeeDetails.FindControl("editAddressTextBox")
  Dim newCityTextBox As TextBox = _
      employeeDetails.FindControl("editCityTextBox")
  Dim newAddress As String = newAddressTextBox.Text
  Dim newCity As String = newCityTextBox.Text
  Dim conn As SqlConnection
  Dim comm As SqlCommand
  Dim connectionString As String = _
      ConfigurationManager.ConnectionStrings( _
      "Dorknozzle").ConnectionString
  conn = New SqlConnection(connectionString)
  comm = New SqlCommand("UpdateEmployeeDetails", conn)
  comm.CommandType = Data.CommandType.StoredProcedure
  comm.Parameters.Add("@EmployeeID", Data.SqlDbType.Int)
  comm.Parameters("@EmployeeID").Value = employeeId
```

```
  comm.Parameters.Add("@NewAddress", Data.SqlDbType.NVarChar, 50)
  comm.Parameters("@NewAddress").Value = newAddress
  comm.Parameters.Add("@NewCity", Data.SqlDbType.NVarChar, 50)
  comm.Parameters("@NewCity").Value = newCity
  Try
    conn.Open()
    comm.ExecuteNonQuery()
  Finally
    conn.Close()
  End Try
  employeeDetails.ChangeMode(DetailsViewMode.ReadOnly)
  BindGrid()
  BindDetails()
End Sub
```

C#	Dorknozzle\CS\19_AddressBook.aspx.cs *(excerpt)*

```
protected void employeeDetails_ItemUpdating(object sender,
    DetailsViewUpdateEventArgs e)
  {
    int employeeId = (int)employeeDetails.DataKey.Value;
    TextBox newAddressTextBox =
      (TextBox)employeeDetails.FindControl("editAddressTextBox");
    TextBox newCityTextBox =
      (TextBox)employeeDetails.FindControl("editCityTextBox");
    string newAddress = newAddressTextBox.Text;
    string newCity = newCityTextBox.Text;
    SqlConnection conn;
    SqlCommand comm;
    string connectionString =
        ConfigurationManager.ConnectionStrings[
        "Dorknozzle"].ConnectionString;
    conn = new SqlConnection(connectionString);
    comm = new SqlCommand("UpdateEmployeeDetails", conn);
    comm.CommandType = CommandType.StoredProcedure;
    comm.Parameters.Add("EmployeeID", SqlDbType.Int);
    comm.Parameters["EmployeeID"].Value = employeeId;
    comm.Parameters.Add("NewAddress", SqlDbType.NVarChar, 50);
    comm.Parameters["NewAddress"].Value = newAddress;
    comm.Parameters.Add("NewCity", SqlDbType.NVarChar, 50);
    comm.Parameters["NewCity"].Value = newCity;
    try
    {
      conn.Open();
      comm.ExecuteNonQuery();
```

```
    }
    finally
    {
      conn.Close();
    }
    employeeDetails.ChangeMode(DetailsViewMode.ReadOnly);
    BindGrid();
    BindDetails();
  }
```

This code is fairly straightforward. It starts by reading the value of the DataKey of the DetailsView object. As we saw earlier, the DetailsView, like the GridView, is able to store the ID of the record (or records) it's displaying. You'll remember that we made the DetailsView object aware of the EmployeeID data key when we bound the DetailsView to its data source in the BindDetails method. We read this information in the ItemUpdating event handler, like so:

Visual Basic	Dorknozzle\VB\19_AddressBook.aspx.vb *(excerpt)*

```
Dim employeeId As Integer = employeeDetails.DataKey.Value
```

C#	Dorknozzle\CS\19_AddressBook.aspx.cs *(excerpt)*

```
int employeeId = (int) employeeDetails.DataKey.Value;
```

The next step is to find the TextBox objects that contain the updated data. We do this using the FindControl method, as we've seen previously. After we obtain the control references, we obtain the string values that we're interested in simply by reading their Text properties, as you can see in the following code snippets:

Visual Basic	Dorknozzle\VB\19_AddressBook.aspx.vb *(excerpt)*

```
Dim newAddressTextBox As TextBox = _
    employeeDetails.FindControl("editAddressTextBox")
Dim newCityTextBox As TextBox = _
    employeeDetails.FindControl("editCityTextBox")
Dim newAddress As String = newAddressTextBox.Text
Dim newCity As String = newCityTextBox.Text
```

```
C#                                    Dorknozzle\CS\19_AddressBook.aspx.cs (excerpt)
TextBox newAddressTextBox =
    (TextBox)employeeDetails.FindControl("editAddressTextBox");
TextBox newCityTextBox =
    (TextBox)employeeDetails.FindControl("editCityTextBox");
string newAddress = newAddressTextBox.Text;
string newCity = newCityTextBox.Text;
```

After we obtain the data we wish to insert into the database, we call the UpdateEmployeeDetails stored procedure we created earlier. The database connection and
command code is identical to the code we've used previously, so we don't need to
examine it again.

In the last part of employeeDetails_ItemUpdating, we rebind both the GridView
and the DetailsView with the updated information, and switch the DetailsView
back to its read-only state:

```
Visual Basic                          Dorknozzle\VB\19_AddressBook.aspx.vb (excerpt)
employeeDetails.ChangeMode(DetailsViewMode.ReadOnly)
BindGrid()
BindDetails()
```

```
C#                                    Dorknozzle\CS\19_AddressBook.aspx.cs (excerpt)
employeeDetails.ChangeMode(DetailsViewMode.ReadOnly);
BindGrid();
BindDetails();
```

The code is ready to be executed! Try updating the addresses of your employees to
ensure the feature works correctly—it should display as shown in Figure 11.18.

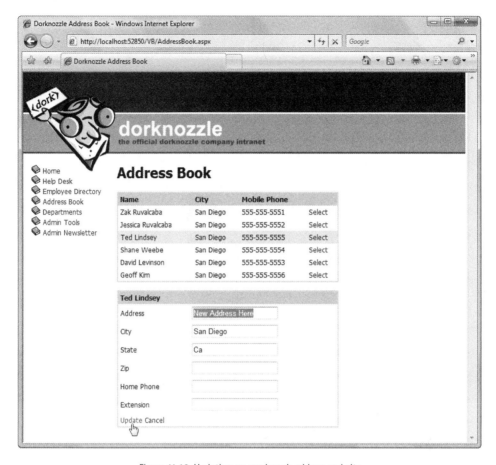

Figure 11.18. Updating an employee's address and city

Summary

As we've seen throughout this chapter, GridViews and DetailsViews provide enormous flexibility and power in terms of presenting database data dynamically within the browser. In these pages, we learned how to create both of these data controls and bind data to them. We also learned how to customize the appearance of elements using templates and styles, and saw how various commands allow us to select and update items. You can use these techniques to add new records, and update existing ones.

The next chapter will begin to introduce you to advanced programming topics, as we investigate even more possibilities for data binding the DetailsView control to allow for the editing, updating, and insertion of new records with minimal coding effort. We'll also have a chance to explore the topic of code-free data binding in that chapter.

Chapter 12

Advanced Data Access

In the last three chapters, you learned some of the important concepts of data access and presentation. You learned how to use the `SqlConnection` class to establish a connection to the database, you learned how to use the `SqlCommand` class to execute a query on a database table, and you learned how to return the results of the command into an `SqlDataReader` for use within the application.

In this chapter, we'll discuss the alternatives to using the `SqlDataReader` object for retrieving data from your database. For starters, it's important to understand that `SqlDataReader` has both advantages and disadvantages. The two main points you need to keep in mind about `SqlDataReader` are:

- It represents the fastest method available to read data from the data source.
- It allows read-only, forward-only access to data.

In other words, the `SqlDataReader` achieves very high performance at the cost of providing a direct connection to the data source. It doesn't store the data locally, so after it reads one record and moves to the next, there's no way to go back. The `SqlDataReader` basically offers an input data stream that you can read in the order in which it was sent, but which you are unable to modify.

However, `SqlDataReader` isn't the only way to access your data, and in many scenarios, it makes sense to use one of the two popular alternatives:

1. The first option involves using the new ADO.NET data source controls, which are tightly integrated with the `GridView` and `DetailsView` controls. They allow you to implement reading, updating, deleting, inserting, paging, and sorting features very easily—for the most part, you don't even need to write any code!

2. The second approach involves using the `SqlDataAdapter` class in conjunction with the `DataTable`, `DataView`, and `DataSet` classes, which are able to read data from the database and store it locally, allowing you to browse, filter, and sort data in your code without leaving a connection to the database open. This method occupies more memory on the server that runs your application, and means that fewer of Visual Web Developer's automated features are available to you (you have to write more code!), but it does give you more flexibility in terms of what you can do with your data.

In this chapter, you'll learn how to use both of these data access methods.

Using Data Source Controls

The .NET framework offers seven **data source controls**: `SqlDataSource`, `AccessDataSource`, `LinqDataSource`, `ObjectDataSource`, `XmlDataSource`, `EntityDataSource` and `SiteMapDataSource`. These objects enable automatic connection to various data sources and provide easy ways to read or modify your database using data-bound controls:

- `SqlDataSource` allows you to connect to any data source that has an ADO.NET data provider. The default providers are `SqlClient`, `OracleClient`, `OleDb`, and `Odbc`. Even though the name of the class is `SqlDataSource`, the fact that its name begins with *Sql* doesn't mean it works only with SQL Server—it's really very flexible. This is the data source we'll work with in this chapter.

- `AccessDataSource` is the data source object we use to connect to Access databases.

- `LinqDataSource` is the data source object you can use to connect to Language-Integrated Query (LINQ) data sources. This is an advanced ADO.NET feature that we will cover later in this book.

- `ObjectDataSource` allows us to connect to custom data access classes, and is appropriate when we're creating complex application architectures.

- `XmlDataSource` knows how to connect to XML files.

- `EntityDataSource` is the data source object that connects to objects using the Entity Framework. Data access using the Entity Framework is outside the scope of this book, but it is heavily similar to LINQ-To-SQL which we will cover.

- `SiteMapDataSource` knows how to connect to a site map data source, and can be used to generate site maps. We worked a little with this data source control in Chapter 4.

You can find these controls in the **Data** tab of Visual Web Developer's Toolbox, as Figure 12.1 shows.

Figure 12.1. The Data Source Controls in the Toolbox

In Chapter 11, we implemented the functionality required to show employee details in the Dorknozzle Address Book page (**AddressBook.aspx**). We used the `SqlDataReader` class for the task, which means we've achieved the best possible performance. However, we wrote quite a bit of code to implement the viewing and editing features for that page, and we'd need to do even more hand coding to implement paging, sorting, and inserting features.

This time, to make it easier on our fingers, we'll use the `SqlDataSource` object instead. This object can automate many tasks for us, and while it may not always provide the best performance or the greatest flexibility, it's important that we know how to use it, because it can come in very handy for quick programming tasks.

Binding the `GridView` to a `SqlDataSource`

We'll start by binding the `GridView` control in **AddressBook.aspx** to a `SqlDataSource`; we'll deal with the `DetailsView` control later. Since the data sources work with different SQL queries, we'll need to create two data sources: one that reads all employees (to populate the `GridView`), and one that reads the details of one employee (to populate the `DetailsView`).

Let's start by deleting all the code in the code-behind file (**AddressBooks.aspx.vb** or **AddressBook.aspx.cs**). Yes, you've read this correctly: we're starting from scratch! As you'll see, we can implement a large number of features without any code at all when we use the `SqlDataSource` class. Leave your code-behind files like this:

Visual Basic	Dorknozzle\VB\01_AddressBook.aspx.vb *(excerpt)*

```vb
Imports System.Data.SqlClient

Partial Class AddressBook
    Inherits System.Web.UI.Page

End Class
```

C#	Dorknozzle\CS\01_AddressBook.aspx.cs *(excerpt)*

```csharp
using System;
using System.Collections;
using System.Configuration;
using System.Data;
using System.Linq;
using System.Web;
using System.Web.Security;
using System.Web.UI;
using System.Web.UI.HtmlControls;
using System.Web.UI.WebControls;
```

```
using System.Web.UI.WebControls.WebParts;
using System.Xml.Linq;
using System.Data.SqlClient;


public partial class AddressBook : System.Web.UI.Page
{

}
```

If you're using C#, you'll also need to delete the event handler declarations from **AddressBook.aspx**. Remove the OnSelectedIndexChanged property from the GridView control, and the OnModeChanging and OnItemUpdating properties from the DetailsView control.

Open **AddressBook.aspx** in **Design** view, and drag the SqlDataSource control from the Toolbox (it's located under the **Data** tab) onto the form. You can place it anywhere you like—the location isn't relevant because the control doesn't display in the browser. Of course, it will appear in the **Design** view, as Figure 12.2 shows.

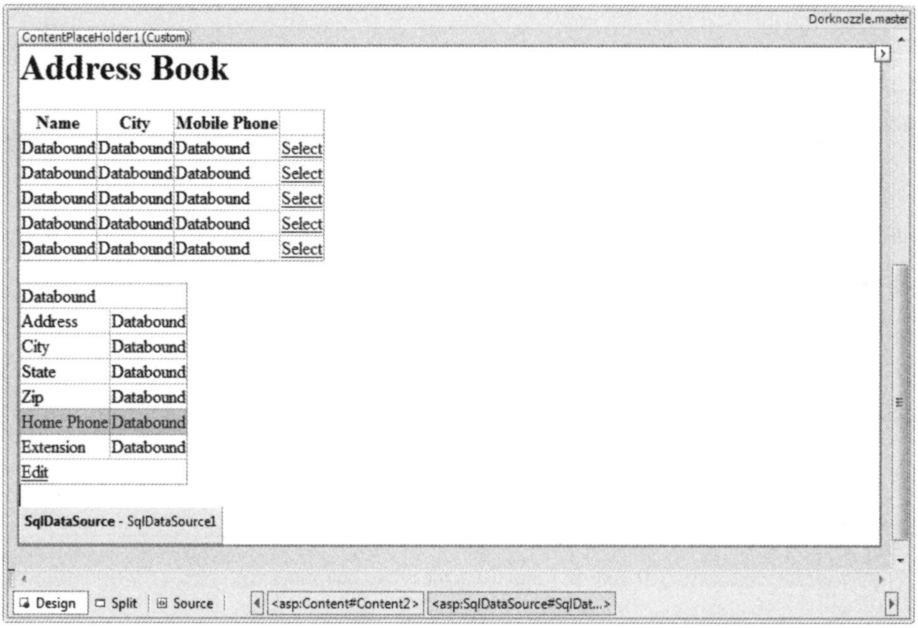

Figure 12.2. **AddressBook.aspx** with an SqlDataSource control

Rename the object `employeesDataSource`. In **Source** view, the code for the new control should look like this:

Dorknozzle\VB\02_AddressBook.aspx *(excerpt)*

```
<asp:SqlDataSource id="employeesDataSource" runat="server">
</asp:SqlDataSource>
```

Switch back to **Design** view, click the `SqlDataSource` control's smart tag, and select **Configure Data Source**. A dialog will appear, giving us the opportunity to provide the details of the data source. In the first page of the dialog, we specify the data connection we want to use. If we hadn't already added the Dorknozzle connection string to the **Web.config** file, we could have clicked the **New Connection…** button, and used the wizard to add a connection string to **Web.config**. However, as we've already set up the connection string, we simply choose it from the drop-down list, as shown in Figure 12.3.

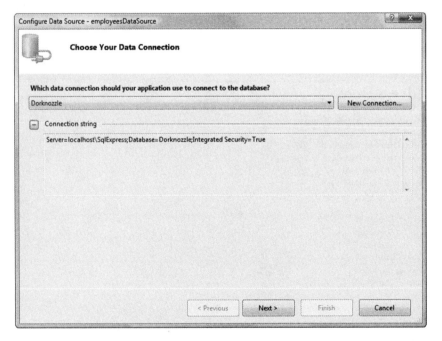

Figure 12.3. Specifying the connection string

After we've selected the **Dorknozzle** connection, we click **Next**. This is where the fun begins!

In the next screen, we can specify the database table and the columns that we want our data source object to handle. Select the `Employees` table and check the `EmployeeID`, `Name`, `City`, and `MobilePhone` columns, as depicted in Figure 12.4.

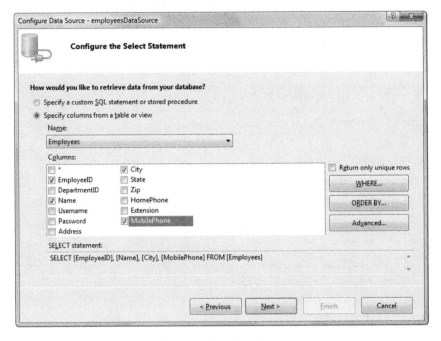

Figure 12.4. Choosing columns

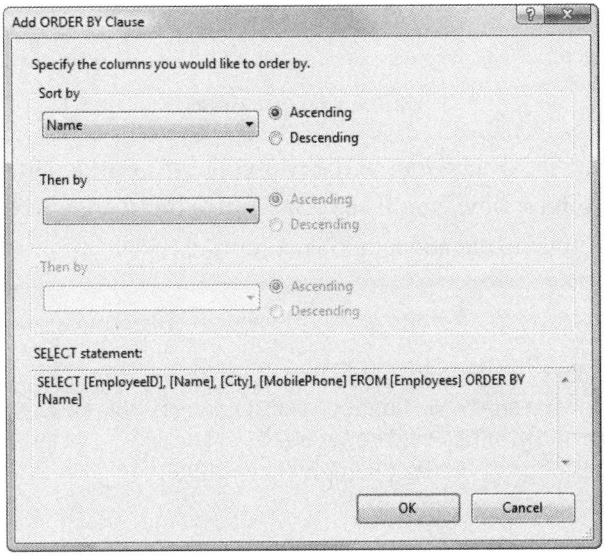

Figure 12.5. Specifying an ORDER BY clause

Click the **ORDER BY...** button and select the Name column (or any other column by which you want to sort your employees), as illustrated in Figure 12.5.

Click **OK**, then **Next**. In the dialog that appears, press the **Test Query** button to test that the query will work with this data source. If everything worked well, you should be shown a list of employees similar to the one depicted in Figure 12.6. Finally, click **Finish**.

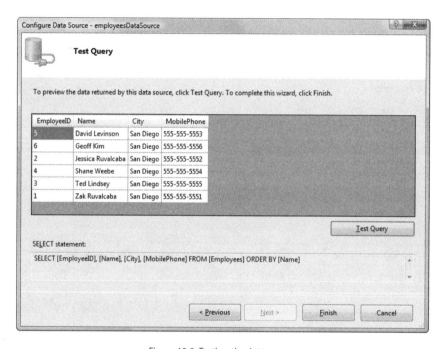

Figure 12.6. Testing the data source

Before we move on, let's take a look at the new code we've added to **AddressBook.aspx**. If you switch to **Source** view, you'll see that quite a bit of code has been created for you. Let's look at the SqlDataSource object first:

Dorknozzle\VB\03_AddressBook.aspx *(excerpt)*

```
<asp:SqlDataSource ID="employeesDataSource" runat="server"
    ConnectionString="<%$ ConnectionStrings:Dorknozzle %>"
    SelectCommand="SELECT [EmployeeID], [Name], [City],
        [MobilePhone] FROM [Employees] ORDER BY [Name]">
</asp:SqlDataSource>
```

This object is amazing in its simplicity, yet the `GridView` can connect to it and display the required data with very little additional effort. Let's use this `SqlDataSource` object to populate the `GridView`.

In **AddressBook.aspx**, use either **Source** view or the **Properties** window in **Design** view to set the properties of the `GridView` control to those outlined in Table 12.1.

Table 12.1. Properties to Set for the `GridView` Control

Property	Value
DataSourceID	employeesDataSource
DataKeyNames	EmployeeID
AllowPaging	True
PageSize	3
AllowSorting	True

Don't Overwrite the Columns!

If you set the `DataSourceID` property in **Design** view, Visual Web Developer will ask if you'd like to clear the column data and replace it with that from the data source, as Figure 12.7 illustrates. Make sure you choose **No**, because we're happy with the columns we decided to display when creating the grid in Chapter 11.

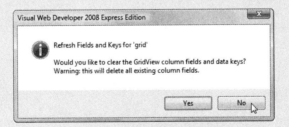

Figure 12.7. We're not refreshing the `GridView` fields

`PageSize` specifies the number of records the `GridView` should display on every product page. Normally, we'd want this number to be greater than three, but we've set it to a low number here so that we can test the paging functionality with our sample data. `AllowPaging` enables `GridView`'s paging functionality, which will cause paging links to be displayed. When we set `AllowSorting` to `True`, it will allow us to change the column names into links that users can click to sort the data on the basis of that field; we'll do this in a moment.

After the above properties have been set, the `GridView` control source should look like this:

```
                                    Dorknozzle\VB\04_AddressBook.aspx (excerpt)

<asp:GridView id="grid" runat="server" AutoGenerateColumns="False"
    AllowPaging="True" AllowSorting="True" DataKeyNames="EmployeeID"
    DataSourceID="employeesDataSource" PageSize="3">
  <Columns>
    ⋮
  </Columns>
</asp:GridView>
```

Let's also deal with style issues by adding the lines below to the skin file, **SkinFile.skin**. The `PagerStyle` defines the style used by the cells that contain the paging buttons; we'll see these buttons in a moment:

```
                                       Dorknozzle\VB\05_SkinFile.skin (excerpt)

<asp:GridView runat="server" CssClass="GridMain" CellPadding="4"
    GridLines="None">
  <RowStyle CssClass="GridRow" />
  <SelectedRowStyle CssClass="GridSelectedRow" />
  <HeaderStyle CssClass="GridHeader" />
  <PagerStyle CssClass="GridRow" />
</asp:GridView>

<asp:DetailsView runat="server" CssClass="GridMain"
    CellPadding="4" GridLines="None">
  <RowStyle CssClass="GridRow" />
  <HeaderStyle CssClass="GridHeader" />
  <PagerStyle CssClass="GridRow" />
</asp:DetailsView>
```

To enable column sorting, you need to click the grid's smart tag in **Design** view and choose **Edit Columns…**. We want to allow sorting by name and by city, so we'll alter these columns only. Start by selecting the `Name` column from the **Selected fields** box. Then, from its properties box on the right, choose `Name` for its `SortExpression` property as depicted in Figure 12.8.

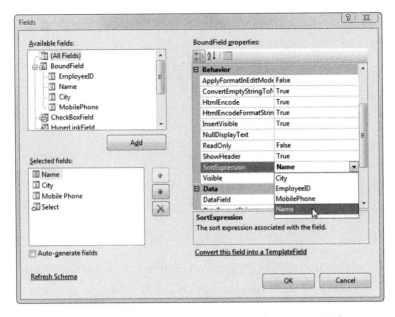

Figure 12.8. Selecting a `SortExpression` value for column sorting\

Then select the `City` column and set its `SortExpression` property to `City`.
`SortExpression` property to `City`.. If the SortExpression field is blank, be sure to
click the **Refresh Schema** link in the lower left-hand corner. After clicking **OK**, the
`Name` and `City` column headers should appear as links in Visual Web Developer's
Design view, as shown in Figure 12.9.

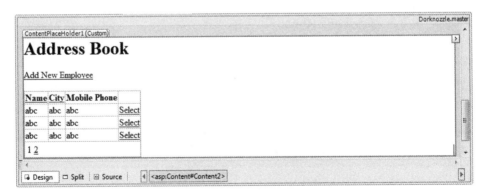

Figure 12.9. Column headers as links in Visual Web Developer

Finally, use Visual Web Developer to generate the signature for the grid's `Sorting`
event, and add the following single line to the generated code:

Visual Basic	Dorknozzle\VB\06_AddressBook.aspx.vb *(excerpt)*

```
Protected Sub grid_Sorting(ByVal sender As Object,
➥    ByVal e As System.Web.UI.WebControls.GridViewSortEventArgs)
➥    Handles grid.Sorting
    grid.DataBind()
End Sub
```

C#	Dorknozzle\CS\06_AddressBook.aspx.cs *(excerpt)*

```
protected void grid_Sorting(object sender, GridViewSortEventArgs e)
{
    grid.DataBind();
}
```

Execute the project. If everything goes well, you should see a functional `GridView`, with working paging buttons, like the one in Figure 12.10.

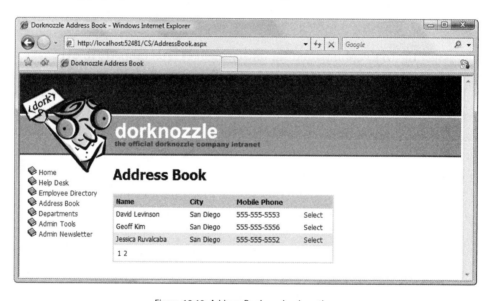

Figure 12.10. Address Book paging in action

Yes, paging works, and you didn't write a single line of C# or VB code to implement it! You can even select rows—although when you do, nothing happens (other than the appearance of shading that acts as a visual cue that the row has been selected), because we haven't implemented any functionality for the `DetailsView` control as yet. (Remember that at the beginning of the chapter, we deleted all the code.)

Binding the `DetailsView` to a `SqlDataSource`

Here, our aim is to replicate the functionality the `DetailsView` gave us in Chapter 11, and to add functionality that will allow users to add and delete employees' records.

Let's start by adding another `SqlDataSource` control, either next to or below the existing one, in **AddressBook.aspx**. Give the new `SqlDataSource` the name `employeeDataSource`. Click its smart tag, and select **Configure Data Source**. The Configure Data Source wizard will appear again.

In the first screen, choose the **Dorknozzle** connection string. Click **Next**, and you'll be taken to the second screen, where there's a bit more work to do. Start by specifying the `Employees` table and checking all of its columns, as shown in Figure 12.11.

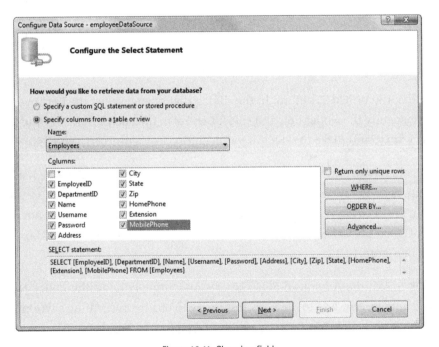

Figure 12.11. Choosing fields

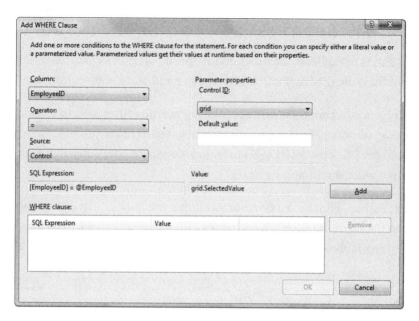

Figure 12.12. Creating a new condition

Next, click the **WHERE...** button. In the dialog that opens, select the `EmployeeID` column, specify the = operator, and select **Control** in the **Source** field. For the **Control ID** select `grid`, and leave the default value empty, as Figure 12.12 shows.

Finally, click **Add**, and the expression will be added to the **WHERE clause** list. The SQL expression that's generated will filter the results on the basis of the value selected in the `GridView` control. Click **OK** to close the dialog, then click the **Advanced...** button. Check the **Generate INSERT, UPDATE, and DELETE statements** checkbox, as shown in Figure 12.13.

Click **OK** to exit the Advanced SQL Generation Options dialog, then click **Next**. In the next screen, feel free to click on **Test Query** to ensure everything's working as expected. If you click **Test Query**, you'll be asked for the Employee ID's type and value. Enter **1** for the value, leave the type as **Int32**, then click **OK**. The row should display as it does in Figure 12.14.

Click **Finish**.

Congratulations! Your new `SqlDataSource` is ready to fill your `DetailsView`. Next, we need to tie this `SqlDataSource` to the `DetailsView` and specify how we want

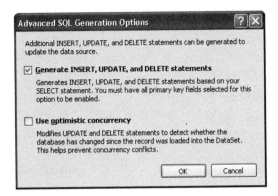

Figure 12.13. Generating `INSERT`, `UPDATE`, and `DELETE` statements

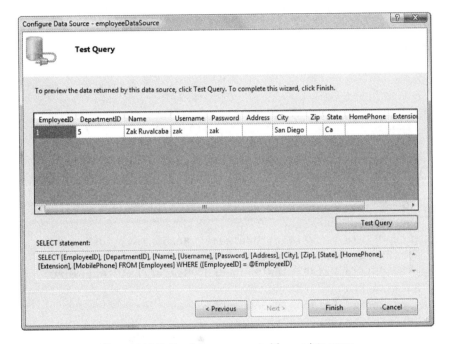

Figure 12.14. Testing the query generated for our data source

the `DetailsView` to behave. Locate the `DetailsView` control and set the properties as outlined in Table 12.2.

Table 12.2. Properties to Set for the `DetailsView` Control

Property	Value
AutoGenerateDeleteButton	True
AutoGenerateEditButton	True
AutoGenerateInsertButton	True
AllowPaging	False
DataSourceID	employeeDataSource
DataKeyNames	EmployeeID

If you're using **Design** view, make sure you choose **Yes** when you're asked about re-creating the `DetailsView` rows and data keys. If you're not using **Design** view, set the columns as shown here:

Dorknozzle\VB\07_AddressBook.aspx *(excerpt)*

```
<Fields>
  <asp:BoundField DataField="EmployeeID" HeaderText="EmployeeID"
      InsertVisible="False" ReadOnly="True"
      SortExpression="EmployeeID" />
  <asp:BoundField DataField="DepartmentID"
      HeaderText="DepartmentID" SortExpression="DepartmentID" />
  <asp:BoundField DataField="Name" HeaderText="Name"
      SortExpression="Name" />
  <asp:BoundField DataField="Username" HeaderText="Username"
      SortExpression="Username" />
  <asp:BoundField DataField="Password" HeaderText="Password"
      SortExpression="Password" />
  <asp:BoundField DataField="Address" HeaderText="Address"
      SortExpression="Address" />
  <asp:BoundField DataField="City" HeaderText="City"
      SortExpression="City" />
  <asp:BoundField DataField="MobilePhone" HeaderText="MobilePhone"
      SortExpression="MobilePhone" />
  <asp:BoundField DataField="State" HeaderText="State"
      SortExpression="State" />
  <asp:BoundField DataField="Zip" HeaderText="Zip"
      SortExpression="Zip" />
  <asp:BoundField DataField="HomePhone" HeaderText="HomePhone"
      SortExpression="HomePhone" />
```

```
    <asp:BoundField DataField="Extension" HeaderText="Extension"
        SortExpression="Extension" />
</Fields>
```

You're ready! Execute the project, and enjoy the new functionality that you implemented without writing a single line of code. Take it for a quick spin to ensure that the features for editing and deleting users are perfectly functional.

Right now, if you select an employee from the list, you'll see the page shown in Figure 12.15.

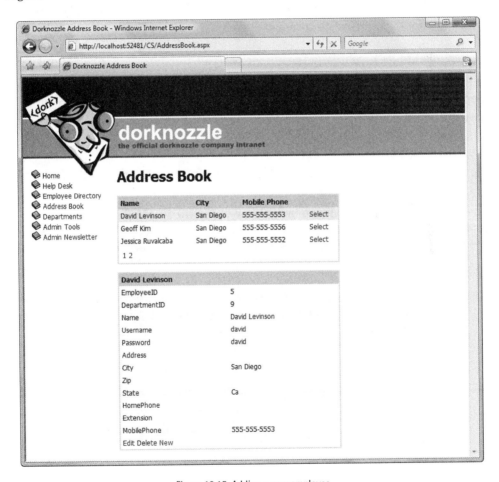

Figure 12.15. Adding a new employee

When you click on **New** to add a new employee, the form becomes editable, allowing you to create a new employee record.

Adding Users the Easy Way

If you want to be able to use this form to add new employees to the database, the easiest way to do so is to leave in all the required columns; otherwise, you'll get an error when you try to add a new employee without specifying values for the NOT NULL columns. If you don't want to give intranet administrators the ability to add new employee records to the database with this form, and you want to keep the list of details short, you can simply remove the unwanted columns from the list.

Before we discuss exactly what's happening here, and how the functionality works, let's implement a few small improvements.

If you agreed to let Visual Web Developer generate the DetailsView columns for you, it will automatically have rewritten the templates we developed in the last chapter, and added BoundField controls for each of the columns you're reading from the data source.

The HeaderTemplate is still intact, but we want to update it to show a different display when we're inserting details for a new employee. Currently, the header is set to display the Name field of the selected employee, which means it will be empty when we insert a new employee (as we saw in Figure 12.15). To change this, modify the HeaderTemplate of your DetailsView as follows:

Visual Basic   Dorknozzle\VB\08_AddressBook.aspx *(excerpt)*

```
<HeaderTemplate>
  <%#IIf(Eval("Name") = Nothing, "Adding New Employee", _
    Eval("Name"))%>
</HeaderTemplate>
```

C#   Dorknozzle\CS\08_AddressBook.aspx *(excerpt)*

```
<HeaderTemplate>
  <%#Eval("Name") == null ? "Adding New Employee" :
    Eval("Name")%>
</HeaderTemplate>
```

Now, when we insert a new employee record, `DetailsView` will display the words **Adding New Employee** in its header; when we're editing or displaying an existing employee's details, it will display the name of that employee, as Figure 12.16 shows.

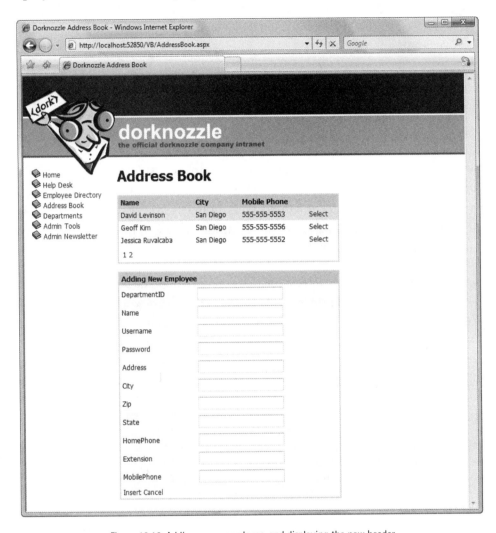

Figure 12.16. Adding a new employee, and displaying the new header

IIf and the Ternary Operator

IIf (in VB) and the ternary operator (in C#) receive as parameters one conditional expression (which returns True or False), and two values. If the condition is True, the first value is returned, and if the condition is False, the second value is returned.

In our case, the conditional expression verifies whether the Name field is empty, which will be the case if we're inserting a new row. So, when we're inserting a new row, we display **Adding New Employee** in the DetailsView's header; otherwise, we display the name of the employee whose details are being edited.

One minor hitch with this solution is that the GridView isn't instantly updated when we make a change using the DetailsView control. Try modifying the name of a user; even after you click the **Update** link in the DetailsView, the GridView will show the old value. Only after you reload the page will the data be displayed correctly by the GridView.

This issue occurs because the GridView is populated before the DetailsView updates the database. To avoid this problem, we could use a simple workaround that forces the GridView to update itself in response to the occurrence of certain events raised by the DetailsView control. These events are ItemUpdated, ItemDeleted, and ItemInserted. Use Visual Web Developer to generate the event handlers for these events, and update the code like this:

Visual Basic	Dorknozzle\VB\09_AddressBook.aspx.vb *(excerpt)*

```
Protected Sub employeeDetails_ItemUpdated(
➥   ByVal sender As Object, ByVal e As
➥   System.Web.UI.WebControls.DetailsViewUpdatedEventArgs)
➥   Handles employeeDetails.ItemUpdated
  grid.DataBind()
End Sub
Protected Sub employeeDetails_ItemDeleted(
➥   ByVal sender As Object, ByVal e As
➥   System.Web.UI.WebControls.DetailsViewDeletedEventArgs)
➥   Handles employeeDetails.ItemDeleted
  grid.DataBind()
End Sub
Protected Sub employeeDetails_ItemInserted(
➥   ByVal sender As Object, ByVal e As
```

```
➡    System.Web.UI.WebControls.DetailsViewInsertedEventArgs)
➡    Handles employeeDetails.ItemInserted
     grid.DataBind()
End Sub
```

C#	Dorknozzle\CS\09_AddressBook.aspx.cs *(excerpt)*

```
protected void employeeDetails_ItemUpdated(object sender,
    DetailsViewUpdatedEventArgs e)
{
  grid.DataBind();
}
protected void employeeDetails_ItemDeleted(object sender,
    DetailsViewDeletedEventArgs e)
{
  grid.DataBind();
}
protected void employeeDetails_ItemInserted(object sender,
    DetailsViewInsertedEventArgs e)
{
  grid.DataBind();
}
```

Now your GridView and DetailsView controls will be synchronized permanently.

The last improvement we'll make is to add an **Add New Employee** button to the page—you can see how it will look in Figure 12.17. Right now, we can only add new employees if we select an employee from the GridView, but this isn't exactly an intuitive way to work. Let's add a button that will make the DetailsView control display in insert mode when it's clicked by a user.

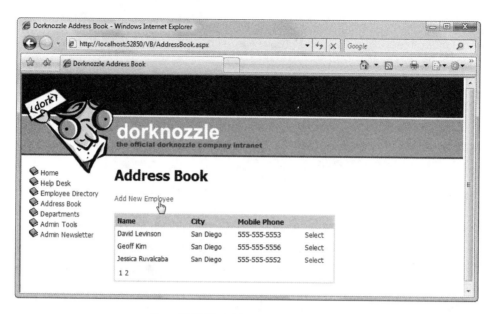

Figure 12.17. The **Add New Employee** button

Add the new button above the grid like this:

```
                                      Dorknozzle\VB\10_AddressBook.aspx (excerpt)

<h1>Address Book</h1>
<p>
  <asp:LinkButton id="addEmployeeButton" runat="server"
    Text="Add New Employee" />
</p>
<asp:GridView id="grid" runat="server"… >
  ⋮
</asp:GridView>
```

Double-click the button in **Design** view, and fill in its `Click` event handler like this:

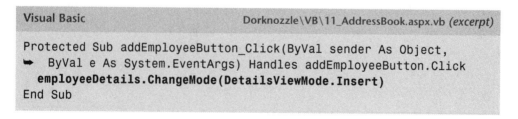

```
Visual Basic                    Dorknozzle\VB\11_AddressBook.aspx.vb (excerpt)

Protected Sub addEmployeeButton_Click(ByVal sender As Object,
➥   ByVal e As System.EventArgs) Handles addEmployeeButton.Click
    employeeDetails.ChangeMode(DetailsViewMode.Insert)
End Sub
```

```
C#                                    Dorknozzle\CS\11_AddressBook.aspx.cs (excerpt)

protected void addEmployeeButton_Click(object sender, EventArgs e)
{
  employeeDetails.ChangeMode(DetailsViewMode.Insert);
}
```

Our new button will cause the `DetailsView` to display in insert mode when clicked. Your Address Book is now fully featured, and ready for production!

What's really interesting about the code that was generated for us in this section is the definition of the `employeeDataSource`. Since this data source needs to store the details of selecting, deleting, updating, and inserting rows, it looks significantly bigger than the `employeesDataSource`:

```
                                    Dorknozzle\VB\10_AddressBook.aspx (excerpt)

<asp:SqlDataSource ID="employeeDataSource" runat="server"
    ConnectionString="<%$ ConnectionStrings:Dorknozzle %>"
    DeleteCommand="DELETE FROM [Employees]
        WHERE [EmployeeID] = @EmployeeID"
    InsertCommand="INSERT INTO [Employees] ([DepartmentID], [Name],
        [Username], [Password], [Address], [City], [MobilePhone],
        [State], [Zip], [HomePhone], [Extension])
        VALUES (@DepartmentID, @Name, @Username, @Password,
        @Address, @City, @MobilePhone, @State, @Zip, @HomePhone,
        @Extension)"
    SelectCommand="SELECT [EmployeeID], [DepartmentID], [Name],
        [Username], [Password], [Address], [City], [MobilePhone],
        [State], [Zip], [HomePhone], [Extension] FROM [Employees]
        WHERE ([EmployeeID] = @EmployeeID)"
    UpdateCommand="UPDATE [Employees]
        SET [DepartmentID] = @DepartmentID, [Name] = @Name,
        [Username] = @Username, [Password] = @Password,
        [Address] = @Address, [City] = @City,
        [MobilePhone] = @MobilePhone, [State] = @State,
        [Zip] = @Zip, [HomePhone] = @HomePhone,
        [Extension] = @Extension
        WHERE [EmployeeID] = @EmployeeID">
    <SelectParameters>
      <asp:ControlParameter ControlID="grid" Name="EmployeeID"
        PropertyName="SelectedValue" Type="Int32" />
    </SelectParameters>
    <DeleteParameters>
```

```
            <asp:Parameter Name="EmployeeID" Type="Int32" />
        </DeleteParameters>
        <UpdateParameters>
          <asp:Parameter Name="DepartmentID" Type="Int32" />
          <asp:Parameter Name="Name" Type="String" />
          <asp:Parameter Name="Username" Type="String" />
          <asp:Parameter Name="Password" Type="String" />
          <asp:Parameter Name="Address" Type="String" />
          <asp:Parameter Name="City" Type="String" />
          <asp:Parameter Name="MobilePhone" Type="String" />
          <asp:Parameter Name="State" Type="String" />
          <asp:Parameter Name="Zip" Type="String" />
          <asp:Parameter Name="HomePhone" Type="String" />
          <asp:Parameter Name="Extension" Type="String" />
          <asp:Parameter Name="EmployeeID" Type="Int32" />
        </UpdateParameters>
        <InsertParameters>
          <asp:Parameter Name="DepartmentID" Type="Int32" />
          <asp:Parameter Name="Name" Type="String" />
          <asp:Parameter Name="Username" Type="String" />
          <asp:Parameter Name="Password" Type="String" />
          <asp:Parameter Name="Address" Type="String" />
          <asp:Parameter Name="City" Type="String" />
          <asp:Parameter Name="MobilePhone" Type="String" />
          <asp:Parameter Name="State" Type="String" />
          <asp:Parameter Name="Zip" Type="String" />
          <asp:Parameter Name="HomePhone" Type="String" />
          <asp:Parameter Name="Extension" Type="String" />
        </InsertParameters>
      </asp:SqlDataSource>
```

The `SqlDataSource` produces the necessary queries for the database for UPDATE, DELETE, and INSERT operations. Look, we didn't even have to write any database code! One more important feature, the code generated uses parameterized queries. A parameterized query is where the data type is known ahead of time and also secures the query against any possible SQL Injection attack. It is good practice to use parameterized queries or stored procedures whenever possible for this security precaution. You should also notice the use of square brackets ([and]) surrounding the fields and table names. These are to help distinguish these database objects from any conflicting keyword. Although our example doesn't use any conflicting keywords as it is an object name, it is always a good habit to develop.

I'm sure you can now immediately see the benefits of us using `SqlDataSource` to create data-entry forms, such as our address book, for smaller projects like the Dorknozzle intranet. The `SqlDataSource` produces secure ASP.NET code and database SQL queries for both the `DetailsView` and `GridView` controls without much interaction from the developer. Yet, we still retain the power and flexibility to edit these SQL queries or controls to improve functionality, introduce styling using our templates, and even interact with the grid controls if we wish to do so.

Displaying Lists in `DetailsView`

We want to improve on our `DetailsView` by making it show a list of department names instead of department IDs. This makes sense, as it's much easier for users to select the name of a department than a department ID when they're updating or inserting the details of an employee. Figure 12.18 shows how the page will look once we've created this functionality.

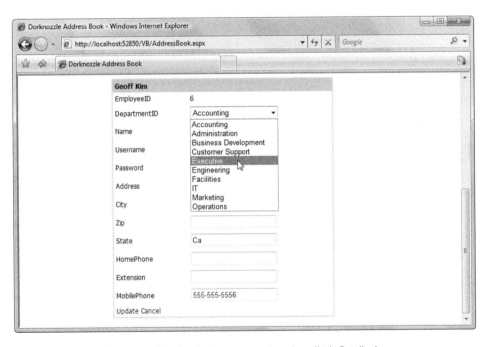

Figure 12.18. Viewing the **Department** drop-down list in Details view

Start by adding a new `SqlDataSource` control beside the two existing data source controls in **AddressBook.aspx**. Name the control `departmentsDataSource`, click its smart tag, and select **Configure Data Source**. In the first screen, select the **Dorknozzle** connection, then click **Next**. Specify the `Departments` table and select both of its columns, as shown in Figure 12.19.

Click **Next**, then **Finish** to save the data source configuration. The definition of your new data source control will look like this:

Dorknozzle\VB\12_AddressBook.aspx *(excerpt)*

```
<asp:SqlDataSource ID="departmentsDataSource" runat="server"
    ConnectionString="<%$ ConnectionStrings:Dorknozzle %>"
    SelectCommand="SELECT [DepartmentID], [Department]
    FROM [Departments]">
</asp:SqlDataSource>
```

Now, with **AddressBook.aspx** open in **Design** view, click the `DetailsView` control's smart tag, select **Edit Fields**, and transform the Department ID `BoundField` into a `TemplateField` (you learned how to do this back in Chapter 11). Now, switch to Source view, and locate the Department ID `TemplateField` that you just generated. It should look something like this:

```
<asp:TemplateField HeaderText="DepartmentID"
    SortExpression="DepartmentID">
  <EditItemTemplate>
    <asp:TextBox ID="TextBox1" runat="server"
        Text='<%# Bind("DepartmentID") %>'></asp:TextBox>
  </EditItemTemplate>
  <InsertItemTemplate>
    <asp:TextBox ID="TextBox1" runat="server"
        Text='<%# Bind("DepartmentID") %>'></asp:TextBox>
  </InsertItemTemplate>
  <ItemTemplate>
    <asp:Label ID="Label1" runat="server"
        Text='<%# Bind("DepartmentID") %>'></asp:Label>
  </ItemTemplate>
</asp:TemplateField>
```

Modify this generated template as highlighted below:

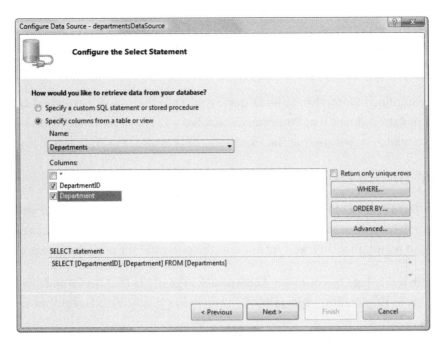

Figure 12.19. Selecting the columns from the Departments table

Dorknozzle\VB\13_AddressBook.aspx *(excerpt)*

```
<asp:TemplateField HeaderText="Department"
    SortExpression="DepartmentID">
  <EditItemTemplate>
    <asp:DropDownList id="didDdl" runat="server"
        DataSourceID="departmentsDataSource"
        DataTextField="Department" DataValueField="DepartmentID"
        SelectedValue='<%# Bind("DepartmentID") %>' />
  </EditItemTemplate>
  <InsertItemTemplate>
    <asp:DropDownList ID="didDdl" runat="server"
        DataSourceID="departmentsDataSource"
        DataTextField="Department"
        DataValueField="DepartmentID"
        SelectedValue='<%# Bind("DepartmentID") %>' />
  </InsertItemTemplate>
  <ItemTemplate>
    <asp:DropDownList ID="didDdl" runat="server"
        DataSourceID="departmentsDataSource"
        DataTextField="Department"
        DataValueField="DepartmentID"
        SelectedValue='<%# Bind("DepartmentID") %>'
```

```
        Enabled="False" />
  </ItemTemplate>
</asp:TemplateField>
```

When you reload your address book now, you'll see that the departments are displayed in a drop-down list. You can use that list when you're inserting and editing employee data—a feature that the intranet's users are sure to find very helpful!

More on `SqlDataSource`

The `SqlDataSource` object can make programming easier when it's used correctly and responsibly. However, the simplicity of the `SqlDataSource` control comes at the cost of maintainability, and introduces the potential for performance problems.

The main advantage of your new **AddressBook.aspx** file is that it's incredibly easy and quick to implement, especially if you're using Visual Web Developer.

However, embedding SQL queries right into your **.aspx** files does have a major disadvantage if you intend to grow your web site: in more complex applications containing many forms that perform data-related tasks, an approach that sees you storing all of your SQL queries inside different `SqlDataSource` controls can degenerate very quickly into a system that's very difficult to maintain. Why does this matter? In the real-world, you'll probably want to store your SQL queries as stored procedures on the database, where they can easily be changed without having to recompile and deploy your code to the web server. Your code logic for handling all data access will most likely also reside in a standalone class, that makes the database calls to these SQL queries without affecting the user interface in case of a database design change. Trust me, no matter how often you believe a screen is complete, somebody will always need an additional field or column. This would require manually updating every control on every page that uses a SqlDataSource.

Another disadvantage of using the `SqlDataSource` is that its sorting and paging features usually aren't as fast and efficient as they could be if you used a custom SQL query that returned the data already paged and/or sorted from the database. When we use the `GridView`'s paging feature, for example, the `SqlDataSource` control doesn't limit the number of records we read from the database. Even if only a small subset of data needs to be shown, unless customizations are implemented, the entire table will be read from the database, and a subset of the data displayed. Even if only three records need to be displayed, *all* of the records in the table will be returned.

An interesting property of `SqlDataSource` that's worth noting is `DataSourceMode`, whose possible values are `DataSet` or `SqlDataReader`. The `DataSet` mode is the default mode, and implies that the `SqlDataSource` will use a `DataSet` object to retrieve its data. We'll analyze the `DataSet` class next. The other mode is `SqlDataReader`, which makes the `SqlDataSource` use your old friend, the `SqlDataReader`, behind the scenes.

So, what is this `DataSet` class? Since version 1.0, the .NET Framework has come with a number of objects—`DataSet`, `DataTable`, `DataView`, `SqlDataAdapter`, and others—that provide **disconnected** data access. So, instead of having the database return the exact data you need for a certain task in the exact order in which you need it, you can use these objects to delegate some of the responsibility of filtering and ordering the data to your C# or VB code.

Both the `DataSet` and `SqlDataReader` settings of `DataSourceMode` have advantages and disadvantages, and the optimum approach for any task will depend on the task itself. There are circumstances in which it makes sense to store the data locally, and you need to be aware of all the possibilities in order to be able to make an informed decision about which mode to use.

Working with Data Sets and Data Tables

We've been working with databases for a while now. Initially, you learned about the `SqlDataReader`, and used it to populate your controls. Then, in the first half of this chapter, we gained first-hand experience with the data source controls, which can automate many features for you. Let's learn about one more technique you can use to get data to your visitors.

I know that all these options can be confusing at first, but hang in there. You need to play around with all of them before you can become an experienced ASP.NET developer!

The `DataSet` object is at the center of Microsoft's model for presenting **disconnected data**. Disconnected data—data that resides in memory and is completely independent of the data source—gives us a raft of new opportunities of developing desktop and web apps.

In Chapter 9, you learned about the role that data readers play in relation to applications and database data. Whenever we need to access data from a database, we create a connection object and a command object. These two objects are used together to create a data reader object, which we can use within our application by binding it to a data control for presentation purposes. Figure 12.20 illustrates this process.

So, what's the problem? Well, while they're the fastest way to retrieve data from a database, data readers can't be used to carry out any significant work—you can't use them to sort, filter, or page through the data. As the arrows in Figure 12.20 show, data readers present a forward-only stream of data to the application: you can't go back to a previous record, or reuse that data reader somewhere else. Moreover, a data reader object isn't reusable. This means that you can't make multiple requests to a database using the same data reader to fetch more data.

Data sets, on the other hand, are much more flexible. Imagine your own in-memory representation of your database containing your data tables that you're free to use in code whenever and however you wish. That's a data set. As we'll see in the next section, data sets have all the bells and whistles that databases offer, including tables, columns, rows, relationships, and even queries! A data set is a memory-resident copy of database data, so, once a data set has been created, it is stored in memory and its ties to the database will have been broken. Then, when you need to work with the data, you don't need to re-query the database—you simply retrieve the data from the data set again and again. From your data set, you can filter, sort, edit, or page data as you choose without ever having to call the database again. Figure 12.21 illustrates this point.

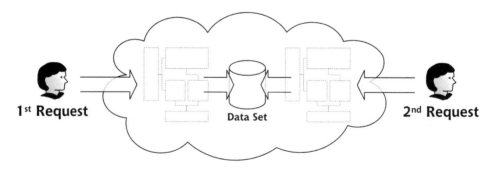

Figure 12.22. Multiple pages making multiple requests from the same data set

An even greater advantage of data sets is that they can be shared among multiple requests, as illustrated in Figure 12.22.

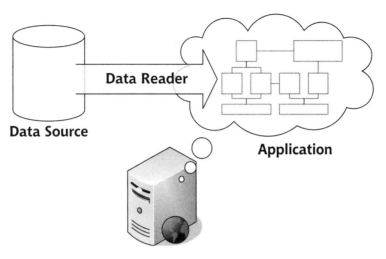

Figure 12.20. Retrieving data using a data reader

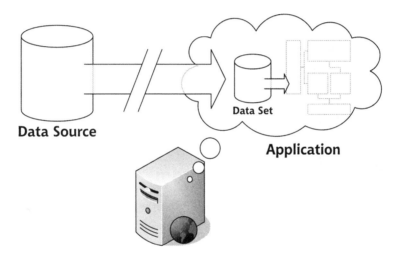

Figure 12.21. Breaking the data set's ties to the data source once it has been created

What this means is that you simply need to create the data set once per request. Once the data set has been created, it can be used by many different pages, all of which may make multiple—and even different—requests to that data set.

However, data sets require more memory resources than do data readers. A data reader simply keeps track of its position within the results of a query, whereas a data set can contain a local copy of an entire database. However, in practice you shouldn't do this of course, as the larger the amount of data kept in the data set, the more memory the data set uses.

If you're only reading the data, using a data reader can make sense—especially if you've gotten yourself familiar with reading from a data reader object. If you also need to update, insert, or delete data, or you need to process the data within your code, data sets might be of more help. However, if you need to perform other operations, such as adding, editing, or deleting data then using a data set is your only choice.

When you're deciding whether to use data readers or data sets, you need to consider the purpose for which you need the data. This decision is important, because it affects:

- resources consumed on the database server
- resources consumed on the web server
- the overall application architecture
- Maintainability for future enhancements

If you're only reading the data, using a data reader can make sense. If you also need to update, insert, or delete data, or you need to process the data within your code, data sets might be of more help.

This section will teach you everything you need to know to begin working with data sets.

What Is a Data Set Made From?

A data set comprises many parts, all of which are required for its usage. We'll meet and discuss the following classes in this section:

- `DataSet`
- `DbDataAdapter`and its derivative, `SqlDataAdapter`
- `DataTable`
- `DataColumn`
- `DataRow`
- `DataRelation`
- `DataView`

We need to use most of these classes in order to work with data sets. The `DbDataAdapter` is an abstract class that handles the communication between a `DataSet` and the database server itself. It knows how to fill the `DataSet` with data, and it also knows how to handle any request for add, edit, or delete operations from your `DataSet` back to the database server. Because we are using SQL Server we then use the `SqlDataAdapter` for all of our communications.

Data Adapters

`SqlDataAdapter` is one of the many available data providers available now in ASP.NET 4. `SqlDataAdapter` can only be used with Microsoft SQL Server, and isn't interchangeable with other database servers. Microsoft has cataloged several data providers at http://msdn.microsoft.com/en-us/data/dd363565 including popular database servers such as Oracle, MySQL, and Sybase. Included in the .NET 4.0 Framework is the `OdbcDbDataAdapter` and `OleDbDataAdapter` for generic access to custom data sources that support ODBC or OLE respectively. Going forward we will use only the `SqlDataAdapter` for our examples, however the code should be the same when using a different data provider.

A `DataSet` will always contain at least one `DataTable`, but it can contain many. DataTables can contain a reference back to the DataSet object, but they can standalone.These `DataTables` contain `DataColumns` and `DataRows`. If we needed to establish a relationship between multiple `DataTables` within a `DataSet`, we'd use `DataRelations`. Finally, we'd create `DataViews` to query the `DataSet`.These `DataViews` represent sorted or filtered data from the `DataSet`.

A `DataSet` mirrors the structure of a relational database, as Figure 12.23 shows.

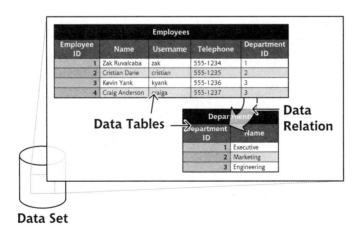

Figure 12.23. The structure of a `DataSet`, which closely resembles that of a database

You can see the parallel between the `DataSet`'s structure and that of a database. A database contains tables; here, the `DataSet` contains `DataTables`. Tables in a database have columns and rows; our `DataTables` have `DataColumns` and `DataRows`. When we work in a database, we establish relationships between tables; here, we'd create `DataRelations`. The major difference between `DataSets` and databases is that `DataSets` are memory-resident, while a centralized database resides inside a database management system.

Let's see how we can create a `DataSet` within code.

Binding `DataSets` to Controls

Now that you have some understanding of the structure of a typical `DataSet`, let's look at the process involved in creating a `DataSet` in code, and binding a `DataTable` to a control. To illustrate this example, we'll create a simple page that displays the Dorknozzle departments; we'll call this page **Departments.aspx**.

Create a new web form called **Departments.aspx**, as you have for the other pages in the Dorknozzle project. Update the generated code like this:

```
                                    Dorknozzle\VB\14_Departments.aspx (excerpt)

<%@ Page Language="VB" MasterPageFile="~/Dorknozzle.master"
    AutoEventWireup="false" CodeFile="Departments.aspx.vb"
    Inherits="Departments" title="Dorknozzle Departments" %>

<asp:Content ID="Content1" ContentPlaceHolderID="head" Runat="Server">
</asp:Content>
<asp:Content ID="Content2"
    ContentPlaceHolderID="ContentPlaceHolder1" Runat="Server">
  <h1>Dorknozzle Departments</h1>
  <asp:GridView id="departmentsGrid" runat="server">
  </asp:GridView>
</asp:Content>
```

So far, everything looks familiar. We have a blank page based on **Dorknozzle.master**, with an empty `GridView` control called `departmentsGrid`. Our goal through the rest of this chapter is to learn how to use the `DataSet` and related objects to give life to the `GridView` control.

Switch to **Design** view, and double-click on an empty part of the form to generate the `Page_Load` event handler. Add references to the `System.Data.SqlClient` namespace (which contains the `SqlDataAdapter` class), and, the `System.Data` namespace (which contains classes such as `DataSet`, `DataTable`, and so on) and the `System.Configuration` namespace (which contains the `ConfigurationManager` class, used for reading connection strings from **Web.config**). Here's how the code should look:

Visual Basic	Dorknozzle\VB\15_Departments.aspx.vb *(excerpt)*

```
Imports System.Data.SqlClient
Imports System.Data
Imports System.Configuration

Partial Class Departments
    Inherits System.Web.UI.Page

Protected Sub Page_Load(ByVal sender As Object,
➥   ByVal e As System.EventArgs) Handles Me.Load
    ⋮
End Sub
⋮
End Class
```

C#	Dorknozzle\CS\15_Departments.aspx.cs *(excerpt)*

```
using System;
using System.Collections;
using System.Configuration;
using System.Data;
using System.Linq;
using System.Web;
using System.Web.Security;
using System.Web.UI;
using System.Web.UI.HtmlControls;
using System.Web.UI.WebControls;
using System.Web.UI.WebControls.WebParts;
using System.Xml.Linq;
using System.Data.SqlClient;

public partial class Departments : System.Web.UI.Page
{
  protected void Page_Load(object sender, EventArgs e)
```

```
    {
        ⋮
    }
    ⋮
}
```

Next, we'll add a method called `BindGrid`, which populates the `GridView` control using an `SqlDataAdapter` and a `DataSet`. We'll call `BindGrid` from `Page_Load` only when the page is loaded for the first time. We assume that any postback events won't affect the data that's to be displayed by the grid, so we populate the grid just once, when the page loads:

Visual Basic   *Dorknozzle\VB\15_Departments.aspx.vb (excerpt)*

```vbnet
Protected Sub Page_Load(ByVal sender As Object,
➥ ByVal e As System.EventArgs) Handles Me.Load
  If Not Page.IsPostBack Then
    BindGrid()
  End If
End Sub

Private Sub BindGrid()
  Dim conn As SqlConnection
  Dim dataSet As New DataSet
  Dim adapter As SqlDataAdapter
  Dim connectionString As String = _
      ConfigurationManager.ConnectionStrings( _
      "Dorknozzle").ConnectionString
  conn = New SqlConnection(connectionString)
  adapter = New SqlDataAdapter( _
      "SELECT DepartmentID, Department FROM Departments", _
      conn)
  adapter.Fill(dataSet, "Departments")
  departmentsGrid.DataSource = dataSet
  departmentsGrid.DataBind()
End Sub
```

C#   *Dorknozzle\CS\15_Departments.aspx.cs (excerpt)*

```csharp
protected void Page_Load(object sender, EventArgs e)
{
  if (!IsPostBack)
  {
```

```
    BindGrid();
  }
}
private void BindGrid()
{
  SqlConnection conn;
  DataSet dataSet = new DataSet();
  SqlDataAdapter adapter;
  string connectionString =
      ConfigurationManager.ConnectionStrings[
      "Dorknozzle"].ConnectionString;
  conn = new SqlConnection(connectionString);
  adapter = new SqlDataAdapter(
      "SELECT DepartmentID, Department FROM Departments",
      conn);
  adapter.Fill(dataSet, "Departments");
  departmentsGrid.DataSource = dataSet;
  departmentsGrid.DataBind();
}
```

Execute the project, and browse to your Departments page. You should see a display that's similar to Figure 12.24.

The grid is already styled because we have a GridView skin in place. At this point, we've achieved a level of functionality that you might otherwise have reached using SqlCommand and SqlDataReader, or the SqlDataSource; the difference is that, this time, we've used an SqlDataAdapter and a DataSet.

An SqlDataAdapter object is created in much the same way as an SqlCommand object. We simply provide it with an SQL statement and an SqlConnection object. However, it's the line that immediately follows the creation of the adapter that does all the work. The Fill method of the SqlDataAdapter fills our DataSet with the data returned by the SQL query. The Fill method accepts two parameters: the first is the DataSet object that needs to be filled, the second is the name of the table that we want to create within the DataSet.

Once the DataSet has been filled with data, it's simply a matter of binding the DataSet to the GridView, which we do using the same approach we'd use to bind an SqlDataReader.

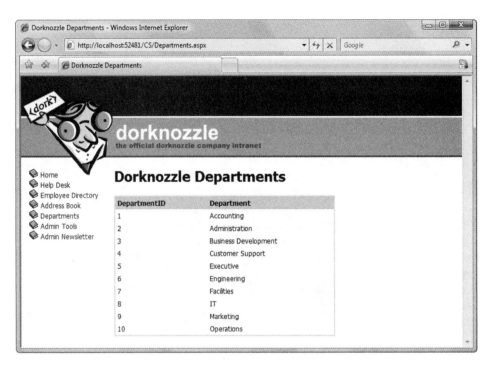

Figure 12.24. The Departments page

Moving on, let's see how we can add another `DataTable` to our `DataSet`. The following code uses the `SelectCommand` property of the `SqlDataAdapter` object to create a new command on the fly, and fill the same `DataSet` with a new `DataTable` called `Employees`:

Visual Basic

```
⋮
adapter = New SqlDataAdapter( _
    "SELECT DepartmentID, Department FROM Departments", conn)
adapter.Fill(dataSet, "Departments")
adapter.SelectCommand = New SqlCommand(_
    "SELECT EmployeeID, Name, MobilePhone FROM Employees", conn)
adapter.Fill(dataSet, "Employees")
departmentsGrid.DataSource = dataSet
departmentsGrid.DataMember = "Employees"
departmentsGrid.DataBind()
⋮
```

C#

```
⋮
adapter = new SqlDataAdapter(
    "SELECT DepartmentID, Department FROM Departments", conn);
adapter.Fill(dataSet, "Departments");
adapter.SelectCommand = new SqlCommand(
    "SELECT EmployeeID, Name, MobilePhone FROM Employees", conn);
adapter.Fill(dataSet, "Employees");
departmentsGrid.DataSource = dataSet;
departmentsGrid.DataMember = "Employees";
departmentsGrid.DataBind();
⋮
```

This code binds the Employees table of the DataSet to the GridView control by setting the GridView's DataMember property. The GridView will now appear as shown in Figure 12.25.

EmployeeID	Name	MobilePhone
1	Zak Ruvalcaba	555-555-5551
2	Jessica Ruvalcaba	555-555-5552
3	Ted Lindsey	555-555-5555
4	Shane Weebe	555-555-5554
5	David Levinson	555-555-5553
6	Geoff Kim	555-555-5556

Figure 12.25. Displaying data from a `DataTable` in a `GridView`

It's easy to imagine how quickly you could fill a page containing many `GridViews` using only one `DataSet` as the source.

As you've learned thus far, `DataTables` are elements that hold data within a `DataSet`. Just like tables in a database, `DataTables` are built from columns and rows. However, unlike tables in databases, `DataTables` reside in memory, which gives us the ability to page, sort, and filter the data in ways that just wouldn't be possible with an `SqlDataReader` without having to wait for additional data to load from the database.

Implementing Paging

We saw the `GridView`'s paging functionality in action earlier in this chapter. When we bound the `GridView` to the `SqlDataProvider`, the paging functionality was automatically implemented. Now that we're binding the `GridView` to a `DataSet`, there's a little more work involved in getting paging up and running. However, the effort will be more than worthwhile if performance is an issue for your application.

The task of implementing paging in a `GridView` that has been bound to an `SqlDataAdapter` involves a two-step process. First, we need to set the `AllowPaging` property of the `GridView` to `True`, and set its `PageSize` value to reflect the number of items we want to see on every page. Open **Departments.aspx** in Visual Web Developer and set `AllowPaging` to `True`, and `PageSize` to 4 on the `departmentsGrid` control, as shown below:

```
                                        Dorknozzle\VB\16_Departments.aspx (excerpt)

<asp:GridView id="departmentsGrid" runat="server"
    AllowPaging="True" PageSize="4">
</asp:GridView>
```

Next, we need to handle the `PageIndexChanging` event of the `GridView` control. This event is fired when the user clicks one of the paging controls; we'll need to update the data displayed in the grid accordingly.

Double-click the `PageIndexChanging` entry in the **Properties** window, as shown in Figure 12.26, to have Visual Web Developer generate an empty event handler for you.

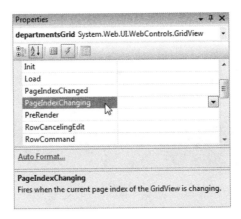

Figure 12.26. Creating the `PageIndexChanging` event handler

Finally, fill in the generated event handler as shown below:

```
Visual Basic                          Dorknozzle\VB\17_Departments.aspx.vb (excerpt)

Protected Sub departmentsGrid_PageIndexChanging(
➥   ByVal sender As Object,
➥   ByVal e As System.Web.UI.WebControls.GridViewPageEventArgs)
➥   Handles departmentsGrid.PageIndexChanging
  Dim newPageIndex As Integer = e.NewPageIndex
  departmentsGrid.PageIndex = newPageIndex
  BindGrid()
End Sub
```

```
C#                                    Dorknozzle\CS\17_Departments.aspx.cs (excerpt)

protected void departmentsGrid_PageIndexChanging(object sender,
    GridViewPageEventArgs e)
{
  int newPageIndex = e.NewPageIndex;
```

```
  departmentsGrid.PageIndex = newPageIndex;
  BindGrid();
}
```

In this code, we've retrieved the index of the requested page from `e.NewPageIndex` parameter, and used its value to set the `PageIndex` property of the `GridView`. We've then bound the grid to its data source once more.

Execute the project again. When you click a paging link within the grid, the display should update quickly, as Figure 12.27 shows.

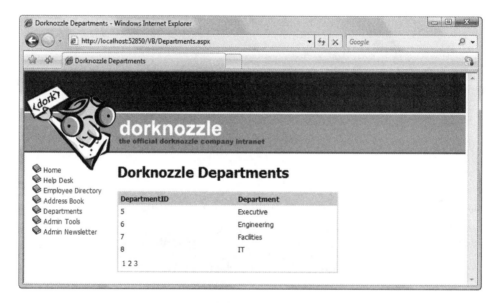

Figure 12.27. Viewing Departments with paging functionality

Storing Data Sets in View State

Now, we're able to page through our list of departments, but the code isn't anywhere near as efficient as it could be. Every time we display another page of departments in our `GridView`, we call the `BindData` method, which executes the following code in order to retrieve a list of departments:

Visual Basic   Dorknozzle\VB\15_Departments.aspx.vb *(excerpt)*

```vb
conn = New SqlConnection(connectionString)
adapter = New SqlDataAdapter( _
    "SELECT DepartmentID, Department FROM Departments", conn)
adapter.Fill(dataSet, "Departments")
```

C#   Dorknozzle\CS\15_Departments.aspx.cs *(excerpt)*

```csharp
conn = new SqlConnection(connectionString);
adapter = new SqlDataAdapter(
    "SELECT DepartmentID, Department FROM Departments", conn);
adapter.Fill(dataSet, "Departments");
```

Given that this list of departments is unlikely to change while we're browsing through its pages, wouldn't it be better if we had to query the database only once? Well, given that we now have a complete copy of the data in the Departments table, we can! Modify the BindGrid method as shown below:

Visual Basic   Dorknozzle\VB\18_Departments.aspx.vb *(excerpt)*

```vb
Private Sub BindGrid()
  Dim conn As SqlConnection
  Dim dataSet As New DataSet
  Dim adapter As SqlDataAdapter
  If ViewState("DepartmentsDataSet") Is Nothing Then
    Dim connectionString As String = _
        ConfigurationManager.ConnectionStrings( _
        "Dorknozzle").ConnectionString
    conn = New SqlConnection(connectionString)
    adapter = New SqlDataAdapter( _
        "SELECT DepartmentID, Department FROM Departments", _
        conn)
    adapter.Fill(dataSet, "Departments")
    ViewState("DepartmentsDataSet") = dataSet
  Else
    dataSet = ViewState("DepartmentsDataSet")
  End If
  departmentsGrid.DataSource = dataSet
  departmentsGrid.DataBind()
End Sub
```

```
C#                                          Dorknozzle\CS\18_Departments.aspx.cs (excerpt)

private void BindGrid()
{
  SqlConnection conn;
  DataSet dataSet = new DataSet();
  SqlDataAdapter adapter;
  if(ViewState["DepartmentsDataSet"] == null)
  {
    string connectionString =
        ConfigurationManager.ConnectionStrings[
        "Dorknozzle"].ConnectionString;
    conn = new SqlConnection(connectionString);
    adapter = new SqlDataAdapter(
        "SELECT DepartmentID, Department FROM Departments",
        conn);
    adapter.Fill(dataSet, "Departments");
    ViewState["DepartmentsDataSet"] = dataSet;
  }
  else
  {
    dataSet = (DataSet)ViewState["DepartmentsDataSet"];
  }
  departmentsGrid.DataSource = dataSet;
  departmentsGrid.DataBind();
}
```

Here, we're using the `ViewState` collection to store our `DataSet`. The `ViewState` collection works a lot like the `Session` collection, except that instead of storing data for access by the entire application, `ViewState` stores data for just this one page while the user is interacting with it. If the users navigate away from this page, the data in `ViewState` will be lost—even if they return to the page within the same session. But, be careful trying to store too much data in the ViewState, it comes at a cost of increasing the page size for the browser which can negatively affect your page load times. In our final chapter, we'll talk about potential ways we can store these `DataSet`son the server to increase our performance. In the meantime, using the ViewState is sufficient for our smaller result sets.

In this revised version of `BindGrid`, we start by checking the `ViewState` collection for an item named `DepartmentsDataSet`. If no such item exists, we create a new `DataSet`, fill it with data from the database, as before, and store it in `ViewState`. If an item named `DepartmentsDataSet` does exist in `ViewState`, we simply save that item into our local variable, dataSet. Regardless of how the DataSet is loaded, we bind it to our GridView as we did before.

If you save your work and load the Departments page in your browser, you should see that the page runs exactly as it did previously, except that now the database is accessed only once, the first time the page loads.

Implementing Sorting

To implement sorting functionality, we need to understand a few details of the inner workings of data binding.

Technically, you can't bind a DataSet to a GridView control, because a DataSet can contain many tables, whereas the GridView control can only handle one set of rows and columns. However, by virtue of the fact that your DataSet has, so far, only contained a single DataTable, the GridView control has been smart enough to figure out that what you probably meant was the following:

Visual Basic

```
departmentsGrid.DataSource = dataSet.Tables("Departments")
departmentsGrid.DataBind()
```

C#

```
departmentsGrid.DataSource = dataSet.Tables["Departments"];
departmentsGrid.DataBind();
```

However, the above code isn't technically correct in the strictest sense. All of the GridView's data binding is actually achieved through DataView objects. Thankfully, each DataTable has a DefaultView property, which the GridView will automatically use whenever you bind it to a DataTable. So, the following code listings have the same functionality as those we saw above:

Visual Basic

```
departmentsGrid.DataSource = _
    dataSet.Tables("Departments").DefaultView
departmentsGrid.DataBind()
```

```
C#
```

```
departmentsGrid.DataSource =
    dataSet.Tables["Departments"].DefaultView;
departmentsGrid.DataBind();
```

 DefaultView Does Not Apply when Binding to a DataSet

It's interesting to note that if you bind directly to a `DataSet` that contains only one table, that table's `DefaultView` will not be used; the `GridView` will generate a separate `DataView` itself.

`DataViews` represent a customized view of a `DataSet` for sorting, filtering, searching, editing, and navigation. When binding a `GridView` directly to a `DataTable`, the `DefaultView` property, which is a `DataView` object, is accessed automatically for us. However, if we want to enable sorting, we need to access the `DataView` and set its sorting parameters.

The first step to enabling sorting is to set the `AllowSorting` property to `True`. When we do that, the grid's column headings become hyperlinks. Before we make those hyperlinks work, we need to handle the grid's `Sorting` event, in which we teach the grid what to do when those links are clicked.

Set the `AllowSorting` property of the `GridView` control in **Departments.aspx** to `True`, then use the designer to generate the handler for the `GridView`'s `Sorting` event. Now, complete the code as shown here:

Visual Basic   Dorknozzle\VB\19_Departments.aspx.vb *(excerpt)*

```
Protected Sub departmentsGrid_Sorting(ByVal sender As Object,
➥  ByVal e As System.Web.UI.WebControls.GridViewSortEventArgs)
➥  Handles departmentsGrid.Sorting
  Dim sortExpression As String = e.SortExpression
  If (sortExpression = gridSortExpression) Then
    If gridSortDirection = SortDirection.Ascending Then
      gridSortDirection = SortDirection.Descending
    Else
      gridSortDirection = SortDirection.Ascending
    End If
  Else
    gridSortDirection = WebControls.SortDirection.Ascending
```

```
  End If
  gridSortExpression = sortExpression
  BindGrid()
End Sub

Private Property gridSortDirection() As SortDirection
  Get
    If (ViewState("GridSortDirection") Is Nothing) Then
      ViewState("GridSortDirection") = SortDirection.Ascending
    End If
    Return ViewState("GridSortDirection")
  End Get

  Set(ByVal value As SortDirection)
    ViewState("GridSortDirection") = value
  End Set
End Property

Private Property gridSortExpression() As String
  Get
    If (ViewState("GridSortExpression") Is Nothing) Then
      ViewState("GridSortExpression") = "DepartmentID"
    End If
    Return ViewState("GridSortExpression")
  End Get

  Set(ByVal value As String)
    ViewState("GridSortExpression") = value
  End Set
End Property
```

C#   Dorknozzle\CS\19_Departments.aspx.cs *(excerpt)*

```csharp
protected void departmentsGrid_Sorting(object sender,
    GridViewSortEventArgs e)
{
  string sortExpression = e.SortExpression;
  if (sortExpression == gridSortExpression)
  {
    if(gridSortDirection == SortDirection.Ascending)
    {
      gridSortDirection = SortDirection.Descending;
    }
    else
    {
```

```
        gridSortDirection = SortDirection.Ascending;
    }
  }
  else
  {
    gridSortDirection = SortDirection.Ascending;
  }
  gridSortExpression = sortExpression;
  BindGrid();
}

private SortDirection gridSortDirection
{
  get
  {
    if (ViewState["GridSortDirection"] == null)
    {
      ViewState["GridSortDirection"] = SortDirection.Ascending;
    }
    return (SortDirection) ViewState["GridSortDirection"];
  }

  set
  {
    ViewState["GridSortDirection"] = value;
  }
}

private string gridSortExpression
{
  get
  {
    if (ViewState["GridSortExpression"] == null)
    {
      ViewState["GridSortExpression"] = "DepartmentID";
    }
    return (string) ViewState["GridSortExpression"];
  }

  set
  {
    ViewState["GridSortExpression"] = value;
  }
}
```

Properties

We haven't really discussed the task of defining your own properties since Chapter 4, so now might be a good time for a quick refresher. By now, you should be fairly comfortable with the idea that each of your web forms is its own class, and inherits a great deal of functionality from its parent class, `Page`. You've already dealt with quite a few of that class's features, such as its `Load` event and its `IsPostBack` property.

You can define for your class properties that can be read-only, write-only, or are able to be both read and written to. When you read data from a property, its `Get` code is executed. Most of the time, this code will be quite simple, but it can be as complex as you choose to make it. In the same way, when a value is written to a property, its `Set` code is executed, which can also be quite complex if you choose to make it so.

Finally, update the `BindGrid` method to apply the sorting:

Visual Basic   Dorknozzle\VB\19_Departments.aspx.vb *(excerpt)*

```vb
Private Sub BindGrid()
  Dim conn As SqlConnection
  Dim dataSet As New DataSet
  Dim adapter As SqlDataAdapter
  If ViewState("DepartmentsDataSet") Is Nothing Then
    Dim connectionString As String = _
        ConfigurationManager.ConnectionStrings( _
        "Dorknozzle").ConnectionString
    conn = New SqlConnection(connectionString)
    adapter = New SqlDataAdapter( _
        "SELECT DepartmentID, Department FROM Departments", _
        conn)
    adapter.Fill(dataSet, "Departments")
    ViewState("DepartmentsDataSet") = dataSet
  Else
    dataSet = ViewState("DepartmentsDataSet")
  End If
  Dim sortExpression As String
  If gridSortDirection = SortDirection.Ascending Then
    sortExpression = gridSortExpression & " ASC"
  Else
    sortExpression = gridSortExpression & " DESC"
  End If
```

```
    dataSet.Tables("Departments").DefaultView.Sort = sortExpression
    departmentsGrid.DataSource = _
        dataSet.Tables("Departments").DefaultView
    departmentsGrid.DataBind()
End Sub
```

C#   Dorknozzle\CS\19_Departments.aspx.cs (excerpt)

```
private void BindGrid()
{
  SqlConnection conn;
  DataSet dataSet = new DataSet();
  SqlDataAdapter adapter;
  if(ViewState["DepartmentsDataSet"] == null)
  {
    string connectionString =
        ConfigurationManager.ConnectionStrings[
        "Dorknozzle"].ConnectionString;
    conn = new SqlConnection(connectionString);
    adapter = new SqlDataAdapter(
        "SELECT DepartmentID, Department FROM Departments",
        conn);
    adapter.Fill(dataSet, "Departments");
    ViewState["DepartmentsDataSet"] = dataSet;
  }
  else
  {
    dataSet = (DataSet)ViewState["DepartmentsDataSet"];
  }

  string sortExpression;
  if(gridSortDirection == SortDirection.Ascending)
  {
    sortExpression = gridSortExpression + " ASC";
  }
  else
  {
    sortExpression = gridSortExpression + " DESC";
  }
  dataSet.Tables["Departments"].DefaultView.Sort = sortExpression;
  departmentsGrid.DataSource =
      dataSet.Tables["Departments"].DefaultView;
  departmentsGrid.DataBind();
}
```

Execute the project again, and test that sorting by column works as shown in Figure 12.28.

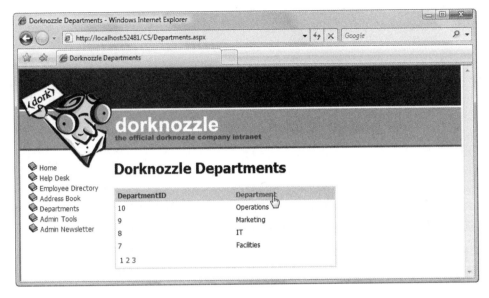

Figure 12.28. Sorting Dorknozzle's departments

We've written a lot of code here! Let's take a look at how it works.

In order to sort the data in the grid, all we need to do is set the Sort property of the view we're displaying to *ColumnNameSortOrder*, where *ColumnName* is, of course, the name of the column we're sorting, and *SortOrder* is either ASC (for ascending) or DESC (for descending). So, if you were sorting the DepartmentID column, the Sort property would need to be set to DepartmentID ASC or Department DESC.

This property must be set before the data binding is performed, as is shown in the following code, which will sort the data by DepartmentID in descending numeric order:

Visual Basic

```
dataTable.DefaultView.Sort = "DepartmentID DESC"
departmentsGrid.DataSource = dataTable.DefaultView
departmentsGrid.DataBind()
```

```
C#
```

```
dataTable.DefaultView.Sort = "Department DESC";
departmentsGrid.DataSource = dataTable.DefaultView;
departmentsGrid.DataBind();
```

It's a pretty simple task to sort a `DataView` in code like this, but if we want to let users sort the data on the basis of any column, in any direction, things get a little bit more complicated. In this case, we need to remember the previous sort method between requests.

In order to be truly user-friendly, our grid should behave like this:

- The first time a column header is clicked, the grid should sort the data in ascending order, based on that column.

- When the same column header is clicked multiple times, the grid should alternate between sorting the data in that column in ascending and descending modes.

When a column heading is clicked, the grid's `Sorting` event is fired. In our case, the `Sorting` event handler (which we'll look at in a moment) saves the details of the sort column and direction in two properties:

- `gridSortExpression` retains the name of the column on which we're sorting the data (such as `Department`).

- `gridSortDirection` can be either `SortDirection.Ascending` or `SortDirection.Descending`.

We create a sorting expression using these properties in `BindGrid`:

```
Visual Basic                        Dorknozzle\VB\18_Departments.aspx.vb (excerpt)
Dim sortExpression As String
If gridSortDirection = SortDirection.Ascending Then
  sortExpression = gridSortExpression & " ASC"
Else
  sortExpression = gridSortExpression & " DESC"
End If
```

C#   Dorknozzle\CS\18_Departments.aspx.cs *(excerpt)*

```csharp
string sortExpression;
if(gridSortDirection == SortDirection.Ascending)
{
  sortExpression = gridSortExpression + " ASC";
}
else
{
  sortExpression = gridSortExpression + " DESC";
}
```

In order to implement the sorting functionality as explained above, we need to remember between client requests which column is being sorted, and whether it's being sorted in ascending or descending order. That's what the properties gridSortExpression and gridSortDirection do:

Visual Basic   Dorknozzle\VB\18_Departments.aspx.vb *(excerpt)*

```vbnet
Private Property gridSortDirection() As SortDirection
  Get
    If (ViewState("GridSortDirection") Is Nothing) Then
      ViewState("GridSortDirection") = SortDirection.Ascending
    End If
    Return ViewState("GridSortDirection")
  End Get

  Set(ByVal value As SortDirection)
    ViewState("GridSortDirection") = value
  End Set
End Property

Private Property gridSortExpression() As String
  Get
    If (ViewState("GridSortExpression") Is Nothing) Then
      ViewState("GridSortExpression") = "DepartmentID"
    End If
    Return ViewState("GridSortExpression")
  End Get

  Set(ByVal value As String)
    ViewState("GridSortExpression") = value
  End Set
End Property
```

```csharp
private SortDirection gridSortDirection
{
  get
  {
    if (ViewState["GridSortDirection"] == null)
    {
      ViewState["GridSortDirection"] = SortDirection.Ascending;
    }
    return (SortDirection) ViewState["GridSortDirection"];
  }

  set
  {
    ViewState["GridSortDirection"] = value;
  }
}

private string gridSortExpression
{
  get
  {
    if (ViewState["GridSortExpression"] == null)
    {
      ViewState["GridSortExpression"] = "DepartmentID";
    }
    return (string) ViewState["GridSortExpression"];
  }

  set
  {
    ViewState["GridSortExpression"] = value;
  }
}
```

Here, we use the ViewState collection to store information about which column is being sorted, and the direction in which it's being sorted.

When the Sorting event handler fires, we set the gridSortExpression and gridSortDirection properties. The method starts by retrieving the name of the clicked column:

Visual Basic   Dorknozzle\VB\18_Departments.aspx.vb *(excerpt)*

```
Protected Sub departmentsGrid_Sorting(ByVal sender As Object,
➥  ByVal e As System.Web.UI.WebControls.GridViewSortEventArgs)
➥  Handles departmentsGrid.Sorting
  Dim sortExpression As String = e.SortExpression
```

C#   Dorknozzle\CS\18_Departments.aspx.cs *(excerpt)*

```
protected void departmentsGrid_Sorting(object sender,
    GridViewSortEventArgs e)
{
  string sortExpression = e.SortExpression;
```

Next, we check whether the previously clicked column is the same as the newly clicked column. If it is, we need to toggle the sorting direction. Otherwise, we set the sort direction to ascending:

Visual Basic   Dorknozzle\VB\18_Departments.aspx.vb *(excerpt)*

```
If (sortExpression = gridSortExpression) Then
  If gridSortDirection = SortDirection.Ascending Then
    gridSortDirection = SortDirection.Descending
  Else
    gridSortDirection = SortDirection.Ascending
  End If
Else
  gridSortDirection = WebControls.SortDirection.Ascending
End If
```

C#   Dorknozzle\CS\18_Departments.aspx.cs *(excerpt)*

```
if (sortExpression == gridSortExpression)
{
  if(gridSortDirection == SortDirection.Ascending)
  {
    gridSortDirection = SortDirection.Descending;
  }
  else
  {
    gridSortDirection = SortDirection.Ascending;
  }
}
else
```

```
{
  gridSortDirection = SortDirection.Ascending;
}
```

Finally, we save the new sort expression to the `gridSortExpression` property, whose value will be retained in case the user keeps working (and changing sort modes) on the page:

Visual Basic	Dorknozzle\VB\18_Departments.aspx.vb *(excerpt)*

```
gridSortExpression = sortExpression
BindGrid()
```

C#	Dorknozzle\CS\18_Departments.aspx.cs *(excerpt)*

```
gridSortExpression = sortExpression;
BindGrid();
```

After we store the sort expression, we rebind the grid to its data source so that the expression will reflect the changes we've made to the `gridSortExpression` and `gridSortDirection` properties.

Filtering Data

Although we're not using the `DataView` control in the Dorknozzle project, it's interesting to note that this control can filter data. Normally you'd have to apply `WHERE` clauses to filter the data before it reaches your application, but in certain cases you may prefer to filter data on the client.

Imagine that you wanted to display employees or departments whose names started with a certain letter. You could retrieve the complete list of employees or departments from the database using a single request, then let the user filter the list locally.

The `DataView` class has a property named `RowFilter` that allows you to specify an expression similar to that of an SQL statement's `WHERE` clause. For instance, the following filter selects all departments whose names start with "a":

Visual Basic	

```
dataTable.DefaultView.RowFilter = "Department LIKE 'a%'"
```

```csharp
C#
dataTable.DefaultView.RowFilter = "Department LIKE 'a%'";
```

Updating a Database from a Modified `DataSet`

So far, we've used the `DataSet` exclusively for retrieving and binding database data to controls such as the `GridView`. The reverse operation—updating data within a database from a `DataSet`—is also possible using the `Update` method of the `SqlDataAdapter`.

The `SqlDataAdapter` has the following four properties, which represent the main database commands:

- `SelectCommand`
- `InsertCommand`
- `UpdateCommand`
- `DeleteCommand`

The `SelectCommand` contains the command that's executed when we call `Fill`. The other properties are quite similar, except that, to execute them, you must call the `Update` method instead.

If we want to insert, update, or remove records in a database, we simply make modifications to the data in the `DataSet` or `DataTable`, then call the `Update` method of the `SqlDataAdapter`. This will automatically execute the SQL queries specified in the `InsertCommand`, `UpdateCommand`, and `DeleteCommand` properties as appropriate.

The excellent news is that ADO.NET also provides an object named `SqlCommandBuilder`, which creates the UPDATE, DELETE, and INSERT code for us. Basically, we just need to populate the `DataSet` or `DataTable` objects (usually by performing a SELECT query), then use `SqlDataAdapter` and `SqlCommandBuilder` to do the rest of the work for us.

In the example below, we'll see a modified version of `BindGrid` that adds a new department, called New Department, to the database. The new lines are highlighted (note that I've simplified `BindGrid` by removing the code that stores and retrieves the `DataSet` from view state, as well as the code that sorts the results):

Visual Basic

```
Private Sub BindGrid()
  Dim conn As SqlConnection
  Dim dataSet As New DataSet
  Dim adapter As SqlDataAdapter
  Dim dataRow As DataRow
  Dim commandBuilder As SqlCommandBuilder
  Dim connectionString As String = _
      ConfigurationManager.ConnectionStrings( _
      "Dorknozzle").ConnectionString
  conn = New SqlConnection(connectionString)
  adapter = New SqlDataAdapter( _
      "SELECT DepartmentID, Department FROM Departments", _
      conn)
  adapter.Fill(dataSet, "Departments")
  dataRow = dataSet.Tables("Departments").NewRow()
  dataRow("Department") = "New Department"
  dataSet.Tables("Departments").Rows.Add(dataRow)
  commandBuilder = New SqlCommandBuilder(adapter)
  adapter.Update(dataSet.Tables("Departments"))
  departmentsGrid.DataSource = _
      dataSet.Tables("Departments").DefaultView
  departmentsGrid.DataBind()
End Sub
```

C#

```
private void BindGrid()
{
  SqlConnection conn;
  DataSet dataSet = new DataSet();
  SqlDataAdapter adapter;
  DataRow dataRow ;
  SqlCommandBuilder commandBuilder;
  string connectionString =
      ConfigurationManager.ConnectionStrings[
      "Dorknozzle"].ConnectionString;
  conn = new SqlConnection(connectionString);
  adapter = new SqlDataAdapter(
      "SELECT DepartmentID, Department FROM Departments",
```

```
        conn);
    adapter.Fill(dataSet, "Departments");
    dataRow = dataSet.Tables["Departments"].NewRow();
    dataRow["Department"] = "New Department";
    dataSet.Tables["Departments"].Rows.Add(dataRow);
    commandBuilder = new SqlCommandBuilder(adapter);
    adapter.Update(dataSet.Tables["Departments"]);
    departmentsGrid.DataSource =
        dataSet.Tables["Departments"].DefaultView;
    departmentsGrid.DataBind();
}
```

If you run this code a few times, lots of departments titled New Department will be added to the database, as shown in Figure 12.29.

As you can see, adding a new record is a trivial task. The work that's required to submit the changes to the database requires us to write just two rows of code. The rest of the new code creates the new row that was inserted.

We create an `SqlCommandBuilder` object, passing in our `SqlDataAdapter`. The `SqlCommandBuilder` class is responsible for detecting modifications to the `DataSet` and deciding what needs to be inserted, updated, or deleted to apply those changes to the database. Having done this, `SqlCommandBuilder` generates the necessary SQL queries and stores them in the `SqlDataAdapter` for the `Update` method to use. It should be no surprise, then, that our next action is to call the `Update` method of the `SqlDataAdapter` object, passing in the `DataTable` that needs updating.

Deleting all of these new departments is also an easy task. The following code browses the `Departments` `DataTable` and deletes all departments with the name `New Department`:

Visual Basic

```
Private Sub BindGrid()
    Dim conn As SqlConnection
    Dim dataSet As New DataSet
    Dim adapter As SqlDataAdapter
    Dim commandBuilder As SqlCommandBuilder
    Dim connectionString As String = _
        ConfigurationManager.ConnectionStrings( _
        "Dorknozzle").ConnectionString
```

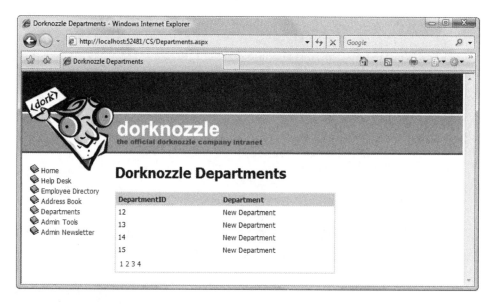

Figure 12.29. Adding many new departments

```
conn = New SqlConnection(connectionString)
adapter = New SqlDataAdapter( _
    "SELECT DepartmentID, Department FROM Departments", _
    conn)
adapter.Fill(dataSet, "Departments")
For Each dataRow As DataRow In _
    dataSet.Tables("Departments").Rows
  If dataRow("Department") = "New Department" Then
    dataRow.Delete()
  End If
Next
commandBuilder = New SqlCommandBuilder(adapter)
adapter.Update(dataSet.Tables("Departments"))
departmentsGrid.DataSource = _
    dataSet.Tables("Departments").DefaultView
departmentsGrid.DataBind()
End Sub
```

Note that in the C# version the conversion to string needs to be performed explicitly:

```csharp
C#

private void BindGrid()
{
  SqlConnection conn;
  DataSet dataSet = new DataSet();
  SqlDataAdapter adapter;
  SqlCommandBuilder commandBuilder;
  string connectionString =
      ConfigurationManager.ConnectionStrings[
      "Dorknozzle"].ConnectionString;
  conn = new SqlConnection(connectionString);
  adapter = new SqlDataAdapter(
      "SELECT DepartmentID, Department FROM Departments", conn);
  adapter.Fill(dataSet, "Departments");
  foreach (DataRow dataRow in
      dataSet.Tables["Departments"].Rows)
  {
    if(dataRow["Department"].ToString() == "New Department")
    {
      dataRow.Delete();
    }
  }
  commandBuilder = new SqlCommandBuilder(adapter);
  adapter.Update(dataSet.Tables["Departments"]);
  departmentsGrid.DataSource =
      dataSet.Tables["Departments"].DefaultView;
  departmentsGrid.DataBind();
}
```

Execute this command, and all departments called New Department will be removed. We use the ToString() method just as we did during our discussion of data readers. In the real-world, if you're using VB, you'll probably want to explicitly call any conversions to the data types just as C# requires. This helps in the readability of code without having to go back to the database to refresh your memory on the data types.

Summary

This chapter has given us the chance to explore some more important concepts of ADO.NET. First, you learned about the data source controls, and how they can be used to build code-free data binding. With just a few mouse clicks, you were able to build editable grids of data!

We also investigated the `DataSet` class, and learned how to use it in our intranet application. We then moved on to learn about the constructs of `DataSets`, including `DataTables` and `DataViews`. We also learned how to populate `DataSets` using `SqlDataAdapters`. Finally, we looked at sorting, paging, and filtering data using `DataViews`, and updated a data source from a modified `DataSet` using the `SqlCommandBuilder`.

In the next chapter, we'll be looking at ASP.NET's security features. Using ASP.NET's form-based security capabilities, we'll learn how to restrict each user's access to the specific web forms we want them to be able to use, while still allowing public access to other parts of the site. We'll also take a look at some controls that make building login and logout mechanisms a snap.

Chapter 13

Security and User Authentication

The issue of security is important in many facets of information technology, but it's especially relevant in web development. While you'll want to make sure that your web site users are able to go where they need to go and see what they're allowed to see, you'll also want to prevent unauthorized and malicious users from getting into your system.

One common approach is to require your site's visitors to log in before they can view certain pages and to ensure that restricted pages cannot be accessed by simply typing in the correct URLs, unless the user has been specifically allowed to view those pages. Although different solutions exist for the various applications you may create—for instance, IIS could provide certain pages to users who have been authenticated by Windows within an intranet environment—this chapter focuses on the more straightforward tasks of form- and script-based authentication.

In this chapter, we'll learn some simple coding techniques and discover just how easy it is to secure your web applications using ASP.NET. Security is a huge topic, and several books have been written on the subject. If you're serious about developing secure complex applications, we recommend that you check out some additional resources, such as *Professional ASP.NET 2.0 Security, Membership, and Role*

Management with C# and VB (Wrox Press, 2006),[1] and *Writing Secure Code, Second Edition* (Microsoft Press, 2003).[2]

In this chapter, you will:

- Learn how to authenticate your visitors using ASP.NET Forms Authentication.
- Use ASP.NET Memberships and Roles.
- Create users and roles.
- Use the ASP.NET login controls.

Let's get moving!

Basic Security Guidelines

The primary and most important element of building secure applications is to consider and plan an application's security from the early stages of its development. Of course, we must know the potential internal and external threats to which an application will be exposed before we can plan the security aspects of that system. Generally speaking, ASP.NET web application security involves—but is not limited to—the following considerations:

validating user input

Back in Chapter 6, you learned how to use validation controls to enable the client-side validation of user input, and how to double-check that validation on the server side.

Since the input your application receives from web browsers is ultimately under users' control, there's always a possibility that the submitted data will not be what you expect. The submission of invalid data can generate errors in your web application, potentially compromising its security.

protecting your database

The database is quite often the most important asset you need to protect—after all, it's there that most of the information your application relies upon is stored.

---

[1] Stefan Schackow, *Professional ASP.NET 2.0 Security, Membership, and Role Management with C# and VB* (New Jersey: Wrox Press, 2006). A new version updated for ASP.NET 3.5 is due out in November 2008.

[2] Michael Howard and David LeBlanc, *Writing Secure Code, Second Edition* (Washington: Microsoft Press, 2003)

SQL injection attacks, which target the database, are a common threat to web application security. If the app builds SQL commands by naively assembling text strings that include data received from user input, an attacker can alter the meaning of the commands the application produces simply by including malicious code in the user input.[3]

You've already learned how to use ADO.NET to make use of command parameters, and parameterized stored procedures, in order to include user input in SQL queries. If you use the practices you've learned in this book, ADO.NET will protect your against injection attacks.

displaying data correctly

If your web application produces HTML output, you should always bear in mind that any text you include in that output will also be interpreted as HTML by your visitors' browsers. As such, you need to escape special characters (such as < and &) correctly, using the `HttpUtility.HtmlEncode` method.

This consideration is especially important when you're outputting a string that was originally received as user input. If that user input were to contain HTML code, that code might disrupt the appearance or functionality of your application when it was displayed. For example, if you want to display the text "`<script>`" using a `Label` control, you should set your label's `Text` property to `HttpUtility.HtmlEncode("<script>")`.

Note that the fields or columns of data-bound controls such as `GridView` and `DetailsView` have a property called `HtmlEncode`, the default value of which is `True`. As such, any values that are displayed by these controls are automatically HTML-encoded unless you set this property to `False`.

keeping sensitive data to yourself

Even though it may not be visible in the browser window, any output that your application produces is ultimately accessible to the end user. Consequently, you should never include sensitive data (such as user passwords, credit card data, and so on) in JavaScript code, HTML hidden fields, or the `ViewState` collection. (Unlike the `Application`, `Session`, or `Cache` collections, `ViewState`

---

[3] You'll find a detailed article on SQL injection attacks at
http://www.unixwiz.net/techtips/sql-injection.html.

isn't stored on the server, but is passed back and forth between the client and the server on every request in an easily decipherable format.)

using encryption or hashing whenever necessary

As we'll see later in this chapter, ASP.NET also supports hashing, an irreversible form of encryption that you can use to encrypt passwords and store them safely on your server.

using secure communication channels whenever necessary

You can always use the HTTPS (HTTP Secure) protocol to secure the communication between your visitors and your site. If you use this protocol, an attacker who intercepts the data being passed back and forth between your application and its users won't obtain any meaningful data.

This approach is particularly useful when you're transferring very sensitive data such as user passwords, credit card information, and so on. However, HTTPS isn't used in scenarios where the extra security doesn't bring benefits, because it consumes significant processing power on the server—especially when many users access the site simultaneously.

In this chapter, we'll explore the basic ASP.NET features for implementing user authentication and authorization to protect the sensitive areas of your web site.

Securing ASP.NET Applications

The ASP.NET server model offers several robust options for storing user information. In securing the sensitive pages of a web site, you'll need to deal with two basic security-related concepts: **authentication** and **authorization**.

authentication

Authentication is the process by which an anonymous user is identified as a particular user of your system.

Authentication mechanisms include providing a username/password combination, using a fingerprint reader, and so on. As a result of this process, the person (or process, or computer) accessing your web site is associated with a security token (such as a username) which identifies the user into your system.

authorization

Authorization establishes the resources an authenticated user can access, and the actions that user is allowed to perform. For example, you'll probably want to give different permissions to anonymous users, to registered users, and to site administrators.

To ease the administrative work, modern authorization systems, including those supported by ASP.NET, support the notion of **authorization roles** (or **groups**). A role represents a set of permissions that can be associated with any user who needs all the permissions associated with that role. For example, you could build a role called Administrators, and associate the permissions typically required by an administrator to that role. Then, when you need to give administrative permissions to a user, you simply assign that user to the Administrators role, instead of supplying all the related permissions manually.

With older versions of ASP, usernames and passwords were either hard-coded into the ASP file, or stored in an external data store such as a database. ASP.NET offers a better way to implement these old techniques, and also adds new user authentication methods:

Windows authentication

Windows authentication uses IIS in conjunction with the users' operating system user accounts to allow or deny those users access to certain parts of your web application.

forms authentication

Offering the greatest flexibility, forms authentication provides the maximum control and customization abilities to the developer. Using forms authentication, you can authenticate your users against hard-coded credentials, credentials stored in your **Web.config** file, user account details stored in a database, or a combination of these.

Windows Live ID authentication

The newest addition to user authentication methods, **Windows Live ID authentication** (also known as **Passport authentication**) is a centralized authentication service provided by Microsoft. It allows users to sign in to multiple web sites using Windows Live accounts, which are associated with the users' email addresses. Developers who use this authentication method don't need to worry about storing credential information on their own servers.

When users log in to a site that has Windows Live ID authentication enabled, they are redirected to the Windows Live ID web site, which prompts them for their email addresses and passwords. After the information is validated, the users are automatically redirected back to the original site.

This method sounds good, but it has one major downside: it requires users to have a Windows Live account in order to use your site, and it ties your application to Microsoft's proprietary system.

We'll spend the rest of this chapter exploring forms authentication—the most popular authentication method supported by ASP.NET.

Working with Forms Authentication

By far the most popular authentication method, forms authentication is extremely flexible. With forms authentication, you get to choose where the usernames and passwords are stored: in the **Web.config** file, in a separate XML file, in a database, or in any combination of the three.

Forms authentication is cookie-based—each user's login is maintained with a cookie. A browser may not access protected pages of the site unless it has a cookie that corresponds to the successful authentication of an authorized user.

You'll most frequently use three classes from the System.Web.Security namespace as you work with forms authentication:

FormsAuthentication
contains several methods for working with forms authentication

FormsAuthenticationTicket
represents the **authentication ticket** that's stored in the user's cookie

FormsIdentity
represents the authenticated user's identity

Let's walk through an example that explains how a basic Login page is constructed.

Adding a Login Page to Dorknozzle

In this chapter, we talk about security and the final goal is to establish in the site a number of secure zones that can be accessed only by certain users. We start by adding a Login page to Dorknozzle. Whenever an anonymous user tries to access those secured zones, he or she will be redirected to this Login page. In the following few pages, we will:

1. Configure the authentication mode for the application within the **Web.config** file.

2. Configure the authorization section to allow or deny certain users within the **Web.config** file.

3. Create the Login page that your visitors use.

The first step is to configure the authentication mode for the application.

To do so, we must edit the application configuration file, **Web.config**. Open this file in Visual Web Developer and add the `<authentication>` tag shown in the following code snippet. Visual Web Developer may already have created an `<authentication>` tag for you with the default `mode` of `Windows`—in this case, just change the value to `Forms`:

```
                                            DorkNozzle\VB\01_web.config (excerpt)
<configuration>
  <system.web>
    ⋮
    <authentication mode="Forms"/>
    ⋮
  </system.web>
</configuration>
```

The `mode` attribute has four possible values: `Forms`, `Windows`, `Passport`, and `None`. Since we're working with forms authentication, we set the `mode` to `Forms`.

Next, set up the authorization scheme by adding the `<authorization>` tag:

DorkNozzle\VB\02_web.config *(excerpt)*

```
<authentication mode="Forms" />
<authorization>
  <deny users="?" />
</authorization>
```

As you'll see in more detail in the next few sections, the question mark symbol (?) represents all anonymous users—that is, users who have not logged in. Essentially, this configuration reads: "Deny all non-logged-in users." If a user tries to access a page controlled by this **Web.config** file without logging in, he or she will be redirected to the Login page. Unfortunately, this has the side-effect of denying all unauthenticated users access to our style sheet and image files as well. Thankfully, ASP.NET provides a way to override **Web.config** settings for particular directories of your web site—the <location> tag.

To allow anonymous users access to your **App_Themes** and **Images** folders, add the following to **Web.config**:

DorkNozzle\VB\03_web.config *(excerpt)*

```
<system.web>
  ⋮
</system.web>

<!-- Allow access to App_Themes directory -->
<location path="App_Themes">
  <system.web>
    <authorization>
      <allow users="?"/>
    </authorization>
  </system.web>
</location>

<!-- Allow access to Images directory -->
<location path="Images">
  <system.web>
    <authorization>
      <allow users="?"/>
    </authorization>
  </system.web>
</location>
```

Now, all you need do is create that Login page.

Create a new page named **Login.aspx**, which uses a code-behind file, and is based on the **Dorknozzle.master** master page. Then, modify its title and content placeholders like this:

```
                                              DorkNozzle\VB\04_Login.aspx
<%@ Page Language="VB" MasterPageFile="~/DorkNozzle.master"
    AutoEventWireup="false" CodeFile="Login.aspx.vb"
    Inherits="Login" Title="Dorknozzle Login" %>

<asp:Content ID="Content1" ContentPlaceHolderID="head"
    Runat="Server">
</asp:Content>
<asp:Content ID="Content2"
    ContentPlaceHolderID="ContentPlaceHolder1" Runat="Server">
  <h1>Login</h1>
</asp:Content>
```

If you execute the project now, you'll notice that no matter which link you click, you'll be redirected to the blank Login page shown in Figure 13.1.

Naming the Login Page

How did ASP.NET know that our login form was named **Login.aspx**? We didn't specify the name anywhere. By default, unless you specify another form name, ASP.NET will assume that the Login page is called **Login.aspx**. This is configurable in the web.config by editing the loginUrl attribute on the `<forms>` tag.

Authenticating Users

You're secured! Anonymous users can't see your application's pages, and are automatically redirected to the Login page. Now what? How can you create users, give them privileges, store their settings, and so on? Well, it depends.

All versions of ASP.NET can store user account data, and details of the resources each user can access, in the **Web.config** file. However, relying only on the **Web.config** file isn't particularly helpful when the users' account settings need to be easily configurable: you can't keep modifying the configuration file to register new users, modify user passwords, and so on.

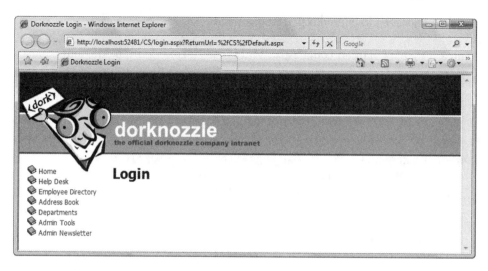

Figure 13.1. The Login page

As you probably already suspect, a real user management solution must use the database somehow. Storing authentication and authorization data—such as user accounts, roles, and privileges—in the database gives you much greater flexibility in the long run.

A third solution is to store the user data in the code-behind file. This solution should *never, ever* be used in *any* application, but it will make things easier for us as we work through the first few examples.

To start off, let's update our login form by adding a TextBox into which the user can enter a username, another TextBox for the password, and a Button for submitting the data to the server. Add this code after the Login heading in **Login.aspx**:

```
                                          DorkNozzle\VB\05_Login.aspx (excerpt)
<h1>Login</h1>
<p>Username:<br />
  <asp:TextBox id="username" runat="server" />
</p>
<p>Password:<br />
  <asp:TextBox id="password" runat="server" TextMode="Password" />
</p>
<p><asp:Button id="submitButton" runat="server" Text="Login"
      OnClick="LoginUser" /></p>
```

As you can see, the page contains two `TextBox` controls, one of which has the `TextMode` set to `Password`, which means that an asterisk will display for each character that a user types into this field. The other is a `Button` control, the `OnClick` attribute for which calls the `LoginUser` method. Of course you'll want to include validator controls to validate input from the user. To do that, you can add RequiredFieldValidators for the both textboxes, however we'll leave that step up to you. Next, we'll add the server-side script for this method, which will validate the login credentials. Add the following code to your code-behind file:

Visual Basic	DorkNozzle\VB\06_Login.aspx.vb

```vb
Partial Class Login
    Inherits System.Web.UI.Page
Sub LoginUser(ByVal s As Object, ByVal e As EventArgs)
  If (username.Text = "username" And _
      password.Text = "password") Then
    FormsAuthentication.RedirectFromLoginPage(username.Text, False)
  End If
End Sub
End Class
```

C#	DorkNozzle\CS\06_Login.aspx.cs

```csharp
public partial class Login : System.Web.UI.Page
{
  protected void Page_Load(object sender, EventArgs e)
  {

  }
  protected void LoginUser(Object s, EventArgs e)
  {
    if (username.Text == "username" &&
        password.Text == "password")
    {
      FormsAuthentication.RedirectFromLoginPage(username.Text,
          false);
    }
  }
}
```

Execute your project and you'll see the simple, yet functional, Login page shown in Figure 13.2.

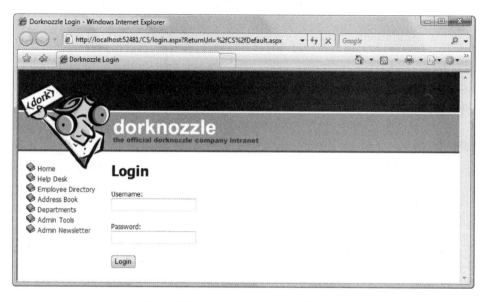

Figure 13.2. The simple Dorknozzle Login page

In the code above, the `If` statement is used to check whether or not the user typed in the correct username and password. If the username and password entered were **username** and **password**, respectively, we call the `FormsAuthentication` class's `RedirectFromLoginPage` method, passing in two parameters.

The first parameter is the username that will be stored in the authentication ticket (the cookie that's sent to the user's browser). We'll simply use the username entered into the form for this example. The second parameter is a Boolean value that indicates whether a persistent cookie should be created. By setting this value to `True`, you allow your users to close their browsers, open them again, navigate back to your site, and still be logged in to the application. Setting this value to `False` allows users to be logged in only as long as their browsers remain open. If they close their browsers, reopen them, and navigate to your site, they'll have to log in again.[4]

Once you enter the correct name and password, you'll be forwarded to the page you initially requested—by default, this is the homepage.

---

[4] You could add a **Remember Me** checkbox, and decide the value of the second parameter based on the user's preference.

Configuring Forms Authentication

In the previous section, we created a basic Login page. We also modified the **Web.config** file to enable the forms authentication mode. In this section, we'll explore the forms authentication section of the **Web.config** file in greater detail.

Aside from the basic authentication mode, the `<authentication>` tag within the **Web.config** file may contain a `<forms>` tag. The `<forms>` tag accepts the following attributes:

loginUrl

This attribute specifies the page that the user is redirected to when authentication is necessary. By default, this page is called **login.aspx**. Using this attribute, you can modify the filename to anything you like.

name

This attribute specifies the name of the cookie to be stored on the user's machine. By default, the name is set to `.ASPXAUTH`.

timeout

This attribute specifies the amount of time in minutes before the cookie expires. By default, this value is set to 30 minutes.

path

This attribute specifies the path to the location at which the cookie is stored. By default, this value is set to `/`.

protection

This attribute controls the way(s) in which the cookie data is protected. Values include `All`, `None`, `Encryption`, and `Validation`. The default value is `All`.

cookieless attribute

A new ASP.NET feature, this attribute forces your application to use the URL instead of a cookie to identify the logged-in user. The possible values are `UseCookies` (use the cookie to identify the user), `UseUri` (use the URL to store identification data), `AutoDetect` (try to detect if the user client supports cookies), and `UseDeviceProfile` (use cookies if the user client is known to support them). The default is `UseDeviceProfile`.

Applying the cookieless authentication mode is similar to using cookieless sessions, and can be used to support visitors who have cookies disabled. When the URL is used to identify the visitor, the links in your website will automatically be modified to include the identification information, and will look like this:

```
http://localhost/Dorknozzle/(F(oyVZpBZ3w7Iz_LEFRukBigAf
nxM5QzvMY374YdcVjfcfgKJt8SJ3x9pVlrvUSUKbAiMuTP4rylvvNi7
HQH3ta9kMmQWQmZM5aT13GkenHPk1))/Default.aspx
```

slidingExpiration

This attribute specifies whether the cookie's expiration date (which is specified using the `timeout` attribute) should be reset on subsequent requests of a user's session. The default value in ASP.NET 1.x was `True`, and the default value in ASP.NET is `False`.

An example **Web.config** file to which the `<forms>` tag has been applied might look like this:

```
<configuration>
  <system.web>
    <authentication mode="Forms">
      <forms name=".LoginCookie" loginUrl="Login.aspx"
          protection="All" timeout="40" path="/"
          cookieless="UseUri"/>
    </authentication>
    ⋮
  </system.web>
</configuration>
```

Configuring Forms Authorization

As is the case with the `authentication` section of the **Web.config** file, the `<authorization>` tag can be modified to provide or deny certain users access to your application, allowing you to make extremely specific decisions regarding who is, and is not, accepted into the app. For instance, the following code allows all authenticated (non-anonymous) users except for `andrei`:

```
<configuration>
  <system.web>
    <authentication mode="Forms"/>
    <authorization>
      <deny users="?"/>
      <deny users="andrei"/>
    </authorization>
  </system.web>
</configuration>
```

Here, we again use the question mark (?) to force users to log in, thus denying anonymous users access to our application. We've also added another <deny> tag, for the user andrei. In a nutshell, the two deny elements will allow everyone except andrei to log in.

In addition to <deny> tags, the <authorization> tag may contain <allow> tags—we'll see an example of this in a moment. For each user who attempts to access the application, ASP.NET will read through the tags in <authorization> and find the first tag that matches that user. If it turns out to be a <deny> tag, that user will be denied access to the application; if it's an <allow> tag, or if no matching tag is found, the user will be granted access.

The users attribute of <allow> and <deny> will accept three types of values:

?

Use this value to allow or deny all anonymous users. This is the most common value used with forms authentication.

*

Use this value to allow or deny all users, including users who are logged in.

user, …

As with andrei above, we can allow or deny access to a specific user via this attribute. We can list several users by separating their names with commas.

We could modify the code a bit further in an effort to allow only specific users:

```
<configuration>
  <system.web>
    <authentication mode="Forms"/>
```

```
      <authorization>
        <allow users="john,jane" />
        <deny users="*" />
      </authorization>
    </system.web>
  </configuration>
```

In this case, the users with the login names of john and jane are allowed access to the application, but all other users (whether they're logged in or not) will be denied access.

Now that you have a basic understanding of the ways in which user access is configured within the **Web.config** file, let's see how we can use **Web.config** to store a list of users for our application.

Storing Users in Web.config

The great thing about the **Web.config** file is that it is secure enough for us to store usernames and passwords in it with confidence. For now, we'll leave it in plain text, however in the next section we will cover the recommended approach of hashing the password in case someone gets access to the web.config file. The <credentials> tag, shown here within the forms element of the **Web.config** file, defines login credentials for two users:

DorkNozzle\VB\07_web.config

```
<authentication mode="Forms">
  <forms>
    <credentials passwordFormat="Clear" >
      <user name="john" password="john" />
      <user name="jane" password="jane" />
    </credentials>
  </forms>
</authentication>
<authorization>
  <deny users="?" />
</authorization>
```

As we want to prevent users from browsing the site if they're not logged in, we use the appropriate <deny> tag in our <authorization> tag. The names and passwords of the users we will permit can then simply be specified in the <credentials> tag.

Change your **Web.config** file to match the one shown above, and we'll try another example.

Let's modify the code in the code-behind file for the **Login.aspx** page to validate the usernames and passwords based on the **Web.config** file. Here's what this change looks like:

```
Visual Basic                              DorkNozzle\VB\08_Login.aspx.vb (excerpt)

Sub LoginUser(s As Object, e As EventArgs)
  If FormsAuthentication.Authenticate(username.Text, _
      password.Text) Then
    FormsAuthentication.RedirectFromLoginPage(username.Text, True)
  End If
End Sub
```

```
C#                                        DorkNozzle\CS\08_Login.aspx.cs (excerpt)

void LoginUser(Object s, EventArgs e)
{
  if (FormsAuthentication.Authenticate(username.Text,
      password.Text))
  {
    FormsAuthentication.RedirectFromLoginPage(username.Text,
        true);
  }
}
```

In this case, we use the `Authenticate` method of the `FormsAuthentication` class, which checks a username and password against the users defined in the `<credentials>` tag within the **Web.config** file. Save your work and test the results in the browser. Again, when you enter credentials that match those in the **Web.config** file, you'll be redirected to the page you requested.

In order to make this solution easier to maintain, you *could* write code that checked the username and password against a database. However, as it turns out, ASP.NET has built-in features that do all this work for you. We'll look at them a little later in this chapter.

Hashing Passwords

You can provide an increased level of protection for your users' passwords by storing them in a hashed format.

A **hashing** algorithm is an algorithm that performs an irreversible but reproducible transformation on some input data. If we hash a user's password before storing it, then, when that user tries to log in, we can simply apply the same hashing algorithm to the password the user has entered, and compare the results with the stored value.

You can store hashed versions of passwords in your database—you can even store hashed passwords in **Web.config**. If you choose the latter option, you'll obviously need a means of hashing your passwords when you add new users to the file. For a quick test, you can use an online hashing tool.[5] Simply supply the tool with a **cleartext** string (the desired password in its original unencoded state) and a hashing algorithm, and it will give you the hashed version of the string.

The built-in hashing algorithms that ASP.NET supports are MD5 and SHA1. If you were to hash the string "cristian" using MD5, the hashed version would be B08C8C585B6D67164C163767076445D6. Here's what your **Web.config** file would look like if you wanted to assign the password "cristian" to the user "cristian":

```
<authentication mode="Forms">
  <forms>
    <credentials passwordFormat="MD5">
      <user name="cristian"
            password="B08C8C585B6D67164C163767076445D6" />
    </credentials>
  </forms>
</authentication>
```

After you make this change, execute your project again. When the login form appears, enter **cristian** for the username, and **cristian** for the password, and you should be redirected to the requested page (which, by default, is the homepage).

---

[5] Try the one at http://aspnetresources.com/tools/pwdhash.aspx.

Hashing Passwords Programatically

I won't insist on using `Web.config` because ASP.NET offers the much more powerful option of storing credentials in the database. However, if you want to hash passwords yourself without using an online tool, you can use the `HashForStoringInConfigFile` method of the `FormsAuthentication` class, which takes as parameters the cleartext password, and the hashing algorithm you want to use—MD5 or SHA1.

Logging Users Out

You'll usually want to provide users with the ability to log out once they've finished browsing your site. People gain security from the knowledge that they have successfully logged out, and rightly so, since it's possible for a hacker to take over (or spoof) an existing login while it remains active. The first step to take in order to create logout functionality for your application is to insert a suitable control that users can click on when they finish browsing.

The method that lets you sign out current users is the `FormsAuthentication` class's `SignOut` method. You could call this method in the `Click` event handler of a **Sign Out** button, like this:

```vb
Visual Basic

Sub Logout(s As Object, e As EventArgs)
  FormsAuthentication.SignOut()
  Response.Redirect("Default.aspx")
End Sub
```

```csharp
C#

void Logout(Object s, EventArgs e) {
  FormsAuthentication.SignOut();
  Response.Redirect("Default.aspx");
}
```

The `SignOut` method shown above is used to clear the authentication cookie. The next line simply redirects the user to the homepage.

In the next section we'll be learning about ASP.NET Memberships and Roles and using our database to store user credentials. This means that now is a good opportunity to remove the user credentials for John and Jane (and anyone else you may have added) from our **Web.config** file before we progress.

ASP.NET Memberships and Roles

The ASP.NET team made a big step forward by implementing common functionality that previously needed to be coded from scratch for every new web application. This functionality includes a **membership system**, which supports the management of customer accounts, login forms, user registration forms, and so on, and is divided into several layers, each of which can be extended or modified to suit your needs.

In particular, this new membership system offers a rich set of **login controls**, which you find in the **Login** tab of the Toolbox in Visual Web Developer. That's right—you can add a form for the creation of new user accounts simply by dragging a CreateUserWizard control into a web form! ASP.NET makes implementing many such features extremely easy, but in order to take full advantage of these controls, we'll need to learn about the framework on which they're built.

Creating the Membership Data Structures

ASP.NET's membership system stores user profile data, including membership and personalization information, in a structured data store consisting of a set of tables, views, and stored procedures. We'll call these **membership data structures**, although that name doesn't take into account the complete range of data they contain.

To manipulate this data, Visual Web Developer provides the **ASP.NET Web Site Administration Tool**, which lets you add and edit users and their roles, and perform other administrative tasks.

We can use two procedures to create the necessary data structures. The first option is simply to open the ASP.NET Web Site Administration Tool, and click the **Security** tab. When you do this for the first time, the Web Site Administration Tool will create a database called ASPNETDB in the **App_Data** folder of your Web Application. This database will consist of two files: **ASPNETDB.MDF** (the database file) and **ASPNETDB_LOG.LDF** (the database log file).

Let's give this a try. With the Dorknozzle web site project loaded in Visual Web Developer, select **Website > ASP.NET Configuration**. This will load a page like that shown in Figure 13.3.

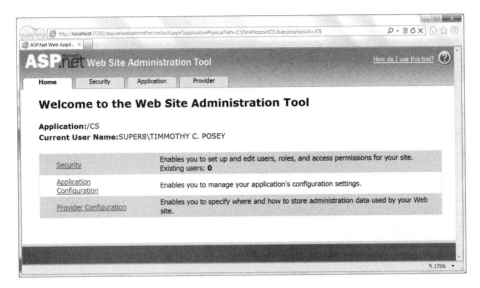

Figure 13.3. The ASP.NET Web Site Administration Tool

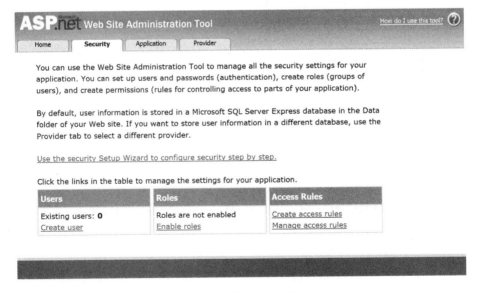

Figure 13.4. The **Security** tab

Click the **Security** tab to access the page shown in Figure 13.4.

At this point you can open the **Dorknozzle\App_Data** folder, where you'll be able to see your new database files, as Figure 13.5 indicates.

The ASPNETDB database is what's called a **User Instance database**, whose files are stored locally inside your application's folder. User instance databases are new to Microsoft SQL Server 2005; they allow you to access database files without attaching them to an SQL Server instance. These databases can easily be copied or transferred, and your application can connect to them as needed.

The new ASP.NET login controls, the ASP.NET Web Site Administration Tool, and a number of related classes are able to access the ASPNETDB database automatically, without any configuration. Should you need to access this database through your own code (for example, to customize the data structures), you can do so using the special connection string LocalSqlServer.

There are two things you need to be aware of when you're using the ASPNETDB database:

- Although User Instance databases were designed to be easy to move between systems, you can't always easily upload them to a hosting server.

- This approach will cause your application to have to work with two databases.

  In our case, the Dorknozzle site would need to use both the ASPNETDB database and our old friend, the Dorknozzle database. Whether this is a wise choice or not depends on the specifics of your project, and whether your site's other data structures need to relate to the membership data of your users.

Fortunately, you have the option to create the necessary data structures within your existing database.

Using Your Database to Store Membership Data

In many cases, it's more beneficial to store the membership data structures in your own database than in the default ASPNETDB database. Indeed, for the purposes of our application, it would be preferable to keep that data inside the existing Dorknozzle database. This way, when we launch the project, we'll need to transfer only one database to the production machine, rather than having to migrate two separate databases.

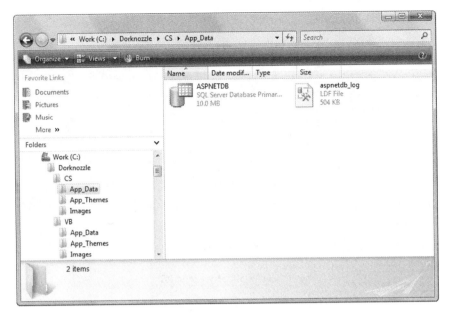

Figure 13.5. The `ASPNETDB` database files

In order to use your database to store membership data, you need to complete two tasks:

- Create the necessary data structures in `Dorknozzle`.

- Edit **Web.config** to specify the new location of these structures, overriding the default configuration that uses the `ASPNETDB` database.

You can use a tool that ships with ASP.NET, **aspnet_regsql.exe**, to customize the data store and add the necessary structures to your own database. This tool can be executed at the Windows command prompt, where you can include various parameters to configure it instantly for your database; alternatively, it can be run in Wizard mode, allowing you to set those options one at a time. To execute the tool, open **aspnet_regsql.exe**, which is located in
C:\Windows\Microsoft.NET\Framework\v2.0.nnnnn.

The wizard should open with a Welcome screen, where you'll just need to click **Next**. In the next window, which is shown in Figure 13.6, you can choose between adding the data structures to an existing database (or to a new database that can be created for you), or removing the data structures.

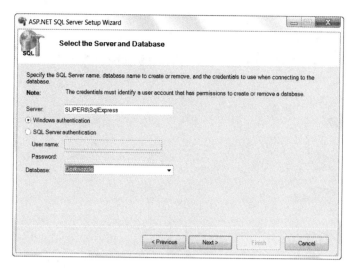

Figure 13.6. The SQL Server Setup Wizard

Leave the first option selected and hit **Next**—you'll see the dialog shown in Figure 13.7. Here, you'll need to tell the wizard which server and database you want to connect to in order to create those structures. The **Server** should be *LOCAL* \ `SqlExpress` (where *LOCAL* is the network name of your current machine), and the **Database** should be `Dorknozzle`.

Using Remote Servers

You can enter any local or remote server into the **Server** field. You might use this tool to configure a remote server, for example, when you're choosing to move the application from your development machine to a remote production machine. In that case, you'd need to select **SQL Server Authentication** and supply the username and password provided by the server's administrator.

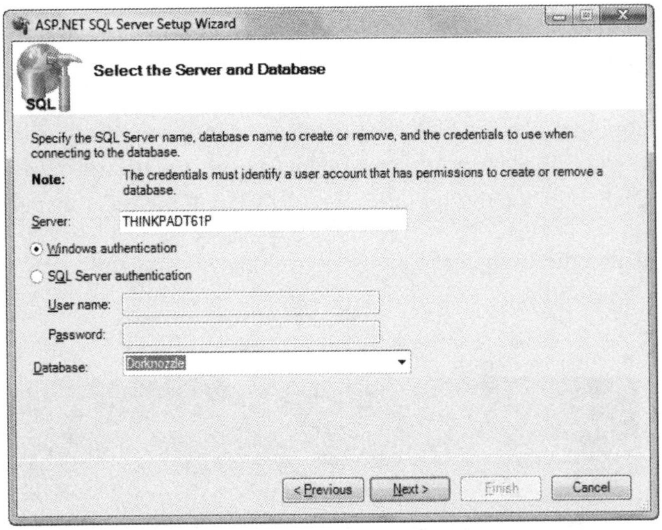

Figure 13.7. Selecting the **Server** and **Database**

Click **Next**, and you'll be asked to confirm the data you've entered. Hit **Next** again, and expect a delay while the tool finishes setting up the database for you. When it's done, click **Finish** to close the wizard; then, when **aspnet_regsql.exe** finishes executing and a new prompt is displayed, you can close the SDK Command Prompt window.

Once your database is ready, you'll need to modify **Web.config** to configure a new connection string named `LocalSqlServer`, which points to your database. As we mentioned earlier, this is the default connection string used by the built-in controls and tools that need access to the membership data.

More on aspnet_regsql.exe

You can customize or automate this process by supplying parameters to the **aspnet_regsql.exe** program at the command prompt. For example, instead of running the wizard using the steps above, you could have executed this command at the SDK Command Prompt:

```
aspnet_regsql -S LOCAL\SqlExpress -E -A all
      -d Dorknozzle
```

To have the tool connect using SQL Server Authentication instead of the integrated Windows Authentication, you'd use a slightly different command:

```
aspnet_regsql -S LOCAL\SqlExpress -U username
    -P password -A all -d Dorknozzle
```

Keep in mind that you can also use this tool to configure a remote database, in which case you'd need to mention the remote server address and database instance name instead of the local machine name and local SQL Server instance name.

If you executed the commands shown above, the output would look like that shown in Figure 13.8.

Figure 13.8. Using **aspnet_regsql.exe** at the command prompt

LocalSqlServer Definition In machine.config

Should you ever want to see or modify the default definition of the `LocalSqlServer` connection string, you can find it in the file **\Windows\Microsoft.NET\Framework**_version_**\CONFIG\machine.config**.

The **machine.config** file contains default machine-wide settings, which can be customized by each application's **Web.config** file. Here's the default definition of `LocalSqlServer`; this snippet also shows you how to connect to a disconnected database, such as **ASPNETDB**:

```
<connectionStrings>
  <add name="LocalSqlServer" connectionString="
      data source=.\SQLEXPRESS;
      Integrated Security=SSPI;
      AttachDBFilename=|DataDirectory|aspnetdb.mdf;
```

```
        User Instance=true"
        providerName="System.Data.SqlClient"/>
  </connectionStrings>
```

Modify **Web.config** so that it removes the default `LocalSqlServer` connection string, then redefines it with the same connection data as `DorknozzleConnectionString`:

Dorknozzle\VB\09_web.config (excerpt)

```
<connectionStrings>
  <add name="Dorknozzle"
      connectionString="Server=localhost\SqlExpress;
          Database=Dorknozzle;Integrated Security=True"
      providerName="System.Data.SqlClient"/>
  <remove name="LocalSqlServer"/>
  <add name="LocalSqlServer"
      connectionString="Server=localhost\SqlExpress;
          Database=Dorknozzle;Integrated Security=True"
      providerName="System.Data.SqlClient" />
</connectionStrings>
```

At this point, if you experimented with the auto-generated `ASPNETDB` database, you can delete the two database files, **aspnetdb.mdf** and **aspnetdb_log.ldf**, from your application's **App_Data** folder.[6]

If you're curious, open the `Dorknozzle` database using the tool of your choice to see the new tables that have been created—they're shown in Figure 13.9. You'll notice that your database now has 11 new tables whose names start with `aspnet`.

---

[6] It's interesting to note that if your application isn't using the **ASPNETDB** database, you're free to simply delete its files. This is possible because, as we explained earlier, **ASPNETDB** is a User Instance database, the files of which are opened and read only when needed.

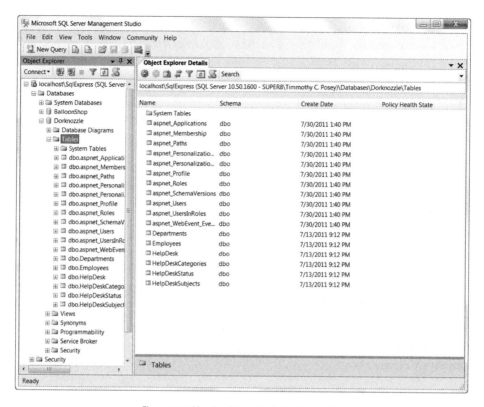

Figure 13.9. Membership tables in `Dorknozzle`

Using the ASP.NET Web Site Configuration Tool

After making the configuration changes we mentioned earlier, run the ASP.NET
Web Site Configuration Tool and click the **Security** tab again. If you look into the
App_Data folder, you'll notice that the tool didn't create the ASPNETDB database. In-
stead, it's using the Dorknozzle database.

Before you start to add users and roles, it's worth taking a look around. While you're
viewing the **Security** tab, click the **Select authentication type** link. You'll see two options:

From the Internet

You would normally have to select this option to enable forms authentication,
but since you have already selected that type of authentication by editing your
application's **Web.config** file, you'll find this option is already selected. However,
in future, you might want to use this tool to set your preferred authentication
type, instead of editing the file manually.

From a local network

Had we not specified forms authentication in the **Web.config** file, this option, which selects Windows authentication—ASP.NET's default—would have been selected. If you were to re-select this option at this stage, the tool would remove the <authentication> tag from your **Web.config** file, restoring the default setting.

Leave the **From the Internet** option selected, and click **Done** to return to the **Security** tab.

The **Provider** tab allows you to change the data provider that's used to store the security data. Currently, you can only choose AspNetSqlProvider, which uses SQL Server to store the membership data.

The **Application** tab shown in Figure 13.10 lets you create and manage application settings. You will find particularly useful the Application Settings tab, which lets you define name-value pairs to be stored in the **Web.config** file. For example, you might want to add a setting named AdminEmail, which contains an email address that can be used by your application to send important administration messages, as shown in Figure 13.11.

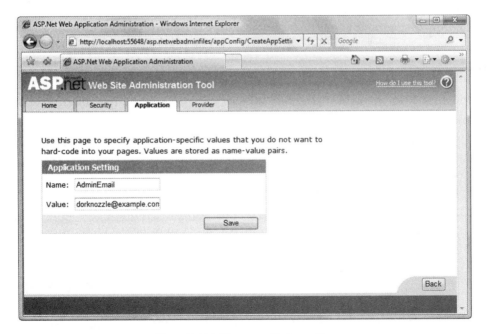

Figure 13.11. Adding an application setting

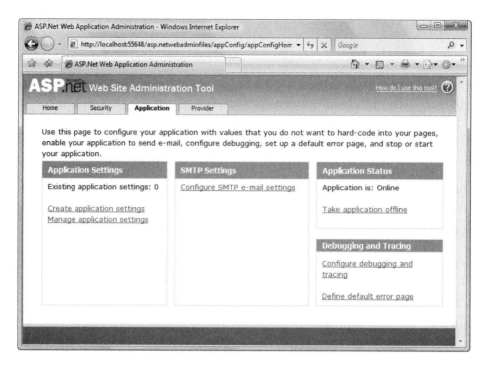

Figure 13.10. Managing application settings

We've already learned to use **Web.config** to store connection strings within a dedicated <connectionStrings> tag. Similarly, ASP.NET supports an <appSettings> tag in the same file for the purpose of storing general application settings.

If you click **Save**, the administration tool will store the setting in your application's **Web.config** file:

```
<appSettings>
  <add key="AdminEmail" value="dorknozzle@example.com" />
</appSettings>
```

To access this data, you need to use the ConfigurationManager class, which is located in the System.Configuration namespace, like this:

Visual Basic

```
adminEmail = ConfigurationManager.AppSettings("AdminEmail")
```

```
C#
```

```
adminEmail = ConfigurationManager.AppSettings["AdminEmail"];
```

Creating Users and Roles

Open the ASP.NET web site, click the **Security** tab, and click **Enable Roles** under the **Roles** section. This will add the following line to your **Web.config** file:

Dorknozzle\VB\10_web.config (excerpt)

```
<roleManager enabled="true" />
```

Two new links will appear under **Roles: Disable Roles**, and **Create or Manage Roles**. Click **Create or Manage Roles**, and use the form shown in Figure 13.12 to create two roles: one named **Users**, and another named **Administrators**.

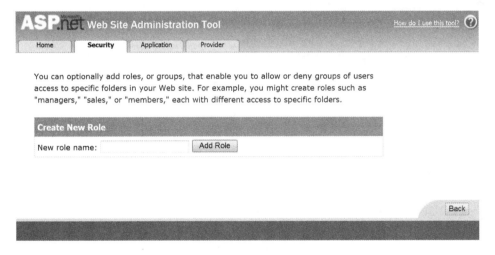

Figure 13.12. Creating roles

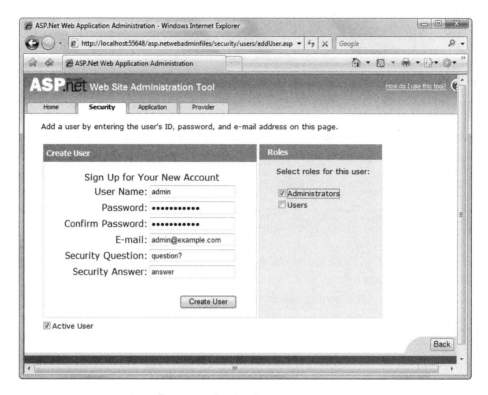

Figure 13.13. Creating the `admin` account

Click the **Security** tab to return to the main **Security** window. Now click the **Create user** link and add a user named **admin**, whose password is **Dorknozzle!**. Check the checkbox to assign this user the **Administrators** role, and complete the other fields shown in Figure 13.13, which are not optional.

Previously, the settings you specified using the ASP.NET Web Site Administration Tool always affected the **Web.config** file. Not this time, though! In accordance with the connection string in **Web.config**, roles and users are stored directly in the membership data structures that we added to the `Dorknozzle` database.

Changing Password Strength Requirements

By default, you won't be allowed to enter passwords that aren't considered sufficiently secure. The default security requirements for `AspNetSqlMembershipProvider`, as defined in **machine.config**, require the password to be at least seven characters long, and to include at least one non-alphanumeric character (which is why the exclamation mark was included in the example above). Also, passwords are stored in a hashed format by default.

To change the password strength requirements, we must override the default settings for the `AspNetSqlMembershipProvider` by adding a `<membership>` tag to the **Web.config** file. As you might expect, we must first remove the default settings inherited from **machine.config**, then define our own settings:

Dorknozzle\VB\11_web.config *(excerpt)*

```
<system.web>
  ⋮
  <membership>
    <providers>
      <remove name="AspNetSqlMembershipProvider" />
      <add name="AspNetSqlMembershipProvider"
          type="System.Web.Security.SqlMembershipProvider"
          connectionStringName="LocalSqlServer"
          enablePasswordRetrieval="false"
          enablePasswordReset="true"
          requiresQuestionAndAnswer="false"
          applicationName="/"
          requiresUniqueEmail="false"
          passwordFormat="Hashed"
          maxInvalidPasswordAttempts="10"
          minRequiredPasswordLength="7"
          minRequiredNonalphanumericCharacters="0"
          passwordAttemptWindow="10" />
    </providers>
  </membership>
  ⋮
</system.web>
```

The settings in the example above are self-explanatory. For example, we've increased the `maxInvalidPasswordAttempts` from the default of 5 to 10, to help many users avoid being locked out of their accounts if they repeatedly enter an incorrect password. We've also removed the constraint that required us to have at least one alphanumeric character in the password, and the function that facilitated lost password retrieval by means of a secret question and answer.

What Does Your Project Need?

Don't take these security settings as recommendations for your own projects. These kinds of decisions need to be taken seriously, and the choices you make should relate directly to the specific needs of your project.

Using Regular Expressions

Advanced programmers can make use of an additional setting, `passwordStrengthRegularExpression`, which can be used to describe complex rules that ensure password strength.

After you make this change in **Web.config**, start the ASP.NET Web Site Configuration Tool again and add another user named **cristian** with the password **cristian**; assign this user the **Users** role.[7] As Figure 13.14 illustrates, the fields for specifying a security question and answer no longer appear in the form.

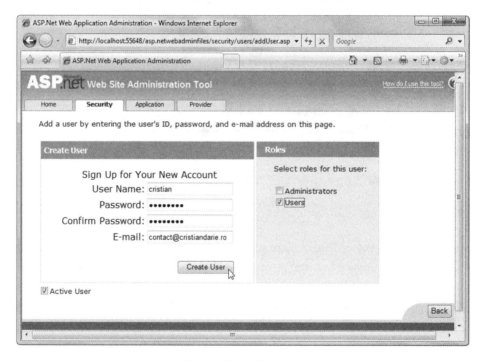

Figure 13.14. Creating a user

---

[7] Feel free to use another username and password combination that matches the new password strength requirements—the purpose of this exercise is to see for yourself that the new settings are in place.

Securing Your Web Application

Now we have two roles, and two users (admin and cristian), but we still need to secure the application. You should have restricted access to the app earlier in this chapter by modifying **Web.config** like this:

Dorknozzle\VB\11_web.config *(excerpt)*

```
<authorization>
  <deny users="?" />
</authorization>
```

If you haven't already done so, you can add this code now, or use Visual Web Developer to add it for you. Open the ASP.NET Web Site Administration Tool, click the **Security** tab, and click **Create access rules**. Create a new access rule for the **Dorknozzle** directory, as shown in Figure 13.15, to **Deny** all **Anonymous users.**

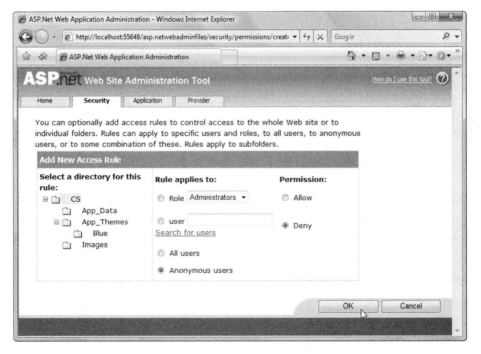

Figure 13.15. No anonymous users can access Dorknozzle!

Check the options indicated in Figure 13.15 and click **OK**. If you look at your updated **Web.config** file, you'll see the new `authorization` element that denies anonymous access.

Creating Access Rules Using the Administration Tool

Note that, while it's useful, this tool can be misleading. When you add a new access rule using the ASP.NET Web Site Administration Tool, the new rule is added to **Web.config**—even if it existed before! If you used the tool multiple times in the previous example, you could end up with repetitions like this:

```
<authorization>
  <deny users="?" />
  <deny users="?" />
  <deny users="?" />
</authorization>
```

Also, keep in mind that the new rules you add using the tool are appended to the bottom of the list. This is important because these rules are applied in sequence! For example, adding a new rule that allows anonymous users doesn't change the line created previously. Instead, it creates a new entry:

```
<authorization>
  <deny users="?" />
  <allow users="?" />
</authorization>
```

As these rules are processed in sequence, all anonymous users would be rejected even after we added the new rule. The tool isn't smart enough to detect such logical contradictions, so you must be careful with your rule-setting.

Before moving on, make sure your `authorization` element looks like this:

Dorknozzle\VB\11_web.config *(excerpt)*

```
<authorization>
  <deny users="?" />
</authorization>
```

At this point, no unauthenticated users can access your application. Since this is an intranet application that's supposed to be accessed only by Dorknozzle's employees, this security requirement makes sense.

However, we'd like to impose more severe security restrictions to the **AdminTools.aspx** file, which is supposed to be accessed only by administrators. Unfortunately, the

ASP.NET Web Site Application Configuration tool can't help you set permissions for individual files in your project, so you'll either need to place all admin-related functionality into a separate folder (which would allow you to continue using the tool to configure security options), or modify **Web.config** by hand.

You can set individual access rules for files using the `location` element, which can contain a `system.web` sub-element, which, in turn, can contain settings customized for the location. Add this code to your **Web.config** file:

```
Dorknozzle\VB\12_web.config (excerpt)

<!-- Allow access to Images directory -->
<location path="Images">
  <system.web>
    <authorization>
      <allow users="?"/>
    </authorization>
  </system.web>
</location>
<!-- Only administrators may access AdminTools.aspx -->
<location path="AdminTools.aspx">
  <system.web>
    <authorization>
      <allow roles="Administrators" />
      <deny users="*" />
    </authorization>
  </system.web>
</location>
</configuration>
```

Now, administrators are allowed to access **AdminTools.aspx**, as this rule comes first under the `authorization` element. If you switched the order of the `allow` and `deny` elements, *no one* would be allowed to access **AdminTools.aspx**.

Now your site is accessible only to authenticated users, with the exception of the Administration page, which is accessible only to users in the Administrator role. Now we just need to let users log in into the system.

Using the ASP.NET Login Controls

As we mentioned earlier in this chapter, ASP.NET delivers a range of very useful controls for managing users on your site:

Login

This control displays a login form that contains a **User Name** text box, a **Password** text box, a **Remember me next time** checkbox, and a **Log In** button. It's integrated with the membership API, and performs the login functionality without requiring you to write any code. The layout is customizable through templates and multiple properties.

LoginStatus

This is a simple yet useful control that displays a **Login** link if the user isn't logged in; otherwise, it displays a **Logout** link. Again, this control requires no additional coding in order to work with your application's membership data.

LoginView

This control contains templates that display different data depending on whether or not the user is logged in. It can also display different templates for authenticated users depending on their roles.

LoginName

This control displays the name of the logged-in user.

PasswordRecovery

If the user has provided an email address and a secret question and answer during registration, this control will use them to recover the user's password.

ChangePassword

This control displays a form that requests the user's existing password and a new password, and includes the functionality to change the user's password automatically, without requiring you to write additional code.

CreateUserWizard

This control displays a wizard for creating a new user account.

Let's see a few of these controls in action in our own application. In the following pages, we'll undertake these tasks:

1. Use a Login control in the **Login.aspx** page to give users a means of logging in to our application.

2. Use LoginStatus and LoginView controls to display **Login** and **Logout** links, and ensure that the **Admin Tools** link is displayed only to site administrators.

Authenticating Users

Earlier in this chapter, we created a web form based on the **Dorknozzle.master** master page, called **Login.aspx**. Remove the existing controls from the form's `ContentPlaceHolder`, and also remove the `LoginUser` method from the code-behind file.

Using the ASP.NET login controls, we can easily make the authentication work. If you're using Visual Web Developer, simply drag a `Login` control from the **Login** section of the Toolbox to just below the **Login** header in **Login.aspx**. If you'd prefer to add the control manually, here's the code:

```
                                    Dorknozzle\VB\13_Login.aspx (excerpt)
<asp:Content ID="Content2"
    ContentPlaceHolderID="ContentPlaceHolder1" Runat="Server">
  <h1>Login</h1>
  <asp:Login ID="Login1" runat="server">
  </asp:Login>
</asp:Content>
```

If you switch to **Design** view, you should see a display like the one depicted in Figure 13.16.

Figure 13.16. Using the `Login` control

Yes, that's all you have to do! Start your project, and you'll be sent to the Login page. First, log in with the regular user details that you created earlier (not with the admin account), then browse through the links to see that they can indeed be accessed, with the exception of the **Admin Tools** link. When you click **Admin Tools**, you should be sent back to the Login page. This time, log in with the admin user details, and *voilà*! You'll gain access to the Admin Tools page as well.

Let's take a few moments to customize the look of your login controls. Stop the execution of the project, and switch back to **Login.aspx** in **Design** view. Select the Login control and click its smart tag to see the three very useful options shown in Figure 13.17.

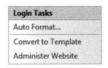

Figure 13.17. Options for the `Login` control

The **Administer Website** menu option launches the ASP.NET Web Site Administration Tool. The **Convert to Template** option transforms the current layout of your control into templates, which you can customize down to the smallest detail. The **Auto Format...** link lets you select a predefined style to apply to this control.

If you were working in a production scenario, I'd advise you to select **Convert to Template** and use CSS to fine-tune the appearance of your control, as we did with the `GridView` and `DetailsView` controls in Chapter 11. However, for the purposes of this exercise, let's just set the `BorderStyle` property of the `Login` control to `Solid`, and the `BorderWidth` property to `1px`.

It was very simple to add login functionality—we even changed its appearance with just a few mouse clicks! There are just one or two more things that we need to take care of before we can continue to add features to our site. First, let's deal with personalization.

Customizing User Display

The next feature we want to implement is functionality that gives the user a way to log out of the application. After you perform the changes that we're about to implement, logged-in users will have the option to log out, as Figure 13.18 illustrates.

On the other hand, users that aren't logged in won't see the menu at all, as Figure 13.19 indicates.

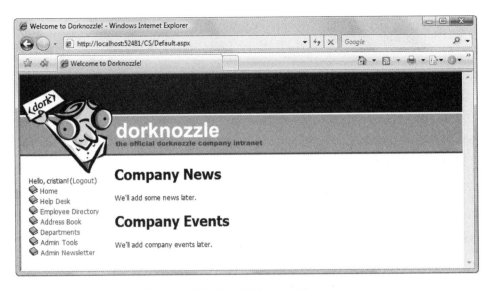

Figure 13.18. The view that the logged-in user sees

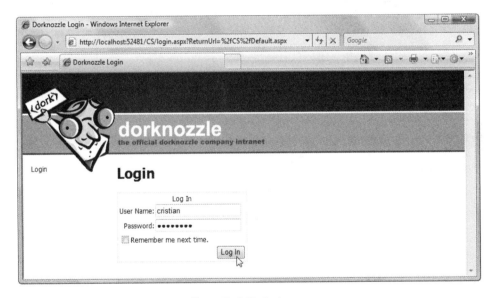

Figure 13.19. The Login page

To implement the logout link functionality, we'll need to modify the menu in the
Dorknozzle.master master page.

Using Master Pages

At this point, you should appreciate the extraordinary flexibility that master pages offer us. If you didn't use master pages or web user controls, you'd have to modify *all* of the pages on your site to implement this new functionality.

Open **Dorknozzle.master**, and change the code between `<!-- Menu -->` and `<!-- Content -->` as indicated here:

Dorknozzle\VB\14_Dorknozzle.master (excerpt)

```
<!-- Menu -->
<div class="Menu">
  <asp:LoginView ID="loginView" runat="server">
    <LoggedInTemplate>
      <asp:LoginName ID="loginName" runat="server"
        FormatString="Hello, {0}!" />
      (<asp:LoginStatus ID="loginStatus" runat="server" />)
      <asp:SiteMapDataSource ID="dorknozzleSiteMap" runat="server"
        ShowStartingNode="false" />
      <asp:Menu ID="dorknozzleMenu" runat="server"
        DataSourceID="dorknozzleSiteMap">
        <StaticItemTemplate>
          <img src="Images/book_closed.gif" border="0" width="16"
            height="16" alt="+" />
          <%# Eval("Text") %>
        </StaticItemTemplate>
      </asp:Menu>
    </LoggedInTemplate>
    <AnonymousTemplate>
      <asp:LoginStatus ID="loginStatus" runat="server" />
    </AnonymousTemplate>
  </asp:LoginView>
</div>
<!-- Content -->
```

Also modify the **Dorknozzle.css** file to accommodate the new control:

Dorknozzle\VB\15_Dorknozzle.css (excerpt)

```
.Menu
{
  top: 180px;
```

```
  left: 15px;
  width: 195px;
  position: absolute;
}
```

Don't let this code scare you; it's actually quite simple. The root control here is a `LoginView` control, which displays different templates depending on whether or not the user is logged in (it also knows how to display different templates depending on the roles of the user).

If the site is loaded by an anonymous (unauthenticated) user, we don't want to display the navigation menu; we want to display only the **Login** link. The output that's to be shown to anonymous users by the `LoginView` control is placed inside its `AnonymousTemplate` template. There, we use a `LoginStatus` control that displays a **Login** link for anonymous users, and a **Logout** link for logged-in users. Note that with the current Dorknozzle configuration, the contents of the `AnonymousTemplate` are never actually used—all anonymous users are simply redirected to the Login page. However, it's best to include the `LoginStatus` control here anyway, just in case we should ever reconfigure the site to include some pages that are accessible to anonymous users:

Dorknozzle\VB\14_Dorknozzle.master *(excerpt)*

```
<AnonymousTemplate>
  <asp:LoginStatus ID="loginStatus" runat="server" />
</AnonymousTemplate>
```

The output that will be displayed to authenticated users is placed inside the `LoggedInTemplate` template of the `LoginView` control. The `LoggedInTemplate` starts by displaying a welcome message:

Dorknozzle\VB\14_Dorknozzle.master *(excerpt)*

```
<LoggedInTemplate>
  <asp:LoginName ID="loginName" runat="server"
    FormatString="Hello, {0}!" />
```

By default, the `LoginName` control displays just the username. However, you can customize it by setting its `FormatString` property to a custom string, where {0} is a placeholder for the username. Our FormatString value, Hello, {0}! will output "Hello, cristian!" if the logged in user's username is cristian.

Immediately after this welcome message, we have a **Logout** link generated by another LoginStatus control which, as we discussed earlier, displays a **Logout** link to logged-in users:

Dorknozzle\VB\14_Dorknozzle.master *(excerpt)*

```
(<asp:LoginStatus ID="loginStatus" runat="server" />)
```

Just below the welcome message and the **Logout** link sits our old friend, Menu, which displays the navigation menu. Since the Menu is now part of the LoggedInTemplate of the LoginView, it's displayed only for logged-in users, as we planned.

Finally, it's worth noting that you can use Visual Web Developer to edit the various templates (and the controls they house). Open **Dorknozzle.master** in the designer, and click the smart tag of the LoginView control. The options that display, which are shown in Figure 13.20, are certainly interesting.

Figure 13.20. Viewing **LoginView Tasks**

The **Edit RoleGroups…** link lets you administer the templates that are shown to users who are assigned particular roles. This facility is useful when you want to display to users specific content that's relevant to their roles. For example, if you wanted to display to administrators different menus than you show to regular users, you could create a group for users within the Users role, and another group for users in the Administrators role, then create different views for these groups using templates.

To check in your code whether or not the current user is authenticated (that is, logged in), you must check the value of HttpContext.Current.User.Identity.IsAuthenticated. To check the role of the logged-in user, you must use the HttpContext.Current.User.IsInRole method, as shown here:

Visual Basic

```
If HttpContext.Current.User.IsInRole("Administrators") Then
    ⋮
```

C#

```
if (HttpContext.Current.User.IsInRole("Administrators"))
{
    ⋮
```

This method returns True if the current user is a member of the specified role, and False if he or she is not.

Summary

In this chapter, we examined the approaches you can use to secure your ASP.NET applications. You learned how to create a simple Login page, configure the **Web.config** file to handle authentication and authorization, and check for usernames and passwords using a database.

ASP.NET's membership features provide extraordinary built-in functionality, and we have explored a number of these features through this chapter. The complete list of features is much larger, and, as we mentioned at the beginning of this chapter, there are entire books that deal solely with this topic.

In Chapter 14, we'll learn to work with files and directories, and send email messages using ASP.NET.

Working with Files and Email

The .NET Framework exposes a set of classes for working with text files, drives, and directories, through the System.IO namespace. This namespace exposes functionality that allows you to read from, write to, and update content within directories and text files. On occasion, you will want to read from and write to a text file. Text files almost always use a format that's based on the ASCII standard, which is perhaps the most widely accepted cross-platform file format, having been around since the 1960s. This makes it a very useful way of exchanging information between programs—even if they're running on different platforms and operating systems.

As we'll see in the course of this chapter, we can use the set of classes exposed by the System.IO namespace to complete the following tasks:

Write to text files.
The sales department within our fictitious company may want to write sales and forecast information to a text file.

Read from text files.

As a member of the web development team, you may want to use the data within a text file to create dynamic graphs to display sales and revenue forecasts on the Web.

Upload files from the client to the server.

You may want to create an interface that allows staff from the Human Resources department to upload company documentation for reference by employees.

Access directories and directory information.

You may want to let the Human Resources department choose the drive to which staff will upload files. For instance, you may have one drive dedicated to spreadsheets, and another just for Word documents.

Once you have a firm grasp on the intricacies of working with text files and directory information, you'll learn how to send email in ASP.NET using the System.Net.Mail namespace. We'll finish the chapter with a quick introduction to serialization.

Writing and Reading Text Files

The System.IO namespace contains three different groups of classes:

- classes for working with files
- classes for working with streams
- classes for working with directories

As we progress through this chapter, we'll look at each of these groups. However, let's begin by discussing the tasks of writing to and reading from text files with the aid of the classes that work with files and streams. These classes include:

File

contains methods for working with files

FileStream

represents a stream for reading and writing to files

StreamReader

reads characters from a text file

StreamWriter

   writes characters to a text file

Path

   contains methods for manipulating a file or directory

For the most part, we read from and write to text files by using the `File` class to return a stream. If we want to write to a text file, we use the `StreamWriter` class; conversely, we use the `StreamReader` class to read from a text file.

Setting Up Permissions

Before our ASP.NET page can read and write files to your hard disk, the ASP.NET page must have permissions to access the file we're trying to read or write. The task of setting the permissions depends on our context. Here's a couple of possible scenarios:

- If you're running the page using Cassini (Visual Web Developer's integrated web server), the code will run under the credentials of your user account, so it will inherit all your permissions. For example, if you're a computer administrator, then your page will be able to access any resource on your computer.

- If you're running the page using IIS, the code will run under the credentials of the ASPNET user account, or the Network Service user account, depending on your operating system. By default, this account has access to any folder that's part of an IIS application.

 Running Under IIS

   The IIS scenario is particularly relevant because your web application will run under IIS when it's hosted on a production server. Also of note is the fact that, while you may fine-tune the permission rules on your development machine, on a hosting server you probably won't be allowed to access folders outside your application's virtual directory.

On your own machine, you'll need to set special permissions only if you use IIS, and you want to write in a folder that's not part of an existing IIS application. If you're in this situation, read on. Otherwise, feel free to skip to the next section, in which we'll create within your application's folder structure a file that will be accessible under the default configuration of either IIS or Cassini.

Detailed instructions are provided only for Windows XP, which requires an extra step compared to Windows Vista. If you run Windows Vista, follow the exercise, but exclude Step 2. At Step 5, you should add the account **Network Service** instead of **ASPNET**.

1. Create a new folder called **WritingTest** somewhere on your disk. For the purposes of this discussion, I'll assume it's at **C:\WritingTest**.

2. In Windows XP, simple file sharing is enabled by default. This hides the **Security** tab you'll need to select in Step 4, preventing you from granting web applications write access to this directory. To disable simple file sharing, open the Windows Control Panel and double-click the **Folder Options** icon. In the **View** tab, uncheck **Use simple file sharing (Recommended)** (as Figure 14.1 indicates, this should be the last option on the list).

3. Open the **C:** drive with the Windows Explorer (not the IIS control panel), right-click on the **WritingText** directory and select **Properties**.

4. Select the **Security** tab.

5. Add the **ASPNET** account (**Network Service** if you run Vista) to the **Group or user names** list by clicking **Add...**, and typing it into the **Select Users or Groups** dialog as shown in Figure 14.2. A new entry called **ASP.NET Machine Account** (*machinename***ASPNET**) will be added to the list.

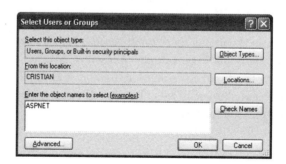

Figure 14.2. Adding the ASPNET account

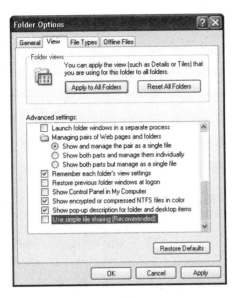

Figure 14.1. Disabling simple file sharing in Windows XP

6. Select the new user in the list, and click on the **Write** checkbox under **Allow** in the permissions list, as shown in Figure 14.3.

7. Click **OK**.

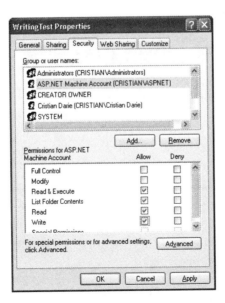

Figure 14.3. Giving write access to ASPNET

Writing Content to a Text File

For the purposes of the next few exercises, let's work again with our old friend, the **LearningASP** folder. Start Visual Web Developer, open the **LearningASP\CS** or **LearningASP\VB** folder, and create a new web form called **WriteFile.aspx**. Make sure you *aren't* using a code-behind file or a master page. Next, enter the code shown here in bold:

LearningASP\VB\WriteFile_1.aspx (excerpt)

```
<%@ Page Language="VB" %>
<%@ Import Namespace="System.IO" %>
<!DOCTYPE html PUBLIC "-//W3C//DTD XHTML 1.0 Transitional//EN"
    "http://www.w3.org/TR/xhtml1/DTD/xhtml1-transitional.dtd">

<script runat="server">

</script>

<html xmlns="http://www.w3.org/1999/xhtml">
  <head runat="server">
    <title>Writing to Text Files</title>
  </head>
  <body>
    <form id="form1" runat="server">
      <div>
        <p>Write the following text within a text file:</p>
        <asp:TextBox ID="myText" runat="server" />
        <asp:Button ID="writeButton" Text="Write" runat="server"
            OnClick="WriteText" />
      </div>
    </form>
  </body>
</html>
```

As you can see, we import the System.IO namespace—the namespace that contains the classes for working with text files—first. Next, we add a TextBox control to handle collection of the user-entered text, and a Button control to send the information to the server for processing.

Next, in the <head> tag, we'll create the WriteText method mentioned in the OnClick attribute of the Button. This method will write the contents of the TextBox to the text file:

Visual Basic   LearningASP\VB\WriteFile_2.aspx *(excerpt)*

```
<script runat="server">
  Sub WriteText(ByVal s As Object, ByVal e As EventArgs)
    Using streamWriter As StreamWriter = File.CreateText( _
        "C:\LearningASP\VB\myText.txt")
      streamWriter.WriteLine(myText.Text)
    End Using
  End Sub
</script>
```

C#   LearningASP\CS\WriteFile_2.aspx *(excerpt)*

```
<script runat="server">
  void WriteText(Object s, EventArgs e)
  {
    using (StreamWriter streamWriter = File.CreateText(
        @"C:\LearningASP\CS\myText.txt"))
    {
      streamWriter.WriteLine(myText.Text);
    }
  }
</script>
```

Apart from the new `Using` construct, the code is fairly straightforward. First, we create a `StreamWriter` variable called `streamWriter`. To obtain the variable's value, we call the `CreateText` method of the `File` class, passing in the location of the text file, which returns a new `StreamWriter`. Don't forget that C# needs to escape back-slashes when they're used in strings, so the path to our file must use \\ to separate folder names, or use the @ character in front of the string so that backslashes are automatically ignored.

What about `Using`, then? Similarly to database connections, streams are something that we need to close when we're finished working with them, so they don't occupy resources unnecessarily. The `Using` construct is a common means of ensuring that the stream is closed and **disposed of** after we work with it.

 ### Disposing of Objects

Technically, when we work with `Using`, the object is disposed of, rather than simply closed. The action is identical to explicitly calling its `Dispose` method.

When the code enclosed by `Using` finishes executing, `streamWriter`'s `Dispose` method is called automatically for you. This ensures that it doesn't keep any resources locked, and that *the object itself* is removed from memory immediately.

In the world of .NET, closed objects are cleared from memory at regular intervals by .NET's Garbage Collector, but for classes that support the `Dispose` method (such as `StreamWriter`), you can use this method (or the `Using` construct) to remove an object from memory immediately.

It's also interesting to note the way we used the `File` class's `CreateText` method in the code above. Normally, when we need to call a method of a particular class, we create an object of that class first. How was it possible to call the `CreateText` method using a class name, without creating an object of the `File` class first?

The `CreateText` method is what Visual Basic calls a **shared method**, and what's known in C# as a **static method**. Shared or static methods can be called without our having to create an actual instance of the class. In the above code, `CreateText` is a shared or static method, because we can call it directly from the `File` class, without having to create an instance of that class.

We worked with shared/static class members earlier, when we read the connection string. In that case, you didn't need to create an object of the `ConfigurationManager` class in order to read your connection string:

Visual Basic

```
string connectionString =
    ConfigurationManager.ConnectionStrings( _
    "Dorknozzle").ConnectionString
```

Instance methods, on the other hand, are those with which you're familiar—they may only be called on an instance (object) of the class. Instance methods are most commonly used, but shared/static methods can be useful for providing generic functionality that doesn't need to be tied to a particular class instance.

Now, test the page in your browser. Initially, all you'll see is an interface that's similar to Figure 14.4.

Type some text into the text box, and click the **Write** button to submit your text for processing. Browse to and open the **C:\LearningASP\VB\myText.txt** or

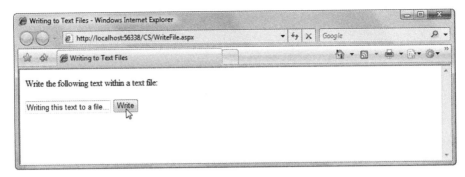

Figure 14.4. Writing text to a file

C:\LearningASP\CS\myText.txt file in Notepad, and as in Figure 14.5, you'll see the
newly added text.

If you try to enter a different value into the `TextBox` control and click the **Write**
button, the existing text will be overwritten with the new content. To prevent this
from happening, you can replace the call to the `CreateText` method with a call to
`AppendText`. As Figure 14.6 shows, the `AppendText` method adds to existing text,
rather than replacing it.

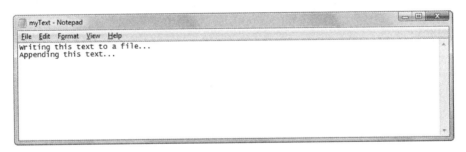

Figure 14.6. Appending text

Also note that, rather than specifying the full path to the text file, you can use the
`MapPath` method to generate the full path to the text file automatically. All you need
to do is give the method a path that's relative to the current directory, as follows:

Visual Basic   *LearningASP\VB\WriteFile_3.aspx (excerpt)*

```
Using streamWriter As StreamWriter = File.AppendText( _
    MapPath("myText.txt"))
```

Figure 14.5. Viewing your new file in Notepad

C#	LearningASP\CS\WriteFile_3.aspx *(excerpt)*

```
using (StreamWriter streamWriter = File.AppendText(
    MapPath("myText.txt")))
```

The `MapPath` method returns the full path to the filename that you pass in as a parameter, and can make for cleaner code that's easier to read.

Reading Content from a Text File

Just as you used the `CreateText` and `AppendText` methods of the `File` class to return a new `StreamWriter` object, you can use the `OpenText` method of the `File` class to return a new `StreamReader`. Once the `StreamReader` has been established, you can loop through the text file using a `While` loop in conjunction with the object's `ReadLine` method to examine the contents of the text file.

To experiment with the process of reading from text files, create a new web form named **ReadFile.aspx** in the same way that you created **WriteFile.aspx**, and add this code to it:

Visual Basic	LearningASP\VB\ReadFile_1.aspx *(excerpt)*

```
<%@ Page Language="VB" %>
<%@ Import Namespace="System.IO" %>
<!DOCTYPE html PUBLIC "-//W3C//DTD XHTML 1.0 Transitional//EN"
    "http://www.w3.org/TR/xhtml1/DTD/xhtml1-transitional.dtd">

<script runat="server">

</script>

<html xmlns="http://www.w3.org/1999/xhtml">
```

```
<head runat="server">
  <title>Reading from Text Files</title>
</head>
<body>
  <form id="form1" runat="server">
    <div>
      <asp:Button ID="readButton" Text="Read" runat="server"
          OnClick="ReadText" />
      <br />
      <asp:Label ID="resultLabel" runat="server" />
    </div>
  </form>
</body>
</html>
```

As you can see, we've simply added a Button and Label to the page. When the user clicks the button, the Click event will be raised and the ReadText method will be called. Let's add this method next. It will read the text from the text file and write it out to the Label control:

Visual Basic   LearningASP\VB\ReadFile_2.aspx *(excerpt)*

```
<script runat="server">
  Sub ReadText(ByVal s As Object, ByVal e As EventArgs)
    Dim inputString As String
    resultLabel.Text = ""
    Using streamReader As StreamReader = _
        File.OpenText(MapPath("myText.txt"))
      inputString = streamReader.ReadLine()
      While (inputString <> Nothing)
        resultLabel.Text &= inputString & "<br />"
        inputString = streamReader.ReadLine()
      End While
    End Using
  End Sub
</script>
```

C#   LearningASP\CS\ReadFile_2.aspx *(excerpt)*

```
<script runat="server">
  void ReadText(Object s, EventArgs e)
  {
    string inputString;
```

```
    resultLabel.Text = "";
    using (StreamReader streamReader =
        File.OpenText(MapPath("myText.txt")))
    {
      inputString = streamReader.ReadLine();
      while (inputString != null)
      {
        resultLabel.Text += inputString + "<br />";
        inputString = streamReader.ReadLine();
      }
    }
  }
}
</script>
```

We declare a new string variable named inputString to hold the text we'll read from the text file. Next, we set the text value of the Label control to an empty string. We do this in case the user presses the **Read** button when the Label already contains text from a previous click.

The next thing our method has to do is call the OpenText method of the File class to return a new StreamReader, again passing in the full path to the text file. And, once again, we're using the Using construct to ensure the stream object is disposed of after we finish working with it:

Visual Basic   LearningASP\VB\ReadFile_2.aspx *(excerpt)*

```
  Using streamReader As StreamReader = _
      File.OpenText(MapPath("myText.txt"))
```

C#   LearningASP\CS\ReadFile_2.aspx *(excerpt)*

```
  using (StreamReader streamReader =
      File.OpenText(MapPath("myText.txt")))
  {
```

Next, we call the ReadLine method of the streamReader object to get the first line of the file:

Visual Basic   LearningASP\VB\ReadFile_2.aspx *(excerpt)*

```
    inputString = streamReader.ReadLine()
```

```
C#                                    LearningASP\CS\ReadFile_2.aspx (excerpt)

    inputString = streamReader.ReadLine();
```

Now we loop through the file, reading each line and adding it, in turn, to the end of the text in the `Label`:

```
Visual Basic                          LearningASP\VB\ReadFile_2.aspx (excerpt)

    While (inputString <> Nothing)
      resultLabel.Text &= inputString & "<br />"
      inputString = streamReader.ReadLine()
    End While
```

```
C#                                    LearningASP\CS\ReadFile_2.aspx (excerpt)

    while (inputString != null)
    {
      resultLabel.Text += inputString + "<br />";
      inputString = streamReader.ReadLine();
    }
```

Remember, `While` loops are used when you want to repeat the loop while a condition remains `True`. In this case, we want to loop through the file, reading in lines from it until the `ReadLine` method returns the value `Nothing` (`null` in C#), which indicates that we've reached the end of the file. Within the loop, we simply append the value of `inputString` to the `Label` control's `Text` property using the `&=` operator (`+=` in C#), then read the next line from `streamReader` into `inputString`.

Save your work and test the results in the browser. Figure 14.7 shows the contents of the text file, as displayed by **ReadFile.aspx**.

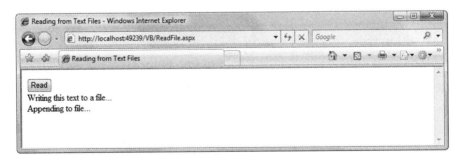

Figure 14.7. Reading a file using `StreamReader`

Accessing Directories and Directory Information

Now that you have some understanding of writing to and reading from text files, let's look at accessing the directories in which those files are located. The classes that are available in the System.IO namespace for working with directories and directory information are as follows:

Directory

contains shared/static methods for creating, moving, and retrieving the contents of directories

DirectoryInfo

contains instance methods for creating, moving, and retrieving the contents of directories

Just like the File class, the Directory class contains shared/static methods, which we can call without instantiating the class. The DirectoryInfo class, on the other hand, requires instantiation, as it contains only instance methods. The Directory class contains the following useful methods:

GetDirectories

returns a string array of directory names

GetFiles

returns a string array of filenames from a specific drive or directory

GetFileSystemEntries

returns a string array of directory and filenames

Let's build an example page with a DropDownList control to display the directories and files within the server's **C:** drive. In the same **Learning** folder, create a web form named **Directories.aspx**, without a code-behind file, then add to it the code shown here in bold:

| Visual Basic | LearningASP\VB\Directories_1.aspx *(excerpt)* |

```
<%@ Page Language="VB" %>
<%@ Import Namespace="System.IO" %>
<!DOCTYPE html PUBLIC "-//W3C//DTD XHTML 1.0 Transitional//EN"
    "http://www.w3.org/TR/xhtml1/DTD/xhtml1-transitional.dtd">

<script runat="server">

</script>

<html xmlns="http://www.w3.org/1999/xhtml">
  <head runat="server">
    <title>Directory Info</title>
  </head>
  <body>
    <form id="form1" runat="server">
      <div>
        <p>What do you want to view:</p>
        <asp:DropDownList ID="dirDropDown" runat="server"
            OnSelectedIndexChanged="ViewDriveInfo"
            AutoPostBack="true">
          <asp:ListItem Text="Select..." />
          <asp:ListItem Text="Directories" />
          <asp:ListItem Text="Files" />
          <asp:ListItem Text="Directories/Files" />
        </asp:DropDownList>
        <asp:GridView ID="grid" runat="server" />
      </div>
    </form>
  </body>
</html>
```

As you can see, our interface consists of a DropDownList control containing the three choices from which the user can select (**Directories**, **Files**, or **Directories/Files**). When a user selects an item from the DropDownList control, the SelectedIndex-Changed event is raised, and ViewDriveInfo is called.

Now, let's write the ViewDriveInfo method, which will write the specified information to the GridView control:

Visual Basic   LearningASP\VB\Directories_2.aspx *(excerpt)*

```vb
<script runat="server">
  Sub ViewDriveInfo(ByVal s As Object, ByVal e As EventArgs)
    Select Case dirDropDown.SelectedItem.Text
      Case "Directories"
        grid.DataSource = Directory.GetDirectories("C:\")
      Case "Files"
        grid.DataSource = Directory.GetFiles("C:\")
      Case "Directories/Files"
        grid.DataSource = Directory.GetFileSystemEntries("C:\")
    End Select
    grid.DataBind()
  End Sub
</script>
```

C#   LearningASP\CS\Directories_2.aspx *(excerpt)*

```csharp
<script runat="server">
  void ViewDriveInfo(Object s, EventArgs e)
  {
    switch (dirDropDown.SelectedItem.Text)
    {
      case "Directories":
        grid.DataSource = Directory.GetDirectories("C:\\");
        break;
      case "Files":
        grid.DataSource = Directory.GetFiles("C:\\");
        break;
      case "Directories/Files":
        grid.DataSource = Directory.GetFileSystemEntries("C:\\");
        break;
    }
    grid.DataBind();
  }
</script>
```

You might remember from Chapter 3 that we use Select Case (VB) or switch (C#)
statements to check for the possibility of multiple values of an object, rather than
just one. The Select Case or switch specifies the value that is to be checked (in
this case, the Text property of the selected list item):

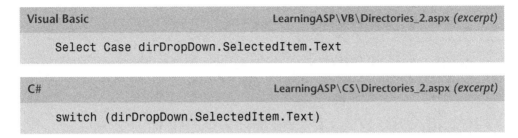

Visual Basic   *LearningASP\VB\Directories_2.aspx (excerpt)*

```
Select Case dirDropDown.SelectedItem.Text
```

C#   *LearningASP\CS\Directories_2.aspx (excerpt)*

```
switch (dirDropDown.SelectedItem.Text)
```

Next, we use `Case` to specify the action to be performed for each significant value.

The data retrieved by the , `GetFiles`, or `GetFileSystemEntries` method of `Directory` can be fed to the `GridView` as its `DataSource`. After we specify the `DataSource`, we need to call the control's `DataBind` method, as if we were reading from a database, to fetch and display the data from the data source.

Save your work and test the results in your browser. Figure 14.8 shows within the `GridView` the kind of results that display when the user selects an item from the `DropDownList`.

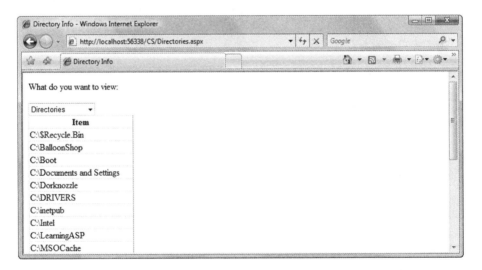

Figure 14.8. Using the `Directory` class to view specific files, directories, or both, from a given drive

 More Options

The `GetDirectories`, `GetFiles`, and `GetFileSystemEntries` methods accept more than simple drive or directory names. For instance, if you wanted to view only text files, you could use the following VB code:

```
Directory.GetFiles("C:\", "*.txt")
```

In this example, the `GetFiles` method would retrieve from the root of the `C:` drive all files that have the **.txt** extension.

Working with Directory and File Paths

The System.IO namespace includes a utility class named `Path` that contains methods for retrieving path information from files and directories. As an example, let's build a simple application that retrieves the directory and path information for a text file. Create a new web form named **PathInfo.aspx** in the **Learning** directory, then add to it the code shown here in bold:

Visual Basic	LearningASP\VB\PathInfo_1.aspx

```
<%@ Page Language="VB" %>
<%@ Import Namespace="System.IO" %>
<!DOCTYPE html PUBLIC "-//W3C//DTD XHTML 1.0 Transitional//EN"
    "http://www.w3.org/TR/xhtml1/DTD/xhtml1-transitional.dtd">

<script runat="server">

</script>

<html xmlns="http://www.w3.org/1999/xhtml">
  <head runat="server">
    <title>Directory and Path Information</title>
  </head>
  <body>
    <form id="form1" runat="server">
      <div>
        <asp:Label ID="resultLabel" runat="server" />
      </div>
    </form>
  </body>
</html>
```

The page contains a simple `Label` control, which we'll use to show all the directory and path information. Next, let's add the code that actually returns the path and directory information:

| Visual Basic | LearningASP\VB\PathInfo_2.aspx *(excerpt)* |

```
<script runat="server">
  Sub Page_Load(ByVal s As Object, ByVal e As EventArgs)
    Dim strPath As String
    strPath = MapPath("myText.txt")
    resultLabel.Text &= "File Path: " & strPath & "<br />"
    resultLabel.Text &= "File name: " & _
        Path.GetFileName(strPath) & "<br />"
    resultLabel.Text &= "Directory: " & _
        Path.GetDirectoryName(strPath) & "<br />"
    resultLabel.Text &= "Extension: " & _
        Path.GetExtension(strPath) & "<br />"
    resultLabel.Text &= "Name without Extension: " & _
        Path.GetFileNameWithoutExtension(strPath)
  End Sub
</script>
```

| C# | LearningASP\CS\PathInfo_2.aspx *(excerpt)* |

```
<script runat="server">
  void Page_Load(Object s, EventArgs e)
  {
    string strPath;
    strPath = MapPath("myText.txt");
    resultLabel.Text += "File Path: " + strPath + "<br />";
    resultLabel.Text += "File name: " +
        Path.GetFileName(strPath) + "<br />";
    resultLabel.Text += "Directory: " +
        Path.GetDirectoryName(strPath) + "<br />";
    resultLabel.Text += "Extension: " +
        Path.GetExtension(strPath) + "<br />";
    resultLabel.Text += "Name w/out Extension: " +
        Path.GetFileNameWithoutExtension(strPath);
  }
</script>
```

Initially, we create a new string variable and set it equal to the full path of the text
file:

| Visual Basic | LearningASP\VB\PathInfo_2.aspx *(excerpt)* |

```
    Dim strPath As String
    strPath = MapPath("myText.txt")
```

Next, we write into the `Label` control the complete file path, filename with extension, directory, extension, and filename without extension, by using the `Path` class's `GetFileName`, `GetDirectoryName`, `GetExtension`, and `GetFileNameWithoutExtension` methods, respectively.

Save your work and test the results in your browser. Figure 14.9 shows how all the information for the text file is displayed.

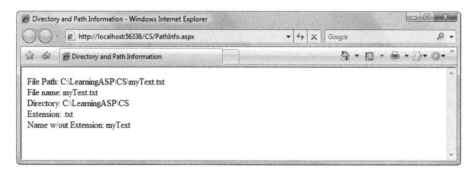

Figure 14.9. Retrieving the path, filename, directory, file extension, and filename without extension for the text file

However, those aren't the only methods to which the `Path` class gives us access. Here's a list of all of the methods you can use:

ChangeExtension
modifies a file's extension

Combine
joins two file paths

GetDirectoryName
returns the directory part of a complete file path

GetExtension
returns the file extension from a file path

GetFileName
returns the filename from a file path

GetFileNameWithoutExtension
returns the filename without the file extension from a file path

GetFullPath

expands the supplied file path with a fully qualified file path

GetPathRoot

returns the root of the current path

GetTempFileName

creates a uniquely named file and returns the name of the new file

GetTempPath

returns the path to the server's **temp** directory

HasExtension

returns True when a file path contains a file extension

IsPathRooted

returns True when a file path makes reference to a root directory or network share

See the .NET Framework SDK documentation for full details on all of these methods.

Uploading Files

There are many situations in which you'll want your web application to allow users to upload files to the server. For example, you could create a photo album site to which users could upload images for others to view.

ASP.NET offers the FileUpload control for uploading files; it provides a text box and **Browse** button to allow users to select files from their own computers and transfer them to the server with ease. The FileUpload control can be found in the **Standard** tab of the Toolbox; Figure 14.10 shows how it looks in Visual Web Developer's **Design** view.

Figure 14.10. The `FileUpload` control in Visual Web Developer

The `FileUpload` control has the following read-only properties:

HasFile

is `True` if the user has uploaded a file, `False` otherwise

FileName

the name of the file as a string

FileContent

a stream that can be used to read the contents of the file

FileBytes

an array of bytes that can be used to read the contents of the file

PostedFile

an `HttpPostedFile` object for the uploaded file; this object has properties that can be used to obtain additional data about the file, such as:

ContentLength   the file length in bytes

ContentType   the MIME type of the file (such as `image/gif` for a .**gif** file)[1]

The `FileUpload` control also has a method that you'll find very useful: `SaveAs`. Although you can get the contents of an uploaded file using the `FileContent` and `FileBytes` properties described above, it's usually more convenient to use the `SaveAs` method to save files uploaded by users, but not before checking that `HasFile` is `True`. The `SaveAs` method takes as a parameter a string containing the path and the name of the target file.

---

[1] View the complete list of MIME types at http://www.w3schools.com/media/media_mimeref.asp. Note that there's no guarantee the MIME type is correct, as it's easily manipulated by the client.

Let's test this control out. Create a new web form named **FileUpload.aspx** in the
LearningASP\VB or **LearningASP\CS** folder, and populate it with this code:

Visual Basic	LearningASP\VB\FileUpload.aspx *(excerpt)*

```
<%@ Page Language="VB" %>
<%@ Import Namespace="System.IO" %>
<!DOCTYPE html PUBLIC "-//W3C//DTD XHTML 1.0 Transitional//EN"
    "http://www.w3.org/TR/xhtml1/DTD/xhtml1-transitional.dtd">

<script runat="server">
  Sub UploadFile(ByVal s As Object, ByVal e As EventArgs)
    If fileUpload.HasFile Then
      Dim fileName As String = fileUpload.FileName
      fileUpload.SaveAs(MapPath(fileName))
      label.Text = "File " & fileName & " uploaded."
    Else
      label.Text = "No file uploaded!"
    End If
  End Sub
</script>

<html xmlns="http://www.w3.org/1999/xhtml">
  <head runat="server">
    <title>File Upload</title>
  </head>
<body>
  <form id="form1" runat="server">
    <div>
      <asp:FileUpload ID="fileUpload" runat="server" />
      <asp:Button ID="uploadButton" runat="server" Text="Upload!"
        OnClick="UploadFile" />
      <br />
      <asp:Label ID="label" runat="server"></asp:Label>
    </div>
  </form>
</body>
</html>
```

If you're using C#, you should place the following code in the `<script
runat="server">` tag:

```
C#                                              LearningASP\CS\FileUpload.aspx (excerpt)
<script runat="server">
  void UploadFile(Object s, EventArgs e)
  {
    if (fileUpload.HasFile)
    {
      string fileName = fileUpload.FileName;
      fileUpload.SaveAs(MapPath(fileName));
      label.Text = "File " + fileName + " uploaded.";
    }
    else
      label.Text = "No file uploaded!";
  }
</script>
```

Load the script, and click the **Upload!** button without selecting a file. The message
"No file uploaded!" is displayed, as shown in Figure 14.11.

Figure 14.11. An error arising as a file has not been specified

Now, click the **Browse...** button, select a file from your system, and click **Upload!**
again. Some basic file information, like that shown in Figure 14.12, is displayed.

Figure 14.12. Uploading a file

After you've uploaded a file successfully, check the **LearningASP\VB** or **LearningASP\CS** folder to ensure that the new file has indeed been saved there. As you can see, handling file uploads in ASP.NET is very easy.

Sending Email with ASP.NET

Suppose for a moment that you're the webmaster for an online store, and you want to send an email confirmation to each customer who places an order. Rather than manually typing an email to every customer about every order, you could automate the process using ASP.NET.

The namespace that groups the .NET mail-related classes is System.Net.Mail. The most useful classes in this namespace are:

SmtpClient
>contains functionality for sending email

MailMessage
>represents an email message

Attachment
>represents an email attachment

AttachmentCollection
>represents a collection of Attachment objects

MailAddress
>represents an email address

MailAddressCollection
>represents a collection of email addresses

A core set of features is common to most email programs. For instance, they all enable you to send an email to someone by typing the recipient's email address in a **To** field. You are also able to specify who the email is from, the subject of the message, and the body content of the email. All these properties—and more—are available through the MailMessage class. Here's a partial list of the properties that MailMessage supports:

From

specifies the address from which the email message is to be sent

To

specifies the address to which the email message is to be sent

CC

specifies the carbon copy field of the email message

Bcc

specifies the blind carbon copy field of the email message

Attachments

a collection of items or files attached to the email message

Subject

specifies the subject of the email message

Body

defines the body of the email message

IsBodyHtml

`True` if the message is in HTML format; `False` otherwise (defaults to `False`)

Other properties of `MailMessage` that you may need to use include `AlternateViews`, `BodyEncoding`, `DeliveryNotificationOptions`, `Headers`, `Priority`, `ReplyTo`, `Sender`, and `SubjectEncoding`.

The `From` field has the `MailAddress` type which represents an email address. The `To`, `CC`, and `Bcc` properties are of the `MailAddressCollection` type, and represent a collection of `MailAddress` objects.

As you can see, there are lots of classes and properties that let you define email messages. However, to be able to send these messages, you need access to a SMTP server.

The standard email protocol of the Internet is **Simple Mail Transfer Protocol** (SMTP). When you use ASP.NET to send an email, the message is relayed through one or more SMTP servers on the way to its final destination. Most ISPs provide an SMTP server for customers' use; alternatively, if you're using IIS, you can make use of Windows' built-in SMTP Server.

Sending a Test Email

Later, we'll add a newsletter section to the Dorknozzle site; first, let's write a very simple page to test that everything's working as it should.

Create a new file named **SendEmail.aspx** in the **LearningASP\VB** or **LearningASP\CS** folder. Don't use a code-behind file. Open it for editing and add the code highlighted in bold here:

```
                                              LearningASP\VB\SendEmail_1.aspx
<%@ Page Language="VB" %>
<%@ Import Namespace="System.Net.Mail" %>
<!DOCTYPE html PUBLIC "-//W3C//DTD XHTML 1.0 Transitional//EN"
    "http://www.w3.org/TR/xhtml1/DTD/xhtml1-transitional.dtd">

<script runat="server">

</script>

<html xmlns="http://www.w3.org/1999/xhtml">
  <head runat="server">
    <title>Sending Emails with ASP.NET</title>
  </head>
  <body>
    <form id="form1" runat="server">
      <div>
        <asp:Button ID="sendEmailButton" runat="server"
          Text="Send Email!" OnClick="SendEmail" />
        <br />
        <asp:Label ID="statusLabel" runat="server" />
      </div>
    </form>
  </body>
</html>
```

Add the following code, making sure you change the To email address to your own, and that you set the Host property to your SMTP server's address:

```
<script runat="server">
  Sub SendEmail(ByVal s As Object, ByVal e As EventArgs)
    Dim smtpClient As SmtpClient = New SmtpClient()
    Dim message As MailMessage = New MailMessage()
    Try
      Dim fromAddress As New MailAddress( _
          "from@example.com", "From Me")
      Dim toAddress As New MailAddress( _
          "to@example.com", "To You")
      message.From = fromAddress
      message.To.Add(toAddress)
      message.Subject = "Testing!"
      message.Body = "This is the body of a sample message"
      smtpClient.Host = "mailserver.example.com"
      smtpClient.Credentials = _
          New System.Net.NetworkCredential("username", "password")
      smtpClient.Send(message)
      statusLabel.Text = "Email sent."
    Catch ex As Exception
      statusLabel.Text = "Coudn't send the message!"
    End Try
  End Sub
</script>
```

```
<script runat="server">
  protected void SendEmail(object sender, EventArgs e)
  {
    SmtpClient smtpClient = new SmtpClient();
    MailMessage message = new MailMessage();
    try
    {
      MailAddress fromAddress = new MailAddress(
          "from@example.com", "From Me");
      MailAddress toAddress = new MailAddress(
          "to@example.com", "To You");
      message.From = fromAddress;
      message.To.Add(toAddress);
      message.Subject = "Testing!";
      message.Body = "This is the body of a sample message";
      smtpClient.Host = "mailserver.example.com";
      smtpClient.Credentials = new System.Net.NetworkCredential(
```

```
            "username", "password");
        smtpClient.Send(message);
        statusLabel.Text = "Email sent.";
    }
    catch (Exception ex)
    {
        statusLabel.Text = "Coudn't send the message!";
    }
    }
</script>
```

This script simply creates a new `MailMessage` object to hold the email contents and a new `SmtpClient` object that will handle the job of creating a connecting to the server and sending the email. We've also set the `Credentials` property of the `SmtpClient` object, but this is only necessary if the SMTP server requires a username and password to establish a connection. We wrap the code in a `Try-Catch` block in order to catch any potential email errors.

Execute the script, and press the **Send Email** button, as shown in Figure 14.13.

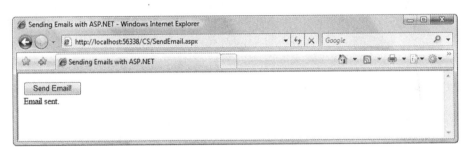

Figure 14.13. Sending the email

The email should arrive successfully at its destination, looking something like Figure 14.14.

Now you're ready to update the Dorknozzle site!

Creating the Company Newsletters Page

Let's now extend the Dorknozzle site structure by adding a Newsletters page. This page will be accessible only to the site administrator, and will provide tools with which a customized newsletter can be sent to a list of recipients.

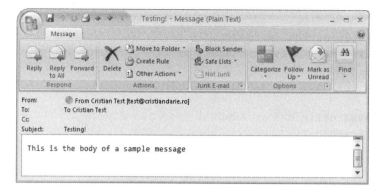

Figure 14.14. Viewing the email

Open the Dorknozzle project in Visual Web Developer, and add to it a new web form named **AdminNewsletter.aspx**, making sure both the **Select master page** and **Create code in a separate file** checkboxes are checked. When prompted, select the **Dorknozzle.master** master page.

Complete the generated code like this:

```
                                    Dorknozzle\VB\01_AdminNewsletter.aspx
<%@ Page Language="VB" MasterPageFile="~/Dorknozzle.master"
    AutoEventWireup="false" CodeFile="AdminNewsletter.aspx.vb"
    Inherits="AdminNewsletter" title="Dorknozzle Admin Newsletter"
%>

<asp:Content ID="Content1" ContentPlaceHolderID="head"
    Runat="Server">
</asp:Content>
<asp:Content ID="Content2"
    ContentPlaceHolderID="ContentPlaceHolder1" Runat="Server">
  <h1>Create Newsletter</h1>
  <p>
    <asp:Label ID="resultLabel" runat="server" ForeColor="Red"/>
  </p>
  <p>
    To:<br />
    <asp:TextBox ID="toTextBox" runat="server" />
  </p>
  <p>
    Subject:<br />
    <asp:TextBox ID="subjectTextBox" runat="server" />
  </p>
```

```
<p>
  Introduction:<br />
  <asp:TextBox ID="introTextBox" runat="server"
      TextMode="MultiLine" Width="300" Height="100" />
</p>
<p>
  Employee Of The Month:<br />
  <asp:TextBox ID="employeeTextBox" runat="server" />
</p>
<p>
  Featured Event:<br />
  <asp:TextBox ID="eventTextBox" runat="server" />
</p>
<p>
  <asp:Button ID="sendNewsletterButton" runat="server"
      Text="Send Newsletter" />
</p>
</asp:Content>
```

Switch to **Design** view. The form should look like the one shown in Figure 14.15.

As you can see, the form contains five TextBox controls, plus a Button and a Label. The boxes will allow the administrator to specify who the email is to be sent to and what the subject is, enter a simple introduction, identify the employee of the month, and feature a company event. The Button control is used to submit the form, while the Label control will display a confirmation message once the email has been sent.

To ensure that only administrators can send email messages, add the XML code below, which we've already discussed in detail in Chapter 13, to **Web.config**:

Dorknozzle\VB\02_web.config *(excerpt)*

```
<!-- Only administrators are allowed to send emails -->
<location path="AdminNewsletter.aspx">
  <system.web>
    <authorization>
      <allow roles="Administrators" />
      <deny users="*" />
    </authorization>
  </system.web>
</location>
```

\

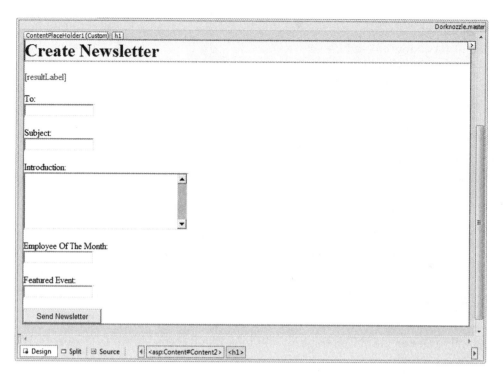

Figure 14.15. The **Create Newsletter** form

One hurdle that we need to overcome is that we want to include an image to be displayed as part of the HTML content of the message. We can use either of two approaches to solve this problem:

▦ Host the image on our web server and reference it in an `<img>` tag in the HTML code of the message (for example, `<img src="http://www.dorknozzle.com/Images/Newsletter.jpg" …>`).

▦ Embed the image data in the email.

We'll apply the first technique, as it has the benefit of simplicity, and keeps the message as small as possible. If you want readers to see the image even when they're not connected to the Internet, you should look into the second option. Developer Mike Pope explains image embedding, and provides sample code, in a post on his blog, titled "System.Net.Mail and embedded images."[2]

---

[2] http://www.mikepope.com/blog/DisplayBlog.aspx?permalink=1264

All we need to do is handle the **Send Newsletter** button's `Click` event. While in **Design** view, double-click the button to generate the event handler signature. In the code-behind file, we'll first need to import the System.Net.Mail namespace:

Visual Basic	Dorknozzle\VB\03_AdminNewsletter.aspx.vb *(excerpt)*

```vb
Imports System.Net.Mail
```

C#	Dorknozzle\CS\03_AdminNewsletter.aspx.cs *(excerpt)*

```csharp
using System.Net.Mail;
```

Then, complete the code of `sendNewsletterButton_Click` to send your newsletter:

Visual Basic	Dorknozzle\VB\03_AdminNewsletter.aspx.vb *(excerpt)*

```vb
Protected Sub sendNewsletterButton_Click(
➥  ByVal sender As Object, ByVal e As System.EventArgs)
➥  Handles sendNewsletterButton.Click
  Dim smtpClient As SmtpClient = New SmtpClient()
  Dim message As MailMessage = New MailMessage()
  Try
    Dim fromAddress As New MailAddress( _
        "dorknozzle@example.com", "Your Friends at Dorknozzle")
    Dim toAddress As New MailAddress(toTextBox.Text)
    message.From = fromAddress
    message.To.Add(toAddress)
    message.Subject = subjectTextBox.Text
    message.IsBodyHtml = True
    message.Body = _
        "<html><head><title>" & _
        HttpUtility.HtmlEncode(subjectTextBox.Text) & _
        "</title></head><body>" & _
        "<img src=""http://www.cristiandarie.ro/Dorknozzle" & _
        "/Images/newsletter_header.gif"" />" & _
        "<p>" & _
        HttpUtility.HtmlEncode(introTextBox.Text) & "</p>" & _
        "<p>Employee of the month: " & _
        HttpUtility.HtmlEncode(employeeTextBox.Text) & "</p>" & _
        "<p>This months featured event: " & _
        HttpUtility.HtmlEncode(eventTextBox.Text) & "</p>" & _
        "</body></html>"
    smtpClient.Host = "localhost"
    smtpClient.Credentials = _
```

```
        New System.Net.NetworkCredential("username", "password")
      smtpClient.Send(message)
      resultLabel.Text = "Email sent!<br />"
    Catch ex As Exception
      resultLabel.Text = "Couldn't send the message!"
    End Try
End Sub
```

C#   Dorknozzle\CS\03_AdminNewsletter.aspx.cs *(excerpt)*

```csharp
protected void sendNewsletterButton_Click(
    object sender, EventArgs e)
{
  SmtpClient smtpClient = new SmtpClient();
  MailMessage message = new MailMessage();
  try
  {
    MailAddress fromAddress = new MailAddress(
        "dorknozzle@example.com", "Your Friends at Dorknozzle"
    );
    MailAddress toAddress = new MailAddress(toTextBox.Text);
    message.From = fromAddress;
    message.To.Add(toAddress);
    message.Subject = subjectTextBox.Text;
    message.IsBodyHtml = true;
    message.Body =
        "<html><head><title>" +
        HttpUtility.HtmlEncode(subjectTextBox.Text) +
        "</title></head><body>" +
        "<img src=\"http://www.cristiandarie.ro/Dorknozzle" +
        "/Images/newsletter_header.gif\" />" +
        "<p>" +
        HttpUtility.HtmlEncode(introTextBox.Text) + "</p>" +
        "<p>Employee of the month: " +
        HttpUtility.HtmlEncode(employeeTextBox.Text) + "</p>" +
        "<p>This months featured event: " +
        HttpUtility.HtmlEncode(eventTextBox.Text) + "</p>" +
        "</body></html>";
    smtpClient.Host = "localhost";
    smtpClient.Credentials =
        new System.Net.NetworkCredential("username", "password");
    smtpClient.Send(message);
    resultLabel.Text = "Email sent!<br />";
  }
  catch (Exception ex)
```

```
  {
    resultLabel.Text = "Couldn\'t send the message!";
  }
}
```

That's a pretty large chunk of code, so let's break it down. Initially, we create a new instance of the `MailMessage` class, called `message`:

Visual Basic   Dorknozzle\VB\03_AdminNewsletter.aspx.vb *(excerpt)*

```
Dim message As MailMessage = New MailMessage()
```

C#   Dorknozzle\CS\03_AdminNewsletter.aspx.cs *(excerpt)*

```
MailMessage message = new MailMessage();
```

Next, we begin to define the email message by setting some of the properties that the `MailMessage` class exposes:

Visual Basic   Dorknozzle\VB\03_AdminNewsletter.aspx.vb *(excerpt)*

```
Dim fromAddress As New MailAddress( _
    "newsletter@dorknozzle.com", "Your Friends at Dorknozzle")
Dim toAddress As New MailAddress(toTextBox.Text)
message.From = fromAddress
message.To.Add(toAddress)
message.Subject = subjectTextBox.Text
message.IsBodyHtml = True
```

C#   Dorknozzle\CS\03_AdminNewsletter.aspx.cs *(excerpt)*

```
MailAddress fromAddress = new MailAddress(
    "newsletter@dorknozzle.com", "Your Friends at Dorknozzle"
);
MailAddress toAddress = new MailAddress(toTextBox.Text);
message.From = fromAddress;
message.To.Add(toAddress);
message.Subject = subjectTextBox.Text;
message.IsBodyHtml = true;
```

You'll notice we've set the `IsBodyHtml` property to `True` because we're creating an HTML email message. By default, this property is set to `False`.

Next, we need to create the body of the message, which, essentially, will be an HTML document:

```vb
Visual Basic                          Dorknozzle\VB\03_AdminNewsletter.aspx.vb (excerpt)

message.Body = _
    "<html><head><title>" & _
    HttpUtility.HtmlEncode(subjectTextBox.Text) & _
    "</title></head><body>" & _
    "<img src=""http://www.cristiandarie.ro/Dorknozzle" & _
    "/Images/newsletter_header.gif"" />" & _
    "<p>" & _
    HttpUtility.HtmlEncode(introTextBox.Text) & "</p>" & _
    "<p>Employee of the month: " & _
    HttpUtility.HtmlEncode(employeeTextBox.Text) & "</p>" & _
    "<p>This month's featured event: " & _
    HttpUtility.HtmlEncode(eventTextBox.Text) & "</p>" & _
    "</body></html>"
```

```csharp
C#                                    Dorknozzle\CS\03_AdminNewsletter.aspx.cs (excerpt)

message.Body =
    "<html><head><title>" +
    HttpUtility.HtmlEncode(subjectTextBox.Text) +
    "</title></head><body>" +
    "<img src=\"http://www.cristiandarie.ro/Dorknozzle" +
    "/Images/newsletter_header.gif\" />" +
    "<p>" +
    HttpUtility.HtmlEncode(introTextBox.Text) + "</p>" +
    "<p>Employee of the month: " +
    HttpUtility.HtmlEncode(employeeTextBox.Text) + "</p>" +
    "<p>This month's featured event: " +
    HttpUtility.HtmlEncode(eventTextBox.Text) + "</p>" +
    "</body></html>";
```

As we're building an HTML document, we need to take care to convert special characters (including <, >, and &) into their character entity equivalents (<, >, &, and so on). The HtmlEncode method of the HttpUtility class does this for us.

Also note that the image we'll use in the email has to be hosted on a site somewhere. In the code above, I've used an example URL. To get this example to work properly, you'll need to host the image on your web site, and use the appropriate URL in your code.

We set the Host property of the smtpClient object to localhost, indicating that the computer that's acting as our ASP.NET server should also act as our outgoing mail server—you'll need to change this if you're using another SMTP server. Finally, we call the Send method, pass in the message object, and display a confirmation message to the user within the resultLabel control:

Dorknozzle\VB\03_AdminNewsletter.aspx.vb *(excerpt)*

```
smtpClient.Host = "localhost"
smtpClient.Send(message)
resultLabel.Text = "Email sent!<br />"
```

Dorknozzle\CS\03_AdminNewsletter.aspx.cs *(excerpt)*

```
smtpClient.Host = "localhost";
smtpClient.Send(message);
resultLabel.Text = "Email sent!<br />";
```

Save your work and run the page in your browser. Enter all the necessary information into the Newsletters page and click the **Send Newsletter** button, as shown in Figure 14.16.

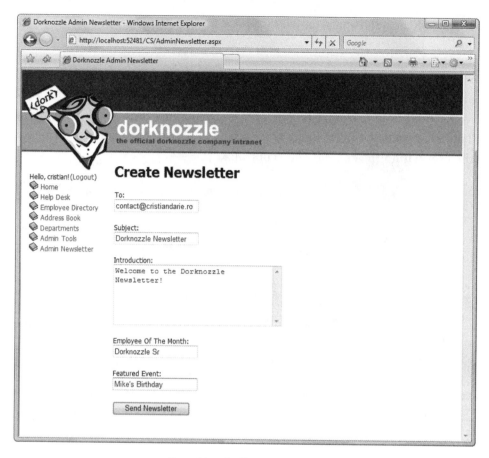

Figure 14.16. Sending the newsletter

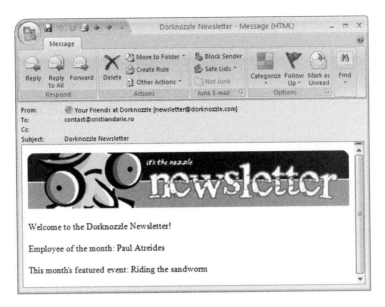

Figure 14.17. Receiving the newsletter

You should receive the message once the email is sent. Check your email account for the new email message. The message should look like the one shown in Figure 14.17.

Summary

This chapter introduced you to some useful topics relating to files and email; it gave you the ability to read and write to files, access directory information, upload files from the client to the server, and send email messages in ASP.NET.

The topics we covered in this chapter will prove invaluable as you develop applications with ASP.NET. Although, strictly speaking, they're not core features of ASP.NET, these tools enable you to implement many of the common requirements of ASP.NET applications. Stick 'em in your mental tool belt for now—I guarantee they won't gather much dust!

Chapter 5

Introduction to LINQ

LINQ—Language-Integrated Query—is a new data-access feature that enables the querying of data sources from within the language itself. Typically in .NET we use a technology such as ADO.NET to directly query a relational database management server, such as SQL Server or MySQL. LINQ is a new language construct that allows us to query relational data from different sources and interact with it just like any other object or class. With LINQ we get access to compile-time syntax checking, the use of IntelliSense, and the ability to access other data sources such as XML or just about any custom data sources. There are many LINQ extensions, such as LINQ-to-SQL, LINQ-to-Sharepoint, LINQ-to-MySQL, LINQ-to-Entities, and so on

Let's get started with LINQ to give you an immediate feel for the syntax. We present this in C# since it's the easiest to use with LINQ, although VB fans can rest assured that VB code samples are provided.

```
// create an array of integers
  int[] sampleNumbers = { 1, 2, 3 };


  IEnumerable<int> doubledNumbers = from i in sampleNumbers
                                    select i * 2;
```

```
// produces "2, 4, 6";
foreach (int number in doubledNumbers)
Response.Write(number + "<br />");
```

Our IEnumerable variable called doubledNumbers contains the output from the query expression. As you can see the syntax is similar to SQL. However Microsoft introduces **selectors** (the "I" in our case). As we dig deeper into the LINQ syntax, these selectors will become more obvious. This sample only shows a collection of numbers. In our case we know we are expecting the return of integers. However, to help in the cases where we may not know the exact return type at compile-time , Microsoft has introduced the var keyword.

```
// create an array of integers
int[] sampleNumbers = { 1, 2, 3 };


var squaredNumbers = from i in sampleNumbers
                     select i * i;

// produces "1, 4, 9";
foreach (int number in squaredNumbers)
Response.Write(number + "<br />");
```

So like most lazy programmers, we will use the var keyword going forward to allow the compiler to determine the type where appropriate.

Let's do another example of LINQ syntax to introduce WHERE clauses since we often need a subset of data.

```
// create an array of random fruits
string[] fruits = { "Blueberry", "Banana", "Orange", "Peach",➡
                    "Kiwi", "Blackberry" };


var fruitsStartingWithB = from f in fruits
                          where f.StartsWith("B") && ➡
                             f.Contains("berry")
                          select f;
```

```
// produces "Blueberry, Blackberry"
foreach (var fruit in fruitsStartingWithB)
Response.Write(fruit + "<br />");
```

Here we use the standard "AND" (&&) operator as part of C#. Also available is the "OR" (||) operator within the WHERE clause.

Extension Methods

LINQ makes heavy use of extension methods in order to manipulate the data into what we need. One of these features is the First extension method. This takes the first item in the result and returns it. It can be used as follows:

```
string[] fruits = { "Blueberry", "Banana", "Orange", "Peach",➡
                    "Kiwi", "Blackberry" };


string berry  = (from f in fruits
                where f.StartsWith("B") && ➡
                    f.Contains("berry")
                select f).First<string>();

// Output is "Blueberry"
Response.Write(berry);
```

In a subsequent article, we will discuss more extension methods that allow us to have more control over our result set as well as fine-tune the LINQ capabilities.

LINQ to SQL

How does this help us when dealing with a non-objected oriented data structure? Let's see how LINQ can help us when dealing with relational data.

We'll need a new sample database with plenty more records and tables to query. The Microsoft sample database called **AdventureWorks** is perfect for our SQL Server 2008 Express Edition installation. You can get the AdventureWorks sample database at the Microsoft CodePlex, available directly at http://msftdbprodsamples.codeplex.com/releases/view/4004#DownloadId=11753.

You will want to "attach" the AdventureWorks sample database. To do this, open the SQL Server 2008 Management Studio. Right click on **Databases** and select **Tasks**

-> **Attach Database**. Select the **.mdf** file from the location you installed it, and then you will be ready to begin the sample exercises.

Next, we create a server connection within Visual Studio with the Server Explorer toolbar window, as shown in Figure 15.1 and Figure 15.2

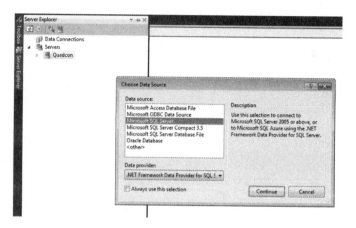

Figure 15.1. Creating a connection with Visual Studio

Figure 15.2. Connecting to the database

To connect to our SQL Express instance, we choose the **Microsoft SQL Server** data source option. Then we simply select the **SQLEXPRESS** instance and the **Adventure-Works database** as the default database option.

Next, we add a new item to our project, as in Figure 15.3. To utilize LINQ with a SQL data source we choose to create a LINQ-to-SQL data class. In the simplest explanation, LINQ-to-SQL maps object-oriented classes with a SQL database table, otherwise called an object relational mapper. There are other ORM frameworks available, such as nHibernate, Entity Framework, or SubSonic. Each of these has their own strengths and weaknesses, but for the sake of this writing we concentrate on the features found in LINQ-to-SQL.

Figure 15.3. Adding a new item to our project

We name this **.dbml** file **AdventureWorks.dbml**. Once you create this, you begin with a blank slate where you have the ability to create **entities**. An entity is a strongly-typed data structure typically used to represent a business relationship or object. Microsoft has introduced the ADO.NET Entity Framework that takes these advanced concepts further. These topics are beyond the scope of our current discussion and may be discoursed at a future date.

In our example, we want an entity called "Employee" that represents a single instance of an employee within the AdventureWorks corporation. The on-screen details show that you can use the Toolbox to create a new entity, but we want to utilize the power of the created data source connection to our SQL Express instance by opening the Server Explorer to drag-and-drop the Employees table.

The result is a new entity object called "Employee" (take note that it is the singular wording of the 'Employees' table name, these are auto-named by Visual Studio). Visual Studio not only creates the entity for us, it also auto-generates code for a `DataContext` object. This `DataContext` object represents the connection with the data source, in our case the SQL Express database connection. The `DataContext` also keeps track of all changes to all entities and serves as the reference point to insert, update, or delete an entity record back to its main data source (the "Employees" database table). These objects are designed to be used once as they are lightweight and have no discernible impact when creating thousands of instances. Furthermore, the `DataContext` is different from the standard ADO.NET way of opening a SqlConnection and then executing queries; the SQL generated when performing LINQ queries are performed at run-time as well as the connection management. A `DataContext` is created in one line:

```
AdventureWorksDataContext dataContext = ➡
    new AdventureWorksDataContext();
```

The `DataContext` is created and named after the DBML file created earlier. If you created your DBML as **Sample.dbml** then your `DataContext` would be named `SampleDataContext`.

Everything at this point has been connected by Visual Studio using auto-generated code for the DBML class. From the Solution Explorer window, you can explore this auto-generated code for the **AdventureWorks.dbml** file by right clicking on the file to **View Code**. Be sure not to make any permanent changes here, as any changes with the designer will automatically overwrite any changes in the auto-generated code files. We can now query the Employees data table using LINQ. As an example we will look for only female employees. For the purpose of these exercises, you can assume we are using the same reference namespaces in the "using" section at the top of the source code. All code samples should be run from within the `Page_Load` event of an ASP.NET page:

```
using System;
using System.Collections.Generic;
using System.Linq;
using System.Text;

AdventureWorksDataContext dataContext = ➥
  new AdventureWorksDataContext();

var employees = from emp in dataContext.Employees
                where e.Gender == 'F'
                select emp;

// produces a list of employee IDs for all female employees
foreach (var employee in employees)
Response.Write(employee.EmployeeID + "<br />");
```

Updating Data

One of the columns in the Employees table is the MaritalStatus column. This is
a character field that has an "S" for a single employee or "M" for a married employee.
Due to a rash outbreak of women getting married, HR has decided to just have
everyone marked as being married. Our example is then to perform this update using
LINQ-to-SQL.

```
using (AdventureWorksDataContext dataContext = ➥
  new AdventureWorksDataContext())
{
var employees = from e in dataContext.Employees
                where e.Gender == 'F'
                select e;

// produces a list of employee IDs for all female employees
foreach (var employee in employees)
{
  employee.MaritalStatus = 'M'; // all changes have not been ➥
    persisted to the database.
  Response.Write(employee.EmployeeID + " is now married.<br />");

}

      // Send changes to the database.
```

```
                  dataContext.SubmitChanges();

}
```

The change here seems simple enough, but one thing to take note of is that the changes to the Employee entity record is not saved (persisted) to the database until the `DataContext`'s `SubmitChanges`method is called.

You may also notice that we create our `DataContext` object within a using statement. This is a feature of C# that will automatically call close our `DataContext` object and dispose of it properly, without having to specifically call it. This is done by the closing brace. Anything inside the braces is run, and once it is finished, the object is disposed of by calling its `Dispose` method. We will use this using keyword to ensure our database connections have been properly taken care of when we're done with them.

Relationships

sSo far we have dealt with only one single Employees table. Our Employee entity has a `ContactID` property that is the reference key for the Contacts table. Visual Studio's DBML designer tool will automatically recognize foreign keys within the database. We simply drag-and-drop the Contacts table from the Server Explorer window for the SQL Express connection (just as we did for the Employees table) onto the DBML designer to have Visual Studio create the Contact entity object for us. The designer view now looks like Figure 15.4:

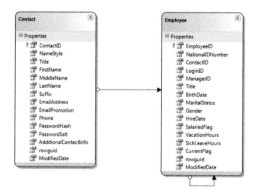

Figure 15.4. Dropping the contacts table onto DBML designer

We can now reference the personally identifiable information for each of the employees. Let's prepare a report for HR listing employees hired after 2002.

```
using (AdventureWorksDataContext dataContext = ➡
    new AdventureWorksDataContext())
{
    var employees = from e in dataContext.Employees
        where e.HireDate > DateTime.Parse("2002-01-01")
            select e;

    foreach (var employee in employees)
        Response.Write(employee.Contact.FirstName + ➡
            " " + employee.Contact.LastName + "<br />");

}
```

Directly Executing Queries from the DataContext

At this point, you may most likely be familiar with directly calling standard ANSI SQL to the database via ADO.NET and/or stored procedures. LINQ-to-SQL supports these direct queries via the ExecuteQuerymethod call. This method has two overridden parameters, a standard version that takes a Type as its first parameter, or a generic version that returns the generic input type given.

▨ ExecuteQuery<ResultType>(String SqlQuery, Object[] Parameters)

▨ ExecuteQuery(Type result, String sqlQuery, Object[] Parameters)

When using ExecuteQuerywith the generic version, we intend to use the Employee entity type so we can access the relationship with the Contact entity to get the employee's first and last name. Thus, it is in our interest to use the generic method signature for the ExecuteQuerycall.

```
using (AdventureWorksDataContext dataContext = ➡
    new AdventureWorksDataContext())
{

    var employees = from e in dataContext.Employees
    where e.HireDate > DateTime.Parse("2002-01-01")
                select e;

    var emps = dataContext.ExecuteQuery<Employee>➡
```

```
  ("SELECT * FROM HumanResources.Employee
    WHERE HireDate > '2002-01-01'");

  foreach (var currentEmployee in emps)
  Response.Write(currentEmployee.Contact.FirstName ➡
    + " " + currentEmployee.Contact.LastName);

Response.Write("----------------");

  foreach (var employee in employees)
    Response.Write(employee.Contact.FirstName ➡
    + " " + employee.Contact.LastName + "<br />");

}
```

When running this example, you should receive the same results for both query executions. Furthermore, LINQ-to-SQL also supports direct query execution where there aren't any return parameters expected from the SQL execution, such as deleting records, manually inserting or updating records with the Execute method.

HR has asked us to reverse a prior policy of making all female employees married. Now they want us to make them all single. We will do this using direct query execution with LINQ-to-SQL.

```
using (AdventureWorksDataContext dataContext = ➡
  new AdventureWorksDataContext())
 {
     int rowsAffected = dataContext.ExecuteCommand➡
     ("UPDATE HumanResources.Employee WITH(ROWLOCK)
       SET MaritalStatus = 'S' WHERE Gender = 'F' ");

     // should display "Execution completed, ➡
         84 rows affected."
     Response.Write("Execution completed, {0} rows ➡
       affected", rowsAffected);


 }
```

Stored Procedures with LINQ-to-SQL

One of the features of LINQ-to-SQL is the **stored procedure** support for LINQ. LINQ-to-SQL treats stored procedures as standard method calls. As part of the Adventure-Works database, there is a stored procedure called `uspGetManagerEmployees`. To enable LINQ-to-SQL to integrate this stored procedure call, we perform a drag-and-drop from the Server Explorer window, where we select the Stored Procedure from our SQL Express connection onto the right-pane of our DBML designer. Have a look at Figure 15.5

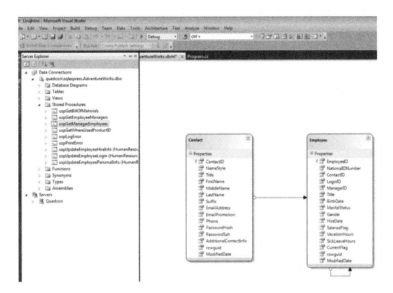

Figure 15.5. Dropping the stored procedure onto DBML designer

Visual Studio will now create the method called `uspGetManagerEmployees`. Because the "usp" prefix isn't necessary for method calls, we right-click on this to choose **Properties** and rename it as simply `GetManagerEmployees`.We can now call this procedure in our code:

```
using (AdventureWorksDataContext dataContext = ➡
   new AdventureWorksDataContext())
   {
        var employees = dataContext.➡
          GetManagerEmployees(185);

        foreach (var currentEmployee in employees)
            Response.Write(currentEmployee.FirstName ➡
```

```
                    + " " + currentEmployee.LastName);


    }
```

Notice the return type from the `GetManagerEmployees` call is a `ISingleResult<us-pGetManagerEmployees1>` object. This is where the `var` keyword becomes useful since we may not know the full return type. The properties for the procedure call in the Designer View show us that the result type is auto-generated. However, what if we want the designer to strongly-type this return to one of the known entity types? To conduct this sample, we first create a new stored procedure called `uspGetEmploy-eeByID`:

```sql
CREATE PROCEDURE uspGetEmployeeByID
-- Add the parameters for the stored procedure here
@EmployeeID int = 0

AS
BEGIN
-- SET NOCOUNT ON added to prevent extra result sets from
-- interfering with SELECT statements.
SET NOCOUNT ON;

    -- Insert statements for procedure here
SELECT * FROM HumanResources.Employee where EmployeeID = @EmployeeID
END
GO
```

From the designer view, we drag-and-drop this procedure call to the right-side pane of the Designer View. We then rename the method call to remove the "usp" prefix. Furthermore, we intend to change the return type to the Employee entity, as in Figure 15.6.

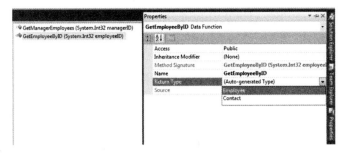

Figure 15.6. Selecting 'Employee' as the return type

When you make this selection, you will see a warning alerting you to the one-way nature of this change (see Figure 15.7. You cannot undo this change. If you need to make adjustments to the stored procedure, you must delete the method call, and then re-add it using drag-and-drop from the Server Explorer window.

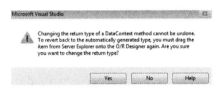

Figure 15.7. Changing the return type

Once we are satisfied with the changes that have been made, we can make a call to this new stored procedure by using the `DataContext` object.

```
using (AdventureWorksDataContext dataContext = ➥
    new AdventureWorksDataContext())
{

    Employee jefferyFord = dataContext.➥
        GetEmployeeByID(15).First<Employee>();

    Response.Write(jefferyFord.Contact.FirstName ➥
        + " " + jefferyFord.Contact.LastName);

}
```

Using ASP.NET and LINQ-to-SQL

LINQ allows fully bindable objects as a data source. This allows us to build fully-functional datagrids with a `LINQDataSource`. To get started, we drag-and-drop a

`LinqDataSource` from the Visual Studio Toolbox side bar menu onto a standard ASP.NET Web Forms **.aspx** page. After highlighting this new object on the page, we can now configure this `DataSource` to use our `DataContext` object for the AdventureWorks database. Take a look at Figure 15.8

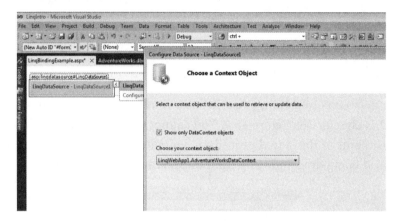

Figure 15.8. Choosing a Context Object

For the purposes of this sample, we simply want a read-only data source for a standard ASP.NET datagrid control. We configure our `LinqDataSource` object as shown in Figure 15.9:

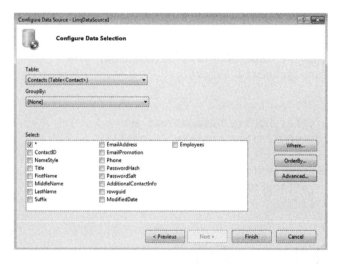

Figure 15.9. Configuring the data selection

By selecting all columns, we have enough information to display the first and last names for the employee records we wish to display. More advanced features are available when configuring the data source, such as a custom query or custom order by clause which pre-sorts the records when they are returned from the LINQ query. Furthermore, the `LinqDataSource` allows automatic editing, insertion, and deletion commands to be configured. These advanced topics are outside the scope of this current lesson and may be discussed at a future date.

Next, we continue by adding a standard `GridView` control to our page. We can now configure this grid to use our `LinqDataSource` that we created earlier; this is shown in Figure 15.10.

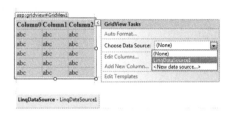

Figure 15.10. Using our LinqDataSource in GridView

We select our newly created `LinqDataSource1` object as the data source for the Grid View. The GridView control will change to reflect the new schema of the `LinqData-Source` object. You are now ready to view the page in the browser. Be aware that the pay may take some time to fully load, as the `LinqDataSource` is currently configured to return all rows and columns from the Contacts table from the Adventure-Works database. To prepare a report for HR that shows a list of all employees and their email addresses, we can choose the **Edit Columns**task from the SmartTag popup for the GridView and select only the columns we wish to show. The full HTML of the **.aspx** page should look as follows:

```
<!DOCTYPE html PUBLIC "-//W3C//DTD XHTML 1.0 Transitional//EN" ➥
  "http://www.w3.org/TR/xhtml1/DTD/xhtml1-transitional.dtd">
<html xmlns="http://www.w3.org/1999/xhtml">
<head runat="server">
    <title></title>
</head>
<body>
    <form id="form1" runat="server">
    <div>
        <asp:GridView ID="GridView1" runat="server" ➥
            AutoGenerateColumns="False"
            DataKeyNames="ContactID" DataSourceID="LinqDataSource1">
```

```
                    <Columns>
                        <asp:BoundField DataField="ContactID" ➥
                          HeaderText="ContactID"
                            InsertVisible="False" ReadOnly="True" ➥
                              SortExpression="ContactID" />
                        <asp:CheckBoxField DataField="NameStyle" ➥
                            HeaderText="NameStyle"
                            SortExpression="NameStyle" />
                        <asp:BoundField DataField="Title" ➥
                            HeaderText="Title" ➥
                            SortExpression="Title" />
                        <asp:BoundField DataField="FirstName" ➥
                            HeaderText="FirstName"
                            SortExpression="FirstName" />
                        <asp:BoundField DataField="MiddleName" ➥
                            HeaderText="MiddleName"
                            SortExpression="MiddleName" />
                        <asp:BoundField DataField="LastName" ➥
                            HeaderText="LastName"
                            SortExpression="LastName" />
                        <asp:BoundField DataField="Suffix" ➥
                            HeaderText="Suffix"
                            SortExpression="Suffix" />
                        <asp:BoundField DataField="EmailAddress" ➥
                            HeaderText="EmailAddress"
                            SortExpression="EmailAddress" />
                    </Columns>
                </asp:GridView>
                <br />
            </div>
            <asp:LinqDataSource ID="LinqDataSource1" runat="server"
                ContextTypeName="LinqWebApp1.AdventureWorksDataContext" ➥
                EntityTypeName=""
                TableName="Contacts">
            </asp:LinqDataSource>
        </form>
</body>
</html>
```

Overall, LINQ is a powerful tool that allows you to rapidly develop your code and spend less time focused on the data management aspects of it. This increases our productivity because we can query all data within Visual Studio without the need for knowing the underlying structure of how a database server is configured, or even knowing the data source itself.

Introduction to MVC

ASP.NET **MVC (Model-View-Controller) Framework** is the invention of Scott Guthrie of Microsoft's ASP.NET team, built upon a common software design principle to solve many common problems that software developers face. In the real world, software is a living design that requires many changes after the original features are developed.

The benefits of using MVC include:

- the Separation of Concerns between the HTML markup, data classes, and user workflow

- there's no more need for server-side forms, or view state, as we have full control over HTML output

- easy integration with Visual Web Developer to create views, controllers, models, and scaffolding template support

- razor scripting engine support to easily mix HTML markup with C#/VB code

- search engine optimized (SEO) URLs and URL Routing

The benefits of using standard ASP.NET Web Forms are:

- it's an event-driven programming model

- access to view state and server-side web forms for processing data and preserving the state between pages

- out-of-the-box access to use repeaters and other ASP.NET and third-party controls with minimal code

- ability to create websites rapidly

Nearly every software development project will undergo significant changes from the original scope. *Maintenance* is typically the largest phase of the software life cycle, with the addition of new features and the modification of business rules in regards to the ever changing environment of a company. Each change often requires updates to the three major components of a software product:

1. Business rules—the code that manages logic and functionality customized to the business for which you are developing.

2. User interface—how these new features are presented and how the user interacts with them.

3. Control flow—managing what is shown on the user interface screens and when.

These components are not universal to software development in general, but we run across them very often in a corporate web development environment. If you break down the individual components of our Dorknozzle intranet site, you'll see that the majority of what we've done is manage these components, referred to as the Model-View-Controller software design pattern. A **software design pattern** is simply a common way of solving a problem in software development and mainten-ance. There are several useful design patterns, all of which are probably outside the scope of this book, but we would highly recommend *Design Patterns: Elements of Reusable Object-Oriented Software by the Gang of Four.*[1] The Model-View-Controller pattern as shown in Figure 16.1 fits our use for the Dorknozzle project. First, we have some sort of business logic, which is displaying employee records that we want to see for the Employee Directory page. Then we have the View itself, the

---

[1] Gamma, Eric, Helm, Richard, Johnson, Ralph, Vlissides, John (New Jersey: Pearson, 2010).

HTML markup used to display the page along with CSS styling to make it look pretty. Lastly, we have the Controller, the mediator between the Model and the View as it handles *actions* requested by the user, such as whether to edit an existing employee's record or to add a new one, and which employee ID we are editing or deleting.

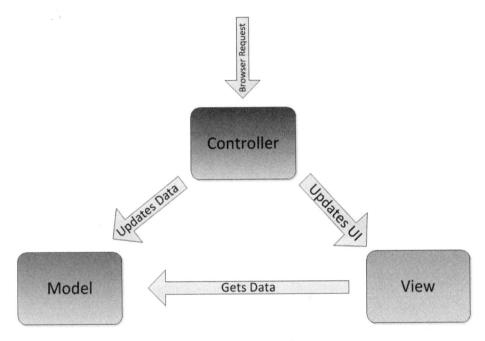

Figure 16.1. Model-View-Controller pattern

Don't worry, it can take a bit of time to fully grasp this concept. We'll be exploring the third iteration of MVC for the ASP.NET framework, called MVC3 for short. We'll give you the main concepts, skipping past the items discussed in earlier chapters and leaving it up to you to implement the rest of the Dorknozzle intranet project in MVC3. Now, let's jump into some code so that you can get a feel for how the Visual Web Developer processes this. First, we want to create a brand new web application project. To do this, we choose **File > New Project > ASP.NET MVC 3 Web Application**, as seen in Figure 16.2.

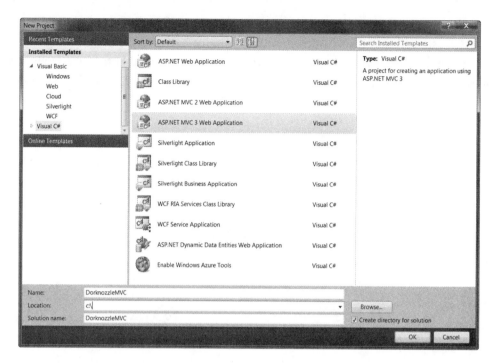

Figure 16.2. Creating a new project

We'll name this one **DorknozzleMVC** to distinguish it from our previous Dorknozzle intranet project. On the next screen you'll be prompted to choose the MVC project type; we'll go with an empty project here and use the ASPX view engine, as shown in Figure 16.3.

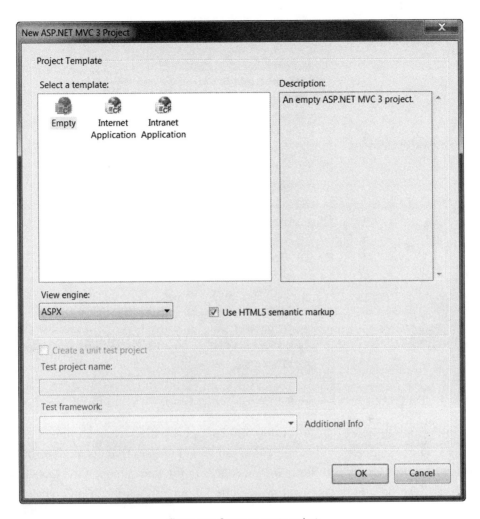

Figure 16.3. Create an empty project

Once you create the new project, you'll notice several folders and files in the Solution Explorer, similar to Figure 16.4.

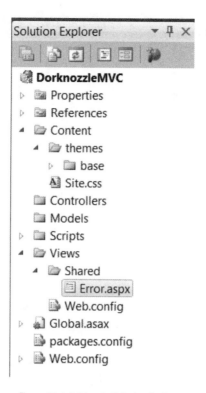

Figure 16.4. Folders in Solution Explorer

The folders are necessary for full integration support with our development environment. The folders for Controllers will store all our classes that act as Controllers; the same for the Models and Views folder. At this point, you can open the **Global.asax** file to see how the default URL routing is set up for our application, as in Figure 16.5.

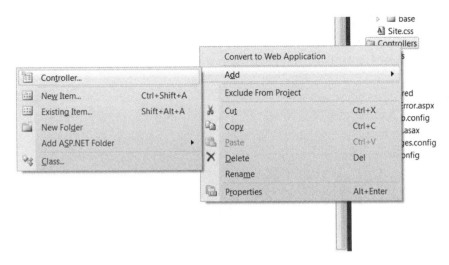

Figure 16.5. Adding a controller

One of the features that is supported out of the box with MVC is the use of search engine optimized URLs. These URLs are in a clean format, without question marks and ampersands that clutter the URL and make it hard for search engines to determine which page you are on. Most search engines will rank a URL higher in the format of http://www.myDomain.com/Products/iPad/12345, rather than http://www.myDomain.com/products.aspx?id=12345.

As part of ASP.NET 4, the URL Routing feature is available for use in non-MVC projects, but it is required for MVC3 to work properly. This is done in the **global.asax** file that was generated when we created the project.

In the `RegisterRoutes` method, the URL that is expected is the controller name, followed by a slash, and then the action. For instance, a URL request with http://MyServer/Home/Index will have ASP.NET load the Home controller and call the Index action within that controller. Optionally, an ID parameter can be passed for any actions that will use it. An example of the ID parameter would be http://MyServer/Products/Details/5 having ASP.NET load the Products controller and call the Details action with a parameter of 5. What's neat about the use of parameters here in MVC is that they are strongly typed, as we will see shortly. In this file, the default route is set to the Home controller calling the Index action with no parameter.

This exercise will essentially replicate the Employee Directory of the earlier chapters, but using MVC and LINQ. To get started, let's right-click on the Controllers folder to create a new Controller called `EmployeesController`, as in Figure 16.6.

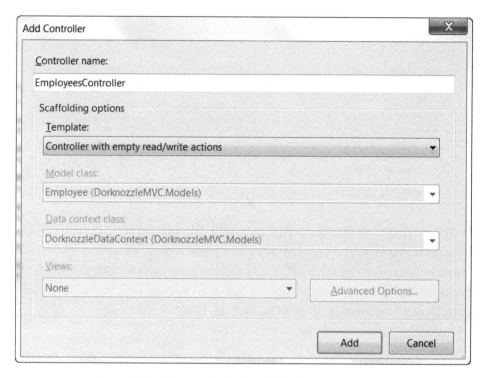

Figure 16.6. Creating a new Controller called `EmployeesController`

As you can see, Visual Web Developer automatically recognizes the folder is called `Controller` and prompts you to add a new controller in that directory.

In the recent version of MVC3, Visual Web Developer included support for scaffolding. **Scaffolding** is using the IDE to quickly generate code samples on how to do popular tasks. We use the scaffolding feature to create our Controller, seen in Figure 16.7.

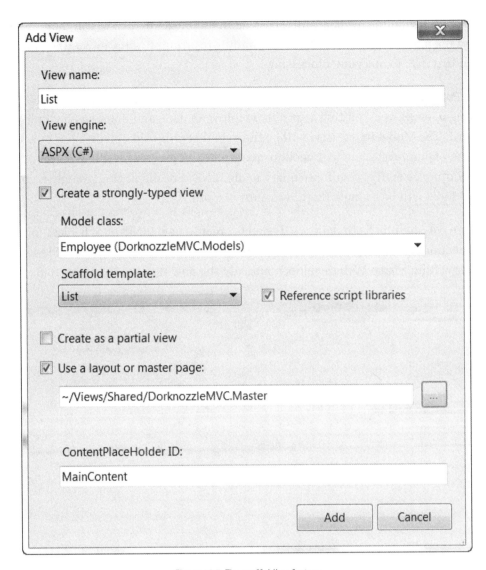

Figure 16.7. The scaffolding feature

Once created, you'll see several **Actions** that make up the use of the controller. Actions are similar to events called to the controller. Most of these are separated into GETs and POSTs. When the web server is requesting data, it'll send a GET request to ASP.NET along with the Action. One of the default Actions created by the scaffolding template is Details, along with an *id* parameter. To call this from the browser, your URL would be http://myserver/Employee/Details/10 to get the details where the ID is 10. In other URLs, you may have seen something like Details.aspx?id=10". With the URL Routing part of MVC, ASP.NET will automatically route the `Details`

Action to the Employee controller, passing in an integer of 10. We can then implement the method to get the data corresponding to an employee with an ID of 10 and send this data to our view processing.

The `EmployeesController` will process various Actions such as showing a full listing of employees, editing a specific employee's data, and deleting an employee record. The Model in our case will be the data that will be displayed. For our full listing of employees, we will need to create a Model containing a List object of all the Employee entity records we query using LINQ. For displaying a single record, our Model will be a single Employee entity record.

Before we can fully fetch data, we'll need to create a new LINQ-to-SQL class for our connection to the Dorknozzle database. To do that, we right-click on the Models folder within Visual Web Developer, and add the new item, as in Figure 16.8.

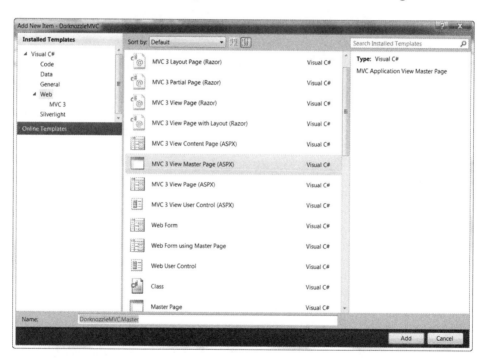

Figure 16.8. Adding the new item

Within the **Dorknozzle.dbml** file, you'll want to drag-and-drop the Employees table from the Database Explorer for our Dorknozzle database (your local SQL Express instance) to our DBML pane.

Now that we have our database connectivity set up, our next task is to create a new Action for `Details`. This Action should display the list of all available employees. To do so, we create a new method in the `EmployeeController` class:

```
// GET: /Employee/List
public ActionResult List()
{
    DorknozzleDataContext dorkDC = new DorknozzleDataContext();

    List<Employee> listEmployees = dorkDC.Employees.➥
      ToList<Employee>();

    return View(listEmployees);
}
```

As you can see, the first two lines of code are standard LINQ data access code, which will return a generic list of all Employee entity records. The last line of code tells ASP.NET to render the View with the generic list to be used as the Model. You can specify the name of a View manually, but if you do not, ASP.NET assumes it to look for a View named after your Action, within a folder for your controller in the Views folder.

Phew! That sounds like a lot, but in our example, this basically means that we need to have another folder called "Employees" within our Views folder. Then we create a new View called **List.aspx**. So if our `EmployeesController` class has an action for "List", it will automatically render the **List.aspx** in the Views/Employees folder. Alternatively, there are method overloads where you can manually specify the view name.

Before we start creating our view, we'll want to add in a new master page and stylesheet. Master pages often go in the Views/Shared directory since it will be used across multiple controllers and actions. To add a new master page, right click on the Shared folder within "Views" and select "Add New Item". You'll create a new **Dorknozzle.master** file, as we've done in previous chapters. Our master page file will give us the same layout as its web forms version, but without a server-side ASP.NET controls and no required forms:

```
<%@ Master Language="C#" Inherits="System.Web.Mvc.ViewMasterPage" %>
```

```
<!DOCTYPE html PUBLIC "-//W3C//DTD XHTML 1.0 Transitional//EN"
  "http://www.w3.org/TR/xhtml1/DTD/xhtml1-transitional.dtd">

<html xmlns="http://www.w3.org/1999/xhtml">
<head id="Head1" runat="server">
    <title></title>
    <asp:ContentPlaceHolder id="head" runat="server">
    </asp:ContentPlaceHolder>



    <link type="text/css" href="~/Content/Dorknozzle.css"
        rel="Stylesheet" />
    <link type="text/css" href="~/Content/Site.css"
        rel="Stylesheet" />
</head>
<body>

    <!-- Header -->
    <div class="Header">
      <asp:Image id="Image1" runat="server"
          ImageUrl="~/Content/Images/header.gif" Width="450"
          Height="174"
          AlternateText="The Official Dorknozzle Company
          Intranet" />
    </div>
    <!-- Menu -->
   <div class="Menu">
     <div id="dorknozzleMenu">
<ul class="level1">
<li><a title="Dorknozzle Home" class="level1"➥
          href="/Employees/List">
          <img src="/Content/Images/book_closed.gif" alt="+" />
          Home</a></li>
          <li><a title="Dorknozzle Help Desk" class="level1"
          href="/HelpDesk">
          <img src="/Content/Images/book_closed.gif" alt="+" />
          Help Desk</a></li>
          <li><a title="Dorknozzle Employee Directory"
          class="level1" href="/Employees/List">
          <img src="/Content/Images/book_closed.gif" alt="+" />
          Employee Directory</a></li>
          <li><a title="Dorknozzle Address Book" class="level1"
          href="/AddressBook">
          <img src="/Content/Images/book_closed.gif" alt="+" />
```

```
                    Address Book</a></li>
                <li><a title="Dorknozzle Departments" class="level1"
                    href="/Departments">
                <img src="/Content/Images/book_closed.gif" alt="+" />
                    Departments</a></li>
                <li><a title="Admin Tools" class="level1"
                    href="/AdminTools">
                <img src="/Content/Images/book_closed.gif" alt="+" />
                    Admin Tools</a></li>
                <li><a title="Dorknozzle Admin Newsletter"
                    class="level1" href="/AdminNewsletter">
                <img src="/Content/Images/book_closed.gif" alt="+" />
                    Admin Newsletter</a></li>
</ul>
</div>
        </div>

        <!-- Content -->
        <div class="Content">
            <asp:ContentPlaceHolder id="MainContent"
                runat="server" />
        </div>
    </body>
</html>
```

Focus on MVC

We removed the `SiteMapDataSource` object here because it is a server-side control that did not fit in with the MVC pattern, and chose to hard-code the links instead with search engine optimized URLs. We won't implement the Views for each of the links here, although it would be a good exercise for you to do. If you want a MVC-compatible sitemap control, you can try taking a look at `MvcSiteMapProvider` at mvcsitemap.codeplex.com.

If you have downloaded the code files, you can **Add Existing Item** rather than create a new file. When you **Add Existing Item** to that folder, it'll prompt you to indicate where the file is located, and then copy the file to the solutions directory with the rest of the project. Static content, such as images and stylesheets, go into the Content folder. You'll want to create an "Images" folder within /Content and add the existing images to it; then simply add Dorknozzle.css to the base of the **/Content** directory. You can delete the existing **Site.css** that was created when the initial MVC project was created. If this folder structure is a little foreign to you or you are unsure of how it should look, refer to the code files for this chapter.

Now that our asset files are in place, we are now ready to create our view. We start by right-clicking on the Views folder to **Create New Folder**. Name this folder Employ-ees. In the real world, most developers create a new folder for each one of their controllers to separate the MVC pattern. Within the Employees folder, right-click to **Add > View** with the settings on the next dialog screen shown in Figure 16.9:

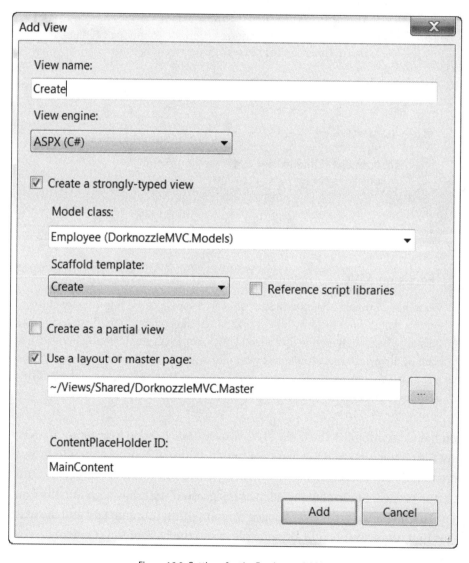

Figure 16.9. Settings for the Employees folder

The scaffolding template here is helpful, as it generates the Add, Edit, Details, Delete links for us. However the auto selected Model needs to be a generic `List<>` of Employees, which we can change on our own. So we correct it in the `Inherits` attribute in the Page Declaration, along with minor formatting changes:

```
<%@ Page Title="" Language="C#" MasterPageFile="~/Views/Shared/➥
    DorknozzleMVC.Master" Inherits="System.Web.Mvc.ViewPage➥
    <List<Employee>>" %>
<%@ Import Namespace="DorknozzleMVC.Models" %>
<asp:Content ID="Content1" ContentPlaceHolderID="MainContent"
    runat="server">

<h2>Employee List</h2>

<p>
    <%: Html.ActionLink("Create New", "Create") %>
</p>
<table class="mvcTable">

   <thead>
   <tr><td>Name</td><td colspan="3">Action</td></tr>


   </thead>
<% foreach (Employee emp in Model) { %>
   <tr>
       <td>
           <%: emp.Name %>

       </td>
       <td><%: Html.ActionLink("Edit", "Edit", new { id =➥
           emp.EmployeeID }) %></td>
       <td><%: Html.ActionLink("Details", "Details", new { id =➥
           emp.EmployeeID })%></td>
       <td><%: Html.ActionLink("Delete", "Delete", new { id =➥
           emp.EmployeeID })%></td>

   </tr>
<% } %>

</table>

</asp:Content>
```

```
<asp:Content ID="Content2" ContentPlaceHolderID="head"
  runat="server">
</asp:Content>
```

Notice the Html.ActionLink code blocks? These are helper methods that are useful in MVC3 as we can easily generate new Html items (hyperlinks in this case), without messy code integration blocks. Html.ActionLink() simply creates a new hyperlink to call a new Action for our current controller, and optionally passes in a parameter. In our case, it now passes in the EmployeeID as the URL parameter. In the Web Forms way of using the repeater, we often had a server-side HyperLink control that managed these links.

These integrated code blocks within the View may remind you of other web development languages, such as PHP. You can find additional helper methods to generate standard HTML controls such as text boxes or drop-down boxes, such as Html.TextBox or Html.DropDownList. These have the added benefit of not requiring a server-side postback like typical controls in ASP.NET Web Forms, which helps the performance of our application.

Let's go ahead and give our project a run. Take a look at Figure 16.10.

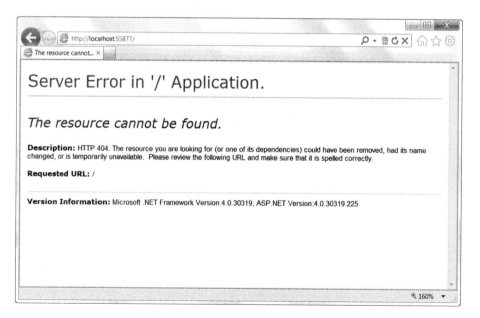

Figure 16.10. Something amiss when we run our project

Don't be alarmed if you get a 404 error the first time around. You simply need to specify the URL. In this case, it will be http://localhost:port/Employees/List.

The Specifics

You can permanently set the URL by right-clicking on the solution, and going to **Properties**; now select the **Web** tab and enter "Employees/List" as the start Action for a "specific page."

This will call the `List` action within the `EmployeesController` class. Your page should show up as in Figure 16.11:

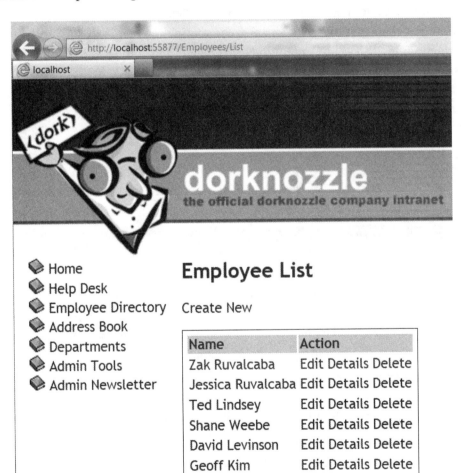

Figure 16.11. Dorknozzle employee list

Look familiar? Take a look at the HTML source code from the browser. You'll notice that the HTML being output is much cleaner: no forms are needed, no extra view state was added, and the HTML from the view and the master page is essentially what the server outputs. With MVC, you have full control over the way HTML is rendered. This is extremely useful in accessibility situations—such as developing a website geared for mobile devices.

You can verify that the ActionLinks are being created properly by hovering over the links and verifying that they are calling the EmployeesController with the Edit, Details, or Delete Action, along with the correct Employee ID parameter.

Let's continue by adding the Details Action to our EmployeesController. Our Details Action was already stubbed for us using the scaffolding template. We just have to make minor modifications to pull the exact data of the employee ID from the database:

```
public ActionResult Details(int id)
        {
                DorknozzleDataContext dorkDC = new ➥
                  DorknozzleDataContext();

                Employee currentEmployee = dorkDC.Employees.Where➥
                  (e => e.EmployeeID == id).First<Employee>();

                return View(currentEmployee);
        }
```

This is fairly simple LINQ-to-SQL code to get the first Employee entity record that matches based on the employee ID passed as a parameter. This Employee record will be the Model passed to the Details View. MVC handles the URL parameter passed from the URL to this Action call here. Coincidentally, the same code will be used for our Edit Action.

 Getting Some HTTP Action

There are two methods for the Edit actions. One has a standard parameter of *id*, which is the HTTP GET Action. Then there is an HTTP POST Action, where the parameter is a *FormsCollection* object. The first GET Action is when the user chooses to begin editing a user. This should load the user's existing data in writable fields. When the user finishes editing and clicks the **submit** button, the browser

sends the information contained in these form fields to ASP.NET with an HTTP
POST, essentially telling the server to process the information:

```
public ActionResult Edit(int id)
    {
        DorknozzleDataContext dorkDC = new➡
          DorknozzleDataContext();

        Employee currentEmployee = dorkDC.Employees.Where➡
          (e => e.EmployeeID == id).First<Employee>();

        return View(currentEmployee);
    }
```

Now we're at the point where we can create our views for Edit and Details.

Right-click on the Employees folder under **Views** and add a new View called "Details"
as in Figure 16.12. Select the Employee LINQ entity as your Model, `Details`as your
scaffolding template, and select the Master Page we added earlier.

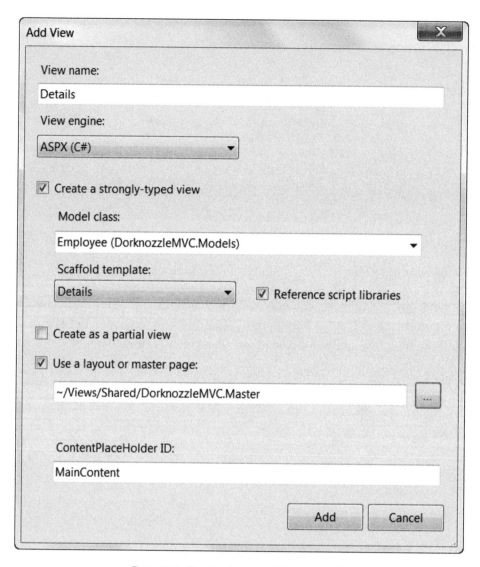

Figure 16.12. Choosing Employee LINQ as the model

We'll also add a new View called Edit (seen in Figure 16.13) using the same options, except using Edit as the scaffolding template option. For this, we'll specifically skip the script libraries referencing, as our master page is not yet ready for jQuery validation for the editable fields.

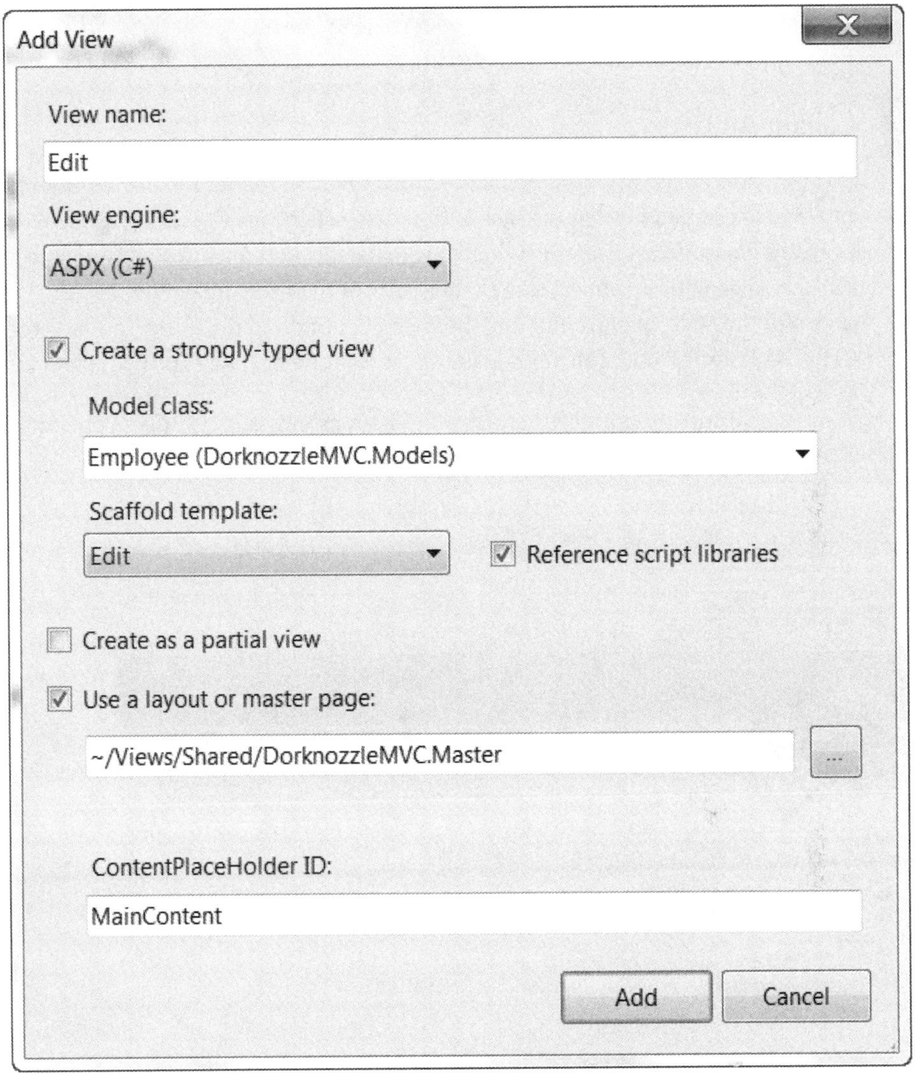

Figure 16.13. Adding a new View called "Edit"

The HTML used for the Details and Edit template are enough to get us going. The only minor bit we need to change is at the bottom of both Views: we want to use the "List" Action when we return our user to the main page. An excerpt is below:

```
<%: Html.ActionLink("Back to List", "Index") %>
```

It should now be:

```
<%: Html.ActionLink("Back to List", "List") %>
```

 Calling All Lists

We could have create a new Action called Index here to render the List view, but since we have already coded the List Action, we just change our user interface to call List. This is a great example where our Separation of Concerns allows us to make a change without affecting the other parts of the code, one of the useful features of the MVC pattern. But one thing you could do in the Index action is to call the `RedirectToAction` method as: return `RedirectToAction("List");`.

Let's go ahead and test our new Actions and Views by navigating to them, clicking on **Edit** or **Details** from the List view.

The Details View looks like Figure 16.14:

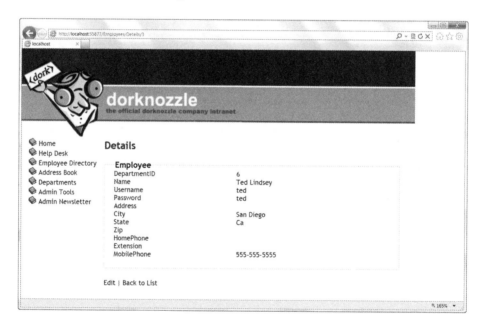

Figure 16.14. The Details View

The Edit View looks like Figure 16.15.

Figure 16.15. The Edit View

So with very little code written on our side thanks to the scaffolding templating, we can see the Details and the Edit view for our application. The POST Action isn't implemented, so the edit feature is yet to fully work. Let's do that now!

The method parameters for our Action for handling the POST of our Edit Action will give us the ID being edited, as well as a `FormsCollection` object. This is simply a name-value pair containing the new items that the end-user entered. So if you wanted to reference the "Name" field, we'd access it through the `FormsCollection` object as:

```
collection["Name"]; // returns "Ted Lindsey" if you're editing ID 3
```

We can now go ahead and edit the Employee record with the new data being submitted:

```
[HttpPost]
        public ActionResult Edit(int id, FormCollection collection)
        {

                using (DorknozzleDataContext dorkDC = new➡
                DorknozzleDataContext())
```

```
              {
                  Employee currentEmployee = dorkDC.Employees.➥
                    Where(e => e.EmployeeID == id).➥
                      First<Employee>();

                  currentEmployee.Address = collection["Address"];
                  currentEmployee.City = collection["City"];
                  currentEmployee.DepartmentID = Convert.ToInt32➥
                    (collection["DepartmentID"]);
                  currentEmployee.Extension = ➥
                    collection["Extension"];
                  currentEmployee.HomePhone = ➥
                    collection["HomePhone"];
                  currentEmployee.MobilePhone = ➥
                    collection["MobilePhone"];
                  currentEmployee.Name = collection["Name"];
                  currentEmployee.Password = ➥
                    collection["Password"];
                  currentEmployee.State = collection["State"];
                  currentEmployee.Username = ➥
                    collection["Username"];
                  currentEmployee.Zip = collection["Zip"];

                  dorkDC.SubmitChanges();
              }
              return RedirectToAction("List");
          }
```

Compile your application and give it a test run by editing an Employee record. After editing, it should return you to the List view. For deleting a user, it's similar:

```
public ActionResult Delete(int id)
    {
        using (DorknozzleDataContext dorkDC = new➥
          DorknozzleDataContext())
        {
            var employee = dorkDC.Employees.Where(emp => ➥
              emp.EmployeeID == id).First<Employee>();

            dorkDC.Employees.DeleteOnSubmit(employee);

        }
```

```
        return RedirectToAction("List");
}
```

Finally, we can implement the "Create" Action and View to fulfill our final requirement for this application, as in Figure 16.16. Since the "Create" Action is already
stubbed out for us, we can begin with creating the Create view, also using the scaffolding template. We don't need the reference script libraries here either.

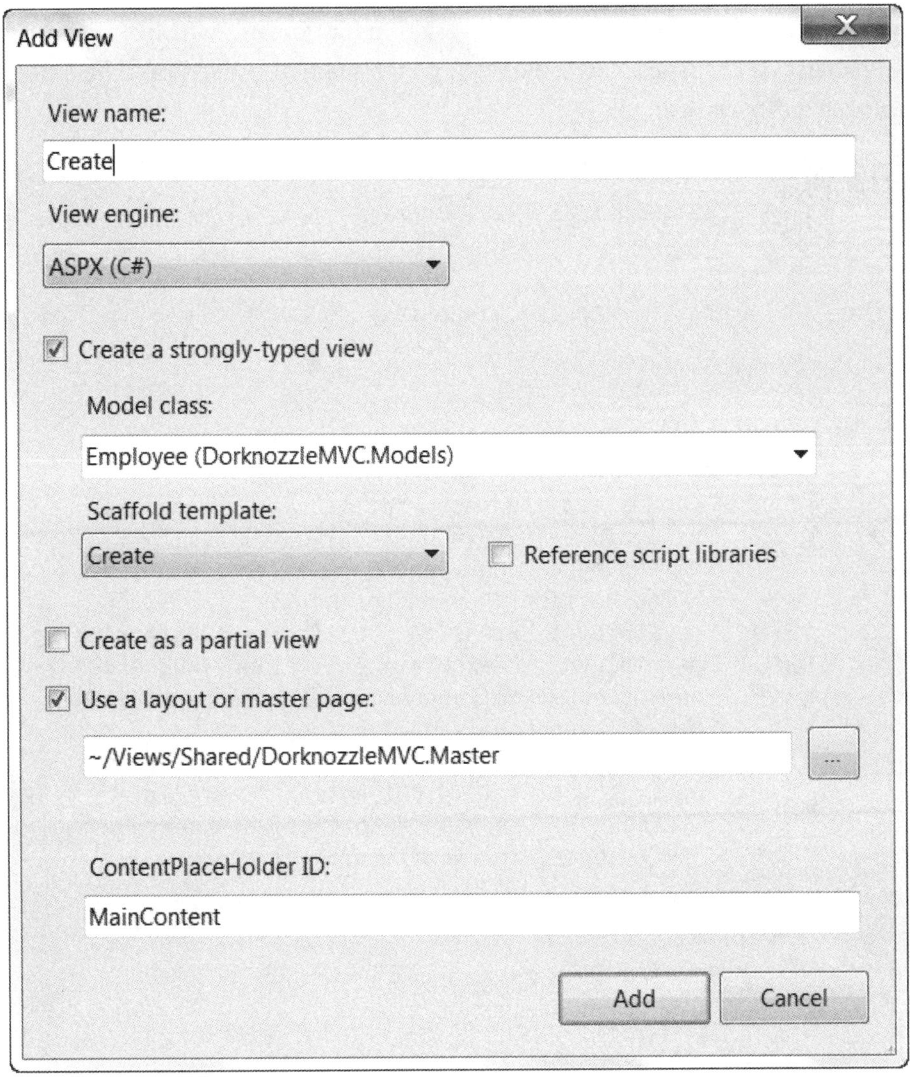

Figure 16.16. Creating the Create view

The View comes ready for us with no changes, except the link to return to the main List:

```
<%: Html.ActionLink("Back to List", "Index") %>
```

It becomes:

```
<%: Html.ActionLink("Back to List", "List") %>
```

Now, all we have to do is handle the POST action for "Create" within our controller. This also uses a `FormsCollection` object, which we will use to populate a new Employee entity record:

```
[HttpPost]
    public ActionResult Create(FormCollection collection)
    {

        using (DorknozzleDataContext dorkDC = new ➥
            DorknozzleDataContext())
        {

            Employee newEmployee = new Employee();

            newEmployee.Address = collection["Address"];
            newEmployee.City = collection["City"];
            newEmployee.DepartmentID = Convert.ToInt32➥
              (collection["DepartmentID"]);
            newEmployee.Extension = collection["Extension"];
            newEmployee.HomePhone = collection["HomePhone"];
            newEmployee.MobilePhone = collection["MobilePhone"];
            newEmployee.Name = collection["Name"];
            newEmployee.Password = collection["Password"];
            newEmployee.State = collection["State"];
            newEmployee.Username = collection["Username"];
            newEmployee.Zip = collection["Zip"];

            dorkDC.Employees.InsertOnSubmit(newEmployee);

            dorkDC.SubmitChanges();
        }
```

```
            return RedirectToAction("List");

    }
```

That's it! Give it a compile and view your application. You can now add, edit, delete, and view details for the employees of the Dorknozzle Corporation as in Figure 16.17.

Figure 16.17. Employee detail page of the Dorknozzle Corporation

Our listing with the newly created employee can be seen in Figure 16.18.

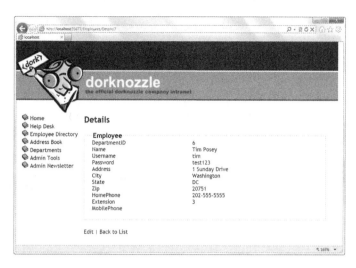

Figure 16.18. Our newly created employee

Summary

Is MVC a replacement for the Web Forms that we've used throughout this book? No—it's another tool in the web developer's arsenal to choose, depending on the project. MVC is a powerful framework for ASP.NET that solves many of the original issues we discussed earlier—namely the ability to more easily maintain complex applications by separating the three main sections of the project. Many of the features that were once previously available for ASP.NET MVC are now available for Web Forms, such as the URL Routing features and SEO-friendly URLs. jQuery integration is also now shipping with Visual Web Developer—previously it was once a mainstay of the MVC Framework. The choice is ultimately up to you as the developer, but it is important to understand what tools are available, and MVC is yet another tool to help you accomplish your tasks.

We have seen the full power of MVC, from creating a new web application without the need for server-side web controls or `ViewState`. We've also seen LINQ-to-SQL in a real-example setting, and how easy it is to use LINQ-to-SQL to promptly query data from the database without needing to worry about data sets or connection strings.

One of the major benefits here from MVC is the ability for multiple programmers to work on the same project using different files. The programmer whose strengths are in HTML design can now work on the View, while a back-end developer can handle the Model and Controller. The principle of Separation of Concerns allows us to also make changes without affecting most of the other working parts of the application. We also have full control over the HTML being output by the server, so if we needed to target other browsers or devices, we could easily accommodate those changes.

Lastly, we saw the usefulness of the scaffolding templates to add functionality for our Controller, in order to stub out Action methods for adding, editing, deleting, and viewing the details on our Model. This scaffolding template also generated the majority of our HTML layout with very little changes on our side to make it fully functional.

17

ASP.NET AJAX

Throughout this book, we've been building ASP.NET Web Forms that, after any user interaction, send all of the page's data back to the server. You may not really notice any problems with this approach if you're developing locally on a fast computer, but once your application is deployed to the Internet, it may appear to be quite slow and unresponsive to users. However, by harnessing ASP.NET AJAX, you can take a slow and clunky web application and make it sing with surprisingly little effort.

In this chapter we'll learn about:

- what Ajax is and how it works
- ASP.NET AJAX
- the `UpdatePanel` and `UpdateProgress` controls
- using triggers
- the ASP.NET AJAX Control Toolkit
- the `ValidatorCalloutExtender` control extender
- jQuery and how it fits in with Visual Web Developer

What is Ajax?

What is **Ajax**, you ask? The acronym itself, coined by Jesse James Garret in 2005, stands for Asynchronous JavaScript and XML.[1] In a nutshell, the term represents the methodologies and technologies that allow developers to make web applications feel far more interactive and responsive. Notable examples of applications that utilize Ajax include Gmail, Google Maps, Yahoo! Mail, Kayak, Flickr, and Facebook. Moreover, just about every significant web site you interact with today probably takes advantage of some Ajax concepts to improve the user experience in some way.

On a technical level, Ajax uses a few key technologies:

- The most critical piece is the JavaScript `XmlHttpRequest` object. Originally invented by Microsoft for Internet Explorer 4, it's now a standard feature of all browsers. This very powerful object allows developers to use JavaScript to make HTTP `GET` and `POST` requests without submitting the whole page, and to then access the content of the server response. Note that the `Xml` part of the name is a bit misleading. In practice, you're free to choose the format of the response data—XML, JSON,[2] an HTML snippet, or just about any format that can be sent over HTTP.

- The second most important technology is browser DOM scripting: Document Object Model manipulation using JavaScript. JavaScript is required to create the `XmlHttpRequest` object and make the request, but also to take the raw data returned from the request, parse it, and integrate it back into the page for the user.

- The final leg on which Ajax applications stand is standards–based HTML and CSS. HTML provides the structure and the content, while CSS is used to control the presentation of the interface.

Like any technology, Ajax is not without its challenges. First and foremost, to do anything with Ajax, you need to have JavaScript enabled in the browser. From an accessibility viewpoint, heavily interactive web sites can be very difficult for people using assistive technology like screen readers to use. The application of Ajax within

---

[1] "Ajax: A New Approach to Web Applications," http://www.adaptivepath.com/ideas/essays/archives/000385.php

[2] JavaScript Object Notation, a lightweight data transfer format for use with JavaScript. See http://www.json.org/ for further information.

a web site can subtly alter the behavior of the browser in ways that users can find confusing—for example, they may be unable to use the **Back** button, or accurately bookmark pages. Finally, if your web site content can't be accessed by any means other than JavaScript, search engines won't be able to index your content.

Ajax may sound intimidating, and for the original trail blazers there were a number of complex problems to solve. But, as Ajax has matured and become a standard component of modern web development, a number of tools have been created to make "Ajaxifying" your application very easy. You may have heard of—or even used—some of these tools, including jQuery,[3] Prototype,[4] and MooTools.[5] However, as a budding ASP.NET developer, you really need to familiarize yourself with one tool in particular: Microsoft's ASP.NET AJAX.

ASP.NET AJAX

ASP.NET AJAX, originally called ASP.NET Atlas, is a core part of ASP.NET 4.[6] The library itself has three components. The first is a set of client-side JavaScript libraries, known as the Microsoft AJAX Library, which provide the framework of cross-browser functionality that's used by the ASP.NET AJAX server-side components. Second, on the server-side, Microsoft developed a set of HTTP handlers and modules to wrap the standard XML-based web services and allow them to respond to Ajax requests using JSON. Finally, there's the component we'll focus on in this chapter—the server-side controls that make Ajaxifying your application incredibly easy.

Included in the core ASP.NET AJAX library are just a few key server controls:

1. The `ScriptManager` control is rather boring and unsung, but it's absolutely critical.[7] As its name indicates, it manages the registration of client scripts on your web page, handling mundane tasks like making certain that your Ajax controls have the scripts they need and, more importantly, that these scripts are included only once.

---

[3] http://jquery.com/

[4] http://www.prototypejs.org/

[5] http://mootools.net/

[6] http://www.asp.net/ajax/

[7] http://www.asp.net/AJAX/Documentation/Live/overview/ScriptManagerOverview.aspx

2. The `Timer` control provides the plumbing to perform postback operations at defined intervals.[8] Again, it's a straightforward, often-overlooked control, but it's very handy for those operations.

3. The final components are the interrelated `UpdatePanel` and `UpdateProgress` controls.[9] The `UpdatePanel`, when used with a `ScriptManager`, allows a developer to use **partial rendering**—a procedure by which different sections of a page are updated independently, without requiring the browser to refresh the entire page. The `UpdateProgress` control informs users that a partial rendering operation is in progress.

While it probably doesn't seem like there's much variety in the way of server controls, these provide the core functionality to let us very quickly and easily add Ajax functionality to just about any web site that uses ASP.NET 2.0 or later versions.

Using the `UpdatePanel` Control

The most exciting control included in the core of ASP.NET AJAX is the `UpdatePanel`. It's been called the "gateway drug" to Ajax, and rightly so—it can be added to nearly any ASP.NET page to instantly, and almost magically, make it feel "Ajaxy." In most cases, this goal can be achieved without making material changes to the code. Let's try a simple example: wrapping a `GridView` in an `UpdatePanel`.

The `GridView` on our **Departments.aspx** page currently requires a complete page reload for every interaction. That seems a bit wasteful for simple user actions such as sorting columns and clicking the paging links. This page is a perfect candidate for a little Ajax magic!

To get started, let's add an `UpdatePanel` to the **Departments.aspx** page. Open your **Departments.aspx** page and make the changes shown below:

```
                                   Dorknozzle\VB\01_Departments.aspx (excerpt)

<asp:Content ID="Content2"
    ContentPlaceHolderID="ContentPlaceHolder1" Runat="Server">
  <asp:ScriptManager runat="server" ID="DepartmentsScriptManager"
      EnablePartialRendering="True" />
```

---

[8] http://www.asp.net/AJAX/Documentation/Live/overview/UsingTimerControlTutorial.aspx
[9] http://www.asp.net/AJAX/Documentation/Live/overview/PartialUpdates.aspx

```
<h1>Dorknozzle Departments</h1>
<p>Page rendered at <%= DateTime.Now.ToLongTimeString() %>.</p>
<asp:UpdatePanel runat="server" ID="DepartmentsUpdatePanel">
  <ContentTemplate>
    <asp:GridView id="departmentsGrid" runat="server"
        AllowPaging="True" PageSize="4" AllowSorting="True"
        onpageindexchanging="departmentsGrid_PageIndexChanging"
        onsorting="departmentsGrid_Sorting">
    </asp:GridView>
    <p>Grid rendered at <%= DateTime.Now.ToLongTimeString() %>
    </p>
  </ContentTemplate>
</asp:UpdatePanel>
</asp:Content>
```

Hit **F5** to execute the site and if everything goes well, you should see a rather familiar Dorknozzle Departments page with a few extra lines of text, as shown in Figure 17.1.

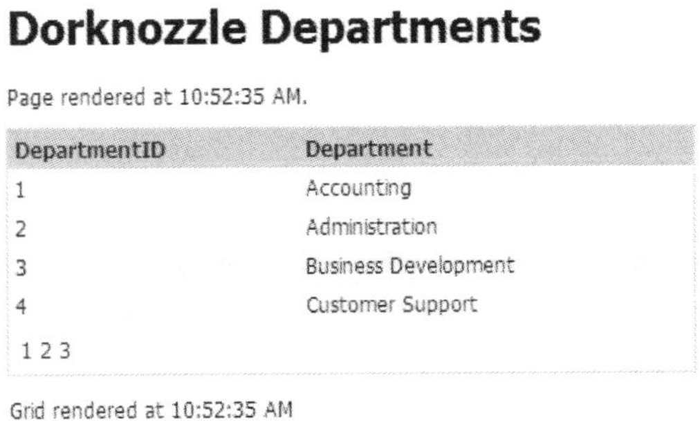

Dorknozzle Departments

Page rendered at 10:52:35 AM.

DepartmentID	Department
1	Accounting
2	Administration
3	Business Development
4	Customer Support
1 2 3	

Grid rendered at 10:52:35 AM

Figure 17.1. The Departments `GridView` within an `UpdatePanel`

Now click on the paging buttons to change the `GridView` display. You should notice two things: first, the page doesn't flicker nor completely refresh—only the contents of the `GridView` change; second, the time output in the bottom paragraph will be updated each time you click, while the time output in the top paragraph will stay the same. Congratulations, you just Ajax-enabled your page! Now let's take a look at how this all works.

We added the time output only to underline the fact that this page is being partially rendered—you probably won't do that in a real application. The top paragraph is output when the page is first rendered, while the bottom one is changed using Ajax.

However, the Ajax wouldn't work at all if we didn't add the `ScriptManager` control to the page. We also made sure that the `EnablePartialRendering` property was set to `True` to enable partial rendering. This invisible control also provides the key plumbing for the other Ajax controls we're going to use in the chapter, so don't leave home without it!

With the `ScriptManager` control in place, we can add our Ajax controls. We've wrapped the `GridView` in an `UpdatePanel` control, making sure the `GridView` is within the `<ContentTemplate>` tags. The `UpdatePanel` allows the content within its `<ContentTemplate>` tags to be partially rendered and updated using Ajax.

Now let's expand on this functionality using one of the other controls included in ASP.NET AJAX—the `UpdateProgress` control. You're probably fairly familiar with the little spinning animations on sites such as Facebook. The animation serves as an indicator that although the page itself isn't refreshing, some aspect of the page is being loaded or updated. In our case, since this application is running locally and the data sets are limited, we're going to need to fake a time delay in order to see the effect. Open the **Departments.aspx** code-behind file (**Departments.aspx.vb** or **Departments.aspx.cs**) and add the following line to the `BindGrid` method:

Visual Basic

```
departmentsGrid.DataSource = _
    dataSet.Tables("Departments").DefaultView
System.Threading.Thread.Sleep(2500)
departmentsGrid.DataBind()
```

C#

```
departmentsGrid.DataSource =
    dataSet.Tables["Departments"].DefaultView;
System.Threading.Thread.Sleep(2500);
departmentsGrid.DataBind();
```

The `System.Threading.Thread` class represents the current `Thread` in which our application is running, and this trick simply tells the thread to halt for 2500 milliseconds. This isn't something you should do in production, but it can help with examples like this, and with testing.

Now that we've added a time delay, let's add an UpdateProgress control to our GridView. Make the following changes to **Departments.aspx**:

```
Dorknozzle\VB\02_Departments.aspx (excerpt)

<asp:UpdatePanel runat="server" ID="DepartmentsUpdatePanel" >
  <ContentTemplate>
    <asp:UpdateProgress ID="DepartmentsUpdateProgress"
        DynamicLayout="true" runat="server">
      <ProgressTemplate>
        <p class="UpdateProgress">Updating...</p>
      </ProgressTemplate>
    </asp:UpdateProgress>
    ⋮
  </ContentTemplate>
</asp:UpdatePanel>
```

Examine the code and you'll see that all we've done is add an UpdateProgress control with the an id value of DepartmentsUpdateProgress, set the DynamicLayout property to True, and added some HTML: a <p> tag within the <ProgressTemplate> tags. Whatever content we place within those tags will be visible while the UpdatePanel is updating; you can add just about anything you can dream up. The DynamicLayout property is handy—if we left it as False, space would always be reserved on the page for the UpdateProgress control's content.

Let's give our update indicator a little style. Add the following CSS rule to the Dorknozzle CSS file:

```
Dorknozzle\VB\03_Dorknozzle.css (excerpt)

.UpdateProgress {
  background-color: Black;
  color: White;
  font-weight: bold;
  padding: 5px;
  text-transform: uppercase;
}
```

Save the changes and execute the page to see our new UpdateProgress control in action. Now, when you click on a different page number, you should see the UPDAT- ING... message shown in Figure 17.2.

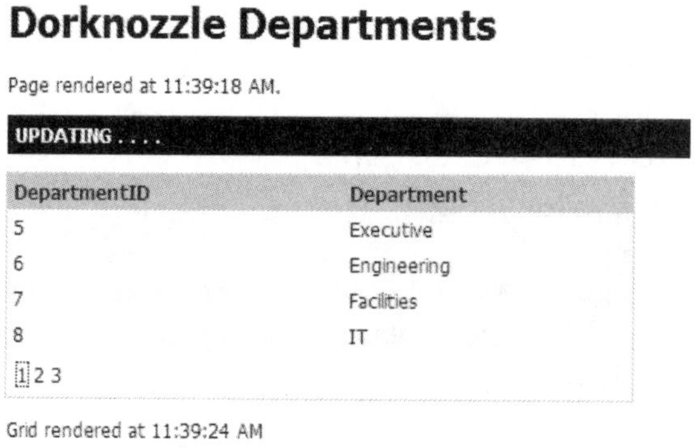

Dorknozzle Departments

Page rendered at 11:39:18 AM.

UPDATING	
DepartmentID	**Department**
5	Executive
6	Engineering
7	Facilities
8	IT
[1] 2 3	

Grid rendered at 11:39:24 AM

Figure 17.2. The `UpdateProgress` control at work

Managing the `ScriptManager` Control

As we saw above, one thing that all ASP.NET pages with Ajax controls need in order to work is the `ScriptManager` control. In the first example, we added the `ScriptManager` directly to our page. But since we have a well-structured project including a master page, and we intend to use ASP.NET AJAX controls on multiple pages, it would be handy to add the `ScriptManager` control to our master page. Open **Dorknozzle.master** in **Design** mode. Look in the toolbox for the **AJAX Extensions** section and drag a `ScriptManager` to the top of the form. Right-click on the new `ScriptManager` control and choose **Properties**—let's give our control a good name, like **DorknozzleScriptManager**, by editing the **(ID)** property. If you save the file and then click on **Source** view, you should see this code:

```
                                  Dorknozzle\VB\04_Dorknozzle.master (excerpt)
<!-- Header -->
<div class="Header">
  <asp:ScriptManager ID="DorknozzleScriptManager" runat="server">
  </asp:ScriptManager>
  ⋮
</div>
```

If you try to execute the **Departments.aspx** page we modified previously, you'll see an error—the dreaded yellow screen of death, which states that, "Only one instance of ScriptManager can be added to the page." Go back and remove the `ScriptManager` control from that page to restore normal functionality.

There's one downside to adding the `ScriptManager` control to the master page: sometimes you need to reference it from your web forms. That won't be a problem in this book, but if you do ever need to access a `ScriptManager` control, ASP.NET AJAX has you covered. Just add a `ScriptManagerProxy` control to the web form, and you can access the master page's `ScriptManager` as if it lived on that page.

Using Triggers to Update an UpdatePanel

Our first example was rather simple—we just wrapped the Departments page's `GridView` in an `UpdatePanel` and let ASP.NET AJAX handle the rest. Unfortunately, real-life web applications aren't often so simple. Sometimes you need to use a control that's located separately from the `UpdatePanel` to trigger the partial rendering process, instead of allowing the default behaviour of reloading every single `UpdatePanel` with every asynchronous postback.

The Departments page was a great starting point, but in this example, we're going to work with a more complex page. Open the **AddressBook.aspx** file in your Dorknozzle project. To begin our work with triggers, we'll need to add some basic plumbing to the page:

1. We'll need two `UpdatePanel`s: one for the `GridView` control, and one for the `DetailsView` control.

2. We'll need to add bit of instrumentation—an output of the current server time—for the sake of the demonstration.

In **AddressBook.aspx**, modify the code as shown below:

```
                                          Dorknozzle\VB\05_AddressBook.aspx (excerpt)

<h1>Address Book</h1>
<p>Page rendered at <%= DateTime.Now.ToLongTimeString() %>.
</p>
<p>
<asp:LinkButton id="addEmployeeButton" runat="server"
  Text="Add New Employee" />
</p>
<asp:UpdatePanel runat="server" ID="AddressGridViewUpdatePanel"
    UpdateMode="Conditional" ChildrenAsTriggers="True">
  <ContentTemplate>
    <asp:GridView …>
```

```
      ⋮ GridView control markup…
     </asp:GridView>
     <p>Grid rendered at <%= DateTime.Now.ToLongTimeString() %>.
     </p>
   </ContentTemplate>
 </asp:UpdatePanel>
 <br />
 <asp:UpdatePanel runat="server" ID="DetailsViewUpdatePanel"
     UpdateMode="Conditional" ChildrenAsTriggers="True">
   <ContentTemplate>
     <p>Details rendered at <%= DateTime.Now.ToLongTimeString() %>.
     </p>
     <asp:DetailsView …>
       ⋮ DetailsView control markup…
     </asp:DetailsView>
   </ContentTemplate>
 </asp:UpdatePanel>
```

The instrumentation should look familiar—we used the same technique in the first example, when we output the current time inside the `UpdatePanel` controls. This time, we need to track three items: the page and the two `UpdatePanels`. For the `UpdatePanel` controls, we use a new property—we set the `UpdateMode` property to `Conditional`, which tells the panel to refresh only when it's triggered.

Execute the page in your browser to check out the results. The new page shouldn't look appreciably different than the previous version, but it should display a few new lines of text to indicate the rendering times of different parts of the page. If you click on the page numbers or sorting controls in the `GridView`, you'll notice that the refresh lacks any of the flashing associated with a complete page refresh, and it's only the rendering time display for the `GridView` that changes.

Next, try to click on the **Select** `LinkButton` for one of the employees. Shockingly, nothing happens! Remember that the **Select** button opens the `employeeDetails` `DetailsView` control that's now invisible. Now that each control is in a distinct `UpdatePanel`, and the `UpdatePanel` controls have their respective `UpdateMode` set to `Conditional`, a postback in one control—clicking **Select**, in this case—doesn't let ASP.NET AJAX know enough to refresh the other `UpdatePanel` control. We need to use another element to make this happen: a trigger.

ASP.NET AJAX triggers come in two fashions: `AsyncPostBackTriggers` and `PostBackTriggers`. The former trigger performs an asynchronous Ajax postback, while the latter triggers a normal, full-page postback operation. In most cases you'd want to use `AsyncPostBackTriggers`—after all, we *are* making Ajax applications! Yet there are some cases in which you'll need to use an explicit `PostBackTrigger`. A common scenario is the uploading of files. For security reasons, ASP.NET AJAX doesn't handle file uploads—any posted file is ignored. But if you use a `PostBackTrigger` on a control that triggers a file upload, the upload can be made to work.

In order to make the page that contains multiple `UpdatePanels` work properly, we're going to have to add a few `AsyncPostBackTrigger` controls to our `UpdatePanels`. Switch **AddressBook.aspx** to **Design** mode and select the `AddressGridUpdatePanel` first. Spotting an `UpdatePanel` can be tricky at first—they're invisible controls that are difficult to see on the design canvas. The easiest way to find them is to select a child control, so click on the `employeeDetails DetailsView`. From there, the label for the containing `UpdatePanel` should appear as it does in Figure 17.3.

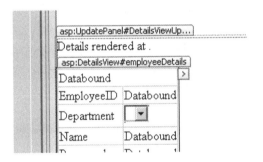

Figure 17.3. Finding the `UpdatePanel` in **Design** view

Click on the label to select the `UpdatePanel`, then and look at the **Properties** window. Edit the **Triggers** collection by selecting its entry in the **Properties** window and clicking on the … button that appears next to it. Add a new `AsyncPostBackTrigger` by clicking on the **Add** button. Select **grid** for the **ControlID** field and select **SelectedIndexChanged** for the **EventName** field. Click **OK** to add the trigger to your page, then save it and view it in your browser.

Once the page renders, try clicking the **Select** button on any row. Hey presto—the `DetailsView` appears as it should! Look at the timestamps and you'll see that both the `UpdatePanel` controls now update, but the page itself isn't being reloaded.

Not all of our problems are solved, though; in fact, we've created a new issue. Click **Edit** on an employee's record, change the **City** field to **Beijing**, then click **Save**. The

DetailsView updates correctly, but the GridView doesn't register the update. If you look at the timestamp, you'll see that the GridView wasn't refreshed when you clicked **Save**. If you think we need another trigger, you're quite correct. In fact, we're going to need a few triggers to make this happen.

Switch back to Visual Web Developer and let's add four AsyncPostBack triggers to the AddressViewGridView using the **Properties** dialog as we did before. We'll need one trigger for each of the following events: ItemCreated, ItemDeleted, ItemInserted, and ItemUpdated. For each, choose **employeeDetails** for the **ControlID**.

Next, select the employeeDetails GridView. Add one more trigger for the Click event and choose **addEmployeeButton** for the **ControlID**.

If you switch to **Source** view, you'll see the source code of your new triggers, which looks like this:

```
                              Dorknozzle\VB\06_AddressBook.aspx (excerpt)

<asp:UpdatePanel runat="server" ID="AddressGridViewUpdatePanel"
    UpdateMode="Conditional">
  <ContentTemplate>
  ⋮
  </ContentTemplate>
  <Triggers>
    <asp:AsyncPostBackTrigger ControlID="employeeDetails"
        EventName="ItemCreated" />
    <asp:AsyncPostBackTrigger ControlID="employeeDetails"
        EventName="ItemDeleted" />
    <asp:AsyncPostBackTrigger ControlID="employeeDetails"
        EventName="ItemInserted" />
    <asp:AsyncPostBackTrigger ControlID="employeeDetails"
        EventName="ItemUpdated" />
  </Triggers>
</asp:UpdatePanel>
<br />
<asp:UpdatePanel runat="server" ID="DetailsViewUpdatePanel"
    UpdateMode="Conditional">
  <ContentTemplate>
  ⋮
  </ContentTemplate>
  <Triggers>
    <asp:AsyncPostBackTrigger ControlID="grid"
        EventName="SelectedIndexChanged" />
```

```
    <asp:AsyncPostBackTrigger ControlID="addEmployeeButton"
        EventName="Click" />
  </Triggers>
</asp:UpdatePanel>
```

Now, execute the page and edit an employee's **City** field again. You'll see the change reflected in the GridView. Click the **Add Employee** LinkButton to create a new employee, and the new item will appear in the GridView. If you want to live dangerously, delete the new employee and note how the item disappears from the GridView. Finally, note that even with all these changes, the page itself has never been wholly reloaded—that page's timestamp should remain the same.

Now, you might ask "Why bother setting up all these triggers? If we just leave the UpdateMode property of all the UpdatePanel controls set to the default value of Always, we'll never have to deal with this." Technically, that's correct, but that idea's not without its drawbacks. UpdatePanels can be quite expensive in terms of server capacity. In order to properly maintain state, the controls must submit the entire view state back to the server. The server must then process this mass of data and push the content of all the UpdatePanel controls back to the browser. By only triggering the updates on the panels we wished to change in this example, we saved significant amounts of bandwidth per request.

The ASP.NET AJAX Control Toolkit

So far, we've explored the basic ASP.NET AJAX Server Controls—the ScriptManager, the UpdatePanel, and the UpdateProgress controls. They're very handy, but they have no flair, and today's users expect a little glitz in their web applications. With the ASP.NET AJAX Control Toolkit, adding a touch of glamour to your ASP.NET AJAX application becomes a simple matter of applying a few control extenders to your page.

The ASP.NET AJAX Control Toolkit is a Microsoft-supported open source project. It's a good example of a very well-designed, well-tested control library that you can include in any of your projects. Unlike many of the libraries you might wish to use in the future, this one is totally free of charge. Check out the sample project at http://www.asp.net/ajax/ajaxcontroltoolkit/samples/, play around with some of the controls, and think about how we can spice up Dorknozzle a little. Pay special attention to the `Animation` and the `ValidatorCallout`—we'll see these controls in action shortly.

In order to best use the Toolkit, we need to integrate it into Visual Web Developer Express. The first step is to acquire the Toolkit itself. Visit the project's home page at http://www.codeplex.com/AjaxControlToolkit and click on the **Releases** tab. Select the **AjaxControlToolkit-Framework3.5-NoSource.zip** file, download it, and extract it to a temporary folder on your hard drive. In the extracted folders, open the **SampleWebSite\Bin** folder. You should see a number of localized language folders and also a key file: **AjaxControlToolkit.dll**.

Grab the **AjaxControlToolkit.dll** file and stash it somewhere permanent so we can reference it from Visual Web Developer to integrate it into the designer. I recommend that you create a folder within your **My Documents** folder to handle this:

1. Click on **Start**, and then **Run**.

2. Type in **My Documents**.

3. Double-click on the **Visual Studio 2008** folder.

4. Create a new folder called **Add-Ins**.

5. In this new folder, create a folder called **Ajax Control Toolkit**.

6. Get the **AjaxControlToolkit.dll** from the location we established above, and copy it to the **Ajax Control Toolkit** folder we just created.

7. In Visual Web Developer, expand the **Toolbox**, right-click on an empty area, and choose **Add Tab**. Call the new tab **AJAX Control Toolkit**.

8. Right-click on the text in the empty tab and select **Choose Items...**.

9. Click **Browse** to add a new file, and then head to the location where you saved the **AjaxControlToolkit.dll** file. Double-click on the file to select it.

10. You should see a few new, highlighted lines in the **Choose Toolbox Items** dialog with the namespace value of `AjaxControlToolkit`. Click **OK** to continue.

11. Two dozen or so new items should load into your new toolbar tab, ranging from `Accordian` all the way to `ValidatorCalloutExtender`.

The `ValidatorCalloutExtender` Control Extender

ASP.NET's built-in validation controls are very effective, but they're visually boring—especially when they're compared to many modern web applications. The ASP.NET AJAX Control Toolkit has a solution: the `ValidatorCalloutExtender`. This control extender takes the plain old ASP.NET validator controls we learned about in Chapter 6 and extends them. It adapts their rendering to take advantage of the tools ASP.NET AJAX provides to make them more user friendly and visually appealing.

Once you have the toolkit set up, open **HelpDesk.aspx**, go into **Design** mode, and click on the red text message that reads, **You must enter station number**. This will select the simple `RequiredFieldValidator` control and show a smart tag indicating that we can add something to it. Click on the smart tag and choose **Add Extender...**, as shown in Figure 17.4, to start the **Extender Wizard**. Select the `ValidatorCallout` and click **OK**. Repeat this process with three remaining validation controls on this page.

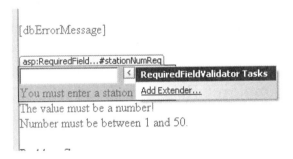

Figure 17.4. Adding the `ValidatorCalloutExtender` control

One thing to note—the first time you added an extender to the page, you might have seen a new **Bin** folder appear in your **Solution Explorer**. This folder contains the familiar **AjaxControlToolkit.dll** file, which is known as an **assembly**—a logical unit of code that can actually contain one or more files as a package. If you click on the file in **Solution Explorer** and look at the **Properties** panel, you'll notice that the value of the `Auto-refresh Path` property is the same as the location in which we parked the assembly file. Once we incorporated the functionality into Dorknozzle, Visual Web Developer added the referenced assembly to our solution for our convenience. Visual Web Developer also registered the assembly on the Help Desk page. If we switch to **Source** mode, we'll see the following new code near the beginning of our file:

```
<%@ Register assembly="AjaxControlToolkit"
    namespace="AjaxControlToolkit" tagprefix="cc1" %>
```

And, if we look at the first `ValidatorCalloutExtender` extender we added, we'll see the following code:

```
<cc1:ValidatorCalloutExtender
    ID="stationNumReq_ValidatorCalloutExtender"
    runat="server" Enabled="True"
    TargetControlID="stationNumReq">
</cc1:ValidatorCalloutExtender>
```

That snippet of code tells the compiler and Visual Web Developer to look for tags from the **AjaxControlToolkit.dll** when we add an element with the prefix cc1. Now, let's run the page and see how it looks when we input some invalid data. Click on the **Submit Request** button and you should see a validation message like the one displayed in Figure 17.5.

This isn't quite what we wanted. First, why are those red error messages appearing? Second, how can we highlight the fields in error?

Figure 17.5. Both validation messages displaying

Let's tackle the redundant validation text first. When we first built the page in Chapter 6, we used the validation controls' dynamic rendering functionality to improve the usability of the page. Now, since we're going to use callouts to highlight the fields in error, this dynamically generated error message is interfering with our much prettier callouts. To eliminate this problem, we could hunt down each of the four validator controls on the page and set their `Display` properties to `None`. Alternatively, we can take advantage of Visual Web Developer's find-and-replace functionality:

1. Open **HelpDesk.aspx** in **Source** view.
2. Open the **Quick Replace** dialog by pressing **Ctrl+h**.
3. Make absolutely certain that **Look in** is set to **Current Document**.
4. Enter **Display="Dynamic"** into **Find What**.
5. Enter **Display="None"** into **Replace With**.
6. Click **Replace All**.
7. You should see four replacements made.

Our next task is to enable some kind of highlight on the fields that have errors. Conveniently, the `ValidationCalloutExtender` extender has a property just for this purpose: `HighlightCssClass`. This class is applied via JavaScript manipulation when a field is in error. To use it, we need to add the following piece of CSS to our Dorknozzle CSS file:

Dorknozzle\VB\07_Dorknozzle.css*(excerpt)*

```
.fieldError {
  background-color: pink;
  color: White;
}
```

Next, add the `HighlightCssClass` attribute to each of the four `ValidatorCalloutExtender` extenders you added to the page, and give each instance the value `fieldError`. If you're using **Design** view, the extenders can be very hard to find—the only way is to grab them from the drop-down list in the **Properties** panel. In **Source** view, on the other hand, you can just type the code directly into the relevant tag. Each of your `ValidatorCalloutExtender` extenders should have a new attribute like the one below:

Dorknozzle\VB\08_HelpDesk.aspx *(excerpt)*

```
<cc1:ValidatorCalloutExtender
    ID="stationNumReq_ValidatorCalloutExtender"
    runat="server" Enabled="True" TargetControlID="stationNumReq"
    HighlightCssClass="fieldError">
</cc1:ValidatorCalloutExtender>
```

View the page in your browser again, and click **Submit Request** without entering any data. The red error messages should have been replaced with pink highlights and yellow validation callouts like the ones in Figure 17.6.

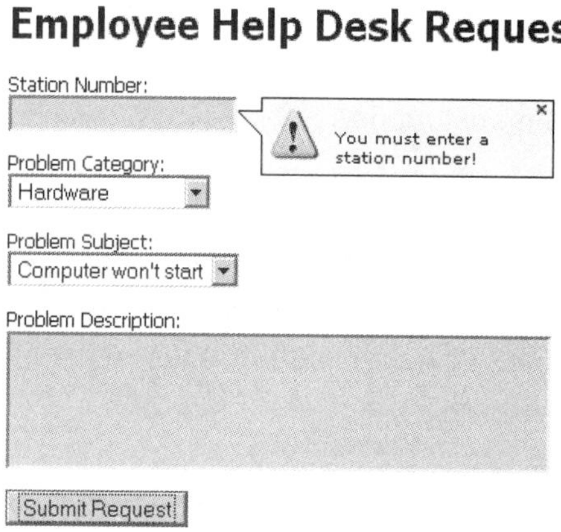

Figure 17.6. The completed validation display

Getting Started with Animation

ValidatorCalloutExtender extenders are fun, but we all know that the marketing department is always demanding the kind of pop and pizzaz that's powered by animation.

We're going to take our old **Departments.aspx** page and spice it up—we'll use some animation to indicate that it's updating, rather than relying on a plain old UpdateProgress control. However, before we get started on this, we're going to have to enable the AJAX Control Toolkit to be used project-wide. Open the Dorknozzle **Web.config** file, find the <controls> node within the <pages>, and make the following addition:

```
                                          Dorknozzle\VB\09_web.config (excerpt)

<pages theme="Blue">
  <controls>
    ⋮
    <add tagPrefix="atk" namespace="AjaxControlToolkit"
        assembly="AjaxControlToolkit" />
  </controls>
</pages>
```

You might notice that this is quite similar to the @Register directive that was created in the **HelpDesk.aspx** file when we dragged the ValidationCalloutExtender extender onto the design canvas. However, rather than applying only to a single page, as the directive does, this configuration applies to the entire project. This is a handy way to globally enable a library that you plan to use liberally throughout your project.

Now that we've registered the library, we can add our animation. Open the **Departments.aspx** page in **Source** view and remove the UpdateProgress control we added previously. If you didn't remove the ScriptManager control earlier, do that now—it will conflict with the global ScriptManager control we added to **Dorknozzle.master** file.

Next, make the following changes to your **Departments.aspx** file:

```
                                    Dorknozzle\VB\10_Departments.aspx (excerpt)

<asp:UpdatePanel runat="server" ID="DepartmentsUpdatePanel">
  <ContentTemplate>
    <div id="gridContainer">
    <asp:GridView id="departmentsGrid" runat="server"
        AllowPaging="True"
        PageSize="4" AllowSorting="True"
        onpageindexchanging="departmentsGrid_PageIndexChanging"
        onsorting="departmentsGrid_Sorting">
    </asp:GridView>
    <p>Grid rendered at <%= DateTime.Now.ToLongTimeString() %></p>
    </div>
  </ContentTemplate>
</asp:UpdatePanel>
s<atk:UpdatePanelAnimationExtender
    ID="UpdatePanelAnimationExtender1" runat="server"
    TargetControlID="DepartmentsUpdatePanel"
    BehaviorID="Animation">
```

```
<Animations>
  <OnUpdating>
    <FadeOut AnimationTarget="gridContainer"
        minimumOpacity=".2" />
  </OnUpdating>
  <OnUpdated>
    <FadeIn AnimationTarget="gridContainer"
        minimumOpacity=".2" />
  </OnUpdated>
</Animations>
</atk:UpdatePanelAnimationExtender>
```

In this code, we first wrapped the grid in a `div` element, which is required for the animation. Then we added an `UpdatePanelAnimationExtender` extender targeting the `DepartmentsUpdatePanel`. The extender handles two events—`OnUpdating` and `OnUpdated`. We specify a fade-out animation to appear while the page is updating, and a fade-in animation to appear when it's finished updating. Execute the page in your browser and click on a few of the paging and sorting controls to enjoy the effect.

Animations can be far more complex than this simple example, but this should be enough to get you going.

jQuery

When performing some of the examples in this book, you may have noticed a **jQuery.js** file in the Scripts folder that comes by default with most created projects within Visual Web Developer. jQuery is a popular open-source JavaScript framework used by many websites to easily perform AJAX operations, animations, and other web development tasks. jQuery and JavaScript are both beyond the scope of this book, but it is important to note that Visual Web Developer includes a recent version of jQuery.

The three files here represent different outputs for version 1.6.2 of jQuery. The **vsdoc** file is for Visual Studio IntelliSense to work correctly if you choose to use jQuery within Visual Studio. The **min** file is a deployable file that represents the smallest possible format so browsers can easily download this file very quickly. Finally, the main **jquery-1.6.2.js** file is the human readable form.

To include jQuery in your presentation, you'll want to reference the script as such:

```
<script type="text/javascript" src="jquery-1.6.2-vsdoc.js"></script>
```

The website at http://www.jquery.com is the best resource to see examples and tutorials for using jQuery, as well as for getting the latest version. jQuery runs on a fast release schedule—currently at v1.6.2.

Summary

In this chapter, we started out by learning a bit about Ajax technology, and what ASP.NET AJAX has to offer. We used the UpdatePanel and the UpdateProgress controls on our Departments GridView to improve the user experience. We then employed AsyncPostBackTriggers and multiple UpdatePanels in our Address Book page to explore a more advanced, multi-UpdatePanel scenario.

Shifting gears, we examined the ASP.NET AJAX Control Toolkit and added it to Visual Web Developer. We then added some ValidationCallout control extenders to our Help Desk form before going on a short foray into the wonderful world of animation. While we didn't have the space here to fully examine every feature of ASP.NET AJAX or the ASP.NET AJAX Control Toolkit, you should now have the knowledge to start employing them in your own projects.

Appendix A: Web Control Reference

The following reference includes a list of important properties, methods, and events for some of the useful controls you'll find in the Visual Web Developer Toolbox.

We've grouped the lists of controls on the basis of their locations within the Toolbox:

- standard controls
- validation controls
- navigation controls
- Ajax controls

As well as the controls listed below, don't forget that any HTML element can be used with a `runat="server"` attribute value to access server-side features. We covered this capability in the section called "HTML Server Controls" in Chapter 4.

As almost all the web controls listed here are based on (or, more specifically, derived from) the `WebControl` class, they inherit its properties and methods. First up, let's review the more useful of these, which can be used with any of the web controls.

The `WebControl` Class

Properties

`AccessKey`	specifies a shortcut key that quickly selects a control without the user needing to use a mouse; the shortcut command is usually **Alt** plus a letter or number
`Attributes`	allows the accessing and manipulation of the attributes of the HTML code rendered by the control
`BackColor`	the control's current background color
`BorderColor`	color for the border
`BorderStyle`	style of border drawn around the web control; default is `NotSet`; other values are `None`, `Solid`, `Double`, `Groove`, `Ridge`, `Dotted`, `Dashed`, `Inset`, and `Outset`

`BorderWidth`	width of the border
`Controls`	a collection of all the controls contained within the web control (its child controls)
`CssClass`	indicates the style class within the current CSS stylesheet that should be applied to the web control
`Enabled`	determines whether the web control is active and able to receive user input
`EnableTheming`	determines whether the control uses themes
`Font`	a `FontInfo` object representing the control's current font; properties of `FontInfo` include `Bold`, `Italic`, `Name`, `Names`, `Overline`, `Size`, `Strikeout`, and `Underline`
`ForeColor`	the control's current foreground color
`Height`	the current height of the control
`SkinID`	the ID of the skin to be used by the control
`Style`	allows the manipulation of the CSS style elements through the returned `CssStyleCollection` object
`TabIndex`	defines the order in which controls on the page are selected when the user presses **Tab**; the lowest value is selected first
`Tooltip`	the text that appears in a popup when the cursor is hovered over the control
`Visible`	determines whether the control appears onscreen in the user's browser
`Width`	the current width of the control

Methods

`ApplyStyle`	copies an element of a `Style` object to a control

MergeStyle	copies an element of a `Style` object to a control but does not overwrite existing styles
DataBind	binds the web control to its data source

As well as the properties and methods described here, web controls offer additional properties and methods specific to each control. These are listed in the following sections.

Standard Web Controls

AdRotator

Properties

AdvertisementFile	specifies the path to the XML file that contains the list of banner advertisements
KeywordFilter	returns only advertisements that match a specific filter when the property is set
Target	displays the page in this window or frame; possible values are _child, _self, _parent, and _blank

Events

AdCreated	raised after an ad is retrieved from the advertisement file, but before the ad is rendered

BulletedList

Properties

BulletImageUrl	specifies the URL of the image used to display the bullets
BulletStyle	identifies the style of the bulleted list; can take one of the `BulletStyle` enumeration values: `Numbered` (1, 2, 3, ...), `LowerAlpha` (a, b, c, ...), `UpperAlpha` (A, B, C, ...), `LowerRoman` (i, ii, iii, ...), `UpperRoman` (I, II, III, ...), `Circle`, `CustomImage`, `Disc`, and `Square`

DisplayMode	determines the display mode, which can be Text (the default), or HyperLink (if you want the list to be formed of links)
FirstBulletNumber	specifies the value of the first bullet
SelectedIndex	the index of the selected item
SelectedItem	specifies the currently selected item as a ListItem object
SelectedValue	the Value of the selected ListItem object
Target	specifies the target window or frame in which new content should be displayed when a link is clicked; possible values are _blank, _parent, _search, _self, and _top
Text	the text of the BulletedList control

Events

Click	raised when the Button is clicked and the form is submitted to the server for processing

Button

Properties

CommandName	passes a value to the Command event when the Button is clicked
CommandArgument	passes a value to the Command event when the Button is clicked
CausesValidation	allows interaction with client-side validation controls; when False, validation does not occur
Text	specifies the text displayed by the Button
Visible	controls the visibility of the Button

Events

Click   raised when the Button is clicked and the form is submitted to the server for processing

Command   raised when the Button is clicked and the form is submitted to the server for processing; passes the values of the CommandName and CommandArgument properties

Calendar

Properties

CellPadding   specifies the number of pixels between a cell and border

CellSpacing   specifies the number of pixels between cells

DayHeaderStyle   specifies the style of the weekdays listed at the top of the calendar

DayNameFormat   sets the format of day names; possible values are FirstLetter, FirstTwoLetters, Full, and Short

DayStyle   specifies the style applied to each day in the calendar

FirstDayOfWeek   specifies which day of the week is displayed in the first column

NextMonthText   if ShowNextPrevMonth is True, specifies the text for the next month hyperlink

NextPrevFormat   specifies the format for the next and previous hyperlinks

NextPrevStyle   specifies the style to use for next and previous month links

OtherMonthDayStyle   specifies the style to use to display days of adjacent months within the current month's calendar

PrevMonthText   if ShowNextPrevMonth is True, specifies the text for the previous month hyperlink

SelectedDate	contains a date-and-time value that specifies a highlighted day
SelectedDates	contains a collection of date-and-time values that specify the highlighted days
SelectedDayStyle	specifies the style to use for the currently selected day
SelectionMode	determines whether or not days, weeks, or months can be selected; possible values are `Day`, `DayWeek`, `DayWeek-Month`, and `None`
SelectMonthText	contains the HTML text displayed in the month selector column; default value is `&gt;&gt;`, rendered as >>
SelectorStyle	specifies the style to be applied to the link for selecting week and month
SelectWeekText	contains HTML text displayed for selecting weeks when `SelectionMode` has the value `DayWeek` or `DayWeekMonth`
ShowDayHeader	if `True`, displays the names of the days of the week
ShowGridLines	if `True`, renders the calendar with a border around each day's cell
ShowNextPrevMonth	if `True`, displays links to the next and previous months
ShowTitle	if `True`, displays the calendar's title
TitleFormat	determines how the month name appears in the title bar; possible values are `Month` and `MonthYear`
TitleStyle	specifies the style to use for text within the title bar
TodayDayStyle	specifies the style to use for the current day
TodaysDate	specifies a `DateTime` value that sets the calendar's current date
VisibleDate	specifies a `DateTime` value that sets the month to display

`WeekendDayStyle`	specifies the style to use for weekend days

Events

`DayRender`	raised before each day cell is rendered on the calendar
`SelectionChanged`	raised when a new day, month, or week is selected
`VisibleMonthChanged`	raised by clicking the next or previous month links

CheckBox

Properties

`AutoPostBack`	when `True`, automatically posts the form containing the `CheckBox` whenever it's checked or unchecked
`Checked`	shows the `CheckBox` as checked if set to `True`
`Text`	specifies the text displayed next to the `CheckBox`
`TextAlign`	determines how the text associated with the `CheckBox` is aligned; possible values are `Left` and `Right`

Events

`CheckedChanged`	raised when the `CheckBox` is checked or unchecked

CheckBoxList

Properties

`AutoPostBack`	if `True`, automatically posts the form containing the `CheckBoxList` whenever a `CheckBox` is checked or unchecked
`CellPadding`	sets the number of pixels between the border and a particular `CheckBox`
`CellSpacing`	sets the number of pixels between individual `CheckBoxes` within the `CheckBoxList`

`DataMember`	represents the particular table within the data source
`DataSource`	represents the actual data source to use when binding to a `CheckBoxList`
`DataTextField`	represents the field within the data source to use with the `CheckBoxList` text label
`DataTextFormatString`	a format string that determines how the data is displayed
`DataValueField`	represents the field within the data source to use with the `CheckBoxList`'s value
`Items`	the collection of items within the `CheckBoxList`
`RepeatColumns`	determines the number of columns to use when displaying the `CheckBoxList`
`RepeatDirection`	indicates the direction in which the `CheckBoxes` should repeat; possible values are `Horizontal` and `Vertical`
`RepeatLayout`	determines how the checkboxes are formatted; possible values are `Table` and `Flow`; default is `Table`
`SelectedIndex`	represents the index selected within the `CheckBoxList`
`SelectedItem`	represents the item selected within the `CheckBoxList`

Events

`SelectedIndexChanged`	raised when a `CheckBox` within the `CheckBoxList` is selected

DropDownList

Properties

`AutoPostBack`	automatically posts the form containing the `DropDownList` whenever the selection in the list is changed
`DataMember`	represents the particular table within the data source

DataSource	represents the actual data source to use when binding to a DropDownList
DataTextField	represents the field within the data source to use with the DropDownList's text label
DataTextFormatString	specifies a format string that determines how the DropDownList is displayed
DataValueField	represents the field within the data source to use with the DropDownList's value
Items	the collection of items within the DropDownList
SelectedIndex	represents the index selected within the DropDownList
SelectedItem	represents the item selected within the DropDownList

Events

SelectedIndexChanged	raised when an item within the DropDownList is selected

FileUpload

Properties

FileBytes	returns the contents of the uploaded file as an array of bytes
FileContent	returns the contents of the uploaded file as a stream
FileName	returns the name of the file
HasFile	returns True if the control has loaded a file, and False otherwise
PostedFile	returns for the uploaded file an HttpPostedFile object whose properties can be used to obtain additional data about the file

Methods

SaveAs   saves the uploaded file to disk

HiddenField

Properties

Value   specifies the value of the hidden field

HyperLink

Properties

ImageURL   specifies the location of the image to use

NavigateURL   specifies the URL to navigate to when the hyperlink is clicked

Target   specifies the target window or frame to display for the URL; the possible values are _top, _blank, _self, and _parent

Text   specifies the text displayed by the HyperLink

Visible   controls the visibility of the HyperLink

Image

Properties

AlternateText   specifies the text to display within browsers that do not support images

ImageAlign   specifies one of ten possible values for image alignment; possible values include AbsBottom, AbsMiddle, Baseline, Bottom, Left, Middle, NotSet, Right, TextTop, and Top

ImageURL   specifies the location of the image to use

Visible   controls the visibility of the image

ImageButton

Properties

AlternateText	specifies the text to display within browsers that do not support images
CommandName	passes a value to the Command event when the ImageButton is clicked
CommandArgument	passes a value to the Command event when the ImageButton is clicked
CausesValidation	allows interaction with client-side validation controls; when False, validation does not occur
ImageAlign	specifies one of ten possible values for image alignment; possible values include AbsBottom, AbsMiddle, Baseline, Bottom, Left, Middle, NotSet, Right, TextTop, and Top
ImageURL	specifies the location of the image to use
Visible	controls the visibility of the ImageButton

Events

Click	raised when the ImageButton is clicked and the form is submitted to the server for processing
Command	raised when the ImageButton is clicked and the form is submitted to the server for processing; values of the CommandName and CommandArgument properties are provided with the event

ImageMap

Properties

Enabled	enables or disables the control

HotSpotMode   defines the behavior when a hot spot is clicked; possible values are `Inactive`, `Navigate`, `NotSet`, and `PostBack`

HotSpots   the `HotSpotCollection` object containing the `ImageMap`'s hot spots; hot spots are defined using three controls that generate hot spots of different shapes: `CircleHotSpot`, `RectangleHotSpot`, and `PolygonHotSpot`

Target   specifies the target window or frame where new content should be displayed when a link is clicked; the possible values are `_blank`, `_parent`, `_search`, `_self`, and `_top`

Events

Click   raised when a `HotSpot` object in the `ImageMap` is clicked and the form is submitted to the server for processing

Label

Properties

AssociatedControlID   specifies the ID of the server control with which the `Label` is associated and, if set, causes the control to be rendered as an HTML `label` element

Text   specifies the text displayed by the `Label`

Visible   controls the visibility of the `Label`

LinkButton

Properties

Text   specifies the text displayed by the `LinkButton`

CommandName   passes a value to the `Command` event when the `LinkButton` is clicked

CommandArgument   passes a value to the `Command` event when the `LinkButton` is clicked

CausesValidation	allows interaction with client-side validation controls; when `False`, validation does not occur
Visible	controls the visibility of the `LinkButton`

Events

Click	raised when the `LinkButton` is clicked and the form is submitted to the server for processing
Command	raised when the `LinkButton` is clicked and the form is submitted to the server for processing; values of the `CommandName` and `CommandArgument` properties are passed

ListBox

Properties

AutoPostBack	when `True`, automatically posts the form containing the `ListBox` whenever an item is selected
DataMember	specifies the particular table within the data source to use when binding
DataSource	represents the actual data source to use when binding
DataTextField	represents the field within the data source to use with the `ListBox`'s text label
DataTextFormatString	specifies a format string that determines how the `ListBox` is displayed
DataValueField	represents the field within the data source to use with the `ListBox`'s value
Items	the collection of items within the `ListBox`
Rows	indicates the number of rows to display within the `ListBox`; default value is 4
SelectedIndex	represents the index selected within the `ListBox`

SelectedItem	represents the item selected within the `ListBox`
SelectionMode	determines whether or not a user can select more than one item at a time; possible values are `Multiple` and `Single`

Events

SelectedIndexChanged	raised when an item within the `ListBox` is selected

Literal

Properties

Text	specifies the text displayed by the control

MultiView

Properties

ActiveViewIndex	specifies the index of the active view
Views	represents the `ViewCollection` object representing the collection of views

Methods

GetActiveView	returns the active view as a `View` object
SetActiveView	sets the active view to the `View` received as parameter

Events

ActiveViewChanged	fires when the active view of the `MultiView` changes

Panel

Properties

BackImageURL	the URL of the background image to use within the `Panel`

DefaultButton	specifies the ID of a button contained within the Panel that is the default button that's clicked should the user press the **Enter** key while the Panel has focus
HorizontalAlign	sets the horizontal alignment of the Panel; possible values are Center, Justify, Left, NotSet, and Right
Wrap	wraps the contents within the Panel when True; default value is True
Visible	controls the visibility of the Panel

PlaceHolder

Properties

Visible	controls the visibility of the PlaceHolder

RadioButton

Properties

AutoPostBack	automatically posts the form containing the RadioButton whenever checked or unchecked is True
Checked	shows the RadioButton as checked if set to True
GroupName	determines the name of the group to which the RadioButton belongs
Text	specifies the text displayed next to the RadioButton
TextAlign	determines how the text associated with the RadioButton is aligned; possible values are Left and Right

Events

CheckedChanged	raised when the RadioButton is checked or unchecked

RadioButtonList

Properties

AutoPostBack	automatically posts the form containing the RadioButtonList whenever checked or unchecked is True
DataMember	represents the particular table within the data source
DataSource	represents the actual data source to use when binding to a RadioButtonList
DataTextField	represents the field within the data source to use with the RadioButtonList's text label
DataTextFormatString	specifies a format string that determines how the RadioButtonList is displayed
DataValueField	represents the field within the data source to use with the RadioButtonList's value
RepeatColumns	the collection of items within the RadioButtonList
Items	determines the number of columns to use when displaying the radio buttons
RepeatDirection	indicates the direction in which the radio buttons should repeat; possible values are Horizontal and Vertical
RepeatLayout	determines how the radio buttons should repeat; possible values are Horizontal and Vertical
SelectedIndex	represents the index selected within the RadioButtonList
SelectedItem	represents the item selected within the RadioButtonList
SelectedItem	represents the item selected within the RadioButtonList

| TextAlign | determines how the text associated with the RadioButtonList is aligned; possible values are Left and Right |

Events

| SelectedIndexChanged | raised when a radio button within the RadioButtonList is selected |

TextBox

Properties

AutoPostBack	automatically posts the form containing the TextBox whenever a change is made to the contents of the TextBox
Columns	sets the horizontal size of the TextBox in characters
MaxLength	sets the maximum number of characters that may be entered
Rows	sets the vertical size of the multiline TextBox
Text	specifies the text displayed by the TextBox
TextMode	determines whether the TextBox should render as SingleLine, Password, or MultiLine
Visible	controls the visibility of the TextBox
Wrap	determines how a multiline TextBox wraps; if set to True, word wrapping is enabled

Events

| TextChanged | raised when the contents of the TextBox have changed |

Wizard

Properties

ActiveStep

represents the step that is currently displayed to the user

ActiveStepIndex

specifies the index of the current step

CancelButtonImageUrl

specifies the URL of the image displayed for the **Cancel** button

CancelButtonStyle

represents the style properties of the **Cancel** button

CancelButtonText

specifies the text for the **Cancel** button

CancelButtonType

specifies the type of button that's displayed as the **Cancel** button; possible values are Button, Image, or Link

CancelDestinationPageUrl

specifies the URL that the user is directed to when he or she clicks the **Cancel** button

CellPadding

specifies the amount of cell padding

CellSpacing

specifies the amount of cell spacing

DisplayCancelButton

enables or disables the display of a **Cancel** button

DisplaySideBar

enables or disables the display of the sidebar area

FinishCompleteButtonImageUrl

specifies the URL of the image displayed for the **Finish** button

FinishCompleteButtonStyle

represents the style properties of the **Finish** button

FinishCompleteButtonText

specifies the text for the **Finish** button

FinishCompleteButtonType

specifies the type of button that's displayed as the **Finish** button; possible values are `Button`, `Image`, or `Link`

FinishDestinationPageUrl

specifies the URL that the user is directed to when he or she clicks the **Finish** button

FinishNavigationTemplate

specifies the template used to display the navigation area on the **Finish** step

FinishPreviousButtonImageUrl

specifies the URL of the image displayed for the **Previous** button on the **Finish** step

FinishPreviousButtonStyle

represents the style properties of the **Previous** button on the **Finish** step

FinishPreviousButtonText

specifies the text for the **Previous** button on the **Finish** step

FinishPreviousButtonType

specifies the type of button that's displayed as the **Previous** button on the **Finish** step; possible values are `Button`, `Image`, or `Link`

HeaderStyle

represents the style properties of the header area

HeaderTemplate

specifies the template that's used to display the header area

HeaderText

specifies the text caption that's displayed for the header area

NavigationButtonStyle

represents the style properties for the buttons in the navigation area

NavigationStyle

represents the style properties for the navigation area

SideBarButtonStyle

represents the style properties for the buttons on the sidebar

SideBarStyle

represents the style properties for the sidebar area

SideBarTemplate

specifies the template that's used to display the sidebar area

SkipLinkText

specifies alternative text that notifies screen readers to skip the content in the sidebar

StartNavigationTemplate

specifies the template that's used to display the navigation area on the **Start** step

StartNextButtonImageUrl

specifies the URL of the image displayed for the **Next** button on the **Start** step

StartNextButtonStyle

represents the style properties of the **Next** button on the **Start** step

StartNextButtonText

specifies the text for the **Next** button on the **Start** step

StartNextButtonType

specifies the type of button that's displayed as the **Next** button on the **Start** step; possible values are `Button`, `Image`, or `Link`

StepNavigationTemplate

specifies the template that's used to display the navigation area on any step other than the **Start**, **Finish**, or **Complete** step

StepNextButtonImageUrl

specifies the URL of the image displayed for the **Next** button

StepNextButtonStyle

represents the style properties of the **Next** button

StepNextButtonText

specifies the text for the **Next** button

StepNextButtonType

specifies the type of button that's displayed as the **Next** button; possible values are Button, Image, or Link

StepPreviousButtonImageUrl

specifies the URL of the image displayed for the **Previous** button

StepPreviousButtonStyle

represents the style properties of the **Previous** button

StepPreviousButtonText

specifies the text for the **Previous** button

StepPreviousButtonType

specifies the type of button that's displayed as the **Previous** button; possible values are Button, Image, or Link

StepStyle

represents the style properties of the steps that are defined for the Wizard

WizardSteps

represents the steps that are defined for the Wizard control as a collection of WizardStepBase objects

Methods

GetHistory	returns all the steps that have already been accessed as a collection of WizardStepBase objects
GetStepType	returns the WizardStepType value for the specified WizardStepBase object
MoveTo	sets the ActiveStep property of the Wizard control to the specified WizardStepBase-derived object

Events

ActiveStepChanged   raised when the user switches to a new step

CancelButtonClick   raised when the **Cancel** button is clicked

FinishButtonClick   raised when the **Finish** button is clicked

NextButtonClick   raised when the **Next** button is clicked

PreviousButtonClick   raised when the **Previous** button is clicked

SideBarButtonClick   raised when a button in the sidebar is clicked

Xml

Properties

Document   specifies the `System.Xml.XmlDocument` object to display

DocumentContent   specifies a string representing the XML document to display

DocumentSource   specifies the URL of a document to display

Transform   specifies the `System.Xml.Xsl.XslTransform` object used to format the XML document

TransformArgumentList   specifies the `XsltArgumentList` used to format the XML document

TransformSource   specifies the URL of an XSLT stylesheet used to format the XML document

Validation Controls

The following reference includes a list of important properties, methods, and events for each of the validation controls. These controls ultimately derive from the `WebControl` class, meaning that they, like the web controls themselves, inherit its properties and methods. The more useful of these properties and methods are listed at the start of this appendix.

CompareValidator

Properties

ControlToCompare	specifies the ID of the control to use for comparing values
ControlToValidate	specifies the ID of the control that you want to validate
Display	shows how the error message within the validation control will be displayed; possible values are Static, Dynamic, and None; default is Static
EnableClientScript	enables or disables client-side validation; by default, is set to Enabled
Enabled	enables or disables client and server-side validation; the default is Enabled
ErrorMessage	specifies the error message that will be displayed to the user in any associated validation summary control; if no value is set for the Text property, this message also appears in the control itself
IsValid	has the value True when the validation check succeeds, and False otherwise
Operator	specifies the operator to use when performing comparisons; possible values are Equal, NotEqual, GreaterThan, GreaterThanEqual, LessThan, LessThanEqual, DataTypeCheck
Text	sets the error message displayed by the control when validation fails
Type	specifies the data type to use when comparing values; possible values are Currency, Date, Double, Integer, and String
ValueToCompare	specifies the value used when performing the comparison

Methods

Validate   performs validation and modifies the `IsValid` property

CustomValidator

ClientValidationFunction

specifies the name of the client-side function to use for validation

ControlToValidate

specifies the ID of the control that you want to validate

Display

shows how the error message within the validation control will be displayed; possible values are `Static`, `Dynamic`, and `None`; default is `Static`

EnableClientScript

enables or disables client-side validation; by default, is set as `Enabled`

Enabled

enables or disables client and server-side validation; by default, is set as `Enabled`

ErrorMessage

specifies the error message that will be displayed to the user

IsValid

has the value `True` when the validation check succeeds, and `False` otherwise

Text

sets the error message displayed by the control when validation fails

Methods

Validate   performs validation and modifies the `IsValid` property

Events

ServerValidate   the function for performing server-side validation

RangeValidator

Properties

`ControlToValidate`	specifies the ID of the control that you want to validate
`Display`	shows how the error message within the validation control will be displayed; possible values are `Static`, `Dynamic`, and `None`; default is `Static`
`EnableClientScript`	enables or disables client-side validation; set as `Enabled` by default
`Enabled`	enables or disables client and server-side validation; set as `Enabled` by default
`ErrorMessage`	specifies the error message that will be displayed to the user in any associated validation summary control; if no value is set for the `Text` property, this message also appears in the control itself
`IsValid`	has the value `True` when the validation check succeeds, and `False` otherwise
`MaximumValue`	sets the maximum value in the range of permissible values
`MinimumValue`	sets the minimum value in the range of permissible values
`Text`	sets the error message displayed by the control when validation fails
`Type`	specifies the data type to use when comparing values; possible values are `Currency`, `Date`, `Double`, `Integer`, and `String`

Methods

`Validate`	performs validation and modifies the `IsValid` property

RegularExpressionValidator

Properties

ControlToValidate specifies the ID of the control that you want to validate

Display shows how the error message within the validation control will be displayed; possible values are Static, Dynamic, and None; default is Static

EnableClientScript enables or disables client-side validation; set as Enabled by default

Enabled enables or disables client and server-side validation; by default, is set as Enabled

ErrorMessage specifies the error message that will be displayed to the user

InitialValue specifies the initial value by the ControlToValidate property

IsValid has the value True when the validation check succeeds, and False otherwise

Text sets the error message displayed by the control

ValidateExpression specifies the regular expression to use when performing validation

Methods

Validate performs validation and modifies the IsValid property

RequiredFieldValidator

Properties

ControlToValidate specifies the ID of the control that you want to validate

Display	shows how the error message within the validation control will be displayed; possible values are `Static`, `Dynamic`, and `None`; default is `Static`
EnableClientScript	enables or disables client-side validation; set as `Enabled` by default
Enabled	enables or disables client and server-side validation; by default, it is enabled
ErrorMessage	specifies the error message that will be displayed to the user in any associated validation summary control; if no value is set for the `Text` property, this message also appears in the control itself
InitialValue	specifies the initial value by the `ControlToValidate` property
IsValid	has the value `True` when the validation check succeeds, and `False` otherwise
Text	sets the error message displayed by the control when validation fails

Methods

Validate	performs validation and modifies the `IsValid` property

ValidationSummary

Properties

DisplayMode	sets the formatting for the error messages that are displayed within the page; possible values are `BulletList`, `List`, and `SingleParagraph`; these messages are the `ErrorMessage` properties of all validation controls for which validation has failed
EnableClientScript	enables or disables client-side validation; by default, is set as `Enabled`

`Enabled`	enables or disables client and server-side validation; by default, is set as `Enabled`
`HeaderText`	sets the text that is displayed to the user at the top of the summary
`ShowMessageBox`	when the value is set to `True`, an alert box listing form fields that caused errors is presented to the user
`ShowSummary`	enables or disables the summary of error messages

Navigation Web Controls

SiteMapPath

Properties

`CurrentNodeStyle`	the style used to display the current node
`CurrentNodeTemplate`	the template used to display the current node
`NodeStyle`	the style used to display `SiteMapPath` nodes
`NodeTemplate`	the template used to display nodes
`ParentLevelsDisplayed`	the maximum number of parent nodes to display
`PathDirection`	specifies the path direction display; possible values are `PathDirection.CurrentToRoot` and `PathDirection.RootToCurrent`
`PathSeparator`	the string used to separate path nodes
`PathSeparatorStyle`	the styles used to display the path separator
`PathSeparatorTemplate`	the template used to display the separator
`Provider`	the `SiteMapProvider` object associated with the `SiteMapPath`; the default site map provider is `XmlSiteMapProvider`, which reads its data from the **Web.sitemap** file

RenderCurrentNodeAsLink	when set to `True`, the current site map will be displayed as a link; default value is `False`
RootNodeStyle	the style used to display the root node
RootNodeTemplate	the template used to display the root node
ShowToolTips	specifies whether the node links should display tooltips when the cursor hovers over them
SiteMapProvider	a string representing the name of the `SiteMapProvider` object associated with the `SiteMapPath`
SkipLinkText	a string that describes a link to allow screen reader users to skip the control's content

Methods

DataBind	binds the `SiteMapPath` to its data source

Events

ItemCreated	fires when a new `SiteMapNodeItem` object is created
ItemDataBound	fires after a node item has been bound to the data source

Menu

Properties

Controls

returns a `ControlColection` object containing the menu's child controls

DisappearAfter

an integer representing how long, in milliseconds, a dynamic menu continues to display after the cursor ceases to hover over it; the default is `500`; when `DisappearAfter` is set to `-1`, the menu won't disappear automatically

DynamicBottomSeparatorImageUrl

a string representing the URL of an image to be displayed at the bottom of a dynamic menu item; this is usually a line that separates the dynamic item from the other items; value is empty (an empty string) by default

DynamicEnableDefaultPopOutImage

a Boolean value representing whether a dynamic menu that contains a submenu should be enhanced with the image specified by `DynamicPopOutImageUrl`; default value is `True`

DynamicHorizontalOffset

an integer representing the number of pixels by which a dynamic menu should be shifted horizontally relative to the parent menu item

DynamicHoverStyle

a `MenuItemStyle` object that allows you to control the appearance of a dynamic menu item when the cursor hovers over it

DynamicItemFormatString

a string used to set the text to be displayed for dynamic menu items on mobile devices that don't support templates

DynamicItemTemplate

the template to be used to render dynamic menu items

DynamicMenuItemStyle

the `MenuItemStyle` object that represents the styles used to render dynamic menu items

DynamicMenuStyle

the `SubMenuStyle` object that represents the styles used for rendering the dynamic menu

DynamicPopOutImageTextFormatString

a string representing the alternate text to be displayed instead of the image specified by `DynamicPopOutImageUrl`

DynamicPopOutImageUrl

a string representing the URL for the image to be displayed for a dynamic menu item that has a submenu when `DynamicEnableDefaultPopOutImage` is `True`

DynamicSelectedStyle

a `MenuItemStyle` object representing the style of a selected dynamic menu item

DynamicTopSeparatorImageUrl

a string representing the URL for an image to be displayed at the top of a dynamic menu item; this is usually a line that separates the dynamic item from the other items; the value is empty (an empty string) by default

DynamicVerticalOffset

an integer representing the number of pixels by which a dynamic menu should be shifted vertically relative to the parent menu item

Items

a `MenuItemCollection` that contains `MenuItem` objects, representing all the menu items

ItemWrap

a Boolean value representing whether the menu items' text should wrap

LevelMenuItemStyles

a `MenuItemStyleCollection` representing a collection of `MenuItemStyle` objects that define the styles to be applied to menu items, depending on their levels in the menu (the first object in the collection defines the style for the first menu level, the second object in the collection defines the style for the second menu level, and so on)

LevelSelectedStyles

similar to `LevelMenuItemStyles`, but applies to selected menu items

LevelSubMenuStyles

similar to `LevelMenuItemStyles`, but applies to submenu items

MaximumDynamicDisplayLevels

specifies the maximum number of dynamic menu levels to display; the default value is 3

Orientation

specifies the direction in which to display the menu items; can be set either to `Orientation.Horizontal` or `Orientation.Vertical`

PathSeparator

a Char value representing the character used to delimit the path of a menu item

ScrollDownImageUrl

a string representing the URL for an image to be displayed in a dynamic menu to indicate that the user can scroll down to see more menu items

ScrollDownText

alternate text for the image defined by ScrollDownImageUrl

ScrollUpImageUrl

a string representing the URL for an image to be displayed in a dynamic menu to indicate that the user can scroll up to see more menu items

ScrollUpText

alternate text for the image defined by ScrollUpImageUrl

SelectedItem

a MenuItem object representing the selected menu item

SelectedValue

a string representing the text of the selected menu item

SkipLinkText

a string representing alternate text to be used by screen readers to allow screen reader users to skip the list of links

StaticBottomSeparatorImageUrl

a string representing the URL for an image to be displayed at the bottom of a static menu item—usually a line that separates the static item from the other items; value is empty (an empty string), by default

StaticDisplayLevels

an integer representing the maximum number of levels to display for a static menu; default is 1

StaticEnableDefaultPopOutImage

a Boolean value representing whether a static menu that contains a submenu should be enhanced with the image specified by StaticPopOutImageUrl; default is True

StaticHoverStyle

a MenuItemStyle object that allows you to control the appearance of a static menu item when the cursor is hovered over it

StaticItemFormatString

a string used to set the text for static menu items displayed on mobile devices that don't support templates

StaticItemTemplate

the template to be used to render static menu items

StaticMenuItemStyle

the MenuItemStyle object that represents the styles used to render static menu items

StaticMenuStyle

the SubMenuStyle object that represents the styles used to render the static menu

StaticPopOutImageTextFormatString

a string representing the alternative text to be displayed instead of the image specified by StaticPopOutImageUrl

StaticPopOutImageUrl

a string representing the URL for the image to be displayed for a dynamic menu item that has a submenu, when StaticEnableDefaultPopOutImage is True

StaticSelectedStyle

a MenuItemStyle object representing the style of a selected static menu item

StaticSubMenuIndent

a Unit value representing the number of pixels by which submenus should be indented in a static menu

StaticTopSeparatorImageUrl

a string representing the URL for an image to be displayed at the top of a static menu item; this is usually a line that separates the static item from the other items; value is empty (an empty string) by default

Target

specifies the target window or frame in which content associated with a menu item should be displayed when the item is clicked; possible values are _blank, _parent, _search, _self, and _top

Methods

DataBind   binds the menu to its data source

FindItem   returns the MenuItem located at the path specified by the *valuePath* string parameter; that path must also contain the path separator, which is retrieved through the PathSeparator property

Events

MenuItemClick   fires when a menu item is clicked

MenuItemDataBound   fires when a menu item is bound to its data source

TreeView

Properties

AutoGenerateDataBindings

a Boolean value specifying whether the TreeView should automatically generate tree node bindings; default is True

CheckedNodes

a collection of TreeNode objects representing the checked TreeView nodes

CollapseImageToolTip

the tooltip for the image displayed for the "collapse" node indicator

CollapseImageUrl

a string representing the URL for a custom image to be used as the "collapse" node indicator

EnableClientScript

a Boolean value that specifies whether or not the `TreeView` should generate client-side JavaScript that expands or collapses nodes; `True` by default; when the value is `False`, a server postback needs to be performed every time the user expands or collapses a node

ExpandDepth

an integer representing the number of `TreeView` levels that are expanded when the control is displayed for the first time; default is `-1`, which displays all the nodes

ExpandImageToolTip

the tooltip for the image displayed for the "expand" node indicator

ExpandImageUrl

a string representing the URL for a custom image to be used as the "expand" node indicator

HoverNodeStyle

a `TreeNodeStyle` object used to define the styles of a node when the cursor is hovered over it

ImageSet

a `TreeViewImageSet` value representing the set of images to be used when displaying `TreeView` nodes; default values are `Arrows`, `BulletedList`, `Bulleted-List2`, `BulletedList3`, `BulletedList4`, `Contacts`, `Custom`, `Events`, `Faq`, `Inbox`, `News`, `Simple`, `Simple2`, `Msdn`, `WindowsHelp`, and `XPFileExplorer`; when not using one of these predefined sets, you should define these properties instead: `CollapseImageUrl`, `ExpandImageUrl`, `LineImagesFolder`, and `NoExpandImageUrl`

LeafNodeStyle

a `TreeNodeStyle` representing the style used to render leaf nodes

LevelStyles

a `TreeNodeStyleCollection` that contains the styles used to render the items in each `TreeView` level

LineImagesFolder

a string containing the path to a web-accessible folder that holds the image files used to connect child nodes to parent nodes; that folder must include these files: **Dash.gif**, **Dashminus.gif**, **Dashplus.gif**, **I.gif**, **L.gif**, **Lminus.gif**, **Lplus.gif**, **Minus.gif**, **Noexpand.gif**, **Plus.gif**, **R.gif**, **Rminus.gif**, **Rplus.gif**, **T.gif**, **Tminus.gif**, and **Tplus.gif**

MaxDataBindDepth

defines the maximum number of tree levels to bind to the `TreeView` control

NodeIndent

an integer representing the number of pixels by which child nodes in the tree will be indented

Nodes

a `TreeNodeCollection` containing the root nodes of the tree

NodeStyle

the `TreeNodeStyle` object that defines the default appearance of all tree nodes

NodeWrap

a Boolean value indicating whether the text in a node wraps

NoExpandImageUrl

a string representing the URL for a custom image that indicates nodes that cannot be expanded

ParentNodeStyle

the `TreeNodeStyle` object that defines the appearance of parent nodes

PathSeparator

the character used to delimit node values in the `ValuePath` property

PopulateNodesFromClient

a Boolean value that specifies whether or not node data should be populated dynamically when necessary, without posting back to the server; default value is `True`

RootNodeStyle

a `TreeNodeStyle` object that defines the appearance of the root node

SelectedNode

a string containing the value of the selected node

SelectedNodeStyle

a `TreeNodeStyle` object that defines the appearance of the selected node

ShowCheckBoxes

a `TreeNodeTypes` value that defines which tree nodes should be associated with text boxes; possible values are `All`, `Leaf`, `None`, `Parent`, and `Root`

ShowExpandCollapse

a Boolean value that determines whether or not expansion node indicators should be displayed

ShowLines

a Boolean value that determines whether or not linking lines between parent nodes and child nodes should be displayed

SkipLinkText

a string that describes the link that allows screen reader users to skip the content of this element

Target

specifies the target window or frame in which content associated with a menu item should be displayed when that item is clicked; possible values are `_blank`, `_parent`, `_search`, `_self`, and `_top`

Methods

CollapseAll	collapses all nodes
DataBind	binds the control to its data source
ExpandAll	expands all nodes
FindNode	returns the `TreeNode` object located at the path specified by the string parameter

Events

SelectedNodeChanged	fires when the currently selected item changes

TreeNodeCheckChanged   fires when a checkbox changes state

TreeNodeCollapsed   fires when a node is collapsed

TreeNodeExpanded   fires when a node is expanded

TreeNodePopulate   fires when a node that has its `PopulateOnDemand` property set to `True` is expanded

Ajax Web Extensions

ScriptManager

Properties

AllowCustomErrorsRedirect

specifies whether or not the custom errors section of the **Web.config** file is used in the case of an error occurring during an asynchronous postback request

AsyncPostBackErrorMessage

specifies the error message that's sent to the client browser when an unhandled error occurs during an asynchronous postback request

AsyncPostBackSourceElementID

specifies the ID of the control that initiated the asynchronous postback request

AsyncPostBackTimeout

specifies the time-out period in seconds for asynchronous postback requests

EnablePartialRendering

if set to `True`, allows the use of `UpdatePanel` controls to implement partial page updates

LoadScriptsBeforeUI

specifies if scripts are loaded before or after the page markup is loaded

ScriptPath

sets the root path of the location of ASP.NET AJAX or custom script files

Events

AsyncPostBackError	raised when an error occurs during an asynchronous postback request

Timer

Properties

Enabled	specifies if the Timer is active
Interval	specifies the length of the delay in milliseconds before a postback request will be initiated

UpdatePanel

Properties

ChildrenAsTriggers

specifies whether immediate child controls of the UpdatePanel can trigger an update of the panel

ContentTemplate

the template that defines the content of the panel

ContentTemplateContainer

a control object to which you can add child controls

Controls

a ControlCollection object containing the child controls for the UpdatePanel

IsInPartialRendering

indicates the UpdatePanel is currently being updated by an asynchronous postback request

RenderMode

specifies whether the UpdatePanel will be rendered as an HTML div (if set to Block) or span (if set to Inline) element

Triggers

an UpdatePanelTriggerCollection object containing all the registered triggers for the UpdatePanel

UpdateMode

specifies when the contents of the UpdatePanel are updated; possible values are Always or Conditional

Methods

Update   causes an update of the contents of the UpdatePanel

UpdateProgress

Properties

AssociatedUpdatePanelID

specifies the ID of the associated UpdatePanel

DisplayAfter

specifies the amount of time in milliseconds before the UpdateProgress control is displayed

DynamicLayout

specifies if the control is rendered dynamically

ProgressTemplate

the template that defines the content of the UpdateProgress control

Appendix B: Deploying ASP.NET Websites

One of the trickier parts of working with ASP.NET is deploying your application. First, unlike many traditional scripting languages such as PHP or classic ASP, ASP.NET is compiled. Second, SQL Server databases are not as easily transportable as other database like MySQL, for example, which many developers grew up with. Third, the complex nature of the framework may lead to many cases where things that work in development on your local machine fail on your remote web server, where you don't have nearly as many tools available to debug the issues.

But don't be intimidated—it's still possible to deploy ASP.NET applications quite easily using Visual Web Developer Express and the SQL Server Hosting Toolkit.

ASP.NET Hosting Considerations

Before worrying about how to deploy our applications, we should find a web host. Feel free to skip this section if you already have a host that you're satisfied with; if not, read on for some handy tips on how to choose a host. Given the bewildering array of ASP.NET hosting options available these days, you might find it helpful to remember these key points while you shop:

- You are first and foremost choosing a service provider. If you can't get quick answers to sales questions, don't delude yourself that the service department will be any better—it won't. Trust us, you *will* need to use the service department at some point.

- Making the decision solely on the basis of price is pure folly. Yes, you could save $2 a month or so with the cheapest options, but you generally get what you pay for in this world. Web hosting is a very low-margin business these days, and bargain-basement hosting is almost a no-margin business. Remember, your hosting fees are not dead money; they're paying for the equipment your site is running on, as well as the engineers looking after that equipment.

- Choose a service that has an upgrade path of some sort. It should offer semi-dedicated hosting, virtual private servers and/or dedicated boxes, along with run-of-the-mill shared hosting.

■ Make sure the host supports the version of the framework you're using in development. You may be surprised that at the time of writing, there are still some less reputable hosts that don't support ASP.NET 4 or even ASP.NET AJAX on .NET 2.0, both of which have long been released to manufacturing with Microsoft's full support. In addition, make certain the host provides the sort of database server you wish to use in your project.

■ Peruse the host's online troubleshooting documentation. Be wary if you can't find any documentation at all; but, if it exists, walk through some typical scenarios—such as deploying a database—to see if there's any guidance, and if such guidance is clear and intelligible. Good documentation general indicates a well-run operation with the resources to create such documentation, rather than a fly-by-night shop with limited resources.

■ If at all possible, choose a Windows Server 2008-based host. Windows Server 2008 has a new version of IIS with many features that are designed to make working with a remotely hosted ASP.NET website much, much easier. The early adoption of new technology by a host usually indicates that it's better funded, and has access to a larger skill base than the guys milking yet another year out of old equipment and operating systems.

■ Definitely visit online communities to ask any questions before you reach for the plastic, such as the hosting section of SitePoint forums.[1]

Using Visual Web Developer Express to Deploy ASP.NET Websites

The principal tool that Visual Web Developer Express offers to help you deploy your website is the **Copy Website** feature. It can be found through the **Solution Explorer** (it's the second button from the left) or via the **Website** menu's **Copy Website**... item. The deployment tools also support the deployment of the file system, a local IIS instance, a remote IIS instance using Front Page Server extensions, and/or a remote server via FTP. You'll probably use the FTP option to deploy your site, but we're going to use the local file system functionality in our example. This isn't to say that

---

[1] http://www.sitepoint.com/forums/forumdisplay.php?f=95

you can't use your favorite FTP client to push your files to your site, but Visual Web Developer Express's tool has a few advantages that we'll explore.

The time has come! Fire up Visual Web Developer Express, open your Dorknozzle project, and let's get started:

1. Click on the **Website** menu and select **Copy Website…** to open the website copy tool.

2. Click on the **Connect** button and leave **File System** selected. It's here that, when transferring your website to a remote host, you'd choose **FTP** and configure the connection using the credentials provided by your host or your network administrator. For now, we'll practice the process using the local file system.

3. Select a folder to deploy to. Since we're just practicing, and we'll remove it later, let's create a temporary folder for the time being. Type **C:\DorknozzleTemp** into the **Folder** field and click **Open**. Click **Yes** when prompted, to create the folder. Your screen should now look like Figure B.1.

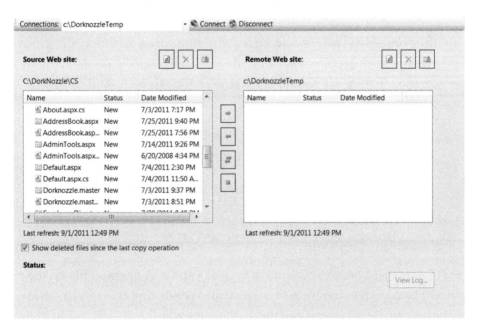

Figure B.1. Opening the remote website

4. Select all the files in your **Source Web site** panel and click on the double arrow button to synchronize all selected files. There should now be an identical list in both panes of the display.

Congratulations—you've just deployed the site with Visual Web Developer Express!

If you know anything about websites, you'll realize that changes and updates occur often and the challenge is keeping the live website synchronized and up to date. This is exactly where the **Copy Website** tool shines. Let's update the home page to see this in action. Open **Default.aspx**, and add a line of text like the one shown in bold here:

```
<h1>Company News</h1>
<p>We'll add some news later.</p>
<p>We added some news.</p>
<h1>Company Events</h1>
<p>We'll add company events later.</p>
```

Save the file and open the **Copy Website** tool again. Note that there is now a blue arrow next to the **Default.aspx** file icon and the status is now listed as **Changed**. Select everything, as we did earlier, and click the double-arrow button again. Since we're working locally, the action will be a little too quick for us to catch, but if we click the **View Log…** button, we should see that, even though we had all the files selected, only the **Default.aspx** has been updated:

```
Synchronize between 'C:\Dorknozzle\VB' and 'C:\DorknozzleTemp'
    started at date and time.

            Copy file Default.aspx from source to remote Web site.

Synchronize between 'C:\Dorknozzle\VB' and 'C:\DorknozzleTemp'
    is finished. Completed at date and time.
```

Don't forget that synchronization is a two-way street. A changed file on the remote site will be copied to the local site. The **Copy Website** tool will indicate when files on the remote site have been updated in the same way that it indicates local updates. Now that we're done, feel free to delete the **C:\DorknozzleTemp** folder at your leisure.

Do take care when using this tool—it can easily lead to accidental file overwrites if you're not careful. For example, your **Web.config** file is likely to be different in production than it is in your development setting and you don't want one overwriting the other. There isn't an **Undo** button, so be certain before you synchronize.

Deploying MVC Sites and Web Applications

One of the main differences between *websites* and *web applications* is how they are deployed. Websites will deploy all the code files, including the source code, to your hosting server. The first browser request for a page on your site will cause IIS to compile your **.cs** or **.vb** files. Subsequent requests don't have this compilation step unless your code files have changed. If you need to make a change on the server, you can do so quite quickly. You do not have an **App_Code** folder as part of Web Applications, as your project is compiled into a single DLL for deployment, along with only your **designer .aspx** files. There are many minor differences between the two project types, but our Dorknozzle MVC site was built as an application, to take advantage of our model, view, and controller design pattern. When you built the DorknozzleMVC project, you will have noticed that a single DLL was created.

One of the newer features of Visual Web Developer 2010 is the ability to *publish* these web applications automatically to the server or to a file system. This is very similar to the Copy Web Site feature we talked about above, but this will include the step for compiling your site into the DLL and copying the views only. To do this for our DorknozzleMVC project, we simply right-click on the project and select **Publish**. You will see a similar screen such as the one in Figure B.2

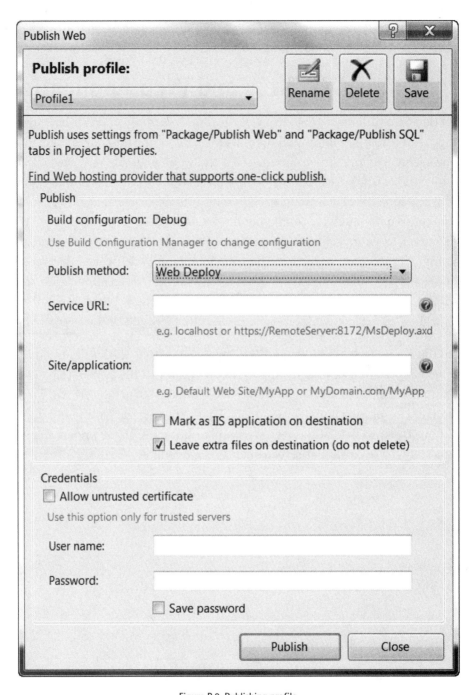

Figure B.2. Publishing profile

The publish feature can configure IIS on your host if it supports one-click deployments. Not all hosting providers allow for this, so click on the link provided on the

Publish screen to see a list of Microsoft-endorsed providers with this feature. If your host is without this feature, you can select to have the site deployed via file system or FTP as in the `Copy Web Site` feature by changing the Publish method on the same screen.

After publishing, your Build Window will contain notification that the **DorknozzleMVC.dll** file was compiled. The Publish system will also deploy the `asset` files, such as JavaScript files, CSS stylesheets, and images that have been included with your project. Figure B.3 shows the resulting output after publishing to the file system for our DorknozzleMVC project.

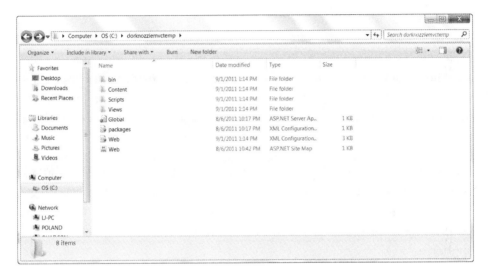

Figure B.3. Output after publishing to the file system

ASP.NET Deployment "Gotchas"

Deploying ASP.NET sites can be frustrating at times. Here are a few gotchas that could save you some time, some hair, your liver, or all three:

1. If you have disabled custom errors, it can be annoying receiving the following error message: `An application error occurred on the server. The current custom error settings for this application prevent the details of the application error from being viewed remotely (for security reasons). It could, however, be viewed by browsers running on the local server machine.` It usually indicates that the website you're using is configured

to use a version of ASP.NET that's different from the one your **Web.config** file wants. Be sure to double-check that with your host.

2. Most shared hosts run at a security level of Medium trust. You'll probably figure this out when you try to either access a file outside of the web root or access a remote URL and get the dreaded System.Security.SecurityException. The best solution is to run your application locally at the same security level, so that you can discover any issues ahead of time. To do so, add the following line to the system.web section of your **Web.config**:

```
<trust level="Medium" originUrl="" />
```

3. This issue isn't especially ASP.NET-specific, but it's worth remembering that you should never do anything in production without having a backup of the website's previous state in case something goes wrong when you push it to production. The previous working state of the website is often better than a non-functional website.

4. Hard-coded file paths will come back to bite you. Remember to resolve all paths using Server.MapPath (we used this method in the section called "Writing Content to a Text File" in Chapter 14), or handle the issue with configuration values. To assume that your site will always run in **C:\MyApplication** is not a wise approach.

5. Be certain that your host supports the features you wish to use. A good example would be ASP.NET AJAX support on ASP.NET 4.0, which some hosts are yet to install, even though it's been a production release for some time.

This is not a complete list of everything that can go wrong. It's probably worthwhile to look at the Microsoft recommended hosting providers conviently linked from within Visual Web Developer, or at Microsoft.com/web/hosting/. But remember: if you run into an insurmountable issue, contact your host or the server administrators. They're there to help you—in theory, at least!

Using the SQL Server Hosting Toolkit

As we saw above, deploying the website is fun and easy—it simply involves copying some files. By contrast, getting your database going can be very difficult if you're not careful. In this book, we've been using SQL Server Express, which has one very easy deployment option—user database instances in which the database file itself is included and deployed with the project. Unfortunately, many hosts don't support this feature, preferring to push users to a dedicated SQL Server instance, which renders this easy deployment and management option useless.

That said, SQL Server databases are notoriously hard to transfer if you don't have direct access to the server, which is even harder to obtain! Rather, you need a tool that can generate an SQL script that can be executed either from SQL Management Studio, or via an ASP.NET web page if you can't access even the database server directly. Your first approach might be to use the Generate Scripts functionality in SQL Server Management Studio Express, which works to some extent. It does a fine job of generating the scripts you'll use to create your database objects—the tables and stored procedures we made in this book. But it doesn't know what to do with your data, which is often a key feature in a database-driven web application.

Conveniently, Microsoft has created a very handy tool that's designed to help non-database administrators deploy SQL Server Databases: the SQL Server Hosting Toolkit. The software can be found on the Microsoft CodePlex website at http://sqlhost.codeplex.com/. Click on the **Database Publishing Wizard** link to grab the current release. Once you've downloaded the file, close all running Visual Web Developer Express instances and install the product with the default options.

Running the wizard is a piece of cake. Find **Microsoft SQL Server Database Publishing Wizard** in your **Start** menu, and then run the **Database Publishing Wizard**:

1. Click **Next** to get past the introductory page.

2. Specify **localhost\SqlExpress** in the **Server** field and leave **Use Windows Authentication** selected.

3. Select the Dorknozzle database, leave the **Script all objects in the selected database** box checked, and click **Next**.

4. Choose the **Script to file** option and select a handy location for the generated SQL file. Click **Next** to continue.

5. The **Select Publishing Options** page is a bit more interesting than the last few. Examine the options, but make sure you leave them set to the defaults before you

click **Next**. Be especially careful about the first option. If you're making an update to your database, you probably don't want to generate DROP statements, unless you actually want to delete your data.

6. Click **Finish** and let the tool create your SQL script.

Now browse to the location you chose in step 4 and open the script file with SQL Server Management Studio Express. You'll notice this is a rather obtuse mess of SQL code, but you should see a number of INSERT statements among the other SQL statements. In any case, given proper credentials, you'll be able to connect to your host's SQL server and execute this file to deploy your database.

There's one big potential land mine here: the script we created could include DROP statements. So, if we were pushing this into an existing database, we could very easily destroy all the existing data. And if there's one thing that will cost you dearly in the software development field, it's losing people's data. The rule of thumb is that before touching the production data, make absolutely certain you have a good backup of the database. Your host or database administrator should be able to help you with this problem. In its current version, this tool is better suited to initial deployments than it is to updating your application. Your own hand-crafted SQL ALTER scripts still rule the day on that front.

For further reading about the Hosting Toolkit, head over to the CodePlex site.[2] You'll also find a discussion forum[3] as well as several good tutorials and demonstrations that show how to make the best use of this tool to deploy your application in various scenarios.

Dealing with SQL Security

Another issue that drives many novice developers crazy is dealing with SQL Server security. We've not really had to touch on the subject in this book, as we've been relying on a default feature of SQL Server security, whereby local administrators are automatically granted full access to all databases and database objects. And, since we were using Visual Web Developer's built-in web server and Integrated Security features, our application was accessing the database in our context with

---

[2] http://www.codeplex.com/
[3] http://www.codeplex.com/sqlhost/Thread/List.aspx

full privileges. Running your application in the cold, hard world of the Internet will make things a bit more complex.

Your first resource should be your host or database administrator. They hold the keys to the bank—specifically, they can tell you which account you should be using to access your database. We explored the use of SQL Server authentication in the section called "Setting Up Database Authentication" in Chapter 9. In many cases with most web hosts, you'll have a single SQL user account to access the database, and that account will have database owner privileges to your database. However, depending on the host, your database account might be a bit more restricted.

To work around this issue, first ensure that the account in question has been created on the SQL Server and granted a login to your database. From there, you could take the easy way out by simply adding this account to the **db_owners** role. But beware—in this context, users can do just about anything they want to your database should they find a way to execute arbitrary commands. A better method is to assign only the required permissions. In most cases, you can achieve this by using a statement to grant the account privileges on the DBO schema:[4]

```
GRANT SELECT, INSERT, UPDATE, DELETE on SCHEMA :: DBO to account
```

This will allow the SQL user account to run SELECT, INSERT, UPDATE, and DELETE statements, while granting the account the powers necessary to execute stored procedures. However, it will not allow users to complete nefarious actions such as dropping or creating database objects.

---

[4] Note that in many shared hosting environments, your database might not be using the default DBO schema. If you examine the table names in SQL Server Management Studio Express, the name of the schema should be visible—your employee table will be called *xxx*.Employees rather than dbo.Employees.

Index

Symbols

!!, 68
!=, 68
$, 258
%, 332, 341
&, 68
&&, 68
', 34
( ), 62, 258
*, 68, 258, 324, 339
+, 68, 258, 339
++, 73
+=, 73
., 81, 258, 337
.NET Framework, 4–5, 6
/, 68, 339
/*, 34
//, 34
/>, 108
<, 68, 339
<!--, 37
<%--, 37
<%@, 32
<=, 68, 340
<>, 340
=, 68
==, 68, 69
>, 68, 339
>=, 68, 340
?, 258
@, 356, 380
[ ], 62, 530
\, 368

\\, 368
\d, 258
\s, 258
\S, 258
^, 258
_, 69, 332, 341
{ }, 22, 258
−, 339

A

About.aspx file, 164
ABS function, 342
access
    file-level, 605
    folder-level, 576, 616, 617, 628–632
    restricting (*see* forms authentication;
        memberships)
access modifiers, 83
AccessDataSource control, 508
AccessingData.aspx file, 366
accessors, 140–142
Account folder, 164
ActionLinks, 686–688
ActiveViewIndex property, 133
Add method, 380
addition, 68, 339
Admin Tools link, 606, 607
Administer Website, 608
AdminTools.aspx file, 604
ADO.NET
    about, 363–365
    building queries, 368–369
    connecting to ODBC, 365
    connecting to OLE DB, 365

connecting to Oracle, 365
connecting to SQL Server, 365
database authentication, 371–372, 373
DELETE, 428–431
displaying data, 375–376, 377
Entity Framework, 659
error handling, 385–387, 406, 408
ExecuteNonQuery method, 370
ExecuteReader method, 369, 370–371
ExecuteScalar method, 370
executing queries, 369–371
importing the SqlClient namespace, 366
initializing database connection, 367–368
INSERT, 405–411
selecting with parameters, 377–383
setting database owner, 374
SqlCommand, 365, 368–369
SqlCommandBuilder, 563
SqlConnection, 365, 367–368
SqlDataReader, 365, 375–376
storing procedures, 431–433
UPDATE, 411–428
user authentication, 373–375
ADO.NET Entity Framework, 659
AdRotator control, 124–128
ads.xml file, 126–127
aggregate functions, 348, 351–352
Ajax
about, 702–703
ASP.NET and, 703–704
jQuery and, 720–721
ScriptManager control, 703, 706, 708–709
ScriptManagerProxy control, 709
triggers, 710–713

UpdatePanel control, 704–706, 709–713
UpdateProgress control, 707, 708
Ajax Control Toolkit
about, 713–714
creating animations, 719–720
enabling for project, 718–719
ValidatorCalloutExtender, 715–718
AjaxControlToolkit.dll file, 715
alert box, 253, 254
allow tag, 583–584
AllowPaging property, 515, 522
AllowSorting property, 515, 552
ALTER PROCEDURE function, 358
AlternateViews property, 640
AlternatingItemStyle property, 460
AlternatingItemTemplate, 389, 439
and, 68
AND operator, 341
AndAlso, 68
animation, using Ajax Control Toolkit, 719–720
anonymous users, 576
AnonymousTemplate, 610, 611
App_Data folder, 13, 164
AppendText method, 623
Application object, 182, 188
application settings, configuring, 597–599
application state
about, 182–184
hit counter, 184–191
locking, 189–191
loss of data, 182
application variables, 182, 184
Application_AuthenticateRequest handler, 180

Application_AuthorizeRequest handler, 181

Application_BeginRequest handler, 180

Application_End handler, 180

Application_EndRequest handler, 180

Application_Error handler, 180

Application_PreSendRequestContent handler, 180

Application_PreSendRequestHeaders handler, 180

Application_Start handler, 180

appSettings tag, 598

arithmetic functions (T-SQL), 342–343

arrays, 60–63, 68, 75–76, 221–222

as keyword, 183

ASP, vs ASP.NET, 40–41, 192

ASP.NET
    about, 2–4
    Ajax and (see Ajax)
    ASP vs, 40–41, 192
    benefits of, 4–5
    client-side validation and, 239
    controls (see controls)
    deployment issues (see deployment)
    object oriented programming in, 140
    object-oriented programming in, 85–86
    pages (see ASP.NET pages)
    required software, 5–11
    resources, 25

ASP.NET Atlas (see Ajax)

ASP.NET controls (see controls)

ASP.NET pages
    about, 98–99
    code declaration blocks, 33–35
    code render blocks, 35–36
    creating new, 12–15, 31
    directives, 32–33, 44–45
    HTML in, 39–40
    life cycle, 28
    opening in browser, 22
    server-side comments, 37–39
    text in, 39–40

ASP.NET runtime, 28, 227

ASP.NET Web Site Administration Tool
    about, 588, 589
    configuring application settings, 597–599
    configuring authentication, 596–597, 598
    launching, 608

asp: prefix, 107

ASPNET account, 618, 619

aspnet_regsql.exe, 591–594

ASPNETDB database, 588–590, 591

aspnetdb.mdf, 595

aspnetdb_log.ldf, 595

AspNetSqlMembershipProvider, 600

AsyncPostBackTrigger, 710–713

Attachment class, 639

AttachmentCollection class, 639

Attachments property, 640

attachments, sending, 639

Authenticate method, 585

authentication
    about, 572
    configuring for site, 596–597
    cookieless, 581–582
    database, 367
    methods of, 573–574
    of users, 164, 179, 180–181, 373–375
    SQL Server, 371–372, 373
    of users, 164, 179, 180–181, 373–375

(*see also* forms authentication;
memberships)
authentication section, 179
authentication tag, 575–576, 581
authorization, 573
authorization section, 179
authorization tag, 582–584
Auto Format, 458, 459
autocompletion, of code, 169–170
AutoEventWireup attribute, 212
AutoGenerateDeleteButton property, 522
AutoGenerateEditButton property, 522
AutoGenerateInsertButton property, 522
AutoGenerateRows property, 486
AVG function, 352

B

background properties, 153
banner ads (*see* AdRotator)
Bcc property, 640
BETWEEN keyword, 330–331
BindGrid method, 483, 549
birthdate, validating, 251–252
bit data type, 285
block properties, 153
Body property, 640
BodyEncoding property, 640
boolean data type, 58
border properties, 154
BoundField control, 472, 477
box properties, 153
breadcrumb navigation, 131–132
break, 76
breakpoints, 222–223
browsers
    disabling JavaScript, 241–242
    JavaScript support, 239

setting default, 17, 174
BulletedList control, 118–119
BulletStyle property, 119
BulletStyleImageUrl property, 119
Button class, 81
Button control
    about, 111–112
    attributes, 51
    events, 48
    LinkButton, 442
    OnClick attribute, 48
ButtonField control, 477, 478–479

C

C#
    about, 46
    case sensitivity, 21, 70
    comments, 34
    data typing, 59, 453
    declaring variables, 57
    default page code, 18
    marking code blocks, 22
    setting with Language attribute, 33
    specifying in Visual Web Developer,
        12
cache dependencies, 193
Cache object, 192–194
Calendar control, 119–124, 204
call stack, 229
Camel Casing, 107
candidate key, 289
cascading style sheets (CSS)
    about, 149–150
    associating, 150–151
    declaring, 152–153
    properties, 153–156
case sensitivity, 21, 70, 286

case statements, 70

Cassini, 172, 173, 617

casting, 183

catch (errors), 220, 231, 406, 408

categoryComm, 404

CausesValidation property, 244

CC property, 640

CEILING function, 342

ChangeExtension, 634

ChangePassword control, 606

char data type, 286

character data type, 58

CHARINDEX function, 345

CheckBox control, 113

CheckBoxField control, 477

CheckBoxList control, 118

CheckChanged event, 113, 114

Choose Data Source, 458

CircleHotSpot, 114

class libraries, 87

classes, 78–80, 82, 93

clearing fields, 420

Click event, 48, 50, 51, 104

closing tags, 108

Codd, E.F., 273

code blocks

    in C#, 22

    in VB, 22

code declaration blocks, 33–35

code editor, 166–168

Code Project, 67

code regions, 168

code render blocks, 35–36

code-behind files

    about, 88

    creating, 89–91

    inheritance and, 85, 93

script tags vs., 92

storing user data in, 578

viewing, 166–168

working with, 17, 91–94

CodeFile attribute, 212

Combine, 634

CommandArgument property, 442

CommandField control, 477, 492–494

CommandName property, 442

CommandType property, 433

comments

    C#, 34

    HTML, 38

    server-side, 37–39

    SQL, 356

    VB, 34

CompareValidator control, 248–251

compilation errors, 225

compilation section, 179

compiling, 28

concatenation, 68, 69

conditional logic, 69–71

CONFIG folder, 176

configuration element, 178

configuration errors, 224

configuration files

    Global.asax, 164, 180–182, 192

    Machine.config, 176, 182, 594, 600

    Web.config (see Web.config file)

configuration section groups, 178

configuration section handlers, 179

configuration sections, 178–180

ConfigurationManager, 398

ConfigurationManager class, 598

connection strings

    for LocalSqlServer, 593, 594, 595

    for SQL Server Express, 367

for SqlDataSource, 512

storing in Web.config, 397–398

constraints, database, 289, 301, 355

constructors, 82

Content control, 147

ContentLength property, 636

ContentPlaceHolder control, 145–149

ContentType property, 636

control events, 48–53

controls

about, 99

data (*see* DetailsView control; Grid-
View control)

data retention, 448

extending, 715–718

HTML server, 99–106

in templates, 447

validator (*see* validator controls)

web server (*see* web controls)

web user (*see* web user controls)

ControlToCompare property, 249

ControlToValidate property, 248, 249

conversion, of data types, 58–60, 66–67,
183, 453, 667

Convert.ToInt32, 454

cookieless attribute, 581–582

cookies, 195–197, 574, 581–582, 587

Cookies property, 195

Copy Website tool, 766

COUNT function, 348

CREATE PROCEDURE function, 356–358

CreateTables.sql file, 295

CreateText method, 622

CreateUserWizard control, 588, 606

credentials tag, 584–585

CSS style sheets

creating, 201–203

location of, 164

setting width property, 138

styling GridView, 474–475

styling validation controls, 248, 717–
718

styling web server controls, 204

themes, 200–201, 206

CssClass attribute, 248

CssClass property, 138, 154–156

currency data type, 285, 286

customErrors element, 226–227

customErrors section, 179

CustomValidator control, 258–261

D

data adapters, 539

data binding

about, 37, 388

DataBind method, 398–405

in DataList, 444–445

to DataSets, 540–545, 551–562

drop-down list using, 400

HtmlEncode property, 571

OnDataBinding attribute, 51

to SqlDataSource, 510–516, 519–521

to LINQDataSource, 667–670

data controls (*see* DetailsView control;
GridView control)

data keys, 483, 503

data readers, 536, 537

data sets

about, 535–538

classes required, 538–539

filtering, 562–563

handling multiple requests, 536

storing in view state, 548–551

updating database with, 563–567

data source controls
  about, 508–509
  AccessDataSource, 508
  EntityDataSource, 509
  LinqDataSource, 508
  ObjectDataSource, 509
  SiteMapDataSource, 509
  SqlDataSource (*see* SqlDataSource)
  XmlDataSource, 509
data storage
  (*see also* application state*;* session
      state)
  application state vs session state, 182
  Cache object, 192–194
  cookies, 195–197
data types
  (*see also* specific data types, e.g. char
      or int)
  about, 56
  converting, 58–60, 66–67, 183, 453,
      667
  list of, 58
  for parameters, 380–381
  in SQL Server, 285–286
  Type property, 250
  validating, 250–251, 383, 384
data typing
  in JavaScript, 59
  in LINQ, 666, 667
  in VB and C#, 59, 453
database authentication, 371–372, 373
database design, 280–285, 299–301
database diagrams
  about, 304
  creating, 304–308
  creating relationships, 308–311
  diagram editor, 307

one-to-many relationships, 313
Database Publishing Wizard, 771
database servers, 274
database tables
  (*see also* keys)
  about, 275–276
  adding data, 352–353, 405–411
  constraints, 289, 301
  creating, 290–293
  creating with SQL scripts, 295
  data types, 285–286
  DEFAULT property, 287
  default values, 287, 288
  deleting data, 354–355, 428–431
  IDENTITY property, 287, 289–290,
      291
  mapping tables, 315–316
  NULL property, 287, 288
  outputting as HTML tables, 391, 435
  populating, 296
  querying (*see* LINQ*;* MVC*;* SQL)
  relationships between (*see* relation-
      ships)
  setting properties, 291, 292
  updating data, 314, 353–354, 411–428
databases
  about, 274–275
  creating, 276–280
  data sets vs, 540
  design phase, 280–285
  location of files, 164
  normalizing, 284
  querying (*see* ADO.NET*;* LINQ*;* MVC*;*
      SQL)
  relational, 299–301
  security issues, 570
  setting owner, 374

setting permissions, 773
updating using data sets, 563–567
User Instance, 590
DataBind method, 398
DataColumn class, 538
DataContext object, 660
DataField property, 472
DataKeyNames property, 515, 522
DataList control
   about, 435–436
   accessing controls, 447
   accessing events, 440, 442
   basic format, 436–438
   data binding in, 444–445
   editing items, 448–456
   editing templates, 457–458
   ItemCommand event, 442–444
   refreshing, 449
   Repeater vs, 438
   smart tags, 458
   styling, 458–461
DataRelation class, 538
DataRow class, 538
DataSet class
   about, 538
   binding to GridView, 540–545
   paging, 546–548
   selecting data, 543
   sorting with GridView, 551–562
   storing in view state, 548–551
   structure, 539–540
DataSource property, 398
DataSourceID property, 515, 522
DataTable class, 538, 544–546, 551–552
DataView class, 538, 551–552, 562
date formats, 251
date functions, 346–347

DATEADD function, 347
DATEDIFF function, 347
DATEPART function, 347
DateTime class, 23
datetime data type, 285
DAY function, 347
DayNameFormat property, 122
DbDataAdapter class, 538
DBML designer, 662
debugging
   breakpoints, 222–223
   compilation errors, 225
   configuration errors, 224
   custom errors, 226–227
   enabling, 176–177
   handling exceptions, 227–232
   in Internet Explorer, 16, 173
   Locals window, 222, 224
   parser errors, 224
   run-time errors, 219–221
   setting start page, 213
   starting, 218
   stopping, 198
   syntax errors, 224–225
   toolbar options, 223–224
   in Visual Web Developer, 15–16, 172–175
   Watch window, 221–222, 224
decimal data type, 58
DEFAULT property, 287
Default.aspx
   about, 164
   adding master page, 210
   C# version, 18, 168
   creating, 13–15, 211
   deleting, 211
   VB version, 19, 167, 168

defaultRedirect attribute, 227

DefaultView property, 551–552

DELETE query, 428–431

DELETE statement, 354–355

DeleteCommand property, 563

DeliveryNotificationOptions property, 640

deny tag, 576, 583–584

deployment

  ASP.NET issues, 763

  choosing a host, 763–764

  of MVC sites, 767–769

  security issues, 772–773

  with SQL Server Hosting Toolkit, 770–772

  troubleshooting, 769–770

  with Visual Web Developer Express, 764–767

Design view, 166

DetailsView control

  about, 482–483

  adding data, 527–529

  basic format, 483–486, 487

  binding to SqlDataSource, 519–521

  customizing fields, 486

  default fields, 488

  display mode, 495–496

  drop-down lists, 531–534

  edit mode, 488–490, 492–496

  editing fields, 496–498

  events, 490–492

  properties, 522

  refreshing, 709–713

  storing record data, 503

  styling, 487

  synchronizing with GridView, 526–527

  templates, 498

  updating header, 524–525

  updating items, 500–504

dictionaries, 182

Dim keyword, 57, 79

directives, 32–33, 44–45

directories, accessing, 576, 616, 617, 628–635

Directory class, 628

DirectoryInfo class, 628

disconnected data, 535, 537

Display property, 245–246

DisplayMode property, 118

Dispose method, 621–622

DISTINCT keyword, 326–329

div element, 116

division, 68, 339

Do loops, 71–74

DROP statement, 772

drop-down lists, in DetailsView, 531–534

DropDownList control, 74, 117, 217, 399–405, 628–631

E

EditItemIndex property, 439, 449

EditItemStyle property, 461

EditItemTemplate, 439, 498

EditItemTemplate template, 448–456

email

  classes, 639

  creating, 643–645, 646, 649–650

  images in, 646–647, 650

  properties, 639–640

  restricting sender, 645

  sending group messages, 647–649

  sending single message, 641–643

  storing addresses, 177

EnableViewState property, 43
encryption, 572
End Sub, 22
entities, 280, 659
EntityDataSource control, 509
equals, 68
Equals method, 86
error messages
  customizing, 226–227, 248
  in ADO.NET, 406, 408
  summarizing, 252–253
ErrorMessage property, 248
errors (*see* debugging)
  catching, 220, 231, 406, 408
  in deployment, 769–770
escaping (of special characters), 571
event handlers
  about, 48–50
  components of, 51–53
  for page events, 55
  generating code for, 270
  in Global.asax, 181
event receivers, 84
event senders, 84
EventArgs, 53
events
  (*see also* specific events, e.g. Click
    event)
  about, 48
  application-wide, 180–181
  control, 48–53
  in templates, 440, 442
  page, 53–56, 57
  senders and receivers, 84
Exception class, 220, 231–232
exceptions, handling, 227–232
  (*see also* errors)

Execute method, 664
ExecuteNonQuery method, 370, 405, 410
ExecuteQuerymethod, 663–664
ExecuteReader method, 369, 370–371
ExecuteScalar method, 370
Exit, 76
exponents, 343
extension methods, 657

F

File class, 616
file length, retrieving, 636
FileBytes property, 636
FileContent property, 636
FileName property, 636, 637, 638
filenames, retrieving, 628, 629, 631–632,
    634
filenames, retrieving property, 636
files
  allowing access to, 605
  manipulating (*see* text files)
  reading, 636
  sharing, 617–619
  text (*see* text files)
  uploading, 616, 635–639
file-sharing, 617–619
FileStream class, 616
FileUpload control, 135, 635–638
Fill method, 543
FindControl method, 447
Firefox
  disabling JavaScript, 241
  width property, 138
First method, 657
FirstDayOfWeek property, 122
float data type, 285, 286
FLOOR function, 343

folders, accessing, 576, 616, 617, 628–632

font properties, 153

footers, setting, 148

FooterStyle property, 461

FooterTemplate, 389, 439

For Each loops, 75–76

For loops, 71, 74–75, 76

foreign keys, 301–302, 308–311, 312–314, 354

form tag, 31, 37, 98

forms authentication

    (*see also* memberships)

    about, 573, 574

    configuring, 581–582

    enabling in Web.config, 575–576

    logging users out, 587

    performing, 577–580

    selecting, 596

    storing user data, 584–587

    user login, 577, 578, 580

    using URL, 581

forms authorization, 582–584

forms tag, 581–582

Friedl, Jeffrey E., 256

From property, 640

Function keyword, 63

functions, 63–66, 70

G

GET, 688

Get accessor, 141–142

GETDATE function, 347

GetDirectories method, 628

GetDirectoryName, 633, 634

GetExtension, 633, 634

GetFileName, 633, 634

GetFileNameWithoutExtension, 633, 634

GetFiles, 631–632

GetFiles method, 628

GetFileSystemEntries, 631–632

GetFileSystemEntries method, 628

GetFullPath, 635

GetHashCode method, 86

GetPathRoot, 635

GetTempFileName, 635

GetTempPath, 635

GetType method, 86

Global.asax file, 164, 180–182, 192

globalization section, 179

graphic, as button, 112

greater than (>), 68

greater than or equal to (>=), 68

greater-than, 339

greater-than or equal-to (>=), 340

gridSortDirection property, 558–561

gridSortExpression property, 558–561

GridView control

    about, 464

    adding columns, 478–479

    adding fields, 479

    basic format, 464–468

    binding to DataSet, 540–545, 546

    binding to SqlDataSource, 510–516

    combining with DetailsView, 483–486

    customizing display, 471–472, 473

    default display, 469–470

    edit mode, 488–490, 492–496

    editing columns, 496

    events, 490, 491–492

    paging, with DataSets, 546–548

    paging, with SqlDataSource, 515, 518

    properties, 515

    refreshing, 515, 704–707, 709–713

Repeater vs, 465
selecting records, 477–482
smart tags, 473
sorting columns, 516–518
sorting DataSets, 551–562
storing record data, 483
styling, 472–477, 516
synchronizing with DetailsView, 526–527
templates, 498
UpdatePanel and, 705
GROUP BY clause, 347, 349–350
Guthrie, Scott, 671

H

Handles keyword, 269
HasExtension, 635
HasFile property, 636, 637
HashForStoringInConfigFile method, 587
hashing, 572, 586–587, 601
HAVING clause, 347, 350–351
Headers property, 640
headers, setting, 148
HeaderStyle property, 460
HeaderTemplate, 389, 439, 524–525
hidden fields, 43, 571
HiddenField control, 111
HighlightCssClass property, 717–718
hit counter, 184–191
Host property, 641, 651
host, choosing, 763–764
hot spots, 114–115
HotSpotMode property, 115
HTML
    comments, 38
    div element, 116
    img tag, 114, 646, 650

in ASP.NET pages, 39–40
ol element, 118
select element, 117
for server controls, 99
special characters, 650
tables, 391, 435, 469
ul element, 118
viewing source, 24
web controls and, 107
HTML server controls, 99–106
HtmlAnchor control, 100
HtmlButton, 101
HtmlButton control, 100
HtmlEncode property, 571
HtmlForm control, 100, 101
HtmlGenericControl, 100
HtmlImage control, 100
HtmlInputButton control, 100
HtmlInputCheckBox control, 100
HtmlInputFile control, 100
HtmlInputHidden control, 100
HtmlInputImage control, 100
HtmlInputRadioButton control, 100
HtmlInputText, 101
HtmlInputText control, 100
HtmlSelect, 101
HtmlSelect control, 100
HtmlTable control, 100
HtmlTableCell control, 100
HtmlTableRow control, 100
HtmlTextArea control, 100
HttpCookie class, 195
HttpPostedFile object, 636
HTTPS protocol, 572
HttpUtility.HtmlEncode method, 571
HyperLink control, 113
HyperLinkField control, 478

I

identity columns, 287, 290, 296, 299

identity increment, 287

IDENTITY property, 287, 289–290, 291, 410

identity seed, 287

If statements, 69

IIf statement, 526

IIS, permissions, 617–618

Image control, 114

ImageButton control, 112–113

ImageField control, 478

ImageMap control, 114–115

images, in emails, 646–647, 650

ImageUrl attribute, 113

img tag, 114, 646, 650

Import directive, 32, 45, 92

IN, 341

IN operator, 332–333

Inactive mode, 115

incrementing variables, 73

IndexOutOfRangeException, 220

inheritance, 84–85, 93

initialization, 57

inline code, 35–36

inline expressions, 35, 36

Insert method, 193

INSERT query, 405–411

INSERT statement, 352–353

InsertCommand property, 563

inserting elements, 115

InsertItemTemplate, 498

instance methods, 622

instantiating a class, 82

int data type, 285

integer data type, 58

Integrated Security attribute, 367, 371

IntelliSense, 169–170

Internet Explorer

debugging in, 16, 173

disabling JavaScript, 242

setting as default, 17

Is Nothing, 188

IsBodyHtml property, 640, 649

IsPathRooted, 635

IsPostBack property, 403–404

IsValid property, 242–244, 265

ItemCommand event, 442–444

ItemDeleted event, 491

ItemDeleting event, 491

ItemInserted event, 491

ItemInserting event, 491

ItemStyle property, 460

ItemTemplate, 389, 438, 439, 498

ItemUpdated event, 491

ItemUpdating event, 491, 500

ItemUpdating method, 501

J

JavaScript

AJAX library, 703

browser support, 239

data typing, 59

disabling, 241–242

DOM scripting and, 702

file location, 164

in script tags, 35

security issues, 571

validation and, 236–237

joining tables, 337–338

jQuery, 164, 720–721

K

keys
  data, 483, 503
  foreign, 301–302, 308–311, 312–314,
    354
  multi-column, 289, 316
  numeric vs non-numeric, 289
  primary, 288–290, 292
KeywordFilter property, 127

L

Label control
  about, 15
  adding in Design view, 184–185, 186
  adding text using, 107, 110
  namespace differences, 109
  with Button control, 111
Language attribute (Page directive), 33,
    212
language attribute (script tag), 34–35
language, specifying in Visual Web De-
    veloper, 162, 206
LEN function, 345
less than (<), 68
less than or equal to (<=), 68
less-than (<), 339
less-than or equal-to (<=), 340
libraries, 87
LIKE keyword, 331–332
limiting query results, 334–335
line continuation symbol, 69
LinkButton control, 113, 442
LINQ (Language-Integrated Query)
  about, 655–657
  binding to GridView, 667–670
  connecting to database, 657–660

data typing, 666, 667
direct queries, 663–664
editing data, 669
extension methods, 657
querying database, 660–661
relationship, 662–663
storing procedures, 665–667
updating data, 661–662
LinqDataSource control, 508
LINQ-to-SQL data classes, 659
list controls
  (see also DataList)
  BulletedList, 118–119
  CheckBoxList, 118
  DropDownList, 74, 117, 217, 399–405,
    628–631
  ListBox, 117
  RadioButtonList, 118
list properties, 154
ListBox control, 117
Literal control, 110, 442
localhost port, 173
Locals window, 222
LocalSqlServer, 593, 594, 595
Lock method, 189–191
locking
  application state, 189–191
  session state, 191
LoggedInTemplate, 611–612
login attempts, 601
Login control, 606, 607–608
login page, 577–580
Login.aspx, 577
LoginName control, 606, 611
LoginStatus control, 606, 611–612
loginUrl attribute, 581
LoginUser method, 579

LoginView control, 606, 611–612
logout functionality, 587
Logout link, 611
loops
    Do or While, 71–74
    exiting, 76–77
    For, 71, 74–75, 76
    For Each, 75–76
LOWER function, 343
LTRIM function, 344

M

Machine.config file, 176, 182, 594, 600
MailAddress class, 639
MailAddressCollection class, 639
MailMessage class, 639–640, 649
MailMessage object, 643
many-to-many relationships, 314–316
MapPath method, 623–624
mapping tables, 315–316
Master Page template, 146, 147
master pages
    about, 144–149, 165
    adding ScriptManager, 708–709
    benefits of, 610
    creating, 147, 148, 149, 206–210
    in MVC, 681–683
    template, 146
    using, 210–213, 214
MAX function, 352
MaximumValue property, 251
memberships
    about, 588
    authenticating users, 607–608
    creating roles, 599
    creating users, 599–600, 602

customizing user display, 605–606, 608–613
    password strength requirements, 600–601
    restricting access, 603–605
    storing in ASPNETDB, 588–590
    storing in your database, 590, 596
    user management, 606
Menu control, 133, 208
menu, building, 208
methods
    about, 81–82
    extension, 657
    instance, 622
    shared, 622
    static, 622
MIME type, retrieving, 636
MIN function, 352
MinimumValue property, 251
MOD function, 343
mode attribute, 227
ModeChanged event, 491
ModeChanging event, 491
ModeChanging event signature, 494–495
money data type, 285, 286
MONTH function, 347
multi-column keys, 316
multiplication, 68, 339
MultiView control, 133–134, 135
MVC
    about, 671–672
    ActionLinks, 686–688
    adding controllers, 677, 678
    connecting to database, 680–681
    Create, 695–696
    deployment issues, 767–769
    Details, 688

Edit, 688
file locations, 683
master pages and, 681–683
scaffolding, 679
SiteMapDataSource and, 683
Views, 672, 684–686
mySubName(), 52

N

name attribute, 581
namespaces
.NET Framework Class Library, 87–88
in Default.aspx, 168
importing, 92, 620
System.Configuration, 398, 541, 598
System.Data, 541
System.Data.SqlClient, 364, 366, 541
System.IO, 615–616, 620, 628
System.Net.Mail, 639
System.Web.Security, 574
System.Web.UI.WebControls, 109
System.Windows.Forms, 109
Navigate mode, 115
nchar data type, 286
.NET Framework, 4–5, 6
.NET Framework Class Library, 23, 87–88
.NET Framework Class Library, 23, 87–88
new keyword, 62
new operator, 68
NextPrevFormat property, 122
normalization, 284
not equal to, 68, 340
NOT operator, 341
NotSet mode, 115
Now property, 23

NULL property, 287, 288
nvarchar data type, 286, 380

O

Object class, 86
Object control, 53
object data type, 58
object oriented programming
about, 77–78
classes, 78–80, 82
constructors, 82
disposing of objects, 621–622
inheritance, 84–85, 93
methods (see methods)
namespaces (see namespaces)
in .NET, 85–86, 140
objects, 78–80
partial classes, 93
properties, 80–81 (see properties)
scope, 83–84
ObjectDataSource control, 509
objects, 78–80, 621–622
ODBC, and ADO.NET, 365
offset, 60
ol element, 118
OLE DB, and ADO.NET, 365
OnCheckChanged attribute, 113, 114
OnClick attribute, 48, 51, 111
OnCommand attribute, 51
OnDataBinding attribute, 51
OnDisposed attribute, 51
one-to-many relationships, 312–313
one-to-one relationship, 312
OnInit attribute, 51
onitemcommand property, 443
onitemupdating property, 501
OnLoad attribute, 51

OnPreRender attribute, 51
OpenText method, 624, 626
Opera, disabling JavaScript, 242
Operator property, 250
operators
    ASP.NET, 67–69
    SQL, 338–341
or, 68
OR operator, 340
Oracle, and ADO.NET, 365
ORDER BY clause, 333–334, 513, 514
OrElse, 68
out parameters, 383

P

Page class, 85–86
Page directive, 32–33, 43, 45, 92, 147
page events, 53–56, 57
Page.Validate method, 265
Page_Init event, 54
Page_Load event, 54, 56
Page_Load method, 19–22, 185–187
Page_PreRender event, 54
Page_UnLoad event, 54, 56
PageIndexChanged event, 491
PageIndexChanging event, 491
pages
    master (see master pages)
    storing multiple, 133, 135
    switching, 134
pages section, 179
PageSize property, 515
Panel control, 116–117
parameterized queries, 530
parameters
    in ADO.NET, 377–383
    in MVC, 677

    in subroutines, 53
parser errors, 224
partial classes, 93
partial rendering, 704
Pascal Casing, 107
Password mode, 579
password strength, 600–601
PasswordRecovery control, 606
passwords
    changing, 606
    hashing, 586–587, 601
    recovering, 606
    storing, 584–585
    strength requirements, 600–601
    validating, 247–249
path attribute, 581
Path class, 617, 632–635
path, specifying, 621, 623–624
paths, hard-coded, 770
performance, enhancing (see Ajax)
persistence of data (see session state;
    view state)
PlaceHolder control, 115–116
PolygonHotSpot, 114
positioning properties, 154
POST, 688, 693
post back, 403
PostBack event, 444, 448, 710
PostBack mode, 115
PostBackTrigger, 710
PostedFile object, 636
POWER function, 343
primary keys, 288–290, 292
Priority property, 640
Private access, 83
private keyword, 52

procedures, storing, 355–360, 431–433, 500–501, 534, 665–667

propagation, of exceptions, 229

properties

  about, 80–81

  creating, 138–142

  custom, 555

  in CSS, 153–156

  setting in Visual Web Developer, 171–172

  setting permissions, 140, 555

Properties window, 171–172

Property Builder, 458

Protected access, 83

protection attribute, 581

Public access, 83

public interface, 84

public keyword, 52

publishing (a website) (*see* deployment)

Q

queries (*see* ADO.NET; MVC; SQL)

R

RadioButton control, 114

RadioButtonList control, 118

RangeValidator control, 251–252

Read method, 375–376

ReadLine method, 624, 626–627

ReadOnly property, 141, 498

ReadText method, 625–626

RecordSet, 364

RectangleHotSpot, 114

Redirect method, 411

RedirectFromLoginPage method, 580

RedirectToAction method, 692

ReferenceEquals method, 86

refreshing

  DetailsView, 709–713

  GridView, 704–707, 709–713

Register directive, 45, 142–143

RegisterRoutes method, 677

regular expressions, 254–258, 602

RegularExpressionValidator control, 254–255, 256

relationships

  about, 312

  creating, 308–311

  design phase, 282

  importance of, 299–301

  in data sets, 540

  in LINQ, 662–663

  many-to-many, 314–316

  mapping tables, 315–316

  one-to-many, 312–313

  one-to-one, 312

  table joins and, 337

remainder, 343

remote servers, 592

Remove method, 183

RemoveAll method, 184

Repeater control, 387–392, 393, 394–397, 435, 438, 465

REPLACE function, 344

ReplyTo property, 640

Request object, 195

RequiredFieldValidator control, 238, 244, 245, 247–248, 715

Response object, 195

Response.Write function, 36

Response.Write method, 77

return types, 65–66

roles, 599

rounding, 342–343

RowDeleted event, 491

RowDeleting event, 491

RowFilter property, 562

RTRIM function, 344

runat attribute, 33, 34–35, 99

run-time errors, 219–221

S

SaveAs method, 636, 637, 638

scope, 83–84

scope_identity function, 353

Script folder, 164

script tag
    basic format, 29–31

script tag
    JavaScript in, 35

    language attribute, 34–35

    runat attribute, 33, 34–35

    src attribute, 35

ScriptManager control, 703, 706, 708–709

ScriptManagerProxy control, 709

Scripts folder, 13

scripts, registering, 703

security
    Account folder, 164

    deployment issues, 772–773

    guidelines, 570–572

    JavaScript issues, 571

security guidelines, 602

Select Case, 70, 630

SELECT DISTINCT statement, 326–329

select element, 117

SELECT statement, 321–324

SelectCommand property, 544, 563

SelectedDate property, 122

SelectedIndexChanged event, 117, 480–481, 629

SelectedItemStyle property, 461

SelectedItemTemplate, 439

SelectionChanged event, 123

SelectionMode attribute, 117

SelectionMode property, 122

SelectMonthText property, 122

selectors, 152, 656

SelectWeekText property, 122

Send method, 651

Sender property, 640

sensitive data, protecting, 571–572

SeparatorTemplate, 389, 438, 439

server controls
    HTML (*see* HTML server controls)

    web (*see* web controls)

Server.MapPath method, 770

server-side technologies, 2–3

ServerValidate event, 261

Session object, 191

session state, 182, 191–192

session variables, 192

Session_Start, 192

sessionState section, 179

Set accessor, 141–142

SetFocusOnError property, 239–240

shared methods, 622

ShowDayHeader property, 122

ShowGridLines property, 122

ShowMessageBox property, 253

ShowNextPrevMo propertynth, 122

ShowTitle property, 122

SIGN function, 343

SignOut method, 587

Simple Mail Transfer Protocol (SMTP), 640

Site Map, 129, 198–200

Site.css, 13

Site.master file, 13, 165

SiteMapDataSource control, 129, 130, 131, 208, 509, 683

siteMapNode element, 208

SiteMapPath control, 131–132, 198

SiteName, 182

skins, 150, 204–206, 475–476

slidingExpiration, 582

smart tags

    DataList, 457–458

    GridView, 472, 473

SMTP (Simple Mail Transfer Protocol), 640

SmtpClient class, 639

SmtpClient object, 643, 651

Solution Explorer, 143, 164–165, 715

Sort property, 557

SortExpression property, 516, 517

sorting

    of DataSets, 551–562

    of query results, 333–334

Sorting event, 517, 558

Source view, 166

special characters, escaping, 571

Split view, 166

SQL

    about, 317–318

    aggregate functions, 348

    arithmetic functions (T-SQL), 342–343

    AVG, 352

    BETWEEN, 330–331

    comments, 356

    COUNT, 348

    date/time functions (T-SQL), 346–347

    DELETE statement, 354–355

DISTINCT keyword, 326–329

embedding in .aspx files, 534

filtering groups, 350–351

GROUP BY clause (T-SQL), 347, 349–350

HAVING clause (T-SQL), 347, 350–351

IN, 332–333

INSERT statement, 352–353

LIKE, 331–332

limiting results, 334–335

matching a list of items, 332–333

matching patterns, 331–332

MAX, 352

MIN, 352

operators, 338–341

ORDER BY clause, 333–334, 513, 514

querying a table, 318–321

querying multiple tables, 335–336, 337

row filtering, 329–330

SELECT, 321–324

selecting a range of values, 330–331

selecting all fields, 324

selecting specific fields, 324–325

selecting unique values, 326–329

sorting results, 333–334

storing procedures (T-SQL), 355–360, 500–501

string functions (T-SQL), 343–346

subqueries, 336–337

SUM, 351

table joins, 337–338

TOP, 334–335

UPDATE statement, 353–354

WHERE clause, 329–330, 354, 355, 413

SQL injection attacks, 570

SQL scripts, 295

SQL Server 2008

  about, 6, 274

  ADO.NET connections, 365, 367–368

  case sensitivity, 286

  data types, 285–286

  enabling authentication, 371–372, 373

  installing, 6

  integrated security option, 367

  selecting authentication mode, 7

  Setup Wizard, 591–594

SQL Server Hosting Toolkit, 770–772

SQL Server Management Studio Express

  about, 6

  configuring, 10, 11

  connecting to database, 278–280, 658

  connecting to server, 9, 658

  creating database diagrams, 304, 305

  creating tables, 290, 291

  installing, 8–11

  Object Explorer, 293

  storing queries, 432

  viewing results in plain text, 323

SQL Server Setup Wizard, 591–594

SqlCommand, 364, 365, 368–369, 380

SqlCommandBuilder, 563

SqlConnection, 364, 365, 367–371

SqlDataAdapter class

  about, 539

  adding tables, 544–546

  loading data, 543

  updating data, 563–567

SqlDataReader, 364, 365, 369–371, 375–376, 388, 507–508

SqlDataSource control

  (*see also* DataSet object)

  about, 508

  adding data, 523–524

  binding to DetailsView, 519–521

  binding to GridView, 510–516

  creating conditions, 520

  editing data, 520, 521, 522

  performance issues, 534–535

  selecting data, 513–514, 519, 533

  testing, 514, 521

SQRT function, 343

Src attribute (Register directive), 142–143

src attribute (script tag), 35

start page, 166, 174, 175, 213

static methods, 622

storage, data, 182

StreamReader, 624, 625–627

StreamReader class, 616

StreamWriter class, 617, 621

strict attribute, 177

string data type, 23, 58, 286

string functions, 343–346

String variables, 36

Style Builder, 203

style sheets (*see* CSS style sheets)

Styles folder, 13, 164

Styles.css, 154

Sub keyword, 52

Subject property, 640

subjectComm, 404

SubjectEncoding property, 640

submitButton_Click method, 240, 269

SubmitChangesmethod, 662

subqueries, 336–337

subroutines

  (*see also* event handlers)

  application-level, 180–181

functions vs., 63
SUBSTRING function, 344
subtraction, 68, 339
SUM function, 351
SupportEmail key, 177
switch statement, 70, 630
SwitchPage, 134
syntax errors, 224–225
System.Configuration namespace, 398,
    541, 598
System.Data namespace, 541
System.Data.SqlClient namespace, 364,
    366, 541
System.IO namespace, 615–616, 620, 628
system.net element, 178
System.Net.Mail namespace, 639
System.Security.SecurityException, 770
system.web element, 178
System.Web.Security namespace, 574
System.Web.UI.MasterPage class, 145
System.Web.UI.Page class, 99
System.Web.UI.UserControl class, 136
System.Web.UI.WebControls namespace,
    109
System.Windows.Forms namespace, 109

T

tables, database (*see* database tables)
tables, HTML (*see* DataList; GridView;
    Repeater)
TagName attribute, 142–143
TagPrefix attribute, 142–143
targetFramework attribute, 177
TemplateField control, 478, 498–499,
    500
ternary operators, 526

text
  displaying, 110
  in ASP.NET pages, 39–40
  non-English, 286
text files
  about, 615
  reading from, 616–617
  setting permissions, 617–619
  writing to, 615, 616–617, 620–627
Text property, 23
TextBox control, 107, 110, 579
TextMode attribute, 111
theme attribute, 206
themes, 150, 200–201, 206
time data type, 285
time functions, 346–347
timeout attribute, 581
Timeout property, 192
Timer control, 704
TitleFormat property, 122
To property, 640
TodaysDate property, 122
Toolbox, 170, 171
tooltips, 226
TOP keyword, 334–335
ToString method, 23, 66, 86–87
trace section, 179
Transact-SQL (T-SQL) (*see* T-SQL
    (Transact-SQL))
TreeView control, 129–131
triggers, 710–713
true/false data type, 285
Try-Catch-Finally, 220, 227–228, 385–
    387
TryParse method, 383, 384
T-SQL (Transact-SQL)
  about, 342

arithmetic functions, 342–343
date/time functions, 346–347
GROUP BY clause, 347, 349–350
HAVING clause, 347, 350–351
storing procedures, 355–360
string functions, 343–346
Type property, 250

U

ul element, 118
Unicode, 286
UnLock method, 191
Update method, 563–567
UPDATE query, 411–428
UPDATE statement, 353–354
UpdateCommand property, 563
UpdateItem method, 454
UpdateMode property, 710
UpdatePanel control, 704–706, 709–713
UpdateProgress control, 704, 707, 708
UPPER function, 343
URLs
    as authenticators, 581
User Instance database, 590
user interaction (*see* server controls)
user management, 606
user sessions, 191–192
username, displaying, 606, 611
users
    anonymous, 576
    assigning roles, 599
    authenticating, 164, 179, 180–181,
        373–375
        (*see also* forms authentication;
        memberships)
    creating, 599–600, 602
    logging out, 587

remembering, 606
restricting access, 603–605
storing in Web.config, 584–585
users attribute, 583
Using construct, 621–622
"usp" prefix, 665

V

validation
    client-side, 236, 239
    data type, 250–251, 383, 384
    disabling, 244
    during data insertion, 405
    security and, 570
    server-side, 236, 240–246
validation controls
    about, 236–240, 246–247
    accessing, 170, 247
    CompareValidator, 248–251
    CustomValidator, 258–261
    Display property, 245–246
    extending, 715–718
    in Help Desk page, 268
    RangeValidator, 251–252
    RegularExpressionValidator, 254–255,
        256
    RequiredFieldValidator, 238, 244,
        245, 247–248
    styling, 248, 717–718
    ValidationSummary, 245, 252–253
validation groups, 261–265
validation warnings, 103
ValidationGroup property, 262
ValidationSummary control, 245, 252–
    253
ValidatorCalloutExtender, 715–718
ValueToCompare property, 250

var keyword, 656

varchar data type, 286

variables

(*see also* data types)

about, 56

application, 182, 184

case sensitivity, 70

casting, 183

declaring, 36, 53, 56–60

incrementing, 73

initializing, 57

return types, 65–66

VB

about, 46

case sensitivity, 21, 70

comments, 34

data typing, 59, 453

declaring variables, 57

default page code, 18, 19

marking code blocks, 22

setting with Language attribute, 33

specifying in Visual Web Developer, 12

View Code, 166

View Source, 24

view state, 37, 40, 43, 403, 448, 548–551, 571

Visible property, 116

VisibleDate property, 122

Visual Basic (*see* VB)

Visual Web Developer

about, 5

accessing validation controls, 247

Ajax Control Toolkit, 714

autocomplete (IntelliSense), 169–170

building web forms, 143

choosing data source, 458

code editor, 166–168

connecting to database, 277–278

creating code-behind files, 89–91

creating database diagrams, 304, 305

creating MVC project, 675

creating new pages, 14–15, 31

creating new website, 12–14, 162–163

creating tables, 290

data source controls, 509

Database Explorer, 277, 293

DataList features, 457–458

debugging in, 15–16, 172–175, 176–177, 198, 213 (*see* debugging)

Design mode, 149

executing a page, 16

executing a project, 172

find-and-replace, 717

generating event handler code, 480

generating event handling code, 270

generating ItemCommand code, 443

generating ModeChanging code, 494–495

generating Page_Load code, 367

GridView features, 472, 473

installing, 6–8

loading multiple projects, 266

master pages, 144

Properties window, 171–172

Property Builder, 458

setting default browser, 17, 174

setting file location, 162

setting programming language, 12, 162

setting Start page, 166, 174, 175

Site Map template, 129

Solution Explorer, 164–165

Style Builder, 203

Toolbox, 170, 171, 509

viewing page code, 17
Web Forms Designer, 166, 167
web server, 172, 173
Visual Web Developer Express, 764–767
void keyword, 52

W

Watch window, 221–222
web applications
    about, 3, 159
    security guidelines, 570–572
    websites vs, 767
web controls
    about, 15, 37, 107–108
    AdRotator, 124–128
    associating classes with, 154
    BulletedList, 118–119
    Button (*see* Button control)
    Calendar, 119–124
    CheckBox, 113
    CheckBoxList, 118
    custom, 135–136
    data binding, 388, 398–405
    data retention, 40
    DataList (*see* DataList)
    DropDownList, 117
    FileUpload, 135
    generic, 53
    HiddenField, 111
    HyperLink, 113
    Image, 114
    ImageButton, 112–113
    ImageMap, 114–115
    Label, 110
    Label control, 109, 111
    LinkButton, 113
    ListBox, 117
    Literal, 110
    Menu, 133
    MultiView, 133–134, 135
    Panel, 116–117
    PlaceHolder, 115–116
    RadioButton, 114
    RadioButtonList, 118
    Repeater, 387–392, 393, 394–397,
        435, 438
    SiteMapPath, 131–132
    styling, 204–206
    TextBox, 110
    TreeView, 129–131
    Wizard, 135
Web Form template, 31
web forms (*see* ASP.NET pages)
Web Forms Designer, 166, 167
web server (Cassini), 172, 173, 617
web user controls
    about, 135–136
    creating, 136–142
    using, 142–144
Web.config file
    about, 165, 176–180, 182
    authentication section, 575–576, 577,
        581–582
    authorization section, 582–584, 604
    configuring for local server, 593, 595
    creating, 13
    customErrors element, 226–227
    database connection strings in, 397–
        398
    enabling Ajax Control Toolkit, 718–
        719
    errors in, 224
    interaction with Machine.config, 594
    namespace references in, 93

setting theme, 206

storing application settings, 597–598

storing hashed passwords, 586–587

storing user data, 584–585

system.web section, 770

Web.sitemap file, 129, 208

WHERE clause, 329–330, 354, 355, 413, 656

While loops, 71–74, 624, 627

Width property, 138

wildcard characters, 331, 341

Windows Authentication, 7, 9, 367, 371, 573, 597

Windows Live ID authentication, 573–574

Windows Server 2008, 764

Windows, file-sharing, 618–619

Wizard control, 135

WriteFile.aspx, 620

WriteOnly property, 140–142

WriteText method, 620–621

X

XML, 125–126

XmlDataSource control, 509

XmlHttpRequest, 702

Y

YEAR function, 347

Z

zero-based arrays, 62